THE CAMBRIDGE COMPANION TO

HUSSERL

WEST VANCOUVER MEMORIAL LIBRARY

The Cambridge Companion to

HUSSERL

Edited by

Barry Smith
SUNY, Buffalo

and

David Woodruff Smith
University of California, Irvine

CAMBRIDGE
UNIVERSITY PRESS

Published by the Press Syndicate of the University of Cambridge
The Pitt Building, Trumpington Street, Cambridge CB2 1RP
40 West 20th Street, New York, NY 10011–4211, USA
10 Stamford Road, Oakleigh, Melbourne 3166, Australia

© Cambridge University Press 1995

First published 1995

Printed in the United States of America

Library of Congress Cataloging-in-Publication Data

The Cambridge companion to Husserl / edited by Barry Smith and
David Woodruff Smith.

p.   cm.

Includes bibliographic references and index.

ISBN 0-521-43023-2 (hbk.)   ISBN 0-521-43616-8 (pbk.)

1. Husserl, Edmund, 1859–1938. I. Smith, Barry, 1944. II. Smith,
David Woodruff, 1944–   .

B3279.H94C28   1995
193-dc20
                                                          95-3957
                                                          CIP

A catalog record for this book is available from the British Library.

ISBN 0-521-43023-2 hardback
ISBN 0-521-43616-8 paperback

WEST VAN MEMORIAL LIBRARY

15026784

WEST VANC... ...ARY

Botes
6856
10/95
28.36

Each volume of this series of companions to major philosophers contains specially commissioned essays by an international team of scholars, together with a substantial bibliography, and will serve as a reference work for students and non-specialists. One aim of the series is to dispel the intimidation such readers often feel when faced with the work of a difficult and challenging thinker.

Edmund Husserl (1859–1938) is a seminal figure in the evolution of modern philosophy. His genius derived from his judicious integration of traditional ideas from such thinkers as Aristotle, Descartes, and Hume with a more sophisticated understanding of the mind and conscious experience influenced by Brentano. He has proven to be a powerful influence on many aspects of twentieth-century thought: phenomenology, existentialism, hermeneutics, post-structuralism, and deconstruction, among others.

The essays in this volume explore the full range of Husserl's work and reveal just how systematic his philosophy is. There are treatments of his most important contributions to phenomenology, the theory of intentionality, epistemology, ontology, the philosophy of language, and the philosophy of mathematics. An underlying theme of the volume is a resistance to the idea, current in much intellectual history, of a radical break between modern and postmodern philosophy, with Husserl as the last of the great Cartesians. Husserl is seen in this volume as a philosopher constantly revising his system. The so-called rift between analytic and continental philosophy emerges as an artificial construct.

New readers and non-specialists will find this the most convenient and accessible guide to Husserl currently available. Advanced students and specialists will find a conspectus of recent developments in the interpretation of Husserl's thought.

Withdrawn from Collection

CONTENTS

v

vi   Contents

CONTRIBUTORS

KIT FINE is Flint Professor of Philosophy at the University of California, Los Angeles. He is the author of *Worlds, Times, and Selves* (with A. N. Prior, Duckworth, 1977), *Reasoning with Arbitrary Objects* (Blackwell, 1985), and numerous articles, including "Essence and Modality" (*Philosophical Perspectives*, 1994). His work focusses on metaphysics, logic, and philosophy of language.

JAAKKO HINTIKKA is Professor of Philosophy at Boston University, the University of Helsinki, and the Academy of Finland. He is the author of many books and articles, including *Knowledge and Belief* (Cornell, 1962), *Models for Modalities* (D. Reidel, 1969), *The Intentions of Intentionality* (D. Reidel, 1975), *Investigating Wittgenstein* (with Merrill Hintikka, Blackwell, 1986), and work in the development of game-theoretic semantics. His work ranges over logic, philosophy of language, linguistics, epistemology, phenomenology, and history of philosophy.

JITENDRA NATH MOHANTY is Professor of Philosophy at Temple University. He is the author of *Husserl and Frege* (Indiana University Press, 1982), *Transcendental Philosophy: An Analytic Account* (Blackwell, 1989), and *Reason and Tradition in Indian Thought* (Oxford University Press, 1992), as well as other books and numerous articles on Husserl and phenomenology.

KEVIN MULLIGAN is Professor of Analytic Philosophy at the University of Geneva. He is the editor of *Speech Act and Sachverhalt: Reinach and the Foundations of Realist Phenomenology* (Martinus Nijhoff, 1987) and the author of various articles on ontology, philosophy of language, and phenomenology.

HERMAN PHILIPSE is Professor of Epistemology and Metaphysics at Leyden University in The Netherlands. He is the author of two books (in Dutch), one on Husserl's philosophy of logic and one on

Descartes' moral theory, and numerous articles on phenomenology, epistemology, metaphysics, and history of philosophy.

PETER SIMONS is Professor of Philosophy at the University of Salzburg. As of 1995 he will be Professor of Philosophy at the University of Leeds. He is the author of *Parts: A Study in Ontology* (Oxford University Press, 1987) and *Philosophy and Logic in Central Europe from Bolzano to Tarski* (Kluwer Academic Publishers, 1992), as well as many articles on ontology, logic, philosophy of language, philosophy of mathematics, and the history of philosophy and logic.

BARRY SMITH is Professor of Philosophy and Member of the Center for Cognitive Science at the State University of New York at Buffalo. He the editor of *Parts and Moments: Studies in Logic and Formal Ontology* (Philosophia Verlag, 1982) and the author of *Austrian Philosophy* (Open Court, 1994) and numerous articles on Husserl, formal ontology, and related themes. He is the editor of *The Monist*.

DAVID WOODRUFF SMITH is Professor of Philosophy at the University of California, Irvine. He is the author of *Husserl and Intentionality* (with Ronald McIntyre, D. Reidel, 1982) and *The Circle of Acquaintance: Perception, Consciousness, and Empathy* (Kluwer Academic Publishers, 1989), as well as a variety of articles on phenomenology, philosophy of mind and language, and ontology.

RICHARD TIESZEN is Associate Professor of Philosophy at California State University, San Jose. He is the author of *Mathematical Intuition: Phenomenology and Mathematical Knowledge* (Kluwer Academic Publishers, 1989), "The Philosophy of Arithmetic: Frege and Husserl" (1994), and other works on philosophy of mathematics, logic, and phenomenology.

DALLAS WILLARD is Professor of Philosophy at the University of Southern California. He is the author of *Logic and the Ontology of Knowledge* (Ohio University Press, 1984) and various articles on ontology and cognition. He has translated the most important papers written by Husserl during the 1890s, published as Volume V of Husserl's "Collected Works" (in English) under the title *Early Writings in the Philosophy of Logic and Mathematics* (Kluwer Academic Publishers, 1994).

Introduction

I. HUSSERL'S PLACE IN THE HISTORY OF PHILOSOPHY

Edmund Husserl was born in 1859 in Moravia, then a part of the Habsburg Empire, now a part of the Czech Republic. He studied mathematics in Leipzig and Berlin, where he came into contact with the great German mathematician Karl Weierstrass. Encouraged by his friend and fellow Moravian T. G. Masaryk (also for a time in Leipzig and later first President of the erstwhile Republic of Czechoslovakia), Husserl attended lectures in philosophy given by Franz Brentano in Vienna. He devoted his life thereafter to what, from around 1908, he came to see as his "mission" – to transform philosophy into a rigorous science.

Husserl's philosophy, by the usual account, evolved through three stages. First, he overthrew a purportedly psychologistic position in the foundations of arithmetic, striving instead to establish anti-psychologistic, objective foundations of logic and mathematics. Second, he moved from a conception of philosophy as rooted in Brentanian descriptive psychology to the development of a new discipline of "phenomenology" and a metaphysical position dubbed "transcendental idealism". And third, he transformed this phenomenology, which initially amounted to a form of methodological solipsism, into a phenomenology of intersubjectivity and ultimately (especially in his *Crisis* of 1936) into an ontology of the life-world, embracing the social worlds of culture and history.

This story of three revolutions can provide, at best, a preliminary orientation. Husserl was constantly expanding and revising his philosophical system, integrating views in phenomenology, ontology, epis-

I

temology and logic with views on the nature and tasks of philosophy and science as well as on the nature of culture and the world – in ways that reveal more common elements than violent shifts of direction. Husserl's genius lay in his judicious integration of traditional ideas from Aristotle, Descartes, and Hume with new ideas relating, above all, to a more sophisticated understanding of mind and conscious experience derived from Brentano. Husserl is thus a seminal figure in the evolution from traditional philosophy to the characteristic philosophical concerns of the late twentieth century: concerns with representation and intentionality and with problems at the borderlines of the philosophy of mind, ontology, and cognitive science.

Volumes have been written about Husserl's influence on twentieth-century European thought, an influence which not only extended to phenomenology and existentialism but also embraces hermeneutics, poststructuralism, deconstruction, and other movements defined by the works of Heidegger, Sartre, Merleau-Ponty, Ricoeur, and others – some developing and some reacting against Husserlian ideas. Much has been written, too, about Husserl's relation to Austrian philosophy around the turn of the century (to the work of Bolzano, Brentano, Meinong, Twardowski, and others) and about his relations to analytic philosophers such as Frege, Wittgenstein, Carnap, Sellars, and Quine. The focus of the present set of essays is somewhat different. Following the pattern set by other volumes in this series of *Cambridge Companions to Philosophy*, this volume will study Husserl as a philosopher in his own right, alongside Plato, Aristotle, Descartes, and Leibniz. While there will be some historical treatment of Husserl's work and influence, most of the essays will deal in conceptual interpretation and systematic analysis. We shall look primarily at Husserl's most important philosophical contributions – what is original in them and what seeems most significant in them today.

These essays resist one recent fashion in intellectual history – to think in terms of a radical break between "modern" and "postmodern" philosophy, with Husserl the last of the great Cartesians.[1] Evolution is a piecemeal affair, in philosophy as in nature, and sharp breaks between philosophical epochs are artificial constructs. Descartes shared much with his Aristotelian-Scholastic predecessors, and Kant's break with his "uncritical" predecessors also turns on many shared assumptions. Moreover, as Michael Dummett, among others, has demonstrated (1993), the idea of a radical break in our own century between analytic philosophy in England and America and the work of Husserl and his contemporaries in continental Europe conceals a multitude of shared problems and even shared solutions. Similarly, arguments purporting to establish a radical rejection of Husserlian thought by Heidegger and others often prove, on closer inspection, to rest on the exploitation of ideas worked out in advance by Husserl himself or by his early realist disciples.[2] Such "breaks" serve mainly to give intellectual history an easy handle on continuities and complexities in the slow evolution of ideas.

Husserl was a systematic thinker in the classical tradition of Western philosophy. In his early writings he embraced a view according to which ontology, logic, and psychology would be developed in tandem with each other, none being given precedence over the others. His account of the ontology of universals and particulars and of parts, wholes and dependence goes hand in hand with his account of the analytic/synthetic distinction and of the nature of logical laws and of the ways in which these laws are applied to the actual events of thinking that are studied by psychology.[3] Later, as Karl Schuhmann has shown, Husserl came increasingly to see the need for a single, founding discipline of philosophy. He saw philosophy in the standard sense as divided into *theoretical* disciplines – above all ontology – on the one hand, and *practical* disciplines such as ethics and aesthetics, on the other. Each of these disciplines is then divided in turn into "formal" and "material" or "regional" sub-disciplines. The entire edifice is seen as being founded, in Fichtean vein, on a universal science of consciousness as such – the science of phenomenology. Each of the disciplines resting on this foundation has its own characteristic type of object (things or objects of nature are dealt with by ontology, values by axiology, and so on). The founding discipline, in contrast, deals not with objects but with the acts of consciousness in which objects are given or experienced.[4] The founding discipline therefore has its source of evidence within itself: only thus, Husserl held, can philosophy become a "rigorous science."

Cutting across these disciplinary divisions are classical philosophical concerns – which reappear at difference points in Husserl's writings – with the relations between mind and body, with realism versus idealism, with solipsism and intersubjectivity. The essays which follow address these and related issues as Husserl saw them. The focus, as already mentioned, will be on the conceptual import of Husserl's various theories. Inevitably, the essays will omit some important themes, and this Introduction will address the more important of these in simple terms. Collectively, the essays will offer a unified picture of the most important aspects of Husserl's thinking while acknowledging controversies around his conception of intentionality, his changing focus in methodology, and the unstable combination in his thinking of tendencies toward both realism and idealism.

II. HUSSERL'S LIFE AND CAREER

Husserl was born on April 8, 1859 in Prossnitz (Prostĕjv), a not unimportant town within the territory of the present Czech Republic.[5] His parents were German-speaking liberal Jews (Husserl converted to Protestantism at the age of 27). In 1876 he moved to Leipzig, where he studied astronomy, also attending lectures in mathematics and physics and, to a limited degree, in philosophy (given by Wilhelm Wundt). In 1878 he moved to Berlin, where he concentrated his energies especially on the lectures of Weierstrass. In 1881 he moved on to Vienna in his native Austria, concentrating still on mathematics, in which subject he received the doctorate in 1883 for a dissertation on the theory of variations.

From 1884 to 1886 Husserl attended philosophy lectures given by Franz Brentano in Vienna. The framework of Brentano's philosophy, above all his re-introduction to philosophy of the problem of intentionality and his subtle combination of psychological and ontological concerns, would determine Husserl's thinking to the end of his life. On Brentano's recommendation Husserl transferred to Halle in order to work for the habilitation degree under Carl Stumpf, a member of the first generation of Brentano's students. Husserl's habilitation thesis on the concept of number was completed in 1887; his examiners included not only Stumpf but also Georg Cantor, the inventor of the theory of sets, and Husserl enjoyed friendly relations thereafter not only with Stumpf and Cantor but also with the mathematician Hermann Grassmann, son of the author of the *Ausdehnungslehre*.

In October 1887 Husserl was made *Privatdozent* in the University of Halle and for a period his energies were concentrated on investigations on logic and the foundations of mathematics, most especially on the role of and on the justification of the use of "inauthentic" or "signitive" processes – processes involving the mere manipulation of symbols – in mathematical practice. Like Brentano, Husserl is at this stage unsympathetic to the type of philosophy then predominant in Germany. In his lectures on the philosophy of mathematics he refers to the tradition of German idealism as a "murky vapor of idealistic or better mystical pseudo-philosophy."[6]

In 1891 he published his first book, the *Philosophy of Arithmetic,* a work which was reviewed *inter alia* by Gottlob Frege, who notoriously (and to some degree unfairly) charged it with propounding a doctrine of psychologism. Frege's influence on the development of Husserl's thinking was, in contrast to what is commonly held, far less important than that of Lotze, Bolzano, and Twardowski. It was the combined effect of these three thinkers which served to point Husserl in the direction of the avowed Platonism of the "Prolegomena to Pure Logic" which constitutes the first volume of Husserl's *magnum opus,* the *Logical Investigations* of 1900–01. This Prolegomena comprises a devastating critique of all forms of psychologism in philosophy, i.e. of all attempts to conceive the sub-disciplines of philosophy as branches of empirical psychology. This critique had a wide influence and succeeded in bringing the heyday of psychologism to an end. While Frege's and Husserl's (and Bolzano's) attacks on psychologistic thinking share many points in common, it was Husserl's critique which was most immediate and far-reaching in its effects.

The years from 1895 to 1900 brought Husserl little professional success. In the wake of the publication of his *Logical Investigations,* however, he was appointed to the post of associate professor at the University of Göttingen. Göttingen was at this time a renowned center of mathematical research, not least through the work and influence of David Hilbert, who had hoped to acquire in the person of Husserl a representative of the new logic as colleague. Hilbert would indeed over the coming years share students with Husserl, including Kurt Grelling and Kasimierz Adjukiewicz. However, Hilbert's hopes for serious collaboration were disappointed as a result of Husserl's increasing interest in problems of "subjectivity," "transcendental idealism," and in the methodology of the new discipline of phenomenology – concerns which often overshadowed the sort of detailed analysis of problems at the borderlines of logic, ontology, and descriptive psychology which had characterized the *Logical Investigations* and other early writings.

The importance of Husserl's work in the Göttingen years for the development of phenomenological philosophy has been clearly set out by Mohanty in his essay herein. Husserl's initial influence began to make itself felt however not in Göttingen, but among a group of students of Theodor Lipps in the University of Munich. The members of this group had been inspired to rebel against their teacher Lipps – himself an erstwhile proponent of psychologism – by a certain Johannes Daubert, a talented organizer who had read the *Logical Investigations* already in 1902 and had persuaded his fellow students to accept this work as their philosophical bible. The term "phenomenological movement" was first used by the group around Daubert to describe its activities, which were marked also by an interest in the work of Brentano and his school and in wider associated developments in logic, linguistics, and empirical and theoretical psychology. The Munich phenomenologists were effective propagandists for the new movement. Only after members of the Munich group, especially Adolf Reinach, had moved to join Husserl in Göttingen, did Husserl's teaching there begin to have an effect, and Spiegelberg refers in this connection to the "Munich invasion of Göttingen" which occurred in the summer semester of 1905.[7]

The members of the Munich group propounded what might be called a "realist" phenomenology, drawing especially on those aspects of the *Logical Investigations* which relate to the investigation of the essential structures of acts, meanings, expressions, signs, and entities of other types. Phenomenology, on this account, consists in setting forth in non-reductive fashion and as faithfully as possible the *a priori* laws which govern the relations between these different sorts of objects in different regions of investigations. Reinach exploited this method in relation to the essential structures of legal and quasi-legal uses of language (for example in promises, commands, requests, etc.). In this way he developed a theory of speech acts of exactly the sort which was later worked out by Austin and Searle in the 1950s and 1960s.[8] In other respects, too, Munich phenomenology bears interesting parallels to more recent developments in analytic philosophy,[9] and the Munich phenomenologists, again in the person of Reinach, were among the first in Germany to read the work of Frege.

In 1906 Husserl was promoted to a personal chair in Göttingen. There is detectable in his thinking from about this time an increasing interest in and sympathy for the tradition of *German* philosophy (as contrasted with the *Austrian* philosophy of Bolzano, Brentano, Twardowski, Meinong, or Mach). In the winter semester of 1907/08, Husserl gave a four-hour lecture on "Kant and Post-Kantian Philosophy," and in September 1908 he drafted manuscripts on "transcendental phenomenology and transcendental logic" in which his own method is compared to Kant's "transcendental-logical method."

In 1912 he completed the manuscript of the three books of the *Ideas* and in 1913 the first of these appeared in print in the first volume of the newly founded *Jahrbuch für Philosophie und phänomenologische Forschung*, Husserl's "yearbook" of phenomenological research.[10] With the outbreak of war, Husserl was caught up, like so many others at the time, by feelings of patriotism and military fervour. From this time also one can detect an interest on Husserl's part in the religious works of Fichte. In 1916 Husserl accepted a call to the University of Freiburg where he succeeded the Neo-Kantian idealist Heinrich Rickert. Here he made the acquaintance of one Martin Heidegger, and was joined by students from Göttingen, among them Edith Stein and Roman Ingarden. Stein and Heidegger became involved with the long and still uncompleted project of editing Husserl's many shorthand manuscripts for publication, working above all on the second and third books of the *Ideas* and the work on the phenomenology of the consciousness of internal time.

By the early 1920s Husserl was the leading philosopher in Germany. In 1923, at the age of 64, he received a call to Berlin, but chose to remain in Freiburg in order to be able to complete the many works he still intended to write. Those who attended his lectures in this period include philosophers as important as Günther Anders, Rudolf Carnap, Marvin Farber, Aron Gurwitsch, Charles Hartshorne, William Kneale, Aurel Kolnai, Emmanuel Levinas, Herbert Marcuse and Arnold Metzger. In 1929, an article by Husserl on the topic of "Phenomenology" appeared in the *Encyclopedia Brittanica* in telescoped form. In this year Husserl retired and was succeeded by Heidegger in his professorship in Freiburg. In the same year, Husserl lectured in Paris to an audience which included Gabriel Marcel, Eugène Minkowski, and Jean Cavaillès. He then published, after a long period during which no original major work by Husserl had appeared, the

Formal and Transcendental Logic. In 1931 the French version of the *Cartesian Meditations* was published and in that same year Husserl gave a lecture on "Phenomenology and Anthropology" to a meeting of the *Kantgesellschaft* in Berlin, attended by an audience of some 1600 persons.

From 1933, however, Husserl began to face problems connected with the political conditions in Germany. In 1934, as a Jewish professor emeritus, he was effectively deprived of his library privileges in the university by his former colleague Heidegger. In the same year he began a new phase of work on the concept of the life-world, whose roots trace to the Second Book of the *Ideas.* In 1935 he began negotations with the Prague Philosophical Circle to have his manuscripts transferred to what then seemed like the relative safety of Bohemia. Towards the end of the same year he traveled to Prague with the intention of making arrangements for a return to his former home. In November, he gave lectures in Prague on the topic of the *"Crisis of European Sciences,"* lectures which were published in 1936 as a 100-page article in the Belgrade journal *Philosophia.* In 1937, he was refused permission by the *Reichsministerium* to participate in the International Congress of Philosophy in Paris. On 27 April 1938, Husserl died. His library and manuscripts were smuggled to Belgium where they remained in safekeeping until after the war. One year later his *Experience and Judgment* was published in Prague, though almost the entire edition was destroyed by German troops during their march into the city.

III. HUSSERL'S PHENOMENOLOGY

For over five decades Husserl lectured and published works on ontological, epistemological, phenomenological, and logico-linguistic matters. While his views in ethics, politics, and theology were less evident, he lectured on such matters, and his published work carries implications for these areas also.[11] In this introduction we outline Husserl's philosophy by sketching his basic views in different fields. Within that context, the connections among these views, and thus his methodology and program, will emerge. Our survey is designed to serve as a framework for the more detailed discussions pursued in the essays to follow.

We begin with phenomenology, the study of "phenomena" in the sense of the ways in which things appear to us in different forms of conscious experience. While nowadays generally used as a name for the philosophical movement formed by Daubert, Husserl, Pfänder, Heidegger, among others, the term "phenomenology" has a longer history as the name of a special sub-discipline of philosophy.[12] It was so used in 1736 by the German Pietist Chistoph Friedrich Oetinger to refer to the study of the "divine system of relations" between the things on the surface of the visible world. Later in the eighteenth century, Johann Heinrich Lambert (a mathematician, physicist, and philosopher influenced by Christian Wolff) used *Phänomenologie* for the theory of the appearances fundamental to all empirical knowledge, and Kant adopted the term in a similar sense. Phenomenology in these early manifestations is above all a *descriptive* enterprise, a theory of appearances, of symptoms, as contrasted with those disciplines which deal in *causal explanation*, and with what lies behind the appearances. It was in this sense that Brentano distinguished between "descriptive" and "genetic" psychology, and Husserl's own phenomenology grew precisely out of descriptive psychology in the Brentanian sense.

Husserlian phenomenology seeks the description and structural analysis of consciousness, as opposed to an account of its causal origin in brain activity or elsewhere. Consciousness is to be studied precisely as it is experienced, and accordingly the *objects* of consciousness, too, need to be characterized precisely as they are given in experience, with no metaphysical reinterpretations (inspired by reductive or other motives). It is in this sense that we are to understand Husserl's slogan: "To the things themselves!" Phenomenology is to deal with the phenomena, with the objects as we experience them in consciousness and with our different ways of "relating" to these objects via intentionality.

Husserl officially defined the science of phenomenology as the study of the essence of conscious experience, and especially of intentional experience (*Ideas* I, §§ 33–34). This definition fits Husserl's work as well as that of his successors: Adolf Reinach, Max Scheler, Roman Ingarden, Alfred Schutz, Martin Heidegger, Maurice Merleau-Ponty, Jean-Paul Sartre, and recent analytic phenomenologists such as Dagfinn Føllesdal and Hubert Dreyfus. Different phenomenologists have placed the emphases in different places in giving an account of the structures of experience. Husserl himself emphasized consciousness as "pure" rational, mental activity, and developed a theory of the essential structures of consciousness in terms of the parts and moments of our mental acts. Heidegger moved away from this intellectualistic account of experience and generally avoided the terms "consciousness" and "subject," which he saw as being laden with Cartesian, dualistic assumptions. For the Heidegger of *Being and Time* (1927), phenomenology is concerned with what he calls *being*, and above all with the being (the experience and behavior) of man, and with the different ways in which this human experience and behavior (a matter of our relations to others, to the surrounding world, to tools and equipment, to history) can be "authentic" and "inauthentic." Thus, Heidegger in his own way endorsed Husserl's methodological incantation to return to the things themselves, as did other existentialist phenomenologists such as Sartre (1937, 1943), who emphasized bodily experience while casting aspersions on the Husserlian assumption of a "pure" consciousness and of a "transcendental ego."

Husserlian ideas have also taken root outside the phenomenological tradition, not least in contemporary cognitive science, a movement of thought which first came to prominence through the overthrow of behaviorism by cognitive psychologists in the 1970s. Underlying much of this work is a research strategy which Jerry Fodor, following Carnap, calls "methodological solipsism" and which amounts to the abstraction of mental activity from its physical basis. As Carnap saw, methodological solipsism is equivalent to Husserl's basic method of "phenomenological reduction."[13] Many proponents of the new cognitive science adopted in addition a functionalist model of the mind, arguing that mental activities are to be compared with computational functioning, so that the mind would stand to the brain as the computer's software stands to its hardware. There are even some traces of the computer analogy of mind in Husserl's early writings,[14] though the later Husserl would surely have rejected functionalism and all that goes with it, on the grounds that it does not do justice to "subjectivity," to the ways in which consciousness is given "from the inside." More recently, in his *The Rediscovery of the Mind*, John Searle has argued that it is precisely consciousness, rather than neural or computational function, which defines the mind. Searle argues, as did the later Husserl before him, that consciousness must be studied from the first-person point of view, for only thus is it possible to do justice to its irreducibly subjective structures.

What we might call the phenomenological attitude in philosophy is of course much older than Husserl and his successors, and traces of it can be detected in Berkeley, Hume, and in other British empiricists. With Husserl, however, phenomenology first emerged as a distinctive philosophical discipline, much as – in the eyes of many contemporary philosophers – epistemology first took on sharp contours in the seventeenth century through the work of Descartes. If Husserl did not single-handedly invent phenomenology (any more than Descartes invented epistemology), certainly he brought it into its own as a discipline. In order to grasp the nature of the discipline itself, however, we need to separate it from other doctrines with which it has been associated, including even the specific method which Husserl proposed.

This method consists in what Husserl called the phenomenological reduction or *epoché* (literally: abstention).[15] We are to "bracket," or abstain from positing the existence of, the natural world around us. That is, we put out of action the general thesis of the everyday "natural" standpoint, our background presupposition that there exists a world independent of our experience. We will then, Husserl holds, be in a position to describe "pure" consciousness, abstracting from its embeddedness in the world of nature. By carrying out the reduction we abandon the "natural" or "naturalistic" attitude which takes the world for granted and come to adopt instead the phenomenological or what is sometimes called the "transcendental" attitude.

We grasp in phenomenological reflection that consciousness is *intentional* in the sense of *being directed towards an object*: consciousness is consciousness *of* something. The phenomenologist attends to acts of consciousness and to the objects they "intend" *just as* we experience and intend them. The use of the method of bracketing implies that such attention involves no concern for whether these objects really exist. The method is a technique for focussing on the act and on the correlated object precisely as they are experienced. Each such act may include validity-claims, and these too fall within the scope of reflection, but as claims only: their validity is neutralized. To describe things as we experience them from the first-person point of view is to describe also the forms of consciousness in which we experience objects, their mode of being given. The phenomenologist can apply his method to the things of fiction or mythology as well as to the things of physics, to the things of imagination as well as to the things of perception and memory, the devil as well as the deep blue sea. Through the *epoché* all objects become reduced to their experienceable properties, and all objects are in this respect equal in the eyes of consciousness.

Among Husserl's most interesting results are his concrete phenomenological analyses of various features of experience. These concern analyses of the structures of perception and reasoning, and of the relation between bare ("signitive") linguistic reference to an object and "fulfilled" perceptual experience of the same object. They concern the experience of oneself and of one's body, of others, of objectivity and intersubjectivity in judgment and belief, and of logical and mathematical entities. Husserl's work in these areas is studied in various essays herein.

Husserl used the method of *epoché* (in his *Ideas* and later works), not only for purposes of phenomenological description and analysis of forms of consciousness, but also – according to a common line of interpretation – to ground a foundationalist epistemology and an idealist metaphysics. Husserl himself insists that it is exclusively consciousness (or conscious subjectivity, the "pure ego") that has absolute being; all other forms of being are such as to depend on consciousness for their existence. (See *Ideas* I, §49.) The *epoché* in this way leads to a metaphysical "nullification" of the world, to the dissolution of the world into the realm of consciousness.

On the one hand, then, the Cartesian privileging of the ego – and the Fichtean desire for an absolute epistemological foundation for philosophy – lead to the most radical of changes: to the adoption of a position according to which the world itself is reduced to the status of a mere correlate of consciousness, a move which flows from the conviction that philosophy must have a grounding insight which has its source of evidence within itself. This idealist Husserl is even more radical than Kant, insisting (again with Fichte) that there is no thing-in-itself beyond the reach of possible experience. Even the thing-in-itself is a mere rule for the synthesizing activities of consciousness. Moreover, every sort of thing is associated essentially with a certain sort of conscious experience in which it reaches a most adequate level of givenness.

On the other hand, however, it appears that nothing is changed with the performance of the *epoché:* we simply change our attitude toward the world, suspending all theses as to the latter's existential dependence or independence. Phenomenologists who have carried out the phenomenological reduction continue to believe that the world exists; but they do not make use of this fact in the practice of phenomenological description of experience. Husserl, like Descartes, certainly awarded a privileged role to the evidence we have of our own acts and states of consciousness. But on the question of the existence of the world beyond consciousness, Husserl sought also to do justice to the claims of common-sense realism (claims to the effect that, for example, things like trees exist independently of consciousness and are the objects of our experiences). As the essays below attest, these Cartesian, Fichtean and common-sense realist tendencies in Husserl are subjects of intense controversy.

The approach to Husserl's philosophy as if it were a matter of practicing a special kind of reflection on consciousness is just one among several alternatives. Thus one may use Husserl's work also as the basis for a study of intentionality itself. Where performing the *epoché* requires neutrality about questions of ontology or metaphysics, to pursue the theory of intentionality is to invite ontological questions about mental acts, their contents, and the objects towards which they are directed. Yet another approach is to set out Husserl's own ontology – his theory of part, whole, and dependence – bringing in special considerations pertaining to the ontology of consciousness and intentionality only later. Still another alternative is to develop Husserl's phenomenology as an exercise in epistemology, somewhat as Descartes turns to the mind by way of his quest for certainty: ontology emerges then as an account of the world we know.

In fact, Husserl took all of these approaches, in different works. This fact, again, should lead us to view his philosophy as a unity and to avoid giving total precedence to any single element. To see his philosophy as having its foundations exclusively in either phenomenology or ontology or epistemology (the claims of each have been advanced) is to miss the mutual dependence among the different aspects of his thinking. And because the concept of dependence or foundation itself is used in all his work – in ontology, in epistemology, and in phenomenology, the very question of foundationalism is more complicated in Husserl than it is in most philosophers.

IV. THE PROBLEM OF INTENTIONALITY

Two groups of solutions to the problem of intentionality – the problem of providing a unified account of the directedness towards objects of mental acts – have been advanced in the history of the subject, which we may call the relational and the adverbial solutions respectively.[16] *Relational* accounts, as the name suggests, see intentionality as a relation between a subject or act and an object: thus if John sees a red square, then he or his act of seeing stands in a certain relation to the object he sees. *Adverbial* accounts, by contrast, see intentionality as a mere feature of the subject or act, a feature that may be expressed linguistically by means of adverbial modifiers, as in "John sees redly" or "John sees squarely." Brentano embraced a radical version of the adverbial theory, asserting that the object of consciousness is in every case existent in the mind: the act is affected by the fact that the object is "intentionally inexistent" within it, as Brentano puts it in a famous passage from the *Psychology from an Empirical Standpoint* of 1874.[17] Adverbial accounts have the merit of providing a theory of intentionality which will yield the same structural account for all acts, drawing on those features which acts share in common as they are experienced from the internal, first-person point of view. Such accounts have problems, however, in doing justice to the ways in which, through conscious experience, we are able to transcend the orbit of our own mind and come into genuine contact with objects in the world. Relational theories of intentionality, in contrast, take as their starting point the existence of a genuine relation between act and object, but they are thereby not in a position to provide a uniform structural account of intentionality that would be valid for all acts. This is because some acts are, of course, such as to lack a (genuine) object entirely, yet remain for all that internally indistinguishable from acts of the more normal, veridical sort.

One of Husserl's principal contributions to philosophy is to have provided a new sort of solution to this problem. Certainly in his earlier work there are passages where Husserl treats the problem of intentionality in relational fashion, as a special problem of ontology.[18] But how can there be an intentional relation if in some cases the object of perception or thought does not exist?[19] In Husserl's middle and later work, on the other hand, intentionality appears consistently as a phenomenological property of acts of consciousness, something we immediately experience: we are in every case conscious of an object whether or not such an object actually exists in the world beyond consciousness. With this the adverbial theory once more takes center-stage. When we view his work as a whole, however, we shall see that Husserl provided an account which enables us to join these two sides of intentionality together – to do justice to both the ontological structure of mind and its phenomenological character.

The concept of intentionality has its roots in Aristotle.[20] In perception, Aristotle held, the mind takes on the form but not the matter of the object known. Thus, for example, the eye's matter becomes impressed by the color (form) of what is seen. Arabic philosophers later refined Aristotle's theory. Distinguishing form-in-mind and form-in-object, Avicenna called the former *ma'ná*, i.e., meaning or message. Medieval philosophers translated Avicenna's term by the Latin *intentio*, from the verb meaning to aim or stretch toward something (specifically by pulling in the bowstring): the form-in-mind, the mental content, then *intends* the form-in-object. Notions of intentional content in this sense were a common feature of much Scholastic philosophizing. Through the influence of the British empiricists' notion of "idea" and of German idealist philosophy, both of which tended confusedly to draw all objects into the mind and thus to eliminate the distinction between object and object-of-thought, the classical notion of intentionality became submerged.

While the term – and the problem – were revived by Brentano in 1874, Brentano was still sufficiently influenced by Descartes and the empiricists to find it difficult to break out of the immanentistic (adverbial) view. A step in a more appropriate direction was made by his student Kasimir Twardowski in a work entitled *On the Content and Object of Presentations* of 1894, which drew a sharp distinction among act, content, and object of presentation (*Vorstellung*) – a distinction essential to any adequate theory of intentionality. Every act, Twardowski held, even a hallucination, has both a content and an object, though the latter need not exist. Thus, the way is open for a new sort of relational theory, of a sort which is able to do justice – in its fashion, and at a price – not only to standard (veridical) experiences of the sort which the Scholastic philosophers were comfortable with, but also to non-standard (non-veridical) experiences, which deviate in different ways from the norm. Alexius Meinong, another Brentano-student, extended Twardowski's relational theory of intentionality in systematic fashion, and has since become notorious for the attention he paid to the jungle of non-standard entities apparently created or picked out by cases of deviant intentionality. A uniform structural account of acts is provided on the basis of the Twardowski-Meinong relational theory by postulating that every act has some object of a precisely tailored sort. Meinong's "The Theory of Objects" (1904) at the same time exploits the notion of non-existent object as a basis for a new sort of ontology which would cast off that "prejudice in favor of the actual" which had in his eyes so profoundly affected the work of previous ontologists. Objects themselves, Meinong held, are "beyond being or nonbeing."

In this way, clearly the principal flaw of the relational theory of intentionality could be avoided: a uniform theory of the intentional relation can be provided for all acts of whatever sort. However, the relational theory inherits the principal flaw of adverbialism, since the relation to the standard, existent objects in the world – that real relation which is characteristic of successful veridical acts as we normally conceive them – still remains to be explained. How does that relation differ from the ubiquitous relation which all acts bear to the Meinongian "pure" objects that float in a realm "beyond being and non-being"?

Husserl, too, extended and ramified Twardowski's notion of intentional content, first in an early essay "Intentional Objects" (1894) and then again in the *Logical Investigations*. The conception of content that is defended in this latter work harks back, first of all, to Bernard Bolzano's logic, and through Bolzano to the Stoic conception of the *lekton* as that which is expressed and communicated in language.[21] This notion of *lekton* or objective proposition has reappeared throughout the history of logic. Thus, it is to be found in the fourteenth century in the work of Adam Wodeham and in the seventeenth century Port Royal Logic. Again, the British empiricists (similar in this respect to Descartes and the German idealists) lie outside this tradition, working instead with the confusingly ambiguous notion of "idea" in a way which made it difficult for them to draw a clear distinction between ideas as tokens and as types. As the Stoics distinguished the subjective presentation or *phantasia* from the objective *lekton* that is its communicable content, so Bolzano in his *Theory of Science* (1837) distinguished "subjective" and "objective" ideas. The objective idea he called an "idea in itself" (*Vorstellung an sich*), the objective content that is expressed by a complete sentence he called a "proposition in itself" (*Satz an sich*).

In the first of the *Logical Investigations*, alluding to Bolzano, Husserl held that a linguistic expression intimates a "real" content of thought – a subjective idea – and expresses an "ideal" content. The real content has an internal structure: it divides into the "matter" of the act (what makes it a presentation of such-and-such an object) and the quality of the act (what makes it a judgment, rather than an act of doubt, surmise, etc.).[22] As we know, the same object may be experienced differently in different acts: for instance, Napoleon may be thought of as the victor at Jena or as the vanquished at Waterloo. The matter of an act thus embodies the particular way in which the object is given in that act of consciousness. Moreover, the same matter can be shared by several acts which differ in quality: thus I can wonder, emptily, whether there is food in the larder; I can subsequently see that there is food; I can be happy that there is food, regret that there is food, and so on. Matter and quality stand in a relation of reciprocal dependence: each is such that, as a matter of necessity, it cannot exist without the other. The theory of dependence relations set forth in the third *Logical Investigation* hereby enables Husserl to give an account of the unity of the act which at the same time leaves room for distinct dimensions of variation within its internal structure and thus for the different ways in which it may be intentionally directed towards an object. Real content (including real matter and real quality) are entities existing in time. They are real parts of the conscious act. The ideal content, in contrast, is the *species* which this real content, with its real parts and moments, instantiates. Husserl's treatment of these matters thus comes close to familiar Aristotelian, immanent realist, theories of universals.[23]

Both real and ideal content are to be distinguished further from the object which the act intends, so that an analogue of the distinction between the sense and the referent of an expression is present, with variations in detail and ontology, in Bolzano, in Twardowski, and again in Husserl. Twardowski and Husserl, true to their Brentanian heritage, locate this distinction squarely in the field of psychology: hence sense or meaning and directedness to object pertain primarily to *acts* and only derivatively to *expressions or uses of language*.

V. LOGIC, MEANING, AND REFERENCE

The distinction between meaning and referent in language is, of course, standardly associated with Gottlob Frege and especially with Frege's essay "On Sense and Reference" of 1892. As Angelelli has shown in his work of 1967, however, the distinction has a long prehistory. As Mohanty shows in his *Husserl and Frege* of 1982, Husserl drew the distinction between sense and reference of a term already in 1891, which is to say before the publication of Frege's essay. For present purposes, however, we need only note that, while Frege drew the Bolzanian distinction between idea (*Vorstellung*) and sense (*Sinn*), the idea being subjective and the sense objective, he took ideas as psychological and sense, though "eternal," as somehow bound to language, so that only expressions have sense. In contrast to Bolzano for whom our thinking acts, too, may have objective content, he thus held that linguistic expression is the sole intramundane locus of objective content. Coupled with this is the fact that, because he saw acts of thinking as irreducibly subjective, Frege's attack on psychologism became an attack on all attempts to explain how logic can apply to our psychological experience of reasoning and inferring. In this respect Husserl enjoys a clear advantage. For Husserl drew the distinction between subjective and objective content for acts in general, and not exclusively for acts of linguistic expression. Moreover his account of subjective act-tokens is part and parcel of his account of objective content, so that Husserl was able to show in direct fashion how logical laws can apply to actual thinking events (namely in the way geometrical laws apply to empirical shapes).[24] Thus it was, in fact, Husserl who integrated the (psychological, or phenomenological) theory of intentional content with the logical theory of objective idea or proposition.

Husserl's account of language in the *Logical Investigations* and later is cognitively based. Linguistic expressions have meaning, on this account, only to the extent that they are *given* meaning through cognitive acts or through parts and moments of acts of certain determinate sorts. The latter are not separate, well-demarcated units of

conscious experience but are bound up or fused together with the
other acts and act-moments involved in uses of language in such a
way as to make a single experiential unity.[25] Meaning acts are further such that they are in every case acts in which objects are intended: "To use an expression significantly, and to refer expressively
to an object," Husserl claims, "are one and the same."[26]

In the ontology of the *Logical Investigations*, meanings are species.
To see what this means we must first note that meaning acts are
divided by Husserl into two kinds: those associated with *uses of
names*, which are acts of presentation, and those associated with *uses
of sentences*, which are acts of judgment. The former are directed
toward *objects*, the latter toward *states of affairs*. A meaning act of
the first kind may occur either in isolation or (undergoing a certain
sort of transformation) in the context of a meaning act of the second
kind: "Each meaning is on this doctrine either a nominal meaning or
a propositional meaning, or, still more precisely, either the meaning
of a complete sentence or a possible part of such a meaning" (*Investigation* VI, §1). The meanings of general names, now, which Husserl
calls concepts, are just *species of corresponding presentations* (or
more precisely of the *matters* of presentations); the meanings of sentences, which Husserl calls propositions, are just *species of acts of
judgment*. And the relation between a meaning and an associated *act*
of meaning (between an ideal content and an associated real content)
is in every case the relation of species to instance, exactly as between,
say, the species *red* and some red object. More precisely, we should say
that, just as it is only a certain real part or moment of the red object –
its individual accident of redness – which instantiates the species
red, so it is only a certain real part or moment of the meaning act
which instances any given meaning-species, namely that part or moment which is responsible for the act's intentionality, for its being
directed to an object in just this way.

> In the concrete act of meaning a certain moment corresponds to the mean-
> ing and makes up the essential character of this act, i.e. necessarily belongs
> to each concrete act in which this same meaning is "realised."
> (*Investigation* IV, §7)

The meaning is this moment of directedness considered *in specie*.[27]
The identity of meaning from act to act and from subject to subject
is the *identity of the species*. Husserl is thus able to do justice to the

communicability of meaning through his theory of ideal contents as species of acts. If Erna understands what Hans says, then while Hans's and Erna's thoughts are numerically distinct internally complex events, they are such that, in virtue of the similarity of their matters (and therefore also of their objects), they are instances of one and the same species. When two interlocutors successfully communicate we can describe what this success consists in by appealing to this identity of species, that is, to the existence of a certain constancy or regularity in the space of mental acts of the relevant community of language-using subjects. We can talk of "the same" meaning from speaker to speaker and from occasion to occasion in virtue of the fact that numerically different individual moments of meaning in the relevant acts serve to instantiate identical species. Indeed, to assert that two individual objects or events instantiate one and the same species is simply to assert that the objects or events in question manifest among themselves a certain qualitative identity of real parts or moments – that they are, *in this or that respect*, the same.

It is important to stress that meanings as thus conceived by Husserl are not the *objects* of normal acts of language use. Meanings can however become the objects of special types of reflective act, and it is acts of this sort which form the basis (*inter alia*) of the science of logic. Logic arises when we treat those species which are meanings as special sorts of *proxy objects* (as "ideal singulars"), and investigate the properties of these objects in much the same way that the mathematician investigates the properties of numbers or geometrical figures.

VI. ACT, CONTENT, OBJECT

It is our contention that it was Husserl who first clearly developed an adequate conception of intentional content and of its psychological role in the intentional relation between act (or subject) and object of consciousness as well as of its role in linguistic reference. Only late in this century, in part as a result of developments in the newly burgeoning field of cognitive science, did philosophy of mind in the analytic tradition focus directly on intentionality as a feature of conscious acts, and only recently has it begun to draw the fundamental Husserlian distinctions among acts of consciousness, their intentional content, the objects represented or "intended" in these acts, and the states (of belief, desire, etc.) which underlie them.[28]

Acts of consciousness include experiences of perception, judgment, phantasy, desire, emotion, volition, etc. The term "act" in Husserl's technical sense means not a bodily action but a mental occurrence, not a state or disposition (or "attitude" in familiar analytic parlance) but an actual episode of perceiving, thinking, desiring or what have you. It should not be supposed however that conscious experience divides neatly into unitary act-shaped lumps; rather, the stream of consciousness is so rich and complicated that it can be parsed into acts, their parts and moments, in a variety of different ways. Phenomenology is in no small part the science of such parsings, which are already illustrated in the simple case of an act of judging of the form *S is P*. This can be parsed into constituent acts of presentation (*of S*) and predication (*that such-and-such is P*); alternatively it can be parsed into matter (*S is P*) and quality (*of judging that such and such is the case*), and so on.

The *object* of an act is whatever one is conscious of in that act. When I see that tree, the object of my visual experience is the tree; when I judge that the tide is high, the object of my judging experience is the state of affairs of the tide's being high (at a certain place and time). Clearly, objects, too, may be rich and complicated, and the object of a single act may be parsed into constituent objects in a variety of different ways on different levels. Note, too, that the object always transcends the content of any given act, in that there are always further aspects of the object which are not in any way represented within it.

Every act has a content. An act of hallucination, however, is such that there does not exist an object corresponding to the content, even though it is from the subject's point of view *as if* it has an object. Husserl occasionally talked as if, with Meinong and Twardowski, he allowed non-existent objects, so that intentionality would be a properly relational affair even in hallucination and like cases (the object of Macbeth's vision would be a non-existent dagger). In his more careful moments, however, Husserl talked as if in hallucination there is no object, and in that case intentionality would be an adverbial affair in the sense of our earlier terminology (it would pertain exclusively to special features of act and content), even if one that is otherwise in many ways like the standard case.

From the time of the second edition of the *Logical Investigations* (1913) Husserl's theory also includes as an extra element the subject or *ego* ("I") of an act, i.e., the individual who performs or experiences the act. Thus, on Husserl's modified theory, the intentionality of an act of consciousness consists in an intentional nexus whose terms are ego, act, content, and (in veridical cases) object. Specifically, the ego or act "intends" the object prescribed by the act's content. More precisely, the ego experiences or lives through the act, the act has a certain content, the content directs us to a certain object (if such exists), and the object of the act is that towards which we are directed in the act.

VII. THEORIES OF THE NOEMA

This basic Husserlian view, with these fundamentals, was laid out in the *Logical Investigations*, and on the above points commentators widely agree. There is divergence, however, on how to interpret the notion of content which Husserl introduced in lectures on the theory of meaning in 1908[29] and developed in *Ideas* I (1913). Husserl here revised his theory of intentional content, renaming the content of an intentional act its *noema*, bringing the terminology back to a Greek usage occasionally employed by Aristotle.

As we saw, Husserl distinguished in the *Investigations* between "real" and "ideal" content: the real content of an act is a temporal part or moment of the act, and the ideal content is the corresponding species. (Analytic philosophers today, following Quine, would say that species are "abstract" entities, but Husserl used "abstract," in accordance with an older usage, for what cannot exist in separation except in the weak sense that it can be *abstracted* in thought, viz., a *moment*, which Husserl defined as a dependent or "abstract" part of the object, a part which is of such a nature that it cannot exist apart from the relevant whole.[30]) For the real content of an act Husserl introduced in *Ideas* I the term *noesis* or *noetic moment*. The noesis is then correlated with what is now called the intentional content or *noema* of the act, and intentionality is seen as consisting in this "noetic-noematic correlation."

Husserl called the act's noema a meaning or *sense* (*Sinn*) and characterized it as "the object as intended" as opposed to the object *simpliciter*. The noema too is an ideal entity, but distinct from a species (indeed Husserl recognizes also species of noemata and noeses at lower and higher levels of generality: see *Ideas* I, §128).

Different models of intentionality have emerged in light of differing interpretations and reconstructions of Husserl's theory of the noema of an act. These include (1) the neo-phenomenalist model, developed by Aron Gurwitsch and others in Germany and later in New York at the New School for Social Research; (2) the intentional object model, developed by the Polish philosopher Roman Ingarden; (3) the content-as-sense model, developed by the California school of Dagfinn Føllesdal, Hubert Dreyfus, Ronald McIntyre, Izchak Miller, and David Smith; and (4) the aspect model, developed by Robert Sokolowski, John Drummond, and others on the East Coast of the United States. Finally we might mention (5) the Aristotelian model (referred to already above), which is defended by those, such as Kevin Mulligan, Barry Smith, and Dallas Willard, who have remained loyal to the original account of intentionality that is presented in the first edition of the *Logical Investigations*.

Gurwitsch's neo-phenomenalist model assimilates object to content of consciousness. For Gurwitsch (1967), the noema or intentional content of an act of perception is a perceptual *appearance* of the object perceived, and the object itself is a complex of such appearances, the ideal limit-totality of all possible appearances of the same object. (For other kinds of experience, noemata are non-sensory, "conceptual" appearances.) The object, on this view, is a complex of noemata, and so an act's noema is a *part* of its object. The view thus bears some similarity to Berkeley's idealism (with Gestalt-theoretical admixtures), but it differs importantly in that objects are bundles of noemata (the descendants of Husserl's *ideal* contents), not bundles of sensations, sense data, or other kinds of mental events or event-constituents. The relation of act to noema is one of correlation: to every difference on the side of the real object-directed components of the act there corresponds a difference in the ("ideal") noema. (See *Ideas* I, §128.) The relation of noema to object, on the other hand, is one of part to whole; the intentional relation of act to object is then the composition of these two relations.

The aspect model of Sokolowski, Drummond, and others starts out from a realist view according to which the object of the act is what it is independently of our cognitive relations to it. This object is in any given act however always intended *as* such-and-such. In

Husserl's example, I think of Napoleon as the vanquished at Waterloo rather than as the victor at Jena. Since the same object can be intended in different ways, the object is an "identity" in a "manifold" of ways in which it can be intended. The noema of the act, on this view, is the *object as intended* in the act, and this is something distinguished from the object itself. This much concurs with Gurwitsch. However, on the aspect model, the object-as-intended is seen as an abstract of the real transcendent object, it is the object abstractly considered, something that is capable of being isolated only in a special "phenomenological" or "transcendental" attitude. We might then exploit Husserl's ontology of part, whole, and dependence in order to generate a realist interpretation of the *aspect* theory according to which the noema would prove to be a dependent part of the real transcendent object (for example a visible surface). The intentional relation would then hold between the act and a certain real transcendent moment of the object.[31]

The sense-content model of the California school does not assimilate noema to object or object to noema.[32] Rather, an act's noema is seen as a type of meaning or sense, distinct in kind both from the act and its parts and moments and from the object and its parts and moments. A noema is an abstract (which is to say "ideal") entity, like a concept or a Bolzanian proposition in itself. Thus, it can be shared as the common content of different acts on the part of different subjects. A noema is formed from a sense or content together with a certain "thetic" character (earlier called "act quality") such as that of imagining, perceiving, judging, etc. The role of an act's noema is then to prescribe which object can satisfy the given act in something like the sense of satisfaction that is familiar from logical semantics.[33]

Every act has a noema and is thus intentional. In cases like hallucination, according to the Californian model, the act has a noema but there is no object that satisfies the noema, so the act has no object. In standard cases of veridical experience, however, where the act's noema is satisfied by a single object, then this is the object of the act. Thus, when I see a tree, the object of my act is a certain material object. This same object can be intended in many different ways, through different noemata. But the object itself is categorially distinct from the noemata through which it is intended. The intentional relation between act and object is mediated by a noema. The relation between act and noema is again one of correlation, while the relation between a noema and its object is the semantic relation of a sense prescribing or being satisfied by an object, and the relation of act to object is the composition of these two relations. This model assumes a form of realism, since material objects are independent of mind: they are not composed of either mental acts or their contents. This is combined, however, with a Platonism in regard to meanings in the manner of Frege or Bolzano. It was Føllesdal's idea to describe intentionality on the noemata theory by stressing the analogy with linguistic reference, especially as this was conceived in Frege's model, where reference is effected *via* sense as this is standardly understood by analytic philosophers. Thus, the sense of an expression such as "the President of the United States" determines a referent, viz., whoever happens to serve currently in the mentioned office. An act of consciousness intends whatever is determined by its sense, much as a linguistic expression refers to what its sense determines on the Fregean model. This so-called Fregean model of intentionality has misled some into thinking that linguistic reference is supposed on the given account to be more fundamental than intentional reference. Philosophers such as the later Wittgenstein, Sellars, and Dummett have indeed argued that language is more fundamental in this sense.[34] As we saw, however, Husserl had worked out already in his *Logical Investigations* an account of linguistic reference as founded on intentional acts of consciousness and the account of linguistic reference there spelled out remains valid, in essence, within the new framework of the *Ideas*. As more recently for Chisholm (1984) and Searle (1983), so also for Husserl in all the phases of his thinking, the philosophy of language is subsumed under the philosophy of mind and intentionality. Husserl saw correctly that speech acts and related phenomena borrow their referential power from the intentionality of underlying acts of thought.

The meaning-content model of intentionality is extended by the Husserlian notion of an act's "horizon."[35] Associated with each act of consciousness is a *horizon* of possible further experiences of the same object. The noemata of these further acts are compatible in sense-content with the noema of the given act. These horizon noemata prescribe further properties or "determinations" of the object, say that it has four legs, is made of wood, etc., in addition to those delineated in the act with which one starts. An act's horizon thus maps out an array of possible states of affairs that fill in what is left "open" or "indeterminate" by the noema of the act itself. In this way Husserlian horizon-analysis can be seen as anticipating the analysis of meaning in terms of possible world semantics developed by Saul Kripke, Jaakko Hintikka, and others in the 1950s and 1960s and inspired in part by Rudolf Carnap's method of state descriptions.[36]

As should by now be clear, the theory of intentionality must account for the existence and structure of non-veridical acts, or, in other words, for the fact that we can, for example, imagine things that do not exist or radically misconceive things which do exist. The features of such acts can be accounted for either by assuming intentional contents distinct from the objects they present (there is content but no object of imagination – the subject is merely deluded into thinking that there is such an object), or by assuming appropriate "intentional objects" *sui generis*. Husserl sometimes spoke interchangeably of intentional objects and intentional contents. However, the Polish phenomenologist Roman Ingarden, a student of Husserl and defender of what he saw as the latter's early realism, developed an ontology of intentionality that embraces both these notions while clearly distinguishing them from each other and from the real transcendent object in the world.[37] Real objects, from Ingarden's point of view, exist "autonomously," which is to say independently of mind. But there are also objects which exist "purely intentionally," which is to say in such a way that their existence is dependent upon acts of consciousness. An object represented in a work of art, for instance, exists only in virtue of certain acts of imagination. An act of veridical perception, in contrast, has an object that is an intentional object only *per accidens* since it enjoys an autonomous existence in its own right.

The Aristotelian theory of intentionality, finally, would rest content with the *Logical Investigations* notion of content as act-species. On this theory, mental acts are seen as internally complex events occurring in time, whose parts and moments instantiate species (in the sense of our discussion above). This holds in particular of those acts in which expressions acquire meanings, which are in Husserl's eyes those acts which do the job of supplying *objects* for the expressions in question. These objects are things, events, processes, etc., in the case of nominal expressions, states of affairs in the case of judgments.

On the species theory, as we saw, if Erna understands what Hans says, then this is because Hans's and Erna's thoughts are instances of the same species (at some level of generality), a fact which is itself to be understood in terms of certain kinds of constancy (similarity of parts) in the space of mental acts. On the noema theory as this is conceived on the mediating sense model, in contrast, we are dealing not with constancy amidst real variation, but with abstract meaning-entities outside space and time. Hans succeeds in communicating with Erna, on this account, because the meaning of his utterance, a certain abstract entity becomes the meaning of Erna's act of registering this utterance. It is as if the noemata are stars in an abstract heaven through which our successive acts, and even the successive acts of distinct subjects, may be identically directed. Proponents of the Aristotelian theory are thus able to give an account of the relation between act and meaning that is simpler and more realistic than that offered by proponents of competing theories. The latter, however, can argue that the simpler ontology of the Aristotelian theory is not up to the task of accounting for intentionality in all its richness and divergation.

VIII. ONTOLOGY

Husserl's accounts of intentionality in the *Logical Investigations* and *Ideas* say a great deal about the structure of intentional relations – among ego, act, content, and object – and about the entities so related. As we saw, the intentional relation can be of variable number of terms: in veridical perception, for instance, the intentional relation connects ego, act, and content to object, but in hallucination the intentional relation connects ego, act, and content, but there is no object. As we also saw, Husserl's early phenomenology was allied with a detailed ontology, including especially an ontology of part, whole, and dependence. An act of consciousness, for instance, is not a simple entity: it is a whole with structural parts, and it and its parts may stand in dependence relations to other acts and their parts. We now turn to Husserl's contributions to ontology itself, which has been reconstructed, using formal techniques of the sort employed by analytic philosophy, by Kit Fine, Jean Petitot, Peter Simons, Barry Smith, and others.[38]

Husserl's works include lengthy treatments of universals, categories, meanings, numbers, manifolds, etc. from an ontological perspective. Here, however, we shall concentrate almost exclusively on the *Logical Investigations*, which contain in a clear form the ontological ideas which provided the terminological and theoretical basis both for much of the detailed phenomenological description and for many of the metaphysical theses presented in Husserl's later works.

The ontology of the *Logical Investigations* is of interest first of all because of its clear conception of a *formal* discipline of ontology analogous to formal logic. (Here Husserl's thinking parallels Meinong's development of ontology as a general "theory of objects.") Formal disciplines are set apart from "regional" or "material" disciplines in that they apply to all domains of objects whatsoever, so that they are independent of the peculiarities of any given field of knowledge.

Logic, as Husserl sees it, is concerned in the first place with meanings (propositions, concepts) and with associated meaning-instantiating acts. Most importantly, it is concerned with that sort of deductively closed collection of *meanings* which constitutes a scientific theory. For Husserl, as for Bolzano, logic is a theory of science. Only where we have an appropriate unity and organisation also on the side of the *objects* (states of affairs, properties) to which the relevant acts refer, however, will we have a scientific theory, so that the unity which is characteristic of the latter must involve both (1) an *interconnection of truths* (or of propositional meanings in general), and (2) an *interconnection of the things* to which these truths (and the associated cognitive acts) are directed.

Where formal logic relates in the first place to meaning categories such as *proposition, concept, subject* and *predicate*, its sister discipline of formal ontology relates to object categories such as *object* and *property*, *relation* and *relatum*, *manifold*, *part*, *whole*, *state of affairs*, *existence* and so on. Logic in a broader sense therefore seeks to delimit the concepts which belong to the idea of a unity of theory in relation to both meanings and objects, and the truths of logic are all the necessary truths relating to those categories of constituents, on the side of both meanings and objects, from out of which science as such is necessarily constituted (including what we might think of as bridge-categories such as *identity* and *truth* which span the division between meanings and objects).

Husserl's conception of the science of logic is not an arbitrary one.

For formal-ontological concepts are like the concepts of formal logic in forming complex structures in non-arbitrary, law-governed ("recursive") ways. And because they are independent of any peculiar material of knowledge, we are able to grasp the properties of the given structures in such a way as to establish *in one go* the properties of all formally similar structures.

As Husserl himself points out, certain branches of mathematics are partial realizations of the idea of a formal ontology in this sense. The mathematical theory of manifolds as set forth by Riemann and developed by Grassmann, Hamilton, Lie, and Cantor, was to be a science of the essential types of possible object-domains of scientific theories, so that all actual object-domains would be specializations or singularizations of certain manifold-forms. And then:

If the relevant formal theory has actually been worked out in the theory of manifolds, then all deductive theoretical work in the building up of all actual theories of the same form has been done.   (Prolegomena, §70)

That is to say, once we have worked out the laws governing mathematical manifolds of a certain sort, our results can be applied – by a process of "specialization" – to every individual manifold sharing this same form.

In addition to formal ontology, then, we have also specialized material or regional ontologies which apply to objects of different special kinds. There are material concepts of a dog, of an electron, of a colour (or of this dog, of dogs in general, of electrons in general), and so on. These concepts serve as basis for the reverse process of formalization, whereby we move to the purely formal level of: *a something, this something, something in general,* and so on, by allowing materially determinate concepts to become mere place-holders for any concepts whatsoever.

The twinned operations of formalization and specialization reflect two distinct sorts of organization on the side of reality itself: material organization, on the one hand, which is studied by the special sciences, and formal organizations, on the other, which is what all objects and object-regions have in common and which is studied by formal ontology. Formal organization involves, above all, relations of part to whole and of dependence. It was Husserl who was the first to recognize that the given notions are capable of being applied, in principle, to all varieties of objects, that the proper place for the distinction between dependence and independence is in a "pure (a priori) theory of objects as such" "in the framework of a priori formal ontology."[39]

The notion of dependence can be set forth, very roughly, in terms of the following definition:

a is dependent on b =: a is as a matter of necessity such that it cannot exist unless b exists.

It is not however individuals as such that are dependent or independent, but individuals *qua* instances of certain species. The notions of dependence and independence can therefore be carried over to the species themselves "which can, in a corresponding and somewhat altered sense, be spoken of as 'independent' and 'dependent' " (*Investigation* III, §7a).

On the basis of this simple notion of dependence a whole family of other, associated notions can be defined. Thus, we can distinguish between one-sided and reciprocal dependence, between mediate and immediate dependence, and between the case where an individual is linked by dependence to one and to a multiplicity of founding objects in a range of different ways. The resulting theory has a number of interesting mathematical properties, and it can be compared with an extension of standard whole-part theory obtained by adding notions of connectedness derived from topology. The formal ideas on which it rests have been applied with some success not only in psychology but also in linguistics. Perhaps the most interesting employment of the theory however – if only in view of the almost total neglect of this fact by Husserl's commentators – was by Husserl himself within the discipline of phenomenology. The detailed descriptions of the structures of acts which are provided by Husserl are remarkably often phrased in the terminology of the theory of dependence or foundation, and something similar applies, as we shall see, to Husserl's ideas in epistemology.

We note, first of all, that the theory of dependence, because it relates primarily to species or to individuals *qua* instances of species, is a matter of ideal and therefore necessary laws:

It is not a peculiarity of certain sorts of parts that they should only be parts in general, while it would remain quite indifferent what conglomerates with them, and into what sorts of contexts they are fitted. Rather there obtain firmly determined relations of necessity, *contentually* determinate laws which vary with the species of dependent contents and accordingly prescribe one sort of completion to one of them another sort of completion to another.

                                                            (*Investigation* III, §10)

It is in terms of the theory of dependence that the idea of unity is to be clarified. Every instance of unity – the unity of a sentence, of a thought, of a pattern, even of a material object or of a person – is based, Husserl tells us, on a necessary law asserting, on the level of species, certain relations of dependence and compatibility between the unified parts. Compatibility, too, a sister notion of dependency, pertains not to individuals as such but always to instances of species. Thus the fact that individual instances of redness and roundness may be unified together in a single whole implies that there is a complex species, a form of combination, which can be seen to be capable of being re-instantiated also in other wholes. This complex species is the foundation of the relevant compatibility, which obtains whether empirical union ever occurs or not; or rather, to say that compatibility obtains, is just to say that the corresponding complex species exists. Redness and roundness are compatible in a way that redness and greenness are not. This is why nothing (as one says) can be red and green all over, and Husserl's ontological theory of *a priori* necessity has its origin at this point.

Dependence is at work also in Husserl's account of the structures of acts. Thus act-quality and act-matter (thetic character and noematic sense) are two mutually dependent moments of the act: it is a matter of necessity that each cannot exist without the other. Just as the act-matter is unthinkable without some quality, so each act-quality is unthinkable "as cut free from all matter." "Or should we perhaps hold as possible an experience which would be judgment-quality but not judgment of a determinate matter? The judgment would thereby after all lose the character of an intentional experience, which has been evidently ascribed as essential to it."[40]

IX. EPISTEMOLOGY

Husserl's concern with the theory of knowledge is evident at every stage in his career. In the Prolegomena to the *Logical Investigations*, he defended the objectivity of knowledge in logic and mathematics, and by implication in other domains as well, against the prevailing, subjectivizing program of psychologism. Husserl argued that objective norms of reason are necessary for genuine knowledge – objective norms which science as such, including the science of psychology, must presuppose. Moreover he argued that such norms themselves presuppose certain theoretical truths about knowledge, reason, validity, consistency, and so on, for

[e]very normative proposition of, e.g., the form "An A should be B" implies the theoretical proposition "Only an A which is B has the properties C," in which "C" serves to indicate the constitutive content of the standard-setting predicate "good" (e.g., pleasure, knowledge, whatever, in short, is distinguished as good by the valuation fundamental to our given sphere).

(Prolegomena, §16)

In the three books of the *Ideas*, Husserl argued that to every domain of objects there is correlated a form of "intuition" (*Anschauung*) through which we come to know the given objects in the most adequate achievable way. Objects in nature are known through perception, acts of consciousness are known through phenomenological reflection, values are known through emotions, other people's experiences are known through empathy,[41] ideal species or essences are known through "eidetic variation," and so on. Knowledge about objects in each of the given domains proceeds, Husserl argues, by comparing corresponding intuitive observations and framing more theoretical judgments about what is known, and in principle going back and revising the initial observations. This is quite a natural account of human knowledge, weaving together strands of both empiricism (knowledge begins with observation) and rationalism (knowledge is guided by reason) in a quasi-Kantian synthesis (knowledge centrally involves putting objects under ideal species via conceptual structures of certain sorts).

Husserl's model of knowledge formation is essentially the same as that recounted later, with an eye to science, by Quine.[42] What is unusual in Husserl's scheme, however, is his doctrine of the different varieties of intuition corresponding to the different regions of objects. Most philosophers in the late twentieth century dismiss the idea that there might be faculties of "intuition" beyond the familiar and fallible modes of sensory perception. When the details of

Husserl's account of intuition emerge, however, these kinds of intuition appear less suspicious than they may at first have seemed. For these are in Husserl's eyes merely components of everyday experience. The philosopher's mistake, from Plato on, has been to claim greater evidence from them, and a more exalted status than experience warrants. Husserl's phenomenology of the kinds of evidence already available in everyday experience is thus the cornerstone of his theory of knowledge.

Recent philosophers have sought to amend the Platonic definition of knowledge as justified true belief. Some modify this definition by adding conditions of causal genesis, defeasibility, or even relativity to a scientific paradigm; others seek norms of justification in the fluctuating methods of the community or group; and neo-pragmatists reduce truth to a mere methodological ideal. Quine's model – dubbed the web of belief – puts off the ultimate questions of truth and justification, conceiving our system of knowledge-claims instead as a system of beliefs that posit various entities, organize observations about them, form hypotheses and theories about them, draw inferences from observations by more or less well defined canons of inference (logic), assess observations and hypotheses (in regard to consistency, simplicity, etc.), and thereby form judgments or beliefs (dispositions to assent or to judge), all of which are indefinitely revisable in light of further evidence and further theorizing. Husserl's theory of knowledge is like this.

The theory is discernible from the *Logical Investigations* to *Ideas* I to the posthumous *Experience and Judgment*. The sixth of the *Logical Investigations* contains an elaborate account of the ways in which intuitively empty ("signitive") intentions may be to greater or lesser degree "fulfilled" in different sorts of intuitive experience. Since total fulfillment, or complete evidence, is unattainable for the objects given in perception, perceptual experience is always in this sense partial and revisable.

In the closing chapters of *Ideas* I, Husserl pursues the phenomenology of "theoretical reason": reason begins with "seeing" acts (§136), allows for different kinds of self-evidence (§137), and forms the ideal of a perfectly adequate consciousness of any object (§142). But at the same time Husserl stresses that this perfect adequacy is unattainable for objects in the natural world (§143). In *Experience and Judgment* he holds that a "predicative" act of judging that this is an apple tree rests on a "pre-predicative" experience of seeing the tree: the judgment not only gets its evidence from the perceptual experience, but depends *ontologically* on it, as the judging act rides piggyback on the perceptual act.

It is in the *Cartesian Meditations*, however, that Husserl presents his most focussed account of the central properties of "evidence." Evidence is defined as "an 'experiencing' . . . of something itself" (§5), that is, an intuitive or (self-) evident form of experience. This is what he often calls "intuition" throughout his writings, what in *Ideas* I (§§1, 138) he characterized as "originally giving" experience. (It is also what Bertrand Russell called "acquaintance.") In the *Meditations* (§6) Husserl distinguishes three grades of evidence. An evident experience is "certain" if, in having the experience, one does not doubt the existence of the object or state of affairs posited in the experience. This kind of certainty is found in every intuitive experience; in everyday perception, for instance, one normally posits the existence of what one sees, in a way that doubt simply does not arise (though it could arise in special circumstances). An "apodictic" evidence, however, would be a case of *perfect* evidence in which the object or state of affairs presented is given with "absolute indubitability" – its nonbeing is "absolutely unimaginable." Perhaps, as Descartes held, one's own consciousness is experienced with this kind of apodicticity. An "adequate" evidence, by contrast, is an ideal of *complete* evidence in which there are no "unfulfilled" components of meaning or intending. Sensory perception, again, is inadequate in this sense, since the table one sees is given with a back side whose color is not given in fulfilled manner in sensation – one does not "see" the color of the back side even though the content of perception requires the table to have a back side.

Husserl thus recognizes various kinds of intuition: sensory perception, phenomenological reflection, empathy, and eidetic intuition. But what grades of evidence do they each have? The answers are not simple, and Husserl changed his views in the course of time.[43] Perception is normally certain but never apodictic and never adequate. Eidetic intuition of essences is neither adequate nor apodictic, except for the very simplest sorts of cases, as found for example in geometry. In *Ideas* I (§153) Husserl allows that the essence of a material thing (a plant or animal) always leaves open possibilities for further exploration, so the corresponding intuitions and judgments are inadequate and thus nonapodictic. Phenomenological reflection – introspection, if you will – is certain and, Husserl seems to think in *Cartesian Meditations*, both apodictic (one cannot imagine the nonbeing of one's current experience) and adequate (there are no "hidden sides" of one's experience). However, the earlier *Ideas* II and the posthumous *Crisis* complicate his account of phenomenological reflection *vis-à-vis* our lifeworld experience of our own acts of consciousness, since our experiences may be viewed as "pure" acts-of-consciousness (intentional experiences), as part of the "natural" world (brain events), or as part of the "human" world (cultural practices).[44] Empathy with another's experience may be rather uncertain (she looks sad, but perhaps . . .); and surely it is neither apodictic nor adequate. However, our evidence concerning the intersubjective, social world – from others' experiences to collective actions – is made stronger by the ways in which our other-related experiences coalesce so as to present a coherent public world.

While Husserl analyzed grades of evidence in our knowledge of the world around us and of our own consciousness, his program was nothing like that of Descartes. Even his *Cartesian Meditations* did not seek foundations of knowledge in the absolute certainty of the cogito. For one thing, his practice of phenomenology showed that whatever apodicticity might seem to be present in reflection on experience, all phenomenological analyses of structures of experience are in principle revisable. Furthermore, as his own *Meditations* progress, there is nothing like Descartes' process of building up one's knowledge of first one's own ego, then God and then nature, and finally other egos, via a process of reasoning that would be immune from all possible doubt even under the hypothesis of an evil demon in control of one's mind. By the time we reach the last of Husserl's *Meditations*, on how we experience other egos, it has become clear that there are different grades of evidence in different kinds of knowledge. Moreover, the guiding theme of the *Cartesian Meditations* is not the quest for absolute certainty, but the working out of a phenomenology of one's experience of one's self or ego (which has many aspects: transcendental, bodily, psychological, human), of the natural world around one, and of other human beings and their egos. The driving issue is how we experience these things, and evidence in its different modes is one element in these different forms of consciousness. Intuitions, for Husserl, are revisable: it is not they which might serve as the indubitable bedrock of a foundationalist edifice. A perception in which a material thing is given intuitively with certain properties is neither adequate nor apodictic and can later be "cancelled" on the basis of further perceptions. Revisability is a characteristic feature, too, of Husserl's notion of horizon, which is built centrally around the idea that a thing can be given in further perceptions which may or may not agree with the initial perception.[45]

Husserl's ontology of dependence relations complicates the question of foundationalism even further. Husserl's notion of dependence or foundation is an ontological, not an epistemological notion: as we saw, one thing is founded or dependent on another if the former cannot – as a matter of necessity – exist unless the latter exists. Husserl uses the notion of founding in phenomenological analyses and thus, where evidence is concerned, in epistemological analyses. In *Experience and Judgment* he distinguishes "predicative" acts of judging *that S is P* from "pre-predicative" acts of perceiving *S as P*. The predicative judgment is ontologically founded on the pre-predicative perception. It also draws its evidence, presumably, from the perception on which it is so founded, but this epistemic dependence is different from the relation of ontological foundation. Still, epistemological foundationalism and the theory of ontological foundation interact in Husserl's account, in the sixth of the *Logical Investigations*, of the way higher-level acts of eidetic intuition are founded on the lower-level acts in which, for example, sense-data are experienced.[46]

Finally, we should note that Husserl's theory of knowledge also ties into his metaphysics, from his early realism to his later transcendental idealism. If there is a world independent of consciousness, then knowledge of it is a matter of "truth-making" relations between what is known and our judgments thereof. But if the world is dependent on consciousness, as one version of transcendental idealism has it, then knowledge ultimately consists in just the evidential relations of corroboration among intuitive experience and higher levels of judgment. Indeed, these patterns of corroboration, characteristic of Husserl's analysis of the notion of horizon, obtain whether realism or idealism prevails. The former aspect of Husserl's philosophy has been emphasized by phenomenological realists such as Adolf Reinach, Roman Ingarden, Dagfinn Føllesdal, Dallas Willard, and the authors of this "Introduction." It is the latter aspect which has been stressed in the work of French phenomenologists such as Sartre, Merleau-Ponty, and Ricoeur, and in the United States, above all in the work of Aron Gurwitsch and his followers.

As one sees, the literature on Husserl, and on these competing extrapolations of his views, has reached a point of near unsurveyability. It is hoped that the essays here collected will provide the English-language reader with a first preliminary guide to further exploration.

REFERENCES

Angelelli, Ignacio. 1967. *Studies on Gottlob Frege and Traditional Philosophy*. Dordrecht: Reidel.

Bell, David. 1990. *Husserl* (The Arguments of the Philosophers Series). London: Routledge and Kegan Paul.

Bolzano, Bernard. 1837. *Wissenschaftslehre*, 4 vols. Sulzbach: Seidel. English translation *Theory of Science*, by R. George. Oxford: Blackwell, 1972.

Brentano, Franz. 1874. *Psychologie vom empirischen Standpunkt*, 1st edition. Leipzig: Duncker and Humblot. Reprinted as Vol. I of 2nd edition. Leipzig: Meiner, 1924. English translation of second German edition *Psychology from an Empirical Standpoint* by A. C. Rancurello, D. B. Terrell, and L. L. McAlister. London: Routledge and Kegan Paul, 1974.

Carnap, Rudolf. 1967. *The Logical Structure of the World and Pseudoproblems in Philosophy*. Translated by R. A. George. London: Routledge and Kegan Paul.

Chisholm, Roderick M. 1967. "Intentionality." In *The Encyclopedia of Philosophy*. Edited by Paul Edwards. New York: Macmillan, Vol. 4: 201–204.

———. 1984. "The Primacy of the Intentional." *Synthese* 61: 89–109.

Cobb-Stevens, Richard. 1990. *Husserl and Analytic Philosophy* (Phaenomenologica 116). Dordrecht/Boston/Lancaster: Kluwer.

Dreyfus, Hubert L., ed. 1982. *Husserl, Intentionality and Cognitive Science*. Cambridge: MIT Press.

Drummond, John. 1990. *Husserlian Intentionality and Non-Foundational Realism: Noema and Object*. Dordrecht/Boston/London: Kluwer Academic Publishers.

Dummett, Michael. 1993. *Origins of Analytical Philosophy*. Harvard: Harvard University Press.

Fodor, Jerry. 1975. *The Language of Thought*. New York: Thomas Y. Crowell, Co.

———. 1980. "Methodological Solipsism Considered as a Research Strategy in Cognitive Psychology." *The Behavioral and Brain Sciences* 3:1. Reprinted in Dreyfus, 1982, 277–303.

Føllesdal, Dagfinn. 1969. "Husserl's Notion of Noema." *The Journal of Philosophy* 66: 680–87. Reprinted in Dreyfus, 1982, 73–80.

———. 1979. "Husserl and Heidegger on the Role of Actions in the Constitution of the World." In E. Saarinen, et al., eds., *Essays in Honour of Jaakko Hintikka*. Dordrecht: Reidel, 365–78.

———. 1988. "Husserl on Evidence and Justification." In *Edmund Husserl and the Phenomenological Tradition. Essays in Phenomenology*. Edited by Robert Sokolowski. Washington D. C.: Catholic University of America Press, 107–29.

Frege, Gottlob. 1892. "On Sense and Reference." As translated in P. T. Geach and M. Black, eds., *Philosophical Writings of Gottlob Frege*. Oxford: Blackwell, 1970, 56–78.

Gurwitsch, Aron. 1967. "Husserl's Theory of the Intentionality of Consciousness in Historical Perspective." In *Phenomenology and Existentialism*. Edited by Edward N. Lee and Maurice Mandelbaum. Baltimore: The Johns Hopkins University Press, 25–58.

Heidegger, Martin. 1927. *Sein und Zeit*, 1st edition. Halle: Niemeyer. English translation by John Macquarrie and Edward Robinson as *Being and Time*. Blackwell: Oxford, 1962.

Hintikka, Jaakko. 1962. *Knowledge and Belief*. Ithaca: Cornell University Press.

———. 1969. "Semantics of Propositional Attitudes." In Hintikka, *Models for Modalities*. Dordrecht: D. Reidel.

———. 1975. "The Intentions of Intentionality." In Hintikka, *The Intentions of Intentionality and Other New Models for Modalities*. Dordrecht: D. Reidel.

Holenstein, Elmar. 1988. "Eine Maschine im Geist: Husserlsche Begründung und Begrenzung künstlicher Intelligenz." *Phänomenologische Forschungen* 21: 82–113.

Ingarden, Roman. 1947/48. *Spór o istnienie świata*, 2 vols. Cracow: Polska Akademia Umiejętności.

———. 1964. *Time and Modes of Being*. Translation by Helen R. Michejda of parts of Volume I of Ingarden 1947/48. Springfield: Charles C. Thomas.

———. 1964/65/73. *Der Streit um die Existenz der Welt*, extended German edition of Ingarden 1947/48, 3 vols. Tübingen: Max Niemeyer Verlag.

———. 1973. *The Literary Work of Art* (German original, 1931). Translated by George G. Grabowicz. Evanston: Northwestern University Press.

———. 1973a. *The Cognition of the Literary Work of Art* (Polish original,

1937; enlarged German edition, 1968). Translated from the German
edition by Ruth Ann Crowley and Kenneth R. Olson. Evanston: Northwestern University Press.

———. 1989. *Ontology of the Work of Art.* German original, 1961; translated by Raymond Meyer and John T. Goldthwait. Athens: Ohio
University Press.

Levin, David Michael. 1970. *Reason and Evidence in Husserl's Phenomenology.* Evanston: Northwestern University Press.

Mates, Benson. 1953. *Stoic Logic.* Berkeley: University of California Press.

Meinong, Alexius. 1904. "Theory of Objects." As translated in *Realism and
the Background of Phenomenology.* Edited by R. Chisolm. Glencoe, Ill.:
The Free Press, 1960, 76–117.

Miller, Izchak. 1984. *Husserl, Perception and Temporal Awareness.* Cambridge, Mass.: MIT Press.

Mohanty, J. N. 1982. *Husserl and Frege.* Bloomington and London: Indiana
University Press.

Mulligan, K. 1989. "Judgings: Their Parts and Counterparts." *Topoi Supplement* 2 (La Scuola di Brentano): 117–48.

Mulligan, K., ed. 1987. *Speech Act and Sachverhalt. Reinach and the Foundations of Realist Phenomenology.* The Hague: Nijhoff.

Münch, Dieter. 1990. "The Early Work of Husserl and Artificial Intelligence." *Journal of the British Society for Phenomenology* 21: 107–20.

Petitot, Jean. 1994. "Phenomenology of Perception, Qualitative Physics and
Sheaf Mereology." In *Philosophy and the Cognitive Sciences.* Edited by
Roberto Casati, Barry Smith, and Graham White. Vienna: Hölder-
Pichler-Tempsky.

Quine, W. V. O. 1991. *Pursuit of Truth.* Cambridge, Mass.: Harvard University Press.

Quine, W. V. and Joseph S. Ullian. 1978. *The Web of Belief.* New York:
Random House.

Reinach, A. 1988. *Sämtliche Werke. Kritische Ausgabe, mit Kommentar,* 2
vols. Edited by Karl Schuhmann and Barry Smith. Munich and Vienna:
Philosophia.

Rorty, Amelie and Martha Nussbaum, eds. 1991. *Aristotle's De Anima.*
Oxford: Oxford University Press.

Rorty, Richard. 1979. *Philosophy and the Mirror of Nature.* Princeton:
Princeton University Press.

Sartre, Jean-Paul. 1936/37. "La transcendance de l'égo: Esquisse d'une description phénoménologique." *Récherches philosophiques* 6. English
translation *The Transcendence of the Ego. An Existentialist Theory of
Consciousness* by F. Williams and R. Kirkpatrick. New York: Farrar
Strauss and Giroux, 1957.

———. 1943. *L'être et le néant. Essai d'ontologie phénoménologique*. Paris: Gallimard. English translation by Hazel Barnes, *Being and Nothingness*. London: Methuen, 1957.

Schuhmann, Karl. 1977. *Husserl-Chronik*. The Hague: Martinus Nijhoff.

———. 1988. *Husserls Staatsphilosophie*. Freiburg i. Br.: Alber.

———. 1990. "Husserl's Concept of Philosophy." *Journal of the British Society for Phenomenology* 21: 274–83.

———. 1991. "Die Entwicklung der Sprechakttheorie in der Münchener Phänomenologie." *Phänomenologische Forschungen* 21: 133–66.

Searle, John. 1983. *Intentionality*. Cambridge: Cambridge University Press.

———. 1992. *The Rediscovery of the Mind*. Cambridge, Mass.: MIT Press.

Sellars, Wilfrid, and Roderick M. Chisholm. 1958. "Intentionality and the Mental." In *Concepts, Theories, and the Mind-Body Problem*. Edited by H. Feigl, M. Scriven, and G. Maxwell. Minnesota Studies in the Philosophy of Science, Minneapolis, 507–39.

Simons, P. M. 1982. "The Formalisation of Husserl's Theory of Wholes and Parts." In *Parts and Moments. Studies in Logic and Formal Ontology*. Edited by Barry Smith, 1982. Munich: Philosophia, 113–59.

Smith, Barry. 1987. "Husserl, Language and the Ontology of the Act." In *Speculative Grammar, Universal Grammar, and Philosophical Analysis of Language*. Edited by D. Buzzetti and M. Ferriani. Amsterdam: John Benjamins, 205–27.

———. 1989. "Logic and Formal Ontology." In *Husserl's Phenomenology: A Textbook*. Edited by J. N. Mohanty and W. McKenna. Lanham: University Press of America, 29–67.

———. 1990. "Towards a History of Speech Act Theory." In *Speech Acts, Meanings and Intentions. Critical Approaches to the Philosophy of John R. Searle*. Edited by A. Burkhardt. Berlin/New York: de Gruyter, 29–61.

———. 1994. *Austrian Philosophy. The Legacy of Franz Brentano*. La Salle and Chicago: Open Court.

Smith, Barry, ed. 1982. *Parts and Moments. Studies in Logic and Formal Ontology*. Munich: Philosophia.

Smith, Barry, and Kevin Mulligan. 1982. "Pieces of a Theory." In *Parts and Moments*. Edited by Barry Smith, 1982. Munich: Philosophia, 15–109.

Smith, Barry, and Kevin Mulligan. 1984. "Framework for Formal Ontology." *Topoi* 2: 73–85.

Smith, David Woodruff. 1994. "How to Husserl a Quine – and a Heidegger too." *Synthese* 98: 153–173.

Smith, David Woodruff. 1989. *The Circle of Acquaintance. Perception, Consciousness, and Empathy*. Dordrecht/Boston/London: Kluwer.

Smith, David Woodruff, and Ronald McIntyre. 1982. *Husserl and Intentionality*. Dordrecht: Reidel.

Sokolowski, Robert. 1974. *Husserlian Meditations*. Evanston: Northwestern University Press.

———. 1978. *Presence and Absence*. Bloomington: Indiana University Press.

Sorabji, Richard. 1991. "From Aristotle to Brentano: The Development of the Concept of Intentionality." *Oxford Studies in Ancient Philosophy*, Supplementary Volume 9: 227–59.

Spiegelberg, Herbert. 1967. " 'Linguistic Phenomenology': John L. Austin and Alexander Pfänder," Appendix B of Alexander Pfänder, *Phenomenology of Willing and Motivation*. Evanston: Northwestern University Press, 86–92.

Stein, Edith. 1970. *On the Problem of Empathy* (German original, 1917). Translated by Waltraut Stein. The Hague: Martinus Nijhoff.

Twardowski, Kasimir. 1977. *On the Content and Object of Presentations. A Psychological Investigation*. English translation of the first (German) edition of 1894 by Reinhardt Grossmann. The Hague: Martinus Nijhoff.

Willard, Dallas. 1984. *Logic and the Objectivity of Knowledge*. Athens, Ohio: University of Ohio Press

NOTES

1 See, for example, R. Rorty 1979 and Dreyfus 1991.

2 See, for example, Føllesdal 1979.

3 See, on these topics, Willard 1984 and Barry Smith 1987 and 1989.

4 On the rootedness of Husserl's thinking in the classical concerns of German philosophy see Schuhmann 1990. Note that this Fichtean, metaphysical foundationalist dimension of Husserl's philosophy is absent from the thinking of Heidegger.

5 The account which follows is based primarily on Schuhmann 1977.

6 See Volume XXI, p. 220, of the Husserliana series of Husserl's works, full details of which are supplied in the bibliography at the end of this volume.

7 On the Munich school, see Schuhmann 1991.

8 See Mulligan, ed., 1987 and Barry Smith 1990.

9 See Spiegelberg 1967.

10 Of the five initial editors of this *Jahrbuch*, four – Alexander Pfänder, Moritz Geiger, Max Scheler, and Adolf Reinach – which is to say all except Husserl himself, hailed from Munich.

11 On Husserl's philosophy of politics and its relation to that of Hobbes, see Schuhmann 1988.

12 On this history, see Niels W. Bokhove, *Phänomenologie. Ursprung und Entwicklung des Terminus um 18. Jahrhundert* (Utrecht: Publications of the Department of Philosophy, Utrecht University, 1991).

13 See Carnap 1967, 101f. and Fodor 1980.

14 See Holenstein 1988 and Münch 1990.

15 See *Ideas* I, §§27ff.

16 David Smith and Ronald McIntyre 1982 distinguish "object" and "content" approaches. Here we employ a slightly broader terminology.

17 See pp. 88f. of the English translation. For a detailed discussion of this passage see Barry Smith 1994, especially Chapter 2.

18 See, e.g., *Logical Investigations* IV, §14 and VI, §§30–35 and the discussion of *Logical Investigations* V, §11 in the essay by Mulligan in this volume.

19 Since language can be used to express thoughts, there is a related problem in the theory of linguistic reference. See, e.g., *Logical Investigations* I, §15.

20 Compare Sorabji 1991, who stresses the revisions of the concept of intentionality introduced by interpreters of Aristotle from the ancient philosophers, neoplatonists, Arabic writers, and Medievals to Brentano. The variant interpretations assume the outlines of rather different theories of intentionality, stressing material process, mental process, mental content, intentional object, etc. Controversies about Aristotle's conception of intentionality may be followed in the Rorty and Nussbaum edition of Aristotle's *De Anima*.

21 See Benson Mates. 1953, *Stoic Logic*, Chapter II, which includes a detailed comparison of the original Stoic notions with Frege's ideas.

22 Husserl distinguishes also a third component called "sensory" or "intuitive" representational content, later called *hyletic data*. See §25 of the sixth *Logical Investigation*, and also *Ideas* I, §85.

23 Strictly speaking each Husserlian ideal content is a hierarchy of species at lower and higher levels of generality, from *infima species* at the bottom to highest genus (or "category") at the top. On this, Aristotelian aspect of Husserl's theory, whose presence in the *Logical Investigations* is to some extent obscured through terminological changes in the second edition, see Barry Smith 1987.

24 See Willard 1984.

25 It was in the criticism of this aspect of Husserl's doctrine of meaning acts that his Munich followers were led to develop their theories of speech acts, which recognized that there are ways in which expressions

can acquire meaning other than through reference to an object. See, on this, §§3–4 of Barry Smith 1990.

26 *Logical Investigations* I, §15. The German reads: "einen Ausdruck mit Sinn gebrauchen und sich ausdrückend auf den Gegenstand beziehen (den Gegenstand vorstellen) ist einerlei."

27 Cf. *Investigation* III, Introduction. This is a simplified version of the doctrine not least in that it does not take account of the fact that an act of meaning involves both a token matter and a token quality (it is either a judgment, an expression of doubt, a surmise, and so on).

28 In the 1950s, Wilfrid Sellars and Roderick Chisholm drew attention to intentional mental states, Chisholm proposing linguistic or logical criteria of the intentional (1967). In the 1960s Jaakko Hintikka developed the logic of intentional states as a branch of modal logic using tools derived from the semantics of possible worlds: see Hintikka 1962 and 1969. Also in the 1960s Dagfinn Føllesdal proposed a reading of Husserl's theory of intentionality in terms suggested by Frege's theory of the way in which reference is effected via sense or meaning: see his "Husserl's Notion of Noema" and related essays in Dreyfus, ed., 1982. Finally, John Searle argued a broadly Husserlian view of consciousness in his 1983 and 1992.

29 See *Husserliana*, Volume XXVI.

30 See *Investigation* VI, §17.

31 In his 1990 work, Drummond sets out a clear account of the opposition between the Gurwitsch and Fregean/Californian models of the noema and the Sokolowski-Drummond model. Drummond does not, however, use Husserl's theory of dependence relations in formulating his account of the aspect-model.

32 See again the collection edited by Dreyfus, 1982, which includes Dagfinn Føllesdal's seminal essay of 1969, David Smith and Ronald McIntyre 1982, and Izchak Miller 1984. For criticisms see Drummond 1990 and Bell 1990.

33 A general concept such as *horse* is satisfied by many objects, where an individual concept such as *Duns Scotus* is satisfied by at most one; a perceptual content such as *that horse (visually presented to me now)* is satisfied by at most one object. See David Smith 1989 for a detailed discussion of this issue.

34 See, for example, Chapters 2 and 13 of Dummett 1993: language is an intrinsically social phenomenon from the Wittgensteinian perspective embraced by Dummett.

35 See the discussion of this notion in Chapters Vff. of David Smith and Ronald McIntyre 1982.

36 In the possible-worlds variants of Fregean semantics prominent in the
    1960s, the sense of an expression is identified as a function that assigns
    to any possible world what would be the referent of the expression in
    that world; Husserl would not have accepted this identification, but it
    has proved an instructive parallel. See Hintikka 1962, 1969, and 1975,
    and David Smith and Ronald McIntyre 1982.

37 Ingarden's renown rests primarily on his work in aesthetics and on the
    problems arising in virtue of the types of non-standard intentionality
    that predominate in the field of art. See Ingarden 1973, 1973a, and 1989.
    For Ingarden's wider ontology see the 1964 selection of extracts from
    Volume I of his *magnum opus, The Controversy over the Existence of
    the World*, originally published in Polish in 1947–48 and in an extended
    German version in 1964/65/73.

38 See Petitot 1994, the papers collected in Smith, ed., 1982, and Kit Fine's
    essay herein.

39 *Investigation* III, Introduction; *Investigation* II, §41.

40 *Investigation* V, §20. See Mulligan 1989 for more details of the internal
    structure of acts of judgment.

41 For a summary of the phenomenological account of empathy initiated
    by Husserl and developed in detail by his student Edith Stein in Stein
    1917, see David Woodruff Smith 1989.

42 See Quine and Ullian 1991. Comparisons of Husserl's epistemology
    with Quine's are found in Føllesdal 1988 and in David Woodruff Smith
    1994.

43 A study of Husserl's changing views of adequacy and apodicticity is
    found in Levin 1970.

44 See the essay "Mind and Body" by David Woodruff Smith herein.

45 Three differing views on issues of epistemological foundationalism in
    Husserl are developed in Føllesdal 1988, Cobb-Stevens 1990, and Drum-
    mond 1990.

46 See Barry Smith 1989.

1 The development of Husserl's thought

The works that Husserl published during his lifetime, and in the light of which one is accustomed to write one's account of the development of his thought, are but the tips of an iceberg. By far the larger parts of his work remained as unpublished manuscripts.[1] Now that some of these manuscripts have been published, it is possible to reconstruct a more accurate account of the development of his thought than was possible some years ago.

There is a well-known account of Husserl's thought which, in simple outlines, runs as follows: a psychologistic *Philosophy of Arithmetic* (1891), written under the influence of Brentano and Stumpf, was rejected and superseded, largely owing to Frege's severe criticism of that work; this was followed by an anti-psychologistic and realistic philosophy of logic in two volumes of the *Logical Investigations* (1900–01), which influenced the early Munich school that then gathered around Husserl in Göttingen. However, the *Logical Investigations*, according to this account, already showed interest in analysis of consciousness and presupposed a conception of phenomenology as a psychology whose task is to describe the essential structures of mental life. Thus the anti-psychologism of the *Prolegomena* quickly yielded to an overwhelming concern with the life of consciousness as the source of meanings – a concern that found its expression more than a decade later in *Ideas pertaining to a Pure Phenomenology and Phenemenological Philosophy*, Book I (1913). Phenomenology is still regarded as a rigorous science, but now as a science of the essential structures of consciousness. Combined with the method of phenomenological reduction (first introduced in the *Ideas* I) and the thesis that all objects derive their meanings from structures of consciousness (and in that sense are *constituted* in consciousness), the *Ideas* inaugurated a transcendental-phenomenological idealism. The lectures on time, although mainly preceding the *Ideas*, were published later, but served to radicalize that theory of constitution by showing how even the sensory data as well as the acts were constituted in the flow of the internal lived experience. The *Formal and transcendental Logic* (1929) extended the thesis of constitution to the structures of formal logic. *Experience and Judgment* (1939) traced the logical forms to their origin in pre-predicative experience of individual things. The *Cartesian Meditations* (1931) for the first time expounded a radical transcendental idealism by making the transcendental ego the source of all constitution. They further expanded the idea of constitution to include genetic constitution (i.e., constitution of objectivities in the historically developing experiences of the ego), expounded the process by which the sense "other ego" is constituted in the innermost experiences of the reflecting transcendental ego, and concluded with a Leibnizian sort of monadology as the condition of the possibility of objectivity in the strongest sense. The last published work, *The Crisis of the European Sciences and Transcendental Phenomenology* (1936), brought in two new themes: the idea of the life-world as the foundation of meaning for the idealizations leading up to modern physics, and a historical reflection on the genesis of meanings as a pathway to a radical transcendental philosophy. The thesis of historical genesis, combined with the ideas of "tradition" and "inheritance," also inform the essay "The Origin of Geometry" (1936). In this sweeping account, the crucial turning points occur in 1887–91, 1900–1901, 1913, and 1929–31. The major influences are in this order: Brentano-Stumpf, Bolzano-Lotze-Frege, Paul Natorp, and perhaps, ironically, Heidegger.

However, this account of the development of Husserl's thought must be rejected. First, Husserl's publications do not reflect the actual process of development of his thought. Second, the conceptualizations under the titles "psychologism," "essentialism," "transcendental idealism," or "life-world" do not do justice to the enormous complexity of the problems, motives, and theories with which Husserl was concerned. Third, the account in terms of these generalities, as well as in terms of the alleged "conversions" (from psychologism to anti-psychologism, and back again to a sort of psychologism) does not consider the continuity of his thinking (notwithstanding new insights gained along the way) and the detailed, problem-oriented nature of his concerns.

With these general remarks, I will begin by dividing my exposition into four parts:

    I. 1886–1900, the Halle period
   II. 1900–1916, the Göttingen period
  III. 1916–1928, the Freiburg teaching period
  IV. 1928–1939, the Freiburg years after retirement.

I. HALLE PERIOD, 1886–1900

1. After two years of studying with Brentano in Vienna (1884–86), Husserl went to Halle in 1886 to work with Stumpf, and eventually habilitated the next year with a work on the psychological analysis of the concept of number. This work is incorporated into his *Philosophy of Arithmetic*. In his *Selbstanzeige* of the *Philosophy of Arithmetic*, Husserl says that in that book he undertakes two tasks: an analysis of the basic concepts of arithmetic and a logical clarification of the symbolic methods used in arithmetic. The two parts of the book correspond to these two tasks.[2] In Part I, he undertakes a psychological enquiry into the concepts of plurality, unity and number, insofar as these entities, i.e., plurality, unity and number, are not given in symbolic forms. Part II considers the symbolic representations of the same entities and shows that the logical origin of general arithmetic is limited to symbolic, numerical presentations. (A symbolic representation, for Husserl, contrasts with intuitive representation. In the latter, the thing represented is itself given; in the former, the thing is represented only by a symbol.)

The underlying philosophical and methodological conceptions, derived from Brentano as well as from Husserl's own mathematics professor, Karl Weierstrass, are these: the clarification of a concept consists in determining its psychological origin; mathematics is primarily an art of calculation; arithmetic is primarily concerned with cardinal numbers. In addition to these concepts, there is an epistemological theory derived from Brentano, according to which presentations (*Vorstellungen*) are of two kinds: some are intuitive and some are merely symbolic. Of these two, sometimes called "authentic" and "inauthentic" respectively, the latter presuppose the former. Not all arithmetical thinking can be authentic, for our intuitive grasp must be limited to very small numbers. Most arithmetical thinking, and most arithmetical operations, are rather merely symbolic.

With regard to the theory that number concepts (not, to be sure, numbers themselves) have their origin in psychological processes (i.e., in acts of what Husserl calls "collective combination"), this is to be understood neither in the psychologistic sense (in which Frege understood it[3]) nor in terms of the later idea of constitution (contrary to the way a host of Husserl scholars, Becker, Biemel, and Landgrebe among them, want to interpret it[4]). It is rather Brentanian descriptive psychology, along with the Brentanian theory of part and whole developed by Stumpf, which determines Husserl's theory, since the conceptual tools of the later theory of constitution were not yet at his disposal.

The philosophy of arithmetic that is advanced by Husserl at this stage is empiricistic: although the subject-matter of arithmetic is the formal properties of aggregates formed by the mind, the foundation of arithmetical thinking lies in the concrete intuitions upon which the mind applies its activities of attention, abstraction, collective combination, and reflection. This is not to psychologise the numbers themselves, but rather to give a theory of how our presentations (intuitions and concepts) of numbers arise. Husserl was, in some respects, indecisive between conceiving numbers as objective structures or as mental creations, and he had not as yet found a satisfactory way of reconciling the subjectivity of the mental processes involved and the objectivity of numbers themselves. For this he needed a different concept of intentionality than Brentano's, and especially a different notion of the *content* of an intentional act.

Husserl had planned a second volume of *Philosophy of Arithmetic*, which was to exhibit the arithmetic of cardinal numbers as a member of an entire class of arithmetics, united by an identical algorithm. But this volume never appeared. As late as 1894, he seems to have been working on this volume.[5] Eventually, he abandoned the project, partly because he realized that a universal arithmetic could not begin with cardinal numbers,[6] partly because, under the influences of Klein and Hilbert, he moved away from an "operational" theory of mathematics towards an axiomatic theory.[7] In all his works after 1900, Husserl clearly remained within an axiomatic understanding of mathematics, and developed his own idea of a manifold (*Mannigfaltigkeit*) that is defined through an axiom-system, and – as he says much later,[8] not merely in terms of how to operate with signs. A manifold is a domain of objects which are completely determined by the forms of their interconnections, which themselves are determined by the forms of elementary laws taken to be valid of them. However, it would be too hasty to say that he totally gave up his earlier concept of mathematics in operational terms. It should also be pointed out that he developed his idea of definiteness independently of Hilbert – not, to begin with, for the purpose of founding arithmetic, but for the solution of the problem of extension of the domain of numbers.[9]

Between the *Philosophy of Arithmetic* and the *Logical Investigations* (1900–1901), Husserl continued to be concerned with philosophical questions about logical calculi, with some problems about logical semantics, with a Brentanian descriptive psychology, and finally with geometry and problems about space.

2. In the long critical review of Schröder's *Lectures on the Algebra of Logic*,[10] Husserl distinguishes between a logical calculus and logic of calculus. Schröder, on his view, develops the former, but not the latter. In other words, as Husserl understands it, Schröder's *Algebra* is a mere calculus but does not contain a theory of that calculus, i.e., a theoretical foundation for the calculatory technique. Furthermore, Husserl rejects Schröder's claim that a logical calculus can only be of classes, and himself prefers an intensional interpretation of logic: as a matter of fact, here (as in the essay "Der Folgerungskalkül und die Inhaltslogik" of the same year) Husserl claims that

Exactly in the same sense in which the so-called extensional logic is a valid theory, a "logic of ideal contents" can also be constructed with a technique which is identical with that of the former (i.e. of the extensional logic).[11]

3. The concern with logical semantics finds its expression in the 1894 essay on "Intentionale Gegenstände" as also in a review of Twardowski's *Zur Lehre von Inhalt und Gegenstand der Vorstellungen*, both of which remained unpublished until recent times.[12] The former essay takes up the problems of objectless presentations. The paradox is taken to lie in holding both that every presentation presents an object and that there are presentations (such as "round square" and "the present Emperor of France" – note that these two

are the examples cited by Husserl in 1894 long before the famous Meinong-Russell debate) for which there is no corresponding object. Following suggestions by Brentano, Twardowski solves the paradox by distinguishing between "intentional existence" and "true existence." One can then say that every presentation has an object in the sense of a merely intentionally existing object. True existence holds good only in some cases, and even there true existence presupposes intentional existence. As against this solution, Husserl questions the distinction between the merely intentional or "immanent" object and the truly existing object, and argues that objects do not divide into two classes, some of which truly exist and some of which exist merely intentionally. Lions, he maintains, are not of two kinds, some determinate (the truly existing ones) and some indeterminate. There are not two kinds of lions, but rather two kinds of presentations. The expression "an object" and "an actual, existing object" are fully equivalent. The conclusion to which Husserl is led is this: what essentially belongs to a presentation is its meaning (*Bedeutung*), while the relatedness to an object ("*gegenständliche Beziehung*") points to an interconnectedness of truths or judgments ("*Wahrheits bzw. Urteilszusammenhänge*"). The content (*Inhalt*) of a presentation is not an "immanent" object like a picture, but its meaning. Truth, as correspondence of meaning with its object, is to be understood as the coincidence (*Deckung*) of the meaning and its fulfilling intuition (when, e.g., we say "red" and "as one with it intuit the redness.")[13] It will be clear at a later stage that some of the ideas expressed here will remain permanently with Husserl. It should be noted, at this point, that in the early 1890s Husserl did not yet regard meanings as entities of a sort, but rather as functions possessed by presentations in certain judgmental contexts.[14] The refusal to distinguish between two sorts of objects – intentional and truly existing – continues in the *Logical Investigations*.[15] The underlying idea that the ontological status of the object depends upon, or rather is correlative to the type of presentation and the type of judgment, would be part of Husserl's developed thought.

4. Husserl's work on Brentanian descriptive psychology during this period is concerned with the concept of presentation (*Vorstellung*). Around 1893, Husserl regarded psychic acts, following Brentano and Stumpf, as having a content or an object. But he had not yet arrived at his later idea of intentionality. What is the center

of his attention, however, is the distinction between two kinds of presentation: intuitive and representing (a distinction which neither Brentano nor Stumpf made). Husserl still subscribes to the Brentanian belief that the content of an intuitive act is "immanent" or a real part of the act. Representing acts, e.g., which point to an object "from a distance," through another object, presuppose intuitive acts. In the former, we turn away from the contents of the acts, the contents point beyond themselves, whereas in intuitive acts the object itself is "actually present before us." The specific mode of consciousness characterizing representing acts is called by Husserl "*Meinen*"[16] or intending. It is in these texts of 1893, especially in connection with representing acts, that Husserl first arrives at the concept of intention.[17] But he goes on to say that intention is "tense interest" directed towards a content that is not given. On this matter, Husserl was influenced by Herbart.[18] It is soon afterwards, in the summer of 1894, that, in the context of his concern with Twardowski's book, he arrived at his concept of intentionality as characterizing both representing and intuitive acts.[19]

Around 1894, Husserl's thoughts about "presentation" may be stated, in a tabular form, as in the figure on the following page.

5. Husserl occupied himself with geometry from 1886 to 1903, and his lectures in Halle during the Winter Semester of 1889/90 included topics on geometry. He planned a work on space (the so-called "*Raumbuch*") and kept a diary which he named "*Tagebuch zum Raumbuch*" from 13 October 1893 onwards. In this work, apart from his studies in geometry, the ideas of Brentano and Stumpf on space, William James's theory of space perception, also works of Lipps and Lotze, determined the nature of his questioning. In the writings on space belonging to this period, Husserl distinguishes between four different concepts of space: space of everyday life, i.e., pre-scientific space, space of pure geometry, space of applied geometry, and space of metaphysics. There is a genetic order in this list; the first three lead up to the last. He also distinguishes between a logical and psychological treatment of space, the psychological being divided into a descriptive account of the *content* of the idea of space and a genetic account of the *origin* of the idea of space. Clearly, again, Brentano and Stumpf determine the very mode of Husserl's questioning.

Of these four spaces, even the pre-scientific space is not, in its totality, perceived, so that even this is an ideal entity. The space of

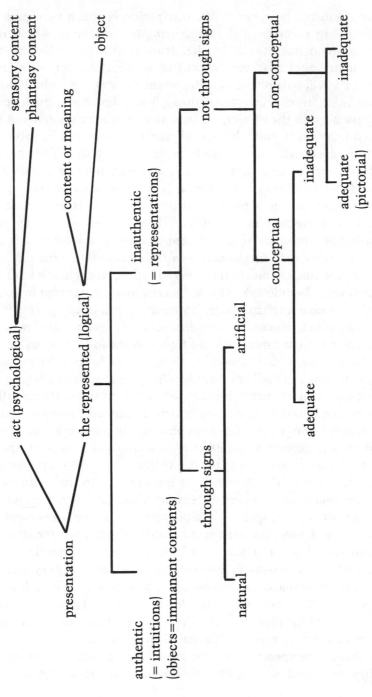

sensory content

phantasy content

act (psychological)

content or meaning

object

presentation

the represented (logical)

authentic
(= intuitions)
(objects=immanent contents)

inauthentic
(= representations)

through signs

not through signs

natural

artificial

conceptual

non-conceptual

adequate

inadequate

adequate
(pictorial)

inadequate

inadequate

52

pure geometry is a logical, conceptual structure, a product of idealization of the perceived space. Thus we have here a position which persists through all Husserl's works right up to the *Crisis*. At this point of time, i.e., early in the 1890s, he seems to have held (a) that the idealization of geometry is not arbitrary but grounded in the nature of things; (b) that the 3-dimensional Euclidean space is the only space in the strict sense; (c) that while the rest of mathematics can be completely formalized, geometry cannot – for it has an irreducibly contentual character;[20] (d) that even if a merely formal determination of the idea of manifold can yield the Euclidean manifold, the Euclidean manifold is not the concrete space; (e) that the 3-dimensionality of space cannot be logically deduced, but is rather an empirical fact; and (f) that a psychological explanation of the privileged status of 3-dimensional space is possible (in terms of the cooperation of visual and motor sensations).

Husserl's views gradually changed. In a letter to Natorp, dated 29 March 1897, he defends a purely deductive theory of geometry which has no essential need for intuition as well as the conception of geometry as a theory of pure manifold. Around 1901, again in a letter to Natorp, he advocates the legitimacy of other space concepts including the idea of *n*-dimensional space, and in a somewhat later manuscript (K I 26) notes that the space of physics is to be understood purely logically and mathematically and may be of a manifold structured differently from the manifold of pure geometry.[21]

Further developments in Husserl's thinking about space took place not in the context of geometry, but rather in the context of the problem of perception.[22]

II. GÖTTINGEN, 1900–1916

1. In 1901, Husserl moved to Göttingen. About the end of the 1890s he had developed the idea of a pure logic. What led Husserl to completely reject psychologism as a theory of logic was not the influence of Frege,[23] but rather his own changing philosophy of mathematics combined with influences of Leibniz, Bolzano and Lotze.[24] He had arrived at an axiomatic understanding of mathematics. Formal mathematics is now taken to be a part of pure logic.

In his *Selbstanzeige* of the *Prolegomena* (1900), Husserl says that he undertook two tasks in that work: first, he wanted to delimit the idea of pure logic as against the ideas of logic as an art (as a *Kunstlehre*, as Brentano had taken it to be), as a technology and as a normative science. Pure logic is rather a system of ideal laws and theories which are grounded purely in the senses of such ideal meaning categories as nominal meanings, propositional meanings, and syllogistic structures. In the second place, he undertook to refute psychologism as a theory of logic which grounds the logical laws in the psychological laws governing the human mind. In its place he propounded the thesis that the epistemological and theoretical foundations of logic lie in the very meanings of the fundamental concepts of logic.

Part II of the *Logical Investigations* consists of six separate investigations. The first, devoted to "Expression and Meaning," distinguishes, on the subjective side, between act of expression, the meaning-intending act, and the meaning-fulfilling act, and, on the object side, between their respective contents, i.e., between the expression, its meaning, and the object it refers to. The meaning is an ideal entity, a species whose instances are the particular acts intending that meaning. In the light of this thesis of the ideality of meanings, Husserl considers indexicals, whose meanings appear to vary depending on who utters them and on what occasion, and argues for the position that indexicals can in every case be replaced by "objective" expressions with ideal meanings. Investigation II defends the thesis that species are universal objects and an irreducible kind of entity, and gives a detailed examination and critique of the empiricist and nominalist theories of abstraction. The positive argument in favor of this thesis involves an appeal to the fact that apprehension of universals is a specific mode of consciousness that cannot be reduced to the modes in which particulars are apprehended. Investigation III develops a theory of whole and part; following Brentano's and Stumpf's distinction between dependent and independent contents, Husserl distinguishes between dependent and independent objects, between various concepts of parts and wholes, between various senses of dependence and independence and of separability and inseparability, between "material" laws obtaining among inseparable essences (i.e., synthetic *a priori* laws such as the law of mutual dependence which obtains between "color" and "extension") and formal-analytic laws. All these concepts and distinctions hold good of the domain of objects in general, and in Husserl's later terminology belong to formal ontology. The synthetic *a priori* laws however belong to regional (material) ontologies.

Investigation IV is devoted to the idea of pure grammar which contains the laws of permissible combinations of meanings, thereby accounting for the distinction between sense and non-sense, which is prior to the logical laws of consistency and non-contradiction. The theme of Investigation V is "intentional experiences and their contents." Beginning with a delimitation of the idea of consciousness to intentional experiences or *acts*, Husserl takes up the structure of intentionality, within which distinctions are made between act-quality and act-matter, between the object that is intended and the object precisely as it is intended, and between the object to which an act in its totality is directed and the objects to which the partial acts (which are parts of the total act) are directed. The act-matter determines the objective reference of an act; it is also called the *Sinn* of the act (and a few years later would be replaced by the "noema" of the act). This investigation also examines the idea of presentation (*Vorstellung*) and the idea of state of affairs (*Sachverhalt*) as the objective correlate of judgments. The sixth Investigation entitled "Elements of a Phenomenological Clarification of Knowledge" further develops the earlier distinction between meaning-intention and meaning-fulfillment. Husserl defines knowledge as synthesis of fulfillment (whereby something emptily taken to be such and such is now intuitively confirmed to be so) and distinguishes between various degrees of fulfillment and defines truth as the evident. An important new theory is introduced, that of categorial intuition as the mode in which categorial objectivities such as states of affairs (that S is P) are given.

It is well known that Husserl continued to look upon the *Logical Investigations* as a work that first made the "break-through" to phenomenology, and so was a beginning and not the end. He was bothered by the fact that the inner unity of the two parts – the Prolegomena and the six investigations – was not appreciated by the readers. His purpose was to bring out the methical principle of correlation research – for which a prior defense of the objectivity of the logical structures was a necessary step to be taken, as against spurious subjectivizations and relativizations. In the preface to the first edition, as well as on many other occasions, he emphasized that his purpose was to bring out the relation, or rather the correlation, between the subjectivity of knowing and the objectivity of the content of knowledge.

At the same time, Husserl also realized that the early work had certain deficiencies which he sought to remove in the second edition. Two of these are most important: first, he realized that the characterization of phenomenology as descriptive psychology was indeed misleading. Phenomenology must be an eidetic science, i.e., a science which enquires into essential structures of consciousness, and much of the *Investigations*, in actual practice, carried out such research – while giving the wrong impression that what he was doing was a descriptive psychology of logical thinking.

The other main defect of the *Investigations*, and especially of the first, as Husserl pointed out in his 1908 Göttingen lectures on theory of meaning,[25] is that the distinction between the noetic (i.e., concerning the act) and the noematic (concerning the objective correlate) had not been drawn. Consequently, the noetic aspect of meaning had been one-sidedly emphasized to the neglect of the noematic side. This led to his eventually rejecting the account of meaning as a species whose instantiations are the particular acts intending that meaning and incorporating (already in his notes on his own copy of the book) the idea of "the meant object precisely as it is meant" into the noematic concept of meaning.[26] A fully developed concept of noema does not seem to have been arrived at before 1907. What was needed for this to be possible was the methodological idea of a phenomenological reduction. Husserl discovered the reduction in the summer of 1905.

Other changes that he made in the second edition of the *Investigations* include rejection of his earlier view that the alleged pure "I" as the origin and the necessary point of reference of all intentional experiences did not exist. Now he wrote: "In the meantime, I have learned to find it [i.e., the pure I]," while not being misled by a metaphysical theory of the ego. The pure ego is now the ego as apprehended in the actual performance of an intentional act.[27] Another tantalizing remark in the Introduction to the second edition of the sixth Investigation leads one to believe that Husserl no longer upheld his earlier view regarding categorial intuition. Which part of the theory of categorial intuition did he reject, and for what reasons?[28]

2. It is clear by now that Husserl's thinking continued to develop immediately following the publication of the *Logical Investigations*. As a matter of fact, the years 1905–10 are the years during which he makes the most important discoveries of his life, discoveries which determined the rest of his thinking. These include the *epoché* and the noema, amongst many others.

During the years 1904–5, Husserl gave a course entitled "Hauptstücke aus der Phänomenologie und Theorie der Erkenntnis." This course had four parts: (i) perception; (ii) attention and specific intendings (*Meinen*); (iii) phantasy and picture consciousness; and (iv) phenomenology of time. In these lectures, Husserl began by saying that until then he had devoted himself to the higher intellectual acts (mathematical operations and logical acts). Now he planned to focus on the underlying acts such as perception, memory, phantasy and pictorial representation.[29] In the summer of 1905, he wrote the pages, now known as the *Seefelder Blätter*, in which one finds the first statement of "reduction." With this discovery, the concept of noema, already implicitly there in his writings, receives an explicit formulation. In the 1906–7 lectures on Logic and Theory of Knowledge,[30] the method of phenomenological reduction (by which all positing of existence is bracketed) is applied for the first time for the purpose of founding a radically presuppositionless science. The concept of "phenomenon" in these lectures is still terminologically restricted to "real immanence," (i.e., what is a real part of mental life) which is distinguished from the intentionally immanent (i.e., what is not a real part, but a correlate of mental acts).[31] Even in 1907, the interest is predominantly in the acts – oriented towards the hyletic data (or sensuous components of the acts) and their interpretive apprehensions (i.e., the acts in so far as they interpret those data). It is in the research manuscripts of September 1907 that the idea of correlation between noesis and noema is to be found explicitly for the first time.[32] Distinction is made between an ontic phenomenology and a noetic phenomenology. In the 1908 Göttingen lectures on "Urteil und Bedeutung,"[33] a distinction is made between a *phänologischer* and a phenomenological concept of meaning as correlates – in order to correct and improve upon the "*zaghaften Halbheiten*" of the theory of meaning of the *Logical Investigations*.

On 25 September 1906, Husserl entered in his diary a note to the effect that for a detailed examination of the idea of phenomenology of reason, it is first necessary to work out "a phenomenology of perception, of phantasy, of time, of thing."[34] Each one of these is a theme which belongs to the pre-predicative level of experience, which, Husserl thought, would eventually provide the needed foundation for logical, mathematical and scientific thinking. Eventually, this is the programme which leads to *Formal and Transcendental Logic* and *Experience and Judgment*. Let us briefly see where he stood with regard to these fields of research by the time the *Ideas* I was written in 1913.

The 1907 lectures on "Thing and Space"[35] take up the first and the last of the four themes listed in his diary. (The introduction to these lectures is now published as five lectures under the title *Idea of Phenomenology.*) On the theory he develops, the thing-appearance (*Dingerscheinung*) has two strata: (a) the thing-schema (*Dingschema*) and (b) the appearing causal properties of the thing. In the 1907 lectures, Husserl confines himself to the thing-schema; after 1907, his interest shifts to substantial and causal reality (in other words, his interest shifts from the *res extensa* to the *res materialis*).[36] The schema, which is not yet the full-blooded thing, is analyzed into the spatial form (without substantiality and causality), the time schema and sensuous filling. All three together constitute what Husserl calls "phantom". This account is supplemented by taking the causal properties into account, in the *Ideen* II.[37]

With regard to space, Husserl introduces the concepts of "visual field" and "tactual field." A field is understood as a 2-dimensional phenomenal manifold, which is neither 3-dimensional space itself nor a plane in that space. As a matter of fact, one of Husserl's questions is: how does the idea of a 3-dimensional space arise from these phenomenal fields? Using Bain's theory that it is muscular sense which connects vision and touch, Husserl suggests (after abstracting from all physiological and anatomical questions) that it is kinaesthetic sensation (understood as consciousness of actual and potential action, of "I move myself" and "I can move") which does the work. This was an important discovery which became a permanent ingredient of his overall theory of the constitution of material objects.

Husserl's researches on phantasy follow from his attempts – again initially following the lead of Brentano and Stumpf – to clarify the

various kinds of intuitive as distinguished from conceptual presentations. Intuitive acts are either perceptions ("*Gegenwärtigungen*") or
phantasy ("*Vergegenwärtigungen*"). What is the difference between
these two? For Stumpf, they are distinguished only by degrees of
intensity and fullness. Here Stumpf is following Hume. Besides,
Stumpf also held that phantasy-presentations are of fleeting character, and permit deliberate supplementation. Stumpf also adds two
more features of phantasy-presentations: perceptual presentations
are immediately taken to be real, while phantasy-presentations are
taken to be real, at least by adults, only on the basis of some other
evidence. Brentano held that phantasy-presentations (a) contain an
intuitive core but (b) are also partly conceptual, and (c) approximate
towards the purely intuitive presentations. Thus they are of a mixed
breed, and belong to the class of what Brentano called inauthentic
presentations.

By 1904–5, Husserl had come to reject the theory of phantasy as a
sort of picture-consciousness. He also rejected Brentano's view that
phantasy-presentation is a mixture of intuition and concept. For
Brentano all differences among the various sorts of presentations
concerned their contents, since on his theory there was no further
differentiation of the act character of presentation. Husserl came to
defend the view that there are different modes of apprehensions
which are also modes of interpretive acts: in the one case, i.e., in
perception, the object is interpreted as being itself-present, in the
other case as merely imagined. Phantasy is now taken to be an
originary mode of intuition (in which the phantasized objects are
presented). But both perception and phantasy have hyletic or sensuous contents: sensations and phantasma respectively. This content-
interpretation (*Inhalt-Auffassung*) schema is now applied to all sorts
of experiences, which entails the view that in every intentional experience, data are interpreted as having some significance or other.

It is in 1909 that Husserl seems to have attempted to overcome
this last distinction.[38] He now writes: "consciousness consists in
nothing but consciousness, and even sensation, even phantasma, is
consciousness." There are no contents, no hyletic data. Perception is
impressional consciousness of the present, phantasy is reproductive
modified presentified consciousness. Phantasy is a modification of
perceptual consciousness, not a mode of consciousness in which
something is "bodily" given.

The researches into perception and phantasy (and thus also into sensation and phantasma) were connected to, and determined by, Husserl's continuing researches into the nature of our experience of time. His explicit focusing on time is later than his researches into space. The first lectures on time were given in Göttingen in early 1905. In *Ideas* I, he refers to the 1905 Göttingen lectures[39] as containing his conclusive results on time-consciousness. Brentano, according to Husserl, reduces the moment of time to "primary content" (i.e., a content which is prior to all interpretation and cannot be reduced to any other content). In 1905, Husserl explains differences in temporality via differences in apprehension or interpretation. However from 1909 onward, time consciousness comes to be conceived by Husserl as a flow of which every phase is also a flow consisting in a continuity of changing profiles (*Abschattungen*). This was a consequence of Husserl's rejection of the content-interpretation schema. Thus, there are two stages in the development of Husserl's thought on time. During the years 1901–7, he understood time-consciousness in terms of the content-apprehension schema: each mode of consciousness, the now perception, the primary memory, and expectation, in this view, has its own appropriate content and its mode of apprehension. The content in each case is non-temporal material, while the apprehensions are either now-apprehensions, past-apprehensions, or future-apprehensions. Each phase of consciousness contains within it all three: the now, the primary memory and expectation. But after the content-apprehension schema is rejected, as just pointed out, consciousness is understood metaphorically as a flow which is not *in* time, but which is the constitutive source of temporality.[40]

The *Ideas Pertaining to a Pure Phenomenology* appeared in 1913. It was the first systematic, published work using the method of reduction discovered in 1905. Now that we know the enormous and varied *detailed* research Husserl had been carrying on since the publication of the *Logical Investigations, Ideas* I would appear to be a work which, although it does incorporate some of that detailed work, does not take into account very much of what Husserl had achieved. As Husserl himself admits, he does not take into account his findings about inner time consciousness. It continues to employ the content-apprehension schema (hyle-noesis) when Husserl had already attempted to overcome it. *Ideas* I is however Husserl's first published work embodying the reduction, the idea of constitution, noema, and transcendental subjectivity – concepts which he had arrived at during the preceding decade. Although in the book Husserl never used the words "transcendental idealism" or "phenomenological idealism," the overall thesis rightly seemed to its readers, including Husserl's students and colleagues, to be a sort of idealism in which consciousness alone possesses absolute being, the world's being is only presumptive, the world derives the sense of its being from the structure of consciousness, and the domain of phenomenology becomes the noesis-noema correlation. The objects of the world are said to be constituted by the overlapping of noemata. The relation of consciousness to object is taken to be a relation within a noema to its innermost core. All these claims are to be understood as being made within the *epoché* which puts within brackets all positings of entities within the world, the very world-belief itself, as well as all naturalistic interpretations of consciousness, leaving pure consciousness alone as the residue, but not as another region of being but rather as the absolute ground of all positing of being.

Husserl's statements about *Ideas* I bear testimony to his dissatisfaction with it as an exposition of his views.[41] Most importantly, he – and many readers – felt that many of the paragraphs and locutions of transcendental phenomenology could mislead one to take his thesis in a psychological sense. This is as much true of the talk of consciousness as what remains after all transcendence is bracketed, as of the thesis of noesis-noema correlation. The transcendental nature of the concept of noema is likely to be missed in favor of a psychological understanding. The radical nature both of the *epoché* and the constitution thesis was not fully developed to the author's satisfaction – partly because of the continuing role of the concept of the *hyle,* partly because of leaving the theme of inner time consciousness (deliberately!) out of consideration, and also because of an inadequate exposition of the concept of transcendental ego as the source of all meanings. The exposition of the *epoché* in the *Ideas* I – as Husserl later recalled in the *Crisis*[42] – made it look too Cartesian, suggesting that one could *all at once* shift gears from the natural to the transcendental standpoint.

At the time Husserl wrote the *Ideas* I, he planned that the *Ideas* was to have three parts. The plan looked like this:[43]

Book I: A general introduction to phenomenology, consisting of fundamental methodological considerations and analysis of pure consciousness.

Book II: Problems connected with the relation of phenomenology to the natural sciences, to psychology and the human sciences, and to all a priori sciences.

Book III: A concluding discussion of the idea of philosophy grounded in phenomenology, as a precondition of all metaphysics.

Book II of the *Ideas* was written by Husserl in 1912 but was never published in his life time. Why did he not publish it? Because, as it appears, the *detailed* problem of constitution increasingly occupied his attention. In 1913 he prepared a large manuscript called "Natur und Geist" devoted to the problem of constitution. The constitution analysis took over the entire Book II, and the relation of phenomenology to the sciences did not find a place in the manuscript. This manuscript itself went through a series of revisions: Edith Stein's two versions, one in 1916 and the other in 1918. Eventually, Landgrebe's typescript of 1924–5 was used for Biemel's Husserliana edition.[44]

Book III was never composed by itself, and its planned theme was taken over in many subsequent projects. The manuscripts devoted to phenomenology's relation to the sciences formed the Third Book, now *Husserliana* V. The *Ideen* III edited by Marlie Biemel is, in reality, part 2 of the manuscript on *Ideen* II.[45] I will take these works up in the next section of this essay. Also in the next section we shall consider Husserl's researches in the problem of intersubjectivity.

For the purpose of keeping in mind the important milestones of Husserl's thinking during the Göttingen period, we note below the following dates:

1905   concern with original time consciousness; first lecture on time; discovery of the epoché;

1906–7   the idea of a radically presuppositionless philosophy; rejection of the *Logical Investigations* theory that meanings are species;

1907–8   correlation between noesis and noema; noematic
         concept of meaning; a new concept of phenome-
         non as incorporating the intended object *qua* in-
         tended; distinction between psychological and
         transcendental subjectivity; the idea of absolute
         constituting consciousness;

1909   first attempts to overcome the content-
         interpretation schema;

1910–11 problem of intersubjectivity.

III. FREIBURG, 1916–1928

Husserl moved to Freiburg in the spring of 1916 and continued to
teach there until 1928. While this was a productive period for him
during which he tried to prepare for publication a ground work of
phenomenology, it must be said that, compared to the host of new
discoveries, insights and beginnings he made during the Göttingen
period, the Freiburg period is marked less by radically new ideas
than by a deepening of the insights already gained. One could ven-
ture the judgment that the years 1905–10 (and preceding it, the years
1894–99) were the most fruitful years of Husserl's life. These were
the years when the distinctive features of his thinking took shape:
the anti-psychologism, the ideality of meanings, the theory of part
and whole, the theories of knowledge and truth, the epoché, the
theory of constitution, the theory of time consciousness, the idea of
radical grounding, and the concept of transcendental subjectivity.

If likewise, one were to list the new innovations and ideas Husserl
arrived at during the Freiburg years, the list would be somewhat as
follows: incorporation of the problem of history within transcendental phenomenology, radicalization of transcendental phenomenology to become an egology and then a monadology, solutions to the
problem of intersubjectivity, the idea of genetic constitution, the
idea of a transcendental logic, the idea of a logic of pre-predicative
experience, the idea of life-world, attempts to solve the problem of
how transcendental subjectivity becomes mundane, and the prob-

lem of a phenomenology of phenomenology. All these may, however, be seen as radicalizing and deepening of the already achieved results. In this sense, there was no radical transformation. Certain motifs and themes of the Göttingen days receded to the background, only to resurface again and again, never to achieve their early prominence: this happens to the earlier essentialism, to the ideal of apodicticity, even to the noematic aspect of experience. The ideas of transcendental fact and transcendental experience, of the open-endedness of phenomenological research and the noetic side of experience, come to the forefront. Not even the theme of life-world was a completely new discovery. That the scientific was an idealization of the pre-scientific is to be found in the early writings on space and geometry; that the logical is based upon the pre-logical experiences (of "perception, phantasy, time and thing", as he tells us in the note of 1906–7 referred to earlier in this essay) was a theme already in 1898.[46] Not even history is a completely new theme (he gave a seminar on it already in the summer of 1905). With these general remarks let us go on to some details, dividing the exposition into the following parts: 1. constitution analysis, 2. First Philosophy, 3. the logic books, 4. intersubjectivity, 5. life-world and history.

Just as between the *Logical Investigations* and *Ideas* I, Husserl published only the programmatic *Logos* essay,[47] so between *Ideas* and *Formal and Transcendental Logic* he published hardly anything. (The unfortunate "Kaizo Essays" on the "Renewal of Culture" appeared in the Japanese magazine *Kaizo* during the years 1922–24.[48] Husserl clearly wrote them for the financial reward Kaizo promised him.) Rather, years of work went into projects that appeared only posthumously. Those that appeared, although results of earlier researches, were composed hastily for specific occasions as they presented themselves.

1. *Constitution Analysis:* Years of Husserl's own work and of his assistants Edith Stein and Ludwig Landgrebe went into the subsequent volumes of *Ideas.* The Second Book undertakes a systematic and detailed account of the constitution of material nature, animal nature and of the spiritual world. Whereas in the *Ideas* I Husserl set out from the everyday world, here he sets out from the idea of nature as the subject matter of natural science as involving a theoretical and objectifying attitude. The theoretical attitude is contrasted with non-theoretical attitudes, the objectifying with non-objectifying

acts. The sensory objects are posited as the primary objects in the order of constitution. The constitution of material things is analyzed, first, in terms of the "thing-schema" or phantom of the 1907 lectures, but then in terms of (causal) relations of dependence on the "real" environment to which the thing belongs. Causality belongs to the essence of material reality. The unity of the thing is said to be constituted in the continuous but unified manifold of sensuous intuitions of an experiencing ego – a manifold of schematic unities, of real states and real unities of various strata. All this is then placed in relation to the lived body of the experiencing subject. The concept of the body that is presented by Husserl in this context is significantly different from the concept of body to be found in the *Ideas* I. In *Ideas* II, body is not, as it was in *Ideas* I, one thing among others, but is the "carrier of the point of orientation," the "zero point," which plays an important role in the constitution of the spatial world through free variation of the systems of kinaesthetic sensations. This leads Husserl to the problem of intersubjectivity, for the experiencing ego, he tells us, is not the solipsistic ego, but one amongst many.[49]

As another stratum of the constituted world, Husserl considers the "psychic reality" or mental life of men and animals, which has real connections to the human or animal body. The pure "I" and the transcendental subjectivity are distinguished from the *real* mental life. Mental life is not real in the sense of material reality, though it acquires the sense of "reality" by its connection to the body of the experiencing human or animal. The sense "mental reality" is constituted through the lived body. Constitution of the "lived body" is exhibited in several stages: first, as carrier of localised sensations; then as the instrument of will and as carrier of free movement; finally as a material thing in contrast to other material things. To the last belongs the role of body as the center of orientation, the manifold of appearances of the body, and the body as a member of causal interconnections. Founded on the constitution of the body is the constitution of mental reality through empathy. This again leads Husserl to the theme of how other animals, other bodies with their inner mental lives, i.e., other men, are given. A preliminary result is that the object *man* is a transcendent, external object of outer intuitive experience which again is two-layered: an outer perception presenting a body is intertwined with an appresenting empathy.[50]

Mental life is then distinguished from the *geistige* or spiritual world. To the spiritual world belongs the ego as a person and as a member of the social world. The spiritual subject is the subject of intentionality. The fundamental law of the spiritual world is motivation which is an unique form of causality (different from physical causality)[51] whose structure has a form like "because-therefore" (*"because* I know it is B, C . . . , I *therefore* suppose it is A").[52] If perceived natural causality is only an appearance underlying which there is the true scientific causality, motivational causality does not point to any such underlying unperceived structure.[53] The personal ego is constituted not only as impulsive, determinate personality, as moved by original instincts, but also as a higher, autonomous, freely active being, guided by rational motives. In this context, Husserl distinguishes between various sorts of "I can" (e.g., between logical possibility and practical possibility, between physical and spiritual possibilities), and discusses how the consciousness of "I can," being the consciousness of freedom, constitutes the spiritual life of a person. "Spirit" is not an abstract ego of position-taking acts, but rather the full personality, the *I*-man. To me belongs a stratum of experiences as well as a stratum of nature.[54] The reality of spirit relates not to real circumstances belonging to nature, but to the personal *Umwelt* and the other spirits, i.e., person in society. The relation to one's body is both spiritual and causal. The body is the field of one's free volition.[55] An important theme is the contrast between the natural standpoint and the personalistic standpoint. Husserl shows that they mutually involve each other. However, after all is said and done, he defends the thesis that nature is a field of relativity while spirit is absolute being[56] (a thesis that is reminiscent of a famed, and much criticized thesis of *Ideas* I). Further, nature is the *X*, and in principle nothing other than the *X* which is to be determined by general determinations, while spirit is not an *X* but what is itself given in the experience of spirits.[57] We have, in another form, the contrast between transcendent being and immanent being, a distinction which supports the corresponding thesis of *Ideas* I. To be noted is that in the constitution analysis of *Ideas* II, the transcendental-phenomenological idealism is kept at a remove. This may be the reason why Husserl never published it even after years of work on it (or it may be that he became convinced that higher order analyses like these need a broader, more elaborately worked out groundwork, a new *First Philosophy*.)

2. *First Philosophy:* Husserl gave the lectures entitled *"Erste Philosophie"* during the years 1923–24.[58] First philosophy, for him, is not metaphysics but a theory of reason. Since he, for whatever reason, did not want to publish the manuscripts of *Ideen* II, he planned another fundamental work on phenomenology which led to these lectures. By "first philosophy," he meant philosophy that derives its justification from ultimate evidence. This leads him, in the first part, called "Critical History of Ideas," to undertake an account of the historical genesis and development of the idea of philosophy. The lectures begin with the idea of Platonic dialectic, move on to the Aristotelian and Stoic conceptions of a logic of consistency with an excursus into his own idea of formal ontology and "logic of truth," then go to the beginnings of a science of subjectivity in Descartes, followed by a longer discussion of British empiricism from his own standpoint, i.e., as anticipating a constitutive phenomenology, finally ending with Leibniz's monadology and Kantian critique of reason. Descartes is recognized as inaugurating the idea of founding all knowledge in the pure immanence of the *ego cogito*, but Descartes was not able to thematise the *ego cogito* as a field of transcendental experience and as the domain for a descriptive science. Likewise, Leibniz is interpreted as having come close to the idea of a science of pure essence of an ego as the subject of a life of consciousness – an *a priori* science of necessary truths. In this regard, Husserl places Leibniz higher than Kant. Kant's *Critique of Pure Reason*, he recognizes, makes a series of discoveries of great importance, but still stops short of the idea of a foundational science of transcendental subjectivity owing to his "regressive methodological procedure" and a mythical conception of transcendental faculties.[59] This historical part of the *Erste Philosophie* is regarded as an introduction to transcendental phenomenology, based on a history of ideas.

The second and systematic part of the lectures develops a theory of phenomenological reduction. Here the idea of transcendental philosophy is executed in a manner that attempts to be far more radical than the *Ideas*. The Cartesian starting point from the mere "I am" is taken to be full of presuppositions, as also of the certainty about the existence of the world. Both certainties are subjected to criticism, and Husserl prefers to begin with "I as beginning philosopher." The method of reduction is then sought to be freed from the claim to apodicticity of transcendental self-knowledge, and transcendental reduction is distinguished from what is called "apodictic reduction."[60] In this sense, transcendental reduction will not aim at arriving at apodictic truths. The Cartesian path of *Ideas* I, as requiring "an immediate ascent to the transcendental attitude," is set aside in favor of a second path – the phenomenological-psychological – where every particular act, each with its own claim to validity, is separately subjected to the *epoché*. This path has the advantage that it seems to open a way from the natural life of consciousness to the transcendental. But does it? How can one reach the transcendental when at least one validity claim has been left out of the scope of the *epoché*? How can this application of the *epoché* to each act separately yield the totality of transcendental life? In order to show this, Husserl makes use of the ideas of intentional implication, horizon (internal and external) and the horizon of validity (*Geltungshorizont*). These lead him to the thesis that every intentional act implies one flowing intentional life and the "horizon of the living-streaming present."[61] This makes possible extension of act-by-act reduction to a universal *epoché*. But not willing to compromise in the radicalness of his reflection, Husserl goes on to suggest the need for an "apodictic critique of transcendental experience," for there is, he tells us, a transcendental naivety as there is a natural naivety.[62] Such a critique will justify the claim that not only does one need to enforce the reduction, but one also needs to have a "phenomenology of phenomenological reduction" – thereby belying Eugen Fink's claim that reduction, for Husserl, remains only an operative concept and is never thematised.[63]

There is another important idea in these lectures which departs from *Ideas* I in a significant respect. If *Ideas* I contained only eidetic descriptions, and the transcendental was taken to be also eidetic (even if the reverse is not true), then Husserl would now speak also of "transcendental experience" (of "transcendentale Empirie"), so that a transcendental science of facts (instead of essences) is taken to be possible.[64] Such a conception would make the thesis, often asserted by him, of parallelism between the empirical and the transcendental more intelligible.

3. *Logic:* During his Freiburg years, Husserl lectured on logic several times. The file in which the manuscripts of the logic courses were kept bore the title "transcendental logic." These manuscripts were

edited and published under the title *Analysen zur passiven Synthesis*.[65] What has "passive synthesis" to do with logic? It is the old idea we met in his 1904–5 lectures, that any account of logical thinking must be founded on an account of pre-predicative, perceptual experience. Husserl's "Logic" in these lectures, therefore, is the same as "Aesthetik" in a Kantian sense (a word he also uses in *Formal and Transcendental Logic*). The thesis of the logic lectures is perception and its allied modes of consciousness that are characterized by passive synthesis. These include remembering, expectation, and phantasy. These experiences are pre-predicative but not pre-logical. The logical – or, as Husserl puts it, *"das Leben des Logos"* – has a two-fold structure: passivity and receptivity form the lower stratum, while spontaneous activity of the ego (in judging, etc.) forms the higher stratum. To the modalities of judgment as they are dealt with in logic (negation, alternation, supposition, etc.) correspond modalizations of the primary perceptual certainty: the expectations aroused by a phase of a perception may be frustrated by the subsequent phases, thereby giving rise to the modality of negation; or two conflicting perceptual apprehensions of the same hyletic datum may be together without any of them being negated, which gives rise to the modality of doubt; or, when a consciousness has lost the mode of certainty and has been transformed into one of uncertainty, there is the modality of possibility. Husserl also devotes attention to the phenomenon of association which belongs to conscious life. "Association" stands for the process of synthesis by which consciousness becomes one, and unified, a process that takes place at the level of sensory data, at the level of affective stimulation of the ego, also at the levels of reproductions and expectations. In this way, consciousness is shown to be an unbroken history of stratified constitutings of higher and higher objectivities in accordance with essential laws.[66]

What was prepared by Husserl himself for publication under the title "Formal and Transcendental Logic" (completed in about two months in the winter of 1928–29)[67] includes this theme of a "transcendental aesthetics," but develops a philosophy of logic in a totally new direction. Although Husserl worked on a logic book for a decade,[68] he also thought that the days of his concern with logic were left far behind him. For a long time, he also wanted to revise his old Göttingen lecture manuscripts on logic so as to make them fit for publication. He also often wanted to use those older manuscripts for his new book on logic. Eventually, the need for producing something for the tenth volume of the *Jahrbuch*, which he was editing, as well as the need of writing an introduction to the *Logical Investigations* which he had Langrebe prepare, led him to write the book rather hastily. Yet this is one of his most mature and well constructed, systematic works. It showed that even at this old age he was able to produce a detailed, original – and not merely programmatic and expository – book on the philosophy of logic.

With regard to formal logic, Husserl was able to develop an idea which he had formulated in the *Prolegomena:* the idea that formal logic is a stratified structure consisting of a pure theory of judgmental forms, a logic of consequence or of non-contradiction, and a logic of truth as the three strata in that order. To each of these strata, Husserl assigned a certain conception of judgment and a certain sort of evidence. The entire discussion is a creative innovation. The idea of formal ontology as the correlate of formal logic (and formal mathematics which for Husserl really belongs to formal logic) is developed by bringing in the notion of a pure deductive theory and the idea of a definite manifold with which Husserl had been concerned since the 1890s.

The transition from formal logic to transcendental logic is effected in several ways: first, by exhibiting the subjective intentional acts in which the logical entities are constituted; then, by bringing out the "idealizing presuppositions" of logic (e.g., of the logical principles such as principle of non-contradiction and excluded middle); by tracing predicative judgments (which form the subject matter of apophantic logic) to pre-predicative experience; by highlighting the fact that traditional logic, even the most abstract formal logic, is world-related (*Weltbezogen*) in the sense that the variables it uses can take as their values entities in some possible world or other; and again, as in the *Analysis of Passive Synthesis* and in *Experience and Judgment*, by tracing the logical forms back to their origin in pre-predicative experience, i.e., in a transcendental aesthetics.

4. *Intersubjectivity:* During all these years and in all the works reviewed, one of Husserl's continuing concerns had been the so-called problem of intersubjectivity. Radicalization of the *epoché* and of transcendental philosophy led to a transcendental solipsism, but Husserl also saw that from within such a transcendental solipsistic stance he should be able to recover the other egos as real others to

the reflecting subject. The chain of thinking reaches its most well known formulation in the fifth *Cartesian Meditation* of 1929. But Husserl's concern with the problem of intersubjectivity goes back to the Göttingen years. Thus, in *Formal and Transcendental Logic* he writes that the main points for the solution of the problem of intersubjectivity and for overcoming transcendental solipsism had been developed in the Göttingen lectures of 1910–11, although an actual execution of these ideas came to a closure much later.[69]

Iso Kern traces the beginnings of Husserl's researches into the problem of intersubjectivity to 1905.[70] Even in the *Logical Investigations*, the function of "intimation" (*Kundgabe*) ascribed to every living speech gives the auditor an insight into the experiences of the speaker. The discovery of the method of *epoché* made the problem more urgent: how, from within phenomenological reduction, can the sense "other ego," and the sense "the life of consciousness of the other" be validated? Now Iso Kern has rightly pointed out that although Husserl continues to speak of "empathy" (*Einfühlung*), he was not using Theodor Lipps's concept of empathy. In a text from 1913, Husserl contrasts his own concern with empathy with that of Lipps.[71] Unlike Lipps, he was not at that time concerned with understanding the expressions of the other's mental life; he was concerned rather with a stratum (of experience of the other) which precedes such understanding. He was asking, how do we come to apprehend the other's body as a field of sensations, as a lived body. This is what Husserl calls that "aesthesiological layer" of the other ego. Even as early as 1909, he was aware of the idea of empathy as constitutive of the other ego.[72] The 1910–11 lectures referred to above were entitled "Grundprobleme der Phänomenologie," but they had a part which Husserl later on called "Über Intersubjektivität." There Husserl says that although I remain in my phenomenological field of experience, this field extends, through empathy, to a sphere of plurality of closed streams of consciousnesses which are connected to mine through "motivational structures" – not through a *real* connection, but through a most peculiar sort of connection made possible by empathetic positing. Consciousnesses which are separated, he goes on to say, remain under the possibility of communication, and communication depends upon perception of the other's lived body as well as on motivations radiating from it.[73]

Although in these 1910–11 lectures Husserl had in principle extended the *epoché* to intersubjectivity,[74] it was not until the *Cartesian Meditations* that he was able to use the second reduction fruitfully. (However, from 1916 onwards, he was using words such as "original sphere," "primordial sphere," "sphere of ownness."[75]) In a note from 1921[76] he writes: "The other's lived body (*Leib*) is not, qua lived body, "bodily given," it is "bodily given" as a thing, its being-a-lived-body is only analogically appresented."[77] In a text from 1922, this analogical appresentation is explained as "appresentation in the mode of an 'expression,' " meaning that thereby a whole world of inner experience is co-posited.[78]

There is also a group of texts from the early twenties in which Husserl discusses the various possible ways of unifying the monads through connecting their ego-subjects – these are social acts, and Husserl goes on to speak of an over-individual "personal unity of a higher order," (an idea which Scheler had much earlier and which is present in *Ideas* II). In 1927, he recognizes that the empathetic appresentation of the other is a "mediate" perception; although its intentions are being continuously fulfilled, it can never amount to an actual perception of the other subjectivity. Various other ideas come to the forefront in the research manuscripts of this year, some of which are: that the representation "as if I were there" is awakened by an external body, and the confirmation of this "as-if interpretation"; that the other is made present as a modification of my ego in the mode "the I who is there"; that the other ego is a modification like the past (which is a present that is a past)[79]; that the appresentative intention of empathy receives its final fulfillment in the synthesis of my original self-experience with the empathized experience of the other by I myself;[80] the idea of "pairing" between a "null-body" (my body which serves as the null-point) and "an external body."[81] Between 15th April and 15th May of 1927, Husserl wrote down the Fifth Cartesian Meditation as a complete structure of the transcendental theory of experience of the other.[82]

It appears, however, that Husserl's thinking about intersubjectivity did not remain at the stage where we find it in the *Cartesian Meditations*.[83] In a text from March 1931, for example, he writes that the other as a transcendental co-subject and as a co-present flux is inseparable from the living present of the ego.[84] In these research manuscripts, he continues to try new ideas. One perhaps should mention a text from April 1932[85] which focusses on the idea of a social act as being essentially a communicative act.

5. *Life-world and History:* The *Crisis,* which Husserl worked on for several years, was his last published work. He was seventy-six years old when he first gave a lecture in Vienna on "Philosophy in the Crisis of European Mankind." The same year he also gave four lectures in Prague. These lectures went into the *Crisis,* Parts I and II of which were published in the journal *Philosophia* of Belgrade. The third part of the work never appeared in Husserl's life time.

Crisis, as soon as it appeared, became famous for its thematic concept of life-world. Many saw in it a completely new turn in Husserl's thinking. But closer reading of Husserl's writings shows that Husserl had this concept long before *Crisis.* As we have pointed out in this essay, the idea that logical thinking and the sciences are idealizations of pre-scientific, perceptual experience had guided Husserl's thinking since the early Göttingen years. The concept of idealization, however, is presented in *Crisis* in a manner ("idealized thinking conquers the infinity of the experiential world") which is reminiscent of a thesis of the *Philosophy of Arithmetic,* that the finite mind, in dealing with what cannot be intuitively grasped, takes to symbolic thinking. With regard to the life-world, what is impressive in *Crisis* is the detailed exposition of the way modern science, and especially Galilean physics, arises out of the life-world which provides its "foundation of sense" (*Sinnesfundament*). What is also novel is the use of this insight to develop a more radical path to transcendental phenomenology. The path begins with the natural sciences, moves on to their underlying ground, namely, to the everyday world, and then exhibits the constitution of that world in the "functioning" or operative intentionalities of transcendental subjectivity.

The true novelty of *Crisis,* however, lies in an attempt on Husserl's part to thematise history and the historicity of the life-world and of the constituting subjectivity within the overall framework of transcendental phenomenology. But history, as Husserl understands it, is from the very beginning "nothing other than the living moment of being-with-one-another and in-one-another of original meaning-constitution and meaning-sedimentation."[86] This is what may also be called "intentional history." And the historicity of the life-world is made possible by the inner historicity of every individual person living in it.[87] This thesis of historicity, however, entails neither historicism (which Husserl had already severely criticized in his 1910 *Logos* essay) nor relativism. History exhibits a historical *a priori* (which assures objectivity of history). The historical *a priori* itself presupposes a certain idealization. History is mastered not by an a-historical apriorism, but by a transcendental stance which shows that the process of constitution worked out in history (like the constitution of modern science, of Galilean physics) can be, in its essential structure, deciphered in reflective thinking by the reflecting ego.

It should be noted that the famous remark of Husserl (dating from the summer of 1935) that "Philosophy as science, as serious, rigorous, indeed apodictically rigorous science – *the dream is over*,"[88] is not a remark about Husserl himself, but is rather about the prevailing anti-rationalism which Husserl thought to be at the root of the crisis of European man.

Early in his life, Husserl caught hold of a few central problems. These problems were continuously deepened as he thought them through. What makes him such an exciting philosopher is that he not only tried to solve these problems at a very general, often methodological level – but again and again returned to test those solutions at the level of detailed execution. Excepting possibly the discovery of the *epoché* in 1905, no major shifts characterize the development of his thought – there is rather a continuous, unceasing attempt to think through the same problems at many different levels.

NOTES

1 In a letter to Natorp, Husserl wrote on 1 February 1992, "Vielleicht arbeite ich, mit aller menschlich möglichen Anspannung der Kräfte, nur für meinen Nachlass" (quoted in the Editor's Introduction to Hua XXIII, xxix–xxx).

2 *Philosophie der Arithmetik* 1970, Hua XII, edited by L. Eley, 287–8.

3 Cf. G. Frege, "Review of Husserl's *Philosophie der Arithmetik*," *Zeitschrift für Philosophie und philosophische Kritik*, 103, 1894, 313–32. English translation by E.W. Kluge, in *Mind* LXXXI (1972): 321–37.

4 O. Becker, "Die Philosophie E. Husserls," *Kant Studien* XXXV 9, 119–50; W. Biemel, "Die entscheidenden Phasen der Entfaltung von Husserls Philosophie," *Zeitschrift für philosophische Forschung*, 1959, 187–213; L. Landgrebe, "Husserls Phänomenologie und die Motive zu ihrer

Umbildung," in Landgrebe, *Der Weg der Phänomenologie* (Gütersloh: G. Mohn, 1966).

5 Cf. Husserl's Letter to Meinong, 22 November 1894.

6 Cf. Husserl's Letter of 1890 to Carl Stumpf.

7 Cf. Letter from Frau Husserl to Albrecht, 28 December 1901.

8 Husserl, *Formale und transzendentale Logik*, edited by P. Janssen, *Husserlian* XVII (The Hague: M. Nijhoff, 1974), §34.

9 Cf. Husserl's Letter to Hermann Weyl, 10 April 1918.

10 Husserl, "Besprechung: E. Schröder, Vorlesungen über die Algebra der Logik, I." *Göttingische gelehrte Anzeigen*, 1891, 243–78.

11 Hua XXII, 18.

12 Hua XXII, 303–48; and Hua XXII, 349–56. A complete edition of Husserl's reviews of Twardowski's book is in Karl Schumann's "Husserl's Abhandlung 'Intentionale Gegenstände': Edition der ursprünglichen Druckfassung" in *Brentano Studien* 3, (1990–1): 137–76.

13 Hua XXII, 345.

14 I have benefitted here from Karl Schumann's "Husserl and Twardowski," a typescript of which was made available to me.

15 Hua XIX/1, 439.

16 Hua XXI, 25, Hua XXII, 284.

17 Cf. K. Schuhmann, "Husserls doppelter Vorstellungsbegriff: Die Texte von 1893," *Brentano Studien* 3 (1990–91): 119–36.

18 Cf. Hua XXII, Editor's Introduction, p. liii, n. 2; also Karl Schumann, ibid., 128.

19 Karl Schuhmann, ibid., 135, especially n. 32.

20 Frege also held a similar view at this time.

21 Hua XXI, p. LXVI, n. 4.

22 Hua XVI.

23 Cf. J.N. Mohanty, *Husserl and Frege* (Bloomington: Indiana University Press, 1982).

24 Cf. Husserl, "Entwurf einer 'Vorrede' zu den Logischen Untersuchungen' [1913]," edited by E. Fink, *Tijdschrift voor Philosophie* I (1936). 106–33, 319–35.

25 E. Husserl, *Vorlesungen über Bedeutungslehre* (Hua XXVI), edited by U. Panzer, (The Hague: M. Nijhoff, 1987).

26 Hua XLX/1, Editor's Introduction, xxxiii–xxxiv.

27 Husserl, *Logical Investigations* Investigation V, § 8, n. 1.

28 On this question, see D. Lohmar, "Wo lag der Fehler der kategorialen Repräsentation? Zu Sinn und Reichweite einer Selbstkritik Husserls," *Husserl Studies* 7 (1990): 179–97.

29 Hua X, Editor's Introduction, p xiii.

30 Husserl, *Einleitung in die Logik und Erkenntnistheorie*, 1906/7.

31 Hua XXIV, especially Beilage V, 424f.
32 Cf. Hua XXIV, Beilagen I–IV.
33 Hua XXIV.
34 Husserl, "Persönliche Aufzeichnungen," edited by W. Biemel, *Philoso-phy and Phenomenological Research* XVI, 1956.
35 Husserl, *Ding und Raum* (1907), edited by U. Claesges, Hua XVI, 1973.
36 Hua XVI, Editor's Introduction, xx–xxi.
37 Husserl, *Ideen zu einer reinen Phänomenologie und phänomenolo-gischen Philosophie*, Zweites Buch, edited by M. Biemel. Hua IV, 1952, especially Chapter 2.
38 Cf. Husserl, *Phantasie, Bildbewusstsein, Erinnerung, 1898–1925*, edited by E. Marbach, Hua XXIII, 1980, especially text no. 8. Also cf. Editor's Introduction, lxii, n. 1. Marbach traces it to August–September 1909 when Husserl was staying in Engadin, Switzerland.
39 *Ideas* I, § 81–§ 86.
40 Cf. John Brough, "The Emergence of an Absolute Consciousness in Husserl's Early Writings on Time-Consciousness," *Man and World*, V, 1972, 298–326. Despite Husserl's attempts to overcome the content-apprehension scheme, that scheme appears in the Bernau manuscripts of 1917/18 and reappears even in manuscripts of the thirties.
41 Karl Schuhmann drew my attention to the fact that the "Boyce Gibson Convolute" shows that Husserl thought it perfectly possible to "raise" the 1913 work to the 1929 level.
42 Husserl, *Die Krisis der europäischen Wissenschaften und die tran-szendentale Phänomenologie*, edited by W. Biemel (The Hague: M. Nijhoff, 1974). Hua VI, § 43, 57–58.
43 Hua IV, Editor's Introduction.
44 Ibid, xvi.
45 Hua VII, Editor's Introduction, xxi.
46 See the plans and mss. for the *Logische Untersuchungen*. Karl Schuh-mann drew my attention to these.
47 Husserl, "Philosophie als strenge Wissenschaft," *Logos* I, 1910–11.
48 The Kaizo essays are now reprinted in Husserl's *Aufsätze und Vorträge* (1922–37), edited by T. Nenon and Hans Rainer Sepp. Husserliana XXVII, (The Hague: Kluwer, 1989).
49 Hua IV, 78.
50 Hua IV, 169.
51 Hua IV, 169.
52 Hua IV, 229.
53 Hua IV, 230–31.
54 Hua IV, 280.
55 Hua IV, 283.

56 Hua IV, 297f.

57 Hua IV, 302.

58 Husserl, *Erste Philosophie* (1923–24), edited by R. Boehm, 2 vols. (Hua VII & VIII), 1959.

59 Hua VII, 197–98.

60 Hua VIII, 80.

61 Hua VIII, 146f.

62 Hua VIII, 169–71.

63 Cf. E. Fink, "Operative Begriffe in Husserls Phänomenologie," *Zeitschrift für philosophishe Forschung* XI (1957), 321–37.

64 Hua VIII, 360f.

65 E. Husserl, *Analysen zur passiven Synthesis*, edited by M. Fleischer, Hua XI (The Hague: M. Nijoff, 1966).

66 *Ibid.*, pp. 218–19.

67 Cf. Husserl's letter to Ingarden, 12 February 1929.

68 Cf. Husserl's letter to Ingarden, 19 March 1930.

69 Hua XVII, § 96(d), n. 1.

70 Husserl, *Zur Phänomenologie der Intersubjektivität*, Bd I–II, edited by Iso Kern, Hua XIII–XV, 1973. Editor's Introduction to Hua XIII, xxii.

71 Hua XIII, 70.

72 See Hua XIII, 44 n.

73 Ibid., 87–88.

74 Cf. Husserl's Letter to Ingarden, 10 December 1925.

75 Cf. Hua XIII, Editor's Introduction, xlv.

76 Text no. 11 in Hua XIV.

77 Hua XIV, 234.

78 Text no. 12 in Hua XIV, especially 249.

79 Text no. 30, Hua XIV.

80 Text no. 31, Hua XIV.

81 Text no. 35, Hua XIV.

82 Cf. Husserl's letter to Ingarden, 26 May 1929.

83 Husserl, *Cartesianische Meditationen und Pariser Vorträge*, edited by S. Strasser, Hua I (The Hague: M. Nijhoff, 1950). See also Iso Kern, Editor's Introduction, Hua XV.

84 Iso Kern quotes this passage on p. xlviii, Hua XV.

85 Text 29, Hua XV.

86 Hua VI, 380.

87 Hua VI, 381, n. 1.

88 Hua VI, Beilage XXVIII.

2   The phenomenological dimension

I. HUSSERL AS A MEANING THEORIST

This essay is addressed to the most general problem confronting a philosopher reading Husserl. How is his approach to philosophy to be understood? What was Husserl trying to do?

One influential answer to such questions is to say that Husserl's phenomenology was a theory of intentionality. That answer aligns Husserl with other theorists of meaning in a sufficiently general sense of the term. For instance, Dagfinn Føllesdal's work on Husserl took off from considerations pertaining to a parallelism between the respective meaning theories of Husserl and Frege, prominently including a partial analogy between on the one hand Frege's distinction between *Sinn* and *Bedeutung* and on the other hand the Husserlian contrast between *noema* and its object. In this parallelism, a noema is construed as the vehicle of intentional meaning in general roughly in the same way as a Fregean *Sinn* is supposed to be the mediator of linguistic meaning. Thus we have the following analogy:

$$\frac{act}{expression} = \frac{noema}{Sinn} = \frac{object}{Bedeutung}$$

(Cf., e.g., Føllesdal, 1969.)

I do not disagree with this type of answer to the question of the character of Husserl's philosophical enterprise when the answer is correctly understood. There is, however, a built-in danger in such an approach to Husserl. For if one envisages Husserl as a kind of generalized meaning theorist, one is easily tempted to concentrate one's attention on the *vehicles, bearers* or *mediators* of that meaning, such as noemata, at the expense of the question of how that meaning operates, i.e., how it is that those meaning entities manage to accomplish their intentional or referential function. More generally there is a temptation to isolate noemata conceptually from their objects far too rigidly, to assume that we can find out all we need to know about intentional meaning by examining the mediators of this meaning, the noemata. I shall refer to this conception as the idea of self-sufficient intentionality.

By studying the vehicles of meaning in their own right we nevertheless cannot come to understand how they are linked up with whatever it is that they in fact mean. For instance, no analysis of the structure of the *noema,* however detailed and accurate, can tell you what its relation is to its object. This does not fault the analysis in the least, but it does show that such an analysis of noema structure is not the whole story of Husserlian phenomenology.

II. REDUCTION, CONSTITUTION, FILLING

The import of this general insight can be made clearer by relating it to various specific features of Husserl's philosophy. For instance, the nature of the famous Husserlian – or, to use the proper term, phenomenological – reductions will be hard to understand if one emphasizes only the vehicles of intentionality themselves. The most important reduction Husserl deals with is the transcendental reduction, which can be described by saying that in it one's belief in factual existence is "bracketed" and one's attention is directed, is fixed "on the sphere of consciousness" and in which we "study what is immanent in it" (*Ideas I,* § 33). Another type of reduction is the eidetic reduction which leads from particulars to general "essences." Here I am considering only the transcendental reduction.

From the viewpoint of a self-sufficient intentionality, the only reasonable sense one can make of these reductions is to aver that what is "bracketed" in them is the very reality which can be intended by means of the vehicles of intentionality. A phenomenologist's entire attention is on this view concentrated on noemata or whatever meaning bearers we are considering.

This way of looking at the phenomenological reductions is mistaken, I shall argue. The main difficulty with an account of phenomenological reductions which sees in them a method of concentrating one's attention exclusively on noemata is that far too much will then end up being bracketed. Such an exclusive concentration inevitably brackets, not merely objects, but the relation of noemata to objects. You simply cannot be aware of a relation's holding between two terms if you are not aware of both of the two terms. If the entire object is in each and every case bracketed in the phenomenological reductions, it therefore becomes literally impossible for a phenomenologist to explain the relation of a noema to its object. For neither the other term of this relation nor this relation itself will be accessible to a phenomenologist.

For instance, it does not help the idea of self-sufficient intentionality to claim that the noema-object relation is a causal relation, as might seem plausible in the case of perception. For causal relations, however direct, are not as such accessible to mere phenomenological reflection. Typically, they must be inferred; they cannot be intuited.

In Husserl's own jargon, my main point can be expressed by saying that the idea of Husserl as a meaning theorist, even if it captures what Husserl wants to exclude ("bracket"), nevertheless fails to account for what survives the transcendental reduction. Husserl himself uses the term *phenomenological residuum* for the purpose. Husserl makes it clear that even the transcendent in a sense partly survives bracketing (*Ideas I*, § 76):

Everything transcendent, in as much as it becomes given in consciousness, is an object for phenomenological investigation not only with respect to the consciousness of it . . . but also, though this is essentially involved with the former, as what is given and accepted in the modes of givenness.

Such statements are incompatible with the idea of the transcendental reduction as a reduction to noemata.

I suspect that the idea of self-sufficient intentionality is due to a confusion between two different things. In Frege, the *Sinn* of an expression was primary, in relation to its reference (*Bedeutung*), and determined the reference completely. *Mutatis mutandis*, the noema of an act can be argued to determine its object. But from such a determination it does not follow that one can understand the noema-object relationship merely by examining noemata. For this purpose, the relationship itself must be made a target of phenomenological reflection.

A related point affects Husserl's concept of constitution. If the entire object is thought of as being bracketed in the phenomenological reductions, how can we hope to understand the processes through which we constitute that object? Husserl claims that what is immediately and primarily given to us in sensory awareness is unarticulated raw material, hyle, which our noeses structure into objects, their properties and interrelations, etc. (The process of such structuring is precisely what Husserl means by his term *noesis*.) But how can we even hope to be able to find out about such constitutive processes, if their input is by definition unavailable to phenomenological reflection?

A special case of the problems I have noted pertains to Husserl's notion of filling. One can compare (admittedly roughly) a noema to the set of expectations concerning the object of the noema. Some substance is lent to this *façon de parler* by Husserl's notion of filling. For what he says is that in certain experiences the noema is "filled" (*erfüllt*). In terms of our analogical explication this means that the expectations associated with the noema are (perfectly or imperfectly) fulfilled.

Not surprisingly, the relation of filling is one of the central notions in Husserl's thinking. But perhaps its central role in phenomenology should come as a surprise if we are viewing Husserl as a meaning theorist. For we will then be faced by the question: What is it that fills a noema? And even more pertinently, whatever it is, does it belong to the sphere of objects or to the sphere of noemata? Either answer lands you in trouble. For if the filling is done by something that belongs to the realm of objects, it must have been bracketed in the phenomenological reductions. This would make the entire phenomenon of filling inaccessible to a phenomenologist. But if the filling is done by something that belongs to the realm of the vehicles of intentionality, that is, to the world of noemata, then filling cannot help to link noemata and reality to each other as it is obviously intended by Husserl to do.

In the last analysis, it seems to me, the idea that we could understand the nature of intentionality by focusing on the vehicles of intentionality is little more than a generalized form of what has been called "the image theory of intentionality," criticized by Husserl himself. We must not, Husserl tells us, think of perception as a reception of an image of what is perceived. By the same token, we must not think of intentionality as a creation of a picture of the intended, even if the picture is abstracted into a noema or "an object as intended."

III. HUSSERL'S QUEST OF THE IMMEDIATELY GIVEN

It is not hard to see what the basic idea of Husserl is that does not find a niche in any interpretation of Husserl as a mere meaning theorist. Husserl repeatedly states loud and clear that what he is trying to do is to find the basis of our conceptual world in *immediate experience*. There may be a sense in which all noemata are equal for Husserl, but if so, some of them are more equal than others, in that they are more closely connected with what is immediately given. It may be that the phenomenological reductions are supposed to bracket objects and focus our attention on noemata, but that move is a mere prolegomenon to a study of the interrelations of the different ingredients of the world of our concepts, culminating in a search for the ultimate foundation of this conceptual world in our direct experience.

It is unmistakable that this search for the basis of our conceptual world in immediate experience is what constitutes the specifically phenomenological element in Husserl's philosophy. It is what was referred to in my title as the phenomenological dimension of Husserl's thought.

It is important to realize what is involved in the Husserlian quest of the immediately given and why it cannot be accommodated by any dichotomy between our consciousness (prominently including its intentional acts) and the intended objects. The idea that something about the actual world is immediately given to me implies that any such sharp dichotomy has to break down. What is immediately given to me will then at the same time be part of the mind-independent reality and an element of my consciousness. There has to be an actual interface or overlap of my consciousness and reality. This is the basic reason why any sharp contrast between the realm of noemata and the world of mind-independent realities ultimately has to be loosened up in Husserl.

It does not change the situation if the noema is renamed and dubbed "an object as intended." For the object as intended is not the same as the intended object. Consequently, all the questions I have been raising are reawakened in the form of questions concerning the relation of the two so-called objects. It is true in a sense that what is directly given to me is the noema or "object as intended." It is the only thing that I can find in my consciousness. But, in this sense, although everything in the noema is given, some facets of it are given in a more fundamental sense than others. And Husserl's "Principle of all Principles" (see § V below) exhorts a phenomenologist to locate that primordial self-givenness. What I am trying to do in this paper is to obey this order.

IV. PHENOMENOLOGY VS. PHENOMENALISM

One reason why the possibility of actual self-givenness in Husserl has been missed is a confusion between phenomenology and phenomenalism. This is one of the most widespread and most invidious mistakes in and about twentieth-century philosophy.

It is indeed a pernicious mistake. What phenomenalism holds is that we have access only to phenomena, not to the real things, be they physical objects or Kantian "things in themselves" or whatever the objects of our experiences may be that Moore distinguished from the experiences themselves in his "Refutation of Idealism." What a phenomenologist like Husserl maintains is that everything must be based on, and traced back to, what is given to me in my direct experience. It is not a part of this position that what is so given to me are mere phenomena. On the contrary, the overall phenomenological project would make little sense unless the phenomenological reductions led us closer to actual realities.

In order to exorcise this mistake it is crucially important to emphasize that, according to Husserl, there is an actual interface of my consciousness and reality, that reality in fact impinges directly on my consciousness.

One way in which one can see that Husserl insisted on a direct access to realities in one's consciousness is his criticism of Kant's idea of "things in themselves," which per definitionem are not so accessible. Here Iso Kern has done us a yeoman's service by collating a great deal of useful evidence (cf. Kern 1964, 120–24). For instance, Kern speaks of Husserl's "thesis of the correlation of being and consciousness" (op. cit., 121). What Kern intends is undoubtedly correct, but it is not the Kernpunkt of Husserl's view. Even Kant could have spoken of a correlation of things in themselves and consciousness. Husserl's distinctive view is that beings can actually be given to us, that "to be capable of being given belongs to the essence of being" (op. cit., 121). Kern provides other impressive quotes to the same realistic effect, e.g.,

If we [try to] speak of objects which are not related to any intuition whatsoever, the result is nonsense.

Another way of seeing the same point is to attend to what Husserl says of the "correlation" (not the best possible term, perhaps) of objects and intuition. Here a *locus classicus* is § 3 of *Ideas I*. There we find statements like the following:

The universalization of the correlatively interrelated concepts "intuition" and "object" is not an arbitrary conceit but compellingly demanded by the nature of the matters in question. Empirical intuition or, specifically, experience, is consciousness of an individual object; and as an intuitive consciousness it "makes this object given," as perception it makes an individual object given originally in the consciousness of seizing upon this object "originally," in its "personal" selfhood.

In order to understand such statements fully, however, we have to have a closer look at Husserl's concept of intuition. That will be done in § VI below.

It is instructive to note that the usage of the term "phenomenological," which is likely to have been most familiar to the young Husserl, conforms neatly to what I just said. It was the use of the term in physics, especially in thermodynamics. There "phenomenological" theories meant those theories which dealt exclusively with directly measurable (observable) variables, in contrast to theories which postulated unobservable entities, e.g., atoms and molecules, as in statistical thermodynamics. There is, of course, no implication here that "phenomenological" theories deal merely with our impressions of realities in contradistinction to the actual realities themselves.

V. THE MEANING OF TRANSCENDENTAL REDUCTION

The fundamental nature of Husserlian phenomenology as the quest of the immediately given also determines the nature of the phenomenological reductions, especially of the transcendental reduction. This reduction is not tantamount to merely bracketing the object of an act and leaving the noema there as the sole object of a phenomenologist's attention. It also invokes bracketing everything in the noema which is not given to us in immediate experience. It separates what is *intended* from what is *given*, and seeks to reduce the former to the latter. As Husserl puts it,

phenomenological reduction . . . entails a limitation to the sphere of things that are *purely self given*, to the sphere of those things which are not merely spoken about, meant, or perceived, but instead to the sphere of those things that are given in just exactly the sense in which they are thought of, and moreover are self-given in the strictest sense – in such a way that nothing which is meant fails to be given.   (*The Idea of Phenomenology*, 48–49.)

What is thus self-given includes the overlap of consciousness and reality, plus of course whatever we do to that immediate experience in order to transform it into the experience of the fully articulated world of objects. This in any case is what I am arguing in this essay. One reason why this point is difficult to see in Husserl's own formulations of what the phenomenological reduction is – one reason why their full import has not always been appreciated – is that he often speaks only about what is excluded by the reduction, not about what it leaves intact. For the purpose of identifying that residuum, we have to turn to other passages in Husserl's writings.

How does Husserl describe his project? I shall quote a few sample passages. In one of them Husserl says that his aim is

to claim nothing that we cannot make essentially transparent to ourselves by reference to consciousness and on purely immanent lines.

In *Ideas I*, § 24, Husserl formulates his "Principle of all Principles" as follows:

that every originary presentive intuition is a legitimizing source of cognition, that everything originary (so to speak, in its "personal" actuality) offered to us in "intuition" is to be accepted simply as what it is presented as being, but also only within the limits in which it is presented there.

Again in *Ideas I*, § 40, we read:

any cognition in physics serves as an index to the course of possible experiences with the things pertaining to the senses and their occurrences found in those experiences.

Such quotations help us to appreciate what Husserlian reductions amount to. In some ways, the import of the phenomenological reductions can be seen more clearly in the realm of logic and mathematics than in sense-experience. Husserl brackets the whole abstract world of logic and mathematics (*Ideas I*, § 59) in so far as it cannot be reduced to "such descriptive analyses as can be resolved into pure intuition". This is in sharp contrast to Frege, who consistently emphasized the independence of logic and arithmetic of intuition.

Next I shall discuss Husserl's notion of intuition. That discussion will clarify further the import of Husserl's views just explained.

VI. INTUITION AS THE MEDIUM OF SELF-GIVENNESS

Husserl makes heavy use of a term whose primary function is to call attention to what is immediately given to us in experience. This term is *intuition* (*Anschauung*). Unfortunately, it is one of the least clearly understood terms in philosophical language. Its semantical history makes it particularly prone to misunderstandings. It is impossible to trace here the entire history of the notion of intuition. Suffice it to indicate the most important precedents of Husserl's usage. They do not include the scholastic usage which some scholars have tried to evoke. The crucial background of Husserl's usage is the early modern use of terms like the Latin *intuitus*, English "intuition," and the German term *Anschauung* which was introduced into German philosophical terminology as a translation of the Latin *intuitus*. (Cf. here Hintikka, 1969.) What is characteristic of this early modern period usage is that intuitions are simply what is directly known to us. It follows that intuitions so understood need not be "intuitive" in our sense, that is, they do not necessarily have much similarity with perceptions or mental images. This usage is illustrated by Locke, who uses as his paradigmatic example of "intuitive truths" that $3 = 1 + 2$.

This older usage is at the bottom of Kant's use of the term *Anschauung*, and it is also what makes it natural for Husserl to use this word as a generic label of everything that is given to us in immediate experience. In fact, Husserl means by an intuition whatever immediately gives us its object, i.e., a "datum" (cf. *Ideas I*, § 19).

This role of intuitions as the basis of all meanings is expressed by Husserl as follows:

> One can say in general, that in order to be quite clear as to the sense of an expression (or as to the content of a concept) one must construct the corresponding intuition: in this intuition one can see what the expression "really means".   (*Logical Investigations* I, Chap. 2, § 21, 306.)

It is thus a serious mistake to attribute to Husserl a view of intuition as a separate source of truth or certainty. Intuition is not a separate epistemological consultant, it is a generic term for whatever any privileged consultant tells me. An expression like "immediate intuitive truth" is for Husserl a pleonasm.

It is sometimes said that phenomenology is the study of acts and of their noemata. It is not; it also includes the study of the relation of noemata to their objects. And this relation is mediated by those "intuitive" experiences in which certain objects are given – "self-given," as Husserl expresses himself – to us.

A small but important semantical word of warning is in order here. In one respect, Husserlian intuition differs markedly from its Kantian precedent. For Kant, intuitions were by definition singular, whereas Husserlian intuition, especially his "eidetic intuition," has an element of generality.

VII. CATEGORIAL INTUITION

So understood (that is, understood as expressing merely self-givenness, not any particular source of knowledge or insight), Husserl's term "intuition" (*Anschauung*) assigns no privileged position to sense-perception or empirical intuition. Immediate sensory awareness is but one species of intuition, nor is the range of non-sensory intuition restricted to imagination in any sense that relates imagination to sensory awareness. Intuitions in Husserl's sense need not be intuitive in the current meaning of the term.

Not only is this possibility of non-sensuous intuitions left open by Husserl. He explicitly recognizes kinds of immediate givenness that are not sensory. Among them is what Husserl terms *categorial intuition*.

It is only when the notion of intuition is taken to this wide sense that it can serve its crucial role as the characteristic of everything that is directly given to us. In *Ideas I*, § 19, Husserl accordingly formulates his leading principle as follows:

Immediate "seeing," not merely sensuous experiential seeing, but *seeing in the universal sense as an originally presentive consciousness of any kind whatever,* is the ultimate source of all rational assertions.

This quote illustrates among other things the wide scope of Husserl's notion of intuition ("seeing in the universal sense") and also shows some of the collateral terminology Husserl used to the same purpose as "intuition," especially the locution "originally presentive" (*originär gebende*).

Another way in which Husserl expresses the same (and closely related) ideas is by speaking of the intuition of *essences* and of seeing essences. (The latter locution obviously involves "seeing in the universal sense.") Examples are found among other places in §§3-4 of *Ideas I*.

VIII.   THERE IS A LEVEL OF SELF-GIVENNESS
IN EXPERIENCE

It is important to heed Husserl's idea of self-givenness illustrated by the quotes above in § IV. For what is in fact given in experience when something is self-given? Not the noema. The noema is simply the sum total of what is thought or meant of an object in an act. The sphere of what is so meant is not the ultimate target of a phenomenological reduction. According to Husserl, the final target is what is *self-given*. And what is self-given must surely be an object, not its *noema*. (In the last analysis, this statement has to be qualified, but that qualification does not affect the present point. For the qualification, see § XVII below.)

Now you can also see in what sense Husserl intended his often-misunderstood slogan "zu den Sachen selbst." This slogan would be as gravely misleading as Husserl's most severe critics have claimed if no facet of actual reality survived the phenomenological reduction.

Another way in which Husserl puts his point is to say that something is (not necessarily that some *things* or some *objects* are) self-given. What he means is that there is a level of consciousness in which reality forces itself on us, which is the interface (not to say overlap) of reality and consciousness. As he expresses his point in *Ideas I*, § 43:

It is therefore fundamentally erroneous to believe that perception (and, after its own fashion, any other kind of intuition of a physical thing) does not reach the physical thing itself.

Even more bluntly Husserl writes in *Ideas I*, § 48:

If there are any worlds, any real physical things whatever, then the empirical motivations constituting them must be able to extend into my experience and into that of each Ego.

The same point can be seen in a variety of ways, perhaps most poignantly when Husserl comments on Brentano (*Ideas I*, § 85) and in that context includes the material moments of experience (sensory data) among physical phenomena (distinguished, of course, from the physical phenomena apprehended by means of noemata).

A closely related notion of immediate givenness reappears in Husserl's later writings, often under the heading of "evidence." Thus we read in the *Cartesian Meditations* (Third Meditation, § 24):

In the broadest sense, evidence denotes a universal primal phenomenon of intentional life, namely . . . the quite preeminent mode of consciousness that consists in the *self-appearance*, the *self-exhibiting*, the *self-giving*, of an affair, an affair-complex (or state of affairs), a universality, a value, or other objectivity in the final mode: "itself there," "immediately intuited," "given originaliter."   (Pp. 92–93 of the original.)

It is important to realize that (according to Husserl) we are here dealing with one particular phenomenon of consciousness. Restricting one's attention to it is therefore fundamentally different from merely focusing one's attention on noemata instead of objects.

Moreover, the "phenomenological residuum" which survives the transcendental reduction is not only an interface with reality. It is the basis of the entire constitution of our conceptualized world. This fact lends the result of the reduction its significance, and it is the reason why Husserl can claim that nothing is lost in the reduction:

That, then, is what is left as the sought-for "*phenomenological residuum*," though we have "excluded" the whole world with all physical things, living beings, and humans, ourselves included. Strictly speaking, we have not lost anything but rather have gained the whole of absolute being which, rightly understood, contains within itself, "constitutes" within itself, all worldly transcendencies.   (*Ideas I*, § 50.)

Such statements would not make any sense if the residuum did not possess a dual citizenship, i.e., if it were not at the same time *both* a denizen of consciousness *and* a denizen of the real world.

X. REDUCTION TO WHAT?

At this point, we run into a major problem. What is the transcendental reduction reduction to? What was intimated above is that the target of this reduction is the interface between consciousness and reality. But what is this interface like? Even more fundamentally, is it even appropriate to speak of *the* interface? Indeed, does the reduction eventually terminate in a rock bottom layer of something completely self-given? If so, what does this layer of the ultimately given consist in? It might seem that the interpretation defended here remains shaky until I have answered these massive questions.

However, the right addressee of these questions is Husserl, not any one of his interpreters. They were problems with which Husserl struggled and to which he proposed different solutions at different times. The problem of the given is in fact very closely related to what is probably the most difficult problem of Husserl exegesis, viz. the question: Was Husserl a realist or an idealist? In one sense of these words, Husserl clearly is a realist to the extent the phenomenological reductions actually take us *zu den Sachen*, and an idealist to the extent that the outcome of even the strictest reduction leaves us with a reduct that is still partly the product of our constitutive and "informing" activities. However, this is not the only relevant sense of "realist" and "idealist" here, and indeed not the most important one. For one of the other senses, compare § XX below.

Obviously, this is not the occasion to try to give a definitive answer to the question of the given. Equally obviously, most of what is said in this paper is independent of the problems of the given and of idealism. The significance of what I am calling the phenomenological dimension does not depend on whether this dimension comes to an end after a finite process of reduction or not. Likewise, the importance of the phenomenological dimension is not affected by the questions of the nature of its possible ultimate product. Does the phenomenological reduction reveal to us a layer of given objects or perhaps facts, or does it merely lead us back to a still unformed raw material for our constitutive processes to work on? And does the reduction process come to an end in either case?

Husserl's plight here is reminiscent of Wittgenstein's desperate search, in working on his *Tractatus*, of his ultimate phenomenological reducts, the simple objects. The difficulty of the task is measured by the fact that Wittgenstein ultimately left in the *Tractatus* the question of his ultimate phenomenological simples open, greatly to the detriment of philosophers' understanding of his work.

I shall leave the question of the ultimate reducts open for the time being. It will be re-opened below in §§ XVII and XX of this essay. Meanwhile, it fortunately turns out to be possible to study many other facets of Husserl's philosophy by means of the framework outlined in this essay, independently of the problem of the termination of the reduction.

XI. NOT THE ENTIRE NOEMA IS SELF-GIVEN

For one thing, we can make several important distinctions in Husserl without prejudicing our answer to the question concerning the possible end-points of reduction. For instance, in the light of what was said in § X we have to distinguish carefully what is contained in a noema and what is self-given in it. For not everything contained in a noema is part and parcel of what direct experience gives to a phenomenologist.

If an example is needed, one component of a noema that is not self-given according to Husserl is the determinable X, which is the element in the noema which makes it the noema of one and the same object. This follows from Husserl's insistence (cf. *Ideas I*, § 131) that the determinable X does not have any properties, any determinations, any *Wie*.

That the determinable X is not self-given is of course not a big surprise. For what is not self-given in a noema is typically contributed to it by the human form-giving and articulating thought-activity. This is seen from the synthetic character of the determinable X according to Husserl (cf. loc. cit.). Now it is well known that it is such human "informing" thought-activity that turns one's sundry impressions into impressions of one and the same enduring object, i.e., sensory matter into something "objective". And the role of the determinable X in a Husserlian noema is precisely to make the noema be of one and the same object.

In general, one is easily misled if one overlooks the distinction between what is self-given in a noema and what the different elements of the given noema are. In other words, this is the distinction between what survives the transcendental reduction in a noema and what does not survive it.

XII. NOEMA, OBJECT AND FILLING

Now we can also see how it is that a noema can do its duty of helping us to intend an object. The basic idea is clear enough, and far from surprising. If the noema is like a set of expectations, it specifies its object by claiming that those expectations will be fulfilled. This idea, suitably generalized, is unproblematic. The problem is how the filling of a noema can be conceptualized in a way which enables the noema so to speak to reach all the way to reality, and not remain within the realm of noemata alone. The picture I have painted now shows how that is possible. The constitution of a noema determines how it is connected with what is given to me in intuition, in Husserl's terminology, how it could be filled. Since the filling is a matter of what is immediately given to me and since what is given to me is part and parcel of the real world, the world of objects, the constitution does constitute a bridge between noemata and objects.

This shows how the problem which was mentioned above and which affected interpretations of Husserl as a meaning theorist can be solved.

XIII. CONSTITUTION

Likewise, Husserl's idea of constitution can be understood within the framework here adumbrated. Constitution is not the inverse of the intentional relation; it is in a certain sense the inverse of the phenomenological reductions. To discuss the constitution of a noema is to discuss the processes through which the given is articulated in one's consciousness.

But how can it make sense, on this view, to speak of the constitution of *objects*, not of their noemata, as Husserl frequently does? Do such locutions mean that according to Husserl we somehow construct the objects? No, they do not. The answer is provided by the insight that the intentional relation between a noema and its object is in the last analysis mediated by what is (or could be) immediately given to me in intuition. What follows is that only such objects can be intended as can manifest themselves through that interface of reality and consciousness that Husserl calls intuition, and that they can so to speak enter my intentional life only via their manifestations in intuition. (Compare the quotations given in §§ IV and V above.) This does not make an object causally or ontologically dependent on its own manifestations in intuition, but it makes it dependent on its actual and possible manifestations conceptually. Only in this sense are objects constituted by us.

XIV. HOW TO RUSSELL A FREGE-HUSSERL

What has been said can be illustrated and put into perspective by means of the same expositional tactic as was used by Føllesdal, to wit, by means of an analogy with another philosopher. However, for the purpose I have in this paper, Frege is almost as bad an object for comparison as one can find. In Frege, there is no trace of a reduction to what is given in intuition. On the contrary, Frege for instance strongly emphasized the independence of logic and mathematics (other than geometry) of intuition.

Instead of an analogy between Frege and Husserl, I propose to consider a partial parallelism between Russell and Husserl. Schematically, it could be presented as in the diagram on the following page.

One interesting facet of this parallelism is that in both philosophers we encounter a Heraclitean identity of the road up and the road down. In other words, in both philosophers, the crucial reduction can also be viewed as a process in the opposite direction, i.e., as a process of constitution (Husserl) or logical construction (Russell).

XV. THE DEEPER PARALLELISM BETWEEN HUSSERL AND RUSSELL

This parallelism is deeper than first might seem to be the case. It has a much more solid basis than the use of the same or similar terms by the two thinkers, such as "reduction," "constitution," and "logical con-

HUSSERL

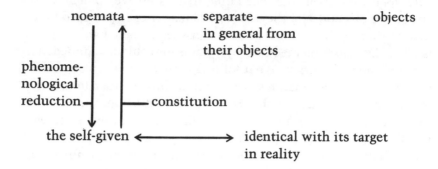

RUSSELL

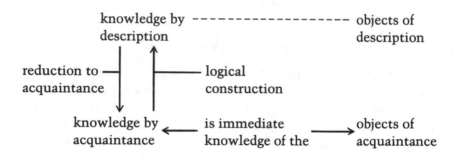

(Cf. here Russell 1912.)

struction," etc. One set of reasons why it is easy to underestimate the analogy is precisely the confusion which was discussed earlier in Section IV. Russell is usually pigeonholed as a realist, and his "reduction to acquaintance" is accordingly thought of as a reduction of one kind of knowledge to another or even of one kind of entity to another. In contrast, the misleading assimilation of phenomenology to phenomenalism has led philosophers to think of Husserlian reductions as intramental. (How else could we perform them by means of *epoché*?) All this easily leads us to underestimate the force of the analogy.

Another ambiguity is operative on both sides of the fence. Neither Husserl nor Russell distinguishes very clearly between an epistemological reduction and a conceptual reduction. Indeed, the best known formulation of Russell's contrast is as a distinction between two kinds of knowledge, knowledge by description and knowledge by acquaintance, while the entities in question are identified typically as the objects of these two different kinds of knowledge. Here we find a difference in degree, for Husserl's terminology was more concept-oriented and even object-oriented. Noemata are conceptual, and often Husserl even refers to them as "objects as intended." These differences are all superficial, however. Perceptive interpreters, such as David Pears or Dagfinn Føllesdal, have in the case of the one or the other of the two men ended up emphasizing the conceptual character of the problems involved in Russell as well as in Husserl. In Russell's case, this is the gist of his often-misunderstood injunction to replace inferences by logical constructions.

In reality, there is a remarkable similarity between the rightly understood overall aims of Husserl and Russell. For instance, most of the same things can be said about Russell's "logical construction" as were said above in § XIII about Husserlian "constitution." It is also instructive to note the similarities between Russellian acquaintance and Husserlian intuition.

In a suitable perspective, what both of them were in the first place trying to do was to see what the cash value of the abstract theories of physics and mathematics was in terms of what is actually given to us. In the case of Russell, this can be seen, e.g., in the chapter on the world of physics of *The Problems of Philosophy* (1912). In the case of Husserl, this is brought out nicely by Charles Harvey in his recent book (1989). Both men would probably have been happy to accept everyday perceptible objects as being among the "objects of acquaintance" at which the reduction ends. Alas, further epistemological arguments, especially arguments concerning sense-perception and its fallibility, persuaded both philosophers that everyday material objects are not given to us directly in the relevant sense. This prompted both analysts to pursue their reduction further. This exposed both of them to the jeopardy of being considered "idealists" or "phenomenalists." For instance, for Russell the true objects of acquaintance came to include prominently sense-data. Even though both Russell and Moore insisted that sense-data are denizens of the world of physics, their status is not clear. In particular, their dependence on the perceiver is hard to avoid. This put Russell under suspicions of phenomenalism not unlike those Husserl was subjected to.

In both cases, the suspicions were unjustified, at least as far as

Russell's and Husserl's ultimate aims are concerned. For instance, when Russell recommends considering objects of description as "logical constructs," he has sometimes been taken to call into question their status as *bona fide* realities. Yet Russell obviously never seriously doubted the reality of such exemplary objects of (mere) description as Bismarck and Julius Caesar. Correctly understood, Russell's aim was exactly the opposite: by showing how our conceptions of such objects are grounded on what is actually given to us, he tried to dispense with awkward questions how their existence and their properties could be inferred. This is analogous to Russell's other major project, which was to safeguard mathematics in the teeth of threatening paradoxes by reducing it to logic.

This is not to say that there remained formidable problems for Russell, especially concerning the precise status of the objects of acquaintance. I shall return to them in § XVII below.

XVI. "CATEGORIAL INTUITION" IN RUSSELL

Meanwhile, it is instructive to note that the analogy between Husserl and Russell can be pushed further. The scope of Husserl's project is seen most clearly in the field of what Frege would have considered pure thought. There, too, Husserl was trying to reduce our conceptual world to what is immediately given to us. But here that giving is not done by sensory intuition. It is done by what Husserl calls categorial intuition.

Likewise, in Russell the range of objects of acquaintance is not restricted to sense-data, which are (in the strict sense of the term) the particulars given to us in sense-perception, nor even to sense-data plus the universals which can be given to us in sense-perception. Russell's theory of acquaintance was supposed to culminate in his 1913 book *Theory of Knowledge*. (Unfortunately, upset by Wittgenstein's criticisms, Russell left the book unpublished, and it saw the light of printer's ink only in 1984 as Volume 7 of Russell's *Collected Papers*.) In it we can find an excellent counterpart to Husserl's categorial intuition. For there Russell maintains that we must assume a further class of objects of acquaintance, viz., logical forms. Our immediate knowledge of them is the "categorial acquaintance" or "logical intuition" (to mix the two gentlemen's terminology) which is a counterpart to Husserl's categorial intuition in Russell.

The idea of logical forms as objects of acquaintance was not a casual suggestion on Russell's part, either. If the idea had turned out to be viable, it would have enabled Russell to construe the entire *Principia* project of reducing mathematics to logic as a facet of his overall philosophical program of a reduction of absolutely everything in our conceptual structure to acquaintance. In terms of my analogy between Husserl and Russell, the upshot would have been to turn Russell's work in logic and in the foundations of mathematics into a counterpart of Husserl's enterprise of phenomenological reduction (or, looked upon from another angle, constitution) in the realm of essences.

Over and above such global analogies, many smaller comparisons between Russell and Husserl are possible. For one example, Russell's somewhat surprising suggestion that sense-data might be identified with the physical states of one's central nervous system can be compared with Husserl's idea (see § VIII above) that sensory data (material moments of experience) are to be pigeonholed among physical in contradistinction to mental phenomena.

XVII. SENSE-DATA VS. HYLE

The analogy between Husserl and Russell throws sharp light on both parties. However, the most intriguing facet of the parallelism is the precise way in which it breaks down.

Earlier, in § X, my interpretational line of thought was left in a state of suspended animation, as far as the targets or end-points of the phenomenological reductions are concerned. A comparison with Russell puts this question in an interesting perspective. In Russell, the end-points of reduction to acquaintance are entities of a well-defined categorial status, and in some cases even having an internal structure. They include particulars (individuals) like sense-data, but they can belong to other well-defined logical types, such as different types of universals, logical forms, etc.

Here the contrast with Husserl could scarcely be sharper. Husserl occasionally also uses the term "sense data" (*Sinnesdaten*), but only as a synonym or near-synonym for his normal term "hyletic data" or simply "hyle." What Husserl means by these terms is radically different from the meaning of Russell's "sense data." Hyletic data are neither particulars nor members of any other logical type. They are what the term suggests, unstructured raw materials for our structuring and form-giving mental activities. In other words, Husserl and Russell entertain radically different views as to what the immediately given is like. For the mature Husserl, unlike Russell, the self-given is not structured categorially into particulars, their properties, their interrelations, etc. For instance, what is given in visual perception is not an articulated structure of visual objects but something like (in Quine's phrase) "a two-dimensional continuum of colors and shades." Only one's articulating and "informing" noesis turns it into perceptions of objects (of different logical types), that is to say, into perceptions of the kinds of objects we can have noemata of.

Moreover, since one cannot turn one's intentional attention to anything without turning it into an object (of a noema), one cannot ever capture hyletic data in their pure unedited form. They can enter into our consciousness only as ingredients of already articulated acts, for instance, as contributing to the filling of a noema.

Here we have discovered a radical difference between Russell and Husserl. Of course this does not reduce the value of the analogy, for the crucial difference could only be seen against the background of the analogy.

XVIII. THE GIVEN CANNOT BE ISOLATED

What is even more important, the difference between Russell and Husserl helps us to answer the question raised above concerning the stopping-points of Husserlian reductions. The answer suggested by the comparison is: there are no absolute stopping-points. Whatever phenomenological reflection can reach has already been structured by form-giving noesis. Apparently no reduction can lead us to objects or other independent entities which are conceptually self-given.

This pervasive contribution of one's mind to everything one can intend according to Husserl is among the reasons why he has sometimes been considered an idealist. It may perhaps explain why Russell the realist and Husserl the alleged idealist have often been viewed in such a different light. However, such "idealism" does not mean that for Husserl the given consists only of phenomena in contradistinction to mind-independent realities or that there is not an actual input from reality into one's consciousness. Whether or not the phenomenological dimension so to speak comes to an end is not the only question relevant to Husserl's status as a realist or idealist. Once these facts have been clarified and acknowledged, it becomes a matter of terminological taste whether or not we should label him a realist or idealist – or neither.

Or does it become a merely "semantical" matter in the vulgar sense of the word? Further light is thrown on this question in §§ XX–XXI below.

XIX. ON HUSSERL'S DEVELOPMENT

The views of the mature Husserl can be appreciated more keenly against the background of the facts of his development. As was pointed out above, the details of this development largely remain to be investigated. The direction of this development is nevertheless clear. An early stage of this development is seen in the so-called "Seefelder Manuskripte über Individuation" from the years 1905–1909 (*Husserliana*, vol. 10, pp. 234–68), and less sharply from his other writings in the same period. In them, we find a view which is very close to Russell's, as illustrated by passages like the following:

I see a beer-bottle, which is brown; I attend to the expanse of brown, "as it is actually given"; I exclude everything that is merely intended in the phenomenon and not given [in it]. There is the beer-bottle; it is such-and-such. I distinguish the beer-bottle-appearances; I turn them into objects. I find a connection between these appearances; I find an awareness [*Bewusstsein*] of an identity which runs through them. I realize that I express it through the words: The beer-bottle is [what is] always appearing; it appears as the same persisting [object]; the appearances are not the beer-bottle, which appears in them. . . . They are different; the beer-bottle is one and the same.

(Op. cit., 237.)

Here it is obvious that Husserl thinks that the immediately given can be assumed to be structured into objects of different kinds not unlike Russell's objects of acquaintance. In fact, the quoted passage continues:

The appearances are themselves objects [*Gegenstände*]. One appearance [means] something that has continued identity. It lasts through a "time span." (Op. cit., 237–38.)

This "Russellian" character of the given according to the Husserl of 1905 is all the more remarkable as he speaks in the same breath of "phänomenologische Wahrnehmung" and even "phänomenologische Reduktion." Such phenomenological objects can also be given to me by memory:

An appearance is fixed in memory; in it one can distinguish such-and-such components [Momente]. They are in turn objects [Gegenstände].

(Op. cit., 238.)

The other side of the same coin is that in Husserl's writings from this period the idea of hyletic data plays no role.

One can also locate in the quoted passages some of the seeds of his subsequent development and to the dissolution of the idea that phenomenological reduction leads us to objects. For what constitutes an object is its permanence in time, and that permanent identity is (according to Husserl's 1905 views) possessed by a phenomenological object as such, without any contribution by the human consciousness. (This is shown by the last two quotes.)

However, Husserl later came to hold that this permanence in time was not actually given to me. This view was a product of the long and intricate analyses which he was beginning around the same time and which culminate in his book *On the Phenomenology of Inner Time Consciousness*. Later, what maintained the persisting identity of the object of a noema was the determinable X, which, I argued above in § xi, is not itself self-given.

One interesting fact about this historical development of Husserl's views is that it affects different concepts differently. In the field of sensory awareness, it is indeed natural to think that what is given to us "originally" are amorphous hyletic data which we cannot ever capture in their unedited state, because they cannot be intended without being subjected to our structure-giving acts. But in the case of intellectual awareness, it is equally natural to think that the basic given comes in the forms of "clear and distinct" ideas, e.g., in categorial intuition. Hence the basic structure of many of Husserl's ideas can be seen more clearly in their application to logic and mathematics rather than in their application to sensory awareness. (Compare § v above.)

Thus, the simplest facts of Husserl's development already serve to illustrate the overall perspective in which I am proposing to consider him in this paper.

XX. EIDETIC REDUCTION AND *WESENSSCHAU*

This perspective can be deepened further. From the absence of an absolute rock bottom of phenomenological reduction it follows that outside purely formal sciences we cannot segregate categorial intuition from sensory intuition. In the phenomenological analysis of our ideas of the sensory world, we encounter more than particular concrete objects. We often, maybe typically, see them as exemplifications of certain general types, e.g., in general laws. These are what Husserl calls essences (*Wesen*). They have to be distinguished in phenomenological analysis from the sensory mass in which they are embedded. They are objectively given to us in experience, not added to experience as an afterthought. (Cf. *Ideas I*, § 22.) Yet they are not always presented to us separately, but can be intertwined with sensory raw material.

Thus in the mature Husserl there is a need of separating the general (the essences) from the particular in intuition. Husserl's response to this challenge was his idea of eidetic reduction. Unlike transcendental reduction, its function is not merely to isolate what is directly given (given in intuition) to me. It serves to focus on what in my complex total experiences is given to me in nonsensory intuition, especially essences.

This kind of nonsensory intuition is called by Husserl *Wesensschau* or *Wesenerschauung*. Its objects are pure essences. In a typical instance of empirical experience they are what Husserl calls material essences. They are analogous to the objects of categorial intuition, which are formal essences. These formal essences have to do with acts of judging in contradistinction to, for instance, acts of perception. Both types of nonsensory intuition are heirs of the notion of abstraction as employed by Husserl in *Logical Investigations*. This transformation of (a kind of) abstraction into *Wesensschau* is part and parcel of the same development of Husserl's thought I have indicated earlier in this paper. If experience came to me already articulated into objects of different categorial sorts, as it came to Russell, no eidetic reduction would be needed, and the objects of categorial intuition would be neatly separated from the objects of sensory intuition.

In the light of these observations, several things become clear. For one thing, even the reduction of empirical intentional complexes has in certain directions ultimate stopping points, of course not in the direction of the sensory raw materials, but in the direction of the essences embodied in that raw material. This helps us to understand what otherwise might appear to be an inconsistency on Husserl's part. He seems to insist on speaking as if *objects* they were given to us in sense-perception, notwithstanding his emphasis on other occasions of the inaccessibility of unedited raw materials of sensation. The explanation is that an essence into which that raw material is articulated can be "given in its purity, wholly and entirely as it is in itself" (*Ideas*, § 67). This puts into a perspective what was said in § xvii above.

At the same time, our observations are relevant to Husserl's relation to idealism. For they imply that, in a sense, the only objects that are completely self-given according to Husserl (albeit only as components of wider intentional complexes) are essences, that is, a sort of "ideas." But the really deep question here is the status of such Husserlian essences. Are they completely given to me in experience, or are they (at least in some cases) contributed by myself as a part of my articulating and editing ("informing") activities? Wittgenstein, for one, opted for the former alternative without any qualifications, at least in his early philosophy. (Small wonder, therefore, that he ended up virtually identifying phenomenology and logic or "grammar," as he later preferred to call it.) But a philosopher who does so is likely to be forced to deny any synthetic *a priori*. What was Husserl's last and final word on this question? Even if I knew the answer, I could not summarize it within the boundaries of this paper.

XXI. WHO IS RIGHT?

Another question which cannot be fully answered here is: Who is right, Husserl or Russell? Does the given come to us categorially prepackaged, as Russell assumes, or does reality impinge on our consciousness only in the form of unstructured raw materials, as

Husserl claimed? At first sight, the answer seems obvious. Husserl's theory is more comprehensive and more flexible. Surely an important part of the activities which we have to perform in order to grasp the world has the character of form-giving or articulation, and surely an adequate theory of concept formation and cognition must therefore deal with the ways in which we impose a categorial structure on the world — or so it seems.

However, the real question is not whether we must try to develop a theory of how we structure the world, but whether such a theory is part of the business of a phenomenologist. And this question turns on whether the articulating and form-giving activities we admittedly perform are accessible to phenomenological reflection or whether they are performed under the surface of our intentional consciousness. And here the testimony of many of the best phenomenological psychologists seems to suggest that our structuring and categorizing activities are inaccessible in a stronger sense than Husserl thought. For instance, they tell us that in the most primitive, unedited sense accessible to our conscious attention, we literally see objects, not a "two-dimensional continuum of colors and shades." For another example, David Katz has written that most people go to their grave without ever seeing purely phenomenological colors (called by Katz "spectral colors") as distinguished from colors already articulated categorially into colors of objects, colors of surfaces, colored areas of space, colors of light-sources, etc.

Be the force of such testimony what it may, much of Husserl's heroic struggle with notions like hyle, filling, and reduction can be viewed as an attempt to do justice to both the facts of constitution and the facts of the immediate givenness of the word's categorial structure.

Last but not least, what are we to say of those ideas that Russell and Husserl shared? Are they right? In order to answer the question, we would have to find the conceptual gist of their shared views, that is, to find the true phenomeno-logic. What, for instance, is the right conceptual analysis of the contrast between acquaintance and description, and does it really have a counterpart in Husserl? I have discussed the first of these two questions on earlier occasions. (See Hintikka 1989.) However, an answer to the second one will have to be left open here.

ACKNOWLEDGEMENT

In working on this essay, I have greatly profited from the comments and criticisms of David W. Smith, Barry Smith, and Martin Kusch. They are not responsible for any of the remaining mistakes or for the views expressed here.

REFERENCES

(Only works actually quoted or referred to are listed here.)

Føllesdal, Dagfinn. "Husserl's notion of noema." *Journal of Philosophy* 66 (1969): 680–87. Also in Dreyfus, ed., 73–80 (cf. below).

――――. "Husserl's theory of perception." In *Husserl, Intentionality and Cognitive Science.* Edited by Hubert Dreyfus. The MIT Press: Cambridge, Mass., 1982, 93–96.

Harvey, Charles W. *Husserl's Phenomenology and the Foundations of Natural Science.* Ohio University Press: Athens, 1989.

Hintikka, Jaakko. "On Kant's notion of intuition. (*Anschauung*)." In *The First Critique: Reflections on Kant's 'Critique of Pure Reason.'* Edited by Terence Pelenhulum and J.J. MacIntosh. Wadsworth, Belmont, Cal., 1969, 38–52.

――――. "The Cartesian *cogito,* epistemic logic and neuroscience: some surprising interrelations." In Jaakko Hintikka and Merrill B. Hintikka, *The Logic of Epistemology and the Epistemology of Logic.* Dordrecht: Kluwer, 1989, 113–36.

Husserl, Edmund. *Cartesian Meditations.* Translated by Dorion Cairns. The Hague: Nijhoff, 1960.

――――. *The Idea of Phenomenology.* Translated by W.P. Alston and George Nakhnikian. The Hague: Nijhoff, 1964.

――――. *Zur Phänomenologie des inneren Zeitbewusstseins* (with supplementary texts). Edited by Rudolf Boehm. *Husserliana* 10. The Hague: Nijhoff, 1966.

――――. *Logical Investigations* I–II. Translated by John Findlay. London: Routledge & Kegan Paul, 1970.

――――. *Ideas Pertaining to a Pure Phenomenology,* First Book. Translated by F. Kersten. Dordrecht: Kluwer Academic, 1982. (Referred to as *Ideas I.*)

Katz, David. *The World of Colour.* London: Kegan Paul, 1935.

Kern, Iso. *Husserl und Kant.* The Hague: Nijhoff, 1964.

Moore, G.E. "Refutation of idealism." In *Philosophical Studies.* London: Routledge & Kegan Paul 1922, 1–30.

Pears, David. *Bertrand Russell and the British Tradition in Philosophy.* London: Collins (The Fontana Library), 1967.

Russell, Bertrand. *The Problems of Philosophy.* London: Home University Library, 1912.

———. "Knowledge by acquaintance and knowledge by description." In *Mysticism and Logic and Other Essays.* London: Longmans, Green, 1918.

———. "The relation of sense data to physics." *Scientia* 16 (1914): 1–27 and supp. 3–34. Also in *Mysticism and Logic and Other Essays,* London: Longmans, Green, 1918.

———. *Theory of Knowledge: The 1913 Manuscript, Collected Papers of Bertrand Russell,* vol. 7. London: George Allen & Unwin, 1984.

Wittgenstein, Ludwig. *Tractatus Logico-Philosophicus.* Translated by David Pears and Brian McGuinness. London: Routledge & Kegan Paul, 1961.

3   Meaning and language

For Alfons Süssbauer

I. INTRODUCTION

Husserl pursued philosophy of language not for its own sake but mainly to support his conception of logic. In particular he wished to refute psychologism, the view that the laws of logic are descriptions of regularities in the way we think, which implies that different ways of thinking may embody distinct but equally acceptable logics. Husserl wishes instead to show there is a single logic which is objectively binding for all. This theory was propounded in the *Logical Investigations* (1900–01), which is where the greater part of Husserl's philosophy of language can be found. Prior to this, Husserl had mentioned language and meaning only in passing in the *Philosophy of Arithmetic* and in an early (1890) manuscript with the title "On the Logic of Signs (Semiotic)"[1] which is mainly concerned with the division between natural signs (like smoke) and artificial signs (like language). This paper will accordingly focus first on the theory of meaning and language in the *Logical Investigations*, it will then consider the changes after 1901. These affect chiefly his view of the nature and status of meanings, which underwent a major modification between the *Investigations* and the *Ideas*. In comparison with other areas of his philosophy, however, Husserl's views on language and meaning were relatively stable, and later developments arise primarily because of his elaboration of other issues adjoining the philosophy of language.

After the direct confrontation with psychologism in the "Prolegomena to Pure Logic," there follows a group of five investigations
dealing with matters arising from Husserl's adoption of a form of
Platonism, the assumption of the existence of abstract entities. In
particular, the laws of logic are viewed as principles governing a timeless realm of abstract, or, to use the term Husserl preferred, *ideal*
meanings. *Investigation* I, "Expression and Meaning," puts forward
the view that meanings themselves are Platonic or ideal entities of a
particular sort, namely the kinds, or, as Husserl says, *ideal species* of
certain aspects of mental acts. The first part of the investigation is
spent in clearly distinguishing meanings in this sense from mental
acts themselves, also from the concomitant mental states of speak-
ers, which have often been confused with meanings, and finally from
the objects to which the speaker refers in using expressions. In the
course of making these distinctions, Husserl sketches a quite comprehensive theory of meaning.[2] The second part of the investigation is
concerned with defending the ideality of meanings in the face of
apparently fluctuating or variable meanings, in particular those of
what Husserl calls *essentially occasional* expressions, but which are
nowadays generally called *indexical expressions*.

Investigation II elaborates Husserl's Platonism of species and attacks the empiricist theory of abstraction. This is the theory, found
especially in Locke, but then popular in Germany, that abstract objects arise by our directing attention to some aspects of what we
experience and overlooking others: the retained features constitute
the abstract object, which is thus dependent on mind for its existence. *Investigation* III sets out Husserl's theory of dependent and
independent parts, a seemingly minor methodological sideline in
the sweep of Husserl's thought, but one which contains his theory of
analytic and synthetic judgements, and outlines the method of
analysing objects into their features, much employed in Husserl's
subsequent philosophy. *Investigation* IV applies the notion of dependent parts to expressions, distinguishing meanings of dependent and
independent categories, and floating an ambitious conception of universal grammar based on the laws governing the combinations of
such meanings. *Investigation* V steps beyond the elaboration of the

programme of pure logic: it is concerned with consciousness and intentionality. Following and at the same time criticising Brentano, Husserl advances an analysis of consciousness, which was to form the basis of philosophical method for him as for Brentano. *Investigation* VI, an extended account of knowledge and evidence, goes far beyond the programme of pure logic and the psychological and ontological analyses supporting it which had originally appeared in 1900–01.

III. EXPRESSION AND MEANING

Husserl prefaces his general theory of meaning with a distinction between signs and expressions. All expressions are signs, but not all signs are expressions. Smoke is a sign of fire; it indicates it in the sense of typically making whoever perceives smoke think there is fire, but it does not express fire or stand for it in the way that *horse* expresses the concept of horse and stands for horses. Expressions are objects employed not just to make one think of something else, but also to carry a meaning. It is the nature of this meaning, its relation to the expressions used to express it, to the mental acts of the speaker who uses it, and to the objects referred to that occupy Husserl in *Investigation* I.

When a sensible physical sign is spoken or written or otherwise uttered and made perceptible to an audience, this occurs in conjunction with certain mental acts of the utterer. These include what the utterer is thinking about when using the sign. Some of the things an utterer is thinking about when uttering an expression will be quite irrelevant to the expression's meaning; for instance, I may say to my neighbour "It is a nice day today" while thinking about an appointment I have in the afternoon. Such incidental accompaniments to an expression will vary quite randomly and will generally remain unknown to the hearer through the fact of utterance. On the other hand, some among the utterer's typical thoughts will be easily inferrable from the fact that the utterance is made. My neighbour will typically take me to believe or judge that it *is* a nice day if I say so, unless there are special clues suggesting I do not mean what I say. Of course the neighbour may be wrong, but typically she will not. Usually we understand what typical concomitants an utterance has in the mind of the utterer without having to be told and without even thinking about it. The utterance thus *intimates* to the hearer a fact about the mental acts of the utterer which the hearer understands spontaneously without need of a special signal. This indicating side to the use of a linguistic expression is not to be confused with its meaning, although expressions have often been said to *express* such mental acts. What my statement to the neighbour *means* is not that *I believe* the day to be nice, but that the day itself is nice, whereas what my uttering intimates is that I believe the day to be nice. And, according to Husserl's view, what the statement refers to is something else again, namely the day's being nice, which is a state of affairs.

Intimation is indeed a regular and important part of language as used communicatively, and Husserl, of course, accepts that the reason for having sensible signs is communicative. He even offers a sketch of what goes on in communication which anticipates in more than one respect the theories of speaker's intentions offered over half a century later by Paul Grice and others:

Expressions were originally framed to fulfil a communicative function . . . The . . . sign . . . first becomes a spoken word or communicative bit of speech, when a speaker produces it with the intention of "expressing himself about something" through its means; he must endow it with a sense in certain acts of mind, a sense he desires to share with his auditors. Such sharing becomes a possibility if the auditor also understands the speaker's intention. He does this inasmuch as he takes the speaker to be a person, who is not merely uttering sounds but *speaking to him*, who is accompanying those sounds with certain sense-giving acts, which the sounds reveal to the hearer, or whose sense they seek to communicate to him.   (*LI* I, § 7)[3]

While accepting the importance of intimation for the establishment and appreciation of communication, Husserl denies that the communicative aspect is essential to every instance of language use, citing the use of language in internal soliloquoy as a decisive counter-instance: "when we live in the understanding of a word, it expresses something, and the same thing whether we address it to anyone or not" (*LI* I, § 8, beginning). Hence communication and intimation, while the *raison d'être* of expressions, is not essential to their use, whereas their being meaningful is essential.

So what is it to be meaningful? One thing it is *not* is perceiving or otherwise being intuitively presented with the object referred to. I may know a lot about someone and use that person's proper name without ever having met, heard, or seen the person. I am nevertheless just as capable of giving expressions referring to that person their *meanings* as someone who met him or her. If I meet the person, then what had been a schematic or abstract way of considering them is filled out by all kinds of perceptual detail, though it remains the same person that I consider. Merely schematically considering someone or something, without benefit of present or past perceptual contact, Husserl calls (mere) *intention* and contrasts it with the intention's perceptual *fulfilment*. The distinction between intention and fulfilment was to be enlarged and play a central role in his theory of knowledge in *Investigation* VI. Fulfilment is therefore also incidental, not essential to meaning, though, as in the case of communicative intimation, there would be no meaningful use of language in general were there not fulfilment in some cases.

The two things that always have to be present when a sign is understood are the sign itself and the person understanding it. Now the sign itself is simply a physical object, whether an event or a thing, even if it is produced for the express purpose of meaning something. Without its being understood or at least being understandable, it is no more a sign than anything else. Hence what breathes life into a sign and makes it a sign are the mental acts of the person or persons who understand it. On the other hand these individual mental acts are not the sign's meaning either. When I say *It is a nice day*, what this *means* when I say it to my neighbour or indeed think it silently to myself is not what is in my head, and Husserl is quite clear about this. Meaning is intersubjective, not subjective:

If I say sincerely . . . "The three perpendiculars of a triangle intersect in a point" this is of course based on the fact that I judge so. If someone hears me and understands my statement, he likewise knows that fact; he apperceives me as someone who judges thus. But is my judging that I here *intimate* the meaning of my statement, is it what my statement *asserts*, and in that sense expresses? Plainly not. . . . What this statement states is *the same* whoever may assert it, and on whatever occasion and in whatever circumstances he may do so, and this same thing stated is precisely this, *that the three perpendiculars of a triangle intersect in a point*, no more and no less. . . . [W]hat we assert . . . involves nothing subjective. My act of judging is a transient experience, but what the statement states, the content ... neither arises nor passes away. It is an identity in the strict sense, one and the same geometrical truth.   (*LI* I, § 11)

If the meaning of an expression is to be distinguished from the mental acts of the utterer, it is likewise to be distinguished from the object(s) referred to. This is fairly obvious in the case of expressions which refer to concrete individuals. A name such as *Julius Caesar* or a description like *The Roman military commander who conquered Gaul* has a meaning which is ideal and immutable, and in proper use the same whoever uses the expression, whereas the referent of these expressions is a man who died violently in 44 B.C. Husserl insists on the distinction for all expressions:

Each expression not merely says something, but says it *of* something: it not only has a meaning, but refers to certain *objects*. . . . But the object never coincides with the meaning.   (*LI* I, § 12)

Expressions with different meanings can refer to the same object: Husserl cites the examples *the victor at Jena* versus *the vanquished at Waterloo* and *the equilateral triangle* versus *the equiangular triangle*. Two expressions can be synonymous – have the same meaning as well as the same object – for instance synonymous words from different languages like *two* and *deux*. Husserl also tries to show that different occurrences of the same word with the same meaning may have different referents, e.g., two occurrences of *horse* in sentences saying of different individual creatures *This is a horse*, but the example is unhappy because the predicative use of the noun need not be referential. Husserl held that common nouns refer to each of the items in the noun's extension, but that does not mean that in predication a particular one is singled out. At best, Husserl's theory here needs considerable elaboration. A similarly unhappy example is that in a sum such as $1 + 1 = 2$ the different "ones" must mean the same but differ in reference. The plurality of *values* of a common noun is however to be distinguished from a plurality of referents for proper names, which can only have more than one referent by being equivocal.

Not only names have referents. In fact, at one point Husserl goes so far as to say "Every expression intimates something, means something and names or otherwise designates something" (*LI* I, § 14). As we have already seen this is false of intimation since when words are uttered in soliloquoy, there is no one there to whom they can intimate anything. Its application to referents is questionable as well. However, declarative sentences for Husserl do have referents: they refer to states of affairs, whether these actually obtain (are facts) or not. Different sentential meanings or propositions may refer to the same state of affairs, e.g., *a is larger than b* and *b is smaller than a*. Husserl prefers in general to call the referents of expressions *objectivities* rather than objects, drawing attention to the fact that the referent is not always an individual thing but may be a higher-order object.

Husserl's theory of meaning and reference is thus quite similar to that of Frege, of which Husserl was aware, since he had read "On Sense and Reference" and disagreed with it, not in the general point that sense and reference should be distinguished, which he upheld, but because he held that the German terms *Sinn* and *Bedeutung* were synonymous and it would be "rather dubious" to use them for different things (*LI* I, § 13). Husserl's linguistic intuition on this point was certainly more secure than Frege's, as subsequent discussions and problems of translation have borne out.

It is thus an interesting historical question how far Husserl's view is merely a variant of Frege's. Certainly at this stage in Husserl's thought the two are different on several points. One is that sentences for Husserl have states of affairs as referents, whereas for Frege they have truth-values. Although logicians have tended to favour Frege's view, it has for almost everyone an initial strangeness which dulls at best with repetition, while Husserl's view, whether right or not, is much more natural. A difference which Frege pointed out is that Husserl accepted that words like *horse* are common names having, as Husserl puts it, a plurality of values, whereas for Frege they are not names at all but undetachable parts of predicates. Again, Husserl's view was not only more generally held at the time, but despite the strictures of Frege[4] and those who thinkingly or unthinkingly followed him, has much to be said in its favour. We have also seen that Husserl allows a single meaning without ambiguity or indexicality to refer now to one referent, now to another, although his arguments are not very convincing. Husserl would therefore not subscribe to the Fregean thesis that sense determines reference.

Perhaps the most striking difference between Frege's theory of meaning and Husserl's lies in the connection between meaning and the mental that Husserl accepts. Whereas for Frege, as for Bolzano, the connection between an abstract meaning and any subjective mental act is an external one of the subject's *grasping* the meaning (Bolzano and Frege even use the same word, *erfassen*), for Husserl the link between meaning and the mental is much more intimate. It is not that meanings *are* mental; that would be the Lockean style of theory that leads to psychologism and that Husserl rejects. Rather, meanings are the abstract *kinds* or *species* of something mental. When I see a green leaf and later think to myself that it is green, then there is an aspect of my mental act of presenting the leaf symbolically, which Husserl calls the act's *matter*, which serves to direct it to the particular individual greenness of this leaf, what Husserl calls a colour-moment, what the scholastics called individual accidents or qualities. The greenness of the leaf is the object of this act, while the act's matter is what Twardowski had called its content. Husserl prefers to use the word "content" not for this psychological moment but for the abstract species of such moments, and this, finally, is the *meaning* of the word "green."

The relation between meaning and the mental is thus not the external one of grasping, but the internal one of an instance's exemplifying its kind. Since all symbolic mental acts, whether self-sufficient or not, have their own matters, and these matters have their own kinds, all such acts instantiate meanings without meaning being thereby hauled down from its Platonic status. Like Frege and Bolzano, Husserl can allow for meanings that never get thought or expressed by accepting a "strongly Platonistic" theory of species whereby a species may exist and be as it is, whether or not it has instances. Husserl thus effects a remarkable economy in the ontology of abstract meaning by employing the relation of instantiation or exemplification, which the realist about universals needs anyway, and at the same time tying meaning internally to the mental, a feat which had eluded his Platonist forebears, Bolzano and Frege. At the same time, Husserl manages to avoid a psychologistic and subjectivistic account of meaning, a feat which had eluded his empiricist forebears. Linguistic reference to the particular instance of greenness or other object is thus effected by a complicated network of relations as follows:

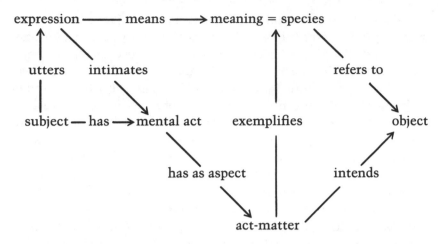

It will be noted from this figure that the apparently simple, semantically central relations of meaning and reference are compounded from other, more fundamental relations in Husserl's theory. The real work done in linking an expression with the object it represents via a meaning is carried out not by the meaning but by the act-matter which is the meaning's instance, which intends the object. This leads the theory of meaning into the general arena of the theory of the intentionality of the mental. It is thus not irrelevant to the theory of meaning that Husserl expends much effort in *Investigation* V on explicating this relation, and Husserl's later adaptations to the theory of meaning always go hand in hand with modifications of the theo.y of intentionality.

Although this is already a fairly complex theory, it still does not overcome all equivocations. For instance, when a subject utters an expression, we should distinguish the act of uttering – which is what really intimates something to a hearer – from the phonic event which is the product of this uttering. Both of these are known as an "utterance," but only the latter is well styled as an "expression." And as an individual event, it is a token to be distinguished from the expression-type, to use Peirce's terms. Husserl also does not enter into detail about the social and conventional side of meaning, whereby certain expression-types are linked by public practice with certain meanings and objects. The emphasis on soliloquoy and the mediating function of the individual's mental acts diverts attention away from this side of meaning, which was later to be stressed, this time to the detriment of the inner, mental aspect, by Wittgenstein. Husserl himself was also to become dissatisfied with his own theory, but for different reasons, as we shall show below.

IV. MEANING AND OBJECT

We have postponed the question whether every meaning has an object. Husserl's Platonist forebears Bolzano and Frege had held that not every meaning has an object, that there are objectless meanings: for example, the expressions *Odysseus* and *the least rapidly converging series*. Husserl's fellow Brentano-pupil Twardowski on the other hand had in 1894 held in opposition to Bolzano that every idea has an object,[5] which, being translated into Husserl's idiom, would imply that every act-quality presents or intends an object. Twardowski did however deny that all such objects exist, and opened up the way thereby for Meinong's theory of objects outside being, which became publicly known as Meinong's position only in 1904. Husserl read Twardowski's monograph carefully,[6] and disagreed with its conclusion that there are non-existing objects, but in language which is dangerously wavering. For Husserl,

the intentional object of a presentation is the same as its actual object, and on occasion as its external object, and . . . it is absurd to distinguish between them. . . . If I present God to myself, or an angel, or an intelligible thing-in-itself, or a physical thing or a round square etc., I mean the transcendent object named in each case, in other words, my intentional object: it makes no difference whether this object exists or is imaginary or absurd. "The object is merely intentional" does not, of course, mean that it exists, but only as an intention, of which it is an actual part, or that some shadow of it exists. It means rather that the intention, the reference to an object so qualified, exists, but not that the object does. If the intentional object exists, the intention, the reference [i.e., the referring, not the referent – PS] does not exist alone, but the thing referred to exists also.

(*LI* V, Appendix to § 11 and § 20, end)

So when Husserl says, as he often does, that an object of consciousness does not exist, is fictitious, absurd, etc., he may sound as though he is endorsing Twardowski's view, but the form of words is misleading. Husserl is quite prepared to say that acts (and names whose meanings are instantiated in them) refer to objects, yet may be objectless: in § 13 of *Investigation* I he says "An act of meaning [*Akt des Bedeutens*] is the determinate way in which we intend [*meinen*] the object in each case," and in § 15 he says "To use an expression significantly, and to refer expressively to an object . . . are one and the same," yet avers shortly thereafter that "countless expressions [have been] shown by mathematicians, in lengthy indirect demonstrations, to be objectless a priori." Husserl endorses what is nowadays called an adverbial account of intentionality when he says:

I have an idea of the god Jupiter: this means that I have a certain presentative experience, the presentation-of-the-god-Jupiter is realized in my consciousness. This intentional experience may be dismembered as one chooses in descriptive analysis, but the god Jupiter naturally will not be found in it. The "immanent," "mental object" is not therefore part of the actual descriptive make-up of the experience, it is in truth not really immanent or mental. But it also does not exist extramentally, it does not exist at all. . . . If, however, the intended object exists, nothing becomes phenomenologically different. It makes no essential difference to an object presented and given to consciousness whether it exists, or is fictitious, or is perhaps completely absurd.   (*LI* V, § 11, middle)

This passage presages the idea of the phenomenological reduction: that it is irrelevant for phenomenological analysis whether an act has an object that exists or not. Does this mean, as David Bell has suggested, that "the intentional object towards which a proper name is directed is not the actual bearer of the name"?[7] The answer must be that it does not. The name "Bismarck" refers to the real man, the Iron Chancellor himself, he is the intentional object of my references to him. Does "Jupiter" refer then to the Greek god? In one sense of "refer," Husserl would say "Yes." But is there an actual bearer of the name as there is in the case of Bismarck? Husserl would say there is not. In other words, if we distinguish between veridical and nonveridical acts, those with and those without suitable objects, the semantics of names is not uniform. Only by ignoring the question of the external object (if any) at all do we get a uniform semantics of names, and in the *Logical Investigations*, despite his acceptance of uniformity in the psychology of presentation, Husserl was not yet prepared to turn his back, at least for certain methodological purposes, on actual, external objects where acts are veridical.

V. EXPRESSIONS WITH VARIABLE MEANINGS

An immediate threat to Husserl's view that the meanings of expressions are immutable Platonic essences comes from expressions whose meaning appears to vary. The plurality of values of a common name is no problem: its fixed meaning and the facts provide it with a fixed extension, comprising all these values. Where there are several such extensions, the names in question can plausibly be considered equivocal, that is, as having more than one meaning, but each separate meaning remains ideal and immutable. Vague or fuzzy expressions likewise offer no serious problem: according to Husserl, they "have no single meaning-content, the same in all cases of their application: their meaning is oriented towards types, only partially conceived with clarity and definiteness" (*LI* I, § 27). While vague concepts form the majority of those used in everyday life, all expressions integral to pure theories and laws, according to Husserl, are exact, a view which may strike one as over-optimistic.[8]

The most serious threat to Husserl's view of the ideality of meanings is posed by expressions whose meaning varies in a regular way according to their context, like "I," "you," "this," "here," "below," "yesterday," "the Kaiser," etc. Because their meaning varies with and depends on the occasion of their use, Husserl calls such expressions *essentially (subjective and) occasional*. They coincide with what are nowadays usually called indexical expressions. It is a mark of Husserl's circumspection as a philosopher of language that these frequently neglected or overlooked expressions should have received careful treatment at his hands.[9] Husserl's theory, which is what we should expect given his other views, is that occasional expressions do not have a single invariable meaning, but on each occasion of use an occasional expression acquires a determinate meaning. In isolation from the circumstances which determine this ideal meaning, occasional expressions have only an incomplete or *indicating* meaning (*LI* I, § 26), whose nature varies from case to case, but which in the circumstances of utterance conspires with these to fix an ideal or *indicated* meaning. The indicating meaning is not a single fixed and objective meaning, but is understood to the extent that it arouses in us the notion of its peculiar function, which may be in part universal and conceptual, as when we know that "here" always refers to some place. Husserl's theory of indexical expressions thus not only demonstrates his flexibility in matters of language, but also succeeds in warding off the threat of subjectivity and fluctuation of meanings.

XI. GRAMMAR OF MEANINGS

Husserl lays stress on the distinction between mere nonsense expressions, which have no meaning at all, and expressions which have a sense, but which could not stand for anything actual, e.g., a sentential contradiction, which could not designate an actual (obtaining) state of affairs, or a name standing for something contradictory, like *round square* or *regular decahedron* (*LI* I, § 15). The latter are, Husserl stresses, not meaningless or senseless, but formally or materially absurd, which is to say that it is *a priori* impossible that the relevant meaning-intentions should be fulfilled. Put more simply, nothing can fall under them, and it is precisely because the expressions in question are meaningful that this is so and that we can realise it. If the impossibility is formal or analytic, Husserl calls it formal absurdity, whereas if the absurdity is synthetic, as it is in the case of *round square* (contrary concepts under a single determinable), it is material absurdity. Husserl accepts and explicates a distinction between analytic and synthetic propositions, though his way of marking the distinction is closer to that of Bolzano than to that of subsequent analytic philosophy (Cf. *LI* III, §§ 11–12).[10]

The job of formal logic in Husserl's view is in the first instance to rule out formal absurdity. That is what the laws of logic in effect do. To affirm and deny the same proposition in a single conjunction is simply the most obvious kind of formal absurdity, so the law *Not (A and not-A)* is the paradigm of a logical law. But before formal absurdity, whether sentential or nominal, can arise, the complex expression in question must form a meaningful whole. A preliminary, pre-logical level of laws must therefore govern how meaningful wholes may be formed, how meanings may combine together. This is the subject of the fourth *Investigation*, called "The Distinction Between Independent and Dependent Meanings and the Idea of Pure Grammar."

The conceptual tools for this investigation were forged in the previous one, "On the Theory of Wholes and Parts." Here Husserl, following his mentor Stumpf but generalizing from psychology to ontology, put forward a distinction between those entities which can exist alone, and those which need others in order to exist, in particular, those which can only exist as parts of a larger whole. Husserl calls such dependent parts *moments*, distinguishing them from parts which could if need be exist alone, which he called *pieces*. Instances of qualities like colour and shape are moments, whereas detachable parts in the common meaning, like a chair's leg, are pieces. The investigation is effectively a modern explication of Aristotle's distinction between substances and accidents, though Husserl, true to the generally antimetaphysical tenor of the time, initially avoided such loaded terms. Investigation III turned out, in fact, to be one of Husserl's most far-reaching pieces, involving him in discussions of analyticity and formal laws and becoming a case study of a discipline with its roots in his early philosophy of arithmetic, one that he was beginning to develop with some confidence, a discipline he called formal ontology.

When a complex whole exists, something must bind its parts into a whole, or else it would be a mere plurality. Husserl's name for the kind of relation which binds is *foundation*, and he insists that in all cases of true complex unity, it is relations of foundation that bind (*LI* III § 22, middle). But these relations cannot, without an infinite regress ensuing, themselves be further constituents of the complex whole. For two things to cohere together by foundation is not for them both to cohere to a third, binding thing, but for them to be of such a type that at least one of them cannot exist without the other. This existential indispensability or ontological dependence has two sides: on the one hand, Husserl holds that cases of it are always instances of a general law, and on the other it is not reducible to anything more fundamental.

Investigation IV applies this analysis to meanings. Whenever we have a unified complex meaning, it is unified by some meanings in the complex being founded on others, maybe one-sidedly, maybe mutually. Husserl's account thus fulfils with much greater theoretical background the same task as Frege's metaphor of the "unsaturatedness" of functions. The general laws, of which the individual combinations are instances, comprise a system which Husserl conceives, by virtue of their applying directly to meanings, to be universal for all languages. He thus confidently calls for the resurrection of the old rationalist ideal of a *grammaire générale et raisonnée*,[11] a call which was paralleled by another Brentano student, Anton

Marty,[12] but which American linguists, still relishing the apparently unbridled variety in natural language thrown up by empirical investigation, were not to follow for another half century. The meanings which can combine with one another according to these universal laws are such that any meaning of one class can be replaced *salva congruitate* by another of that class. Husserl calls these equivalence classes *meaning categories,* and he was the first modern philosopher to formulate the principle of congruous replacement as definitory for such categories. Since Husserl's work was frequently cited by those such as Leśniewski, Ajdukiewicz and Bar-Hillel who were instrumental in developing what has come to be called categorial grammar, it is important to stress that Husserl's categories are not expressions, as in these later theories, but the abstract meanings themselves.

Independent meanings are those which can constitute what Husserl calls "the full, entire meaning of a concrete act of meaning" (*LI* IV, § 7, end). There are complex acts of meaning, made up of other acts of meaning, for example, when I mean someone as *the man over there in the brown suit talking to the manager.* The whole complex act of meaning is concrete, its parts and their meanings are (in this context) dependent. That does not mean that there is a correlation between being a dependent or independent *object* and being something that can be referred to by a dependent or independent meaning, as there is for Frege. On the contrary, Husserl asserts the nameability of anything by an independent meaning (*LI* IV, § 8, beginning). He therefore does not face the problem that Frege brought upon himself by holding that since " – is a horse" is an unsaturated expression which stands for a concept while *the concept Horse* is a saturated expression and so must stand for an object and not a concept, the sentence *The concept Horse is a concept* must be false. For Husserl *the concept Horse* simply names what " – is a horse" expresses as a verb-phrase but does not name.

Husserl's theory of dependent meanings allows him to accept, with Bolzano, that conjunctions, prepositions and other particles have their own meanings, while acknowledging the idea behind the traditional distinction between categorematic and syncategorematic expressions. Whereas traditionally, syncategorematic expressions had no meaning of their own, yet made a regular contribution to propositions in which they occur, Husserl can accommodate the difference as one between independent and dependent meanings, the regular contribution being precisely the syncategorematic expression's own (dependent) meaning. Syncategorematic expressions are then understood in isolation because we are capable of appreciating their making this kind of contribution while leaving formally open what their completing expressions are. Syncategorematic meanings, even those standardly expressed only by morphological fragments and inflexions like *un-* or *-ing*, have their own meanings, even though these are moments.

The fourth *Investigation* is the shortest of all, and Husserl, apart from sketching his conception, does not go into detail. In the course of it, a number of features emerge which remained influential in his philosophy: a level of laws of grammatical well-formedness prior to the laws of logic, a concern to rise above the variability of the empirically given in language and meaning, going hand in hand with a relative indifference to actual empirical research on language.[13] Thus, while Husserl was willing to assert that there are laws of modification, e.g., nominalization of sentences, *suppositio materialis*, iterable adjectival modification, he is not concerned to enter into the details of how these universal features are actually effected in real languages. His vision of a universal science of language was left for others to implement.

In lectures on formal logic given in Göttingen in 1910/11, Husserl returned to these issues. Material from these lectures was published much later in 1929 as the first of three appendices, "Syntactic Forms and Syntactic Matters, Nuclear Forms and Nuclear Matters," to *Formal and Transcendental Logic*.[14] In any judgement or chain of reasoning, there are elements which serve to direct us to the subject-matter in question. Husserl calls the moments which do this *matters* (*Stoffe*) and differentiates them from elements like *because, or is*, which do not of themselves direct us to subject-matter. Again we, in effect, have the categorematic/syncategorematic distinction. The interesting fact is that the division of a sentence into syntactic parts, its parsing, yields a quite different division from its ideal partition into matter and what Husserl calls moments of *pure form* (*FTL*, Appendix I, § 3). The forms like subject-form, object-form, form of a predicative judgement, conjunctive form (using *and*) go to constitute whole judgements, and it is the function of a theory of the combination of such categorial forms (syntax) to indicate how this goes. But beyond these typically programmatic remarks, Husserl in the Appendix does not go.

VII. THE THEORY OF MEANING IN TRANSITION

The success of the *Logical Investigations*, Husserl's increasingly ambitious methodological plans for descriptive psychology, or, as he came increasingly to call it, phenomenology, and his typically thorough reconsideration of his own views, led him within a few years to dissatisfaction with his own theory of meaning in the *Investigations*. In particular he came to regard the identification of meanings with species of act-matters as oversimplified because it fails to take account of a duality in the structure of consciousness which is perhaps latent in the *Investigations* view but which Husserl now believed was inadequately spelled out. The dissatisfaction emerged fully formed for the reading public as a *volte-face* in the *Ideas* of 1913, but it had been in preparation for some time, and the transition from the theory of the *Investigations* to that of the *Ideas* can be witnessed in the *Lectures on the Theory of Meaning* which Husserl delivered in Göttingen in the summer semester of 1908.[15]

These lectures cover to some extent the same ground as the relevant investigations. They also support the analysis of meaning as the species of moments of acts of meaning something. But Husserl now considers that this is not all there is to meaning. He distinguishes between his former concept of meaning, which calls the *phenological* or *phansic* concept, and a new concept which he calls the *phenomenological* or *ontic* concept (*VB*, § 8). Because these terms are ugly and, in the case of ontic meaning, positively misleading, I shall speak instead of *species meaning* and *noematic meaning*, respectively. The argument for species meaning is as in the *Investigations*. Acts of meaning are transitory and individual, whereas the meaning, say that of the expression "lion," is ideal and unmultiplied by repetition. So, Husserl reasons, meaning can be seen as something specific, standing to individual acts as the universal redness stands to individual instances of redness. In meaning, understood as the general way in which an act is directed to an object, reference is constituted. In Investigation I Husserl had said, "An act of meaning is the determinate manner in which we refer to our object of the moment, though this mode of significant reference and the meaning

itself can change while the objective reference remains fixed" (*LI* I, §
13). He now reiterates this in different words, saying, "According to
the specific type of meaning-consciousness we refer in different
ways to objectivities, and ... 'meaning' is thereby seen as that
which is specific to [an act of] meaning, in so far as it establishes a
connection to [an] objectivity and in the way in which it is established" (*VB*, § 8, p. 35).[16]

Husserl is quite prepared to retain this conception of meaning,
but wishes to add another, uncovering what he takes to be yet
another equivocation in the term "meaning." We can introduce it
by considering the problem of apparently objectless acts discussed
above. Recall that Husserl wanted to say in one semantic tone of
voice that "Jupiter" refers to (means) an object, while in another
semantic tone of voice he held (with common sense) that there is
no Jupiter to be referred to. He now (1908) detaches the intentional
object as meant from the actual external object (if any). Discussing
his earlier example of *the victor at Jena* and *the vanquished at
Waterloo*, he now regards the object meant (in one sense of meaning) as being different in each case, calling it "the theme," "the
intentional object as such," and "the object meant as such in the
way in which [it is meant]" (*VB*, § 8, p. 37). When we think of the
victor at Jena we have a quite different theme from when we think
of the vanquished at Waterloo, even though the victor at Jena happens to be the same person as the loser at Waterloo. This new
conception of the ontic meaning of an act, the correlate projected by
it, is that which in *Ideas* Husserl calls an act's *noema*. It is to be
contrasted with the act of meaning itself, which is something real
and transitory, and which Husserl would go on to call the *noesis*.
Husserl goes so far as to regard noematic (ontic) meaning as phenomenologically prior to species (phansic) meaning, on the grounds
that the projecting or reaching out aspect of meaning is immediately present to our phenomenological inspection, whereas the species concept makes itself clear to us only by our reflecting on the
fact that we can repeatedly direct ourselves in the same way to the
same thing.

This new noematic theory is then immediately brought into contact with the dilemma left hanging by the discussion of objectless
acts in the *Investigations*. Husserl puts the dilemma with uncharac-
teristic brevity and clarity. "How can I say in one breath 'the object

presented' and 'that very same thing does not exist'? How can I say, 'There is an object that the idea presents' and at the same time 'in truth there is no such object'?" (VB § 9a, p. 39) Unfortunately the answer is by no means as succinct as Husserl's question, and he effectively spends most of the rest of his lectures working around it. The obvious answer would be to distinguish the noematic meaning, or what I shall now call simply the *noema*, from the actual object, what I shall now, following Guido Küng,[17] call the *referent*, and in the case of propositional acts Husserl does fix this distinction terminologically. Taking the example from the *Investigations*, Husserl now says that the sentences *a is larger than b* and *b is smaller than a*, while they correspond to one and the same *situation* [*Sachlage*], mean different states of affairs [*Sachverhalte*] (VB, § 30b, 98). Thus the same distinction between noema and referent will explain how we mean different things and yet mean the same thing when we speak of the difference between the victor at Jena and the vanquished at Waterloo.

Now it might be thought that Husserl already had the means at his disposal in the *Investigations* to make these distinctions, and that another meaning of "meaning" was unnecessary. For the task of elaborating a semantics of linguistic expressions I think this is true, and that the later theory is unnecessarily complicated. But this point of view does not take into account that Husserl's primary focus of attention lay in phenomenology rather than the theory of linguistic meaning. It is not so much the simple differentiation between noema and referent that gives Husserl trouble, as his wish to give an account of how it may appear to us that we refer to something when we "really" do not, and how we can be aware also that we are referring to the same real person, Napoleon, under different descriptions. Hence, in these 1908 lectures he expounds in considerable phenomenological detail how we can make and understand judgements of identity. From the phenomenological point of view it is quite irrelevant whether there really is a referent or not, or whether the victor at Jena and the vanquished at Waterloo truly are one person. The "inner side" of a false judgement of identity is not different from that of a true one. Husserl refers to a form of judgement about our own acts (e.g., of presentation and judgement) and their objects in which we abstain from considering whether they are veridical or true, but simply take them as they are. He calls it the "assumptive turn" or "assumption" (VB, §§ 28 f., pp. 89 ff.). It is obvious that Husserl is here working towards the method of epoché presented to the world five years later in Ideas.

The Lectures on the Theory of Meaning thus introduce changes which were to have far-reaching effects in Husserl's philosophy, leading in particular to the distinction between noesis and noema and the phenomenological reduction. The dissatisfaction Husserl felt with his analyses of meaning in Logical Investigations thus leads him into a general revision of his theory of consciousness. It shows him taking more account of the phenomenology of the experience of meaning than in the relation of expressions and meanings to referents. The latter are still present in the analysis, but they are increasingly peripheral to Husserl's theoretical focus. Soon they were to be discounted as methodologically irrelevant. The intention towards a referent which characterizes acts of meaning is evidently not confined to them, and Husserl increasingly widened his perspective away from the specifically linguistic, which was to have repercussions both substantial and terminological in his later works.

The Lectures contain further themes which look forward to Husserl's later works. In particular he lays emphasis on the nature of predication and the distinction between subject and predicate as it appears in our experience of meaning, a topic to be worked over at greater length many years later in Experience and Judgment. Another topic of regular interest to Husserl is the device of nominalization, which is required to bring any theme not itself inherently nominal to the point where something can be predicated about it. To an even greater extent than the Investigations, the Lectures show Husserl concentrating on general methodological issues and retreating further from detailed applications of his ideas to actual languages.

VIII. NOEMATIC MEANING

The distinction between the phansic (species) and ontic (noematic) conceptions of meaning, which pervaded the Lectures, was evidently not an isolated distinction but one reflecting a general idea of correlation between real acts of consciousness and their necessary correlates. This distinction was carried forward to the Ideas (1913), Husserl's next major work, as that between noesis and noema. The notorious methodological innovations of this work, in particular the introduction of the transcendental phenomenological reduction, the "bracketing" of all things not in or essentially connected to consciousness, have their bearing on this distinction in that the object-directedness of consciousness turns out to be essentially direction through a noema and only *per accidens* to an independent referent. Every noesis must have its noema, and variations in noesis and noema go hand in hand, but it is incidental and irrelevant to this correlation, now taken as the fundamental "reduced" structure of conscious intentionality, whether or not a noema has a transcendent referent. In fact the shift as far as meaning and language goes is fairly minor compared with the position already adopted in the *Lectures*. The phansic or species meaning of the *Investigations* now drops out of consideration. It is not that Husserl explicitly repudiates it – the act-matters of the *Investigations* are after all still part of Husserl's noeses, and they still have their species – but that his interest has moved on. This procedure of moving on to new themes without always making clear which of the old ones have been rejected and which have simply dropped out of focus is one of the facts which makes Husserl's views so difficult to characterize diachronically. The publication of the *Lectures* however makes it clear that the shift in the theory of meaning from the *Investigations* to the *Ideas*, which seemed so abrupt at the time and for long afterwards, is the product of a process with intermediate stages.

One indisputable effect of the transcendental turn on Husserl's semantics is that questions of actual truth and reference are among those "bracketed" in the phenomenological reductions, so a fully-fledged semantics, a theory designed to explicate the relationship between language and extra-linguistic reality, cannot find a place within transcendental phenomenology. Again, it is not that Husserl would want to deny the possibility of such a discipline, but that it could no longer have the same fundamental place in his philosophical scheme. The theory of ideal meanings anchoring the objectivity of logic in the fashion of Bolzano gives way to a more Kantian view, in which the structure and function of consciousness are to account for this objectivity. This transcendental foundation for logic was to become the object of Husserl's focus some years later in *Formal and Transcendental Logic*.

The *Ideas* are not however completely devoid of innovations in the theory of meaning. While within phenomenological brackets, the referent of an expression or any act of consciousness is present in neutralized form. It is not enough, even for phenomenological analysis, to simply distinguish noesis and noema. The noema is indeed the noesis's correlated "object meant in the way in which it is meant," but even within the reduction account must be taken of experiences in which is becomes clear to us that we have meant the same thing in different ways. In other words, Husserl needs to provide a phenomenological account of our *taking* referents to have objective existence, as when we discover that it was the same commander who both won the Battle of Jena and lost the Battle of Waterloo. Merely to have a succession of qualitatively different noemata is not enough: these have to be tied together as *of one object*. In other words, Husserl has to give an account of how we come to take ourselves to be referring in different manners to one and the same thing, a study inaugurated by Hume and termed "synthesis" by Kant. In fact Husserl had already begun this process in the *Lectures* by stressing identifying judgements and employing the term "constitution" to apply to the way in which our sense of an object as a unified subject of predications may arise.

Much of Husserl's effort now goes into analysing the structure of noemata. In particular, each noema has a kernel or nucleus which consists of three elements: a substratum, a set of qualitative moments, and modes of fulfilment of these qualities. What he calls a pure or empty X is the subject of predicates which are intended in the nucleus and which are more or less intuitively fulfilled. It is that which serves as it were as a peg on which to hang the object's predicative clothing, and which can remain intended as one and the same through a variety of ascriptions. Husserl does not allow an X to be given without some determining content, or vice versa (*Ideas*, § 131). So this X is not a further concrete constituent in the noema; it is an abstract form occurring in it (*Ideas*, § 132). We call it the noema's *substratum* (a term Husserl himself occasionally used) as it fulfils the same rather elusive bearer function as Locke's "something, we know not what." The object meant is also meant in this or that manner, as believed in, as real, or as fictional, or doubted. Husserl calls such variants in the manner of intending *thetic* moments. Finally an object is given as *further determinable*, it has what Husserl calls a *horizon* of possible future determinations (*Ideas*, § 44).

The elaboration of Husserl's account of consciousness thus does not substantially modify his *Lectures* account of linguistic meaning, but, prompted by the greater generality of his analysis of intending, he does take the opportunity to adjust his terminology. Whereas previously he had spoken about the act of meaning (*Akt der Bedeutung*) and what is meant (*Bedeutung*) and had used the word *Sinn* as a synonym for *Bedeutung*, now he opts to use the words non-synonymously. Originally, to mean (noetic) and that which is meant (noematic) were, as Husserl points out, considered solely in connection with language, whereas it is natural, especially for a phenomenologist, to extend them from linguistic to non-linguistic acts (noetic) and items meant (noematic). Husserl elects to henceforth explicitly reserve *Bedeutung* for the noematic side of linguistic acts, allowing *Sinn* to cover both these and non-linguistic noemata (*Ideas*, § 124). The connection is made by Husserl's insistence that in principle,

Everything "intended (*gemeint*) as such," every intending in the noematic sense (as noematic nucleus) of any arbitrary act is expressible by "meanings" (*Bedeutungen*).   (*Ideas*, § 124)

It is important that while not every noema actually is the linguistic meaning of some expression, none is excluded from becoming one. Smith and McIntyre call this the *expressibility thesis*.[18] How it comes about is something on which Husserl expanded in the posthumously published book *Experience and Judgment*.

There is a tradition of Husserl interpretation which assimilates his conception of the noema to Frege's notion of sense, in that noemata are like senses, except that they are assignable to all object-presenting acts. Noemata are abstract entities through which referents are given.[19] In view of the interest this comparison has aroused, to some extent perhaps exaggerated by a wish to restore greater unity to philosophy after the schisms of the past decades, it is worth considering some similarities and differences. Despite a structural similarity between the roles of noema and sense, the theories differ in other respects. Frege's senses come in two ontological sorts: objects and functions, and combine in particular to form abstract propositions or thoughts. The sense of a compound expression is a function of the senses of its parts. Like Husserl's noemata, Fregean senses exist in part to explain how we can be directed to the same thing in more than one way. Senses likewise take the sting out of the problem of objectlessness. They also serve to explain how extensionality applies to language despite the non-substitutivity of clauses and other expressions *salva veritate* in indirect speech and other "intensional" contexts. But other than offering the bald metaphorical idea of our grasping senses, Frege tells us nothing about how we come into cognitive contact with them.

Husserl's account of the grammatico-logical combination of noemata is for its part similarly skeletal, and he is not concerned with such issues as whether noemata can be used to account for the meaning of sentences about propositional attitudes. His principal concern is with the structure of consciousness, and here he finds noemata to be the necessary correlates of noeses, where again, as in the *Investigations*, he takes this as an *internal* (necessary) relation, unlike Frege's *external* (contingent) grasping. Apart from the wider conception of sense Husserl willingly embraces, it is above all the status of noematic entities as correlates of acts of consciousness that severs him from Frege. Whereas a Fregean sense (like an early Husserlian species meaning) can go for ever unthought or ungrasped, a noema without a noesis is *a priori* impossible. There are only noemata in so far as there are acts of consciousness. This correlation thesis is far more important to Husserl than questions of the ontological status of noemata, whether they are abstract or not. Indeed, he at one point seriously entertains the view that noemata are real parts of the acts, rather than something projected by them.[20] Whether this view – which Husserl admits contradicts the *Ideas* – is a temporary catastrophic aberration or his last word on the subject is not so important as the fact that it shows Husserl to be taking the phenomenological *role* of noemata as more important than their ontological status.

IX. THE EXPERIENTIAL BASIS OF PREDICATION

The book *Experience and Judgment*, edited from Husserl's lecture notes by Ludwig Landgrebe and published only after his death, contributes to Husserl's philosophy of language chiefly by examining in more detail than other works the foundation in experience of some aspects of linguistic acts, especially predication. This is founded in what Husserl calls *pre-predicative* experience, which is not inherently formed by language. Husserl not only upholds, by contrast with most analytic philosophers, the view that there is articulate experience which is prior to predication and on which predication and judgement ride, but even undertakes to give a detailed account of the structure of this experience. The book is subtitled "Investigations in a Genealogy of Logic." He wishes to show that the abilities on which the exercise of logical reason depends, in particular judgement and predication, require a suitable experiential basis which can be described in abstraction from the language used to formulate the judgements. The account is notable for its relative freedom from Husserl's typical concern with philosophical methodology, and understanding it does not depend on previously successfully negotiating the phenomenological reduction.

Pre-linguistic experience is not a featureless blur, but is pre-organized – presumably by our innate perceptual faculties – into rough types, which afford a toehold for further development. Drawing on decades of concern with various aspects of the phenomenology of perception, time, synthesis, memory, constitution, Husserl describes how the initial associative clumpiness of experience (the fact, recognized by Locke, that data come in pre-packaged bundles) both lays down expectations on the basis of past perceived similarities, and at the same time invites analysis. Bundles of data are not just spread out in the space and time of perception, they contain independent pieces and dependent moments which can be focussed on attentively. In focussing, we burrow into a complex presented object and highlight a piece or moment, while retaining the whole in implicit grasp. The part is highlighted not just *per se*, but *as part* of the whole. This complex movement back and forth of our attentive grasp contains the germ of predication. Husserl calls it *explication*, trading on the "unfolding" metaphor in that word's etymology. Out of the passively synthesized, pre-given whole, attention picks out a dependent or independent part; for instance in the cup seen I explicate its handle (piece) or its colour (moment). The part is taken as an object in its own right, but one *belonging to and emerging from* the prior whole. We thus have a series: object 1 – (focus inside to) – object 2 – (retain that this is part of) – object 1. Out of this threefold structure: whole, part, and the part-whole relation made clear to us in the to and fro, emerges the basic structure of all predication: subject, attribute, copula. Husserl distinguishes two copulae (as concepts, not as words): *has* for whole-part relations, especially where pieces are in question (e.g., the cup *has* this handle), and *is* for predications where qualities are involved (e.g., the cup *is* blue)(*EJ*, § 52). But the parallel is not perfect: we can just as well say the cup *has* this moment of blue, and it *has* this surface (boundaries are moments or dependent parts too, though they are not qualities). In fact, a predication like *The cup is blue* does not merely set a subject in relation to an individual attribute: it tells us the attribute's type or species, and so brings in predicative generality. Since for Husserl it is moments that are directly perceived, not their types, it would be truer to his theory to interpret *is* predications as implicit existential generalizations: *This cup is blue* would mean *This cup has a blue-moment*, just as we could say *This cup is be-handled*, meaning it *has a* handle.

Once explication has started, its results may be ploughed back into the subject and the procedure may continue. The cup, which I just noted has this handle, I now see is blue, then I note it has a particular shape (for which perhaps I have no name), and so on. This "ploughing back" is at the basis of attributive constructions. From the predicative *S is p* we move to attributive *S, which is p* or simply the adjectival *p S*, and thence to further predications, *S, which is p, is q*, and so on. Each step in the explication process leaves a residue in our conception of the subject, and this provides an enriched subject for further explication (*EJ*, § 28). A further step comes with relational predication. Observing the cup on the table, I may also move to realise that the cup *is on* the table. Typically, that will involve me moving outside the sphere of the cup's determinations, to something else given in the field of experience, and noting the nature of the relationship between them. Husserl is less explicit on what this has to involve, but the basic ingredients of the account are beginning to be clear.

Husserl then goes on to consider how predication is thus structurally apt for the expression of the kinds of experience with which he has dealt. He also returns to several themes of his philosophy which remained more or less constant after the *Investigations:* the way in which the meaning categories available enable one to build up complex meanings, and how these are externalized and communicated in complex expressions; the use of nominalization to make higher-order meanings subjects of further predication. An example of this last is the nominalization of sentences, which allow us to say things like *It is surprising that spring has come so early this year.*

Another constant concern of Husserl's is the nature of essential intuition, the method of controlled imaginative variation whereby we are placed in cognitive contact with universals, or, as Husserl calls them, general essences. That at least some such universals are fed us predigested by language appears not to concern Husserl. Here, as elsewhere in his philosophy of language, the social dimension of language, the fact that it is a community affair which is learnt inter-actively with already competent language users, and the constraints on learning imposed by this fact, are underemphasized. In part this is the result of bracketing other people and the social world, retaining for phenomenological consideration only our *sense* of these things, but for the most part he is simply not interested in anything but individual consciousness. Even the social aspects of experience men-tioned in *Ideas* II and III interest him mainly as aspects of the individ-ual's mental life. The later stress on the intersubjective *Lebenswelt* in the *Crisis* offered a possible way out of the individual's relative isolation which Husserl did not live to exploit in the philosophy of language. In his attitude to the role of the subjectively mental in language he was almost diametrically opposed to Wittgenstein, for whom the mental accompaniments to linguistic behaviour and un-derstanding were of no account. The truth must lie somewhere be-tween the two extremes. However, Husserl's insistence on a pre-predicative basis for predication and thought in general, though speculative and at places naive, points the way to later empirical investigations of psycholinguistics and cognitive science, where a Wittgensteinian would be condemned to silence.

X. LANGUAGE AND ONTOLOGY

In his *Formal and Transcendental Logic* (1929) Husserl returned to the question of the nature of logic and its justification. As the title indicates, he now considered the laws of formal logic to stand in need of a transcendental phenomenological justification. The details of this justification attempt need not concern us here, though in my view it is a sorry affair to try to "justify" something like the law of contradiction on the basis of facts – even transcendental ones – about how consciousness or reason works.

Husserl returns here with renewed emphasis to an idea which he had broached in the *Logical Investigations*, the two-sidedness of logic. Traditionally, logic has to do with judgements or propositions, and inferences. Again traditionally, these are actual mental events.

Logic is concerned not with the way in which they, in fact, are carried out but in how they should be carried out if truth is to be preserved: valid inferences being those which guarantee that with true premises we have a true conclusion. Husserl is perfectly happy with this and calls this study *formal apophantics,* or *apophantic analytics,* from the Greek word *apophansis,* statement. On the other hand, judgements or propositions are about things, and even when emptied of content, they still schematically refer to or range over a domain of entities. Thus in *Every A stands in R to at least two Bs, x is an A, y is a B, and x stands in R to y,* therefore *there is some B, z, different from y, to which x stands in R* (the example is not Husserl's – in his later philosophy Husserl rarely gives examples) we find ourselves reasoning about entities of certain kinds and the relations they stand in, even though we are doing so schematically or "formally." Husserl calls this object-oriented side of reasoning *formal ontology,* and regards it as simply mathematics by another name, citing Leibniz's ambitious project of a *mathesis universalis* as precedent. The account of numbers in *Philosophy of Arithmetic* can be seen as an attempt to illustrate this for that part of mathematics: Husserl's attempts to extend that project to higher numbers, geometry, and other mathematical systems foundered on various difficulties, but the general vision remained with him.

Thus, Husserl's view of the relationship between logic and mathematics is much more akin to that of modern model theory than to that of his logicist contemporaries Frege and Russell. To compare formal apophantics with proof theory and formal ontology with model theory would be overhasty, however, both because Husserl does not provide any account in detail but contents himself with outlining the strategic relationship, and because he does not at any stage question the isomorphic parallelism between thought (apophantics) and the world. Limitative results in metamathematics such as Gödel's incompleteness theorems and the independence of the continuum hypothesis place Husserl's ideal of a perfect (as it were pre-established) harmony between formal laws of inference and formal mathematical structures in jeopardy. Admittedly Husserl was writing shortly before such results began to emerge, but his unquestioning confidence in the isomorphism between thought and reality now seems unduly optimistic.

Formal ontology is not the only kind of ontology: there are also

more restricted regional ontologies, concerned with the laws governing not all objectivities but only those of a certain sphere, such as
the mind, or time. Husserl however nowhere offers a criterion for
distinguishing formal from non-formal concepts, though he more
than once gives lists of formal concepts ending in "and so on." The
theory of part and whole in the third Investigation and the theory of
whole numbers in the *Philosophy of Arithmetic* remain the only
two excursions into formal ontology that Husserl was to make, and
for their time they are both impressive, though modern axiomatic
methods have taken us further both here and in other fields.

The implications of Husserl's idea of the two-sidedness of logic for
formal ontology have been consistently underexploited in modern
philosophy. One aspect of the two-sideness which had been mentioned in the *Investigations* but was stressed more forcibly in the
Formal and Transcendental Logic is the interconnectedness of
propositions in relation to the interconnectedness of a sphere of
correlated objects. While names stand for objects and sentences represent states of affairs, a theory is concerned not with isolated objects and states of affairs but whole *manifolds* of correlated objects
and states. Husserl's conception of a manifold is not only akin to the
logician's conception of a model for a theory, it also represents the
highest ideal of logic, which Husserl construes, following Bolzano,
as a theory of science, a theory of the forms of possible theories, in
particular those which can be true. Although Husserl does not exploit this thought for the philosophy of language, the same thought
leads one from a semantics of isolated sentences to a semantics of
connected discourse. Here, as so often in his writings, Husserl's
philosophy of language, while often sweepingly abstract and uncon-
cerned with details except phenomenological ones, is tantalizingly
suggestive of possible future developments.

REFERENCES

Works by Husserl

Works by Husserl are here listed in chronolgoical order. They are generally
cited in the text by abbreviated title and section number. Standard English
translations have been followed where they exist unless there seemed good
reason to modify them.

Philosophie der Arithmetik. Mit ergänzenden Texten (1890–1901). Edited by Lothar Eley. *Husserliana* XII. The Hague: Nijhoff, 1970. First edition 1891.

Logical Investigations (LI). Translated by J. N. Findlay. London: Routledge & Kegan Paul, 1970. Critical edition: *Logische Untersuchungen.* Bd. 1, edited by Elmar Holenstein. *Husserliana* XVIII. The Hague: Nijhoff, 1975; Bd. II (in 2 parts), edited by Ursula Panzer. *Husserliana* XIX. The Hague: Nijhoff, 1984. First edition 1900 (Vol. I), 1901 (Vol. II).

Vorlesungen über Bedeutungslehre, Sommersemester 1908 (VB). Edited by Ursula Panzer. *Husserliana* XXVI. The Hague: Nijhoff, 1987.

Aufsätze und Rezensionen (1890–1910). Edited by Bernhard Rang. *Husserliana* XXII. The Hague: Nijhoff, 1979.

Ideas. General Introduction to Pure Phenomenology. Translated by W. R. Boyce Gibson. London: Allen & Unwin, 1931. Critical edition: *Ideen zu einer reinen Phänomenologie und phänomenologischen Philosophie.* Erstes Buch, edited by Karl Schuhmann. *Husserliana* III/1. The Hague: Nijhoff, 1976. First edition 1913.

Analysen zur passiven Synthesis. Aus Vorlesungs- und Forschungsmanuskripten 1918–1926. Edited by Margot Fleischer. *Husserliana* XI. The Hague: Nijhoff, 1966.

Formal and Transcendental Logic (FTL). Translated by D. Cairns. The Hague: Nijhoff, 1969. Critical edition: *Formale und transzendentale Logik,* edited by Paul Janssen. *Husserliana* XVII. The Hague: Nijhoff, 1974. First edition 1929.

The Crisis of European Sciences and Transcendental Phenomenology. Translated by David Carr. Evanston: Northwestern University Press. Critical edition: *Die Krisis der europäischen Wissenschaften und die transzendentale Phänomenologie,* edited by Reinhold N. Smid. *Husserliana* XXIX. Dordrecht: Kluwer, 1993.

Experience and Judgment. Investigations in a Genealogy of Logic (EJ). Translated by J. S. Churchill and K. Ameriks. London: Routledge & Kegan Paul, 1973. First German edition: *Erfahrung und Urteil.* Edited by Ludwig Landgrebe. Hamburg: Claassen, 1948. Original edition, Prague: Academia, 1939.

Other works cited

Bell, David A. *Husserl.* London: Routledge & Kegan Paul, 1990.

Føllesdal, Dagfinn. "Husserl's Notion of Noema." *The Journal of Philosophy* 66 (1969): 680–87.

Frege, Gottlob. *Philosophical and Mathematical Correspondence.* Oxford: Blackwell, 1980.

Holenstein. Elmar. *Roman Jakobsons phänomenologischer Strukturalismus.* Frankfurt/Main: Suhrkamp, 1975.

Ingarden, Roman. *Das literarische Kunstwerk.* Halle/Saale: Niemeyer 1931. English translation *The Literary Work of Art,* trans. G. Grabowitz. Evanston: Northwestern University Press, 1973.

Küng, Guido. "The World as Noema and as Referent." *Journal of the British Society for Phenomenology* 3 (1972): 15–26.

Marty, Anton. *Untersuchungen zur Grundlegung der allgemeinen Grammatik und Sprachphilosophie.* Halle/Saale: Niemeyer, 1908.

Simons, Peter. "Wittgenstein, Schlick and the *a priori,*" in his *Philosophy and Logic in Central Europe from Bolzano to Tarski.* Dordrecht, Kluwer, 1992, 361–76.

Smith, Barry. "Husserl, Language, and the Ontology of the Act." In *Speculative Grammar, Universal Grammar and Philosophical Analysis of Language.* Edited by D. Buzzetti and M. Ferriani. Amsterdam: Benjamins, (1987), 205–28.

Smith, David W. "Husserl on Demonstrative Reference and Perception." In *Husserl, Intentionality and Cognitive Science.* Edited by H. L. Dreyfus. Cambridge: MIT Press, 1982, 193–213.

Smith, David W. and Ronald McIntyre. *Husserl and Intentionality.* Dordrecht: Reidel, 1982.

Twardowski, Kasimir. *Zur Lehre vom Inhalt und Gegenstand der Vorstellungen.* Vienna: Hölder, 1894. Reprinted Munich: Philosophia, 1982. English translation *On the Content and Object of Presentations,* trans. R. Grossmann. The Hague: Nijhoff, 1977.

NOTES

1 Printed in Husserl *Philosophie der Arithmetik,* 340–73.

2 There is a continuation and elaboration of this theory in Ingarden 1931.

3 Citations to all works by Husserl will be to sections to enable any edition in any language to be used.

4 See Frege's letter to Husserl of 24 May 1891 in Frege 1980, 63.

5 Twardowski 1894, § 5.

6 See the essay "Intentionale Gegenstände" and the unpublished review of Twardowski's monograph in Husserl *Aufsätze und Rezensionen (1890–1910).*

7 Bell 1990, 133.

8 In *The Crisis of European Sciences and Transcendental Phenomenology,* Husserl came to the more plausible view that exactness is an ideal to which empirical practice only approximates: see § 9.

9 For an account of Husserl's theory and its relation to later views, see Smith, D. W. 1982.

10 See § 4, "Husserl and Bolzano on analyticity," of Simons 1992.

11 See Smith, B. 1987.

12 Marty 1908.

13 Husserl did however himself exercise influence on linguists such as Karl Bühler and especially Roman Jakobson. See Holenstein 1975, 12ff.

14 See *Formal and Transcendental Logic*, Appendix I, § 1, footnote.

15 *Vorlesungen über Bedeutungslehre, Sommersemester 1908* (Husserl 1987). Here cited as *VB*.

16 Although the German is ambiguous, it appears that it is the individual act of meaning, not the species, that "establishes" the relation to an object, as explained in connection with the diagram above.

17 See Küng 1972.

18 Smith and McIntyre 1982, 182ff.

19 The source of this tradition is Føllesdal 1969; it is continued in Smith and McIntyre 1982.

20 *Analysen zur passiven Synthesis*, 332–35.

4   Knowledge

I. ANALYSIS OF KNOWING AS CENTRAL TO HUSSERL'S WORK

Clarification of the nature of knowledge (*Erkenntnis*) is the primary aim of Husserl's philosophical work, at least up to 1913, when he completed Section Four of *Ideas I.* In his earliest work[1] he was concerned with the analysis of specifically mathematical knowledge, but he soon realized that the main issues in that area had to do with knowledge in general rather than with mathematical knowledge as such. Thus, his first major work, the *Logical Investigations* (1900–1901), became an analysis of the nature of knowledge in general and of the conditions of its possibility. Volume II is titled "Investigations in the Phenomenology and Theory of Knowledge" and culminates in the "Sixth Investigation," which is an elaborate statement on what, exactly, knowledge is. That investigation is titled, "Elements of a Phenomenological Clarification of Knowledge," and indicates in its opening words that such clarification has been the aim of the "Investigations" all along. The Sixth Investigation is the counterpart of Section Four in the later *Ideas I* (1913), where, with some novel elements and emphases, he once again gives an account of the nature of knowledge (see note 2 of §145), but now as a phenomenology of reason or noetic phenomenology.

D. F. Pears comments that the question "What is knowledge?" is to be put "more fully and suggestively" as: "What is a piece of knowledge made of, and how is it made?"[2] That is exactly Husserl's view. On his analysis, knowing (in the non-dispositional sense) is fundamentally a matter of finding something to be as it is thought to be. His technical term for this complex type of "finding" is "fulfilment." Thus, for him, "To speak of knowledge of the object and of fulfilment of the meaning of an intention [upon the object] merely expresses the same state of affairs from different viewpoints."[3] And again: "We have equated fulfilment with knowledge (in the more rigorous sense) and have indicated that 'fulfilment' only signifies certain types of re-identification: namely, those which bring us closer to the *goal of knowledge*. What this means may be clarified by saying that in each fulfilment there is a more or less complete '*intuitionalization*' of the relevant subject matter" (*LI* 719–20).

Our task here is to make clear what, for Husserl, the "pieces" are that go into a case of fulfilment, and how they come together. We shall do this by sketching the development of his views on the nature of knowledge, and by emphasizing two major implications of his mature analysis: the independence of the object or objectivity from the act and mind that grasps it in knowledge (epistemological realism), and the possibility of a new, phenomenological "critique of reason" (a setting of the limits of possible knowledge) to replace the Kantian one.

II. SYMBOLIC KNOWING AS GUARANTEED POSSIBLE FULFILMENT

Husserl's concern with the analysis of knowledge developed in three main stages. The first terminated in his articulation of the concept of fulfilment, and was completed in principle by 1894, though vital details remained to be clarified in later years. The second stage terminated in the Fifth Logical Investigation, with its elimination of the "immanent object" from the analysis of the act of consciousness, making possible his realist reconciliation of the objectivity or mind-independence of the object or "content" of knowledge with the subjectivity of the act of knowing. The third stage is the analysis of knowing (Sixth Investigation) as one compound, higher-level act that necessitates its object but does not change it from what it is apart from knowledge.

In his first works, he dealt with the quite specific issue of how to turn the powerful technique of general arithmetic into a body of *knowledge*. The arithmetician's research consists almost totally of work with symbols, with formal languages, involving little or no explicit attention to numbers and number relations themselves. And indeed it is only a vanishingly small group of numbers and number relations that we are capable of attending to "themselves." Still, where do we have better knowledge than in mathematics? He opens an exploratory manuscript written in the aftermath of his *Philosophy of Arithmetic* (1891) with the question: "How is it that one can speak of 'concepts' [generally, 'objects'] which one, nevertheless, does not authentically possess, and how is it not absurd that the most certain of all the sciences, arithmetic, is to be based upon such concepts?"[4]

This question is approached by "a general analysis belonging within the domain of logic," titled, "On the Logic of Signs (Semiotic)." Husserl took logic to be a theory of how the means involved in the attainment of knowledge achieve their purpose, and the main devices utilized by mathematics are obviously systems of symbols.[5] What must be done, then, is to clarify what signs are and how they work for arithmetical knowledge in particular.

The inquiry begins from a distinction that is strongly rooted in common sense: concepts, or contents (objects) in general, come before the mind in one of two ways. In what Husserl calls the *authentic* manner the objects are "given as what they are." Negatively stated, we in this case are not dealing with objects by having something else in mind to which they are in some way related and which deflects our thought to them. But "contents" can also be inauthentically or *symbolically* represented: "Through the mediation of *signs*, signs which are themselves authentically represented." Here we have something authentically present to us – and, for Husserl, in every cognitive act *something*, though not necessarily the act's object, is authentically present – that by natural or acquired dispositions directs us toward something other than itself, the symbolically represented object.

Now the basic question for the understanding of "inauthentic" representation and knowledge, such as that of the arithmetician, concerns *how* symbolic consciousness works. How is it that mere signs can reliably stand in for objects that are not, and perhaps cannot be, within our authentic cognitive grasp? The answer achieved in this early paper is that signs perform their cognitive function:

In virtue of the fact that the deputizing signs (changing from moment to moment in relation to the same object) either include in themselves, as a partial content, precisely the property upon which the momentary interest bears, or at least possess the aptitude to serve as the beginning or connecting point for psychical processes or activities that would lead to this property – or even to the full concept involved – and that we can arouse and produce wherever it may be required.[6]

So the "sign" (inner image, word, even a physical object such as a statue or an exemplary case) either exemplifies, more or less perfectly, the property (concept) to which it directs us, or it simply has the power to elicit in us other mental acts that lead toward an authentic grasp of that property or object. Thus, symbolic representation or knowledge involves authentic consciousness in two ways: it proceeds from it (the "sign" is authentically given), and it tends toward it (for in directing us "beyond" itself, the sign indicates a path through which, ideally, the symbolically indicated object can be authentically given). The heart of the matter is, therefore, not just that, in general, objects may be given in two ways, but that *the same* object can be given in two ways, and that one way has, somehow, an inherent tendency to lead over to the other, the symbolic to the authentic.

Husserl presents this account of how signs work in knowing, not as what must be the case because of what we take signs and knowledge to be – not, as he would later say, as part of a *theory* about knowledge (*LI* 264) – but as a description of the way our thinking actually works, of how signs actually function in thought and, on occasion, proceed to attach themselves indirectly to what has been symbolically represented and judged of. Our thoughts when doing intellectual work consist almost totally of inauthentic representations. "Words or letters, accompanied by indistinct and unclear phantasms, and, in and with these latter, isolated and fragmentary qualities, the rudimentary beginnings of higher psychical activities, and so on . . . ," all in constant fluctuation: "*These* are our thoughts."[7]

Suppose we are working with the concept of a sphere:

Like a flash there appears with the word the representation of a ball, in which the shape alone is specifically attended to. This accompanying representation, whose property crudely approximates to the intended concept and thereby symbolizes it, may then disappear once again, leaving only the word remaining. But its appearance nonetheless suffices to secure us in a confident grasp of the subject involved.   (*Early Writings*, p.32.)

Then, as the line of thought proceeds, various words, concepts or "intuitionalizations" show up to the extent required for the inquiry to continue.

It is, Husserl thinks, only our *experience* of symbolic representations (utilizing inner images, words, abstract properties, and even acts and intentionalities of thought itself) passing over into authentic consciousness of their objects ("contents") that gives us the concept of *sign*, and then makes us "familiar with that practical equivalence between authentic representations and their symbols which makes possible the use of the latter in place of the former."[8]

Once we grasp this equivalence, however, we are able to form "symbolic representations which are not founded through prior authentic representations," and even to deal cognitively with objectivities that can never be "themselves present" to our authentic consciousness.[9] Nearly all numbers and their interrelations are of this nature. Nevertheless, how the symbols stand even to their *permanently* non-present objects is essentially the same as indicated above, and our understanding of this continuity of function is what makes possible symbolic knowledge of subject matters that forever escape intuitive presence.

So, to answer the question that opened Husserl's early inquiry and led toward his mature account of knowledge, we have knowledge of a subject matter that is not in our authentic grasp wherever our understanding of our symbolic representations and judgments concerning it is such as to convey assurance of the possibility, in principle, of an authentic finding of that subject matter to be as we are representing it and judging it to be. It is not enough that a formal or other research procedure actually lead to truth. We have to understand *why it must* lead to truth, when rightly used, before it can provide us with knowledge. "It is only in cases where the procedure itself is a logical one, and where we have logical insight into the fact that, such as it is and because it is so, it must lead to truth, that its result becomes, not a mere *de facto* truth, but rather a knowledge of the truth."[10]

A significant correction of a popular view of what Husserl took knowledge to be emerges from this. The entire point of his early "logical" exploration of the function of signs in knowing is to explain how non-intuitive knowledge is possible. We must, then, permanently set aside the misunderstanding that, for him, knowledge of a truth, a state of affairs or an object either is or requires intuition *of it*. Indeed, intuition of a subject matter is neither a sufficient nor a necessary condition of knowledge of it, on his view. Most of our common sense and scientific knowledge is of things that are never "themselves present" to us, and much of it is of what *cannot* be

present to us, our minds having the limitations that they do (*LI* 201).
Conversely, much that is "itself present" to us is insufficiently conceptualized to be known. Not least, the very mental acts which
make up knowing and other forms of consciousness (*LI* 725). So
things being "themselves present" – the condition which, with certain refinements, he also calls "Evidence" (*Evidenz*) – may remain
fundamental to his analysis of knowledge, but not in the way commonly assumed.

But does not Husserl explicitly state that "Evidence is indeed
nothing other than the character of knowledge as such"? (*LI* 232n.;
cf. 6of.) He does. But it is still not quite true that he thinks you only
know what is given to you with Evidence. It *is* true, for him, that
only that for which Evidence is "in principle" possible can be
known. It is also true, as just noted, that for us to know what is not
itself given we must know on the basis of Evidence why the symbolic or inauthentic procedures we are utilizing in the particular
case must produce truth. But if with reference to a given state of
affairs – e.g., 832 being larger than 764 – Evidence of its obtaining is
"in principle" possible, and we know it to be possible because we
derive the symbolical representation or judgment of that state of
affairs by a method of whose reliability we have Evidence, then we
have knowledge of that state of affairs without intuiting it – which
is out of the question in the example cited anyway.

Husserl, in any case, thought that most commonsense and scientific methods, including those of mathematics, developed "naturally," without logical insight into why they worked. However, they
can be analyzed as to why they produce true results, and thus transformed into genuinely logical techniques that provide knowledge.
This was his goal in his research in the philosophy of arithmetic.
And he held in general that, following the path of logical insight, and
keeping the peculiarities of our mental makeup constantly in view,
"the pioneers of research discover methods which they justify once
and for all. When this has been done, such methods can be used
without insight, so to say *mechanically* . . . , and objectively correct
results are assured" (*LI* 202). But they still will provide *knowledge*
only for those who have insight into why the methods work. And
this insight can come only from phenomenological research, itself
always terminating in intuitions of the essences or natures of the
mental acts and their interconnections involved in the methods.[11]

So significant ground is gained in these early inquiries toward his ultimate clarification of knowing, but Husserl's descriptions of the passage from symbolic to authentic awareness of objects remain very crude. All he has achieved is a general description of certain thought transitions. The finer analysis of inauthentic and authentic cognitions of the same object, and of how they match up to constitute a finding of something to be as it is thought to be, is still lacking. There is not even a mention of "empty" intentions or meanings and of their correlative "fulfilment" at this point. And, with specific reference to the clarification of arithmetical knowledge, Husserl is still far from discovering that parallelism between formal algorithms and categorial structures that logically justifies arithmetical calculations or other uses of formal systems.[12]

Further progress is made in the 1894 paper, "Psychological Studies in the Elements of Logic." It brings to completion the first stage of his analysis of knowledge in general. He is here still puzzled how "a psychical act can reach out beyond its own immanent content to another content [object] which is not really cognized [bewusst] at all."[13] This may seem to be the same question that opened his earlier paper. But he now takes it to be a question about the possibility of knowledge in general, and especially about "scientific knowledge, which is totally based upon the possibility of our being able purposively to prefer such [symbolic] thinking . . . over thought more fully adequated to intuition."

If we keep in mind that what is at issue is how certain mental states (inauthentic) may require the possibility of certain others (authentic), and therewith the relevant objects, it is understandable why Husserl is compelled to inquire how the parts and elements of consciousness necessarily relate to one another. The 1894 paper's first main section is an exploration of how the "abstract" or "dependent" elements of consciousness "require" the "concrete" or "independent" ones. It is presented as a totally disinterested investigation of a fundamental ontological distinction, but the parallel of the "abstract" with symbolic or inauthentic consciousness, and of the "concrete" with the authentic, seems fairly obvious. The second main section of the paper is explicitly focussed upon the passage from symbolic to authentic consciousness. It is a systematic examination of the distinction between representations (inauthentic cognitive acts) and intuitions, and of the relationship of "fulfilment" which may hold between them. There is a striking parallel here with Frege's distinction between *concepts*, which are "unsaturated" or dependent, and the *objects* to which they adhere, although the background assumptions of the two philosophers, and what they take as the fundamental units for analysis, are obviously quite different.

A careful examination of the various ways we speak of intuitions and representations leads Husserl to the following characterizations: "Psychical experiences" which do not "include their objects in themselves as immanent contents (thus as present *within* consciousness)" are called "Representations" (*Repräsentationen*) by him.[14] They "merely intend" a content or object, which means that it is "aimed at, minded, or referred to with understanding, by means of some contents that are given in consciousness" and are used as representatives of the former. In contrast, there are certain other "psychical experiences" that do not merely intend their objects, but "*really include* those objects *within themselves* as their immanent contents." They are called "intuitions."

The real progress beyond what was said in the earlier paper proceeds from the fact that we are now talking about types of representational experiences or acts, whereas in the earlier paper the discussion was about types of contents (or objects). This means that the earlier "contents" are now located within a context of analysis that will permit us to say "what a piece of knowledge is made of, and how it is made." That was impossible so long as we spoke only of contents (as objects), even if some of those contents were symbols.

Husserl is quick to reap the fruits of this transformation of context and proceeds to explain his central concept of fulfilment in terms of relationships between acts of consciousness. We often directly experience an inauthentic or Representational thought of an object finding "satisfaction" in an intuition of that object as thought of. I think my pen is in the desk drawer, and opening the drawer I *find it to be so*. Here I do not merely have two (or more) consecutive mental acts directed upon the same object (*LI* 694f.). I am conscious of the one act, the thought of the pen being in the drawer, being fulfilled through another act in which *its* (the thought's) object is present in a characteristically different manner – intuitively – that satisfies or confirms the earlier act. In Husserl's words, "The immediate psychical experience of the fact that the intuited *is also* the intended shall be designated as consciousness of the *fulfilled intention*."[15] The

intuition and the Representation involved in such a case are reciprocally modified by their union. "Of the intuition . . . we can say that
it is borne upon a consciousness of *fulfilled* intention. Of the Representation we say . . . that it has found its *fulfilment."*

Now the usual case is that a Representation finds its fulfilment,
not immediately, but only by passing through other Representations
that are "closer" to the ultimate object. This is true of me as I leave
the room where I thought of the pen, enter my study, approach the
desk, and begin to open the drawer. For such a thought to find its
fulfilment immediately would, in the usual case, leave us in a state
of shock that could hardly count as knowing anything. With every
subject matter we entertain, whether from the sense-perceptible
world or elsewhere, there is the prospect of getting a *better* view of
it, or examining it more closely, without necessarily fully knowing
it (*LI* 729). In Husserl's language, "we will call the correlative phenomenon most nearly adjoined to the Representation its *proximate
fulfilment.* The *ultimate* fulfilment of any Representation is *the*
intuition proper to it. It is *pure* intuition – a term which expresses
the fact that a content [present to us] bears no Representative function whatsoever."[16]

With this, the underlying structure of an act of knowing, according to Husserl, is in place. We have a sequence of representations of
the same object, arranged in a progression of more or less "close-
ness" or intuitive fulness, up to the point where, ideally, the object is
completely given as it is thought of or conceived to be. In the very
rare case the sequence may shrink to one representation and the
corresponding intuition, and it is even possible to have a static
union of representation with the simultaneous intuition of the object (*LI* 688).

This completes the first stage of Husserl's analysis of the nature of
knowing, though admittedly in this 1894 paper he does not discuss
knowledge (*Erkenntnis*) except right at the end, where he is raising
the question of how it is possible. This paper, after all, is about
representations and their corresponding intuitions, while knowledge is, strictly speaking, a matter of judgments. He here seems
purposively restrained from developing any major conclusions. But
the basic structure of filfilment described is also found in "blind" or
symbolic judgments and the corresponding perceptions or intuitions
in which they are fulfilled. There is, however, a further question

about fulfilment in general that must be dealt with, and that evokes the second main stage of Husserl's analysis of knowledge, terminating in the Fifth Logical Investigation.

III. REACHING THE OBJECTS THEMSELVES

What is most obviously lacking in the account of fulfilment thus far, and so of knowledge, is an account of fulfilment as, ultimately, a relationship of the representation (or judgment) to the object "itself." Certainly the inauthentic representation was never understood by Husserl to be *about* the intuition which "fulfills" it. That would falsify its obvious sense (*LI* 688f., 837ff.). The intuition is not its content or object. But if one reads the 1894 paper without knowing anything else of his works, it is easy to come away with the impression that meaning or intentionality (and as a result, fulfilment) is only a relationship between *experiences* or aspects thereof.

Now this might be agreeable to those who later saw in Husserl's thought a socio-historical form of idealism, as well as to their contemporary "analytic" counterparts such as Quine, Putnam, and Rorty, who all believe that one cannot step "outside" language or consciousness. And when we recall Brentano's influence on Husserl's early development, we can perhaps understand why his early efforts would leave this impression. But all we are really warranted in saying is that the Husserl of the 1894 paper had *not yet* worked out a theory of intentionality that would permit it to reach beyond components of consciousness and join, in fulfilment, with a mind-independent object. Specifically, he had not yet worked his way through the talk of "immanent" or "intentional" objects that was so much a part of the analysis of the mental act presented by Brentano and others of that day.

To get clear of immanent objects was the major achievement of Husserl's work in the mid- and late-1890s. It came to expression in the 1896 review of Twardowski's *Zur Lehre vom Inhalt und Gegenstand der Vorstellungen*, in the research notes drawn together by the *Husserliana* editors under the title "Intentionale Gegenstände," in an essay-length letter of 1901 to Marty,[17] and above all in the fifth Logical Investigation of 1901, §§ 11, 17, and the Appendix to §§ 11 and 20.

The "immanent object" was supposed to be a *part* of the act in which it occurs, while simultaneously being the direct, if not the only, object of that act.[18] It shows up in analyses of the act of consciousness primarily to account for the act's direction upon a specific entity or state of affairs, or for its specific "ofness" or "aboutness," and is especially needed, it seems, in those cases where there exists nothing outside of the act to "serve" as its object. Husserl's rejection of the immanent object is based simply on the insight that a thought does not become *of* a different object, does not shift its intentional direction, nor does its object change into something else, depending upon whether an object "outside" of it exists or not. Adolf Reinach, an early student and collaborator of Husserl's, asks: "Does a gigantic house of five floors, which I suppose myself to be perceiving, by any chance become an element of experience when this perceiving turns out to be an hallucination?"[19]

Another way of putting what is essentially the same point is to insist that it is a distortion of the nature of the representation of anything, existing or not, to say that that representation is of a part of itself. A part of a representation (or judgment) can, of course, be represented (judged of). But that is not what is going on in a representation as such, and in any case what is normally represented – e.g., "a gigantic house of five floors" – is neither a representation nor any part of one. To suppose otherwise is radically to misdescribe the situation. Accordingly, as Husserl says, "We shall do well never to speak of an intentional content where an intentional object is meant" (*LI* 580), and "It will be well to avoid all talk of immanent objectivity" (*LI* 560).

This does not mean that we are in every sense *unaware* of parts or even subordinate acts within a given act in carrying out that act. We are aware of them, as Husserl repeatedly makes clear, and the "apperception" or apprehension of the sensate matter or of distinct acts which *are* parts of a given act is essential to that act having the object which, as a whole act, it has. What is meant, rather, is that the object of the act as a whole, an intentional bearing upon which is essential to its being the act that it is, is not a constituent of *that* act (*LI* 332 and 559).

So the "intentional" object, insofar as we allow ourselves to speak of one, is the same as the "real" object. No act of consciousness is as a whole about two objects, one in the act and one out. If the real object does not exist, neither does the intentional one, and if the intentional one exists, so does the real one, for they are one and the same. To say that an object is "merely intentional" can only mean that the intention bearing upon that object exists, but that the object does not. "If the intentional object exists, the intention, the reference, does not exist alone, but the thing referred to exists also" (*LI* 596). The existence or non-existence of the object is not a matter of the nature and parts of the particular representation or judgment, but of how that representation or judgment fits into the larger context of representations and judgments bearing upon that same object.[20] Roughly, if it possibly fits into a context of fulfilment, however this is to be spelled out, its intentional object is real or actual. If no such context is possible, its intentional object does not exist at all, "in" the mind or out (*LI* 558–59).

This second stage of Husserl's analysis of knowledge, which is really a clarification of the nature of the act of consciousness in general – of how its *object* stands in relation to its *parts* – has the consequence that in representation or judgment my object is not necessarily my own mind or act or any constituent thereof (*LI* 332). Consequently, I am not restricted to comparing my representations or judgments to other representations or judgments. I can, in some cases at least, compare my mental acts with their objects, somewhat as I can compare a wrench to a nut, or a door to a frame, that it may or may not fit. As the wrench and the nut are separate entities that can be compared, so a representation and its object are separate entities that can be compared. My representations can, more or less directly, relate to objects themselves, whether they are mental or not. When thinking of the physical world, or of the various Ideal worlds such as those of numbers, propositions, concepts, or colors, I am, as most people spontaneously assume, dealing with the non-mental. I have stepped outside the "circle of ideas," so far as my subject matter goes, although it is a truism to say that I still think "in ideas," or that my thinking itself is mental. This allows Husserl to extend his treatment of fulfilment to cover the case where what fulfills the thought, in ways and degrees appropriate to the kind of subject matter dealt with, is precisely "the thing itself," and not an experience of it that is just another more or less "proximate" fulfilment. "Consciousness reaches out beyond what is actually lived through" (*LI* 701).

As a result of working out a view of intentionality that at last permits one to speak seriously of the "objectivity" or mind-independence of "contents" (objects), Husserl's question about the nature and possibility of knowledge is no longer stated in terms of what is present and how it enables us to grasp what is not present – though that always remains an issue to be dealt with. Rather, as of 1900 at least, it is in terms of "the relationship between the subjectivity of knowing and the objectivity of the content known." The precise questions to which his mature analysis of knowledge must provide answers are these:

How are we to understand the fact that the "in itself" of the objectivity comes to "representation" – indeed, that in knowledge it falls within our "grasp" [zur "Erfassung" komme] – and so ends up by becoming subjective after all? What does it mean to say that the object is both "in itself" and is "given" in knowledge? How can the Ideality of the universal, in the form of concepts or laws, enter the flux of real psychical Experiences and turn into a knowledge possession of the one thinking? What does the adaequatio rei et intellectus involved in knowing signify in the various types of cases, depending on whether the knowing grasp takes in an individual or universal, a fact or a law, etc.?"   (LI 254)

These constitute the "basic questions of epistemology" (LI 253). "The cardinal question of epistemology" has now become "that of the objectivity of knowledge" (LI 56).

IV. KNOWING AS A HIGHER ORDER ACT

But before we can give Husserl's answer to these questions we must explain the third and final stage in the development of his view of knowledge. This is his clarification of occurrent (non-dispositional) knowing as a distinctive type of higher-order or "founded"[21] act that guarantees its object (no "intentional inexistence" allowed) but does not modify it from what it is "in itself" or apart from knowledge.

   "Talk of knowledge has reference to a relationship between act of thought and fulfilling intuition" (LI 837). Yes, but knowledge is not simply such a relation. Rather, it is an additional act in its own right. An act of knowing consciously incorporates that relation between thought and intuition, along with the related acts of conceptualization and intuition, in the distinctive manner of its own direction

upon the same object. That is, a "peripheral" or "apperceptive" awareness of those two (or more) acts and of their interrelations is what
make possible a knowing of the corresponding object. When I find my
pen in my desk as I thought, the intuition involved is not itself the
fulfilment of the thought. The fulfilment of the thought – the "knowing" involved – is my consciousness of this object, the pen in the
desk, *as* being *as* thought. The thought or "empty intention" is what
is fulfilled, and the intuition is what "gives" the thought its
fulfilment. But fulfilment (knowledge) is still a relation to the object
(*LI* 726 and 728), even though it rests or is "founded" upon a kind of
"gathering up" or "synthesis" of other cognitive acts directed upon
that same object.

The object of knowledge, e.g., the pen in the drawer, is the same as
the object of the conceptualization and the object of the intuition,
but it is not presented in the same way to the act of knowledge. A
fulfilment is one type of "synthesis" of identity or identification.
Hence, "A more or less complete *identity* is the *objective datum
which corresponds to the act of fulfilment* and which 'appears in
it' "(*LI* 697). Accordingly the union of fulfilment, bringing together
meaning (symbol, thought, concept) and intuition within one super-
imposed act, can in its own right "be called an act, since it has its
own peculiar intentional correlate, an objective 'something' to
which it is 'directed'." Conversely, the union of meaning-intention
and intuition "in a fulfilling manner, gives to the *object* the character of a thing known." (Ibid.) A name used in a context of
fulfilment "tangibly adheres to its object" (*LI* 688; cf. 584). A "relation" in the full sense is established between the meaning in the
representational act (and thereby the act itself) and the corresponding object.

It is the *identity* of the intention or "meaning" in the conceptualization, on the one hand, and in the perception (intuition), on the other,
that brings the "fulness" of the object through the perceptual act to
the act of conceptualization or mere meaning. This latter is then
"filled full" of the reality of the object itself. That is, it is *actually
joined to* the object – and, in the ideal case, in every respect that it
"reaches for." "In fulfilment, the object is 'given' intuitively in the
same way in which the mere meaning means it. . . . The ideally conceived [intuiting] element which thus coincides with the [mere] meaning is the *fulfilling sense,* and . . . through this coincidence, the

merely significant intention (or expression) achieves relation to the intuitive object" (*LI* 743). The actual union of the conceptualizing act *with the object*, on the basis of a corresponding intuition of that object together with a recognition of the identity of the object of the concept and of the perception, is *what knowledge is as an act*.

In the dispositional sense we "have" knowledge, are knowledgeable, when we are in a position or are qualified to actualize the path toward the re-cognitive union of concept and object through perception when we choose.

The point not to be missed, for an accurate understanding of Husserl's view of knowledge, concerns what happens to the semantic or intentional essence of the act of "mere thought" that enters into the fulfilment synthesis.[22] In fulfilment as described, it undergoes, according to Husserl, a peculiar modification which is its fulness (*LI* 698f., 728–31). This fulness consists in the peculiar *relation* – by no means mere intentionality – which the act, and hence its essence, achieves to the object itself (*LI* 744). The act (or meaningful word), through the identity of its meaning with that of the corresponding intuition, actually *attaches itself* to the meant (*LI* 691f.). That is why Husserl repeatedly and emphatically speaks of the fulness *of the object itself*, or some part thereof, being imparted to the intention (*LI* 726, 728, 729, 762, 765). As fully given, "the object is fulness itself" (*LI* 766).[23] In its less than perfect degrees, fulfilment of a more or less signitive intention is simply a matter of its matching up (in a "synthesis of identity") to a corresponding act that is *more* of an "intuition" of the same object. But there is possible in many cases, Husserl holds, "the perfection of final fulfilment which presumes this [weaker degree of] fulfilment, and which is an adequation with the 'thing itself' " (*LI* 763; cf. 701, 718, 724, 729).

Of course, by treating one special form of consciousness or language-meaning as being or involving a relation – in the strict sense that conforms to the two axioms, "$Rab \rightarrow (\exists x)Rax$" and "$Rab \rightarrow \breve{R}ba$" (where $\breve{R}$ is the converse relation for R, and the arrow stands for strict implication) – Husserl is not exactly unique. Descartes' "clear and distinct ideas," possibly Hume's vivid impressions, certainly Russell's "acquaintance," denotation and proper names, David Kaplan's "vivid" names, and the "rigid designators" spoken of by many contemporary philosophers, all emphasize the same factor of thought: the "reality hook" as some have called it.

V. DEGREES OF FULFILMENT AND KNOWING

A few more comments must be made with respect to *degrees* of fulfilment if we are to be clear on Husserl's view of "how a piece of knowledge is made." Although all knowing, as a full grasp of "the object itself", is an act of fulfilment, not every act of fulfilment amounts to a knowing of the respective object – just as every act of fulfilment is an identification, but not conversely (*LI* 720). The intuition involved in a fulfilment must be *adequate* if that fulfilment is to be a case of *knowledge,* and it is adequate just in case every aspect of the object as conceived is also directly given (*LI* 745f.). This is the case of the "pure" or complete intuition, already mentioned, where the act contains no intentional bearing upon its object that is not also satisfied by what is given (*LI* 734, 762f.). Such a pure intuition is an option only in a restricted range of objects – mental acts and their components, and certain essences or universals and their connections – and is not possible for the physical world or physical objects (*LI* 831).

The ideal limit of intuitive presence realized in a pure intuition is, as we have noted, also called "Evidence" by Husserl (*LI* 765). He allows us to speak loosely of Evidence – indeed, of knowledge – where there are lower but still significant degrees of intuitive presence. "But the *epistemologically pregnant sense* of Evidence is exclusively concerned with this last and unsurpassable goal, *the act of this most perfect synthesis of fulfilment,* which gives to an intention, e.g., the intention of judgement, the absolute fulness of content, the fulness of the object itself. The object is not merely meant, but in the strictest sense *given,* given as it is meant, and made one with our meaning-reference [*in eins gesetzt mit dem Meinen*]." (Ibid.) Evidence in this strong sense remains exactly the same in character wherever it is possible, whether the objects concerned are individuals (mental acts or their elements), universals or states of affairs, of whatever type.

Now Husserl acknowledges that in most cases where we "confirm" a thought, we do not actually carry through to the Ideal limit of Evidence, but simply assure ourselves that we could do so if we wished. And sometimes we mistakenly assure ourselves. The "really being so" experienced in the grades of fulfilment short of Evidence is then a merely presumed one, which may or may not hold up (*LI* 708). "There are," Husserl observes, "only too many *false and even absurd recognitions* [*Erkenntnisse*]. But these are not 'authentic' recognitions – namely, not logically sound and complete recognitions, recognitions in the strong sense" (*LI* 716f.). *"All inauthentic fulfilment implies authentic fulfilment*, and indeed borrows its character of fulfilment from the authentic case" (*LI* 727). That is, a putative experience of proximate fulfilment is not a fulfilment of any sort unless the corresponding adequate fulfilment is actually possible. The many episodes which are experienced or taken *as* fulfilments, but, in fact, do not have a corresponding object in reality, are therefore not fulfilments at all.

On the scale of degrees of fulfilment, representations or judgments short of full intuitiveness, which Husserl usually refers to as "mediate," always in some measure present their ultimate objects *"as objects of other presentations, or as related to objects so presented."* Objects can of course be presented through their relations to other objects, and these "other objects" may also be presentations. In this latter case "the presentations are *presented presentations* in the relational presentation [of the object]: they belong among its intentional *objects*, not among its constituents" (*LI* 724).

When I see this apple here, for example, an essential part of what my perception is of – and I do see *an apple* – is its back side and its inner and unseen parts, as well as a certain history. These parts are present to me essentially in terms of how my present perception of the apple would develop if I were to proceed to open the apple with a knife, or bite into it, or trace its history, etc., etc. There is possible here, "phenomenologically, a continuous flux of fulfilment or identification, in the steady serialization of the percepts 'pertaining to the same object.' Each individual percept is a mixture of fulfilled and unfilled intentions. To the former corresponds that part of the object which is given in more or less perfect projection in *this* individual percept, to the latter that part of the object that is not yet given, but that new percepts would bring to actual, fulfilling presence" (*LI* 714; cf. 701). The result is a sequence of syntheses of "identifications binding self-manifestations of an object to self-manifestations of the same object." This sequence is governed by a law of essence that *"dictates a determinate order of fulfilment a priori"* (*LI* 724) for every presentation, according to its type.

At the lowest levels of fulfilment we have only an abstract descriptive knowledge of objects that does not even reveal their identity. Progression in fulfilment eventually brings us to a point where the objects are individuated for us – we know *which* entities they are – because they are given in terms of properties that form some significant part of their identity. David Smith and Ronald McIntyre have pointed out the importance of progressive fulfilment, on Husserl's view, for individuative consciousness.[24] He holds that only perception of objects, not any type of symbolic or even imaginative representation, can bring us to this level of comprehension (*LI* 729). But it is only *adequate* perception, or the ultimate degree of fulfilment possible for the given type of object, that guarantees the existence of the corresponding object.

VI. OBJECTS NOT TRANSFORMED BY KNOWING

With this view of occurrent knowing before us, a few matters of special philosophical significance remain to be emphasized.

1. The relation between the act of *knowing* and its object, while a true relation with all that that implies, is an external one. That is, the object may pass into and out of that relationship while retaining its identity. We have seen that, on Husserl's view, the act of knowing requires the existence of the corresponding object, given the precise nature of such an act. The relationship established between the "mere thought" with its meaning and the corresponding object by the fulfilment synthesis is not just intentionality, or basic "of-ness" or "about-ness," though in it intentionality is obviously presupposed in a number of ways. Fulfilment in its ultimate stage, or knowledge in the strict sense, admits no corresponding "inexistence." Knowledge forms a peculiar type of whole, which exists only as its parts do, and one of the parts is the object in question.[25] Some of the parts, on the other hand, may exist without the whole. This is true of the "mere thought" involved, of the intuition involved, and of the object involved, though not of the peculiar synthesizing act of identification, nor of the relation of the thought to the object which is realized on the basis of that synthesis.

Moreover, *in* the relationship to the mere thought that is realized when the thought achieves its object in union with an appropriately corresponding intuition, the object receives a property which it does not have outside of that relationship. That is, the property of being *known* or cognized by a certain person (*LI* 696). But that property in no way distorts or conceals the identity of the object before, during or after the time when it has it, any more than being hit by the bat does so to the ball. Husserl comments with reference to categorial acts, of which knowing is one, that "The object is intellectually grasped by the intellect, and specifically by knowledge (which indeed is itself a categorial function), but is not distorted. . . . Otherwise . . . relational and connective thought and knowledge would not be of what it is, but would be a falsifying transformation into something else" (*LI* 819f.). The property of being hit by bat *x* at time *t* does not produce or destroy the identity of the ball, but, in fact, presupposes that identity as determing *what* is and was hit. It is the same for the property of being known by person *x* at time *t*. Both the relation of hitting and that of knowing are "external," and the properties which they impose upon their relata are contingent, with a coming and going that can, in suitable cases, be *observed*.[26]

Intentionality, by contrast, does not impart a property to its object. That is why "inexistence" of the object is possible for it, and why the two axioms for genuine relations stated above do not hold for it. If it imparted a property to its object, then of course the object would have to exist. For, on a widely accepted understanding of what it means to exist, nothing can both have properties and not exist. And since very often, as we know, intentionality's object does not exist in "the real world" (as with Pegasus, etc.), it would have to exist "immanently," "in the mind." Husserl's final dismissal of immanent objects as a factor in mental acts is based on genuine insight into the nature of intentionality.

2. Given this view of knowing, a new "Critique of Reason" becomes possible. The externality of the knowledge relation or context to its object – and its resultant inability to cast an *inescapable* veil or distortion over that object – opens up the possibility of comparing object with meaning and of observing the agreement or disagreement between the conceptualization and its determinately qualified object. Among philosophers this – the "God's eye view" it is sometimes called – is usually thought to be out of the question because of the widespread assumption that in taking something as our object, and all the more so in *knowing* it, we must necessarily modify it. Thus, we can never grasp it as it is apart from consciousness (language) or "in itself." The "Midas Touch" of the mind transforms the substance of all that it contacts, on such a view. But if Husserl is

right, the object, when appropriately "given," is in itself as we then find it to be. Knowledge is not a modifying but an apprehending function, and nothing stands in the way of comparing the object with our thought of it, and finding them to "agree" (or not). Of course, we must compare the object *as given* with its conceptualizations. That is trivially true. But it does not exclude that the object as given is, under suitable circumstances, the object as it is.

On Husserl's view, accordingly, we, on appropriate occasions, *live through* the agreement between conceptualization and the object as given – including the cases of certain universals ("Ideal objects") and their connections, or certain mental events and their parts, where the object as given is the object itself, every phase of the object being directly united with the meaning directed upon it from the conceptualizing act. And while not every such agreement lived through is viewed, any one of them *can* be viewed by an objectifying act appropriately directed upon it (*LI* 765f.).

Mental acts are not ontologically privileged by Husserl, in such a way that all other things – and even whatever mental acts may be cognized – take their character from their status as objects. A mental act, a representation or judgment, for example, is just one specific type of entity, which may, from time to time, have whatever relations to other entities are made possible by the kind of thing it is and they are. And as entities can in general be observed in their interrelationships, so can a meaningful sign or mental act and its object. It is this fact alone, Husserl thinks, that opens the door to a phenomenology of knowledge and of "Reason," which he treats as the mind's capacity to validly grasp reality.[27]

Now while all of this is clearly assumed in the Sixth Investigation, it is given a completely explicit statement in the 1908 lectures on *The Idea of Phenomenology*. The main issue dealt with in these lectures is precisely how in knowledge the mind enters into relation or "grasps" what is independent of it in existence and nature: the "transcendent," as Husserl usually calls it here and later. "How can knowledge reach the transcendant?" he asks. "What I want to understand is the *possibility* of this 'reaching' " (*IP* 4, cf. 1). And how is it possible to understand this possibility? Husserl's answer is: Only by *seeing* cognition actually reach its object (*IP* 4, 29f.). In seeing the "reach"-become-"grasp" I can abstract its essence and know what it is, thus understanding how it can come about or what makes it possible. Indeed, in appropriate cases – the "dynamic" ones carefully described in the Sixth Investigation (LI 694ff.) – I can see it coming about and thus see how it arises.

The key to Husserl's discussion in this 1908 text is his distinction between two senses of "immanent," with corresponding senses of "transcendent."[28] Something is, of course, immanent to the act or to the mind if it is genuinely (reell) contained in it as a constituent, and correspondingly transcendent if it is not (IP 27f.). This we might call "ontological" immanence/transcendence. But now, in conformity with our discussion of knowledge in the strong sense above, Husserl articulates a second meaning of "immanent" (and "transcendent"). In this case anything is immanent if it is object for the absolute self-givenness of perfect Evidence (IP 28, 47–49). Here the act-intentions or meanings are, as we have seen, directly united – in the full sense related – to all the features and phases of the object as well as to the object as a whole. This we might appropriately call an "epistemological" immanence/transcendence. Something immanent in this latter sense may be transcendent in the first sense, which is exactly so with crucial cases of essences or universals and their laws. And something transcendent in the second sense sense might be immanent in the first sense, as with a thought or valuation not fully focussed on in intuition (LI 725). Physical objects or entities sharing their basic nature are always transcendent in both senses, though they may still be known in a weaker sense.

Now after these clarifications Husserl makes a crucial move. He includes the object of knowledge in the strict sense within the domain left over after the phenomenological reduction. How is this to be warranted? I believe it is to be taken in the following way: He rejects the "naturalist's" error that "[k]nowledge is something apart from the knowledge-object," such that the "knowledge is given, but the knowledge-object is not" (IP 3). The knowledge relation itself is fully present in and to consciousness, and it is also, according to him, directly involved in or attached to its object, whether that object is a part or element of consciousness or not. There is nothing "between" it and its object, and where it is its object also is. Thus: "Phenomenological reduction does not entail a limitation of the investigation to the sphere of genuine (reell) immanence, to the sphere of that which is genuinely contained within the absolute 'this' of the cogitatio. . . . Rather it entails a limitation to the sphere of things that are *purely self-given*, . . . In a word, we are restricted to the sphere of pure Evidence" (*IP* 48f.). We only "bracket the references that go beyond the 'seeing' " (*IP* 50f.).

The upshot is, as we have indicated, that something can now be both transcendent (independent of the mind in character and existence, or not immanent in the ontological sense) and at the same time immanent (fully given to the act conceptualizing and intuiting it). And this is, specifically, true of the "knowledge relation" itself. Evidence can be given in Evidence. It can be fully found in a reflective "seeing" directed upon a case of finding something to be exactly as it was thought to be (*IP* 36; cf. *LI* 165 and 194f.). Thus *it* is epistemologically immanent. But it is also ontologically transcendent, for it is an abstract structure, an essence, which – like all universals – exists and is what it is independently of its cases.[29] Though "in" the concrete act of knowing reflected on – "in" in the manner of universals *viz à viz* their instances – it is not a part of the act. It does not cease to exist, nor is its nature changed, when the exemplifying act, with all *its* parts, does cease.

This provides Husserl with the key to determining the possibility of knowledge in general, for examining fulfilment (knowing) in its cases provides him with knowledge of *what* knowing amounts to. That possibility is just the possibility of the mind fully coming, in the manner described above, into direct relation with what is not a part of, not genuinely (*reell*) contained in, the relevant acts directed upon it. Thus, he says, it would be "senseless, with respect to the essence of cognition and the fundamental structure of cognition, to wonder what its *Sinn* [*nature*] is, provided one is immediately given the paradigmatic phenomena of the type in question in a purely 'seeing' and eidetic reflection within the sphere of phenomenological reduction" (*IP* 45).

So to say that knowledge of *x* is possible is, for Husserl, simply to say that representations or judgements about '*x*' can be incorporated in a synthesis of fulfilment where *x* is intuitively found to be precisely as '*x*' represents it. Accordingly, a "critique" of knowledge and reason – of *Erkenntnis* and *Vernunft* (see *IP* 50 for a brief statement on their interrelationship) – is a matter of determining, as a matter of essence, the precise manner and extent to which objects of specific types that may be in question can be given in a concept-matching intuition. To the extent that they are "in principle" subject to such an intuition, they are knowable.

We can see here that Husserl is substituting "empty intention" for "understanding," and "intuition" for "sensibility," in the familiar Kantian "critique" project. Kant's critique of reason was carried out by limiting knowledge to the sensibly given, shaped by the *a priori* forms of sensibility and understanding. One can easily see how Husserl might have been tempted to compare his critique to Kant's, and on what points Kant's critique would be vulnerable in such a comparison – as well as how Kant might reply.

In fact, Husserl is quite stern in his criticism of Kant. His general point is that Kant simply does not succeed in "clarifying the relationship between *thinking* and *intuiting*," as well as the various matters of principle associated with that relationship (*LI* 832). Certainly, from its earliest appearance, Kant's first *Critique* was hounded by complaints that the relation he hypothesized between sensation and concept – or, more generally, between the various faculties and factors involved in cognition – is hopelessly obscure. That is a historical fact. Moreover, it would seem that his very analysis of knowledge would necessitate that we can have no knowledge of that relation – other, perhaps, than that it must be *there*. For the interaction of sensibility and understanding does not itself fall under the forms of sensibility. It fails, therefore, to be a possible object of knowledge in Kant's own terms, and can only be "deduced" as an alleged transcendental necessity.

Husserl at least is not caught in any such self-imposed bind. He points out that Kant tried to "save" knowledge, show *that* it is possible, before determining *what* it is, "before subjecting it to a clarifying critique and analysis of essence" (*LI* 833). This is further traced to Kant's failure to get clear on the specific nature of "pure Ideation, the adequate survey of conceptual essences, and the laws of universal validity rooted in those essences" (Ibid.). On Husserl's view, such a failure is built into any effort that is not "a critique based on 'seeing' " (*IP* 5of.). Thus, it was naturally impossible for Kant to "investigate the pure, essential laws which govern acts as *intentional* experiences, in all their modes of sense-giving objectivation, and their fulfilling constitution of 'true being.' Only a perspicuous knowledge of these laws of essence could provide us with an absolutely adequate answer to all the questions regarding . . . the 'possibility of knowledge' " (*LI* 834).

Now no doubt Kant's own understanding of intuition and universals (essences) was so very opposed to the one adopted by Husserl that there is little likelihood that he would have been convinced by Husserl's criticisms of his *Critique of Pure Reason*. However, is Kant's position on the relation of the mind to object in knowledge all that attractive? A candid appraisal would have to hold, I think, that it may be a position we are driven to, but it is hardly one we could have hoped for. Kant's answers to the four questions about the objectivity of knowledge posed above by Husserl would seem to simply give away points commonly assumed to distinguish knowledge from other ways our experiences bear upon objects.

VII. SUBJECTIVITY AND OBJECTIVITY RECONCILED

And how does Husserl answer the four questions (listed in Section III above) which, we have said, his mature analysis of knowledge must answer? Let us take them one by one:

1. "How are we to understand the fact that the 'in itself' of the objectivity . . . in knowledge falls within our 'grasp' and thus becomes subjective?"

Answer: The objectivity as it is when unknown, and thus "in itself," is not changed by entering into the knowledge relation. Rather, through the fulfilling synthesis it becomes directly related to the meanings directed upon it, and in that sense only does it "become subjective." It is "possessed" by the act and mind. But it does not take on the nature of the mental, any more than a ball loses its nature and takes on that of the bat or the person who hits it.

2. "What does it mean to say that the object is both 'in itself' *and* is 'given' in knowledge?"

Answer: It is to say that the direct union of the act with the object in the peculiar context of knowledge does not turn the object into something other than what it is outside of that context.

3. "How can the Ideality of the universal, in the form of concepts or laws, enter the flux of real psychical experiences and turn into a knowledge possession of the one thinking?"

Answer: Here we have two distinct cases to consider. Of course, those "universals" that make up theory (*LI* 229 and 232) can "enter" into knowing in the manner of every type of objectivity that is fully given, as signitive or "inauthentic" representations of them progressively give way, in the appropriate manner, up to the point where they are given in *pure* intuition. All said under 1 and 2 applies to them. However, those universals which are concepts and theories also are present (as concepts and propositions) in appropriate thought acts as their *properties* (*LI* 329–31).[31] They are the intentions or meanings of those acts "ideally conceived." In those acts they are "possessed" as the instance possesses its nature or "species" through exemplification or predication. The singular *cases* from which the concepts and propositions that make up theory are "abstracted" to become objects of eidetic insight are *events* of conceptualization and judgment that wholly fall within the ontologically immanent sphere. This perhaps confers upon such universals some significant advantage in becoming epistemically immanent, or the objects of knowledge in the full sense. But it does not, on his analysis of universals, detract from their objectivity, from their independence in existence and nature. And that is what Husserl is really asking about with this third question. The universal/instance relation does not modify the universal any more than the object/knowledge relation modifies the object.

4. "What does the *adaequatio rei et intellectus* involved in knowing signify?"

Answer: It signifies that the components of the object and the intentionalities or meanings involved in the knowledge synthesis are set into direct relation with each other, each meaning being paired intuitively to an objective component and conversely.

VIII. WHAT G.E. MOORE COULD HAVE LEARNED
FROM HUSSERL

G. E. Moore, a contemporary of Husserl's who was engaged with many of the same problems, was also much concerned with undoing the damage he thought Kant and similar thinkers (such as F. H. Bradley and A. E. Taylor) had done to the prospects of knowledge. In "The Refutation of Idealism"[32] (p. 5), he argued for the distinctness of consciousness from its object, and thought that, were he successful, a vast and astonishing effect on philosophy for good would be secured: "It will indeed follow that all the most striking results of philosophy – Sensationalism [Empiricism], Agnosticism, and Idealism alike – have, for all that has hitherto been urged in their favor, no more foundation than the supposition that a chimera lives in the moon. It will follow that . . . all the most important philosophic doctrines have as little claim to assent as the most superstitious beliefs of the lowest savages."

If Moore could have *established* his claim that "I am as directly aware of the existence of material things in space as of my own sensations" (p. 30), he *would* have established something with every bit of the significance for philosophy that he thought. However, he did not establish it, it seems, even to his own mind, and he later adopted an apologetic tone with reference to his "Refutation of Idealism." I think the root of his failure lay in his inability to lend a workable "substance" to consciousness, to intentionality, and, of course, also to knowledge. It remained for him, in an ironically Kantian manner, only something that "must be there" to make a certain difference.

Does Husserl fare any better? At least he has an interesting and coherent story to tell about what consciousness is like and how it, as "mere thought" or empty meaning, can "reach" toward and even seize the corresponding objects as they are in themselves. That it is not a story that can be told within an Empiricist or Naturalist framework is, I think, no automatically devastating objection, though many today will take it to be such. I think he would be on firm ground to reply that that would only beg the question as to the nature of knowledge, and push us back to the higher-level question of how we are to know the nature of knowledge. There again Husserl has an interesting and coherent story to tell, and one which, for my part, seems much more plausible than its well-known alternatives. But it is one which we cannot take up here.[32]

NOTES

1 See Husserl's "Ueber den Begriff der Zahl" (1887) and *Philosophie der Arithmetik* (1891), both in *Husserliana* XII (The Hague: Martinus Nijhoff, 1970). An English translation of the former, "On the Concept of Number: Psychological Analyses," is in *Husserl: Shorter Works*, edited by Peter McCormick and Frederick Elliston (Notre Dame, Ind.: University of Notre Dame Press, 1981), 92–119.

2 David Pears, *What is Knowledge?* (New York: Harper and Row, 1971), 5.

3 *LI*, 695. "*LI*" refers here to Husserl's *Logical Investigations*, translated by J. N. Findlay (New York, Humanities Press, 1970). Although it is necessary to refer to the Findlay translation, I do not always simply quote his version, for it frequently seems to me unperspicuous. Findlay usually translates "*Erkenntnis*" with "recognition." William P. Alston and George Nakhnikian rely mainly on "cognition" in their translation of *The Idea of Phenomenology* (The Hague: Martinus Nijhoff, 1964). Various disadvantageous nuances in these terms have led me to utilize "knowledge," for the most part, and to re-introduce the German term itself occasionally, as a reminder of what is being translated.

4 Edmund Husserl, *Early Writings in the Philosophy of Logic and Mathematics*, translated by Dallas Willard (Dordrecht: Kluwer Academic Publishers, 1994), 20. Husserl uses the term *concept* (*Begriff*) in his early writings in such a way that numbers are spoken of as concepts, and concepts are often treated as objects.

5 *Philosophie der Arithmetik*, 239f.

6 *Early Writings*, 31f. This account closely resembles the accounts by Berkeley and Hume of how concrete images and words become general in their application. The parallel is no accident. Brentano and his students studied the British Empiricists closely, and Husserl acknowledged the profound influence of Hume on his own thought. It is, I believe, seen here as elsewhere.

7 See the remainder of the remarkable descriptions on pp. 31ff. of *Early Writings*. He does not use the term "fulfilment" here.

8 *Early Writings*, 35. Cf. *LI* 695 on this point: "It is a primitive phenomenological fact, that acts of signification and acts of intuition can enter into this peculiar relation. Where they do so, where some act of meaning-intention fulfils itself in an intuition, we also say: 'The object of intuition is known through its concept' or 'The correct name has been applied to the object appearing before us'."

9 *Ibid.*, 35; cf. 33.

10 *Ibid.*, 47; cf. *LI* 61–63.

11 It is not by chance that Husserl later presents Phenomenology as an interdisciplinary methodology that offers the possibility of clarification of methods in each cognitive area, to make clear what should and should not count as knowledge and method in its domain. See the publisher's announcement for the *Jahrbuch für Philosophie und phänomenologische Forschung*, published at the opening of volume one and reprinted at page 124 in volume one of Herbert Spiegelberg, *The Phenomenological Movement: A Historical Introduction*, 2nd edition, two volumes (The Hague: Martinus Nijhoff, 1969).

12 See Dallas Willard, *Logic and the Objectivity of Knowledge* (Athens, Ohio: Ohio University Press, 1984), 194f.; and *LI* 185–86, 237 and 662.

13 *Early Writings*, 166. See also p. 20, and for the "answer" to the "how," see *LI* 701.

14 *Ibid.*, 154.

15 *Ibid.*, 156. The Sixth *Logical Investigation* is Husserl's definitive treatment of fulfilment. See also the discussion of "originary" or ultimate givenness in Section Four of *Ideas* I.

16 *Loc. cit.*; cf. *LI* 724 and 729.

17 These are all contained in *Early Writings*.

18 The clearest exposition of the "immanent object" theory of intentionality that I know of is in Chapter II of David W. Smith and Ronald McIntyre, *Husserl and Intentionality* (Dordrecht: D. Reidel Publishing Co., 1982).

19 Adolf Reinach, "Concerning Phenomenology," translated by Dallas Willard, *The Personalist*, L, Spring 1996: 198. Cf. on the "house" case *LI* 578.

20 *Early Writings*, 376–78.

21 The concept of *foundation*, as it applies to cognitive acts and their components, is crucial to Husserl's philosophy of mind and knowledge – indeed, his ontology. His formal statement of this concept is: "*A content of the species A is founded upon a content of the species B*, if an *A* can by its essence not exist, unless a *B* also exists" in a certain union with it (*LI* 475). If, now, an *act* is in this sense founded upon another act it is said to be an act of "higher-order."

22 Husserl distinguishes the intentional, the semantic and the epistemic essence of acts. *LI* 590ff., 694, 745, 766. The *epistemic* essence of the act is what is present in cases of knowing.

23 See also *Ideas* I, §144, 398 on this crucial point.

24 *Husserl and Intentionality*, 392–93.

25 For further development of this idea of occurrent knowledge as a whole with the object as part, see my *Logic and the Objectivity of Knowledge*, Chapter V, especially § 5. Husserl complained that the importance of his theory of whole and part (Third Investigation) for his account of knowledge was inadequately appreciated (*LI* 49).

26 The American New Realists understood the externality of the cognitive relation. See Section VI, written by E. G. Spaulding, of "The Program and First Platform of Six Realists," first published in *The Journal of Philosophy* VII, #15 (July 1910): 393–401, and republished in Herbert W. Schneider, editor, *Sources of Contemporary Philosophical Realism in America*, (Indianapolis: Bobbs-Merrill, Library of Liberal Arts, 1964), 35–46. Indeed, this entire "platform" statement admirably expresses

much of what Husserl arrived at in his phenomenological analyses of the *Erkenntnis* context. This is no accident, for they were well aware of Husserl's work. Walter B. Pitkin, one of the six who studied with Husserl in Göttingen in 1904 and afterwards, seems to have made a complete English translation of the *Logical Investigations*, which was left unpublished because of a negative recommendation to the American publisher by William James. (See p. 112 of Herbert Spiegelberg, *The Phenomenological Movement: A Historical Introduction*, Volume 1.)

Unfortunately the New Realists, mainly under the influence of E. B. Holt, wanted to interpret consciousness naturalistically – even scientistically – and that prevented them from having an account of what consciousness and knowledge was made up of. Among other things they could not deal with all of the "objects" which presented themselves in "illusions" and in the variabilities of perceptual consciousness (elliptical pennies, train-tracks that run together in the distance, and the like). So they were branded by the term "Naive," while their main opponents took the high ground as "Critical Realists." And they *were* naive, for they tried to characterize the "relation" of cognition without an adequate account of the terms which founded it. In this, they have had much company throughout the history of philosophy. The attempt to characterize the mental in terms of the "inexistence" of objects, for example, in Brentano and others, does not get to the heart of the matter. What is it about the nature of the mental act, what goes into its make-up, that allows it to be "about" something which may or may not exist? I owe James Heanue the observation that one cannot make anything out of "inexistence" taken by itself.

27 *IP* 33 and 46. *IP* refers to the English edition of Husserl's *The Idea of Phenomenology*, translated by Alston and Nakhnikian (The Hague: Martinus Nijhoff, 1964). On the "Phenomenology of Reason" or Noetic Phenomenology see the fourth section of *Ideas* I, especially the second chapter. On the absolute centrality of a Critique of Reason (based upon the Phenomenology of Reason) in Husserl's view of his own work, see *Early Writings*, 493ff.: "In the first place I mention the general problem which I must solve if I am to be able to call myself a philosopher. I mean: a *critique of reason*, a critique of logical and practical reason, of normative reason in general."

28 See the subtle and thorough discussion of this matter in Jacques Taminiaux, "Immanence, Transcendence, and Being in Husserl's *Idea of Phenomenology*," in *The Collegium Phaenomenologicum: The First Ten Years*, edited by Sallis, Moneta, and Taminiaux (Dordrecht: Kluwer Academic Publishers, 1988), 47–75. To me, the effects of the distinctions dealt with for the clarification of Husserl's views on *Erkenntnis* are

somewhat confused by giving Heidegger the last word in the concluding part of Taminiaux's excellent paper.

29 Husserl's view of universals or "Ideal objects" is central to his account of knowledge, especially when he speaks of himself as advocating idealism. One must keep in mind that, for him, "To talk of 'idealism' is of course not to talk of a metaphysical doctrine, but of a theory of knowledge which recognizes the 'ideal' as a condition for the possibility of objective knowledge in general, and does not 'interpret it away' in psychologistic fashion" (LI 338; cf. 193). The entire second Logical Investigation deals with the nature and ontological status of universals or "Ideal" entities and their laws.

30 See my "The Paradox of Logical Psychologism: Husserl's Way Out," American Philosophical Quarterly IX, #1 (January 1972): 94–100, as well as Logic and the Objectivity of Knowledge, Chapter IV, §§4 & 5, on the status of concepts, propositions, and theories as universals.

31 In Mind, XII, 1903, and in Moore's Philosophical Studies (London: Kegan Paul, Trench, Trubner & Co., Ltd., 1922).

32 I recognize that many will regard the realist interpretation of Husserl on knowledge presented here as rendered obsolete by his "later philosophy," as it has come to be understood, especially as it bears upon the noema and the life-world. Here I can only state that I must disagree. I have dealt with the noema in other papers, notably in "Finding the Noema," in J. Drummond and L. Embree, eds., Phenomeology of the Noema (Dordrecht: Kluwer Academic Pubishers, 1992) and in "A Critical study of Husserl and Intentionality," in The Journal of the British Society for Phenomenology, XIX, (1988), 186–198 and 311–322. The amount of exposition required to make Husserl's view of knowledge at all intelligible ruled out dealing with many issues it raises, both within the field of Husserl interpretation and within the theory of knowledge generally.

KEVIN MULLIGAN

KEVIN MULLIGAN

---

5 Perception

I. ON THE DESCRIPTION OF PERCEPTION

Husserl seems to have devoted roughly equal amounts of energy and pages to the description of perception, judgement, and imagination. By "description," he meant the analysis of the traits and components of mental states or acts and their objects. As his views changed over the years about the nature of intentionality and philosophy, the descriptive psychology of the *Logical Investigations* (1900/01) gave way to descriptive programmes in which the objects of perception and of judgement were conceived of in terms of a new, analytic framework; in particular Husserl lost interest in describing the things and processes in the real world that are the objects of perception and judgement and so too in describing their relations to these acts. His new analytic framework, particularly as it applies to perception, has been thoroughly expounded and discussed in the literature.[1] My aim here is to expound Husserl's first descriptions of perception within the framework of the *Investigations* and to incorporate as far as possible his later descriptive results to the extent that these are separable from his later turn to idealism. I shall therefore be concentrating on the *Investigations* and on the 1907 lectures on *Ding und Raum* (*Thing and Space*) which, in their descriptive parts, are relatively free of the mysteries of Husserl's transcendental and idealist turns.[2] I shall also refer to the large body of work stimulated by Husserl's early analyses of perception[3] which expounds, develops, and criticizes Husserl's early ideas about perception. Together with the analyses of Husserl on which they draw, these early contributions to phenomenology constitute perhaps the most impressive body of work within the phenomenological tradition. They are, needless to say, almost completely unknown, particularly to phenomenologists.[4]

Early and late Husserl remained convinced of the importance of description, as opposed to explanation, in philosophy. This has not been a fashionable view, but it was shared by Wittgenstein. Each of these Austrian philosophers thought that description was difficult, that what we see is "hard to describe"[5] and that failure to describe correctly leads to disaster.

Husserl's descriptions of perceptions fall under three headings: what we see, the way we see, and how we see. His central thesis concerning *what we see* is that the primary object of perception is public things, the things we all think we see most of the time, which stand before us *in propria persona* (*LI* V §11, §14, §2). In this respect Husserl is decidedly a naive realist. But he also wants to claim that this direct, straightforward perception of public things is mediated by what he calls *perceptual content*: we always see what we see in a particular way (LI I §23). A critical realist or representationalist may feel that there is only a verbal difference between Husserl's view and his view that we are aware of perceptual contents and infer to the existence of public objects, or that we see public objects by being aware of private objects. For such a representationalist, the very application to perception of the act-content-object schema is enough to make perception an indirect affair. But if Husserl is right (see section X herein) his endorsement of naive realism marks a decisive break with the critical realisms of Brentano's other students and heirs up to and including the Berlin Gestalt psychologists.

His account of *how we see* amounts to a second major difference between his analysis of perception and that of the other heirs of Brentano as well as most subsequent analyses of perception in the English-speaking world. For perceptual states, Husserl thinks, normally form part of wider psychological and behavioural wholes and only an analysis of the role of perceptual acts within such contexts will allow us to make sense of the perceptions of a subject in motion, of perceptions of dynamic objects and of the connection between perceptual states and the sets appropriate to different types of activity. If Husserl is right, most philosophies of perception have failed to appreciate the importance of dynamic perceptual content.

In Husserl's account of what we perceive, the way we perceive and how we perceive the first is the most important, not simply because it contains the details of Husserl's naive realism but also because it enjoys a certain logical priority in view of Husserl's adherence to a principle of *indirect classification*. We provide descriptions of the way we see and of how we see via descriptions of what we see; as Meinong puts it, we cannot avoid the "detour via the object."[6]

Husserl's analysis of perception develops a line of thought that can be traced back to Hering,[7] Stumpf, and Brentano and prepares the way for Gestalt psychology. This approach typically insists on the claim that perception and its objects have a rich structure that is not due to judgement and conceptualization. It is thus opposed to Kantian traditions in philosophy and to traditions in psychology influenced by Helmholtz.

II. TO PERCEIVE IS TO PERCEIVE EITHER SIMPLY OR PROPOSITIONALLY

The now familiar distinction between simple seeing and *seeing that* is clear enough at the level of the grammatical form of perceptual reports. As Husserl puts it: "we do not merely say 'I see this paper, an inkpot, several books' and so on, but also 'I see that the paper has been written on, that there is a bronze inkpot standing here, that several books are lying open' and so on" (*LI* VI §40). He takes this grammatical distinction to be correlated with four further distinctions which are needed to describe the truth-makers of such reports:

  (i)   to see is to see either simply or propositionally;
  (ii) to see particulars is not to mean, is not to exercise a concept, neither an individual nor a general concept;
  (iii) to see particulars is not to judge;
  (iv) to see is to see particulars or states of affairs.

(iii) concerns the type of act or state to which seeings belong, (i) and (ii) the nature of their contents and (iv) that of their objects.

Husserl calls that aspect of an act that makes it an act of judging *that p* rather than seeing or supposing *that p*, or an act of seeing *a* rather than of imagining *a*, the quality or mode of an act. Modes may be independent of other modes (independent of any other modes or of modes of the same type), as is the case in seeing *a*, seeing *that p*, visually imagining *a*, visually imagining *that p*, supposing *that p* and judging *that p*. Or they may be dependent on other modes, as is the case in admiring *a*, regretting or desiring *that p*, etc., each of which requires some cognitive basis. Independent modes are either positing – seeing *a*, judging *that p*, referring to *a* in the context of a judging – or non-positing – visually imagining *a*, supposing *that p*. Their contents are either propositionally articulated – seeing or judging *that p* – or non-propositional – seeing *a*, referring to *a* (*LI* VI §§22–43).

What does Husserl mean by "mean" in (ii), to see particulars is not to mean? He often describes the content of a judging, like that of an act of supposing, as an act of "meaning" (*Bedeuten, Meinen*), used as a gerund. Meaning, so understood, is complex, consisting of acts of naming and predicating. This is a somewhat unusual way of using "meaning," which is most often used as a noun (*Bedeutung*). Husserl also uses "meaning" in this second way to describe the types or species instantiated by namings and predicatings and by the propositional wholes they make up. Husserl argues that seeing particulars is not any sort of meaning, neither naming (whether descriptive or not) nor predicating, because of the independent variability of perceptions, on the one hand, and perceptual judgements, on the other hand.

> I have just looked out into the garden and now give expression to my perception in the words, "There flies a blackbird!" What is here the act in which my meaning resides? I think we may say . . . that it does not reside in perception, at least not in perception alone . . . [W]e could base quite different statements on the same perception, and thereby unfold quite different senses. I could, e.g., have remarked: "That is black!," "That is a black bird!," "There flies that black bird!," "There it soars!" and so forth. And conversely, the sound of my words and their sense might have remained the same, though my perception varied in a number of ways. Every chance alteration of the perceiver's relative position alters his perception, and different persons, who perceive the same object simultaneously, never have exactly the same perceptions. No such differences are relevant to the meaning of a perceptual statement. (*LI* VI §4)

To see particulars is not to mean but to see simply, to see propositionally is to see that some state of affairs obtains. "As the sensible object stands to sense-perception so the state of affairs stands . . . to perception of it (*Sachverhaltswahrnehmung*)" (*LI* VI §44). In the first case, "the 'external' thing appears 'in one blow,' as soon as our glance falls upon it. The manner in which it makes the thing appear present is *straightforward* (*schlicht*)," "simple, immediate" (*LI* VI §46).

The manner in which we perceive states of affairs, on the other hand, follows, according to Husserl, from the nature of states of affairs. We can distinguish in Husserl's account both a relatively uncontroversial and a controversial strand. Since states of affairs are ideal entities (*LI* VI §47), unlike the temporal individuals they may contain, and since they are complex, they can be grasped in judgings and – since the sense or content of a judging is complex – they are then given in a conceptually complex way. More controversially, Husserl notoriously thinks there is a type of non-sensory perception of ideal entities such as numbers and states of affairs (*LI* VI §45) distinct from reference to numbers and judgements that states of affairs obtain. Indeed, because of his endeavour to be as systematic as possible, his use of "perception" is often ambiguous as between perception of ideal entities and between perception of temporal entities (and between external and "internal" perception). This is due, in part, to his ambition to defend a thorough-going parallelism between, on the one hand, reference to and perception of temporal particulars such as tables and birds and, on the other hand, between reference to and "perception" of ideal entities. The reader is therefore easily misled (especially since Husserl also thinks that there is yet another parallelism between meaning and perception, between propositions and melodies). In what follows I studiously ignore what Husserl says about non-sensory perception of states of affairs and concentrate on the relatively uncontroversial strands in his account of our grasp of states of affairs. These are his claims that judgements based on simple perceptions of particulars have as their objects states of affairs (*LI* VI §44) and are conceptually mediated. To see that the gold is yellow is to have visually present the gold and its being yellow and to apprehend this "through judging."[8]

Although Husserl rarely stresses that the two positing, non-propositional modes, naming (as part of a judgement, say) and simple seeing, are distinct, this follows from his premises. Were they not distinct then a simple seeing could be a part of an act of judging, but since simple seeing is not associated with any meaning act it cannot occur in judging. In addition, the essentially non-intuitive nature of judging and of all its parts means that no judgement can include a perception, although a judgement may be based on perceptions in much the same way in which dependent acts such as regret are based on other acts.[9]

Husserl's view that simple seeing and meaning are to be distinguished, is now familiar, thanks to Warnock, Chisholm, Dretske, and Jackson. In particular, Dretske's demonstration of the differences in quantity and quality between perceptally articulated (analogue) information and conceptually vehiculed (digital) information has made clear just why judgings and seeings are independently variable.[10]

Before attempting to set out Husserl's positive views about the nature of perceptual content we shall look at his account of what we see in accordance with the principle of indirect classification already mentioned. For it is by reference to the complexity of what we see that Husserl describes the complexity of the sensorial and interpretative features of perceptual content.

III. WHAT WE PERCEIVE

The distinction between simple perception of particulars and doxastic perception of states of affairs is no more than the beginning of Husserl's analysis, which advances a number of claims concerning not only the different types of particular we simply see but also the different relations between them.

3.1 To perceive simply is to perceive particulars

Things vs. monadic moments. It is tempting to think that simple seeing is just seeing things, and many discussions of the subject content themselves with this case. But the slogans with which Husserl announces his naive realism indicate that his own view is more complicated. We see coloured things (*LI* V §11), trees, houses, but also the events bound up with things such as a flight of birds (*LI* I §23). We hear the barking of the dog (ibid.), the singer's song (*LI* V §11), the adagio of the violin, the twittering of the birds (*LI* V §14), the tones of the barrel organ (*LI* VI, Appendix 4). Thus, we simply see not only things, but also what he calls *moments* (*Momente*) or features (*Merkmale*) and determinations (*Bestimmtheiten*). An important sub-class of moments is what have traditionally been called accidents. A moment is a dependent particular, as non-repeatable as is the thing it depends on.[11] For obscure Australo-American reasons, moments are now often called "tropes." Within a nominalist ontology, moments do all the jobs which ideal, repeatable properties are supposed to do. In Husserl's ontology, every moment instantiates an ideal kind or "species," an ideal object or attribute. He also conceives of things as structured wholes consisting of static, monadic moments.

Like other Brentanians, Husserl seems to have become enamoured of moments first of all in the context of perception. And indeed traditional talk of qualities works with one of the traditional Aristotelian determinations of accidents. To say that a primary quality is, but a secondary quality is not "in" a thing is to work with the idea that there is something which is in a thing without being a part of it in the ordinary sense. Similarly, one analysis of secondary qualities makes them out to be relational accidents.

Husserl's moments, as the examples of perceived objects mentioned above show, may be either static or dynamic. Perceived *monadic moments* are introduced in the context of the critical discussion of the British empiricists in the second *Investigation:* "If we are struck by an 'individual' " [i.e., temporal] " 'trait' or moment of an object, by its peculiar colouring, e.g., or by its noble form etc., we pay special attention to this trait, and yet have no general presentation" (*LI* II §21), and the same is true of perception of a concrete thing. Yet there is a neo-Humean objection to this point, which rejects both moments and ideal properties and allows only things and resemblance relations. Husserl describes it as follows:

Features . . . are not truly immanent in the objects that have them. The distinct mutually inseparable . . . moments of an intuitive content [object], e.g., its colour, form etc., that we think we apprehend as being present in it, are not really in it at all. There is really only one kind of real parts, those which can appear by themselves, in other words the thing's *pieces*. [Moments], of which it is said that they can indeed not be on their own account, (or be so intuited), but that they can be attended to by themselves, are to some extent a mere fiction *cum fundamento in re*. There is neither colour in a coloured thing, nor form in a formed thing, but there are really only circles of resemblance in which the object in question has its place, and certain *habits*.   (*LI* II §36)

We have already seen what Husserl's objection would have been to the attempt to analyze perception of a redness moment in terms of subsuming an object under the concept *red*[12] – simple seeing involves neither naming nor predicating. But Husserl objects, too, to the neo-Humean account of perceptual reports. If these attribute only perceptions of things, their pieces and relations of resemblance among things, then, Husserl points out, we will be led to give an Ersatz-semantics for such propositions. In the light of later neo-Humeanisms (Russell, Nicod, Carnap), the following remark is remarkably prescient:

Naturally the expressions "A tone is faint" and "A tone belongs to the set of objects which resemble one another with respect to faintness" are semantically equivalent. But equivalence is not identity. If someone says that talk about faintness of tones could only arise if we had noticed similarities amongst faint tones . . . he may be right. But what has all this to do with what we *mean* by our words?   (Appendix to *LI* II §39).

Husserl's objection to neo-Humean scepticism about the perceivability of moments is that this position leads to a regress.

Should anyone wish to declare *all* talk of the intuitive presentation of abstract, objective determinations to be senseless, and to maintain that when we perceive, e.g., the property white, we really only perceive, or otherwise present to ourselves, a resemblance between the appearing object and other perceived or otherwise presented objects, then such a man has involved himself in an infinite regress, since talk of this presented resemblance calls for a corresponding reinterpretation.   (*LI* II §37).

If the white moment of a thing is reduced to a similarity between it and other things, then the ascertainment of this connection or relation would have to be explained by recourse to a "group of similar similarities such as subsist among" white objects. "The explanatory principle would have to be applied to this further similarity and so on" (ibid.).[13]

Colour moments and form moments – shapes, extents, etc. – are the two central categories of perceivable static monadic moments. Two points about them should be borne in mind: their inseparability, which Husserl describes in terms of the obtaining between them of a formal or internal relation of dependence and the fact that the shape-moment of a concrete thing is distinct from the region of space the thing occupies (an external relation). An internal relation is a relation that must hold between its terms, an external relation one that need not always hold between them.

Thus if, as Berkeley and Husserl claim, moments of sensory quality such as colour moments always occur together with extent moments their relation is internal. If a thing need not occupy a given location then occupation is said to be an external relation. The internal relations in the perceptual world on which Husserl concentrates are invariably relations between moments and between their species or types.

The point about the inseparability of quality and extent, together with the claim that this is seen, illustrate the thesis that what is given has a structure that is not imposed by the mind and is not due to conceptualization.

Dynamic moments. The category of dynamic moments – events, processes or episodes – is relatively familiar from contemporary work on perception, perceptual reports and, indeed, the psychology of event perception. The sounds and melodies we hear and the movements we see fall into this category. In particular, perceptual reports employing naked infinitives ("Sam saw Mary jump") and "how" ("Sam saw how Mary jumped") are best understood as attributing direct perceptions of events and processes. Since Husserl thinks that to perceive movement is to perceive a continuously changing occupation of places there is an important sense in which, for him, such moments are relational moments. It is to this relatively unfamiliar category that we now turn.[14]

Relational Moments. There is a tendency to assume that simple seeing is of things and monadic moments only, whereas to see a relation is to see that two or more particulars stand in the relation. Husserl, however, to whom we owe the very distinction between simple seeing and seeing that, did not make this assumption.

Relational particulars, or "moments of unity" as Husserl calls them, are objects that are founded on two or more other objects, that is objects that cannot exist without these fundamenta (*LI* III §22). Moments of unity are either *figural moments*, such as melodies and gardens, or they belong to a category of which *spatial contact* is perhaps the clearest example. They are also either temporal or spatial.

The simplest type of figural moment is a group of objects that resemble one another more or less completely, as when we have

"straightforward perceptions of sensuously unified manifolds, series, flights [of birds]" (*LI* VI §51, III §4). A configuration of trian-
gles is a static figural moment of unity, "a static distribution of
objects in the visual field"; but "every sort of movement or qualitative change of particular objects also gives to the whole an immediately noticeable quasi-qualitative character": a flight of birds is a
dynamic figural moment of unity (*PdA* 208). Husserl had described
this category in the *Philosophy of Arithmetic*. "Experience" testi-
fies to the

existence of quasi-qualitative moments . . . One speaks for example of a line
of soldiers, a heap of apples, an avenue of trees, a line of chickens, a flock of
birds, a flight of geese, etc. In each of these examples we have a sensory
manifold [*Menge*, set] of objects that resemble each other, named according
to their type. But this is not all that is thereby expressed – the plural of the
common noun would suffice for that – but rather a certain *characteristic
nature* [*Beschaffenheit*] of the unified total intuition of the manifold, that
can be grasped in one glance and which, in its well-distinguished forms,
constitutes the essential part of the meaning of the expressions that introduce plurals, "series, heaps, avenue, flock, flight" etc.

(*PdA* 203–4; my quotation marks)

In the *Logical Investigations*, he describes a basic feature of the
terms of such relational particulars:

Wherever connecting forms can be demonstrated as peculiar moments in
intuition, that which is connected is always relatively independent parts,
such as the tones in the unity of a melody, colours picked out piecemeal in
the unity of a colour pattern, or partial shapes taken out from the unity of a
complete shape.   (*LI* III §22)

The ontological difference between the two types of relational
particular, figural moments such as melodies and the category to
which spatial contact belongs, is that in the former but not the latter
case the relational moment *contains* its terms.

We directly see not only groups, but also the relation of spatial
contact and other "sensory-relational moments" such as "standing
out from" (*PdA* 207) and the "sensory moment of likeness" (*PdA*
208, *LI* III §23 fn., II §37) as well as relations between such
moments[15] and positional relations (*PdA* 206, 207).[16] In general,
wherever there is phenomenal discontinuity there are perceived
relations.

3.2 (Dis)continuity vs. (in)dependence

The classification of what we perceive has so far been in terms of the distinction between perception of independent and of dependent particulars and, within the latter category, between perception of relational and of monadic particulars, and between perception of static – redness and squareness moments – and dynamic particulars – screamings and hittings. Skew to all of these is the distinction between the visually differentiated and undifferentiated.[17] What is visually differentiated may be independent, a "concretum," or dependent, e.g., a moment of shape. Husserl seems to have thought that it is one of the functions of the interpretative element in perceptual content (see section V) in perception to determine whether an array of discontinuities is seen as belonging to one thing or two. Another function of interpretation is to bring us to distinguish between the relevant and the irrelevant internal relations exhibited in any given visual array: the moments of sensory likeness, distance and contrast that are relevant to the perceptual project in question.[18]

3.3 Perception of states of affairs

A state of affairs is not something that can appear in a sensory fashion even if one or more of the individuals in it is seen (*LI* V §28). We directly see "sensory or real forms of connection," but we see *that* "categorial or ideal connections" – that is, formal or topic-neutral connections – obtain between particulars and properties (*LI* VI §48).

I can see colour, but not *being*-coloured, I can feel smoothness, but not *being*-smooth. I can hear a sound, but not that something *is* sounding. Being is nothing *in* the object, no part of it, no figure of it, no internal form whatsoever, no constitutive feature of it however conceived. But being is also nothing attaching to an object: as it is no real internal feature, so also it is no external feature, and therefore is not, in the *real* sense, a "feature" at all. For it has nothing to do with the *real* forms of unity which bind objects into more comprehensive objects, tones into harmonies, things into more comprehensive things or arrangements of things (gardens, streets, the phenomenal external world). On these real forms of unity the external features of objects, the right and the left, the high and the low, the loud and the soft etc., are founded. Among these anything like an "is" is naturally not to be found.   (*LI* VI §43)[19]

We directly see "sensorily unified groups, series" such as a flock of birds or a group of dots but we see *that* there is this or that conjunctive or disjunctive entity (*LI* VI §51). Sensory connection-moments differ from relations such as exemplification, part-whole relations, dependence and other internal relations. The former [*Verknüpfungen*] are material and perceptible, the latter [*Beziehungen*] formal and invisible.

Of spatio-temporal "objects, their constitutive features, their factual connections with other objects, through which more comprehensive objects are created and . . . external features in the part objects," Husserl says that they "exhaust the possible range of what can be perceived" (*LI* VI §43). Here "perceived" presumably means perceived directly by the senses without the help of judgement or concepts.

What, then, is the relation between the perceptual judgements reported by "see that" and simple, direct perception of particulars? Husserl correctly notes that one can perceive a monadic moment, such as a smell or a sound, without perceiving the whole it belongs to and so, too, see that a state of affairs obtains without seeing all of its components. Indeed, more generally, it is possible to see that aRb without seeing a, or without seeing b, or without seeing the relational particular, r, that falls under the relational concept. As Jackson puts it, I may see that the petrol tank is empty by looking at the gauge. And I may see Mary's jump although I see only an extremely small part of Mary.[20]

Nevertheless it is clear from Husserl's analyses of verification and abstraction (see sections 7.4 and 10.2 herein) that in the optimal and so fundamental case of fully justified true perceptual belief, he thinks that to see that aRb is to see directly a, b and some r and to judge that aRb on the basis of these direct perceptions.[21] In such a case, to use one of his favourite expressions, the perceptual judgement is built up on the basis of the different direct perceptions. It would therefore be in the spirit of Husserl's analysis of the optimal case to say that the subject believes or judges of a, b and r, on the basis of perceptions thereof, that aRb. Judgements that aRb which lack this anchoring in direct perception, such as judgements arrived at via inference or via testimony, would then fall short of this optimal case.

Independently of his analysis of abstraction and verification, Husserl has two further reasons for wanting to relate direct perception of particulars to perception of states of affairs in the ways just described. One of these is epistemological, the other ontological. Ontologically, Husserl seems to have been tempted by a coincidence principle of the sort to be found in Meinong and in logical atomism. An obtaining, positive state of affairs, such as that the square is red, is an ideal entity. But this ideal entity is correlated with an entity that is wholly particular, the square, and "contains" a shape moment and a colour moment. The epistemological consideration is that since direct perception is not normally of simples, the perceived complexity of what we directly see must be allowed for without invoking perception that. This Husserl does by claiming that those parts of what we directly see which are also directly seen are implicitly seen (VI §48). Clearly, too, the "real forms of unity" already described must also be implicitly seen if they are not to be assimilated to the category of correlates of perceptual judgements, to states of affairs such as that *a* has property *P* or contains *b*.

We can now use this account of what we see to introduce Husserl's account of the *way* we see, of perceptual content. This is, in the first instance, an account of what we may call static content and then of dynamic content. The description of dynamic content is, roughly, a description of the way we see when we move or of the way we perceive dynamic moments and things, or both. We shall look first at static content. Husserl's account has two strands: a description of the sensations we have when we see, and a description of the interpretation of these sensations. I give his account of sensations in section IV, and of interpretation and its relation to sensations in section V.

IV. CONTENT: TO PERCEIVE IS TO HAVE SENSATIONS

The way we see particulars is no less complicated or varied than are the objects we see. The parallelism between Husserl's description of what we see and his description of sensations, between his argument for perceived moments, monadic and relational, and his argument for sensational counterparts to these, is striking and thorough.

Thus, the argument above, that if colour moments are rejected then the similarity relations between things that are supposed to replace them must be reinvoked ad infinitum, applies to any attempt to reject sensations of colour. As Husserl points out, if there are no sensations of colour then there can be no "connection and relational contents in the intuition of a whole [*Inbegriff*] with a corresponding form of unity" (*LI* II §37).

Nevertheless, the roles of sensations and perceived public particulars are radically different. "I do not see colour-sensations but coloured things, I do not hear tone-sensations but the singer's song" (*LI* V §11, cf. §14).

To each of the different types of visible particulars described in III, there correspond types of sensations. The description of visual differentiation and continuity given (in §3.2) is actually, Husserl adds, two descriptions: of the complexities of sensations of spatial form and of the spatial traits of physical things (*LI* III §9). To "the *objective* moments of unity, which belong to the intentional objects and parts of objects, which in general transcend the experiential sphere" there correspond the *phenomenological* moments of unity, which give unity to the experiences or parts of experiences (the real phenomenological data) (*LI* III §4).[22] Thus, to the different moments of colour in perceived things, there correspond, for example, colour sensations; to the monadic and relational moments of form, there correspond form sensations (*LI* II §37). And to the way moments hang together in and between what we see, there correspond sensations which are relational. Sensations "form a unique highest genus, which divides into many species" (*LI* VI §58).

This relation of correspondence between visual sensations and the moments and things they help present is conceived of in a very traditional fashion: there are types of visual sensations which "are in a particular sense analogous to types found amongst properties." Husserl notes the problems associated with the thesis that sensations and qualities in objects are analogous: "we make an equivocal use of the same words to refer to the sensuously apparent determinations of things and to the (re)presenting moments in perception and thus speak of 'colour,' 'smoothness,' 'shape' etc. in the sense of objective properties and in the sense of sensations" (*LI* II §10).[23]

Just as Husserl conceives of the thing seen as made up of moments or abstract parts, so too he conceives of sensations as being real parts (*V* §2), parts of the content (I §23) of states of perceptual awareness.

A phenomenological moment of unity, such as a sensation of an avenue of trees is a relational moment, it relates sensations of trees, just as sensations corresponding to the colour and form of an individual tree are linked by relational sensations.[24]

A philosopher who denies the distinction between the visual sensations we have and the objects (moments and things) we see is, Husserl argues, overlooking the phenomenon of perceptual constancy, the "difference between the red of this ball, objectively seen as uniform, and the indubitable indeed necessary shading [Abschattung] of the subjective colour sensations." I see the ball as having a uniform red colour, in spite of noticeable variations due to the play of light on it. I do not see it as having one dark red colour here, another light red colour there. Colour-constancy amidst variations of light and shadow is the phenomenon that the colour sensation/colour quality distinction is intended to do justice to.

Husserl repeatedly claims that we see objects by virtue of the fact that we have, but do not see, sensations. This thesis involves rejecting an assumption shared by Brentano, Russell, and Moore. For them, the relation between sensing and what is sensed, the sensation, is simply a special case of the act-object relation. Husserl, however, denies this. Sensations, on his account, may belong to intentional experiences, but they are not themselves intentional. Husserl generalises the distinction defended by Stumpf between feelings such as a localised pain, which require no cognitive basis, and emotions such as joy or regret, which do have such a cognitive underpinning, so that it applies to perception. Visual sensations – of redness and of form – and tactile sensations – of roughness and smoothness – differ from acts of seeing and touching in the same way in which a localised pain differs from regret. Perceptual sensations and localised pains are non-intentional. Seeing and regret are intentional. Husserl "identifies sensation and its 'content'," since he "does not recognise sensing acts" (LI V §15) (b)).[25]

Husserl's claim that visual sensations belong to perceptions but, unlike these, have neither contents nor objects, has two important consequences. First, it clears the way for the claim that to perceive is to perceive things. For if, as for Brentano and Russell, to see is to have sensations and the latter necessarily have objects, then seeing becomes a relation whose second term cannot be a material thing. Husserl denies any object to sensing and is thereby able to say that the object of perception is a public thing. Second, consider the case of someone who wants to reidentify tokens of a certain visual or pain sensation, perhaps because he wants to note their occurrence in his diary. Since for something to be such a sensation is just for someone to have it, and since the occurrence of the sensation involves no mode or content of presentation (it is not an act), the relevant tokens can only be reidentified via the sense of a suitable description. Thus, private sensations are reidentifiable only via public senses. As we shall see below, public visible items present themselves from different sides. But mental phenomena are not so given.[26]

V. CONTENT: TO PERCEIVE IS TO INTERPRET SENSATIONS

Although a world is conceivable in which creatures would have sensations but would not interpret them, such creatures would not, Husserl claims, be capable of perception (*LI* I §23). Husserl's labels for sensations – he calls them "intuitively presentative" or "representative" contents – may easily mislead. By themselves such sensations do not present or represent: it is these sensations "*in* their interpretations" which have the "relation to corresponding objective determinations," which is (re)presentation (*LI* VI §22). By themselves, sensations stand only in relations of causality and similarity – simple or brute, and structural – to objects and their features.

What, then, is it to interpret sensations? An interpreted sensation is a way of seeing, we said. But if to see simply is not to judge or exercise concepts, then it is clear that Husserl cannot explain the difference between two ways in which one object is seen, for example from below and above, along the lines of his explanation of the difference in sense between two descriptions of the same object. The term of art of Frege, Cantor, and Husserl for the sense of an expression, "the way of being given" (*die Art des Gegebenseins*), seems to be taken from the perceptual domain. But the difference between the two ways of referring accomplished with the help of "the evening star" and "the morning star" and the two ways of seeing one and the same star, in the evening and in the morning, is a difference in kind.[27] Although Husserl describes the *role* of the non-conceptual interpretation of sensations and the *relation* between interpretation and sensations, he has surprisingly little to say about the *nature* of such interpretation. The *role* of interpretation is to be the surplus which, when combined with raw sensations, "makes us perceive this or that object, e.g. see this tree, hear this ringing, smell this scent of flowers etc." But this is just to say that interpretation plays the same *rôle* in perception as sense in judgement which, since perceptual content is not conceptual, is not very illuminating.

Husserl's four most informative claims about the roles and nature of interpretation concern the organisation of sensations, the distinction between seeing an object and seeing one of its sides, perceptual constancy and perceptual identification.

5.1 Interpretation and organisation

The first of these claims is introduced via discussion of examples of the dawning on us of different interpretations. Husserl mentions (a) the case where we suddenly see a figure as a sign and (b) the case where what is seen as a woman turns out to be a waxwork figure. He also (c) contrasts hearing a word first as a mere sound and then with its meaning.

But these three examples do not tell us what it is to interpret visual sensations in two different visual "ways" (*LI* V §14, §27). To come to hear or see a word with its meaning is to understand what was previously merely heard or seen. But, as we have seen, to interpret visual or auditory sensations is not to mean. Similarly, to come to take what seemed to be a woman in the Panopticum Waxworks as a waxwork figure representing a lady is to pass from the perceptual mode to a combination of this with the mode of imagination. As Husserl himself puts it, the difference here lies in the act qualities, i.e., modes (*LI* V §27). In each of these cases, then, the switch of aspect is a switch from the mode of perception to a complex mode that is more than merely perceptual. But what is required is an account of what it is to switch from one way of perceiving to another way of perceiving the same object. There are, doubtless, changes in perceptual interpretation involved in each of Husserl's examples, but he does not describe them. If, for example, "the same tone is at one moment heard close at hand, at another far away" (*LI* V §14), in what respects have we here more than a difference in sensations? So far we have merely the bare claim:

Different acts can perceive the same object and yet involve quite different sensations . . . The same sensational contents are . . . "taken" now in this and now in that manner . . . Interpretation itself can never be reduced to an influx of new sensations; it is an act-character, a way of being conscious, of "mindedness."   (*LI* V §14)

Husserl does, however, make two interesting claims about taking sensations in different ways. First, what remains constant across a switch of aspects is not just the visual sensations I have but also the visual properties these present; thus, both when I seem to see a woman and when I come to see what I am looking at as a wax figure, "identically the same phenomenal determinations" are involved (*LI* V §27). Second, Husserl occasionally hints at a correlation between relational moments of organization in what is seen and the modifications of sensation through which these moments are presented. When "contents are considered in their connections with other contents, as parts knit into wholes," they undergo a modification and differ from the same contents "considered by themselves."

Connections would not connect if they made no difference to what they connected. Certain changes necessarily occur and these are naturally such specific connectednesses as constitute the phenomenological correlatives of what are objectively *relational* properties. Consider, for example, a line set apart, perhaps on a bare white background, and the same line as part of a figure. In the latter case, it *impinges* on other lines, is *touched, cut* by them etc. . . . [T]hese are phenomenological characters that help to determine the impression of the appearance of linearity. The same stretch – the same with respect to its internal content – appears ever different according as it enters into this or that phenomenal context, and, if incorporated in a line or surface qualitatively identical with it, melts indistiguishably into this back ground, losing its phenomenal separateness and independence.   (*LI* VI §9)

The moments or aspects of organisation here called "objectively relational properties" are the counterparts of what, in a perceptual state, is the moment of interpretation. The dependent moments we perceive are "not merely parts but we must also grasp them as parts in a certain manner (that is not mediated by concepts)" (*LI* III §8). What Husserl deals with under the rubric of what is perceptually salient or outstanding, of what does and does not go together, is what the Berlin Gestalt psychologists came to call visual units. *Touching* and *cutting* are the first items on the list of functional features such as being an end-point, being a centre, etc., which the Gestalt psychologists were to extend considerably. Since to interpret is not to bring under concepts, a change in interpretation is, we may say, in a sense, a sensory change.[28] But it is not a sensory change of the same sort as a transition from a redness to an orange sensation. And since sensations alone do not determine which parts of what is seen are grasped "as parts in a certain manner," a level of interpretation in content must, Husserl seems to suggest, be allowed. He also clearly regards aspect switches as bringing to light something that is always present in ordinary perception. Simple seeing is, to use Wittgenstein's expression, continuous aspect perception, that is, interpretation.[29]

5.2 Gestalten and the constancy hypothesis

When Husserl turns to the *relation* between sensations and interpretation, he is somewhat more forthcoming. In simple perception content ("interpretative sense (matter)") and sensations ("representing content") are intimately united, mutually related, and not quite independently variable, although the sensory representative can stay the same while the interpretative sense alters and can vary while the latter remains constant (*LI* VI §54). He calls the combination of matter and sensation in every perceptual act its "intuitive content" (*LI* VI §22). Between visual sensations and matter there is "an internal, necessary connection." Since sensations can occur independently of interpretation, the necessary connection alluded to here must refer to the dependence of types of interpretation on types of complexes of sensations. "Only those contents can be intuitive representatives of an object" – but not by themselves, as we have seen –

that resemble it or are like it. Only we are not wholly free to interpret a content as this or that (or in this or that interpretative sense); and the reasons for this are not merely empirical . . . since the content to be interpreted sets limits to us through a certain sphere of similarity and exact likeness . . . The internal nature of the relation does not merely forge a link between *the interpretative matter as a whole* and *the whole content*: it links their parts on each side *piece by piece*.   [*LI* VI §26].

The "homogenous unity of the perceptual sense pervades the total representation [representative content]," it has definite relations to each distinguishable part of the representing content, without seeming to inner reflection to be a composite of distinct partial interpretations (*LI* VI §55).

Husserl's account of the relation between sensations and interpretation and of interpretation's role as the representation of aspects of organisation will become somewhat clearer if we compare his view with two other accounts and with a common if mistaken criticism of his view. The alternative accounts are the Graz and the Berlin analyses of form (Gestalt) perception; the criticism, inspired by the Berlin analysis, is that Husserl adhered to (a counterpart of) the Constancy Hypothesis.

On the account of Gestalt perception developed by Meinong and his pupils such as Ehrenfels, perception of a complex object is a two-tier mental state corresponding to a two-tier object. The state involves perceptions of the object's parts and features and, built on top of these, a judgement to the effect that these parts stand in certain relations to one another or that they have this or that ideal property. This view embodies two claims: first, a change of aspects is an intellectual change; second, relations, in the final analysis, require independent non-relational terms.

Now Husserl, as we have seen, is definitely a friend of higher-order objects such as states of affairs. But he is not of the opinion that these or any other ideal entities are given in simple perception of what is complex. Nor a fortiori does he think that simple seeing of what is complex, unlike seeing that, is a two-tier affair. He conceives of the states of affairs *that the ball is round and white* as built up out of an individual and two ideal attributes. But he distinguishes an ideal state of affairs from the ball together with its particular whiteness and roundness moments.

In sense-perception, the "external" thing appears "in one blow," as soon as our glance falls upon it. The manner in which it makes the thing appear present is *straightforward*; it requires no apparatus of founding or founded acts . . . We are not here ignoring the obvious complexity that can be shown to exist in the phenomenological content of the straightforward perceptual act, and particularly in its unitary intention.

Husserl's unpacking of this claim makes use of the two distinctions we have already come across – between dependence and independence, and between phenomenal continuity and discontinuity. The unity of a perception of a complex object, at a time or throughout an interval of time is due to (a) the relations of continuity (fusion) between the partial perceptual acts and (b) to the fact that the perception is founded on the partial acts that compose it. This foundation relation is not, however, a relation between a supervenient perceptual or intellecual act and a series of underlying perceptual acts. The relation between the perception of a complex object and the partial acts that merge into one another is not like the relation between my regret that *p* and my judgement that *p*. Husserl describes the difference as follows:

In the continuous running on of individual perceptions we continuously perceive the single, selfsame object. Can we now call this continuous perception, since it is built up out of individual perceptions, a perception which is *founded* on them? It is of course founded on them in the sense in which a whole is founded on its parts, not however in the sense here relevant, according to which a founded act manifests a new act-character, grounded in the act-characters that underlie it . . . In the case before us perception is merely, as it were, extended: it allows parts to be broken off from itself which can function as complete, independent perceptions. But the unification of these perceptions into a continuous perception is not the performance of some peculiar act, through which the consciousness of something new is set up.

(*LI* VI §47)[30]

We have already come across the distinction between foundation with and without containment in our taxonomy of perceptual objects (3.1 above): a flock of birds depends on and contains the individual birds, a hit depends on but does not contain its terms.

The Berlin account of continuous Gestalt perception simply denied the validity of the distinctions central to the Graz analysis: between dependent, ideal higher-order objects and their independent bases, and between the corresponding types of perceptual state. On the Berlin view, to see a Gestalt is not to see an ideal, higher-order entity. Everything that we see is both sensory and dependent. A change of aspect is a sensory change in just the way in which perception of a change of colour is a sensory change. And the Graz view that what is seen is built up from perceptions of independent items is rejected.

Husserl, however, rejects a premiss common to both the Graz and Berlin accounts – their critical realism, as well as claims peculiar to each account. Against the Graz and Berlin views he holds that what we are aware of are public items, not private phenomena. Consider again Husserl's description, quoted above, of perception of a line in different contexts. When the Berlin Gestalt psychologists considered such examples they drew the conclusion that the perceived line could not be an independent entity, that indeed everything we see is dependent. This was a reasonable conclusion given the critical realism they espoused. If everything one sees is a phenomenal item, then the notion of reidentification of such items makes little sense and no sense can be given to the notion that a phenomenal item is independent. It cannot exist outside the phenomenal context in which it occurs. On Husserl's view the line seen in the two different contexts is the same and in each situation it is independent of the relations it stands in. But it *appears* differently in each case. "A line, which with other lines, founds a configuration, is an independent content," wrote Husserl in 1894 (*Husserl* 1979, 96). But, says Koffka (1925, 533), although it may seem natural to say that the sides of a right angle are lines, in fact "a line by itself is phenomenally and functionally different" from the side of a right angle. "The latter has . . . an inside and an outside, the former on the other hand, two completely similar sides." Husserl's description above of perception of lines draws attention to facts of just this sort. But because he does not run together the independence-dependence and the discontinuity-continuity distinctions and because of his naive realism, Husserl's account of these facts differs completely from that of Koffka.

On Husserl's view, we can draw no conclusion as to an item's status as an independent or dependent object from the fact that it does or does not appear to be continuous with other objects, or from the fact that it seems or does not seem to fit or go with other objects. Consider two red boxes which are moved together in such a way that each red surface appears to be continuous with the other. It is nevertheless the case that each red box is independent of the other (and that the spatial relation of contact depends on them).[31] In other words, like the Graz philosophers, Husserl holds fast to the view that relations require independent terms.

Husserl's position, therefore, differs from that of other philosopher-psychologists in the tradition of descriptive psychology brought into being by Brentano. Like Meinong, and unlike Koffka, he thinks that the terms of a perceived relation are independent of it. But unlike both Meinong and Koffka, he thinks that what we see are non-phenomenal, public items.[32] Unlike Meinong Husserl thinks that perception of complex objects does not require judgement and conception. Unlike Koffka, he distinguishes between content and object.

The criticism of Husserl that he falls foul of the constancy hypothesis goes back to Scheler[33] and has been made many times since. But it is either unfounded or impossibly vague. The constancy hypothesis is the thesis that there is a constant correlation between stimuli and sensations. Apparent exceptions to the hypothesis were often dealt with by introducing auxiliary hypotheses such as the existence of unnoticed sensations, of unnoticed judgements about sensations, or the influence of past experience. Both the hypothesis and the auxiliary hypotheses were the subject of a famous attack by Köhler in 1913.[34] Husserl suggests that what was to be called the Constancy Hypothesis, whether true or false, with or without any auxiliary hypotheses, was irrelevant to his analysis:

> What is most emphasised in the doctrine of "apperception" is generally the fact that sameness of stimulus [*Reiz*] does not always involve sameness of sensational content; what the stimulus really provokes is said to be overlaid by features stemming from the actualisations of dispositions left behind them by previous experience. Such notions are, however, inadequate, and, above all, phenomenologically irrelevant.   (*LI* V §14)

No thesis about the relation between stimuli and sensations can have consequences for a descriptive thesis about the relation between interpretation and sensations. In what sense, then, is Husserl supposed to accept the constancy hypothesis? Consider Koffka, who rejects a distinction between sensations and interpretation like that of Husserl and assumes that the sensations we have are what we see, and makes the following claim about aspect-switches:

> Lines that at first lay unconnected side by side, because they were parts of different Gestalten, because they belonged to the ornamental foliage, to a gable, etc., suddenly spring together to form a face and so look quite different. To assert that here . . . nothing changed in the sensations is an assertion that is based not on observation but on the constancy hypothesis.
>   (*Koffka* 1925, 533)[35]

Now the view here criticized is indeed held by Husserl. As we have seen, he thinks that in such a case the sensations do not change (although the perceptual content does). Holenstein calls the view criticized the intellectualist version of the constancy hypothesis,[36] distinguishing it from the empiricist version which, as we have seen, is rejected by Husserl. The latter, unlike the former, makes a claim about relations between stimuli and sensations. What error, interestingly similar to the empiricist version of the constancy hypothesis, is Husserl supposed to have been guilty of? Perhaps the criticism is simply that perceptual content does not display two levels, sensations and interpretation. But Husserl's critics provide no argument for this. Perhaps they have in mind the following view of perception which does indeed deserve to be described as an intellectualist version of the constancy hypothesis. On this view sensations are simple and qualitative and display no structure. Structure is introduced by interpretation or judgement. But this is not Husserl's view. As we have seen, sensations, according to Husserl, are of qualities and of spatial forms. It is by virtue of this that they belong to fields. The creatures imagined by Husserl who enjoy only visual sensations but no interpretative content would enjoy structured sensations in fields. It would be with them as though they were aware of rich arrays of qualitative discontinuities and coloured expanses. They would simply lack representations of what were called above aspects of organisation, of experiences as of tables and chairs.

Husserl's claim that perceptual acts have sensational parts or properties that are irreducible to the parts of properties of interpretative matter and can remain constant while the latter vary was one that he held on to throughout different writings. It was regularly criticised by phenomenologists and psychologists influenced by descriptive psychology. It resembles in some respects Anglo-Saxon sense-data theories, which have likewise been the object of much criticism. But this resemblance is merely superficial in view of Husserl's claim that we do not see sensations and his views about their complex organisation. Husserl himself, however, occasionally had doubts about his account of sensations.[37]

VI. INTERPRETATION, CONSTANCY, AND PROFILES

6.1 Constancy phenomena

We noted previously that Husserl used the phenomenon of colour constancy – not to be confused with the constancy hypothesis – to justify his distinction between sensations and the qualities and things they represent. The phenomena of colour, shape, size, form, and thing constancy play another role in his account. The interpretative stratum in perceptual content has not only the role of representing what we called aspects of organisation (see 5.1) but also that of representing colours, shapes, sizes, etc., as constant moments or features, of representing things as constant things in spite of widespread variation in the sensory level of content. The distinction "betweeen the red of this ball, objectively seen as uniform, and the indubitable indeed necessary shading [*Abschattung*] of the subjective colour sensations," is matched by a number of other three-way distinctions between varying sensations, representation as of some constant feature and the objective feature itself. The difference between constant forms and colours, on the one hand, and the continuously varying sensations thereof, on the other hand, is "a difference repeated in all sorts of objective properties and the complexes of sensations that correspond to them." "What is true of the individual determinations" of particulars, Husserl continues, "carries over to concrete wholes."[38]

The word "*Abschattung*," often translated as shading or adumbration, refers in the first instance to the way one and the same colour appears in a certain context, in a certain light, etc. It seems likely that Husserl was influenced here by Hering's distinction between the way we see colours and colours themselves, and his generalisation of this as a distinction betweeen "*Sehdinge*" and things.[39] For Husserl, too, generalises from the case of colours and subsumes under the term "adumbration" not just the way colours shadow themselves forth, but also the way a shape appears or is shadowed forth. There is a

difference . . . that we sought to cover by our talk of perceptual adumbration, a difference that does not concern . . . sensuous stuff, its internal character, but means . . . the interpretative character of the act.   (*LI* VI §37)

Perception is invariably perception via "adumbrations of colour, perspectival foreshortenings." An adumbration is a sensation that is interpreted as being as of some constant feature, or a complex of sensations that is interpreted as being of some constant thing.

6.2 To perceive a particular is for a profile to appear

To observe a three-dimensional object is, in another sense of "observe," to observe only one or some of its sides. I see an object via one adumbration of its form, but I may see two sides of it at once. Husserl sometimes uses the term "side" to refer to the single profile presented via one adumbration[40] as when he talks of the "one-sidedness" (*DR* §16) of perception. When I look at a house, three features of my perception can be distinguished: my perception of the side that faces me, my awareness of the other sides of the house, the whole perception of the house. Husserl calls the appearance of the side that faces me a "genuine appearance," for it is based on the sensations that correspond to the moments of colour and form making up this side; and he calls the awareness of the other sides "non-genuine" or "inauthentic," meaning thereby that this awareness is not based on any sensation. Each of these two aspects is inseparable from the other, just as my entire perception of the house must contain appearances belonging to these two categories (*DR* §16, §24).

Three ways of construing these distinctions are rejected. First is the temptation to say that I *expect* the house to have sides that are currently invisible. The mode of expectation is future-directed and so cannot explain that feature of my present perception that is my awareness of the sides of the house with which I am not presented. There are certainly, as we shall see, relations of indication and motivation between my present perception and possible future perceptions, but these are much more primitive than expectations – though they may of course ground such expectations, which are more important in the case of dynamic perception than in the case of static perception (*LI* VI §10).

A second temptation, one to which Moore succumbs in his elegant application of Russell's theory of descriptions to perception, is to introduce the notion of judgement into the analysis of the one-sidedness of perception. On Moore's account, for me to see the house is for me to judge that there is exactly one house of which this side is a part.[41] Now the difference between such an account and that of Husserl is not merely that for him to see is not to judge, but a consequence of this point. On Husserl's account my perceptual relation to the house is like the relation between my use of a proper name and its bearer (on Husserl's account of this relation): it is not mediated by any general concept or presentation. And the same is true of the two types of perceptual awareness that constitute the entire perception: my relation to this side of the house and my relation to that invisible side. My perception of the house is a single perception with at least two single partial acts (*DR* §18).

Third, the way in which the hidden sides of the house and its constituent features are "given" is not that of imagination, although imagination may well combine with perception. Husserl's argument for this point is a simple one. Since imagination in the simplest case is a modification of or parasitic on perceptual experience, to imagine (visually) a house is to have an experience which itself displays the two aspects which are a "full" and an "empty" imaginative presentation of a house. But it would be absurd to say that the "empty" imaginative presentation of the far side of the house is a phantasy presentation within the original act of imagination (DR §18).

Unfortunately Husserl does not characterise positively the awareness in perception of the invisible side of the house. What is clear is that, unlike Meinong, he does not wish to introduce a supervenient act of imagination into perception, either to explain perception of visual organisation or to explain awareness of what is currently invisible. On Husserl's view, then, perception is entirely direct and necessarily incomplete.[42] Once again interpretation is introduced in a black box fashion. It is what turns visual sensations into a part of a unified perceptual awareness of a three-dimensional object by orchestrating the combination of genuine and non-genuine awareness of its sides.

6.3 To perceive is to identify

Variations at the level of sensations may be caused by movement of the subject or of the object or both. Husserl's full account of the role of interpretation in such cases will emerge when we consider his account of dynamic content. On that account static perception turns out to be a mere abstraction from dynamic perception. But in order to present a further role played by interpretation we shall assume that dynamic perception is built up out of static perception.

Interpretation is responsible for the fact that one and the same object continues to be perceived as the same although the sensations the subject has vary, perhaps because he is walking round the object. The very different sensations I may have while looking at the same object are interpreted "in the same sense." What I see with the help of one set of sensations is apparently identical to what I see with the help of a quite different set (LI V §14). Where we have such an apparent identity over time, we have coincidence of matter. But, Husserl adds, such apparent identities should not be confused with judgements of identity: to perceive is to identify, to perform an identification, but not to mean any identity (*LI* VI §§8, 25, 47). When two perceptual senses or matters or interpretations overlap or coincide ("*übereinstimmen*," "*sich decken*"), then an identification has been performed. The role and nature of interpretation in such identifications can only be understood by turning to the dynamics of perception.

Husserl never discusses explicitly the relations between the four roles of interpretation distinguished so far: to be responsible for awareness of aspects of organisation, for perceptual constancy, for the orchestration of our awareness of three-dimensional objects and for the performance of identification. It is worth noting that in each case perceptual content turns out to have the property of transposability, that is, of being a whole which remains constant in spite of variation among its parts. Transposability is the property of *Gestalten* such as melodies, actions, and substances that was noted by Ehrenfels when he launched Gestalt psychology. Thus we may say that, on Husserl's view, perceptual content has the same type of structure as that enjoyed by its objects.

VII. DYNAMIC CONTENT: HOW TO PERCEIVE

We are now familiar with the two strata, sensory and interpretative, that make up perceptual content. But the type of content that has been described so far is static content. And this is, on Husserl's view, a mere abstraction from dynamic content. Failure to realize that this is the case is largely responsible for the tendency to conceive of the coloured shapes we are presented with as two-dimensional private entities. Thanks to the work of J. J. Gibson and G. Evans (and indeed of Merleau-Ponty), this point is now becoming as familiar as it was to Husserl and his pupils around 1907.

Husserl's account of dynamic content – that is, of the content of the perceptual states of a subject who is either looking at moving objects or is moving with respect to the objects he is looking at or both – contains (7.1) an analysis of the relation between static and dynamic perception and (7.2) a detailed description of the ways visual and kinaesthetic sensations cooperate to make perception possible.

7.1 The connection between static and dynamic content

Consider a possible world containing creatures whose capacities for general thoughts resemble ours, but whose sensory capacities are limited in the following way: they are always immobile when they perceive and they never perceive objects as being in motion. In other words, although the objects they perceive retain their identity over time, two perceptions of two qualitatively identical sides of one object and two perceptions of two sides of two different objects would be, as far their sensory input is concerned, four of a kind. Such creatures would be incapable of "dynamic thoughts" if such thoughts are taken to be thoughts that cannot occur without dynamic content, for example demonstrative thoughts about objects in movement. Thus, even their conceptual capacities would differ from ours – they would lack singular, perception-based thoughts.[43] The difference between their perceptual experiences and ours would be that the identity over time of objects would not be "given" to them, they would not have our identificational capacities, would not be able to keep track of objects over time[44] in spite of occasional occlusions, etc. Their perceptions would be only "one-sided and singular"; ours are also "many-sided and diverse" (*DR* §42). Only if a "continuous transition from one perception to the other is guaranteed is . . . identity given. . . . [A]n identical-unchanged spatial body can only certify itself ("*ausweisen*") as such in a kinetic perceptual series that continuously yields appearances of its different sides" (*DR* §44).

The continuous transition from one appearance to the next of the same object is not itself any sort of judgement of identity. Rather, such transitions are the basis of perceptual judgements of identity.[45] Continuous perceptual tracking of an object involves variations in sensory input but, Husserl stresses, there is no necessary discontinuity at the levels of mode and content.[46] Similarly, increasing perceptual specification and determination of the way an object looks is not any sort of conceptual specification or determination but an analogue thereof (*DR* §29).

It is important to distinguish two senses of "dynamic," or of what Husserl, talking of dynamic thoughts, calls the "dynamic unity between expression and expressed intuition" (*LI* VI §8): (a) both static and dynamic perceptual contents, "unchanged" and "changed" perceptions (DR §42), can precede or accompany perceptual judgements in the unity of the "temporal Gestalt" (LI VI §8) of verification; (b) but when the sense of a perceptual judgement is not only verified by an ongoing perception but is also individuated by the latter, as in the case of a demonstrative thought,[47] then the temporal Gestalt is much *stronger* than in (a). Then the "dynamic coincidence between meaning and intuition" (ibid.) is not merely verification over time but the perceptual determination of sense over time. The assertion "That is a blackbird" is verified by the perception of a blackbird as a blackbird; the linguistic singular term it contains, "that," is incomplete without perception of the blackbird and does not refer without this. The ambiguity between (a) and (b) carries over to such favourite expressions of Husserl as "experience of transition", "dynamic fulfilment or cognition."

What is the connection between Husserl's account of static perceptual content and his account of dynamic perceptual content? I suggested above that on his account static perceptual content was an abstraction from dynamic content. It suffices to introduce here a principle to which Husserl was much attached to see why he arrived at this conclusion. The principle is that all distinctions have their roots in perceptual experience. Now we have seen that all static perceptual content, indeed all perceptual content, is characterised by two distinct but complementary aspects: the "full" awareness of the side of the object facing me, mediated by the sensations I have that correspond to its constituent features, and the "empty" awareness of its far side(s). What is the origin of this distinction?

It comes to light in every transition from what was an empty awareness of the far side of an object to a "full" perception thereof and correlatively from what was a "full" perception to an "empty" perception. That is to say, in every dynamic perception. If this is the case one might predict that creatures to whom dynamic perception is foreign would have perceptual experience as of sides of objects and not of objects (even though what they see is the side of an object). And that their philosophy of perception would tend to make of these sides private phenomenal entities intervening between the subject and public things (cf. DR §17). And indeed those philosophers – critical realists or representationalists – who have notoriously been unable to see that we see things have indeed tended to ignore dynamic perception.

7.2 Kinaesthetic sensations and motivation

There is another reason for thinking that static perception is a mere abstraction from dynamic perception. Not only is my awarenesss of the side of the house facing me normally accompanied by a perception of it as having other sides, but it is also felt to point forward to a determinate range of possible continuations and verifications.[48] This relation of "pointing to" or indication belongs to the family of relations Husserl calls *motivation*. Closely related to purely perceptual motivation is a better known species of the same genus, the criterial relationship between perceptions and judgements or between judgements. Husserl takes such relations to be more than merely contingent and less than narrowly logical[49] or necessary. They are not, he says, causal or probabilistic. But then in virtue of what do the "interpretative components" in a perceptual state "point beyond" the side of the object facing me?

Husserl's answer, developed at length in *Thing and Space*[50], is that creatures with visual organs, but endowed with no active powers, would be incapable of perception of things and processes. To be endowed with active powers is to be capable of intentional and subintentional movement, it is to be the bearer of actual and possible kinaesthetic and postural sensations, to have information about the positions and movements of one's body. The interpretative components in perception point beyond the present moment because of the connection between perception and the actual and possible states of my body. We must therefore determine what these states are and what sort of connection obtains between them on Husserl's account.

Kinaesthetic and postural sensations resemble visual sensations in that we *have* them and thereby achieve contact with objects, houses, and our own bodies and body-parts. They also resemble visual sensations in belonging to "systems" or "spaces." The different types of kinaesthetic space correspond to the different independent "movement systems," those of one eye, of both eyes, of the head, of the upper part of the body, etc., which do not normally flow continuously one into another. Just as visual sensation-fields are always completely filled, so too kinaesthetic and postural sensations fill the space of our body-image, although they do not display themselves in a graduated fashion and have only an indeterminate localisation due to localised sensations.[51]

One major difference between visual and kinaesthetic sensations concerns the ways they form continuous unities.

The kinaesthetic sensations form continuous systems of many dimensions, yet in such a way that, like tone sensations, they form continuous unities only as series, whereby a linear manifold singled out from the total manifold of kinaesthetic sensations coincides with the continuous unity of the preempirical temporal series in the manner of a continuum that fills [it].

By a "preempirical temporal series," Husserl means our awareness of time (so called "immanent" time). "A kinaesthetic manifold"

can only acquire continuous unity as a linear manifold by filling a temporal interval. Since only a continuous linear manifold can function in such a way as to fill time, a many-dimensional system of kinaesthetic sensations cannot achieve a closed temporal unity.[52]

The contrast between the serial unity of kinaesthetic sensations and the simultaneous unity of visual sensations in a visual field[53] has its origins in the fact that, unlike visual sensations, kinaesthetic sensations do not present the objects we see, do not belong to the "projection" of a thing, although we could not perceive such objects without them (DR §§45–46). They represent neither moments of quality nor moments of extension.[54] Visual sensations stand in a less direct relation to their objects than bodily sensations to their objects,[55] because visual sensations present their objects only with the help of visual interpretations or contents which can vary while their object remains constant. But, as we have seen, no such interpretation is needed for my awareness of the pain in my foot or, we may now add, its movement.[56] In particular, my kinaesthetic sensations do not advise me of, or indicate to me, the movement of my foot. They are just my awareness of my foot's movement "from the inside." As Husserl points out (DR §47), such information can found judgements (conceptual interpretations), but then the singular parts of such judgements cannot fail to refer.

Kinaesthetic sensations collaborate with visual sensations. The latter include not merely the sensations of quality and extent in the two-dimensional visual field[57] that we found in our description of static perceptual content. They may also be sensations of displacement, which Husserl also calls "pre-empirical," "pre-spatial," or "quasi"-displacement. Similarly, he talks of quasi-rotation, quasi-contraction, and quasi-expansion.[58]

The two types of sensation are said to collaborate in the following way. They are essential to every perception, but their relation to each other is not that of reciprocal inseparability or dependence – as in the case of quality and extension – but rather the relation of *"functional" dependence*. Kinaesthetic sensations "have no essential connection to visual sensations; they are connected with these functionally" (DR §49).

Thus, to take one of the simplest cases described by Husserl, in monocular vision, if we abstract from rollings of the eye in question, there is a rough correspondence between positions in the visual field and position sensations of the eye; to every visual line along which the glance of the eye passes there corresponds a continuous kinaesthetic series "which differs sensorially (*empfindungsmässig*) from every other such series."[59]

Husserl's claim that kinaesthetic sensations and visual sensations are linked in a merely functional manner is based on the following assumptions. My kinaesthetic and postural state at a given time does not indicate or point to any particular way of appearing, or visual picture, of a thing. "Every [kinaesthetic] sensation, K, is compatible with every visual picture."[60] And quite different kinaesthetic series can "stand in for one another vicariously.[61] What is achieved by a certain movement of the head may be achieved by a movement of the upper part of the body" (DR §83). And finally, although each visual appearance in an extended dynamic look points forward, this is not true of the kinaesthetic sensations that correspond to these appearances (DR §51).

The unity of wholes of kinaesthetic sensations and visual perception only emerges at the level of entire sensory-motor series or sequences consisting of series of each type. A whole series of kinaesthetic circumstances (*Umstände*) corresponds to a determinate series of visual appearances. It is within my power to ensure that I have no visual appearances, but what is not subject to my will is that if I allow a kinaesthetic series to continue, then a determinate series of appearances will be the result.[62] Ordered kinaesthetic series *motivate* (indicate, are criteria for) the continuations of ordered series of appearances. Series of appearances form more or less complicated types; any kinaesthetic series belongs to one of many "unified, familiar possibilities" (*DR* §52, §55, §61).

Consider again the example of an avenue of trees. Instead of simply describing how a group of trees, *a, b, c, d, e,* is perceived at a moment, we can now consider the way the avenue of trees appears when mediated by dynamic content. As we move along the avenue, the sequence of kinaesthetic circumstances motivates the appearance of *b, c, d, e, f,* containing the appearance of the new tree *f,* then of *c, d, e, f, g,* etc. "To the determinate kinaesthetic series belongs the . . . determinate continuous series of changes of the fillings of one and the same field of places by these and those distributions of visual pictures or appearances." At any given moment the unified interpretative character of the perceptual state brings to the corresponding kinaesthetic state, as a result of association, a certain direction in which this state can continue or persist. This is, Husserl adds, more than a mere tendency. His descriptive capacities exhausted, he writes:

From every series of appearances in certain kinaesthetic circumstances there radiate living intentions that are fulfilled from phase to phase. . . . It belongs to the stable course of motivation that at the absolute place position where *a* was, *b'* presents itself . . . , that in its turn is identified with the *b* that had just occupied another position, that the representational series displace themselves in this way. The determinacy of the spatial order and of the order of visibility and of the relevant order of what actually becomes visible belong essentially together. And the being of object parts that are not currently perceived points to possible and indeed motivated ordered series of documenting perceptions and of the representing contents they contain, that bring about connections between not perceived and currently perceived parts.   (*DR* §62)

The internal, phenomenologically immediate connections between perception and action, between the spaces of perceptual input and of behavioural output are, then, analysed by Husserl (as by Evans) as indirect transitions involving kinaesthetic information and body images. Sensory information involving information about orientation properties is linked to behavioural routes via "kinaesthetic paths."[63] This type of account contrasts sharply with that of Gestalt psychologists such as Koffka for whom ideo-motor transitions are completely direct.[64]

7.3 Interpretation, action, and public objects

How does Husserl's account of the motivational connections between our awareness of our actions from the inside and goings on in
our private two-dimensional visual fields help us understand the
claim that dynamic perceptual content represents public objects in
public space as public objects in public space?

The step from visual fields to visual spaces – from a representation as of a two-dimensional field to representation as of an objective
three-dimensional space – is not a step which a perceiving subject
normally takes. Rather, in Husserl's view, the former is an aspect of
or abstraction from the latter, which is the type of perceptual state
we normally enjoy. Certain types of movement, together with the
types of kinaesthetic and visual information these are correlated
with, are responsible for the fact that this is our normal perceptual
condition.

Two of the most important types of movement are moving towards
or away from an object (distancing) and moving around it (orbiting).[65]
Distancing correlates with quasi-expansions and quasi-contractions
in the visual field.[66] These may be uniform or non-uniform and may
concern the whole field or only a part of it (*DR* §67).

"The multiform system of [quasi-] expansions makes possible a
new dimension, that makes a thing out of a [visual] picture, space out
of the oculomotor field" (*DR* §67). For "expansion is a principle of
selection and unification that marks out certain of the manifold de-
limitations in the oculomotor field as belonging to the unity of a
thing." The "different ways in which expansion . . . is distributed
over the different segments of the oculomotor field . . . lend determinacy to our grasp of things" (*DR* §71). Activities of distancing,
when reversed, yield a reversal of the just-experienced series of quasi-
expansions, quasi-contractions, and quasi-coverings, and so motivate
(are cues for) awareness as of a thing occupying a fixed position.[67]
Similarly, quasi-nonuniform expansion and quasi-covering indicate
(are cues for) awareness of things as being at different distances from
the perceiver.

Distance from the subject, that is depth, is a relation between an
object I see and the "origo" or zero-point of my visual space, whereas
the distance between two objects is "genuinely perceived."[68] Husserl
takes items in the visual field to have absolute monadic position

features. "To every distinguishable concrete sensational element corresponds its position, its here. And this here is a moment belonging to
it that grounds relations of distance."[69] He thinks that there is a level
of analysis of peception at which a one-dimensional continuum of
absolute depth moments can be discerned, a continuum which together with the two-dimensional field, on which it is founded, forms a
double-continuum. These depth moments, just like positions in the
two-dimensional field, ground relations of distance (DR §49). In what
sense, Husserl asks, do such depth moments represent relations of
depth between public things and me (ibid.)?

As Drummond suggests, the gist of his answer is that the activity
of distancing, together with the quasi-expansion and quasi-covering
it is bound up with, "reveal that the relation of depth is *relative* to
the position of the percipient, thereby introducing the relationships
of 'nearer to' and 'further from.' " They uncover "a new dimension,
not within the visual field but within the perceptual experience, a
dimension which indicates that the position of the object relative to
the perceiver is not reducible to the position of an appearance in the
percipient's visual field."[70]

The activity of orbiting an object motivates determinate series
of appearances in which we find not quasi-occlusion but quasi-
replacements and quasi-turnings. It is through cyclical appearances, what O'Shaughnessy calls "looks in the round," that we
see public objects as enclosed items in empty space.[71]

Husserl's descriptions of the different varieties of distancing and
orbiting, of the different determinate patterns of appearances they
generate, and of the combinations between these constitute his contribution to a criteriological account of perception. A complete description of this sort would, he thinks, bring out how movement
contributes to the make up of the interpretative level of perceptual
content and to all the roles he attributes to the latter. In particular,
movement "constitutes" orientation space in which I am aware of
things and myself as occupying positions in public space: "all spatiality . . . comes to givenness in movement, in the movement of the
object itself and in the movement of the 'ego' with the change of
orientation this brings with it" (DR §44).[72]

The continuity of the different ways in which we keep track of
objects has so far been explained in terms of the connections between sequences of appearances and kinaesthetic sensations and in

terms of forward-looking and lateral, informational links. But kinaesthetic sensations and the basic acts or bodily movements with which these are connected (as part to whole) belong to larger behavioural unitts bound up with interests and dispositions that colour and steer these units.

7.4 To perceive is to perceive more or less well – optimality, sets, and determinacy

At §36 of *Thing and Space,* on "Optimal Givenness and Direction of Interest," Husserl describes a feature of perception that has increasingly come to interest psychologists and cognitive scientists. His starting point is the distinction between inadequate and adequate perception, which he takes to be fundamental for psychology (Appendix, 7, to *LI* VI). The phrase "perceptions of things" refers to

determinations [of these things], to maximal points or domains, hence in each case to an appearance or narrowly delimited domain of appearances, in which when it is actualised, the relevant determination counts as "completely" given.   (*DR* 126)

The optimal or normal perspective on a thing varies with the interests of the subject. But given such interests, there is an internal relation between the appearances of the thing which is their different distances from the relevant optimal appearance. These relations are of a quite different type than simple distance relations between positions in the visual field or in colour space. They are internal axiological relations: the appearance of this object in this light from here is better than the way it looks from over there. These internal relations announce themselves, Husserl claims, in any given section of a series of appearances as a part of the subject's background awareness and they vary with his interests. "The natural interest in a flower is not that of the botanist."[73]

Leyendecker's elegant development of Husserl's account of the connection between optimality and interest introduces into the philosophy of perception a phenomenon and a term of art for it that had been introduced into psychology by G. E. Mueller and von Kries, "*Einstellung*"[74] or set. A set is a higher-order unity of modes, tendencies, and dispositions which is often the function of determinate types of interest and attention. As Leyendecker points out, those visual features of things that we take in and the aspects under which we see them are a function of our set and its connection to automatised and non-automatised behaviour. The set peculiar to purely perceptual observation is very different from those appropriate to looking, ordering, searching for, counting, collecting, or working with objects. These again are different from an aesthetic set. These different sets "make it possible to overlook everything that does not correspond to them." Sets may help to make us aspect-blind for what we would see in other sets. Sets may be more or less basic. Some practical sets can be changed at will, especially if not already automatised. Others are connected "with a certain way of life, a certain milieu."[75]

Sets function like sieves, selecting certain aspects and discarding others. This feature of perceptual content is to be distinguished from the different determinate ways in which perceptual content is essentially vague and indefinite. Under this heading, Husserl refers not to the equally essential vagueness of sensory properties – as opposed to mathematical idealisations thereof[76] – but to the fact that the series of possible future perceptions that is indicated by a current perception of, say, one side of a thing, leave open a range of different possible fulfilments. It is a determinate feature of this perceptual content that it refers indeterminately to a range of possible completions: "Perception essentially contains indeterminables, but it contains them as determinables" (*Ideas* II, 222).[77] Two sorts of possible completion can be distinguished – "motivated" and "empty" possibilities. It is emptily possible for the desk I am writing on and whose top alone is visible to turn out to have thirty legs; the possibility of the desk having four legs is motivated. One criterion for distinguishing between the two is the occurrence of perceptual surprises. But it does not follow from this that where there are no perceptual surprises, perception is accompanied by feelings of familiarity.

Different possible perceptual series are "prescribed in a law-like way" by any given perception[78]:

When, e.g., a familiar melody begins, it stirs up definite intentions which find their fulfilment in the melody's gradual unfolding ... The regularities governing melody as such, determine intentions ... which find or can find their fulfilments.   (LI VI §10)

Husserl distinguishes this sort of forward-looking information, which is determined both by sets and by behaviour, from the lateral background information that forms the horizon or Jamesian "fringe" of every perception. The simplest type of background is the perceived background of a thing against which it is seen. But Husserl also describes many other types of background ranging from my awareness that the table I am looking at is in a room in a house in a city to background beliefs.[79]

VIII. INTERPRETATION WITHOUT CONCEPTS

The interpretative aspect of perceptual content, then, has a large number of jobs to perform: it is responsible for the organisation which supervenes on the sensations of quality and extent in the subject's two-dimensional visual field; it is responsible for the unity in any perceptual state between awareness of what is in front of me and of what is not; it is the locus of the properties of orientation and distance which determine how what I see seems oriented; it is the locus of the degree of determinacy of the way I see; it points beyond itself to further possible perceptual states, particularly to optimal perceptual states; and it points sideways; it is responsible for our being able to keep track of an object. "The interpretation of a thing as at such a distance, so oriented, so coloured, etc." is, in its turn, due to the motivating force of kinaesthetic sensations and the structures of the spaces to which they belong.[80] And these, in their turn, are a function of our interests, dispositions, and sets.

One (neo-Kantian) reaction to such a description is that it overburdens non-conceptual interpretation. Surely concepts must do some of these jobs, the objection goes. Another, Husserl's, is that it shows how inadequate is any simple act-content-object schema. Content exhibits many more levels and peculiarities than one might at first think. Against the common conviction that many of these levels are concept- or theory-laden, and more generally against ratiomorphic theories of perception, Husserl would object that these often rest on a failure to take seriously the distinction between episodes and dispositions. It is as true that many types of perceptual content can only be enjoyed by creatures that master certain concepts as it is that many types of content can be enjoyed only by creatures with certain needs and interests. But perception does not necessarily involve any exercise of these concepts.

Husserl, in fact, goes some way towards meeting neo-Kantian worries. Although perception is by its very nature an aconceptual affair, it is of course, as a matter of fact, shot through with conceptual episodes. Not just because perception combines with concept involving modes, not just because many visual pictures can only be enjoyed by those possessing a mastery of this or that family of concepts, but also because continuous aspect perception is often a matter of wordless subsumption of what is seen under concepts, particularly in cases of recognition. At *LI* VI §15, Husserl describes cases of wordless recognition of something as a drill, as an ancient inscription, of a person as the adjutant of the Emperor. To see *a* and recognise it as an *n* is for an act of meaning to "extend over" and beyond what is directly perceived. We may therefore distinguish between conceptual and non-conceptual seeing as, each of which may be either continuous or sudden, as in an aspect-switch. "There is an essential difference between 'interpretation' that is sensory and that which is thought involving" (*LI* II §26). To see something as a part of something else, as going with this rather than that "but not via concepts" is an example of the former (*LI* III §8).[81]

With neo-Kantian temptations in mind, Husserl modifies Kant's slogan when he writes that sensory experience alone is blind. For Husserl, but not for Kant, what removes the handicap is non-conceptual interpretation (*LI* VI §57).

IX. WHAT WE PERCEIVE: TO PERCEIVE A PENNY IS TO PERCEIVE A COLOURED SHAPE AND ITS BEHAVIOUR

Our account of what we see in Section III was mainly an account of what we see in virtue of static content. In the light of the description of dynamic content, we can now flesh out our account of what we see by considering the case where one or both of a perceiver and the object of his perception move (or change). The independent "concreta" we see in virtue of static content, together with their constitutive moments of form and colour, are not to be identified with things and their moments unless such static content is understood to be a mere abstraction from actual or possible dynamic content. "More belongs to the unity of a thing than an isolated concretum."[82] The unity of a thing is due to the fact that it exemplifies some of the

different ideally possible continuous transitions from one concretum to another of the same form. These transitions, involving
both change and persistence, are governed by relations of causal
dependence.[83] In the absence of movement, the distinction between
a visual concretum (which Husserl was later to call an "empty phantom") and a thing is not part of what is visually differentiated. Only
such moments as colour and form, being metallic, or roughness are
differentiated in static perception, not such moments as heaviness,
elasticity, and being magnetic. Indeed, even in some cases of movement of the object, the distinction between phantom and thing may
not show itself visually. For this distinction to become apparent, it is
necessary for there to be a relation between my perceptual interpretation, on the one hand, and interactions between the thing and its
circumstances on the other hand. In particular, the thing appears to
me as one and the same thing to the extent that I am presented with
its *functional dependence* on parts of the visual scene. Continuous
variation in a thing's surroundings leads to continuous variation in
the visual concretum, and unchange in the circumstances, the limit
case of change, is accompanied by unchange in the visual concreta.
Above we saw that variations in colour sensations could present one
and the same colour moment; in the present context, Husserl points
out that it is perception of the correlation between different levels of
illumination, for example, and the different appearances of a coloured surface that allow one and the same colour to appear. Unfortunately, Husserl fails to give an account of the relation between perception of light and of colour.[84] He does, however, accept that to be
acquainted with such correlations is to directly see causal relations.
This provides yet another case where Husserl resists the temptation
to introduce judgements about relations such as causality into perception.[85] However, in his descriptions of our awareness of different
"if-then" or "because-so" connections in perception, in which the
objective forms of a thing "announce" themselves, Husserl has
some difficulty in avoiding the claim that this awareness of conditional or dispositional causal properties of things is propositional.[86]

Husserl's account of the relation between that moment of a thing
which is its shaped extent and other sensory qualities labours to
bring out the primacy of the former. Husserl fails to bring out the
source of this primacy although he erects on it a new distinction
between primary and secondary qualities. As he points out, sensible

qualities stand in an asymmetrical relation to extent: the former cover or fill the latter. Husserl fails to uncover the source of this asymmetry because he does not wish to give up the view that extent and sensory quality are reciprocally dependent and because he fails to distinguish between type and token dependence. Once this distinction is made it becomes possible to reformulate his point about the primacy of extension as follows. Consider a particular brownness moment of a penny. It token depends on the extent moment of the penny. If the latter is modified, the brownness moment gives way to a numerically distinct although qualitatively identical brownness moment. The original extent moment is, however, token independent of the brownness moment that covers it; it could be covered by a quite different colour moment.[87]

By the time Husserl came to investigate in detail the relations between the visual information we acquire from visual concreta at a moment and from material things endowed with the causal properties which remain invisible without the help of dynamic content he had lost interest in the questions that trouble any realist. One such question is the following.

We may distinguish, in the light of the foregoing, between those properties of an object "whose types are in a particular sense analogous to types found amongst sensations" (*LI* VI Appendix 5, cf. *LI* I §23) and those properties of an object of which this is not true. Since determinate form and colour sensations correspond to the array of colour and form properties, these sensory properties belong to the first category. In the second category, we find some of the material, causal properties of things that are "announced" or "indicated" in and through perception of the thing's behavior. But there will also belong to this second category such properties as being a mountain. Suppose I see, via a suitably optimal appearance, a complicated array of spatial and qualitative moments which is Mont Blanc with all its snowfields. What does the copula mean here?

Perhaps the simplest answer available to the naive realist is that the "is" here is the "is" of identity. But as Dretske points out, such identities are very peculiar ones, as are their expression in identity statements containing at least one demonstrative.[88] It is variously qualified shaped things, or more simply, qualified shapes that are identical with mountains and tables. But the identity is identity at a time, or alternatively, identity between a qualified shape at a time and a mountain. And in, e.g., "That brown ellipse = Maria's penny" or "That grey triangle = Mont Blanc," the demonstrative functions referentially.

A more complicated case comes into view if we reintroduce the claim already discussed that we can see such relational particulars as spatial contact. One particular contact moment will be identical with a kiss, another with a slap, and so on (cf. EU §34). Consider two senses of the noun "flight." In one sense, a flight is "a group of similar creatures or objects flying through the air together." When Sam simply perceives a group of characteristically shaped specks moving in a certain characteristic way, he simply perceives a flight of birds – and this independently of his exercising the concept of *flight* or of *bird*. In a second sense of the word, a flight is "an act or instance of fleeing." If Sam simply perceives a certain animate shape in movement, he simply sees Mary flee.

It is essential to such an account that what we see are shaped things rather than things with their shapes, where the latter are conceived of as abstract properties. The category of shaped things and moving things figures prominently in Brentano's ontology (and even occurs in Aristotle's ontology, sporadically, and in his account of perception). But not in Husserl's ontology, with one exception. When Husserl describes the different strata of visual information he employs a three-way distinction between what he calls *res temporalis, res extensa,* and *res materialis* (*Ideas* II §15, I §149). These belong to the category of entities that the account above requires. Husserl uses this stratification in his account of the way non-materially qualified things (mountains) depend on sensorially and materially qualified things (coloured things) which depend on extended things (shaped things) which depend on temporal things. Because he thinks these strata stand in relations of dependence to one another, Husserl is committed to the view that they are distinct.

X. THE ANALYTIC FRAMEWORK: SPACES AND INTERNAL RELATIONS

10.1 Spaces, disjunctivism, and internal relations

Husserl's description of perception, its object and their relations, employs an analytic framework which he applies in all his contributions to descriptive psychology and to ontology. It is a framework which assumes the existence of internal relations. The two main sorts of internal relations employed are *dependence* ("*Abhängigkeit*") and *distance* ("*Abstand*") relations.[89] Dependence is understood modally by Husserl: for *a* to depend on *b* is for *a* to be such that it cannot exist or occur without *b*. He often also understands dependence as relative to wholes. Thus, his analysis of the different abstract parts or aspects of perceptual content is a componential analysis. The copula in the headings to sections IV and V above is the copula of constitution. Distance relations such as orderings among qualities in an *n*-dimensional space[90] presuppose dependence relations: if two qualities stand in the internal relation of greater or lesser similarity then they jointly depend on, cannot exist without, this relation.[91] We have come across many examples of such internal relations: the different types of similarity relations between perceptual content and its object,[92] relations in orientation space and in the different sensory fields, relations among forms and qualities.[93] The relation between the two moments of belonging to the foreground and belonging to the background is an internal relation, unlike the corresponding relation between objects. The ordering of more or less optimal appearances of objects, like those among more or less optimal instances of a type of object, and, more generally, among more or less abnormal cases of a kind are also examples of distance relations. And, as we have seen, Husserl distinguishes between (a) dependence relations between aspects of content and between aspects of what is seen, (b) functional dependence relations between the structures of kinaesthetic space and ordered perceptual sequences, and (c) causal dependence relations. Two central internal relations remain to be considered: the "intentional" relation between perception and its object and the relations between perception and judgement (and, hence, assertion) called verification, falsification, fit, and conflict.

What sort of internal relation obtains between perceptual content and its object? Husserl's account of this relation is merely a special case of the account he gives of the relation between acts and their objects in general. It is brief and obscure. But it represents his answer to the thesis of his representationalist critic which was mentioned in Section I: to allow perceptual content and objects together with the possibility of perceptual error is incompatible with the view that we directly see things, their states, and events.

It will be useful to locate his account with respect to two well-known rival accounts of the content-object relation, disjunctivism and conjunctivism. On the conjunctivist account of content, perceptual content is entirely independent of what is the case in the subject's environment. The very same type of perceptual content can be tokened in the context of veridical perception, of perceptual illusion and hallucination. The difference between these cases is explained by the presence or absence of some appropriate causal relation between object and content. On such a view, veridical perception of an *n* as an *n* and a hallucination of an *n* are said to *have something in common*. On a disjunctivist account, there is no such highest common factor – perceptual content is given by a disjunction. Thus, its looking to Sam as though something is a horse amounts to one of two things. Either a horse perceptually manifests itself to him as a horse, or he enjoys a mere appearance as of a horse.[94] Perceptual seemings are either veridical perceptions under the right aspect or hallucinations.

Many passages suggest that Husserl held fast to the common factor account. Indeed, at *Ideas* §49 he gives a well-known statement of a view that Reiner called "methodical solipsism,"[95] and that has since been called "methodological solipsism": no real being is essential for the being of consciousness. And in the *Investigations* Husserl often seems to be making the same point. The existence or non-existence of the object is "irrelevant to the true nature of the perceptual experience" (*LI* V §14). The distinction between normal or veridical perception, on the one hand, and illusion and hallucination, on the other hand, "do not affect the inner, descriptive . . . character of perception" (*LI* V §2).

Husserl wants to assert both that if "nothing is there, then there is nothing to see" and that there are perceptual illusions and hallucinations, and yet deny that we ever see merely phenomenal intermediaries.[96] His brief attempt to meet these requirements is to be found at *LI* V §11 and in the Appendix thereto. At §11, he sketches an account of content attribution, emphasising that the fact that a content occurs is independent of whether or not it has an object, and rejecting all attempts to introduce intermediate mental objects. He suggests that the right way to describe a perceptual seeming is with the help of hyphenated descriptions: Sam sees-Cologne-Cathedral, sees-a-horse. In the Appendix, he nevertheless defends the claim that there is an internal relation between content and object:

The intentional object of a presentation is the same as its real and in certain cases external object ... it is absurd [*widersinnig*, i.e., contradictory] to distinguish between them. The transcendent object would not even be the object of this presentation, were it not its intentional object. And this is of course a merely analytic proposition ... [That] [t]he object is "a merely intentional object" does not of course mean: it exists, but only in the *intentio* ... ; rather, it means: the intention, the subject's meaning an object with this or that property exists, but not the object.

This passage suggests that his view is not straightforwardly conjunctivist. To begin with, the analytic connection Husserl has in mind in clearly distinguished by him, as by disjunctivists, from the bipolarity of propositional content.[97] Bipolarity, the claim that a proposition can be true and can be false, involves no reference to any mental state. The disjunctivist analysis of perception refers to different types of mental mode and content.

But now what is the "analytic" connection between a perceptual report and its object, between perception and its object? Husserl's use of a counterfactual in the passage quoted[98] should perhaps be taken to mean that if a certain perceptual content occurs and a certain object exists – each of these claims is contingent – then a certain internal relation must obtain between them. What relation? The question is easier to answer in the perceptual case than in others. First of all, the internal relations of similarity, structural and otherwise, which have already been mentioned, suggest themselves. But these relations by themselves are not enough. And Husserl's view in the passage quoted may well involve denying that content and object are independent. A Husserlian disjunctivist claim might be put as follows: to enjoy a perceptual presentation is either to have an intentional object or to have a merely intentional object. Here, to have an intentional object is just to have a transcendent object in virtue of a content, and to have a "merely" intentional object is not to be aware of some mental object but to enjoy only a certain type of content, to be in a certain state.

In favour of such an interpretation is the fact that on Husserl's general account of relational moments every such moment stands in an internal relation to its terms. If Sam sees and hugs Maria, then a particular hug depends on Sam and Maria and a particular perceptual episode depends on Sam and Maria. This does not, of course, commit Husserl to the view that the two states of affairs, Sam hugging and seeing Maria, are anything other than contingent. The two terms are independent of each other and of all huggings and seeings.

Notice, finally, that the passages where Husserl seems to adopt the highest common factor idiom are best explained in terms of two of his favourite distinctions. What is common to veridical perception of a horse as a horse and hallucination of a horse is not any separable "piece" of content but rather a moment or inseparable aspect thereof.[99] What sort of moment? Each of the disjuncts proposed by the disjunctivist entails the proposition of which the disjunction is supposed to be the analysis. Just as to be red is to be coloured, so too, for something to be a veridical perception of a horse as a horse is for it to also be a perceptual seeming. But "also" here means more than mere conjunction, just as the way in which something is red and also coloured differs from the way in which it is red and also accelerating.

Husserl calls the relation between redness and being coloured the relation of logical parthood. If we say that the relation between either of our two disjuncts to the proposition being analysed is that of logical parthood, two questions immediately arise. Like red and blue in a two-colour world, the two disjuncts we have been considering are mutually exclusive, but unlike them these disjuncts stand in the following internal relation to one another: perceptual hallucinations are parasitic on veridical perceptions. But what does this mean? At the very least, that the former are abnormal variations on the latter.[100]

A second distinction of Husserl which throws light on his use of the highest common factor idiom is that between normal and "modified" uses of language (between using a name and mentioning it, for example). If – as *LI* V §11 suggests – the proper description of a perceptual seeming is hyphenated, can any account be given of the semantic connection between the internal structure of this description and that of the two disjuncts? On many accounts of hyphenated descriptions the answer would be negative. But on Husserl's account of semantic, syntactic, and psychological "modification," the result of modification and its basis are said to "have something in common."[101]

Disjunctivism may plausibly be held to be implied by a certain view about object-dependent content. On this view, there just are no determinate types of psychological episodes such that some tokens of a type are dependent only on subjects and others on both subjects and objects in the world (such that some are monadic moments and others relational moments). Now although such a claim, indeed even the more general claim about determinate types of episode of any sort, would be in the spirit of Husserl's strongly Aristotelian conviction that everything in time does come in determinate kinds, it is not a claim he ever makes.[102]

But the approach to perception and the mind he came to adopt after 1907 (the second analytic framework mentioned in Section 1 above) can usefully be understood as embracing the view that it is possible to draw a clean line between what is ideal or non-temporal in perception of objects and what is not. The project then becomes that of describing the former. Unfortunately, so single-minded was Husserl in the pursuit of his new project that he never returned to the questions thrown up by this brief passage on the nature of the intentional relation in the *Logical Investigations*.

There is, however, good reason for thinking that Husserl's later project is incompatible with the object-dependence of content. In the *Logical Investigations* he assumed that psychological episodes such as perceivings are in time. As he came increasingly to be impressed by the claim that purely psychological episodes are not in any sense reidentifiable, he came to the conclusion that such episodes are not in time (but only in "immanent time"). The next step was to deny that there could be any internal relation between what is not in time and what is in time, e.g., between my perception as of a man and some concrete man.

10.2 The perception-assertion link: Non-propositional justification

We saw in section IX what a Husserlian account of direct veridical perception looks like, in Section 10.1 what the nature of the link between perceptual content and object might be. Veridical perception is a necessary condition for what Husserl calls perceptual knowledge (verification or confirmation) – the subject of the sixth *Investigation*.[103] A second condition is that direct perceptual reports be justified by perception. Since perception is not concept-involving, this amounts to the claim that what justifies a perceptual judgement is not any sort of judgement. This claim flatly contradicts the popular assumption that both terms of the relation of justification be propositions or sentences, an assumption shared by Davidson and many others who have taken the linguistic turn.[104] The two main pressures leading Husserl to embrace his alternative view are, first, his central claim that to see is not to believe and secondly his conviction that concepts do not come from nowhere but have origins, in other words, that a theory of meaning must contain a theory of abstraction, of concept-formation, and learning.

For a judgement to be perceptually verified, then, it must not only be true, but the objects named and quantified over by the judgement must be perceived. But an object can be perceived in a way that falls short of the ideal of perceptual justification. I can see a duck although my perceptual content is that of a rabbit. I can see Mary's leap into the air although my perceptual content is as of a fall. These merely veridical perceptions make true but do not justify the relevant indirect perceptual reports. In other words, the fullest sort of perceptual justification of a judgement of the form aRb will involve not only perception of a, b, and some static or dynamic relational moment r but also perception of these under the appropriate aspects, appearances or contents.

As the references to ideal justification indicate, this account takes seriously the idea that perceptual justification, like perceptual acquaintance, comes in degrees.[105] Thus, my judgement that Mary is embracing Sam will be verified by my veridical perception of Mary, Sam, and the embrace under the right aspects. But it will be more fully verified by a perceptual circuit of Mary and Sam, by a look in the round.[106] At the other extreme, we have the sort of case already mentioned above in Section 3.3 where some or even all of the constituents of the truth-maker of the judgement are not seen or are seen under the wrong aspects and where what is seen is merely closely linked to the relevant truth-maker – as when I judge that the petrol tank is empty on the basis of my perception of the gauge. In between these extremes are a variety of cases of partial confirmation and disconfirmation.[107]

Husserl repeatedly stresses that the relation between perceptual content and assertion is an internal one. Is it identical with the relation of motivation or indication? An indication, cue, or criterion "prescribes" a range of possible continuations or objects. But Husserl also says that when an indication is given in a determinate context it indicates just one object or state of affairs. Similarly, the sense of a word embraces or comprehends an ideally fixed manifold of possible perceptions (*LI* VI §7). Husserl also says that the relation between what indicates and what is indicated is less than the internal relation of dependence (*LI* I §§1–7). He certainly conceives of episodes of verification as higher-order activities founded on, and linking, perceptions and assertions (*LI* VI §9). But since particular perceptions and assertions are mutually independent of one another, like an indicator and what it indicates, this does not answer our question. His view seems to be that certain types of perceptual content and certain types of propositional sense are such that when they are tokened, then necessarily a relation of justification, of counting as evidence for, holds between them.[108]

Veridical perception is a necessary condition for perceptual knowledge of spatio-temporal items. But are there any constraints at all on the type of appearance under which the object of such a perception must appear for the perception to be veridical?[109] An extreme minimalist view would be that visual differentiation of an item guarantees perception of it. Husserl never considers our question. But in the light of his emphasis on the importance of actual and possible perceptual integration,[110] it seems likely that he would have wanted to impose stronger conditions than that suggested by the extreme view. In this connection, Leyendecker considers a problem that was to be much discussed by later writers. Suppose that what is visually differentiated for me is a small red point against a green background, and suppose it "is" my house. To say "My house is not small", we have seen, is no objection to the claim "That small point is my house"; the description functions referentially. This point about perceptual reports fits the extreme view about the condition to be met by veridical perception. But there is nevertheless, Leyendecker suggests, a reason for rejecting the claim that, in this case, what I see is my house: my perceptual awareness of the small red point involves no "empty" awareness of the other side of my house, as does the perception I have of it when I move closer.[111]

Husserl's silence about the relation between the veridicality of perception and perceptual content is a function of a more thoroughgoing reticence. Although he provides a defence of the nature of the distinction between the way we see and what we see he says relatively little about what falls under which heading. He clearly thinks that properties of orientation are ways objects are seen.[112] But he rarely takes a stand on the validity of the traditional distinction between primary and secondary qualities, on the claim that redness, for example, is the way an object is seen or would be seen, rather than a monadic moment of it. He suggests that his distinction between sensations and the features in and of things that they help present is independent of the position one adopts about the ontological status of secondary qualities:

We may be led by certain reasons to distinguish appearing determinations into merely phenomenal and genuine ones, perhaps in the sense of the traditional distinction between secondary and primary qualities. [But] the subjectivity of secondary qualities can never amount to the absurd assertion that they are real constituents of phenomena. The appearing objects of external intuition are *meant* unities, not "ideas" or complexes of ideas in the Lockean sense of these terms.   (*LI* II §10)

This suggests that, even if colour moments are really "subjective" or mind-dependent, nevertheless they are not identical with sensations and are perceived as being monadic moments of things. But Husserl here considers only two possible views about their actual status, that they are constituents of content or genuinely mind-independent. He overlooks the view that colours are (actual or dispositional) relational moments. Behind his suggestion that, whatever they are, they are not identical with sensations, there is an idea sketched in passing in *Thing and Space* and later. In this work Husserl develops some ideas to be set out by (his occasional student) Katz in his classic work on colours. Like Hering and Katz, Husserl was aware of the fact that philosophers and psychologists systematically underestimate the variety of colours. In addition to the familiar surface colours, Katz distinguished spectral film colours (on which too many philosophies of perception relied), and space colours of different types. Husserl conceives of the relation between "genuine" optimal surface colours and all other colours as a case of the relation between an object of perception and ways these are seen. Thus, he adopts Katz's term for colours other than surface-colours, "the modes of appearance of colours." Of course, a friend of the traditional distinctions between primary and secondary qualities will reply that this distinction between genuine colours and other colours is a distinction *within* perceptual content rather than between perceptual content and its object.[113]

10.3 Applications

Husserl employs his analysis of perception in a number of different areas, many of which have only been mentioned here. It is developed in his analysis of the perception of other living beings and their psychological states.[114] It is essential to his analysis of the way proper names, indexical and demonstrative expressions connect us to the world. On his two-tier account of these terms, they have a sense but a sense which, in the simplest case, must be completed by perceptual acquaintance, the function of which is to fix the reference of these terms. This sense is simple and non-descriptive; the acquaintance it relies on, unlike Russellian acquaintance, is a relation to public objects.[115] His account of what he calls "direct" naming and reference may therefore be thought to escape many of the objections levelled at some better-known theories of reference.

It is essential to his account of how sentences containing such expressions are verified, in particular to his account of the role of non-propositional justification. This account is used to show what the relation is between truth, understood realistically, and verifiability. This, in its turn, is essential to his account of abstraction, of the origin of concepts in our responses to what we see, an account on which such concepts turn out to be response dependent.[116] It is crucial, too, in his account of the "perception" of "ideal objects."

It is at the basis of his account of imagination. Sensory imagination stands in the internal relation of modification to perception. To visually imagine a child is to make-believedly see a child. Similarly, to suppose that p is to make-believedly judge that p, to imagine drowning, is, among other things, to make-believedly have the "internal perceptions" of a drowning person. Thus, Husserl's analyses of judgement, perception, and imagination turn out to be systematically interconnected.[117] And of the three, it is perception that is basic.

REFERENCES

The abbreviations employed in the text and notes for works by Husserl are given below.

Becker, O. "Beiträge zur phänomenologischen Begründung der Geometrie und ihrer physikalischen Anwendungen." *Jahrbuch für Philosophie und phänomenologische Forschung* 6 (1923): 385–560.

————. "Die apriorische Struktur des Anschauungsraumes." *Philosophischer Anzeiger* 4 (1930): 129–62.

Brunswik, E. *Wahrnehmung und Gegenstandswelt. Grundlegung einer Psychologie vom Gegenstand her.* Vienna: Deuticke, 1934.

Campbell, J. "Is Sense Transparent?" *Proceedings of the Artistotelian Society.* 88 (1987): 273–292.

Casati, R. "Considerazioni critiche sulla filosofia del suono di Husserl." *Rivista di Storia della Filosofia* 44 (1989): 725–43.

————. "The Concept of *Sehding* from Hering to Katz." *Gestalt Theory: Its Origins.* Edited by A. Pagnini and S. Poggi. *Foundations and Influence.* Florence: Olschky, 1994, 21–57.

Chambon, Roger. *Le Monde comme perception et réalité.* Paris: Vrin, 1974.

Child, W. "Vision and Experience: The Causal Theory and the Disjunctive Conception." *Philosophical Quarterly* (1992): 297–316.

————. *Causation and Interpretation.* Oxford: Oxford University Press, 1994.

Conrad-Martius, H. "Zur Ontologie und Erscheinungslehre der realen Aussenwelt." *Jahrbuch für Philosophie und phänomenologische Forschung* III (1916): 345–542.

Dokic, J. "Le corps en mouvement: les relations entre l'action, l'intention et le mouvement corporel." *Revue de Théologie et de Philosophie* 124, III (1992): 249–70.

Dretske, F. *Seeing and Knowing.* London: Routledge & Kegan Paul, 1969.

————. *Knowledge and the Flow of Information.* Cambridge, Mass.: MIT Press, 1981.

Drummond, J. J. "On Seeing a Material Thing in Space: the Role of Kinaesthesis in Visual Perception." *Philosophy and Phenomenological Research* 40 (1979): 19–32.

————. "Objects' Optimal Appearances and the Immediate Awareness of Space in Vision." *Man and World* 16 (1983): 177–205.

Dummett, M. *Ursprünge der analytischen Philosophie.* Frankfurt: Suhrkamp, 1988.

Evans, G. *The Varieties of Reference.* Oxford: Oxford University Press, 1982.

————. *Collected Papers.* Oxford: Clarendon, 1985.

Føllesdal, D. "Husserl's Notion of Noema." *Journal of Philosophy* 66 (1969): 680–87.

————. 1974. "Husserl's Theory of Perception." In *Handbook of Perception,* Vol. 1. Edited by E. Carterette and M. Friedman. New York: Academic Press, 377–86.

Goldmeier, E. *Similarity in Visually Perceived Forms.* Psychological Issues, Monograph 29. New York: International Universities Press, 1972.

Gurwitsch, A. *Studies in Phenomenology and Psychology*. Evanston, Illinois: Northwestern University Press, 1966.

Heider, F. "Ding und Medium." *Symposion* I (1926): 109–57

———. "Die Leistung des Wahrnehmungssystems." *Zeitschrift für Psychologie* 114 (1930): 371–94.

Hinton, J. M. *Experiences*. Oxford: Clarendon Press, 1973.

Hochleitner, A. "Die philosophischen Voraussetzungen und Konsequenzen der Gestaltpsychologie." *Archiv für die gesamte Psychologie* 107 (1940): 71–124.

Hoffmann, H. *Untersuchungen über den Empfindungsbegriff*. Dissertation, Göttingen, 1913.

Holenstein, E. *Phänomenologie der Assoziation. Zur Struktur und Funktion eines Grundprinzipes der passiven Genesis*. The Hague: Nijhoff, 1972.

Husserl, E. *Logische Untersuchungen*, 1st ed. Halle: Niemeyer, 1900/01; 2nd ed. 1913/21. *Husserliana* XVIII, XIX/1, XIX/2; translated by J. Findlay as *Logical Investigations*. London: Routledge (*LI*).

———. 1950. *Ideen zu einer reinen Phänomenologie und phänomenologischen Philosophie* I. *Husserliana* III. The Hague: Nijhoff.

———. 1952. *Ideen zu einer reinen Phänomenologie und phänomenologischen Philosophie* II. *Husserliana* IV. The Hague: Nijhoff. (*Ideen* II).

———. 1970. *Philosophie der Arithmetik. Psychologische und logische Untersuchungen*. *Husserliana* XII. The Hague: Nijhoff. (PdA).

———. 1973. *Ding und Raum. Vorlesungen 1907*. *Husserliana* XVI. The Hague: Nijhoff. (*DR*).

———. 1964. *Erfahrung und Urteil*. Hamburg: Claassen. *Experience and Judgement*. London: Routledge & Kegan Paul, 1973 (*EU*).

———. 1979. *Aufsätze und Rezensionen (1890–1910)*. *Husserliana* XXII. The Hague: Nijhoff.

Ingarden, R. *Das literarische Kuntswerk*. Tübingen: Niemeyer, 1931.

———. 1965. "Husserls Betrachtungen zur Konstitution des physikalischen Dinges," *La Phénoménologie et les sciences de la nature*. Archives de l'Institut international des sciences théoriques, 13. Brussels, 1965, 36–87.

Jackson, F. *Perception. A Representative Theory*. Cambridge: Cambridge University Press, 1977.

Janssen, O. *Vorstudien zur Metaphysik* I. Halle: Niemeyer, 1921.

Katz, D. 1911. *Die Erscheinungsweisen der Farben*. Second ed., 1930, *Der Aufbau der Farbwelt*, Leipzig. Partial English translation, *The World of Colour*. London: Kegan Paul, 1935.

Kelley, D. *The Evidence of the Senses. A Realist Theory of Perception*. Baton Rouge: Louisiana State University Press, 1986.

Koffka, K. "Psychologie." In *Lehrbuch der Philosophie*, Vol. II. Edited by M. Dessoir. Berlin: Ullstein, 1925, 497–603.

Köhler, W. *Psychologische Probleme*. Berlin: Springer, 1933.

———. *Gestalt Psychology*. New York: Liveright, 1947.

———. *The Selected Papers of Wolfgang Köhler*. New York: Liveright, 1971.

Kries, J. von. "Die Gesichtsempfindungen," *Nagels Handbuch der Psychologie des Menschen* III. Braunschweig, 1904.

Krueger, F. "Differenztöne und Konsonanz." *Archiv für die gesamte Psychologie*, 1903.

Küng, G. "The World as Noema and Referent." *Journal of the British Society for Phenomenology* 3 (1972): 15–26

———. "Husserl on Pictures and Intentional Objects." *Review of Metaphysics* 26 (1973): 670–80.

Künne, W. "Hybrid Proper Names." *Mind* (1992): 721–30.

Landgrebe, L. "Prinzipien der Empfindungslehre." *Zeitschrift für philosophische Forschung* 8 (1954): 195–209.

Leyendecker, H. *Zur Phänomenologie der Täuschungen*. New York: Garland, 1980. First published 1913.

Linke, P. *Grundfragen der Wahrnehmungslehre*. Munich: Reinhardt, 1929. 1st edition 1918.

McDowell, J. "Criteria, Defeasibility and Knowledge." *Proceedings of the British Academy* 68 (1982): 455–79.

———. "Singular Thought and the Extent of Inner Space." In *Subject, Thought and Context*. Edited by P. Pettit and J. McDowell. Oxford: Clarendon Press, 1986.

McIntyre, R. and D. W. Smith. "Intentionality via Intensions." *Journal of Philosophy*, 68 (1971) 541–561.

———. "Husserl's Identification of Meaning and Noema." *Monist* (1975): 59.

Meinong, A. "Über Gegenstände höherer Ordnung und deren Verhältnis zur inneren Wahrnehmung." *Gesamtausgabe* Vol. II. Graz: Akademische Druck- und Verlagsanstalt, 1971.

Moore, G. E. "Some Judgements of Perception" 1918. As reprinted in Moore's *Philosophical Studies*. Cambridge: Cambridge University Press, 1922 220–51.

———. Review of August Messer, *Empfindung und Denken*. *Mind* 19 (1910): 395–409.

Mulligan, K. "Seeing as and Assimilative Perception." *Brentano Studien* I (1988): 129–52

———. "Judgings: their Parts and Counterparts." In *Topoi Supplement 2, La Scuola di Brentano*, 1989: 117–48. Bologna Brentano Conference 1984.

————. "Husserl on States of Affairs in the *Logical Investigations.*" *Epistemologia*, special number on *Logica e Ontologia* XII, 1989a, 207–34.

————. "Criteria and Indication." In *Wittgenstein – Towards a Reevaluation.* Edited by R. Haller, J. Brandl. Vienna: Verlag Hoelder-Pichler-Tempsky, 1990, 94–105.

————. "Colours, Corners and Complexity: Meinong and Wittgenstein on some Internal Relations." In *Existence and Explanation. Essays Presented in Honor of Karel Lambert.* Edited by W. Spohn et al. Dordrecht: Kluwer, 1991, 77–102.

————. "Internal Relations." *1992 ANU Metaphysics Conference*, ANU Working Papers in Philosophy 2, edited by B. Garrett and P. Menzies, 1993, 1–22

————. "Description's Objects: Austrian Variations," In *Themes from Wittgenstein*, ANU Working Papers in Philosophy. Edited by B. Garrett and K. Mulligan. Australian National University, Canberra, 1993a, 62–85.

————. "Perception, Particulars and Predicates." Forthcoming, 1995.

————. "L'Imagination, sa varieté et son unité." In *Phénoménologie et philosophie analytique.* Forthcoming, 1995a.

Mulligan, K. and B. Smith "A Husserlian Theory of Indexicality." *Grazer Philosophische Studien* 28 (1986): 133–63.

————. "A Relational Theory of the Act." *Topoi* V (1986a): 115–130.

Mulligan, K., B. Smith and P. Simons. "Truth Makers." *Philosophy and Phenomenological Research* 44 (1984): 278–321.

O'Shaughnessy, B. *The Will: a Dual Aspect Theory,* 2 volumes. Cambridge: Cambridge University Press, 1980.

————. "Seeing the Light." *Proceedings of the Aristotelian Society* 85 (1985): 193–218.

————. "The Appearance of a Material Object." *Philosophical Perspectives* 4. *Action Theory and Philosophy of Mind* (1990): 131–51.

Peacocke, C. *Sense and Content.* Oxford: Oxford University Press, 1983.

————. "Analogue Content." *Proceedings of the Aristotelian Society*, Supplementary Volume LX (1986): 1–18.

————. "Perceptual Content." In *Themes from Kaplan.* Edited by J. Almog et al. Oxford University Press, 1989, 297–329.

Petitot. J. "Phenomenology of perception, qualitative physics and sheaf mereology." In *Philosophy and Cognitive Sciences.* Proceedings of the 16th International Wittgenstein Symposium Edited by R. Casati, B. Smith and G. White. Vienna: Hölder-Pichler-Tempsky, 1994, 387–408.

Prinz, W. "Ideo-Motor Action." In *Perspectives on Perception and Action.* Edited by H. Heuer and A. F. Sanders. Hillsdale, N.J., 1987: *LEA.*

Rang, B. *Husserls Phänomenologie der materiellen Natur.* Frankfurt: Klostermann, 1990.

Reinach, A. "On the Theory of the Negative Judgement." In Smith, ed., 1982, 315–78.

Reiner, H. *Phänomenologie und menschliche Existenz.* Halle: Niemeyer, 1931.

Reyer, W. *Einführung in die Phänomenologie.* Meiner: Leipzig, 1926.

Russell, B. *The Problems of Philosophy.* Oxford University Press, 1959.

Schapp, W. *Beiträge zur Phänomenologie der Wahrnehmung.* Halle, 1910. Reprinted in 1976, Wiesbaden: B. Heymann Verlag.

Scheler, M. "Über Selbsttäuschungen." *Zeitschrift für Pathopsychologie* (1911): 87–163; a revised version of this article is now in Scheler 1972, *Vom Umsturz der Werte,* Berne: Francke, *Gesammelte Werke* III.

———. 1921. *Der Formalismus in der Ethik und die materiale Wertethik.* Halle: Niemeyer. First published 1913/1916.

———. *Schriften aus dem Nachlass,* Bd. 1, *Zur Ethik und Erkenntnislehre.* Berne: Francke, 1957.

———. *Erkenntnis und Arbeit.* Berne: Francke, 1960. First published 1926.

Schilder, P. *Image and Appearance of the Human Body.* New York: International University Press, 1950.

Shoemaker, S. *Identity, Cause and Mind. Philosophical Essays.* Cambridge: Cambridge University Press, 1984.

Smith, B. "Gestalt Theory: An Essay in Philosophy." In *Foundations of Gestalt Theory.* Edited by B. Smith. Munich: Philosophia, 1988.

Smith, B., ed. *Parts and Moments. Studies in Logic and Formal Ontology.* Munich: Philosophia, 1982.

Smith, B. and K. Mulligan. "Pieces of a Theory." In Smith, ed., 1982, 15–110.

Smith, D. W. *The Circle of Acquaintance: Perception, Consciousness and Empathy.* Boston and Dordrecht: Kluwer, 1989.

Smith, D. W. and R. McIntyre. *Husserl and Intentionality.* Dordrecht: Reidel, 1982.

Snowdon, P. "The Objects of Perceptual Experience." *Proceedings of the Aristotelian Society,* Supp. Vol. 64 (1990): 121–50.

Speigelberg, H. *Phenomenology in Psychology and Psychiatry. A Historical Introduction.* Evanston: Northwestern University Press, 1972.

Stein, E. *Zum Problem der Einfühlung.* Munich: Kaffke, 1980. First published 1917.

Strawson, P. *Freedom and Resentment.* London: Methuen, 1974.

Stucchi, N. "Seeing and Thinking: Vittorio Benussi and the Graz School." In *Essays on Meinong.* Edited by P. Simons. Forthcoming, 1995.

Tugendhat, E. *Der Wahrheitsbegriff bei Husserl und Heidegger.* Berlin: de Gruyter, 1970.

Warnock, G. "Seeing." *Proceedings of the Aristotelian Society* (1955): 201–18.

NOTES

1 Føllesdal 1969, 1974; Küng 1972, 1973; McIntyre and Smith 1971, 1975; Smith and McIntyre 1982; Smith, D. W. 1989.

2 Like Husserl in these two works, I shall concentrate largely on visual perception. For an excellent account and criticism of Husserl on the perception of sounds, see Casati 1989.

3 Cf. four monographs by students of Husserl in Göttingen, David Katz's *Die Erscheinungsweisen der Farben* (1911), Heinrich Hoffmann's *Untersuchungen über den Empfindungsbegriff* (1913), Wilhelm Schapp's *Beiträge zur Phänomenologie der Wahrnehmung* (1910), and Herbert Leyendecker's *Zur Phänomenologie der Täuschungen*; Max Scheler's "Über Selbsttäuschungen" (1911) and *Erkenntnis und Arbeit* (1926), Paul Linke's *Grundfragen der Wahrnehmungslehre* (1918), Oskar Becker's *Beiträge zur phänomenologischen Begründung der Geometrie und ihrer physikalischen Anwendungen* (1923) and Roman Ingarden's *Das literarische Kunstwerk* (1931). Cf. also Stein 1917; Becker 1930; Conrad-Martius 1916, 1929; Reyer 1926; Landgrebe 1954. Husserl's analyses also influenced parts of Gestalt psychology. Indeed, Husserl anticipated an entire tradition of work on criteria and constancy – Katz 1911, Bühler, Heider 1926, Brunswik 1934. On the connections between Husserl's early philosophy of perception and psychology, cf. Spiegelberg 1972. Schapp's monograph anticipates, and Merleau-Ponty's phenomenologies of perception and behaviour complete, the decline of the tradition within the philosophy of perception which starts with Brentano and his pupils.

4 An ancestor of this paper, "Husserl und die Phänomenologie in Göttingen," was presented in Göttingen in 1987, as part of the series *Die Philosophie in Göttingen*. I am grateful to the many philosophers there and, later, in Italy who provided useful comments.

5 Wittgenstein, *Philosophical Remarks* §208; Husserl, from an unpublished manuscript, quoted in Rang 1990, 176; cf. also *DR* §44. This difficulty is they also thought, connected with the unnaturalness of their approaches to philosophy (cf. Mulligan 1993a).

6 "Umweg über den Gegenstand," Meinong, "Über Gegenstände höherer Ordnung . . .", *GA* II, 385; cf. Husserl, *LI* Vol. II, Part 1, §3.

7 Cf. Casati 1995.

8 *LI* VI §44. Husserl here introduces a wide concept of judgement comprehending not only "the meaning-intentions belonging to statements" but also "the fulfilments that fit them completely," that is, both sensory and non-sensory perceptions. Using this wide concept of judging, he then asserts that "being can only be apprehended through judging." Husserl's

pupil Reinach calls non-sensory perception based on sensory perception "apprehension" ("*Erkennen,*" cognition): "If I discern from afar the approach of a cyclist then speaking purely decriptively this is an apprehension, even if it should be the case that in reality it is not a cyclist at all who is approaching but rather, say, a cow" (Reinach 1982 375). Reinach also points out that apprehension is a punctual act, like judgement, whereas such perceptual presentations as looking at something have duration (Reinach 1982 344, 322). When Husserl talks of visual perception he normally has in mind not punctual seeing but observing, looking at and scrutinising. Thus, perception of horses, colours always "consists in a straightforward looking at the object (*Hinblicken auf*)" (*LI* VI §58). In "visual perception" "I see a thing, e.g., this box . . . I continue to see one and the same box . . ." (*LI* V §14). He occasionally discusses the relations between such punctual events as hearing and seeing and the processes of listening and looking or observing on which they are based (Cf. Hua X, 225, 456, 21).

9 Cf. *LI* V §§27, 29, 34, 38, 40, 41. Husserl's views may be contrasted with those of four unlikely bed-fellows: Searle (*Intentionality*) and Quine (*The Pursuit of Truth*), for whom perception is always propositional; Brentano, for whom to see is always to judge; and Fodor for whom seeing is not doxastic but has a sentence-like content. However, since Brentano's analysis of judgement is non-propositional, seeing, on his account, is not seeing that. Husserl often contradicts his thesis that simple seeing involves no meaning (*Meinen*), e.g., at *LI* I §23 and his thesis that to see is not to judge or believe (since these attitudes require propositionally articulated contents), e.g., at *LI* V§§27, 38. In later texts his habit of describing all positing modes as modes of belief (often using the English word) becomes more pronounced (cf., e.g., *DR* §43). Perhaps this is a result of the tendency to logicise all psychological phenomena that marks his turn to idealism. Perhaps it is a result of the increasing carelessness that accompanied this turn. Husserl is not even consistently clear in *LI* that seeing is not meaning, thus he occasionally talks of our signitively intending the far side of an object we are looking at. This is criticised at *DR* §18. On the move away from the view that to see is to believe within the Meinong school, cf. Stucchi 1995.

10 Dretske 1969, 1981; Warnock 1955; Jackson 1977.

11 Husserl mentions accidents at, e.g., at Hua X, Appendix XI, 125. It should be borne in mind that when he describes moments as "abstract," he means that they are dependent, not that they are ideal. On moments, cf. Smith and Mulligan 1982.

12 The failure to distinguish between seeing a redness moment and applying a concept of redness is, Husserl thinks, a symptom of a wider failure:

"In the theory of abstraction since Locke, the problem of *abstraction in the sense of an emphatic pointing to 'abstract contents'* [moments] has been mixed up with the problem of *abstraction in the sense of concept-formation*" (*LI* II §40).

13 Husserl also argues for ideal species on the basis of a regress argument at *LI* II §3. Unfortunately he does not explain what the relation between the two arguments is. Cf. Russell 1959, 96–97.

14 On direct perception of changes, see Leyendecker 1913, 137.

15 Cf. Goldmeier 1972. On sensational grouping properties cf. Peacocke 1983, 24–26.

16 "[S]ensory connections [*sinnliche Verknüpfungen*] are moments . . . as when in the intuition of a comprehensive whole, *W*, the contact of A and B is sensorily given . . . In the sensible whole, the parts *A* and *B* are brought together by the sensorily connecting moment of contact" (*LI* VI §48).

17 On discontinuities as topological singularities see Becker 1923, 34ff., Petitot 1994.

18 "Discontinuity . . . relates to specifically differing moments in so far as they are *'spread out with common boundaries'* over a continuously varying spatial or temporal moment. It is *at* a spatial or temporal boundary that one visual quality, e.g., leaps over into another. In our continuous progress from spatial part to spatial part there is at the same time no continuous progress in the covering quality: in one place at least the neighbouring qualities are finitely (and not too minutely) distant . . . [N]ot merely qualities, e.g., colours, achieve separation, but whole concreta set bounds to one another, the visual field is split up into parts. The colour-distance in such a context of "covering" (without which there can be no talk of discontinuity) also wins separation for the moments bound up with it, the covered spatial parts of our example. These could not otherwise be free from fusion. Spatiality necessarily varies continuously. A piece of such variation can only become separately noticeable . . . when a discontinuity is provided by the covering moment, and the whole concretum which corresponds to it has thus been separated" (*LI* III §9).

19 For an interesting suggestion that, in a certain sense, perception involves formal or categorial concepts, see *LI* VI §58.

20 *LI* VI §47; cf. Linke 1929, 280, Dretske 1969, Chap. IV, Jackson 1977, 159–67.

21 Husserl's distinction between the way names name objects and the way predicates "hinweisen auf" (*LI* III §2, cf. VI §10) may be an attempt to describe the implicit quantification over monadic and relational moments that judgements contain.

22 "The abundant multiplicity of sense-qualities, of sensible [empfindbare] forms is at the disposal of straightforward sensuous intuition for purposes of representation" (LI VI §55). On the distinction between sensations and qualities, see LI II §36, §41, V §2.

23 LI VI, Appendix 5; cf. LI I §23; cf. "The fulness of the presentation . . . is the sum-total of determinations [Bestimmtheiten] pertaining to the presentation itself, through which it analogically gives presence to its object" (LI VI §21). Sensations represent "through similarity" (LI VI §37). At DR §16 Husserl mentions that he uses "similarity" in a sense that is "not quite natural"; cf. DR §17, Hua X §1. Nevertheless, he remained attached to the thesis without ever explaining just what it is supposed to involve. His use of expressions such as "in a particular sense analogous" and "generically allied but not identical" (LI I §23) suggest perhaps that he had in mind not the ordinary notion of similarity understood as the possession by two objects of the same property but a type of similarity described by Mill and Stumpf which might be called brute similarity and which does not involve any common property. Thus, a hue of redness may be more similar to a second than a third even though this cannot be explained in terms of the first and second hues having more properties in common than the first and the third. Then the claim would be that there is a relation of brute similarity between red sensations and the quality of redness although it is not the case that both the sensation and the object are red. Perhaps he had in mind some much weaker thesis, e.g., that the concept of redness figures essentially in an identifying description of the sensory state of one who sees, in optimal circumstances, something that is red. Tugendhat and Holenstein suggest that after the Investigations Husserl gave up the claim that there is a relation of similarity between sensation and quality (Ideas I §41, §81; Tugendhat 1970, 75f. Holenstein 1972, 97). But Husserl's points in Ideas I to the effect that there is no non-trivial genus to which both sensations and qualities belong had already been made in the Investigations.

24 A mode of analysis that is more familiar than that preferred by Husserl would have us talk, instead, of the "primed properties" of perceptual acts or experiences rather than of the independent and dependent parts of such experiences (cf. Peacocke 1983 20f., 52f.). We may, if we want, talk of an experience which is red', round', etc. But how, in the language of primed properties, should we express the relation between the sensation of a configuration and the sensations of dots that make it up? Between an experience that is configured' and the experiences that are dot-shaped'? We are obliged to introduce a part-whole relation between the experience that is configured' and those of its parts that are dot-shaped'.

But then we have just the relational and non-relational moments of sensation described by Husserl.

25 This difference of opinion between Husserl, on the one hand, and Brentano, Russell, and Moore on the other hand is a consequence of the fact that for Husserl, the act-object schema is incomplete without the dimension of content. The category of content was rejected at times by both Moore and Russell. Thus, in 1918 Moore describes and rejects the view that we have visual sensations that mediate perception but that these sensations are not seen. (Moore 1918 in Moore 1922, 232.) But Frege, in the same year ("The Thought"), argues that we have but do not see sensations. Cf. also Moore's (1910) review of a primer on Husserl's philosophy of mind; Ryle's distinction in the *The Concept of Mind* between sensation and observation; Frege's *Grundlagen* §26.

26 *LI* VI Appendix, 8. On Husserl and Wittgenstein on the reidentifiability of mental items, cf. Mulligan 1993a.

27 In the second edition of the *Investigations* and later, Husserl's awareness that "interpretation" [*Deutung*] might wrongly be taken to involve a reference to conceptual interpretation led him to use instead of *"Deutung"* such terms as *"Auffassung"* (grasp) and *"Apperzeption"* (apperception). (See Rang 1990, 210. Rang describes in great detail Husserl's relation to and criticisms of Helmholtz's account of perception as the interpretation of signs. He seems, however, to underestimate the importance of Husserl's view that to see is not to judge.) To grasp is not to infer since it involves no concepts (Hua XIII, 50).

28 Cf. "If I see an incomplete pattern, e.g., in this carpet partially covered over by furniture, the piece I see seems clothed with intentions pointing to further completions – we feel as if the lines and coloured shapes 'go on' in the sense of what we see" (*LI* VI §10). Thus, whenever such intentions are frustrated, or whenever a switch from one interpretation to another occurs the discontinuity involved is felt. Cf. Köhler 1947, Chap. 5; Goldmeier 1972; B. Smith 1988, §10.

29 Cf. Schapp 1910, 98. When Husserl uses idioms such as "perceiving as," he normally has in mind the interpretation of sensations. But Schapp and other descriptive psychologists talk of seeing *things* as this or that. Husserl, too, occasionally uses this idiom, e.g., when he says that an interlocutor perceives or grasps a speaker *as* a person who expresses this or that without the intervention of any conceptual knowledge or judgement (*LI* I §7).

30 An important application of the claim that perception unifies without the performance of an extra act is the thesis that perception identifies its objects without the help of judgements of identity – cf. VI.3 below.

31 For a good account of the different senses in which all the parts of a visual field may be said to be dependent, see *LI* III §10.

32 Köhler, of course, like the other Berlin Gestalt psychologists, accepts that there are mind-independent physical Gestalten. But because of his critical realism he does not think we see them (Köhler 1933, 16). On the critical realism of the Gestalt psychologists, see Hochleitner 1940. For a good account of the Berlin and Austrian accounts of Gestalt perception, both of which are mistaken, if Husserl is right, see B. Smith 1988. On the view that aspect switches are intermediate between sensory and intellectual changes, see Mulligan 1988.

33 Scheler 1921 II A 3, Scheler 1957, 448f., Scheler 1960, 165f., 171f. Cf. Linke 1929 §68, §76, Nachwort §1; Gurwitsch 1966 §§15–16 and Landgrebe 1954. One reason why the originality of Husserl's view has been insufficiently appreciated is that for him, as for Linke and perhaps for Wittgenstein, perceptual interpretation does not invariably involve judgement whereas the positions criticised by the Berlin school invariably assumed that to see is to judge.

34 An English translation of Köhler's paper, "On unnoticed sensations and errors of judgement," is to be found in Köhler 1971. Köhler's criticisms of the constancy hypothesis had been anticipated by von Kries 1904 and Krueger 1903 and, in philosophy, by Brentano.

35 The quotations here from Husserl and Koffka are discussed by Holenstein (1972, 296) who also defends the view that Husserl was guilty of something like the Constancy Hypothesis. Holenstein acutely criticizes Husserl's views on sensation from the point of view of the rejection of the interpretation-sensation model by Husserl in his writings on time awareness and from the point of view of Gestalt psychology.

36 Holenstein 1972, 284.

37 Holenstein (1972, 95–96) quotes from a revealing manuscript of 1932: "Is not my original view of an immanent sphere with immanent data which in the end only 'come to be interpreted' through the passive achievement of association still a residue of the old psychology and its sensualist empiricism? But how is one otherwise to put the matter? There are therefore no sense data without interpretation, [the property of] being interpreted, 'representation', is innate. But what can be done with this?" (Ms. B I 13 I, p. 8 (1932)). At one point in the *Investigations* Husserl mentions, and does not reject, the view that "sensuous contents are invariably and necessarily objectively interpreted, that they are always bearers of external intuitions, and can only be attended to as contents of such intuitions" (Appendix, 6, to *LI* VI). Recently Peacocke 1983 has defended the irreducibility of sensational to representational properties. But, unlike Husserl, he thinks that perceptual representation is

conceptual and that aspect-changes are changes in representation that
are conceptual.

38 *LI* V §2, cf. II §36; *Ideas* I §41.

39 See Hering 1879, 343; 1905; Hoffmann 1913, §2; Casati 1995, Rang
1990, Chap. V. Husserl occasionally uses Hering's concept of *Sehding*.
Cf. Katz 1913, Hoffmann 1913, §6.

40 Two excellent accounts of the relation between perceptual interpretation and the profiles of the things we see are Hoffmann 1913 and
Leyendecker 1980. See also Linke 1918, especially 75, 378 and Janssen
1921, 24ff. for extensive criticism. Ingarden 1933 contains a clear account of Husserl's views and applies them to a number of aesthetic
problems. On the interpretation of Husserl's changing views of profiles
and their appearances, see Chambon 1974.

41 Moore 1918, 234f. I ignore here Moore's worries about whether the side
in question is or is not a private sense-datum. It should also be noted
that Moore's topic is perceptual judgements not perception and that
much of his account of the former is compatible with a distinction
between the two, a distinction which is not however emphasised in his
paper.

42 Cf. *LI* VI §10, §14(b), §29, §37; *DR* §16, §24; *Ideas* I §41; Husserl also
mentions such cases as partial occlusion of what I am looking at, etc. Cf.
Evans 1982, 176–77. For the evolution of Husserl's ideas before 1907, see
DR §§17–18.

43 Cf. Evans 1982, 195, 174f., "Understanding Demonstratives" in Evans
1985, Dummett 1988 §12 on "proto-thoughts" and their dynamic nature
in a discussion of Husserl on perception. On dynamic content, looks,
etc., cf. Hoffmann 1913, Becker 1923, O'Shaughnessy 1990 and, for an
extension of the idea to the realm of volitive content, Dokic 1992. The
metaphorical character of Merleau-Ponty's occasionally fascinating developments of Husserl's views on dynamic content seem to have killed
the topic until the work of Evans. Pears (*The False Prison*, 1988, II, 332
n., 405 n.) notes the connection between the last phenomenology of
dynamic content and Evans and with pragmatism. An often inspired
treatment of the phenomenology of dynamic perception in the light of
pragmatism is Scheler 1926/1977. Scheler, however, dispenses with perceptual content.

44 Interestingly enough, the German verb *"spüren"* means to perceive,
sense or experience and *"nachspüren"* to track or trail.

45 *DR* §44 (and *LI* VI §8). In spite of his distinction here between perceptual
and logical "synthesis," Husserl unfortunately talks in the same section
of *DR*, as he had occasionally in *LI*, of the "sense" rather than the
content, of a perception; cf. note 9. Note that in addition to perceptual

identification and logical identification, there is the intermediate case where my grasp of "this" and my perceptual state identify the same object and also the case where I make this identification explicit. Adapting a term of Husserl's we might call such identities "hybrid" or "mixed."

46 *LI* VI §29; cf. Campbell 1988, 282f.

47 Cf. *LI* VI §5, §6, and §8.

48 *LI* VI §10. Cf. Smith and McIntyre 1982, Chap. V. On the "unmediated disposition to treat certain present and future informational states" derived from an object, as germane to the evaluation of demonstrative utterances about it, see Evans 1982, 146–47.

49 *LI* I §§1–5, *DR* §51, §54. Cf. Mulligan 1990.

50 Cf. also *Ideas* II §18 (a), §32, §55. A good account of Husserl's views is to be found in Drummond 1978–79.

51 Cf. *Ideas* II, §40, "Each part of the visual field has a sensation value" (O'Shaughnessy 1980, I, 180). On body-images, cf. *Ideas* II §37, *DR* §47, Stein 1980, Schilder 1950, O'Shaughnessy 1980, I, Evans 1982, 163.

52 *DR* §49. Cf. O'Shaughnessy 1980, I, 197–98

53 On this contrast, cf. Evans 1985 283ff.

54 Husserl attempts to distinguish between the (non-projective) way kinaesthetic sensations present parts of my body and the (projective) way visual sensations present parts of a house at *DR* §47 and §83; cf. also Stein 1980 44f. For another full account of the difference, within the framework of a representationalist theory of perception, see O'Shaughnessy 1980 I, 143ff. Husserl's account of intentional movement is a volitionist one. But like the Gestalt psychologists, Scheler and, for example, O'Shaughnessy (ibid.), he rejects the view that trying simply initiates and precedes movement. Rather, trying coexists with and causes movement, an achievement which is made possible by the fact that perception and volition accompany and steer one another; cf. Hua XXVIII, A, §§13–16.

55 Husserl marks the distinction between visual sensations and kinaesthetic sensations by calling the former *Empfindungen* and the latter *Empfindnisse* (*Ideen* II, §40).

56 Husserl *Ideen* II, §37. O'Shaughnessy suggests that the connection between bodily sensations such as kinesthetic or postural sensations, on the one hand, and their objects, body parts, is a direct and immediate relation. The notions of directness and immediacy involved here come out in a contrast he introduces between visual sensations and their objects, on the one hand, and bodily sensations and their objects on the other hand. The visual sensation is simply "red and bright" (say), and is not as such putatively of some physical object (e.g., balloon) but each bodily sensation is

either merely putatively or else actually of a body part (O'Shaughnessy 1980, I, 180). More precisely, in one of his characteristic formulations, "the basic 'given' is, not just feeling, not just feeling-in-a-certain-body-part, but *feeling-in-a-certain-body-part-at-a-position-in-a-body-relative-physical-space*" (O'Shaughnessy 1980, I, 165; cf. 217). Cf. Becker 1923 §§5–7.

57 On the one-dimensional space of depth values and the way it combines with the two-dimensional system of extent to form a double continuum, see *DR* §49.

58 *DR* §48, *LI* III §25.

59 *DR* §49, cf. Becker 1923 §7.

60 *DR* §51; cf. the quite different account of the relation between visual sensations and interpretations above.

61 On the role of vicarious functioning in perception, see Brunswik 1934.

62 *DR* §52, §54; *EU* §19.

63 *DR* §67, *LI* VI §14 (b).

64 Koffka 1925, V, §9. On the two types of account, see Prinz 1987.

65 For a fuller account in English, see Drummond's excellent 1979 and 1983 papers. The sketch given here differs from that given by Drummond mainly in attaching greater importance to the distinction between perceptual contents and objects.

66 *DR* §58, cf. Becker 1923 §7 A.2 & C.

67 *DR* §70 "On pictures that belong to an identical object."

68 Cf. Hoffmann 1913 103ff. and Wittgenstein on distance from my physical eye vs. distance from my geometrical eye in the Blue Book.

69 *DR* §48, cf. Wittgenstein's *Philosophical Remarks* §206.

70 Drummond 1979, 28. Cf. *DR* §64, §69, 311f., 318f., Appendix. 4.

71 *DR* §§72–75, O'Shaughnessy 1990 §2.

72 On the step from orientation space to the homogenous space of physics, cf. Becker 1923.

73 *DR* §§35–37, §32; *Ideen* II, 59f.; Husserl 1979, 273; cf. Rang 1990, 176f., 280f.; on the optimal perception of sounds, see *Ideas* I §43. The axiological nature of perceptual optima and of typical objects is also described in *EU*. Cf. also Barry Smith's contribution to this volume. Current work on optimal forms and objects (e.g., by Rosch) goes back to the descriptions of singular (good, pregnant) forms by the Gestalt psychologists. Although Husserl talks of optimal appearances of objects and the Gestalt psychologists of optimal perceptual forms, since the latter are for the Gestalt psychologists phenomenal entities, they are, in fact, just what Husserl calls appearances.

74 Although this normally translates as "attitude," the latter word has come to be used for what are here called mental modes. The standard

translation by psychologists of *"Einstellung"* as "set" is therefore a happy one. Because of the role of dispositions in sets, the common translation "mental set" is unfortunate.

75 Leyendecker 1980 (1913), 43, 64, 71, 72. Leyendecker's (and Scheler's) use of concepts such as *Milieu, Umwelt* and "set" clearly anticipate many descriptions of Wittgenstein. Wittgenstein writes about one basic set at *Philosophical Investigations* II, iv, about *"Einstellungen"* and *"Stellungnahmen"* in seeing as at II, xi; cf. also *Last Writings on the Philosophy of Psychology*, I, §§667, 670, 772. For a thorough description of the relation between sets and aspect switches, see Leyendecker 1980, 85f. Cf. also on aspect switches Schapp 1910, 98ff. Husserl's use of *"Einstellung"* differs from that of Leyendecker in that it is restricted to a few abstract distinctions between the theoretical, practical, phenomenological and natural "attitudes."

76 *LI* III §9. Jean Petitot (1994) shows that vague sensory types of object and the phenomena of fusion and phenomenal discontinuity are indeed mathematisable within the framework of "morphological geometry."

77 *LI* VI §10, §37. On this, see Tugendhat 1972, 75. See also *DR* §18 and *LI* V §15(b). Wittgenstein, too, returns frequently to the curious way in which a reference to an indeterminate range of possibilities is a determinate feature of propositions and perceptions, cf. *Tractatus* 5.156, *Philosophical Remarks* §§211, 213, *Philosophical Investigations* §98f. ("there must be perfect order in even the vaguest sentence").

78 *Ideas* I §140; cf §103 on the weightings of different possibilities; *LI* VI §10, V §20; II §37, §39. In his analysis of "motivational connections" (see note 49 above), Husserl points out that it is always possible to find a counterpart connection which expresses a relation of probability or causality. On Allers, Bühler and Wittgenstein on motives, criteria, and indication vs. causes, clues, and symptoms, see Mulligan 1990.

79 On what is co-present in perception, see *Ideas* I §27. On internal horizons, see Hua XI §1. On background vs. foreground, see Hua XXV, 31, *Ideas* I §35, §83. On the sense in which many perceptual properties such as bigness are relative to terms that "remain in the background," see *EU* §46. One group of such "absolute impressions" are the properties of orientation that present themselves as being monadic because their connection with, e.g., the "origo" of orientation space also remains in the background; see *DR* §48. A description of background information is given by Leyendecker 1980 §7. Karl Schuhmann has suggested to me that Husserl may have found the influential concept of a *horizon* in Jakob Friedrich Fries, *Grundriss der Logik*, Heidelberg 1827 (3rd edition), 74. On horizons in Husserl, see Smith and McIntyre 1982 Chap. V.

80 *Ideas* II, §18a.

81 Conceptual seeing as, what Leyendecker calls "seeing through a meaning," is, as he points out, compatible with varying degrees of perceptual
fulness. And although such conceptual subsumption is aided by perception of something as belonging to a certain type, the latter is independent of the former. Cf. Leyendecker 1980, 105f., 168f.

82 *LI* III §12 n. This point and the way it is developed are often taken to be a
fruit of Husserl's transcendental turn. But Husserl's full account of the
relation between concreta and things at *Ideas* I §§12–17 had already
been partially sketched out in the first edition of the *Investigations* in a
section (III §12) dropped from the second edition.

83 Cf. *LI* III §25, Shoemaker "Causal Properties" in Shoemaker 1984, 206–
33.

84 Good accounts of awareness of light are given by Meinong's student
Heider (1926, 1930) and O'Shaughnessy (1985).

85 *DR* §20, *Ideen* II, §15 (c)–(d). Cf. Michotte, A. 1982, *The Perception of
Causality*, London: Methuen. An influential analysis of perception
which succumbs to three Kantian temptations by introducing judgement, concepts and imagination into perception is Strawson 1974.

86 *DR*, Appendix 2, 341ff.; *LI* III §9 (first edition), *Ideen* II §15(d)f., §18(a).
Rang 1990, Chaps. II, IV–VI, presents a detailed analysis of Husserl's
account of causal properties. As Ingarden (1965, 48) points out, Husserl's
account in *Ideen* II of the role of conditional properties brings him dangerously close to critical realism.

87 Husserl's account of the primacy of extent and his "new" account of
the distinction between secondary and primary qualities are given in
Ideen II, §§12–15(b). At *DR*, Appendix 3 Husserl appears to give what I
take to be the right account of the relation between quality and extent
moments, although he does not note that this requires a distinction
between two types of dependence. Cf. *DR* §49.

88 Dretske 1969, 60–61. Cf. Mulligan 1995.

89 On dependence, see Kit Fine's contribution to this volume. On the relations between external and internal relations see Mulligan 1991 and 1993.

90 Becker 1923 provides a clear account of the different spaces distinguished by Husserl and their relation to physical space, drawing on
materials now published in *DR*, and *Ideen* II.

91 Cf. "[T]he dependence [Abhängigkeit] of qualitative distance on the
founding qualities . . . is univocally determined by the lowest specific
differences of the latter and hence determined as a lowest difference – in
contrast to mere functional dependence" (*LI* III §10).

92 On the "inner belonging together of perceptual shadowings and things,"
cf. *LI* VI §14b. Similarly, certain emotions fit or are appropriate to certain objects, according to Brentano and many of his heirs.

93 Husserl mentions but does not study in detail the internal relations in colour space (*LI* III §9); on visual fields, see *LI* III §13, V 15 b, and *DR* passim. On Meinong and Wittgenstein on internal relations in colour and other spaces, see Mulligan 1991. A thorough Gestaltist description of one type of internal relation in perception is Goldmeier 1972.

94 On disjunctivist accounts of perception, see Hinton 1973, Snowdon 1981, 1990, McDowell 1982, 1986, Child 1992. McDowell generalises the account beyond the perceptual case.

95 Reiner 1931, 11.

96 Prolegomena §51; cf. "We have . . . no right to assume from the outset that the objects of outer perception really and truly exist as they seem to us to be" (Appendix 2 to *LI* VI).

97 Cf. Prolegomena §§47, 50, 36.

98 Husserl 1979 (340, 341, 336) throws some light on our passage. Husserl here distinguishes between actual properties of a mental state and merely possible relative determinations and sketches the role of suppositions in specifications of semantic connections.

99 The employment of such a distinction between separable ingredients and inseparable aspects in the formulation of disjunctivism is due to William Child 1994.

100 Cf. Leyendecker 1913 §§8–9.

101 Cf. *LI* IV §11, V §§35–36, §§38–40.

102 Husserl describes the view that perceptual content is "object-dependent" in the following passage: "If one makes the reality of a perceived object part of the notion of perception, then outer perception is not, in this strict sense [the sense in which internal perception is perception] perception at all" (Appendix 2 to *LI* VI). For a weak notion of object-dependent content, based on a careful reading of Frege, see Künne 1992; on this see Mulligan and Smith 1986. For a very strong notion thereof see Mulligan and Smith 1986a. The type of object-dependence employed by Evans and McDowell stands between these two extremes.

103 Husserl is an "ideal" verificationist. For a judgement to have a truth-value is for it to be verifiable, but many true judgements are unverified (*LI* VI §39). But in a little noticed passage he asserts that although the Law of Excluded Middle holds unreservedly for all temporal entities "the exclusion of predicates in an *ideal* sphere (e.g., the sphere of meanings, of numbers etc. [and, we may add, states of affairs (cf. *LI* VI §30)]) is by no means obvious, but must be demonstrated afresh in each such sphere, or set up as an axiom" (*LI* VI §30).

104 For a good defence of non-propositional perceptual justification, see Kelley 1986.

105 *LI* VI §§16–29. Cf Russell 1959, Chap. 5.

106 On the correlation between all parts of perceptual content and all parts of the sense of a sentence, see *LI* VI §25, §40.

107 *LI* VI §§30–35. The distinctions between primary and secondary epistemic seeing of Jackson (1977, Chap. 7) and Dretske (1969, 78, 140, 153, 179) clearly lend themselves to redescription in terms of the distinction between optimal and less than optimal perceptual justification.

108 On internal relations between perceptions and assertions, cf. *LI* VI §4, §7. Verification relations are ideal (*LI* VI §24). On the logical connection between assertion and confirmation, cf. *LI* I §9, Prolegomena §51. Notice that wherever there is *Evidenz*, assertoric *Evidenz* – which does not guarantee the veridicality of the information I receive – or apodeictic *Evidenz* – which never concerns the real world – the mode of articulation of the relevant information is that of fit or conflict among parts of a whole. The distinction between an element of identification and an element of predication which is characteristic of the type of articulation of propositions is entirely foreign to it.

109 In Husserl's early accounts of appearance, these are conceived of as being in the first instance complex mental episodes. In *DR* and later, as he tends more and more to use the terminology of "pictures," Husserl comes to conceive of them as universals. This ontological question has, arguably, some important consequences for the way appearances constrain the veridicality of perception. On appearances as universals, see O'Shaughnessy 1990.

110 As noted in n. 10, Husserl talks mainly of visual perception rather than of seeing. It would be in the spirit of his account to say that the punctual achievement reported by "see" is precisely that of integrating a variety of complex perceptual activities.

111 Cf. Leyendecker 1980, 122, and, on the black point which "is" a fly, 110. The problem was discussed later by Blanshard, Austin, and Castañeda, among others.

112 *Ideas* I §150.

113 Cf. *Ideas* II §18(b) and Rang's (1990, 282f.) detailed discussion. Another tack, compatible with what Husserl says: colours are genuine mind-independent monadic properties but as a matter of fact they are not exemplified in our world. I owe this suggestion to Barry Maund.

114 Cf. Husserl Hua XIII, 46–70; Husserl's views on this matter are well developed in Stein, 1980.

115 Cf. *LI* VI §§1–6, IV §3, and Mulligan and Smith 1986. Husserl's changes of mind about the relation between indexically based and indexical-free thought seem to have been prompted by reflection on the difficulties posed by twin-earth fantasies for mentalist and Platonist accounts of

meaning. Cf. Husserl Hua XXVI, Beilage XIX. This led him to the view that all assertions about temporal items are indexical, cf. Preface to the second edition of *LI*. D. W. Smith 1989 is an analysis of acquaintance informed by Husserlian principles.

116 Perception does all the work in Husserl's early account of abstraction. Only later did phenomenologists come to see the importance of fully automatised patterns of action in the acquisition of concepts.

117 One example among many: Husserl's use of supposition or make-believe assertion and make-believe designation in his account of empty names and negative existential sentences at Husserl 1979, 335ff; cf. Evans 1982, Chap. 7, and *EU* §73. On Husserl's analysis of judgement, cf. Mulligan 1989, Mulligan 1989a; on his account of imagination cf. Mulligan 1995a.

6 Transcendental idealism

"Only those who misunderstand the most profound sense of the intentional method or of the transcendental reduction or even of both, may want to separate phenomenology from transcendental idealism" (*CM*, p. 119).

Edmund Husserl is generally considered to be one of the greatest German philosophers of the twentieth century. Even though the influence of his works has waned somewhat on the European continent, his star is rising in the Anglo-Saxon world. Analytic philosophy has assimilated Husserl as a fellow-contributor to the research programme of a theory of meaning. In particular, Husserl's concept of *noema* is often regarded as a richer and generalized alternative to the Fregean notion of *Sinn*.

How should one evaluate Husserl's place in the history of modern philosophy? Seen from an analytical perspective, Husserl may appear to be a transitional thinker, well ahead of his time, who anticipated the linguistic turn. Many passages from his works might be quoted to substantiate this interpretation. Husserl claims, for instance, that "all real unities are unities of sense."[1] Couldn't we take this as an early expression of the post-positivist contention that the real world is revealed to us only through theoretical networks or "versions," so that all perception is theory-laden?[2] Elsewhere, Husserl says that an object should be defined as a pure identical X of many possible predications.[3] Is this not an anticipation of the doctrine from possible-world semantics that individuals have a transworld identity because they are referred to by means of rigid designators?[4] The analytical assimilation of Husserl's philosophy does not seem to be too difficult, if only one knows which doctrines one has to look for in his often obscure writings.

There are, however, philosophers in the English-speaking world

239

who have a different opinion about Husserl's place in history. Husserl often stresses his affinity to Descartes. Husserlian *epoché* is akin to Cartesian doubt, and transcendental idealism is presented as a radicalization of Descartes's foundationalism. This seems to justify the view, endorsed by Richard Rorty in *Philosophy and the Mirror of Nature*, that Husserl was solidly anchored within the tradition of modern Cartesian and Kantian epistemology, a tradition which the linguistic turn and post-positivistic philosophy of science were meant to overcome.[5]

It may be objected to this latter, traditionalist interpretation that it is unfair to Husserl, because the most fertile and exciting ingredients of his philosophy are thereby obscured. Is it not typical for transitional thinkers that they express new and even revolutionary ideas in a misleadingly traditional terminology? Should we not try to disentangle the philosophically valid core of Husserl's thought from the old and worn-out clothes, and to develop it further? The traditionalist interpretation of Husserl's philosophy is unjustified, it may be argued, because one should measure a philosopher's place in history by the number of future possibilities that his works contain. In order to reveal what Husserl really meant, a critical, teleological, and imaginative interpretation of his philosophy is needed.

But unfortunately, the scrupulous historian of philosophy will interject, "critical" interpretations run risks of their own. First, such interpretations often draw upon small selections of Husserl's works, which are easily misinterpreted because the context is neglected. Second, there is the danger of reading modern analytical doctrines into Husserl. In order to avoid these pitfalls, a critical interpretation must be based on a historically accurate reading of Husserl's *entire* oeuvre.

How one defines Husserl's place in history will depend to a large extent on how one regards his transcendental idealism. Transcendental idealism is Husserl's mature philosophical position. It was clearly stated for the first time in *Ideas* I (1913), although Husserl did not yet use the label "transcendental idealism."[6] Transcendental idealism is explicitly defended in Husserl's later works, such as *Formal and Transcendental Logic* (1929), *Cartesian Meditations* (1931), and *Crisis of the European Sciences* (1954).[7] In the *Postscript* to *Ideas* I (1930), Husserl says that on the issue of transcendental idealism he withdraws nothing.[8]

What is the relation between transcendental idealism and Hus serlian phenomenology? Many critical interpreters have argued that in order to obtain a philosophically valid conception of Husserlian phenomenology, it should be disentangled from transcendental idealism. They see transcendental idealism as an untenable dogmatic ontology, which is due to traditional influences on Husserl. This critical strategy presupposes, of course, that Husserl's phenomenological project makes sense apart from transcendental idealism.[9] But we might well be suspicious with regard to attempts to amputate transcendental idealism from Husserl's phenomenology, because Husserl himself rejects this very suggestion. "Only those who misunderstand the most profound sense of the intentional method or of the transcendental reduction or even of both, may want to separate phenomenology from transcendental idealism," Husserl says in § 42 of *Cartesian Meditations*.[10] This clear pronouncement creates a dilemma for philosophers who have invested in Husserlian phenomenology while rejecting idealist ontologies. It seems that they should either abandon the claim to practise *Husserlian* phenomenology or become transcendental idealists.

Husserl's contention that transcendental idealism has nothing to do with traditional idealist ontologies, such as Berkeley's, may seem to provide a way out of this dilemma.[11] One might claim that Husserl's ontological formulae are "potentially misleading characterizations of his position" and that Husserl is guilty of "excessive and misleading formulations of the new idealist standpoint."[12] Accordingly, it has been argued in recent years that Husserl's phenomenology is ontologically neutral, because, for instance, it says like functionalism that there is an ontologically neutral level of description of the ego and its activities,[13] or because it is essentially a science of meanings.[14]

There are many *prima facie* reasons for thinking that Husserl cannot be an idealist in the traditional ontological sense. First, traditional idealisms were a solution to skepticism's problem of the external world, which was implied by the representative theory of perception. Because Husserl rejects this theory, his idealism must mean something different.[15] Second, traditional idealist doctrines seem to be incompatible with the distinction between immanent contents and transcendent objects of intentional acts, which is basic to Husserl's phenomenology. Finally, ontological idealism is thought to be excluded by Husserl's notion of the life-world. It seems plausible to conclude that "Husserl's . . . statements about the relative and dependent nature of 'Reality' versus absolute consciousness . . . cannot be construed as denoting an 'existential' dependence," and that "they refer to a cognitive relationship, a relation of epistemological priority."[16]

In this essay I shall argue that Husserl's transcendental idealism is closer to traditional idealist positions such as Berkeley's or Kant's than is commonly thought. Husserl's idealism is not only epistemological. It is also an ontological and metaphysical position. In the *Postscript* to *Ideas* I, Husserl says that transcendental idealism is the outcome of his reflections on the epistemological "problem of the possibility of objective knowledge."[17] Most interpretations of Husserl's idealism go astray, I contend, because they have not attempted to reconstruct Husserl's problem of the possibility of objective knowledge and the way Husserl argued for idealism on the basis of this problem. In fact, reconstructing this problem and this argument amounts to reconstructing Husserl's development from *Logical Investigations* (1900/1901) to *Ideas* I (1913).

In order to show what was at stake for Husserl with regard to transcendental idealism, I shall first make some observations about naturalism, idealism, and the "natural attitude" (§§ 1–5). Both Husserl's early Platonic idealism and his later transcendental idealism were meant to replace the ontology of naturalism. In §§ 6–7, Husserl's basic argument for transcendental idealism in *Ideas* I will be analyzed, in order to show that it rests on a traditional philosophical assumption. After a short methodological interlude (§ 8), I shall attempt to reconstruct Husserl's development towards transcendental idealism (§§ 9–15). This reconstruction will enable us to determine the relation between Husserl's transcendental idealism and the idealist positions of Berkeley and Kant (§ 16). The remainder of my essay is critical. In §§ 17–20, I discuss the origin of the presuppositions of Husserl's argument for transcendental idealism and try to determine his place in the philosophical tradition. I conclude with some observations concerning Husserl's own view of his place in history and concerning his concept of the life-world (§ 21).[18]

I. IDEALISM VERSUS NATURALISM

Philosophical naturalism, Husserl says in *Philosophy as a Rigorous Science* (1911), reflects the notion of nature as a domain of spatiotemporal being governed by exact natural laws, a notion which was born during the scientific revolution in the seventeenth century. According to the naturalist, everything is nature in this sense, primarily physical nature. The mental is regarded at best as a dependent and secondary ephiphenomenon.[19] In the eyes of the naturalist, philosophy should follow the natural sciences, broadly conceived. It should become empirical psychology, for instance, or cognitive science, as we would say now.

Although Husserl never accepted a naturalist conception of philosophical method, he assumed a Humean variety of the naturalist *ontology* in early works such as *Philosophy of Arithmetic* (1891), an ontology he inherited from Brentano.[20] However, this ontology created difficulties in the philosophy of mathematics and logic, the initial field of Husserl's philosophical research. Husserl never questioned the traditional idea that all sciences, in the broad sense of the German "Wissenschaften," are *about* some *domain of objects*. What, then, are the objects of logic, for instance? Logic is not about physical reality. If the naturalist ontology is correct, one must conclude that logic is about mental phenomena. And indeed psychologism in logic was fashionable in Husserl's time. According to psychologism, the theoretical content of logical norms is derived from (empirical) psychology.[21]

In the *Logical Investigations*, Husserl rejected psychologism, because it could not account for the *a priori* validity of logical laws. If the laws of logic are empirical generalizations about human acts of thinking, one actual fallacy would falsify a logical law. In the first volume of the *Investigations*, the *Prolegomena to a Pure Logic*, Husserl expounded with great precision the flaws in the arguments for psychologism. He argued that psychologism implies relativism and skepticism in the strict sense of holding a theory which says that essential conceptual conditions for the possibility of theories in general do not obtain.[22] And later on, Husserl never tired of pointing out the cultural dangers of skepticism and relativism.

Because of Husserl's assumption about all sciences having a domain of objects, the rejection of psychologism implied the need for a new ontology. If the laws of logic hold independently of time and place, Husserl argues in the *Investigations*, logic has to be about objects which exist outside time and space. Inspired by Lotze, Herbart, and Bolzano, he came to believe that apart from spatiotemporal objects there must be "ideal" objects, the objects of the *priori sciences*.[23] And the doctrine that there are such objects is called idealism.[24] Without idealism, Husserl says, a consistent epistemology is impossible.[25] For without idealism, it would be impossible to account for the *a priori* character of logical laws, so that a pragmatically inconsistent skeptical doctrine (psychologism) would result.[26]

In the *Investigations*, Husserl holds that all ideal objects are "ideal species" of other objects, in last resort of real objects. The ideal meanings which are the object of apophantic logic, for instance, are said to be ideal species of mental acts of meaning.[27] Because Husserl claims that ideal species exist independently of their instances, and because species and instances are related as one to many, we might call the idealism of the *Investigations* "Platonic idealism," even though Husserl rejects Plato's doctrine that Ideas are more perfect than their instances.[28]

Husserl's Platonic idealism is very different from his later transcendental idealism. Transcendental idealism is concerned not with timeless ideal objects but with the relation of consciousness to the natural world. And yet, transcendental idealism is also opposed to naturalism. Whereas naturalism holds that consciousness is a subordinate reality which depends for its existence on certain physical structures, transcendental idealism contends that the entire natural world, including human minds, is nothing but an intentional structure of transcendental consciousness. According to transcendental idealism, the world ontologically depends on transcendental consciousness, which itself exists in absolute independence.[29] Husserl even uses the Cartesian definition of a substance, that something "nulla 're' indiget ad existendum," to characterize the independent existence of transcendental consciousness.[30] And he says that his phenomenological philosophy is "transcendental" in the sense that it rejects the "absolute" interpretation of the natural world endorsed by naturalism or scientific objectivism, and that it regards the existence of the world as the existence of a unity of meaning constituted by transcendental subjectivity.[31]

According to *Philosophy as a Rigorous Science*, there are two problems that shipwreck philosophical naturalism: (1) it is impossible to naturalize norms; (2) naturalist epistemology incurs a vicious circle.[32] It seems plausible to suppose that Husserl developed his transcendental idealism as a solution to these problems. But what precisely are these problems and what was Husserl's argument?

II. A PRIMACY OF THE NORMATIVE?

It has been suggested that the impossibility of naturalizing norms was the main motive which explains Husserl's transcendental turn and his transcendental idealism. The reason Husserl adduced in the *Investigations* for the impossibility of naturalizing norms was that the theoretical content of the norms of logic cannot derive from empirical sciences of nature in the broad sense. In order to account for the *a priori* validity of the laws of logic, we must assume that logic is a "pure" science about timeless objects. This is why Husserl adopted a Platonist ontology of "ideal species." However, it has been argued, this Platonism was not a radical substitute for naturalism at all. It merely supplemented the naturalist ontology with a Platonist superstructure. In the *Investigations*, Husserl still endorsed the naturalist convictions that consciousness is a part of nature, and that mental events may be causally explained.[33]

The resulting naturalist-Platonist ontology was inconsistent, so the interpretation continues, for Husserl assumed in the *Investigations* that consciousness simultaneously stands under the obligation of following norms and is causally determined. This is impossible, because *ought* implies *can*. In other words, Husserl's naturalism in the *Investigations* raised the traditional problem of freedom and determinism. Between 1900 and 1913, Husserl would have realized that, in order to solve this problem, he would have had to overcome naturalism or positivism in a more radical way: he would have had to argue that consciousness, to the extent that it is free, is not part of the causal natural world.[34] And this is a central thesis of transcendental idealism. In short, one should acknowledge a primacy of problems concerning the normative in reconstructing the genesis of transcendental idealism.[35]

It may seem that this genetic reconstruction of Husserl's transcendental idealism is confirmed by the passage in the *Postscript* where Husserl claims that there is a *motivating path* from the problem of the possibility of objective knowledge to transcendental idealism.[36] What is the relation between problems concerning normativity and this problem of the possibility of objective knowledge? In the introduction to the *Prolegomena*, Husserl says that the question concerning the theoretical foundations of logic partly coincides with the crucial question of epistemology, the question of *how objective knowledge is possible*.[37] Knowledge is "objective" in Husserl's sense if it is true of objects. One of the conditions for being objective is that propositional knowledge should satisfy the laws of logic, because a contradiction cannot be true. Therefore, the laws of logic may be called "conditions for the possibility of objective knowledge." In fact, they are ideal or *a priori* conditions for the possibility of objective knowledge.[38] Consequently, in order to solve the problem of how objective knowledge is possible, Husserl had to explain how the laws of logic can be *a priori* valid. This required his Platonist idealism, as we have seen. Furthermore, in order to explain how we may be free to follow or not to follow the norms of logic, he had to argue that consciousness exists outside the deterministic natural world, that is, he had to adopt transcendental idealism. According to these interpretations, then, both Husserl's Platonic idealism and his later transcendental idealism should be seen as a solution to problems of normativity, problems which in part coincide with the epistemological problem of the possibility of objective knowledge.

It is the merit of these interpretations that they stress the ontological import of Husserl's transcendental philosophy. But as a reconstruction of the genesis of Husserl's transcendental idealism they will not do, for at least three reasons. First, although one should acknowledge that transcendental idealism in a sense solved the problem of freedom and determinism,[39] Husserl solved this problem in yet another way, by incorporating freedom and motivation into the natural world.[40] Accordingly, he did not need transcendental idealism in order to solve it. Second, the genetic reconstruction of transcendental idealism as a solution to the problem of freedom and determinism is historically inadequate. It does not reflect Husserl's arguments for transcendental idealism as we find them in his manuscripts and publications between 1900 and 1913, notably from 1903, 1906–1907, 1911, and 1913.[41] Finally, the authority of the passage in the *Postscript* does not support these reconstructions either, for there is yet another epistemological problem of the possibility of objective knowledge, apart from the problem of the *Prolegomena*, which might explain transcendental idealism. This other problem is concerned not with logic or freedom but with experience. It is this problem which Husserl refers to in *Philosophy as a Rigorous Science* and in many other texts written between 1900 and 1913. I shall argue that Husserl developed transcendental idealism as a solution to this second epistemological problem, the problem of the possibility of objective experience.[42]

III. THE EPISTEMOLOGICAL PROBLEM OF THE POSSIBILITY OF OBJECTIVE EXPERIENCE

Naturalism breaks down, Husserl argued in *Philosophy as a Rigorous Science*, because of two problems: (1) it is impossible to naturalize norms, and (2) naturalistic epistemology incurs a vicious circle. Having disposed of the claim that (1) is important for the genesis of transcendental idealism, I now turn to (2). That (2) is relevant for Husserl's transcendental turn is pretty clear in the text of *Philosophy as a Rigorous Science*. For another formulation of (2) is that it is impossible to naturalize consciousness.[43] But why is it impossible to naturalize consciousness and why does naturalistic epistemology incur a circle?

According to Husserl, the empirical sciences of nature, such as physics and psychology, presuppose that nature exists in itself and that it may be known on the basis of experience. Furthermore, they assume that experience, like the mental in general, is a natural phenomenon which depends for its existence on specific physical structures. All psychological determinations are *eo ipso* psychophysical, in the sense that they presuppose physical nature, Husserl stresses.[44] It follows that if there are arguments to the effect that physics cannot be epistemology, psychology cannot be epistemology either.[45] But what are these arguments?

According to Husserl, all sciences of nature are naive as far as experience is concerned, even though experience is their evidential basis and even though they may be critical about their own experimental methods and techniques. Apart from the critique of particular experiences common in scientific research, Husserl argues, there is yet another and very different kind of critique of experience (*Erfahrungskritik*), which questions experience as a whole together with all research based on experience.[46] Husserl expresses this second kind of critical questions concerning experience as follows:

How is it possible that experience as a form of consciousness gives or hits an object; how is it possible that experiences mutually confirm or correct each other, instead of merely subjectively cancelling or reinforcing each other; how can a play of empirico-logical consciousness yield something objectively valid, that is, valid for things which exist in themselves; . . . how should natural science become intelligible in these respects, to the extent that in each of its moves it posits and claims to know nature as it is in itself – as being in itself over against the subjective stream of consciousness – all this becomes an enigma as soon as we seriously reflect on it.[47]

According to Husserl, these questions are the domain of epistemology. And he seems to argue that because the natural sciences, including psychology, *assume* that experience of natural objects which exist in themselves is possible, epistemology cannot be part of natural science, for the reason that it purports to answer critical questions concerning this very possibility. It has to be *first philosophy* in the sense that it does not presuppose any natural knowledge. Naturalist epistemology would incur a vicious circle, for it assumes the possibility of objectively valid knowledge, the very possibility which epistemology questions and investigates.[48] As a consequence, if epistemology analyses experience, it cannot analyze experience as a natural datum in the world. This is why consciousness cannot be naturalized, at least to the extent that it is the subject matter of epistemology. Epistemology is a presuppositionless science, which studies consciousness in some nonnatural sense.

In many papers and lectures written between the *Investigations* and *Ideas* I, Husserl is preoccupied with epistemology conceived of as a discipline which has to solve the problem of how experience can be objectively valid or of how experience can be concerned with the world as it is in itself.[49] But these texts are not very clear to the uninitiated reader. Why is a naturalist cognitive science not able to investigate the "conditions of the possibility of objective experience"? Shouldn't one identify these conditions with our factual cognitive apparatus, which is studied by psychophysics or cognitive science? And what precisely is the special philosophical critique of experience, which justifies Husserl's non-natural conception of consciousness? Finally, what motivates such a philosophical critique?

I shall argue in §§ 9–11 herein that the critique of experience Husserl refers to, and also his concomitant conceptions of epistemology and metaphysics, are based on the theory of perception he held in the *Investigations* and in his later work. I shall contend that Husserl's very problems concerning experience cannot be understood unless one reconstructs them on the basis of this theory of perception. But before doing so, I want briefly to go into Husserl's argument for transcendental idealism in *Ideas* I. For in *Ideas* I, Husserl claims that a theory-free descriptive analysis of perception, an analysis performed entirely on the level of common sense, will convert us to transcendental idealism. If he is able to substantiate this claim, we should not look for theoretical presuppositions of his epistemological problem of experience, nor of his idealist solution to this problem.

IV. TRANSCENDENTAL IDEALISM AS A REVERSAL OF OUR NATURAL ONTOLOGY

Husserl gives his main argument for transcendental idealism in the second part of *Ideas* I, which has the ponderous title "Fundamental Phenomenological Meditation." He starts this Fundamental Meditation with a description of what he calls the "natural attitude." The natural attitude is the sum of implicit natural convictions about ourselves and the world we all have in our daily life (*Ideas* I, §§ 27–29). These convictions, made explicit, might be called our natural or common-sense ontology. Husserl then claims that this natural attitude is in fact a "thesis" that may be subjected to methodical doubt or *epoché* (§§ 30–32). The central question of the *Fundamental Meditation* is what exactly will remain if the whole natural world, including us as human beings, is "bracketed" by the *epoché* (§ 33).[50] Husserl argues that what remains is transcendental consciousness, with the natural world as its intentional correlate (§§ 33–49).

I shall call this argument Husserl's "basic argument for transcendental idealism." It consists of two parts. In the preliminary §§ 33–38, Husserl argues that our stream of consciousness is a unity which is exclusively determined by the essences of its own conscious experiences (*Erlebnisse*).[51] In its central part, which runs from § 39 to § 49, Husserl tries to prove transcendental idealism by means of a descriptive analysis of the differences between outer and inner perception.

Husserl pretends that his description of the natural attitude in §§ 27–29 is entirely pretheoretical.[52] In the natural attitude, he says, we are convinced that we live in a real world which is extended in space and time. We see ourselves as living beings of some kind. We distinguish between material nature and consciousness, and we think that the latter to some extent depends on the former. As long as we are awake, the world is present to us, and we belong to it.

In § 50 of *Ideas* I, looking back on his argument for transcendental idealism, Husserl describes transcendental idealism as a "reversal" of our natural ontology.[53] Whereas according to the common-sense ontology minds are ontologically dependent on physical nature, transcendental idealism claims that nature is nothing but an intentional correlate of consciousness and that it depends on consciousness for its existence, whereas consciousness is an absolutely independent entity.[54] However, this ontological "reversal" or revolution is not a simple inversion of terms, as if transcendental idealism would claim that the physical depends on the mental in the psychological sense. Husserl's argument for transcendental idealism, or the transcendental reduction, as it may also be called, purports to show that consciousness, if interpreted properly, is an absolute existent in which the whole world, including psychological consciousness, is constituted. Thus, Husserl's ontological reversal implies a drastic reinterpretation of the terms of the original relation. Whereas this original relation was concerned with the mental and the physical, the new, transcendental relation is a relation of ontological dependence between transcendental consciousness, which exists in absolute independence, and the whole natural world, including human minds, which exists as an ontologically dependent intentional correlate of transcendental consciousness (§§ 49–55).

This implies in its turn that Husserl's transcendental standpoint in fact preserves the ontology of the natural attitude, although it initially seemed to eliminate this common-sense ontology. For transcendental idealism does not deny that the mental in the psychological sense depends on the physical. What it claims is that the whole natural world, including minds which depend on bodies, is nothing but an intentional correlate of transcendental consciousness. The thesis of the natural world, having been "bracketed" at first, is, in the final analysis, revealed as a constitutional achievement of transcendental consciousness. The natural ontology is "aufgehoben" in transcendental idealism, one might say in a Hegelian vein. If the new ontology of transcendental idealism is meant to be an alternative to another ontology, this other ontology is not the common-sense ontology of the natural attitude but the ontology of naturalism. This is what Husserl means where he writes:

The real world is not "re-interpreted" or even denied, but an absurd interpretation of it, that is, an interpretation which contradicts the proper sense of reality as it is rendered self-evident, is removed. This interpretation is the product of a philosophical hypostatization of the world, which is completely alien to the natural view of the world.[55]

In short, transcendental idealism is a reversal, but not an elimination of the natural attitude. What it eliminates or rejects is the ontology of philosophical naturalism. One may wonder, however, whether naturalism and the natural attitude are not closely related. But before going into this question, a brief digression is needed.

Husserl says in the passage quoted that transcendental idealism is not an interpretation of the real world, but that it only removes an interpretation, to wit the interpretation of naturalism. This denial that it is an interpretation may be taken to support the view that the transcendental reduction is not an ontological revolution at all, but merely a methodological device: it would only shift our attention away from our interest in worldly affairs to the way in which worldly phenomena are given to consciousness. Now transcendental phenomenology surely is a method of describing the ways in which the objects of consciousness are "constituted," but, as I shall argue, this transcendental method is pointless as an exclusive method in epistemology and ontology, unless the ontology of transcendental idealism is correct. This is why Husserl says in § 51 of *Ideas* I that his radical meditation leads to the insight (*zur Erkenntnis durchzudringen*) that *there is* a field of pure consciousness which is not part (*Bestandstück*) of nature, whereas nature is possible only as an intentional unity constituted by pure consciousness, and that the phenomenological (or transcendental) reduction is *not* a pure shift of attention.[56]

What Husserl really means by denying that transcendental idealism is an interpretation of the real world is this: it is not an interpretation because, according to § 24 of *Ideas* I, it is possible to express the data of original intuition exactly as they are, without any theoretical admixture. Phenomenology aims at being such a theory-free descriptive discipline. What Husserl had in common with positivism, then, is the belief in a theory-free observation language.[57] And if transcendental idealism is the result of a theory-free descriptive analysis of the contrast between inner and outer perception, as Husserl claims in the Fundamental Meditation, it is itself not a theory about or an interpretation of the existence of the world and of consciousness: it simply is the true ontological account.

There are, of course, reasons independent of Husserl to doubt this descriptivist claim, and I shall come back to Husserl's descriptivist ideology in §8 following. But there are also reasons internal to Husserl's thought to doubt it, reasons that are concerned with the relation between naturalism and the natural attitude, and that may lead to Heideggerian "destruction" or "deconstruction" of Husserl's text.

V. NATURALISM AND THE NATURAL ATTITUDE

What exactly is the relation between naturalism on the one hand and the natural attitude, as Husserl analyses it, on the other hand? In the passage from §55 of *Ideas* I quoted in the previous section, Husserl says that the naturalist interpretation of reality which is removed by transcendental idealism is completely alien (*durchaus fremd*) to the natural attitude. But this is surprising. According to the common-sense ontology of the natural attitude, we are human beings belonging to the world, and our mental capacities depend on our bodies. We know, for instance, that if we drink too much we get confused in our minds. Moreover, we would never question the fact that the world exists independently of minds, and that it will continue to exist even when humans have perished. What, then, is the difference between the natural ontology and philosophical naturalism on this point? Naturalism seems to express the very same beliefs we all hold in the natural attitude.

Husserl would reply that, in spite of this correspondence, there is an essential distinction between naturalism and the natural attitude. As he says in the passage I quoted, naturalism is a philosophical absolutizing (*philosophischen Verabsolutierung*) of the natural world. And the text continues to say that the natural attitude itself can never become absurd, because it *simply lives* the general thesis of the natural attitude (*sie lebt naiv im Vollzug der . . . Generalthesis*). Absurdities arise only if one philosophizes.[58] What Husserl means is that philosophical naturalism makes the natural world into an absolute, and claims that the natural world is all there is, whereas in the natural attitude we do not make such claims. Transcendental idealism, on the other hand, makes the opposite claim that the natural world is relative to transcendental consciousness.[59] According to Husserl, then, the relation between the natural ontology and philosophical naturalism is that naturalism says that the natural ontology is a complete ontology, whereas transcendental idealism holds that it is incomplete.

However, one might adopt another and more critical explanation of the surprising resemblance between philosophical naturalism and Husserl's "natural attitude." Should one not conclude from this resemblance that Husserl's descriptive analysis of the natural attitude is not theory-free at all, and that it is contaminated by the very naturalist ontology which Husserl wanted to overcome? If so, even his transcendental idealism would be informed by philosophical naturalism. For, as we saw, transcendental idealism is a reversal of the common-sense ontology as Husserl analyses it, and the common-sense ontology is in a sense preserved in transcendental idealism. And if one sticks to Husserl's idea that a theory-free description of the common-sense world is possible, and that philosophical naturalism is alien to common sense, one might conclude that Husserl's philosophy as a whole persists in the self-alienation of philosophical naturalism. Consequently, if one wants to overcome naturalism, one has to take the philosophical project of an articulation of the natural attitude much more seriously than Husserl did. This is the point, or at least one of the points, of Heidegger's hermeneutics of *Dasein* in *Being and Time*. Heidegger would claim that, if one has articulated the natural attitude by an existential analysis of our being-in-the-world, revealing existential characteristics (*Existenziale*) such as *Befindlichkeit, Verstehen, Verfallen, Sorge*, and *Sein zum Tode*, which are not contaminated by the scientific view of the world, one will conclude that there is no natural motivation left for Husserl's turn towards transcendental idealism, and that the epistemological problem of experience Husserl wanted to solve by this transcendental turn is nothing but a symptom of *Verfall*.[60] In short, if one takes seriously Husserl's wish to overcome philosophical naturalism, one may end up with Heidegger's critique of Husserl.

In this essay, I shall be simultaneously more and less radical than

Heidegger's critique. Less radical because I shall not engage in hermeneutics of our being-in-the-world. More radical because I shall argue that, even in Husserl's descriptive analysis of the natural attitude and of the contrast between inner and outer perception, there is no reason for the transcendental turn to idealism. That is, I shall contend that Husserl's argument for transcendental idealism in the Fundamental Phenomenological Meditation is defective, because it rests on a hidden premise that cannot be justified by his descriptive analysis. And I shall indirectly corroborate the Heideggerian diagnosis of traditional epistemology by arguing, in § 19 below, that this hidden premise in fact is a sedimentation of philosophical doctrines born during the scientific revolution.

VI. HUSSERL'S ARGUMENT FOR TRANSCENDENTAL IDEALISM IN *IDEAS* I

In the central part of his basic argument for transcendental idealism, which covers §§ 39–49 of the Fundamental Phenomenological Meditation in *Ideas* I, Husserl discusses the relation between consciousness and the material world. Starting from the natural attitude, he claims that a pre-theoretical descriptive analysis of the ways in which consciousness and material things are "originally given" to us in reflection and perception, respectively, will necessitate the "reversal" of the natural attitude which yields transcendental idealism (cf. § 39). In this way, Husserl purports to show that the "bracketing" of the natural attitude by the phenomenological *epoché* leaves us with a "residuum" of this methodological doubt: transcendental consciousness together with the natural world as its intentional correlate. This residue is the absolute domain for the descriptive investigations of transcendental phenomenology.[61]

The strategy of Husserl's basic argument may seem to support the common interpretation that transcendental idealism is merely an epistemological, and not an ontological doctrine. For how can a descriptive analysis of inner and outer perception yield ontological results, rather than only epistemological conclusions? But this interpretation overlooks an important methodological principle which informs the argument of the Fundamental Meditation, a principle which Husserl derived from British Empiricism. I am referring to the idea that in order to elucidate the meaning of an elementary word, we have to perceive its referent. Husserl seems to assume that we may read off the meaning of a word from its referent.[62] In *Ideas* I, he enlarges the concept of meaning or sense, and applies the empiricist principle to the *ontological sense* of beings. In other words, he analyses the perceptual givenness of material things and of mental experiences (*Erlebnisse*) in order to determine *the sense in which we should say that they exist*.[63] Clearly, then, the apparent gap between Husserl's epistemological analyses of outer and inner perception and his ontological conclusions is bridged by Husserl's version of the empiricist principle of meaning-analysis.

According to Husserl, there is a crucial difference between the way our own consciousness is given to us in reflection, or in immanent perception, as he calls it, and the way in which we perceive a material thing. If we feel pain, for instance, the pain is not more than we feel at a given moment. As long as we abstain from what Husserl calls "transcending apperceptions" of the pain, that is, as long as we do not interpret the pain as pain in some part of our body, but simply feel it, there is no possible difference between the appearance and the reality of the pain: it is exactly what we feel it to be. From this analysis, Husserl concludes that what is given in such an immanent perception must really exist. It is "absolutely given," as he says. He generalizes this conclusion to all immanent perceptions of our own consciousness (§§ 38, 42, 44, 46).

What Husserl means will become clearer if we compare it with the way material things are given in outer perception, such as vision. Material things are always seen from a certain perspective. We see, for instance, the front of a house, and not its sides, back, or roof. The thing is always more than is perceptually given to us at one particular moment. Furthermore, even the perceived aspect of a thing may appear in many different ways, depending on the angle under which it is seen, and on perceptual conditions such as distance, lighting, and the like. A white house may appear red at sunset, its contours may become fuzzy in rain or fog, and a round object may seem elliptical. Husserl tries to capture these complex characteristics of outer perception by saying that a material thing is always perceived in "adumbrations" (*Abschattungen*), such as colour- or space-adumbrations. Because of this adumbrative character of outer perception, he says, outer perception is "presumptive." Later perceptions may show that the existential claim which seemed to be justified by earlier perceptions is, in fact, wrong. From a distance, we thought that a tower was round, but having come nearer, we now see that it is square. Husserl concludes that outer perception must *always* remain presumptive, because it is impossible to have all possible adumbrations of a thing. In his view, the presumption implicitly contained in perceptual acts, that something exists and is a such and such, is never certain in the case of outer perception (§§ 42, 44, 46).

From these considerations, which are akin to the analyses of perception by analytical authors such as Russell, Ayer, Warnock, or Price, Husserl draws far-reaching conclusions: (1) the existence of our own consciousness is indubitably certain as long as we immanently perceive it; (2) the existence of the material world is essentially doubtful or "phenomenal," even though we may have no practical grounds to doubt it. The argument culminates in § 49 of the Fundamental Meditation, where Husserl argues that (3) consciousness may exist even though there is no material world, and that (4) the existence of the material world depends on consciousness. The last two conclusions, if taken together and interpreted properly, form the doctrine of transcendental idealism. Let us, therefore, have a closer look at Husserl's argument in § 49.

VII. THE THOUGHT-EXPERIMENT OF THE DESTRUCTION OF THE WORLD

Husserl's basic argument for transcendental idealism may be criticized on many grounds. For instance, Husserl says in § 39 of *Ideas* I that according to the natural attitude, consciousness is in two ways related to the material world: it depends on its body and it perceives the world. But in his basic argument, Husserl analyzes the perception of an extended thing only, and omits to discuss the embodiment of consciousness. And yet the conclusion of the argument concerns the relation between consciousness and the world in general. Therefore, one might accuse Husserl of implicitly assuming that the relation between consciousness and its body is of the same kind as the perceptual relation between consciousness and a perceived object, and that our body is nothing but a physical object among others.[64] Also, one might wonder what justifies the jump from the thesis that the existential claim inherent in a local outer perception may be presumptive and fallible, to the conclusion that this is also true for the global thesis that there is a physical world.

But it is still too early to criticize Husserl, and it is improbable that he overlooked these possible objections, if only because he extensively analyzed the perceptual role of the body in his lectures of 1907.[65] Instead of taking the objections as a refutation of Husserl's argument, one should use the flaws in the argument as clues for the discovery of deeper suppositions, which, if stated explicitly, would make Husserl's argument for transcendental idealism logically valid. And, in fact, there is such a presupposition, which I shall call the principle of immanence. The principle of immanence explains many steps in the argument which would be invalid without it. Its role is particularly obvious in § 49 of *Ideas* I.

In § 49, Husserl performs a thought-experiment, the experiment of the destruction of the world. The experiment purports to show that (my) consciousness essentially might exist without a material world, so that it is a substance in the Cartesian sense that it *nulla 're' indiget ad existendum*. Husserl starts with the notion that all objects of outer perception are given in adumbrations. This is also true of the world as a whole, including my body. One might say that with each type of material object there correspond specific types of series of adumbrations, depending on the perspectives we take. When, for example, we walk around a house, the different adumbrations of the house succeed each other in an ordered manner. If these ordered sequences of adumbrations are disturbed or broken, we suffer a perceptual illusion or even a hallucination.

Now Husserl claims that an eidetic variation of outer perception admits of the following possibility.[66] We may imagine that the series of adumbrations in outer perception become totally chaotic. If so, we cease to perceive material things, and our perceptual world is "destroyed." But because our consciousness is not given in adumbrations, at least according to Husserl,[67] consciousness survives such a destruction of the world. Husserl concludes that consciousness may exist without anything else, whereas the existence of the world depends on specific and contingent series of adumbrations in (my) consciousness.[68]

This inference shows that Husserl presupposes the principle of immanence. From the possibility that only a chaotic stream of adumbrations is given to consciousness, he concludes that in this case there is nothing present apart from consciousness, so that conscious-ness may exist entirely on its own. Obviously, he assumes that adumbrations exist *in* consciousness and that they are real parts of the stream of conscious experiences. Otherwise he should have in-ferred from the thought-experiment of the destruction of the world that in this case consciousness would exist *together with a chaotic stream of adumbrations*. But this conclusion would fall far short of showing that consciousness might exist on its own, or that it is ontologically independent.

And indeed Husserl argues in *Ideas* I that adumbrations are "really immanent" in consciousness. In the analysis of outer percep-tion, he distinguishes between what is "really immanent" (*reell im-manent*) in consciousness in the sense that it is part of the stream of experiences on the one hand, and what belongs to the intentional object and its (noematic) manifestations on the other hand (the latter is both "intentionally immanent" and "really transcendent"). Con-trarily to what one would expect, he puts adumbrations on the former side of the divide and identifies them with sensations (*Empfindungen*) in consciousness. In contradistinction to Brentano, Husserl holds that sensations are non-intentional mental experi-ences, such as pain. Adumbrations, then, are really immanent in consciousness. This implies that according to Husserl adumbrations of shape or of colour are not spatially extended, because nothing in the stream of consciousness can be spatially extended.[69] Since adum-brations may be considered as the primary data of outer perception, as the "sensual core," so to say, Husserl claims, in fact, that the primary data of outer perception are really immanent in conscious-ness.[70] This is what I call the principle of immanence. In Husserl's case, the principle takes the special form of an identification of adumbrations with sensations in consciousness.

This identification, and the concomitant thesis that adumbrations are really immanent and not spatial, is a presupposition of Husserl's argument which does not at all follow from a theory-free analysis of outer perception. Such a pre-theoretical description does perhaps justify a notion of adumbration. One might call the momentary appearance of something, as it is determined by various perceptual conditions such as perspective, distance, lighting and the like, an "adumbration." But adumbrations of spatial objects in this sense are spatial themselves. They may be painted or photographed, as Monet did in his famous series of paintings of Rouen Cathedral. One might even claim that photographs are essentially of adumbrations. Accordingly, if a pre-theoretical analysis of perception justifies a notion of adumbration, it is not the notion Husserl needs in order to make his argument for transcendental idealism valid. The principle of immanence, we may conclude, is a theoretical assumption of Husserl's, and not a descriptive result. I shall argue that it is a sedimentation of the philosophical tradition which Husserl did not recognize as such (§ 19, below). As we shall see, the principle of immanence is an essential ingredient of the theory of perception Husserl defends in the *Logical Investigations* and his later works. And this theory explains the problems of experience Husserl refers to in *Philosophy as a Rigorous Science*.

VIII. WHY IS A GENETIC RECONSTRUCTION OF TRANSCENDENTAL IDEALISM NEEDED?

In his later works, Husserl tried to improve on the basic argument for transcendental idealism of *Ideas* I by sketching alternative routes to the transcendental reduction and to transcendental consciousness. Apart from the "Cartesian" way of *Ideas* I and *Cartesian Meditations*, he tried to reach transcendental consciousness by tracing the presuppositions of logic in *Formal and Transcendental Logic*, or by a teleological interpretation of the history of philosophy and a radicalization of phenomenological psychology in *Crisis*. But it did not help very much. Husserl's pupils were simply not convinced and refused to become transcendental idealists. And in fact, Husserl's arguments are not compelling indeed. One may object to the argument of *Ideas* I, § 49, for instance, that even if it shows that the perceptual world is destroyed if the series of adumbrations disintegrate, this says nothing about the world as it is in itself. Maybe the disintegration of the series of adumbrations is a symptom of the fact that my brain, as it is in itself, has been damaged, and that I shall die soon. Now Husserl tells us in §§ 40 and 52 of *Ideas* I that it is an absurdity to posit a world in itself "behind" the perceptual world, so that, if the perceptual world were destroyed, there would be no world at all. But again, his arguments are not convincing, and it is hard to make out his claim.

The interesting fact is, however, that Husserl was firmly convinced of his transcendental idealism, in spite of the weaknesses of his arguments. This is at least what we are told by Roman Ingarden, who, after a visit to Husserl in 1927, complains:

As far as the turn to idealism was concerned, it seemed that everything was firmly settled for Husserl. It was hardly possible to convince him that one could have doubts on this point. And again and again he declared that his "older pupils" (i.e., his pupils of the Göttingen period) misunderstood him and that a sense of idealism was attributed to him which was taken from the tradition and which was completely foreign to himself. But it was impossible to persuade Husserl to say to what extent Husserl's transcendental idealism was different from the other idealisms.[71]

Apparently, in Husserl's eyes his transcendental idealism *had* to be true, even though he did not succeed in proving it. This fact calls for an explanation, and, before making recourse to explanations of a psychological kind, one should wonder whether it is not possible rationally to reconstruct Husserl's argument for transcendental idealism, and in this way to explain why idealism seemed inevitable to Husserl.

There is still a second and more fundamental reason why Husserl's philosophy stands in need of a rational reconstruction, a reason which has to do with Husserl's conception of the discipline. In his early period, from the *Habilitationsschrift* on the concept of number (1887) to the first edition of the *Logical Investigations* (1900/01), Husserl shared Brentano's conviction that descriptive psychology had to be the fundamental philosophical discipline. Descriptive psychology is the foundation of normative disciplines such as ethics and of *a priori* disciplines such as mathematics and logic, because, Husserl assumed, the fundamental concepts of these disciplines are abstracted from mental phenomena, so that they can be elucidated by a description of these phenomena. Such an elucidation would also render the axioms of the *a priori* disciplines self-evident, because these axioms are conceptual truths.[72] Even though Husserl in part rejected this "psychologistic" doctrine on the origin of the concepts of mathematics and logic in the second part of the *Investigations*,[73] the conception of descriptive psychology or phenomenology as fundamental philosophy still informed this work.[74]

In 1903, Husserl rejected this conception.[75] He denied that epistemology, or the fundamental philosophical discipline, should be conceived of as descriptive psychology, even though it had to be phenomenology. This was a first step towards transcendental phenomenology and transcendental idealism. Between 1903 and 1913, Husserl's conception of phenomenology gradually deepened, until he reached his final conception in *Ideas* I, a conception which was further developed in his later works. But in spite of the many revisions of the idea of phenomenology between 1900 and Husserl's death, there is one element of the initial notion of phenomenology as descriptive psychology which is always maintained: that phenomenology as a fundamental philosophical discipline is a *description* of consciousness. The principle of principles stated in § 24 of *Ideas* I, which implies that a pre-theoretical description of phenomena is possible, was never really abandoned, not even in Husserl's later "genetic" phenomenology.

Even if such a theory-neutral description were possible in principle, which is of course denied by post-positivist philosophers of science, it may be shown that Husserl's claim to be theory-neutral often is mistaken. Heidegger would hold, for instance, that Husserl's description of the natural attitude is in fact an expression of the theory of naturalism and, in the final analysis, a specimen of the *Ontologie der Vorhandenheit*. Also, I have argued that Husserl's notion of a really immanent sensation and his identification of adumbrations with sensations (in their representing function) cannot be justified by a naive description of perceptual awareness. The point is that Husserl's descriptivist ideology frequently prevented him from explicitly discussing the philosophical problems and assumptions which inform his "descriptive" terminology. In other words, one of the reasons why Husserl's work is so exceedingly difficult and why a rational reconstruction is needed, is that his real problems rarely surface in the text at all, and that, if they do, often they do so inconspicuously in footnotes and appendices. I would contend, for instance, that Husserl's turn to transcendental idealism cannot be really understood, unless one reconstructs the problems which this turn was meant to solve on the basis of a repeated scrutiny of textual passages which, at first sight, seem to be casual and unimportant.

Many of these passages, concerned with the status of the world *an sich* and with the relation between mental and physical phenomena, occur in the *Logical Investigations*. And here, of course, is a special problem, because Husserl deleted or modified most of these passages in the second edition. They had been rendered obsolete by transcendental idealism. But by doing so, Husserl covered up the tracks of the genesis of this doctrine, which was born from tensions in the first edition. I do not think that it is possible for an English reader, who relies exclusively on the Findlay translation of the *Investigations*, which is based on the second edition, to understand fully Husserl's transcendental turn.

Pivotal to my rational reconstruction of transcendental idealism is what I have called the principle of immanence. In a first, "progressive" part of the reconstruction, I shall show how the principle of immanence leads to transcendental idealism (§§ 9–16). The second part of the reconstruction is "regressive": by tracing the origin of the principle of immanence itself, I try to determine Husserl's place in the history of modern philosophy (§§ 17–21).

IX. HUSSERL'S THEORY OF PERCEPTION IN THE *INVESTIGATIONS*

I shall argue in the present and the next section that the theory of perception which Husserl held in the *Investigations*, and which, with some minor modifications, he endorsed also in *Ideas* I, explains the epistemological problem of experience Husserl wanted to solve by means of his transcendental idealism. As we shall see, the principle of immanence is an essential ingredient of this theory of perception. According to the *Investigations*, of course, the theory is not a *theory*, but a description of the essence of perception.

Perception, Husserl says in the Sixth Investigation, taking the visual experience of an ink-well as an example, essentially consists in the fact that

we have a sequence of experiences belonging to the class of sensations, experiences which are unified on the sensual level by their specific interconnection and which are animated by a specific intentional function of "apperception," which confers upon them an objective sense. It is due to this intentional function that an object, this very ink-well, appears to us perceptually.[76]

As in *Ideas* I, Husserl holds in *Investigations* that sensations (*Empfindungen*) are non-intentional mental experiences, which are "really immanent" in consciousness.[77] And as in *Ideas* I, the thesis that there are sensations present in perceptual acts, sensations such as shape- or colour-sensations, is claimed to follow from the adumbrative character of outer perception.[78] Clearly, then, the principle of immanence is the basis of the theory of outer perception in the *Investigations*, because Husserl identifies adumbrations with really immanent sensations.

Apart from immanent sensations, the perceptual act is said to contain "a specific intentional function of 'apperception'," which confers an "objective sense" on the sensations. Because of this intentional apperception, an object appears to us. This is why Husserl also speaks of an "objectifying apperception" (*objektivierende Auffassung*). As equivalents to the term "apperception" he uses "apprehension," "interpretation" (*Deutung, Interpretation*), and *Auffassung*.[79] One may conclude that according to Husserl material objects appear to us perceptually, because sensations, which are immanent in consciousness, are "interpreted" objectively.

This theory seems to be similar to the traditional representative theories of perception, according to which an immanent sensation is interpreted by consciousness as a sign or as an image of an external object. Consequently, one will expect that Husserl's theory of perception raises the very same skeptical questions about the existence of the external world that were raised on the basis of the representative theories, and that his transcendental idealism is a solution to these skeptical problems, a solution similar to Berkeley's or Kant's. But there are fundamental obstacles to this line of interpretation. First, Husserl rejects the sign- and the image- theories of perception in the *Investigations* as well as in *Ideas* I. Furthermore, he stresses that in perception the object *itself* is bodily given to us.[80] Should one not conclude that "Husserl never shared the traditional prejudice of viewing sensible phenomena or appearances as a 'screen' interpolated between consciousness and the real world," so that his transcendental idealism cannot be akin to traditional idealist positions?[81] This conclusion, I shall argue, is mistaken, and it is based on a misinterpretation of what Husserl really says.

In order to reconstruct the problems Husserl wanted to solve by the idealist turn in *Ideas* I, we should concentrate on the first edition of the *Investigations*. Admittedly, Husserl criticizes the traditional sign- and image-theories of perception in the first edition. But this is not at all because he rejects the traditional idea that in perception, immanent sensations are interpreted or apperceived. On the contrary: this traditional idea is essential to his own theory of perception, as we saw above, and in the first Investigation he even compares the perceptual interpretation of a sensation to the interpretation of a physical object as a sign.[82] What Husserl objects to in the traditional representative theories of perception is, first, that the perceptual apperception is not sufficiently analyzed, so that it is confused with image- or sign-apperceptions, or even overlooked altogether, and second, that often the immanent content of the perceptual act, i.e., sum of the present sensations, is taken to be the object of perception. Furthermore, if Husserl stresses that in perception the object *itself* is "bodily given," he does not mean by "the object itself" the object as it is *an sich*, independently of the perceiver, as contrasted to the merely phenomenal object; if he did, the *Investigations* would endorse direct realism. The expression "the object itself" is not meant as an antithesis to "the phenomenal object," but to "signs or images of an object." What Husserl wants to stress is that the interpretations of something as a sign or an image of an object *O* is a mental act which is different from simply perceiving *O*.

To interpret Husserl correctly, one should raise the following question. What, according to the first edition of the *Investigations*, is the ontological status of the "object itself," which is "bodily given" in outer perception, as Husserl says? Since he claims that an ink-well is bodily given in perception because of the "objectifying interpretation" of immanent sensations, this first question is related to a second one: what precisely is the objectifying interpretation which allegedly is essential to the perceptual act? The difficulty is that Husserl does not answer these questions explicitly, so that we have to reconstruct his opinion from a number of casual passages in the first edition, which are all changed or suppressed in the second edition. *This very fact, however, proves that these passages are important for Husserl's philosophical development.*[83]

If one defines "idealism" in the strict sense as the doctrine that the material world is nothing but a series of ideas or sensations in the mind, Husserl's conception of intentionality and the concomitant distinction between the immanent contents of the perceptual act (the sensations and the apperception) and its transcendent intentional object (where "transcendent" means: "not really-immanent") rules out idealism. And indeed Husserl rejects this kind of idealism in § 7 of the Fifth Investigation (deleted in the second edition).[84] Husserl also repudiates phenomenalism, if taken as the claim that the material world consists of actual *and possible* sensations in the mind, although at least one passage in the first edition seems to suggest such a phenomenalism.[85] This kind of phenomenalism cannot be true, Husserl says, because "the appearing properties of things are not . . . sensations. . . . For they are not present in consciousness, as sensations are."[86] And yet, Husserl affirms that "the things of the phenomenal world, that is to say all their characteristics, are constituted *out of the same stuff* which, as sensations, we consider to belong to the content of consciousness."[87] In other words, the "things themselves" which are bodily given in perception, belong to the *phenomenal world*, which is constituted out of *the same stuff* as sensations are.

This latter affirmation fits in well with Husserl's theory of perception. For according to this theory, the perceptual act is an "objectifying interpretation" of really immanent sensations. As a consequence, the phenomenal world must be constituted out of the *stuff* of sensations, even though we are not allowed to say that it *consists of* sensations. It has been argued that, according to the first edition of *Investigations*, the transcendent perceptual "thing itself" is nothing but a complex of *objectified sensations*.[88] This is nearly correct, but not sufficiently clear. For one thing, this claim does not yet specify what the objectifying interpretation of sensations is. And it seems to conflict with Husserl's thesis that the phenomenal world does *not* consist of sensations. How is it possible that an objectifying interpretation of sensations, which are *in* our mind, causes us to perceive an object which is *transcendent to* our mind? How is Husserl able to claim simultaneously that the phenomenal world is constituted out of the same stuff as sensations are and that it does not consist of sensations?

These questions are answered by the hypothesis that Husserl endorsed a theory of outer perception that was popular in the second half of the nineteenth century, the so-called *projective theory of perception*. According to the projective theory, the perceptual apperception is a projective mental function by which the impressions or sensations we have when we perceive an external object, sensations which, in fact, are nothing but subjective mental modifications, are "projected" outside, that is, are localized at a place different from the one in which the perceiving subject localizes itself. This projective function would endow the sensations with the illusory appearance of independent existence.[89] If this hypothesis is correct, Husserl's "objective sense" is nothing but this "illusory appearance of independent existence" of phenomenal objects, which we project or posit on the basis of our sensations, and his "objectifying perceptual apperception" is nothing but projection. In other words, Husserl's key-term "constitution" simply means projective interpretation, at least in the case of outer perception.

This interpretative hypothesis is confirmed by another casual passage, this time in a review from 1903 to which Husserl often refers. For he there characterizes the objectifying apperception in outer perception as an *interpretative externalization (deutende Hinausverlegung)*.[90] The hypothesis also explains why the phenomenal world is constituted out of the same stuff as sensations are, although we cannot say that it consists of sensations, and how Husserl is able to say that the perceived object itself is transcendent to consciousness, even though the fact that it perceptually appears to us is due to an objectifying apperception of sensations which are really immanent in consciousness.[91]

We may conclude, then, that if Husserl says that in perception the object itself is bodily given to us, he means that we do not perceive a sign or an image of the object that we intend to perceive, but this very object itself.[92] However, this does not imply at all that Husserl is a direct realist. For the object we perceive is the phenomenal object, and the phenomenal object is ontologically dependent on consciousness, because it is a projection of the latter. The phenomenal real object may be called a "sense," as Husserl does in § 55 of *Ideas* I, because it is the product of a projective *interpretation* of sensations. Husserl's position here might be called idealist or phenomenalist in the broad sense of a doctrine saying that the object as we perceive it ontologically depends on the perceiving mind. And Husserl explicitly says in the first edition of the *Investigations* that, if phenomenalism takes into account the fundamental distinction between the immanent contents of mental acts and their intentional objects, it might very well be true.[93] If phenomenalism is defined as the doctrine that "the objective grounds for speaking of physical objects and events reside in purely lawlike correlations, which obtain between the mental experiences of the multiple minds," Husserl is indeed a phenomenalist in the *Investigations*.[94] However, this conclusion has to be qualified, and there are good reasons why Husserl in the *Investigations* did not endorse phenomenalism explicitly, as we shall see in the next section.

X. RECONSTRUCTION OF HUSSERL'S EPISTEMOLOGICAL PROBLEM. HIS CONCEPTIONS OF EPISTEMOLOGY AND METAPHYSICS IN THE *INVESTIGATIONS*

Having diagnosed Husserl's theory of perception in the *Investigations* as being a variety of projective theory, we will be able to understand the problem of the possibility of objective experience that haunted Husserl between 1900 and 1913, and that he formulates for example in *Philosophy as a Rigorous Science* (see § 3 herein). Surely, Husserl's theory of perception is not a representative theory in the strict sense. The phenomenal object that is bodily present in perception is not a representation of another object, which exists in itself and at which the perceptual act is really aiming, as the sign- and the image-theory of perception claims. On the contrary, the object itself to which the perceptual "intention" refers is identical with the object which appears to us. And yet, this object is not an object *an sich* in the sense that it exists independently of consciousness. It is the phenomenal object, as Husserl explicitly says, and this phenomenal object is a projection of the mind. The phenomenal world ontologically depends on the perceiving subject, because it is the latter's projection, the product of an objectifying interpretation of subjective sensations. As Husserl says in § 49 of *Ideas* I, specific series of sensations and perceptual interpretations in consciousness are a *sufficient* condition for the existence of the world.[95]

Although Husserl's projective theory of perception is not a representative theory, it raises the same skeptical questions as the representative theories raised. What about the physical causes of the sensations which are "interpreted" in perception? Should we not assume a physical world *an sich* in the strong sense, in order to explain the presence of the sensations in our minds? And what is the relation between this objective world *an sich* and the subjective, phenomenal world? Physics claims to know the objective world *an sich* on the basis of experience. But how can this claim be justified, if what is given in experience is a phenomenal world which is a projection of the perceiving mind? These are the questions raised by the theory of perception in the *Investigations*, and these are the problems Husserl wanted to solve by his transcendental idealism. Before tracing the genesis of Husserl's solution, I shall briefly discuss the conceptions of epistemology and metaphysics Husserl held between 1900 and 1903, for these conceptions confirm my interpretation: they are motivated by the skeptical problems which Husserl's projective theory of perception entails.

A direct realist would never endorse Husserl's claim in § 5 of *Prolegomena*, that the existence of the external world is a "fundamental metaphysical presupposition" of the natural sciences, which is never tested and rarely noticed.[96] For this claim implies that the external world *an sich* is not (even partially) given in outer perception. And this, in its turn, is an implication of the theory of perception in the *Investigations*. Husserl's early distinction between empirical science and metaphysics must also be understood against the background of this theory. As Husserl says in a review from 1903, metaphysics has the task "to elaborate the last and absolutely valid determinations of reality from the confusing mass of provisional and only relatively valid ones pertaining to the empirical sciences."[97] This implies that metaphysics is last philosophy rather than first philosophy, because we will be able really to resolve metaphysical questions only after the sciences have been completed.[98] As a consequence, Husserl provisionally pleads for a physics and a psychology without metaphysical assumptions.[99] Physics and psychology should not posit bodies and minds *an sich*, but content themselves with studying physical and mental *phenomena*. In 1903, Husserl even seems to endorse the Machian idea that the sciences aim merely at finding "purely economical formulae which enable us to calculate the stream of phenomenal being and becoming into the future and into the past," whereas metaphysics "wants to disclose the ultimate meaning of the world."[100] Husserl's distinction between science and metaphysics is very similar to Berkeley's, for instance.

In contradistinction to metaphysics, epistemology might be called first philosophy. It is the fundamental philosophical discipline,[101] which precedes the empirical sciences and metaphysics.[102] Epistemology is a general conceptual investigation concerned with the

possibility of objective knowledge. Although it cannot answer the
scientific and metaphysical question whether we are able to obtain
knowledge about reality *an sich* on the basis of the data we *in fact*
possess, it does investigate *in which legitimate sense* we can speak
about an objectivity *an sich* at all.[103] This is a first reason why
epistemology is more fundamental than the sciences and than
metaphysics.

In the *Investigations*, Husserl accepts the Cartesian predicament
for epistemology. Because the existence of the external world is uncertain,[104] whereas the existence of my own present mental phenomena is absolutely certain,[105] epistemology should be limited to a
descriptive analysis of my present mental phenomena. As a consequence, epistemology is phenomenology or descriptive psychology.
Epistemology has to be presuppositionless. It cannot assume the
validity of the alleged knowledge about the external world, because
it has to investigate the legitimate sense of such knowledge-claims.
This is why a naturalist epistemology, which uses knowledge-claims
about the external world, involves a vicious circle. In the first edition of the *Investigations*, Husserl assumes that descriptive psychology can be a presuppositionless epistemology in this sense.[106]

Like his conception of metaphysics, Husserl's idea of epistemology presupposes his projective theory of perception. It follows from
this theory that only an immanent perception of my own mental
phenomena can be certain and "adequate" in the sense that it does
not involve a projective interpretation, and that all outer perception
is problematical.[107] Both the requirement that epistemology must be
presuppositionless in the sense that it cannot use knowledge-claims
about the external world, and the claim that descriptive psychology
is presuppositionaless in this sense, are motivated by the skeptical
problems which Husserl's theory of perception raises.[108]

We now see why we should qualify the thesis that Husserl is a
phenomenalist (in a broad sense) in the *Investigations*. To the extent
that it is a corollary of Husserl's descriptive analysis of perception,
his phenomenalism is merely an epistemological, and not a metaphysical position. It is concerned with perceptual acts and with the
world as we perceive it, but not with the world *an sich*. Epistemology should be metaphysically neutral, because it is presuppositionless and because it precedes metaphysics. This does not preclude, however, that epistemology has metaphysical implications.

For it fixes the legitimate sense of metaphysical concepts such as the concept of the "an sich."

Although Husserl's epistemological phenomenalism excludes direct realism, it is compatible with hypothetical scientific realism, which was Brentano's position, or with metaphysical realism, which was Kant's.[109] It is also compatible with phenomenalism in the ontological sense of a doctrine saying that even the world *an sich* depends on consciousness. In § 13, I shall argue that this kind of phenomenalism is *implied by* Husserl's epistemology in the *Investigations*.

VI. TWO PROBLEMS OF TRANSCENDENCE

In his later work, Husserl usually says that the main task of epistemology or phenomenology is to solve the "problem of transcendence." Epistemology has to elucidate the claim of consciousness that it relates to objects which are transcendent to it. Central to this problem is the notion of intentionality, because intentionality is the relatedness of consciousness to its objects. Husserl claims that this epistemological problem of the subject-object relation can be solved by analyzing the constitution of different kinds of entities by the transcendental ego.[110] How did this later transcendental conception of epistemology evolve from the conception of the *Investigations*?

In order to answer this question, one should realize that the projective theory of perception, which explains Husserl's conception of epistemology in the *Investigations*, in fact raises two very different "problems of transcendence." Husserl uses the term "transcendent" as short for "transcendent to consciousness," so that everything that does not belong to the really immanent contents of the stream of consciousness may be called "transcendent." If outer perception consists of an objectifying interpretation of immanent sensations, as Husserl's theory of perception has it, a first problem of transcendence may be formulated as follows: what exactly is this objectifying interpretation? How does it differ from other interpretations of immanent sensations, such as the image- or the sign-apperceptions? How does an objectifying interpretation of sensations manage to make us perceive an external object? In other words, how is a transcendent phenomenal object constituted by consciousness? According to the *Investigations*, this problem can be solved by a descriptive analysis of consciousness, that is, by descriptive psychology. I shall call this problem the problem of constitution.

But Husserl's projective theory of perception implies yet another "problem of transcendence," a problem that may be called the problem of the *Ding an sich*. This is the more intractable problem, which I stressed in the previous section and which has haunted Western philosophy since Descartes, or at least since Kant. If what is given in perception is the phenomenal world only, which is a projection of consciousness, how fares the claim of empirical science that it investigates the world as it really is, independently of experience? Kant thought that this claim is simply false, and that science is concerned with the phenomenal world only. He found himself unable to explain the objective validity of synthetic *a priori* principles otherwise. Nevertheless, Kant assumed the existence of an unknowable world *an sich*, in order to explain the presence of the sensations in consciousness out of which the phenomenal world is constituted. However, this assumption did not fit in well with his philosophy and it seemed odd to posit something which is unknowable *per se*. As a consequence, many philosophers in the second half of the nineteenth century became hypothetical scientific realists. Science would be concerned with the world *an sich*, in spite of the fact that the existence of this world had forever to remain a hypothesis, because it is not given in perception. But hypothetical scientific realism is not a more satisfactory position than Kantian metaphysical realism. For our conviction that there is a real world, which exists independently of experience, a conviction we all have in our daily life, does not seem to be a mere hypothesis. As a result, there was a general feeling around the turn of the century that the problem of the *Ding an sich* had to be dispensed with.

Husserl's progress towards transcendental idealism, I suggest, consisted of two major steps. The first was that he eliminated the traditional problem of the *Ding an sich*, by means of a re-interpretation of the concept of an *an sich*. Consequently, the only remaining epistemological problem of transcendence was the problem of constitution, so that Husserl could now claim that constitution-analysis was able to solve all conceivable epistemological problems. The second step was a drastic re-interpretation of consciousness, necessitated by what I shall call the problem of the phenomenological field (or the problem of human subjectivity, as Husserl names it in *Crisis*). This second step explains the transition from descriptive psychological epistemology to transcendental phenomenology. The first step was required by Husserl's conception of epistemology in the *Investigations*.

XII. THE PROBLEM OF THE THING IN ITSELF

Having traced Husserl's conception of epistemology in the first edition of the *Investigations*, we now may wonder how epistemology in Husserl's sense is able to deal with the problem of the *Ding an sich*. For according to the principle of presuppositionlessness, epistemology is restricted to a descriptive analysis of my present mental phenomena. Epistemology is also defined as a conceptual investigation concerned with the sense (*Sinn*) of the epistemic claim that we know objects as they are in themselves. These two characterizations of epistemology may seem incompatible: how can epistemology be both a conceptual investigation and a descriptive psychological analysis? But here, as in the Fundamental Phenomenological Meditation of *Ideas* I, Husserl's empiricist principle of meaning-analysis informs his philosophical programme. In order to elucidate concepts such as knowledge and truth, we have to describe the phenomena from which they are abstracted. And if these phenomena are mental phenomena, as they have to be according to the Cartesian predicament in epistemology, conceptual analysis in epistemology reduces to descriptive psychology.[111]

But this epistemological research programme will seem to be utterly unable to deal with the problem of the *Ding an sich*. Is this problem not concerned with the relation between mental phenomena (acts of thought, of perception) on the one hand and objects as they are in themselves on the other hand? If so, a descriptive analysis merely of mental phenomena will necessarily fall short of solving it. Now Husserl considers this objection in § 7 of the introduction to the second volume of the *Investigations*. In the first edition, he dismisses it by the observation that if mental acts intentionally aim at transcendent, or even non-existent or impossible objects, we nevertheless will be able to determine the *sense* of such an intentional directedness by means of a descriptive-psychological analysis, because the intentional sense is a really immanent descriptive feature of these acts.[112] And indeed Husserl assumes in the *Investigations* that to each characteristic of an object, to the extent that it is meant in consciousness, there corresponds a really immanent characteristic of the relevant act.

The difficulty is, however, that even if this answer were satisfactory as far as the problem of constitution is concerned, it does not explain how epistemology might tackle the problem of the *Ding an sich*. According to Husserl's theory of perception, the *Ding an sich* in the Kantian sense is simply not given to, or meant in, perceptual consciousness. As a consequence, there are no descriptive features of mental acts corresponding to the *Ding an sich*. It is tempting to conclude that the problem of the *Ding an sich* is simply beyond the scope of the phenomenological epistemology of the *Investigations*, so that Husserl evaded rather than solved it.[113]

And yet, this conclusion should be rejected. It is incompatible with the fact that Husserl proposed a new interpretation of the concept of the *Ding an sich* in the sixth *Investigation*. Apparently, Husserl thought that the concept of a *Ding an sich* stood *in need of* a new interpretation, and this, I suggest, was because of the very fact that the traditional concept of a *Ding an sich* could not be validated by the method of Husserl's epistemological analysis. If this interpretation is correct, Husserl applied the empiricist analysis of concepts in a manner no less radical than Hume's. Like Hume, he rejected all concepts that could not be traced back to their origin in experience. And this meant the death-warrant for the traditional concept of a thing in itself. As Husserl says in §§ 43 and 52 of *Ideas* I, it is *absurd* to posit things in themselves which cannot be perceived in principle, because perception (in Husserl's wide sense of "original intuition") is the final justification of all concepts and existence-claims.

XIII. HUSSERL'S RE-INTERPRETATION OF THE NOTION OF A THING IN ITSELF

Husserl's new interpretation of the notion of a *Ding an sich* purports to satisfy the boundary conditions of the epistemological programme in the first edition of the *Investigations*. Epistemology, we saw, is an analysis of the fundamental concepts of knowledge, such as "truth" and "object in itself." Husserl's empiricist principle of meaning-analysis proclaims that, in order to analyze these concepts, we have to describe their referents, i.e., the phenomena from which they are "abstracted." These phenomena are called the *Sachen selbst*.[114] Furthermore, we saw that Husserl in the first edition endorses the Cartesian predicament of epistemology. Epistemology is restricted to a descriptive analysis of what is absolutely certain, to wit my own present mental phenomena as they are adequately perceived in immanent perception.[115] In short, epistemology is conceptual analysis by means of a description of the "origins" of concepts in my present mental experience.

I have already raised the question of how an epistemology of this type will be able to solve the problem of a *Ding an sich*. If the expression "Ding an sich" is taken to refer to something which is radically transcendent in relation to the sphere of consciousness and its intentional objects, the epistemology of the first edition will not be able to account for the concept of a *Ding an sich*. However, I suggested that Husserl took his empiricist analysis of concepts as seriously as Hume did. He assumed that concepts which are beyond the scope of such an analysis simply are not legitimate concepts. This is why the concept of a *Ding an sich* stood in need of a re-interpretation. Such a re-interpretation had to comply with the requirements of epistemological analysis. In other words, the *Ding an sich* in the new sense had to be a possible intentional object of consciousness, so that there would be really immanent features of mental acts corresponding to it. Let me now briefly state this new conception.

In Chapter 3 of the Sixth Investigation, Husserl discusses different stages or degrees of intuitive and perceptual knowledge. We may order the adumbrations of a spatial object, for instance, in series of ever greater completeness, adequacy, and richness. These series point to a limit, which Husserl calls adequate perception. In adequate perception, the object itself would be wholly and fully given.[116] Now Husserl defines a "Ding an sich" in his new sense as the objective intentional correlate of such an adequate perception.[117] In other words, we would perceive an object as it is *an sich* if we perceived it completely and adequately. In the case of outer perception, such an adequate perception is impossible because of the essentially adumbrative character of outer perception. Accordingly, the limit of adequate perception is an *ideal* limit, as Husserl says. Similarly, we might say that the thing in itself in this new sense is an *ideal limit* of the phenomenal thing. And in the first edition, Husserl applies this definition also to the notion of a *world* in itself: the world in itself is the intentional correlate of the ideal community of scientists, i.e., of the community of scientists which possesses a complete science.[118] Clearly, this new concept of a *Ding an sich* is very different from the traditional notion, as Husserl himself stresses. Whereas, according to the traditional notion, the thing in itself is radically different from the phenomenal object, being the cause of the sensations in consciousness which provide the sensuous stuff for the constitution of the phenomenal world, the *Ding an sich* in the new sense is an ideal limit of the phenomenal object. It is not "behind" the phenomenal object, but rather an idealized extension of it.[119]

One might object to this analysis that it does not satisfy Husserl's epistemological requirements, because an adequate outer perception is impossible, as Husserl admits, so that the analysis cannot be based on a really present mental act. But Husserl could have given a Humean response to this objection. Although an adequate outer perception is impossible, the concept of such an act is an idealization of a series of acts which are possible, so that this concept has a sufficient phenomenological justification. As in Hume's case, the empiricist genealogy of concepts may admit of "mental operations" such as "augmenting the materials afforded us by the senses."[120] An empiricist analysis of concepts does not prohibit idealizations on the basis of experience. Another objection would be that even if the concept of an adequate outer perception is phenomenologically justified, the corresponding concept of a *Ding an sich* is not, because it cannot be developed by an idealization of a series of mental acts. Rather it is the idealization of a series of intentional correlates of these acts. In 1901, Husserl would have rejected this objection as well. For it is "simply impossible to describe the intending acts, without referring to the intended objects in the expressions used."[121] However, the only way really to avoid this objection would have been to accept that intentional objects *as such* are as adequately "given" as acts of consciousness, and to enlarge the descriptive domain of epistemology by including the intentional correlates. Instead of a description of what is really immanent in consciousness, phenomenology would then become a description of the noetic-noematic correlation, to use Husserl's later terminology. Although in the first edition of the *Investigations* there is a passage which suggests this move, Husserl made it only in 1907.[122]

As I have claimed, Husserl's new interpretation of the notion of a

Ding an sich is meant to be an elimination of the traditional notion on the basis of the empiricist conception of meaning. This view is confirmed by the fact that in the first edition of the *Investigations* Husserl calls his new notion of the *Ding an sich* "empirically founded," in contrast with what he calls the "mystic" conception.[123] "Mystic," or rather "mythical," became Husserl's later *epitheton ornans* for Kantian conceptions.[124] This text refutes the opinion that Husserl could not deal with the problem of the *Ding an sich* in the *Investigations.* On the contrary, he "solved" it by eliminating the traditional "mystic" notion of an *an sich* and by substituting an "empirically founded" conception for it. What is more important, Husserl never grew dissatisfied with this solution. In the later works, the world in itself is interpreted as an ideal limit of the world which we experience.[125] This new conception of a world *an sich* and the concomitant elimination of the old conception have important consequences. Let me briefly discuss four of them.

1. The first consequence is metaphysical or ontological. Although the phenomenological epistemology of the *Investigations* is "metaphysically neutral" in that it aims at being free from metaphysical *presuppositions*, it certainly has metaphysical *implications*. It is even meant to have such implications, because metaphysics should be based on epistemology (and also on the empirical sciences). As far as the epistemological analysis of the concept of a *Ding an sich* is concerned, the metaphysical implications are drastic indeed. Husserl's theory of perception implies that he is what I have called an "epistemological phenomenalist." The phenomenal world is ontologically dependent on consciousness, because it is a projection of the latter. But if the world in itself is merely an idealization of the phenomenal world, as is the case according to Husserl's re-interpretation of the *an sich*, it follows that Husserl is also an *ontological* phenomenalist or idealist. Even the world in itself is ontologically dependent on the perceiving subject, for it is an idealization of a projection performed by this subject. In short, Husserl's theory of perception, combined with his new conception of a *Ding an sich*, implies the idealist ontology of the real world which Husserl states in *Ideas* I. The real world is nothing but a "sense," constituted by consciousness, because it is the product of a transcending interpretation of really immanent sensations.[126] If Husserl did not conclusively argue for this ontology of the

world in *Ideas* I, this must have been because he reached this conclusion much earlier, that is, in the *Investigations*.

2. A second consequence is concerned with philosophical method and with epistemology. By re-interpreting the *Ding an sich* as an ideal limit of the phenomenal object, Husserl eliminates the second problem of transcendence which I discussed in § 11. What remains is the first problem only, the problem of constitution. This is why Husserl is able to claim in *Ideas* I and the later works that the analysis of constitution will solve all conceivable epistemological problems. In other words, *Husserl's later constitution-analysis does not make sense as an exclusive method in epistemology, unless one accepts his idealist ontology of the world first.* Husserlian phenomenology without transcendental idealism is nonsensical. If one wants to be a phenomenologist without being a transcendental idealist, one should make clear what one's non-Husserlian conception of phenomenology amounts to, and which problems it is meant to solve.

3. Husserl's re-interpretation of the notion of a *Ding an sich* has decisive implications also for the philosophy of science. If the world *an sich* is nothing but an ideal limit of the phenomenal world, hypothetical scientific realists such as Brentano or Stumpf were wrong in thinking that physics is about a hypothetical physical world which exists independently of human experience. The world of human experience, Husserl concludes, is the only real world there is. If so, it is misleading to call it the "phenomenal world," as Husserl did in the *Investigations*. It is simply the world, or the life-world, to use the jargon of *Crisis*.[127] But if the world of human experience is the only real world, what about the theoretical entities of physics? If they cannot be conceived of as the independent causes of the phenomena we experience, there seem to be only two options left for Husserl: either Machian instrumentalism, or the idea that theoretical entities are the product of higher strata of constitution which are based on the constitution of the life-world. Husserl endorsed the first option in 1903 and in *Crisis*, and the second in § 52 of *Ideas* I.[128]

4. Finally, Husserl's re-interpretation of the notion of a *Ding an sich* implies a problem which, I think, is fatal to his claim that constitution analysis will be able to resolve all epistemological difficulties: the problem of the origin of our sensations. If both hypotheti-

cal scientific realism and metaphysical realism are false, how to account for the (alleged) fact that we find in our consciousness coherent series of sensations, which are the *hyletic* basis for the constitution of the world? The real import of this problem can be measured only on the transcendental level. This is why I shall now go on to explain Husserl's transcendental turn. As usual, I shall first try to reconstruct the problem that the transcendental turn was meant to solve.

XIV. THE PROBLEM OF THE PHENOMENOLOGICAL FIELD OR THE PARADOX OF HUMAN SUBJECTIVITY

As I have argued so far, the phenomenology of the *Investigations* already implies the idealist ontology of the world which Husserl explicitly proposes in *Ideas* I. Even though in the latter work the structure of intentional objects receives a much richer articulation, the ontological status of the world remains basically the same. The world is an ontologically dependent phenomenon, constituted on the basis of really immanent sensations.[129] But if both the *Investigations* and *Ideas* I are idealist, what is the difference between the two works as far as idealism is concerned? The answer is that the *Investigations* imply a psychological or mundane idealism, whereas in *Ideas* I the idealist doctrine is transcendental. What exactly is this difference? And what explains Husserl's transcendental turn? I shall argue that Husserl transcendentalized his idealism as a solution to the problem of the phenomenological field (my terminology) and to the paradox of human subjectivity (Husserl's terminology). Let me first briefly introduce these two *dramatis personae*.

According to the *Investigations*, the phenomenal world (the only world there is, as we now know) is a projection of consciousness and it ontologically depends on the latter. But what, one might ask, is the ontological status of consciousness itself? Because consciousness is the subject matter of phenomenology, this question is equivalent to the question as to what the subject-matter of phenomenology precisely is. This is the problem of the phenomenological field.

According to the first edition of the *Investigations*, phenomenology or descriptive psychology is concerned with mental phenomena. It precedes genetic psychology, which aims at causally explaining them.[130] Primarily, phenomenology is concerned with my present mental phenomena as they are adequately perceived, for these make up the epistemologically primary and absolutely certain core of my ego.[131] In the first edition, Husserl endorses a Humean conception of the ego or the self. The self is an empirical unity of mental experiences.[132] This is why we may say just as well that phenomenology studies consciousness in the sense of the phenomenological ego or the mental *I*. Because the mental *I* is the empirical *I*, as Husserl's Humean conception implies, phenomenology investigates a part of the (my) phenomenal world, the part which is isolated from the remainder of the phenomenal world by concentrating my attention on my mental experiences.[133] Ontologically and causally speaking, mental phenomena depend on physical phenomena.[134] According to the first edition of the *Investigations*, then, the phenomenological field is a dependent part of the phenomenal world: it is *mundane* or psychological consciousness. In this sense, Husserl was a naturalist in the *Investigations*.

This naturalist definition of phenomenology and its field, if coupled to the idealist ontology implied by Husserl's theory of perception and by his re-interpretation of the *Ding an sich*, yields a paradox which Husserl later came to call the paradox of human subjectivity.[135] The paradox is stated in many forms in Husserl's later works, and it occurs in all texts where Husserl discusses the transcendental reduction, transcendental idealism, or the difference between phenomenological psychology and transcendental phenomenology.[136] This proves the importance of the paradox for Husserl's transcendental turn. In its most simple form, the paradox is as follows. If, as Husserl's theory of perception implies, the world is a projection of perceptual acts, the world ontologically depends on consciousness. Specific series of sensations and specific objectifying interpretations in consciousness are a sufficient condition for the existence of the world. But if, on the other hand, the perceptual acts which phenomenology investigates are psychological acts of human beings, consciousness as the domain of phenomenology ontologically depends on physical nature. But how is it possible that constituting consciousness both depends on physical nature and is a sufficient condition for the existence of nature? The conjunction of naturalism and idealism in the *Investigations* yields a contradiction, the contradiction of mundane or psychological idealism. In other words, Husserl's projective or constitutive theory of perception is inconsistent with his definition of the phenomenological field in the first edition of the *Investigations*.

In order to solve this paradox, Husserl had to reject either his constitutive theory of perception or his identification of phenomenology with descriptive psychology. In fact, he maintained his theory of perception until the end of his life. As a consequence, he had to redefine the phenomenological field and to argue that the constituting ego is not part of the constituted natural world, but an absolute, which exists independently of nature. And this very doctrine is transcendental idealism.

Let me now summarize the genesis of Husserl's transcendental idealism as I have reconstructed it. Husserl's projective theory of perception implies a variety of epistemological idealism, which says that the phenomenal world is ontologically dependent on consciousness because it is its projection. Husserl's re-interpretation of the notion of a *Ding an sich* turned this epistemological idealism into an ontological idealism: even the world as it is in itself is now said to depend on consciousness. But because Husserl in the *Investigations* (first edition) assumed that consciousness is part of the world, his idealism confronted the paradox of human subjectivity. Mundane or psychological idealism is a contradictory position, because it says that the world as a whole is constituted by one of its dependent parts, human consciousness. In order to solve this paradox, Husserl transcendentalized his idealism. He claimed that consciousness which constitutes the world is not part of the world. Transcendental consciousness is a substance in the Cartesian sense. It can exist even if the world does not. And the world it constitutes contains consciousness in the psychological sense.

Husserl claimed that each of us is able to discover his ultimate transcendental self by reflecting on his or her own consciousness and its relation to the world (cf. the argument of the Fundamental Meditation). This is the so-called transcendental reduction. Because Husserl's idealism interprets the world as constituted by each individual consciousness, he had to confront the familiar problems of transcendental solipsism and of intersubjectivity. In spite of Husserl's claim to the contrary, I do not think that he was able to solve these problems, which are typical of idealist ontologies.

XV. THE GRADUAL IMPLEMENTATION OF TRANSCENDENTAL IDEALISM: HUSSERL AND DESCARTES

Many commentators hold that Husserl's self-professed Cartesianism is an exaggeration, and that Husserl, in fact, broke free from the Cartesian project in modern philosophy.[137] We have seen, however, that Husserl endorsed the Cartesian predicament in epistemology already in the *Investigations*. Epistemology should be based on an analysis of the indubitable sphere of my own consciousness. What is more, Husserl's gradual development towards transcendental idealism between 1900 and 1913 may be seen as a progressive radicalization of the Cartesian requirement of finding an indubitable foundation of knowledge by means of the method of doubting. Summarizing the argument of his lectures in 1907, Husserl wrote that all he wanted was to "grasp purely and develop consistently what was already implied in this very old intention" of Cartesian doubt.[138] And this is what he, in fact, tried to do. Transcendental idealism, then, was implemented by a gradual radicalization of Cartesian doubt, which took place in five or six steps. I shall describe these steps schematically, without discussing the many manuscripts and lecture notes needed to fill in further historical details. Husserl's various radicalizations of Descartes also explain his later criticisms of his predecessor, which I shall briefly indicate.

1. Husserl's first radicalization of Descartes was achieved already in the *Investigations*. It has often been objected to Descartes's second meditation that what resists methodological doubt is not my mental substance, but purely the sum of my present *cogitationes*. The idea that thoughts cannot exist without a thinking substance is an Aristotelian assumption which should be subjected to doubt. Accordingly, Husserl restricts the sphere of Cartesian indubitability to "my" present mental phenomena, and pleads for a psychology without a soul, as we have seen. This first radicalization of Descartes is due to Hume's influence on Husserl.

2. A second Humean radicalization also occurs in the *Investigations*. It consists in doubting the validity of all concepts which cannot be abstracted from the sphere of mental phenomena, such as the traditional concept of a *Ding an sich*. The elimination of this con-

cept disposes of the Cartesian project of proving the existence of the world *an sich*, and transforms epistemology into a descriptive analysis of constitution. Husserl's most fundamental criticism of Descartes is that the latter always assumed the possibility of a world *an sich* in the traditional sense as an unproblematic possibility, and that he tried to prove the existence of such a world.[139] Husserl's empiricist principle of meaning analysis is a radicalization of Cartesian doubt, because it extends methodical doubt to concepts, and implies that concepts are justified only if they can be abstracted from the Cartesian sphere of absolute certainty.

3. In the first edition of the *Investigations*, Husserl identified phenomenology with descriptive psychology. In other words, he thought that the existence of my present mental phenomena, taken as the mental aspect of empirical human beings in the world, meets the Cartesian requirement of indubitability. In 1903, however, Husserl realized that the interpretation of my mental phenomena as phenomena of this human being in the world is a *transcending interpretation* of consciousness, because it implies the existence of my body and of the world. Like all transcending interpretations, this one is presumptive and not apodictically certain. Accordingly, Husserl rejected the identification of phenomenology with descriptive psychology, and proclaimed that one should finally draw "the essential boundary between purely immanent phenomenology and critique of knowledge on the one hand, which excludes all suppositions that transcend the content of what is given, and empirical psychology on the other hand, which, even when it merely describes, makes such suppositions."[140] This third step is necessary for transcendental idealism, but it is far from being sufficient, because it is negative only. It belongs to Cartesian doubt or *epoché*, but it does not show what the residuum of the *epoché* is. For to refrain from affirming that consciousness as the subject-matter of epistemology is identical with the mental aspect of human beings, is still very far from affirming that there is a consciousness which is not identical with the mental and which exists independently of the natural world. In order to substantiate the latter claim, Husserl needed the experiment of the destruction of the world. Nevertheless, the radicalized *epoché* of 1903 already explains Husserl's later criticism of Descartes, that consciousness as a residuum of the *epoché* cannot be interpreted as a part of the natural world.[141]

4. Whereas the first three steps are radicalizations of Cartesian doubt in the sense that the sphere of indubitability was restricted, the fourth radicalization is an enlargement of this sphere. Already in the *Investigations*, Husserl observed that the phenomenal object of perception, if taken precisely as it appears to us, is as indubitably given as the present conscious experiences themselves.[142] But this implies, as Husserl realized in 1907, that it was a mistake to restrict the domain of indubitable knowledge to consciousness in the sense of what is really immanent in the stream of experiences. He now sees that the real domain of indubitability is "this marvellous correlation" of epistemic experiences and their intentional objects as such.[143] If we "bracket" the transcending existential claims implied in our natural perceptual acts, and take the intentional objects exactly as they appear to us, that is, as "noemata" or "noematic structures," we will be able to understand how the transcendent real object may be really known by studying the way in which it is constituted in consciousness.[144] The subject-matter of epistemology is not the stream of consciousness in the sense of what is really immanent only, but the noetic-noematic correlation. This radicalization of Descartes explains that in Husserl's eyes Descartes underestimated the importance of intentionality.[145]

The later notion of a noema, then, was developed purely on "Cartesian" epistemological grounds, and it germinated in Husserl's analysis of perception.[146] In *Ideas* I, Husserl characterizes the noemata as "senses" or "meanings," and from the transcendental perspective, all real unities are also "senses."[147] This terminology may misled one into thinking that the notion of a noema primarily belongs to the philosophy of language. But this popular view is erroneous, even though, on the purely terminological level, Husserl of course extends the term "Sinn," which originally belongs to the sphere of language.[148] Furthermore, the characterization of reality as a "sense" is not a "terminological blunder" either, as one commentator contends.[149] It follows from Husserl's theory of perception that transcendent objects are "senses," for they are the product of a projective *interpretation* of sensations. What is constituted by an *interpretation* can only be a *sense*.

5. In the second Investigation, Husserl already generalized his Platonist philosophy of logic, according to which propositions are "ideal species" or "essences" of specific mental acts (meaning inten-

tions). As a result of this generalization, he claimed that all factual objects and events have their "ideal essences," and that these essences may be "intuited" and studied in synthetic *a priori* sciences. Phenomenology in the sense of descriptive psychology was meant to be such a synthetic *a priori* science. Between 1901 and 1913 Husserl gradually developed his theory of the "eidetic reduction," claiming that all domains of facts have their essential or eidetic structures, that these eidetic structures can be "intuited," and that all factual sciences should be based on eidetic sciences or "regional ontologies." This doctrine is summarized in the first part of *Ideas* I. Now the eidetic reduction is very different from the transcendental reduction. Like empirical consciousness in the psychological sense, transcendental consciousness is a domain of facts, a region of individual being.[150] The transcendental reduction discloses this factual domain. It does not reveal a domain of essences, as the eidetic reduction does. Nevertheless, the transcendental factual domain may also be studied eidetically, and this is the programme of transcendental phenomenology. Transcendental phenomenology is the eidetic ontology of the transcendental domain, whereas Husserl defines metaphysics as the ultimate *factual* analysis of this domain and of the world.[151] Strictly speaking, then, the eidetic reduction is irrelevant to the genesis of transcendental idealism. If I am referring to it here, this is because Husserl saw the eidetic reduction as yet another extension of the Cartesian sphere of indubitable givenness. This is stressed, for instance, in the lectures on phenomenology from 1907.[152] In other words, Husserl conceived his Platonism as an extension of his Cartesianism.

6. Steps 1–5 fall drastically short of resolving the paradox of human subjectivity. In particular, the purely negative third step does not provide the positive ontological re-interpretation of consciousness needed for showing how consciousness can constitute the world in spite of the fact that human consciousness is a subordinate and dependent reality *in* the world.[153] The argument for such a re-interpretation was published for the first time in *Ideas* I, § 49. As Husserl claims, the thought-experiment of the destruction of the world shows that consciousness cannot be a subordinate part of the world, for it survives the destruction of the latter. This is why we have to distinguish between transcendental consciousness, which exists as an ontologically independent absolute

and which constitutes the world, and psychological consciousness, which is constituted by transcendental consciousness as a dependent part of human nature. Husserl's thought-experiment of the destruction of the world resembles the Cartesian supposition that an almighty God could have created my mind without matter. Husserl's conclusion is also similar to that of Descartes. They both conclude that consciousness is a substance. If Husserl differs from Descartes in claiming that consciousness as a substance cannot be identical with consciousness as a part of the world, this is only because Husserl denies the possibility of a world *an sich* first (step 2), and concludes that consciousness as part of the world has to be part of the constituted phenomenal world (cf. step 1). These assumptions yield the paradox of human subjectivity, a paradox which is absent from Descartes's philosophy. We may conclude that even though Husserl's conception of consciousness and his foundational programme in philosophy are different from the Cartesian ones, Husserl remained a Cartesian. For Husserl's very deviations from Descartes are due to radicalizations of the method of Cartesian doubt.

XVI. HUSSERL, KANT, AND BERKELEY

In §§ 9–15, I reconstructed the argument which led Husserl from the epistemological problem of the possibility of objective experience to his transcendental idealism. This rational reconstruction will enable us to discern clearly the nature of Husserl's idealism, and to define its relation to the idealist doctrines of Kant and Berkeley. Like Kant and Berkeley, Husserl argued for his idealism on the basis of the principle of immanence, which excludes direct realism. This principle is fundamental to his projective theory of perception, which implies an idealist ontology of the phenomenal world. Husserl's elimination of the traditional *Ding an sich* and his concomitant definition of the phenomenological field then raised the paradox of human subjectivity, which was solved by transcendenntal idealism. Although Husserl's transcendental idealism differs from the Kantian variety and from Berkeleian immaterialism, the three idealist doctrines are close relatives: they contain the same genetic materials, in particular the principle of immanence. I shall first elucidate Husserl's criticism of Kant, and then argue that Husserl's position is similar to Berkeley's.

In *Crisis*, Husserl claims that Kant's transcendental philosophy implicitly presupposes the life-world.[154] The import of this rather obscure criticism may be clarified against the background of my genetic reconstruction of Husserl's transcendental idealism. Kant implicitly presupposes the life-world, because he assumes that the constituting subject belongs to the world and that in perception it is affected by the world. And indeed Kant supposes that sensations in consciousness, which provide the matter for the constitution of the phenomenal world, are produced by *affections* of the senses. Husserl has to reject this view, for it confronts a dilemma. Either the senses are affected by the *Ding an sich* in the Kantian sense, or they are affected by the phenomenal world. However, the first alternative is unacceptable to Husserl, because the Kantian concept of a *Ding an sich* is "mythical." If, on the other hand, the senses are affected by the phenomenal world, as Husserl himself had to assume in the *Investigations*, the constituting mind must be part of the phenomenal world. In this case, we get caught up in the paradox of human subjectivity. What Husserl reproaches Kant with, then, is that he used a mythical concept of the *an sich* and that he never solved the paradox of human subjectivity. As a consequence, Kant's distinction between empirical and transcendental consciousness was never really clarified, and his transcendental terminology was mythical through and through. Because Husserl's own transcendental idealism was obtained by a radicalization of Cartesian doubt, Husserl reproaches Kant for having never fathomed the "immense depths of the Cartesian fundamental meditation."[155]

What distinguishes Husserl from Kant, to wit his rejection of the latter's notion of a world *an sich*,[156] brings him near to Berkeley. Like Husserl, Berkeley thought that the concept of a material world which exists independently of consciousness is nonsensical. In § 55 of *Ideas* I, Husserl denies that he is a Berkeleian idealist, for the reason that he does not deny the existence of the world. But this attempt to dissociate himself from the unpopular bishop fails, being based on a misunderstanding of Berkeleian immaterialism. Like Husserl, Berkeley claims merely to remove an absurd interpretation of the existence of the world; he does not deny its existence. Like Husserl, Berkeley is a reductive and not an eliminative idealist. And like Husserl, he claims that the material world is constituted by the mind on the basis of its immanent sensations or ideas.

There are two differences between Berkeley and Husserl which, I think, are of minor importance. First, Berkeley did not distinguish clearly between what is really contained in consciousness and its intentional objects.[157] But recent commentators such as Yolton have interpreted Berkeley's 'ideas' as intentional objects, so that this point is a matter of emphasis only.[158] Secondly, Berkeley does not distinguish between empirical and transcendental consciousness. He did not solve Husserl's paradox of human subjectivity.[159] However, Berkeley cannot really be blamed for this, because his views did not imply the paradox. Berkeley never situated the constituting mind within the phenomenal world, because he claimed that the mind could not be a phenomenon in the sense matter is. The mind is known by means of notions, and not by means of ideas. Berkeley distinguished constituting consciousness as radically from the phenomenal world as Husserl did, although in a different manner. Even if this latter difference between Berkeley and Husserl may be thought to be substantial, it is nothing compared to the striking similarities between the two thinkers. They both hold that the material world depends on consciousness and that it is constituted on the basis of sensations or ideas. They both hold that a descriptive study of consciousness will reveal the sense of the existence of the world and that it will clarify its constitution. As we have seen, they both are instrumentalists in the philosophy of science, and they deny that matter may exist independently of consciousness. The most forceful reason for a *rapprochement* between Berkeley and Husserl is implied by this latter point.

Since both Husserl and Berkeley claim that one can not assume an independent physical cause of the presence of sensations in (transcendental) consciousness, they have to explain the existence of these sensations in some other way. In the *Principles*, Berkeley argues that the ideas of perception must be caused by a foreign will, and that we must assume that this will is God's will, because of the magnificent order in these ideas.[160] The "Berkeleian" nature of Husserl's transcendental idealism is shown by the fact that Husserl endorses this same argument from design. As he says in § 58 of *Ideas* I, the contingent regular order in the sensations of transcendental consciousness, which enables it to constitute a world, is a rational ground for assuming the existence of a Divine Being beyond the world.[161] Both for Husserl and for Berkeley, epistemology was the gate to rational theology and metaphysics.[162]

XVII. TRANSCENDENTAL IDEALISM AND THE PHILOSOPHY OF SCIENCE

The rational reconstruction of Husserl's transcendental idealism also enables us to evaluate Husserl's place in the history of modern philosophy. As we have seen, transcendental idealism was the result of a gradual radicalization of Cartesian doubt (§ 15, above). In order to locate Husserl in history, then, I shall briefly discuss the origins of Cartesian doubt and the Quest for Certainty. In §§ 17–18, I focus on the philosophy of science, whereas §§ 19–20 are concerned with the ontological assumptions of Cartesian doubt and with the origin of the principle of immanence.

Contemporary philosophers generally reject the Cartesian quest for certainty. As a consequence, they also reject methodological doubt as a procedure for obtaining absolute certainty. But what was the historical origin of the quest for certainty? In the fifties and sixties, when many analytic philosophers still believed that all philosophical doctrines of the past originated from transcending the bounds of sense, the quest for certainty was often explained as a product of a confusion in logical grammar. Descartes allegedly failed to distinguish between logical and epistemic necessity. From the logical impossibility that a knows that p although p is false, he is held to have inferred that a cannot know that p unless p is epistemically necessary, that is, indubitable.[163] Historians will object, however, that they do not find this confusion in Descartes' writings. In fact, the Cartesian quest for certainty has a different origin. It is an implication of the philosophy of science Aristotle proposed in his *Analytica Posteriora*.

Science, Aristotle thought, should have the form of an axiomatic-deductive system. Aristotle also adhered to a specific epistemological conception of such a system. He assumed that we first accept the axioms of the system as true propositions. After that, we would accept theorems as true for the sole reason that we could deduce them directly or indirectly from the axioms. Imagine an axiomatic-deductive system as a pyramid with the axioms at the top. We then can say that according to Aristotle's philosophy of science, there is a top-down flow of truth and knowledge in scientific theories. This philosophy of science was inspired by the best "theory" the Greeks had: (proto-) Euclidean geometry. Unfortunately, Aristotle general-

ized it into a general philosophy of science, which was claimed to
hold for natural science as well.

If contemporary philosophers of science endorse the ideal of ax-
iomatization, they reject Aristotle's epistemology of axiomatic-
deductive systems. In natural science, for instance, we do not accept a
system because we first know that its axioms are true. Rather, we accept the system as a whole because, in conjunction with background
theories and initial conditions, it yields a set of predictions which is
superior to the sets of its competitors. According to this modern conception, there cannot be a top-down stream of knowledge and truth.
There cannot be a bottom-up stream of truth either, for this would
imply a fallacy of affirming the consequent. As a consequence, scientific theories are essentially hypothetical. We can never prove that
they are true. At best, there is a bottom-up stream of falsity, partly
channelled by strategic decisions, so that theories may be refuted.

In the Aristotelian conception of science there is a fundamental
problem which drops out in the modern conception, the problem of
the first principles. Aristotle defines *epistémé* or scientific knowledge as knowledge by proof. We do not *know p* unless we have deduced *p* from a set of premises. In other words, scientific knowledge is
knowledge of theorems of a system. But this definition implies either
an infinite regress or a circle, that is, it implies skepticism, if there is
not another kind of knowledge, which does not need any proof: knowledge of the first principles or axioms. This kind of knowledge has to be
more certain than that of the theorems, since we accept the theorems
only because we accept the axioms first. The first principles are "better known," says Aristotle. The problem of the first principles is
central to the philosophical tradition from Aristotle to Kant and
Husserl: how are we able to know the first principles with certainty?
Aristotle's conception of science implies that no knowledge will be
possible unless this problem is solved satisfactorily.

The Aristotelian philosophy of science yields the traditional distinction between science (*epistémé*) and (first) philosophy or metaphysics (*sofia*). If knowledge of the first principles is more certain
than, and both logically and epistemically prior to, knowledge of the
theorems, philosophy or *sofia* has to be distinguished from the sciences (*epistémé*). According to Aristotle, there are first principles,
the axioms in the strict sense, which are common to all sciences.
These hold not for specific regions of being only, but for being as

such. Knowledge of these general first principles was later called "ontology." And if the deity is considered as a first principle or first cause as well, first philosophy will be onto-theology. First philosophy or metaphysics, then, is an onto-theology which contains the foundation of the sciences.

Descartes rejected Aristotle's hylomorphistic onto-theology. And yet he endorsed Aristotle's *conception* of first philosophy or metaphysics as onto-theology. As he says in the *lettre-préface* to the *Principles*, Plato and Aristotle did not succeed in providing a certain philosophical foundation to the sciences. Where they failed, Descartes claims to have succeeded. He upgraded the requirement of certainty into one of indubitability, and invented the procedure of methodical doubt for discovering indubitable principles. We may conclude that the Cartesian quest for certainty, the procedure of methodical doubt, and Descartes's foundationalism originate not from confusions in logical grammar, but from the Aristotelian philosophy of science.

Descartes's methodical doubt culminates in doubting the existence of the material world and the propositions of mathematics. And yet it yields an indubitable first principle of metaphysics: the existence of my own consciousness. Reflecting upon consciousness, Descartes formulates a rationalist criterion of truth, which is then validated by a proof of God's existence and veracity. The rationalist criterion of truth in its turn justifies the *a priori* first principles of physics, such as the principle that matter is extension. Although these principles are too weak for the deduction of specific physical theories, they define the essential structure of matter, to which all models for physical explanation must conform. We may say, then, that the Cartesian edifice of knowledge consists of three levels. The most fundamental level is a metaphysical foundation of the first principles of the sciences. Then comes an ontology of nature, which comprises these *a priori* first principles. Finally there is the level of empirical theories, which purport to explain natural phenomena along the lines indicated by the ontology of nature.

XVIII. HUSSERL AS AN EXPONENT OF THE ARISTOTELIAN-CARTESIAN TRADITION

What was the fate of this tripartite conception of knowledge in the modern era? Cartesian foundationalism was undermined when, in the second half of the seventeenth century, direct deductive consequences of the Cartesian first principles of physics were empirically refuted. Because Descartes identified matter and extension, his physics excluded the possibility of a vacuum. Descartes also considered the instantaneous propagation of light as a direct implication of his principles. But Rømer discovered the finite speed of light in 1676, and Pascal contended that the recent experiments with the barometer implied the existence of the vacuum. However, if direct deductive consequences of the first principles of physics may be refuted empirically, these principles cannot be *a priori* and purely rational, as Descartes had claimed. Therefore, Pascal concluded that all science of nature is empirical and hypothetical. About 1700, many thought that empiricism was the only legitimate philosophy of natural science, authorized by the development of physics and by Newton's official adherence.

It is an irony of history that the very successes of Newtonian science, conjoined with Hume's skeptical analysis of empiricism, were the motive for Kant's restoration of the Aristotelian-Cartesian conception of knowledge. Kant thought that, in order to explain Newton's predictive successes, he had to assume the *a priori* nature of some fundamental principles of Newtonian physics, such as the deterministic principle of causality and Euclidean geometry. Kant rejected the Cartesian theological explanation of the objective validity of such synthetic *a priori* principles, and proposed his Copernican revolution instead. Because the phenomenal world is constituted by the knowing subject, it conforms to *a priori* principles contained in this subject. This transcendental theory justifies the metaphysics of nature, which contains the alleged *a priori* principles of physics, and the metaphysics of nature in its turn is the foundation of empirical physics. In Kant, we find again the traditional tripartite architecture of cognition.

Husserl endorsed the axiomatic-deductive conception of knowledge in the *Prolegomena*.[164] In *Ideas* I, he also accepts the traditional tripartite structure of knowledge. The empirical sciences are founded by *a priori* "regional ontologies" which, in their turn, are validated by transcendental phenomenology.[165] However, the nature of this latter validation is different from Kant's or Descartes's. Husserl's transcendental constitution-analysis elucidates the *ontological sense* of the regions of being and, correspondingly, the precise meaning of the essential and empirical truths about them.[166] After having acknowledged the existence of ideal objects in the

Investigations, for instance, Husserl tries to elucidate the ontological sense of this type of existence in *Formal and transcendental Logic* and in the paper on the origin of geometry, by an analysis of its "constitution."[167] And yet, Husserl remained a Cartesian in that he claimed apodictic certainty for his analyses. Both of these features of Husserl's foundationalism are explained by my rational reconstruction of transcendental idealism.

Like Husserl, Heidegger in *Being and Time* (1927) was still under the spell of the traditional tripartite conception of knowledge. According to §§ 3 and 4 of this book, *a priori* regional ontologies are the foundation of the empirical sciences, whereas these ontologies, in their turn, are based on the ontological structure of *Dasein*. Accordingly, the hermeneutics of *Dasein* is called "fundamental ontology." But in 1927, this type of philosophical foundationalism was already refuted by developments in science. The general theory of relativity and quantum mechanics proved that physics can do without the assumptions which Kant mistakenly glorified as synthetic *a priori* principles. As Logical Positivists and Karl Popper concluded, physics does not have an *a priori* philosophical foundation and, indeed, the mistaken belief in such a foundation will be merely an impediment to the development of science. This was fatal to the Aristotelian conception of science, and to the concomitant distinction between science and philosophy. The principles of scientific theories are as hypothetical as these theories themselves. The problem of the first principles disappears, and is replaced by the problem of articulating a scientific methodology which optimizes the *growth* of knowledge. Ontology cannot be an *a priori* foundation of the sciences; it is at best an *a posteriori* corollary of the development of science. The question what there is, is answered by the best scientific theories. And if all knowledge is hypothetical, the Husserlian quest for apodictically certain foundations of knowledge by means of a radicalized methodic doubt must be misguided in principle. From the point of view of the philosophy of science, then, Husserl's foundationalism belongs to a philosophical tradition which is dead and buried.

XIX. THE ONTOLOGICAL ROOTS OF CARTESIAN
DOUBT AND THE PRINCIPLE OF IMMANENCE

It goes without saying that to define Husserl's place in the history of philosophy solely from the point of view of the philosophy of science is one-sided, even though this is an important point of view. Thus far, I have explained the *necessity* of Cartesian doubt within the framework of the Aristotelian conception of science. It is a method for finding the indubitable principles which this conception requires. But I did not explain the *possibility* of Cartesian doubt, nor did I discuss the origin of the principle of immanence, which was at the root of Husserl's transcendental idealism. In this section I shall argue that Cartesian doubt concerning the external world is not possible unless one assumes the principle of immanence. Furthermore, I shall argue that the principle of immanence itself was implied by the anti-Aristotelian ontological revolution in the seventeenth century. It is my aim to locate Husserl also within the history of modern ontology and epistemology.

The question as to the origin of the principle of immanence, or the notion of a sensual core, as it is also called, is crucial both for understanding modern psychology of perception (seventeenth to nineteenth centuries) and modern philosophical epistemology. As we have seen, the principle cannot be justified by a descriptive analysis of perception within the framework of common sense (§ 7, previous). It may be thought that the principle of immanence is an implication of the empirical analysis of visual perception in the sixteenth and seventeenth centuries. After Kepler had discovered the way in which light rays project the three-dimensional world onto our retinae, and when the retina-images of cows had become experimentally available for inspection,[168] it became abundantly clear that the two-dimensional properties of the retina-image are different from the three-dimensional properties of the object perceived. Did this discovery motivate the conception of the *sensory core* as a mental correlate of the retinal image, which, although typically unnoticed, would be interpreted in the perceptual act? Hatfield and Epstein have argued that the historical motivation for assigning to the sensory core a content distinct from the visual world has come from geometrical optics.[169] But clearly, as they also notice, the principle of immanence itself cannot be derived from geometrical optics. The distinction between the physical properties of the retinal image and the perceived physical properties of the object of vision does not at all imply the existence of a *mental* correlate of the retinal image. It could be argued either that the phenomenal character of everyday experience in fact corresponds to the features of the retinal image, or that the information processing that starts with retinal stimulation and ends up with our visual awareness of a three-dimensional world, is wholly "physiological" and inaccessible for consciousness. Hatfield and Epstein conclude that it was not the scientific theory of vision itself that engendered the notion of a sensory core, but rather the introduction of the theory into a new metaphysical context. My account of the origin of the principle of immanence may be seen as a substantiation of this claim.[170]

Let me start with the problem of the possibility of Cartesian doubt concerning the existence of the external world. This doubt is at the root of the "subjectivist bias" of modern philosophy, for it shows that mind is better known than matter, as Descartes says in his Second Meditation. Husserl clearly belongs to the subjectivist tradition. A presupposition of this tradition is that global doubt concerning the external world is at least a conceptual possibility. Philosophers of language have argued, however, that it is not. The concept of doubting, they say, excludes global doubt, just as the concept of lying excludes that everyone always lies. In order to be able to lie, there must be a general practice of speaking the truth. Without such a practice, language breaks down. This very practice enables us to act as if we speak the truth, although in fact we do not. As Kant and Wittgenstein have argued, lying is a parasitic activity. Concepts of parasitic activities do not allow us to infer from "It is sometimes possible to do F" that "It is always possible to do F." In other words, lying is essentially local.

It is argued that this holds also for the concept of a hallucination. To suffer a hallucination means that we are in an exceptional state. It seems that we are perceiving something, whereas in fact we are not. Like the concept of a universal lie, the concept of a global hallucination is incoherent, not because we would never be able to discover that we are suffering a global hallucination, but because "to hallucinate" *means* that we are in an exceptional state which deceptively resembles other, normal states. We would not be able to *have* this concept if we were not normally in these latter states. Therefore, a hallucination is necessarily local. But because Cartesian doubt concerning the existence of the material world is nothing but entertaining the possibility of a global hallucination, Cartesian doubt is conceptually impossible.

A Wittgensteinian philosopher will perhaps conclude that Cartesian doubt originated from a confusion of logical grammar. Descartes would be held to have overlooked the parasitic nature of the concept of a hallucination. His mistake was to think that the inference from "It is sometimes possible to do F" to "It is always possible to do F" is universally valid. But, I would suggest, it is unsatisfactory to stop at this conclusion, even if it were correct. What we want to know is: why did Descartes see no conceptual difficulties at all in doubting the existence of the external world, and why was this doubt such a persistent feature of modern epistemology? The answer is that the possibility or even the necessity of doubting the existence of the external world is implied by the ontological revolution which took place in the seventeenth century and by the then-dominant theory of perception. I shall now briefly spell out this answer.

During the scientific revolution, Aristotelian hylomorphism as a model of explanation was replaced by mechanism. The successes of mechanics as a science of terrestrial and heavenly motions seemed to confirm the bold speculation of the corpuscular ontology, known from Antiquity. Would it not be possible to generalize mechanics into a universal science of nature? But to do so required the hypothesis that phenomena of nature which are not overtly mechanical, such as warmth, colour, light, magnetism, and sound, in fact consist of the operation of mechanical microstructures. These phenomena had to be explained as the macroscopic effects of the mechanical behaviour of very small particles, the *corpuscula*. According to the corpuscular ontology, then, in the final analysis nature as a whole consists of small particles which behave according to the laws of mechanics. As far as the philosophical implications of this physicalist ontology are concerned, it does not matter whether one substitutes waves or fields for particles and refines this ontology as physics develops. For reasons of terminological convenience, I shall simply speak of the "corpuscular" ontology.[171]

The corpuscular revolution in ontology engendered in its turn a revolution in the theory of perception. According to Aristotle, the perceiving mind absorbs the "forms" of the perceived objects, so that perception is a formal or essential identity of perceiver and object perceived. This identity theory of perception does not allow for a general doubt concerning perception. The corpuscular ontology, however, implies a deep cleft between perceptual appearance and physical reality. In order to avoid circular explanations in physics, corpuscular philosophers deny phenomenal or secondary qualities such as colours or temperatures to the particles whose mechanical behaviour accounts for these qualities. And they argue, surprisingly, that if the corpuscles lack colour, for instance, macroscopic objects cannot be really coloured either. For how can a coloured macroscopic object be assembled from colourless particles?[172] Physical reality, then, is very different from its perceptual appearance, because it lacks secondary qualities. The world-view of physics seems to be incompatible with the view of common sense.

This *incompatibility thesis* leads to the principle of immanence and to the representative theories of perception. For if phenomenal qualities do not exist in material nature, what is their ontological status? Galileo replies that they are affections of the perceiving organism. But what if the perceiving organism is itself a purely material mechanism, as Descartes contended? Because the secondary qualities are "direct" objects of perceptual consciousness, it seemed plausible to interpret them as mental entities, once they were expelled from the physical world. The secondary qualities were assimilated to sensations such as pain, and were thought to exist in the mind only. This mentalization of phenomenal qualities or "qualia," allegedly necessitated by corpuscular physics, yields the principle of immanence: it is now claimed that the primary data of perception are really immanent in consciousness. The principle of immanence, in its turn, seems to imply a projective theory of perception. For if we assume that secondary qualities are really sensations in the mind, it has to be explained why we perceive these qualities as being qualities of physical objects in our environment. The answer is that they are "projected" outside, by a mental mechanism of perception.[173] In this manner, the corpuscular ontology leads to a dualist projective theory of perception, according to which physical processes in the world cause sensations in consciousness, which are then "objectively interpreted," as Husserl says. Husserl's principle of immanence, then, is not a purely descriptive phenomenological result, as he himself contends. To use Husserlian terminology, it is a "sedimentation" of traditional seventeenth century philosophy, which Husserl did not recognize as such. This holds also for Husserl's projective theory of perception.

The principle of immanence raises the two problems of transcendence I discussed in § 11. If the primary data of perception are sensations or qualia in the mind, how is our familiar perceptual world constituted out of these data? For instance, how is it possible that we seem to see distance, although the primary data of vision are not at a distance? I called this problem the problem of constitution. Cartesian perceptual judgements and the *géométrie naturelle*, empiricist association mechanisms, and Kantian or Husserlian processes of constitution are all postulated to solve this problem. The principle of immanence also raises the problem of realism, or the problem of the world *an sich*. Does the perceptual world, which depends on the perceiving mind, refer to a world which exists independently of perception? The realist answer implies that one has a representative theory of perception in the strict sense. Idealists are not representationalists, even though they also endorse the principle of immanence and the projective theory of perception.

The possibility of Cartesian doubt concerning the external world is nothing but the second problem of transcendence. The real origin of this possibility of doubting the existence of the external world, then, lies in the corpuscular ontology. This ontology implies the subjectivity of the immediate data of perception (the principle of immanence), which implies the projective theory of perception, which, in its turn, implies skepticism concerning the material world. In this way, the corpuscular ontology annihilates itself, unless the skeptical problem is solved realistically.

In the previous section, I interpreted Cartesian doubt as a necessary means for solving the problem of the first principles, which was implied by the Aristotelian conception of science. If we call this conception "classical foundationalism," Descartes and Husserl are classical foundationalists. Although Descartes merely wanted to solve the problem of the first principles and thereby to construct a scientific metaphysics, the method he used for solving this problem, the method of systematic doubt, made him the father of modern epistemology. For methodological doubt raised the problem of the external world, and showed that mind is better known than matter. Epistemology was defined, in the nineteenth century, as first philosophy, because it had to test the most fundamental assumption of science, that the material world exists. Epistemology in this sense is also foundationalist. We might call it modern foundationalism. We may conclude that Husserl was part of the foundationalist tradition in modern philosophy in two senses: he was both a classical and a modern foundationalist.

XX. EMPIRICISM AND THE PARADOX OF IDEALISM

In the last three sections, I have determined Husserl's place in history by focusing on the origins of his philosophical *problems*. Because Husserl accepts the Aristotelian theory of science, he has to look for absolutely certain first principles. Because he also inherits the principle of immanence and the problem of the external world, these principles have to be found in consciousness. Thus far, I have traced two important origins of Husserl's philosophy: Aristotelian philosophy of science and the assumption that the corpuscular ontology is incompatible with common sense (call it: the incompatibility thesis). The incompatibility thesis implies the principle of immanence and the problem of the external world, because it leads to a mentalization of the primary data of perception. In order to explain Husserl's idealist solution to his problems, however, we need a third important origin of his philosophy: empiricism.

As we have seen, the skeptical problem of the external world is suggested indirectly by the corpuscular ontology, which yields the projective theories of perception. But if a realist view is the starting point of the problem,[174] it is natural to look for a realist solution. As long as philosophers remained rationalists, it was relatively easy to argue for such a realist view. This is because the rational *a priori* principles of science provided an *extra-perceptual* access to the real material world, backed up by God's veracity (Descartes). But as soon as corpuscular philosophers turned empiricist, for the reasons indicated in § 18, above, the problem of the external world became a central problem of epistemology. According to the empiricist, sense-perception leads to corpuscular physics. Corpuscular physics, however, implies that sense-perception is unreliable, for according to the projective theories, perception gives access to a phenomenal world only. Should one not conclude that empiricism is refuted by the corpuscular philosophy and the concomitant theory of perception? It seems, therefore, that one cannot be both an empiricist and a scientific realist concerning corpuscular physics. The first philosopher who saw this was Bishop Berkeley. Berkeley held on to empiricism. He also endorsed the principle of immanence. In order to avoid skepticism, he had to argue that if the primary data of perception are in the mind, as the principle of immanence says, physics must be about this mind-dependent empirical world. As a consequence, it is superfluous and even absurd to posit a material world which exists independently of perception. Husserl is also an empiricist of sorts. Admittedly, he holds that the empirical sciences are based on *a priori* regional ontologies. But because the *a priori* principles of the sciences are concerned with essences of factual domains of the empirical world, which are eidetically abstracted from these domains, the empirical world is the basis of all scientific knowledge. Because Husserl's theory of perception implies that the empirical world is mind-dependent, Husserl became an idealist as well.

If my regressive reconstruction of the principle of immanence is correct, idealist doctrines are paradoxical. In these doctrines, the self-annihilation of the corpuscular ontology becomes a fact. This surely is a paradox, but the real paradox of idealism is as follows. Because the principle of immanence originated from the corpuscular ontology via the incompatibility thesis, the idealist doctrines reject the corpuscular ontology on the grounds of what this ontology itself implies. This means that the idealist position rests on an implication of the ontology it rejects, i.e., on the principle of immanence. As a consequence, idealism will destroy itself in the final analysis. For one cannot reject a doctrine and preserve its implications (unless, of course, one is able to justify these implications differently; see below). Let me call this the paradox of idealism.

I have argued before that Husserl's descriptivist ideology prevents him from seeing that the principle of immanence is a sedimentation from the philosophical tradition and not a descriptive result. We now understand why Husserl *had to* dissimulate the realist antecedents of the principle of immanence. By admitting these antecedents, he would have acknowledged that his idealism was based on the implications of the realist position it rejects, so that he would have been caught in the paradox of idealism. In fact, there is but one way to escape from this paradox. One might attempt to argue that the principle of immanence can be justified in another way than by deriving it from corpuscular physics. Empiricists such as Berkeley, Ayer, and Husserl tried to do this. They contended, for instance, that the occurrence of hallucinations and illusions, or the adumbrative nature of outer perception, imply the existence of mental sensations or qualia in all perceptual acts. It is well known that these arguments are fallacious.[175] If one believes that phenomena such as colours, temperatures, sounds, and odours are subjective sensations, this is because one believes that physics implies this. The paradox of idealism, then, is inescapable. Idealism seems to be a radical alternative to naturalism or corpuscularian realism. But it is less radical than it seems, for it rests on an implication of the doctrine it rejects.

The incompatibility thesis may be considered as one of the deepest assumptions of modern philosophy, including Husserl's philosophy. If the world view of physics, or the scientific image as it is also called, is incompatible with the common-sense view or the manifest image, the philosopher will seem to have two options only. One is to adopt the scientific image as the true one and to explain the manifest image as a subjective phenomenon, an illusion, or a false theory. This is the naturalist strategy of realists such as Descartes, Quine, and Churchland.[176] The alternative is to claim that the common-sense world is the real world, and that the world of science is but a secondary and derived construction. Idealists such as Berkeley and Husserl adopt the second strategy, albeit imperfectly. For their idealist conclusions were based on an implication of the realist position, the principle of immanence. Therefore, idealism does not radically replace naturalism. In order to overcome naturalism radically, one has also to reject the principle of immanence and the epistemological problem of the external world which is implied by it. And one has to develop an account of the world we live in which really reflects common sense and which is in no way contaminated by the ontologies of physics. This is one way of interpreting Heidegger's project in *Sein und Zeit*. According to Heidegger, the entire problematic of the external world is a symptom of *Verfall*, that is, of an interpretation of ourselves and our being-in-the-world due to scientific objectivism and the ontology of presence.[177] And the aim of his philosophy is to argue that there is a more fundamental way of seeing the world than the scientific way, a way which is closer to "being."[178] We may conclude that Heidegger rejected Husserl's transcendental idealism because he wanted to radicalize Husserl's anti-naturalism.

XXI. HUSSERL'S PLACE IN HISTORY: TRANSCENDENTAL IDEALISM AND THE LIFE-WORLD

There are at least two reasons for concluding this essay with some brief observations on Husserl's *Crisis*. First, in *Crisis* the concept of the life-world plays a pivotal role, and it is often thought that this concept is incompatible with transcendental idealism as I have interpreted it. Therefore, the onus of proving that this is not the case falls on me. Second, in *Crisis* (as earlier in the lectures on *First Philosophy*) Husserl attempts to locate transcendental phenomenology within the history of Western philosophy. By means of a reconstruction of the "inner sense" or the "hidden teleology" of this history, he purports to show that his own transcendental phenomenology is the end-point of the philosophical development since Antiquity, because he would finally have realized the dream of a scientific philosophy.[179] Husserl's view of his place in history differs at crucial points from my view of his place in history, and, indeed, his reconstruction of the history of modern philosophy is at variance with mine. What I have to show, then, is that Husserl's reconstruction of history is mistaken.

I argued that Husserl's attempt to overcome naturalism failed, because transcendental idealism still rests on an implication of naturalism. If one really wants to replace naturalism, one should prefer Heidegger to Husserl. As a consequence, assuming that a transcendental critique of naturalism is the aim of history as Husserl saw it, Heidegger came nearer to this aim than Husserl did. This is because Heidegger saw that Husserl's descriptions of the "natural attitude" and of the "life-world" were contaminated by the very naturalist ontology which Husserl wanted to overcome. And because transcendental idealism is a "reversal" of the natural attitude, this is also true for transcendental idealism. Therefore, Heidegger replaced Husserl's ontology of daily life by another one, which is not at all coloured by science.

Furthermore, I argued that the opposition between realism and idealism in modern philosophy is due to the corpuscular ontology, the incompatibility thesis, and the principle of immanence. This analysis opens the possibility of rejecting both traditional idealism and realism by rejecting the principle of immanence, or, even more radically, by rejecting the incompatibility thesis. Of course, one may dismiss traditional realism as based on the principle of immanence, and yet accept the "realist" conviction that the world which we perceive and which we investigate in science exists independently of consciousness. There would then be nothing wrong, from the present standpoint, with "realism" in this sense.

In part II of *Crisis*, Husserl also reconstructs the origin of the modern opposition between "physicalist objectivism" and "transcendental subjectivism," as he calls it. Because Husserl sees himself as the final founding father of transcendental subjectivism, the main objective of his genealogy of modern philosophy is to deconstruct scientific realism or objectivism. In *Crisis*, Husserl deconstructs realism by interpreting it as a hypostatization of the mathematical method. In other words, whereas my historical reconstruction opens the possibility of rejecting the traditional dilemma of subjectivism and objectivism, Husserl accepts the dilemma and acclaims subjectivism. I shall briefly summarize Husserl's reconstruction, which does not refer to the corpuscular ontology at all, and argue that it cannot be correct. Next, I shall elucidate the notion of a life-world as it figures in Part III A of *Crisis*.

In the central § 9 of Part II, Husserl first shows how the ideal objects of Euclidean geometry are constituted on the basis of the life-world, which is the only real world, as he says in § 9h. The history of technology shows that humans gradually brought to perfection artefacts of certain shapes, such as circular wheels. If we order these artifacts in series of ever greater perfection of shape, say circularity, these series point to an ideal limit (*Limesgestalt*), which technology will never be able to realize: the perfect circle. The objects of Euclidean geometry are nothing but such ideal limits, which we conceive by extrapolating series of shapes in the life-world. Clearly, then, the existence of these ideal limits depends on human thought. But when geometry had become an institutionalized science, this life-world "origin" of geometrical objects was forgotten, because pure geometers work with these ideal objects only, and do not need to trace their origin in the life-world. Husserl calls this process of forgetting about ontological sense *Sinnentleerung* (emptying of sense). As a consequence, it was assumed, by Plato and others, that geometrical objects exist *an sich*, independently of human thought.

This analysis of the origin of geometry and of Platonism in the philosophy of mathematics is instructive, but Husserl extends it in a dubious way. For he goes on to argue that the Galilean and Cartesian picture of a material world *an sich*, which is in some sense "mathematical," is the product of a similar hypostatization of the mathematical method. Whereas the shapes of objects in the life-world, if ordered in series of ever greater perfection, point to the ideal limits of geometry, the sensuous contents of life-world objects such as colours and warmth or coldness cannot be ordered in series which point to ideal limits. This means that they cannot be directly "mathematized." In order to apply mathematical physics to these qualities, Husserl argues, Galileo had to assume that variations in sensuous qualities are causally related to variations in shape, so that they might be measured indirectly by directly measuring these shapes. To the extent that this hypothesis was corroborated by the discovery of specific causal relations and by the invention of measuring instruments, physics could be mathematized. But this is a method only, and it does not mean that the world itself is mathematical, as Galileo and Descartes thought. Their conception of a mathematical material world, which causes our perceptions, is also a hypostatization of a mathematical method (§§ 9b–k). From this point onward, Husserl's reconstruction parallels mine, for the mathematical conception of the world excludes secondary qualities and mental aspects of living beings in the same way as the corpuscular conception does. This is why both conceptions lead to a cleft between the subjective and the objective.

It is important to see that Husserl's point in deconstructing the mathematical conception of the world is not merely the criticism, also raised by Wittgenstein, that Galileo and Descartes "predicated of the thing what lies in the method of representing it."[180] According to Husserl, not only the idea that the material world is somehow "mathematical," but also the very notion that there is a material world *an sich* at all is due to a hypostatization of the mathematical method (§ 9h)! As in *Ideas* I, Husserl argues in *Crisis* that the theoretical entities of physics are nothing but intellectual constructs, which derive their real sense from the scientific method. Their ontological status is more or less the same as that of the perfect idealized shapes of pure Euclidean geometry. What Husserl claims, then, is that the notion of an independent physical world is due to a hypostatization of the mathematical method in physics.

There are at least three good reasons for rejecting this claim. The first is that there is nothing wrong with the idea that the material world exists independently of consciousness, and that this idea is as old as philosophy. Accordingly, it does not need a "deconstruction," and it certainly cannot be the product of a hypostatization of the mathematical method in the seventeenth century. Secondly, Husserl's reconstruction is historically inadequate, for it fits at best

Galileo and Descartes only. Most philosophers of the seventeenth century believed that the material world exists independently of consciousness (except in the sense that it was thought to depend on God, of course), but few of them held that the material world is "mathematical." Matter was often thought to possess other "primary" qualities besides the mathematical ones, such as Locke's "solidity." But all progressive philosophers of the seventeenth century endorsed the corpuscular ontology. Accordingly, one should reconstruct the dichotomy of subjectivism and objectivism, which confronted these philosophers, on the basis of the corpuscular ontology. Finally, Husserl's analysis is too vague, because he does not specify what exactly is hypostatized. Admittedly, it would be a mistake to think, for instance, that Newtonian point-masses are real entities. But such a hypostatization of point-masses is a quite incredible mistake, and it is implausible to suggest that the idea of a material world *an sich* is due to it. On the other hand, it is difficult to see how the particles of the corpuscular philosophy could be due to hypostatizations of the mathematical method. The vagueness of Husserl's analysis merely conceals its implausibility, and I conclude that we should reject it.

Husserl's deconstruction of the idea of a material world *an sich* is but the first step in his complex argument in *Crisis*. In this first step, it is assumed that the real world is not the world of physics but the life-world, and Husserl stresses that the life-world is "the only real world."[181] This is why one might think that Husserl is a realist after all, and of course he is a realist in the sense that he does not deny that the life-world exists. But such an "empirical realism" does not conflict with Husserl's transcendental idealism, which claims that the life-world ontologically depends on transcendental consciousness. And indeed the second stage of Husserl's argument (Part IIIA of *Crisis*) purports to show that this is in fact the case. Although the life-world includes the social and the cultural world, its basic stratum is the sensible phenomenal world (*die sinnliche Erscheinungswelt*).[182] The life-world in this sense is "subjective-relative," not only because we always have a definite perspective on it, but also because it is "constituted out of spiritual materials."[183] It is a meaningful construct (*Sinngebilde*) of the ultimate functioning subject.[184] This thesis then leads to the paradox of human subjectivity, because the subject which *produces* the world (*zustandebringen, gestalten)* cannot be a subordinate reality *within* the world. The argument culminates in Husserl's transcendental solution to this paradox (§§ 54–55).

It is not likely, I think, that the uninitiated reader will be able to follow Husserl's argument in *Crisis*, Part IIIA, and even less probable that he or she will be convinced. This is because the argument rests on a concealed premise, the same premise that is presupposed by the argument of *Ideas* I: the projective theory of perception. Although Husserl does not discuss perception in *Crisis*, he hints at this theory where he says that the life-world is constituted out of spiritual materials, i.e., the sensations.

However, against the background of my reconstruction of the genesis of transcendental idealism, Husserl's argument in *Crisis* will be easily understood. The life-world in *Crisis* is identical with the phenomenal world of the *Logical Investigations*, which is subjective-relative because it is a product of an interpretation of subjective sensations. This world is the only world there is, because it does not make sense to posit a material world *an sich* in the traditional sense. Husserl in *Crisis* completes his earlier rejection of this notion of an *an sich* by explaining it as a hypostatization of the mathematical method in physics. Because the life-world depends on the constituting subject, Husserl is faced with the paradox of human subjectivity, which he solves by transcendental idealism. In § 7 of *Crisis*, Husserl says that in this book he merely shows the ways he himself had gone. And this is very true, for the argument in *Crisis* repeats Husserl's development towards transcendental idealism between 1900 and 1913.

REFERENCES AND ABBREVIATIONS

All references to Husserl's works are to the *Husserliana* edition (Edmund Husserl, *Gesammelte Werke*, Den Haag/Dordrecht: Martinus Nijhoff/Kluwer, 1950–   ), abbreviated Hua, followed by volume number, page number, and, if necessary, line number. But there are a few exceptions. I referred to the first edition of the *Logical Investigations* (Halle a.S.: Max Niemeyer, 1900/1901) as *LU A*, and to the second edition (Tübingen: Max Niemeyer, 1913 and 1921) as *LU B* (see also *HUA* XVIII and XIX, vol. 1 and 2). Further, I referred to the pages of *Philosophy as a Rigorous Science* in the original *Logos* edition (see Hua XXV), and I added the page numbers of the *Jahrbuch* edition of *Ideas* I between square brackets. I decided not to use English translations, first, because scholarly interpretations should be based on the German original, and secondly, because translations are not always of the edition I wanted to use (especially in the case of *LU*). However, where possible I referred also to sections, in order to enable those who do not read German to find the relevant passages. In the notes, I used the following abbreviations for Husserl's works:

CM   *Cartesianische Meditationen* (Hua I)
EPh   *Erste Philosophie* (Hua VII–VIII)
FTL   *Formale und transzendentale Logik* (Hua XVII)
Id.I   *Ideen zu einer reinen Phänomenologie und phänomenologischen Philosophie*, Erstes Buch. NB: I used the critical edition by Karl Schuhmann (Hua III/1 and 2), and not the slightly corrupt Biemel edition (Hua III).
Id. II   Idem, zweites Buch (Hua IV)
Id. III   Idem, drittes Buch (Hua V)
IdPhä   *Die Idee der Phänomenologie* (Hua II)
Kr.   *Die Krisis der europäischen Wissenschaften und die transzendentale Phänomenologie* (Hua VI)
LU   *Logische Untersuchungen*. See above.
PhstrW   *Philosophie als strenge Wissenschaft, Logos* I (1911) (Hua XXV)

For a bibliography of Husserl's writings, see Manfred Schmitz, "Bibliographie der bis zum 8 April 1989 veröffentlichten Schriften Edmund Husserls," *Husserl Studies* 6 (1989): 205–26.

NOTES

1 *Id.* I, § 55, Hua III/1, 120, ll. 4–5 (=[106]). I am greatly indebted to the editors of this volume, especially to David Woodruff Smith, for valuable comments on earlier drafts of this paper, and to James McAllister for having corrected my English.

2 Cf. for a critique of this view: H. Philipse, "The Absolute Network Theory of Language and Traditional Epistemology. On the Philosophical Foundations of Paul Churchland's Scientific Realism," *Inquiry* 33 (1990): 127–78.

3 *Id.* I, § 131.
4 This view is developed in D.W. Smith and R. McIntyre, *Husserl and Intentionality.* Dordrecht: Reidel, 1982.
5 *Philosophy and the Mirror of Nature.* Oxford: Blackwell, 1980, 4, 166–169.
6 *Id.* I, §§ 49–55.
7 *FTL,* §§ 62–67, 92–99, and 103–104; *CM,* §§ 11, 40–41, 49, 59 and 62; *Kr.,* §§ 41–43, 48–50, 52–55, and 72–73.
8 Hua V, pp 150–51.
9 See Ernst Tugendhat, *Der Wahrheitsbegriff bei Husserl und Heidegger* (Berlin: Walter de Gruyter, 1967), §§ 9 and 10, especially 194 ff.; David Bell, *Husserl,* (London: Routledge, 1990), 168–71. Cf., for a similar critical strategy concerning Kant's transcendental idealism: Peter Strawson, *The Bounds of Sense,* (London: Methuen, 1966), 1975, 22 and 43.
10 *CM,* Hua I, 119, ll. 8–11. Cf. *EPh* I, 54th lecture, Hua VIII 181, where Husserl says that "die ganze Phänomenologie (ist) nichts anderes als die erste streng wissenschaftliche Gestalt dieses Idealismus."
11 *Id.* I § 55, where Husserl says that his position differs from Berkeley's immaterialism because it does not deny the existence of the world, but only eliminates an absurd interpretation of reality which is alien to common sense: Hua III/1, 120, 1. 21–33 (=[106–107]). Cf. on Berkeley and Husserl § 16 below.
12 Harrison Hall, "Was Husserl a Realist or an Idealist?," in Hubert L. Dreyfus and Harrison Hall, eds., *Husserl, Intentionality and Cognitive Science* (Cambridge Mass.: MIT Press), 1982, 175, and Ingrid M. Wallner, "In Defense of Husserl's Transcendental Idealism: Roman Ingarden's Critique Reexamined," *Husserl Studies* 4 (1987), 14, respectively. Cf. also Elisabeth Ströker, *Husserls transzendentale Phänomenologie* (Frankfurt a/M: V. Klostermann, 1987), 221–22.
13 Ronald McIntyre, "Husserl and the Representational Theory of Mind," *Topoi* 5 (1986): 104; David Woodruff Smith and Ronald McIntyre, *Husserl and Intentionality. A Study of Mind, Meaning, and Language* (Dordrecht: Reidel, 1982), 98–99 and 104.
14 Hall, op. cit., passim.
15 Wallner, op. cit., 22.
16 Wallner, op. cit., 11. Cf. Richard H. Holmes, "Is Transcendental Phenomenology Committed to Idealism?," *The Monist* 59 (1975): 98: "It is my contention that Husserl's transcendental phenomenology, which he labels transcendental idealism, is epistemologically idealistic but metaphysically neutral." Cf. Ronald McIntyre, op. cit., 104.
17 Hua V, 150–51.
18 I hope to publish an expanded version of my interpretation as a mono-

graph, which will contain the full historical credentials of my account of Husserl's transcendental idealism.

19 *PhStrW*, 294.

20 For Brentano's influence on Husserl, see Theodore De Boer, *The Development of Husserl's Thought* (The Hague: Nijhoff, 1978), part 1. This book, which is a slightly abridged English translation of the Dutch original (*De Ontwikkelingsgang in het denken van Husserl* (Assen: Van Gorcum, 1967), is by far the best historical study of Husserl's philosophy that I know of. I shall refer to it as *DHT*. The fact that more of Husserl's manuscript material has become available since 1966 barely necessitates corrections in De Boer's interpretation, although, of course, further details may now be filled in. I disagree with De Boer on some crucial points, but these points concern texts which Husserl himself published. Cf. for Brentano's influence also H. Philipse, "The Concept of Intentionality: Husserl's Development from the Brentano Period to the *Logical Investigations*," *Philosophy Research Archives* 12 (1987): 293–328.

21 For Husserl's notion of the theoretical content of norms, see *LU* I, Chaps. 1–2, and H. Philipse, "Psychologism and the Prescriptive Function of Logic," *Grazer Philosophische Studien* 29 (1987): 13–33 (also in Mark A. Notturno, ed., *Perspectives on Psychologism* (Leiden: Brill, 1989), 58–71).

22 *LU* I, Chap. 7. Cf. *PhstrW*, 295–96.

23 In Prolegomena, Husserl says that Herbart, Leibniz, and Bolzano influenced him most (§§ 58–61, and *Anhang*). But in a draft from 1913 for a preface to the second edition of the *Investigations*, Husserl says: "Die voll bewusste und radikale Umwendung und den mit ihr gegebenen 'Platonismus' verdanke ich dem Studium der Logik Lotzes." See "Entwurf einer 'Vorrede' zu den 'Logischen Untersuchungen'," *Tijdschrift voor filosofie* I (1939), 128.

24 *LU* A I, 79, n. 1, and 136, 164, 188, 212ff. and *LU* A II, 107–108. If, on this later page, Husserl denies that his idealism is a "metaphysical doctrine," he simply means that it is not a speculation but the acknowledgement of a fact. See "Entwurf einer 'Vorrede'," op. cit. 131: "In dem 'Platonismus' liegt keine Erkenntnistheorie, sondern die einfache innerliche Hinnahme eines ganz offenbar Gegebenen." Husserl's argument of course resembles Frege's.

25 *LU* A II, 107: "Dies ist der Punkt, an dem sich der relativistische und empiristische Psychologismus von dem Idealismus unterscheidet, welcher die einzige Möglichkeit einer mit sich einstimmigen Erkenntnistheorie darstellt."

26 I call a theory pragmatically inconsistent if the claim that the theory is true is inconsistent with the content of the theory. Such theories are

"skeptical in the strict sense" according to Husserl's definition in *LU* I, Chap. 7.

27. *LU* II, *First Investigation,* Chaps. 3 and 4; cf. the second *Investigation.* Cf. also Husserl's review of J. Bergmann, *Die Grundprobleme der Logik* (1895), in "Bericht über deutsche Schriften zur Logik in den Jahren 1895–99," I, *Archiv für systematische Philosophie* 9 (1903): 115–16, Hua XXII, 164. Husserl's distinction between ideal species and instance (*Einzelfall*) is parallel to the analytic distinction between type and token.

28. Ideal meanings, for instance, are said to exist *an sich* (§ 35 of the first Investigation), whereas ideality in the ontological sense does not imply ideality in the normative sense (§ 32). For the latter point, cf. Prolegomena, § 59.

29. *Id.* I, §§ 49–55. Terms such as "absolutes Sein" are defined in the third Logical Investigation, and have an ontological sense. Something is absolutely independent if, essentially, it can exist even when nothing else exists. And an entity of the kind *W* depends on *c* if a *W* essentially cannot exist without *c*. See Third Logical Investigation, §§ 5, 7, 10, 11, 13–17, and 21. See also De Boer, *DHT,* 341–57.

30. *Id.* I, § 49.

31. *Kr.,* § 27, Hua VI, 102. Cf. *Id.* I, § 97, Hua III/1 228 (=[204]); "Kant und die Idee der Transzendentalphilosophie," Hua VII, 230–35.

32. *PhStrW,* 294–95 and 298–300.

33. *LU* A I, 183, 186; A II, 332, 336, 356; cf. *LU* B I, 55ff., 119, 237, and B II/1, 145. Husserl assumed also that the mental phenomena described by descriptive psychology may be causally explained by explanatory psychology and psychophysics: *LU* A II, 336 (first paragraph of § 7, 5th. Inv.). But in fact it may be doubted whether Husserl in the *Investigations* really assumed that all reality is subject to deterministic causality, for in § 5 of the *Prolegomena* the idea that all natural processes are subject to causality is called a "metaphysical presupposition" of science, whereas phenomenology should abstain from metaphysical presuppositions (cf. Introd. vol. II, § 7). See § 10, herein.

34. Cf. *Id.* I, § 49, where Husserl says that transcendental consciousness is not subject to causal influences from worldly objects: Hua III/1, 105, ll. 35–39 (=[93]).

35. De Boer, *DHT,* the Conclusion, 494–506.

36. James R. Mensch, *The Question of Being in Husserl's 'Logical Investigations'* (The Hague: Nijhoff, 1981). Mensch endorses De Boer's interpretation, but on different grounds. Cf. his Introduction. See for the passage in the *Postscript* Hua V, 150, ll. 12–23.

37. *LU* A I, 8: "Im wesentlichen deckt sich diese Frage, wenn auch nicht

dem Ganzen, so doch einem Hauptteile nach, mit der Kardinalfrage der Erkenntnistheorie, die Objektivität der Erkenntnis betreffend."

38 See Chap. 11 of *Prolegomena*. Truth and objectivity are linked for Husserl, because he endorses a correspondence theory of truth. Cf. also the 6th Investigation, Chap. 5.

39 In his later work, Husserl often stresses that the transcendental reduction is a *liberation* from the bonds of the natural world. See, for instance, *Kr.*, § 41, Hua VI, 154.

40 This is what he does in *Ideas* II, §§ 54–61.

41 Mensch concludes his introduction, significantly, I think, with the observation that he does not analyze Husserl's argument for transcendental idealism in *Ideas* I. See Mensch, op. cit., 8.

42 As in Kant's case, Husserl's transcendental idealism was invented to solve epistemological problems, and the fact that it also solved the problem of freedom and determinism was, as Kant says with regard to his own case, something like an experimental confirmation of the theory. Cf. *Kritik der reinen Vernunft*, B xviii–xix, footnote. I do not deny, then, that the problems of freedom and of normativity constituted an important motivation for Husserl in developing transcendental idealism. But these problems should not play a role in a rational reconstruction of its genesis, because they do not explain at all the specific features of Husserl's idealist position.

43 *PhstrW*, pp 294–95: "die *Naturalisierung des Bewußtseins.*"

44 *PhstrW*, 298–99.

45 *PhstrW*, 299.

46 *PhstrW*, 299–300.

47 *Phstr W*, 299–300.

48 *PhstrW*, 300.

49 See, for instance, *LU* A/B I, 205–6; *LU* A II, 9, 20, 21, (B II/1, 10, 20–21), the review of Th. Elsenhans, "Das Verhältnis der Logik zur Phychologie" (1897), in "Bericht über deutsche Schriften zur Logik in den Jahren 1895–99," III, *Archiv für systematische Philosophie* IX (1903), 398–401, Hua XXII, 205–8, and the lectures from 1907, edited as *The Idea of Phenomenology*, Hua II, 3ff. The importance of this epistemological problem in Husserl's writings is also stressed by Dallas Willard in his book *Logic and the Objectivity of Knowledge. A Study in Husserl's Early Philosophy* (Athens, Ohio: Ohio University Press, 1984).

50 *Id.* I, § 33, Hua III/1, 66 (=[57]): "Was kann denn übrig bleiben, wenn die ganze Welt, eingerechnet uns selbst mit allem cogitare, ausgeschaltet ist?" This sentence is emphasized in the original text.

51 Cf. *Id.* I, § 38, Hua III/1 79 (=[69]): "Eine rein durch die eigenen Wesen

der Erlebnisse selbst bestimmte Einheit ist ausschließlich die Einheit
des Erlebnisstromes." Also emphasized in the original.

52 *Id.* I, § 30, Hua III/1, 60 (=[52]): "ein Stück reiner Beschreibung *vor aller
    Theorie.*" In other words, Husserl does not believe at all in radical
    theory-ladenness of observation. Therefore, Husserl's *epoché* concern-
    · ing the common-sense ontology is very different from attempts to elimi-
    nate this "folk" ontology by philosophers such as Paul Churchland. See
    my paper on Paul Churchland in *Inquiry* 33 (1990): 127–78.

53 Hua III/1 106, ll. 11–13 (=[93]): "So kehrt sich der gemeine Sinn der
    Seinsrede um. Das Sein, das für uns das Erste ist, ist an sich das Zweite,
    d.h. es ist, was es ist, nur in 'Beziehung' zum Ersten."

54 *Id.* I, § 49, Hua III/1, 104, ll. 23–28 (=[92]): "Das immanente Sein ist also
    zweifellos in dem Sinne absolutes Sein, daß es prinzipiell nulla 're'
    indiget ad existendum. Andererseits ist die Welt der transzendenten 'res'
    durchaus auf Bewußtsein, und zwar nicht auf logisch erdachtes, sondern
    aktuelles angewiesen." In fact, as Husserl says in the next paragraph of
    this text, specific sequences of experiences in transcendental conscious-
    ness are a *sufficient* (and not only a necessary, as interpreters such as
    Sokolowski hold) condition for the existence of the world (Hua III/1, 105,
    ll. 3–10). Consequently, the world is an intentional correlate of transcen-
    dental consciousness and "darüber hinaus ein Nichts" (Hua III/1, 106, l.
    8). Cf. also 109, ll. 5–9: "Existenz einer Natur *kann* Existenz vom
    Bewußtsein nicht bedingen, da sie sich ja selbst als Bewußtseinskorrelat
    herausstellt; sie *ist* nur, als sich in geregelten Bewußtseinszusam-
    menhängen konstituierend." Cf. also § 55, first paragraph, and many
    passages in §§ 49–55, where Husserl makes abundantly clear that the
    transcendental reduction is an ontological revolution. As I said before,
    expressions such as "absolute independence" have the ontological mean-
    ing defined in the 3rd *Logical Investigation.*

55 *Id.* I, § 55, Hua III/1, 120, ll. 28–33 (=[107]).

56 Hua III/1, 107–108 (=[95]) and 108, ll. 15–26 (=[95]), respectively.

57 Although, of course, Husserl differed from the Positivists in his interpre-
    tation of what the "positive" or "the given" consists in. Because he
    believed that the Positivists had a too restricted view of the domain of
    the "positive," he claimed in § 20 of *Id.* I that phenomenologists are the
    "real positivists" (*die echten Positivisten,* Hua III/1, 45, l. 14 (=[38])).
    Whether Husserl's belief in the possibility of a theory-free description is
    consistent with other elements of his philosophy, such as his theory of
    perception, is another matter.

58 *Id.* I, § 55, Hua III/1, 120, l. 33–38 (=[107]).

59 The world "is not something absolute in itself . . . , but it is nothing at

all in the absolute sense . . . , it is essentially something which cannot be but intentional, something we are conscious of, . . . a phenomenon." *Id* I, § 50, Hua III/1, 106, ll. 15–23 (=[93–4]). Cf. §§ 49–55, passim.

60 M. Heidegger, *Sein und Zeit*, § 43a. Indeed, Eugen Fink claimed in his famous paper "Die phänomenologische Philosophie Edmund Husserls in der gegenwärtigen Kritik," *Kantstudien* 38 (1933): 319–83, that there is no natural motivation for the transcendental turn. But I think that this was not Husserl's opinion, and that Fink was influenced by Heidegger.

61 Apart from this "transcendental reduction" there also is the "eidetic reduction": transcendental consciousness may be studied as a factual existent, which is the task of *metaphysics*, or in its essential structures, which we discover by means of the eidetic reduction. This is the task of transcendental phenomenological *ontology*. Because these distinctions are not important for understanding transcendental idealism, I shall not discuss them here. Cf. § XV.5, following.

62 See First Logical Investigation, § XV. The (perception of) the referent is called the "origin" of the concept, because the concept is abstracted from it. And the task of epistemology is to investigate the "origins" of the main epistemic concepts. Cf. Introd. *LU* II, § 2, and § 10, below. In *PhstrW*, 307, Husserl criticizes the traditional empiricist version of the principle for confusing genetic and methodological questions. For Husserl, who used the methodological principle from the *Philosophy of Arithmetic* onwards, the principle was self-evident, and he did not bother to discuss it in the *Fundamental Meditation*. Nevertheless, it emerges in the text, although inconspicuously. See *Ideas* I, §§ 44, 47, 52; Hua III/1, 92, ll. 3–5 (=[80]), 100, ll. 20–27 (=[88]), 101, ll. 2–5 (=[89]) and 111, ll. 4–5 (=[98]). I criticized Husserl's theory of meaning for being an instance of "the Augustinian picture of language" in my paper "Heidegger's Question of Being and the Augustinian Picture of Language," *Philosophy and Phenomenological Research* 52, 1992: 251–87.

63 Cf. *Id*. I, § 55, Hua III/1, 120–21 ([=107]): "daß die Welt selbst ihr ganzes Sein als einen gewissen 'Sinn' hat." In a footnote, Husserl stresses that this means stretching the notion of "sense" or "meaning." Cf. also § 62, where Husserl says that Phenomenology provides "die letzte Sinnbestimmung des 'Seins' ihrer Gegenstände" (Hua III/1, 133, ll. 20–1 (=[118]).

64 De Boer, *DHT*, 383–86.

65 *Ding und Raum. Vorlesungen* 1907, Hua XVI, §§ 44–57.

66 Eidetic variation is Husserl's method for discovering essential structures and relations. See for the doctrine of eidetic variation 3rd Logical Investigation, §§ 4–7; 6th Logical Investigation, § 52; *Id*. I, §§ 1–17, 69–75;

Phänomenologische Psychologie , § 9, Hua IX, 72–87; *Erfahrung und Urteil*, §§ 86–93. I discussed the doctrine critically in a Dutch book on Husserl, *De Fundering van de Logica in Husserl's 'Logische Untersuchungen,'* Leiden: Labor Vincit, 1983, 88–109. Husserl claims in the first part of *Ideas* I, that all facts have their essences, so that synthetic *a priori* ontologies will be at the basis of the empirical sciences. Cf. § 15.5, herein.

67 In *Ideas* I, Husserl always associates the notion of an adumbration with the perception of spatial objects. He does not admit of "time-adumbrations." See *Id.* I, § 41, Hua III/1, 86, ll. 14–28 (=[75–76]).

68 Husserl's method here is his usual procedure of eidetic variation for discovering relations of ontological dependency, as explained in the 3rd Logical Investigation (§§ 4–7). One will have no problems in interpreting Husserl's argument of *Ideas* I, § 49, if only one uses the definitions Husserl gives in this Investigation. Incidentally, I am using "our" as short for "each of us for him/herself." Like Descartes' metaphysical *Meditations*, the argument of Husserl's Fundamental Meditation is essentially performed in the first person singular.

69 *Id.* I, § 41, Hua III/1, 86, ll. 21–28 (=[75–6]): "Abschattung ist Erlebnis. Erlebnis aber ist nur als Erlebnis möglich und nicht als Räumliches. Das Abgeschattete ist aber prinzipiell nur möglich als Räumliches (es ist eben im Wesen räumlich), aber nicht möglich als Erlebnis. Es ist speziell auch ein Widersinn, die Gestaltabschattung (z.B. die eines Dreieckes) für etwas Räumliches und im Raume Mögliches zu halten, und wer das tut, verwechselt sie mit der abgeschatteten, d.i. erscheinenden Gestalt." Cf. also §§ 36, 85, 97, 98, and 128. For further textual support, see my book on Husserl's Transcendental Idealism.

70 See for the notion of a "sensory core": Gary C. Hatfield and William Epstein, "The Sensory Core and the Medieval Foundations of Early Modern Perceptual Theory," *Isis* 70 (1979): 363–84.

71 Roman Ingarden, ed., E. Husserl, *Briefe an Ingarden* (The Hague: Nijhoff, 1968), 156. Ingarden himself has been one of the most tenacious critics of Husserl's transcendental idealism. See for instance "Bemerkungen zum Problem 'Idealismus-Realismus'," in *Festschrift Edmund Husserl zum 70. Geburtstag gewidmet* (1929), 2nd ed. (Tübingen: M. Niemeyer Verlag, 1974); *On the Motives which led Husserl to Transcendental Idealism* (The Hague: Nijhoff, 1975); and "Über den transzendentalen Idealismus bei E. Husserl," in H. L. van Breda and J. Taminiaux, eds., *Husserl und das Denken der Neuzeit* (The Hague: Nijhoff, 1959).

72 *LU* A/B I, 84–85, 133, 232–33, 241–46.

73 See § 44 of the 6th Investigation.

74 *LU* A II, 18–19.

75 See the Elsenhans review, "Bericht über deutsche Schriften zur Logik in den Jahren 1895–99," III, *Archiv für systematische Philosophie* IX (1903): 399–400, Hua XXII, 206–208.

76 *LU* A II, 496–97; B II/2, 24–25. Cf. *LU* B II/1, 30, 74–75, 348–51, 381–83, 385, 392, 407, 504; *LU* B II/2, 57, 77–79, 175, 232–33, 237ff.; *Id.* I, §§ 41, 44, 68, 84, 86, 97, 98, and 135.

77 *LU* B II/1, 76, 194–95, 197, 199, 348–52, 369, 374, 383, 392–94, 507, and II/2, 77–79 and 234. Cf. the corresponding passages in A.

78 Cf. *LU* B II/1, 349 (5th Inv., § 2): "It is sufficient here to stress the difference between the red colour of this sphere, which is objectively seen as the same everywhere, and the momentary adumbration of the subjective colour-sensations, which is indubitably and even necessarily in the perceptual act itself." Cf. 76, 194–95, 197, 199, 220, 381–82, and the corresponding texts in A.

79 See for "apprehension" § 26 of the 6th Investigation. "Interpretation" and "Deutung" are often used in the first edition. See, for instance *LU* A II, 704ff.; Cf. B II/2, 233–34.

80 Husserl criticizes the sign- and the image-theories of perception in the appendix to §§ 11 and 21 of the 5th Investigation and in §§ 43 and 52 of *Ideas* I. He stresses again and again that in perception the object itself is bodily given. See, for instance: *LU* B II/1, 354–55, 442; II/2, 56, 65–66, 116, 143, 145, 162, and *Id.* I, §§ 39 and 43.

81 Ingrid M. Wallner, "In defense of Husserl's Transcendental Idealism: Roman Ingarden's Critique Reexamined," *Husserl Studies* 4 (1987): 22.

82 § 23 of the First Investigation.

83 Cf. De Boer, *DHT*, 161 ff.

84 As he says, "the doctrine of Berkeley and Hume, which reduces the phenomenal bodies to bundles of 'ideas,' does not do justice to the fact that, even if the elements of these bundles of ideas may be really in our minds, the bundles themselves . . . never were nor will be really present in any human consciousness." (*LU* A II, 337). This argument does not rule out phenomenalism in the strict sense.

85 *LU* A II, 345–46, where Husserl says that a mind which would contain sensations only and no interpretative acts, would be "a being of the same kind as the phenomenal external things." Husserl changed this passage in the second edition, but the change made it incoherent.

86 *LU* A II, 706–7 (changed in B).

87 *LU* A II, 706, italics mine.

88 De Boer, *DHT*, 161–66. I agree with the gist of De Boer's argument.

89 Cf. A. Lalande, *Vocabulaire technique et critique de la Philosophie*, Paris, 1976 (12th ed.), 840.

90 Review of Th. Elsenhans, *Das Verhältnis der Logik zur Psychologie*

(1896), in "Bericht über deutsche Schriften zur Logik in den Jahren 1895–99" III, *Archiv für systematische Philosophie* IX (1903), 398–99, Hua XXII, 206, ll. 18–19.

91 The projective interpretation of Husserl's theory of perception is also supported by other arguments, which are concerned with Husserl's notions of adumbration and of adequate perception. See my book on Husserl's Transcendental Idealism. Husserl's theory is somewhat more complex than suggested here: because Husserl identifies sensations with adumbrations, and because he is tempted to say that adumbrations resemble the objective properties of perceived objects, he concludes that the phenomenal object merely resembles the sensations, which are said to provide "analogous building materials" for the constitution of the phenomenal object (§ 23 of the First Investigation; *LU* A II, 75–76; B II/1, pp 75–76). But this is of no importance for the gist of my interpretation.

92 Cf., for instance, § 37 of the 6th Investigation, the first six sentences.

93 *LU* A II, 338–39 (§ 7 of the 5th Investigation, deleted in B).

94 *Ibidem*, Husserl's definition.

95 Hua III/1, 105, ll. 3–10 (=[92]).

96 *LU* A/B I, 11; cf. 113–14.

97 Review of Jul. Bergmann, *Die Grundprobleme der Logik* (1895), in "Bericht über deutsche Schriften zur Logik in den Jahren 1895–99," I, *Archiv für systematische Philosophie* IX (1903): 120, Hua XXII, 168, ll. 26–30.

98 *Ibidem*; cf. § 7 of the 5th Investigation, *LU* A II, 339.

99 *LU* A II, 339.

100 The Bergmann review quoted above, *ibidem*.

101 The "philosophische Fundamentalwissenschaft" as Husserl says in § 61 of *Prolegomena* (*LU* A/B I, 224).

102 *LU* II, Introduction, § 7 (A II 21; B II/1, 21).

103 *Ibidem*, 20 (Husserl rewrote this passage in B). According to *LU* A II, 9, the fundamental epistemological questions (*erkenntnistheoretische Grundfragen*) are questions such as: "how the 'an sich' of objectivity may become represented and in this manner may become subjective again; what it means that the object is 'an sich' and also 'given' in knowledge," etc.

104 In fact, both the existence of the phenomenal external world and of the world *an sich*. The world *an sich* is not given in perception at all. And the existence of the phenomenal world is uncertain, because it is always given in adumbrations, so that the existential claims contained in external perception essentially transcend what is really given, and they may be falsified by future experience. Cf. § 49 of *Id.* I.

105 See the appendix to *LU* II, § 6, *LU* A II 711, B II/2, 239–40, jo. § 7 of the Introduction to *LU* II. "My" means, of course, everyone's own. And Husserl stresses that the content of his investigations does not presuppose the existence of his readers, even though he may address them in his presentation (*LU* A II, 22; B II/1, 22).

106 As Husserl says in § 7 of the Introduction to *LU* II, epistemology investigates in what consists our claim that we have knowledge about objects ("worin sein Rechtsanspruch auf Gegenständlichkeit eigentlich besteht"). Such an investigation can yield knowledge instead of opinion, he claims, only if it is based on a descriptive analysis of given acts of thought and knowledge (*LU* A II, 19). The identification of phenomenology and descriptive psychology (A II, 18) is of course rejected in B (B II/1, 18), and, in fact, already in 1903.

107 In adequate perception, the (mental) phenomenon is simply taken as it is, and not interpreted. Cf. 6th Investigation, §§ 37 ff. and the appendix to Vol. II in A. Cf. also the argument of the Fundamental Phenomenological Meditation in *Id.* I, and Husserl's Principle of all principles in § 24 of *Id.* I.

108 Husserl's conception of epistemology was, of course, quite common in the second half of the nineteenth century, when the epistemological tradition of Locke and Hume was revived in German philosophy. Most interpretations of Husserl's principle of presuppositionlessness are defective in that they neglect the Husserl of the *Investigations* and Husserl's contemporaries. Cf., for instance, Teresa Reed-Downing, "Husserl's Presuppositionless Philosophy," *Research in Phenomenology* 20 (1990): 136–51.

109 According to Brentano, science is concerned with the world *an sich*, which is assumed as a hypothesis in order to explain our sensations. See his *Psychologie vom empirischen Standpunkt* (1874) (Hamburg: F. Meiner, 1924), Bd. I, 2. Buch, 1. Kap., § 9, 138: "Man könnte die wissenschaftliche Aufgabe der Naturwissenschaft etwa so ausdrücken, daß man sagte: die Naturwissenschaft sei jene Wissenschaft, welche die Aufeinanderfolge der physischen Phänomene normaler und reiner (durch keine besonderen psychischen Zustände und Vorgänge mit beeinflußter) Sensationen auf Grund der Annahme der Einwirkung einer raumähnlich in drei Dimensionen ausgebreiteten und zeitähnlich in *einer* Richtung verlaufenden Welt auf unsere Sinnesorgane zu erklären suche." According to Kant, science is concerned with the phenomenal world only, although we have to assume the existence of a world *an sich* on metaphysical or transcendental grounds.

110 Hua II, 3ff.; *PhstrW.*, 299–300; *Id.* I, §§ 97, 128, 135, 146, 150; *CM*, § 23ff.; *FTL*, §§ 94ff.; *Kr.*, §§ 34f., 49, 53–55.

111 Cf. Introd. to *LU* A II, § 7, and § 15.4 of the First Investigation; cf. also *LU* A II, 7–8.

112 *LU* A II 19 (re-written in B). Cf. Husserl's concept of "matter" or "sense of the apperception" in the 5th and 6th Investigation. Between 1907 and 1912, Husserl transformed the *noetic* theory of meaning which he held in the *Investigations*, into a *noematic* theory, which he endorsed also in *Ideas* I. From the standpoint of *Ideas* I, then, one cannot say that meanings (tokens) are really immanent in consciousness.

113 De Boer, *DHT,* 178–202.

114 *LU* A II, 7 (§ 2 of the introduction to vol. II). "Abstraction" means here "eidetic abstraction" and not a mere concentration of attention. See for the development of Husserl's theory of abstraction: De Boer, *DHT,* 63–76 and 234–69.

115 *LU* A II, Introd., § 7, and appendix, § 6 (A II, 19–22 and 708–12).

116 6th Investigation, §§ 23–24, 29, 36–38. Cf. for adequate perception: § 23, last paragraph, *LU* A II, 556 (= B II/2, 84), and § 37. Cf. also *LU* B II/ 1, 355, and II/2, 57–58, 66–67, 83, 116–19, 121.

117 Cf. Appendix to vol. II, § 6, *LU* A II, 708–12 and B II/2, 237–40.

118 *LU* A II, 337 (deleted in B). Husserl's concept of the world in itself is similar to Peirce's. Cf. Peirce's "Some Consequences of Four Incapacities" (1868), in J. Buchler, ed., *Philosophical Writings of Peirce* (New York: Dover, 1955), 247: "The real, then, is that which, sooner or later, information and reasoning would finally result in, and which is therefore independent of the vagaries of me and you. Thus, the very origin of the conception of reality shows that this conception essentially involves the notion of a COMMUNITY, without definite limits, and capable of a definite increase of knowledge."

119 Cf. *LU* A II, 529 = B II/2, 57.

120 David Hume, *An Enquiry Concerning Human Understanding,* § 2.

121 *LU* A II, 11. Husserl re-wrote the sequel to this text in B, adapting it to his notion of a noema: *LU* B II/1, 11.

122 This passage is in *LU* A II, on p. 196. One might think that this move does not really refute the objection, because the *Ding an sich* as such, in Husserl's new sense, is never intuitively given. But Husserl assumes in the Sixth Investigation that it is nevertheless *intended* in some sense, because all knowledge aims at becoming complete: it aims at the *Ding an sich.* Cf. Sixth Investigation, §§ 21 (*das Ideal der Fülle*), 23, 24, 37ff.

123 *LU* A II, 336, deleted in B.

124 *Id* I, § 52; *Kr.,* § 30; "Kant und die Idee der Transzendentalphilosophie," Hua VII, 235.

125 *Id.* I, §§ 143–44, 149; *CM,* § 28; "Kant und die Idee der Transzendentalphilosophie," Hua VII, 274.

126 *Id.* I, §§ 42 (in finem), 49, 50, 51, 54, 55. As he says in § 97, all transcendent objects are "transcendentally constituted by noetic functions on the basis of hyletic data" (Hua III/1, 228, ll. 8–10 = [204]).

127 The life world is "the only real one" (*die einzig wirkliche*), as Husserl says in *Crisis*, § 9h (Hua VI, 49, l. 2).

128 In 1903, Husserl says that the empirical sciences "aim at lawlike formulae facilitating our orientation in the phenomenal world": review of Jul. Bergmann, *Die Grundprobleme der Logik* (1895), "Bericht über deutsche Schriften zur Logik in den Jahren 1895–99," I, *Archiv für systematische Philosophie* IX (1903): 120, Hua XXII, 168, ll. 34–37. This, of course, is an expression of Machian instrumentalism. According to § 52 of *Ideas* I, "the physical thing" is not a hidden hypothetical cause of our experiences or of the thing we experience, but a "higher transcendence," i.e., a layer of "deeper" causal properties of an object constituted on the basis of the phenomenal properties of the same object. In § 9h of *Crisis*, Husserl claims that scientific realists such as Galileo misinterpreted their mathematical method in physics as a description of true being ("daß wir für wahres Sein nehmen, was eine Methode ist," Hua VI, 52, ll. 6–7). This, if anything, is an expression of instrumentalism. Within the framework of constitution-analysis, however, these two views concerning theoretical entities and the world *an sich* of physics may perhaps been reconciled, for even intellectual "instruments" are "constituted." And indeed Husserl says in § 52 of *Ideas* I, that the "ideal ontological thought-constructs, which are expressed in the concepts of physics, derive and must derive their sense exclusively from the scientific method" (Hua III/1. 114, ll. 5–8 = [100–101]).

129 *Id.* I, §§ 49–55 and § 97, Hua III/1, 228, ll. 8–9 (=[204]): "Das 'auf Grund' der stofflichen Erlebnisse 'durch' die noetischen Funktionen 'transzendental Konstituierte'."

130 *LU* A II, 336 (§ 7 of the 5th Investigation).

131 *LU* A II, 335 (§ 6 of the 5th Investigation). Cf. 19–21 and 710–12.

132 *LU* A II, 5th Investigation, §§ 4 and 8.

133 *LU* A II, 5th Investigation, §§ 1, 4, 6, 7, 8; pp. 325, 331, 336, 342. "My" means here: everyone for himself.

134 *LU* A II, 328, 331, 332, 336, 342.

135 *Crisis*, §§ 53–55.

136 *Id.* I, § 53; *Id.* III, §§ 12–15; *EPh.* I, Hua VII, 114; "Kant und die Idee der Transzendentalphilosophie," Hua VII, 243, 277–80; *Phänomenologische Psychologie*, Hua IX, 147–50; Encyclopedia Britannica article, Hua IX, 247–50, 288–95; "Amsterdamer Vorträge," Hua IX, 331–44; "Nachwort," Hua V 150, 154, 160; "Pariser Vorträge," Hua I, 30–34; *CM*, Hua I, 115–19; *FTL*, § 99; *Kr.*, Hua VI, 70–71, 80, 92, 117, 120,

169 note, 182ff., 205, 265–66. Cf. also M. Heidegger, *Prolegomena zur Geschichte des Zeitbegriffs, GA,* Vol. 20, Frankfurt a/M: V. Klostermann, 1988, 139ff.

137 See, for instance, Elisabeth Ströker, *Husserls transzendentale Phänomenologie* (Frankfurt a/M.: V. Klostermann, 1987), 221–22: "Demnach steht die Phänomenologie Husserls schon mit ihrer Grundfragestellung [i.e., to determine the sense of the existence of the world instead of proving its existence] in einem anderen Problemhorizont als Descartes ... Daß Husserl trotz unübersehbarer Unterschiede in Fragestellung und Verfahren in irritierende Nahe zu Descartes geraten konnte, lag vor allem an erheblichen, sogar befremdlichen Konfundierungen, mit denen er selbst seine Darstellung der transzendentalen Reduktion belastete."

138 *IdPhä,* summary, B, in finem, Hua II, 10. Cf. *Id.* I, §§ 46 and 62, Hua III/1, 99, ll. 14–17 (=[87]), and 133, ll. 22–25 (=[118]): "So begreift es sich, daß die Phänomenologie gleichsam die geheime Sehnsucht der ganzen neuzeitlichen Philosophie ist. Zu ihr drängt es schon in der wunderbar tiefsinnigen Cartesianischen Fundamentalbetrachtung hin."

139 *Kr.,* §§ 18–19. According to the title of § 19, this assumption is the "ground" for Descartes' misinterpretation of consciousness. See point 5. Cf. also *EPh* I, Hua VII, 63ff.; *FTL,* § 93b; *CM,* § 10.

140 The Elsenhans review, "Bericht über deutsche Schriften zur Logik in den Jahren 1895–99," III, *Archiv für systematische Philosophie* IX (1903): 400, Hua XXII, 207–8. As Husserl says in *PhstrW,* all psychological description is *eo ipso* psychophysical (299). In his later works, Husserl often refers to this review. Cf. *Id.* I, Introd., note 2; "Entwurf einer 'Vorrede' zu den 'Logischen Untersuchungen,' *Tijdschrift voor Filosofie* I (1939), 330; and *LU* B I, xiii–xiv.

141 *IdPhä,* 5–6, 7 ("Zunächst schon die Cartesianische *cogitatio* bedarf der phänomenologischen Reduktion," etc.), 9–10 ("Aber entdecken und fallen lassen war bei Descartes eines"); *EPh* I, Hua VII, 63ff.; *CM,* § 10; *FTL,* § 93b; *Kr.,* § 18.

142 *LU* A II, 196; cf. the modified text of *LU* B II/1, 198.

143 *IdPhä,* 10 ("Vorurteil der Immanenz als reeller Immanenz") and 12 ("wunderbare Korrelation").

144 *IdPhä,* 12–14. Cf. the later works, passim.

145 Cf. *Kr.,* § 20.

146 This is confirmed by Husserl's lectures from 1906/7 and 1908, on epistemology and theory of meaning, respectively. See Hua XXIV and XXVI, and Rudolf Bernet, "Husserls Begriff des Noema," in S. Ijsseling, ed., *Husserl-Ausgabe und Husserl-Forschung, Phaenomenologica* 115 (Dordrecht: Kluwer, 1990), 61–80. Husserl's early semantics even ex-

cluded the notion of a noema. Cf. H. Philipse, "The Concept of Intentionality: Husserl's Development from the Brentano Period to the *Logical Investigations,*" *Philosophy Research Archives* 12 (1987): 293–328, especially 312–17

147 *Id.* I, §§ 88ff. and § 55.

148 Cf. *Id.* I, § 55, footnote.

149 Bernet, op.cit., p. 75: "einen terminologischen Missgriff."

150 Husserl stresses this in § 33 of *Ideas* I.

151 *Id.* I, Introduction, Hua III/1, 7, ll. 14–18 (=[4–5]); cf. § 51 Anmerkung and § 58. Cf. also the Encyclopedia Britannica article, Hua IX, 298; *CM,* § 64; *Kr.,* § 6. As we saw, in the *Investigations* and in 1903 Husserl defined metaphysics as a factual science concerned with the ultimate meaning of reality.

152 *IdPhä,* 8–10, 51–61. Cf. *PhstrW.,* 314–18 and *Id.* I, § 24. Husserl's distinction between the eidetic and the transcendental (or epistemological) reduction was only gradually clarified. In *IdPhä* and *PhstrW,* the distinction is not yet very clear.

153 *Cf.* Id. I, § 53.

154 *Kr.,* § 28ff.

155 *Kr.,* § 27, Hua VI, 102, ll. 1–3. There are many more criticisms of Kant in Husserl, which however, are less relevant to transcendental idealism. In the *LU,* Husserl criticizes the Kantian definition of the synthetic *a priori.* He blames Kant for not having discovered the eidetic intuition. Furthermore, Kant's transcendental method is reconstructive, starting with the fact of synthetic *a priori* propositions and trying to reconstruct the conditions of their possibility, whereas Husserl claims to be able to intuit and describe transcendental consciousness. According to Kant, the phenomenal world is also the scientific world. Husserl, however, claims that the world of science is constituted on the basis of the life-world, etc. Cf. for a historical account of Husserl's relation to Kant: Iso Kern, *Husserl und Kant. Eine Untersuchung über Husserls Verhältnis zu Kant und zu Neukantianismus* (The Hague: Nijhoff, 1964).

156 If, at least, we assume that Kant's world *an sich* is in part a material world in some sense. But perhaps Kant remained a crypto-Leibnizian and implicitly assumed that the causes of sensations in consciousness are spiritual. If so, Husserl resembles Kant more than it seems.

157 *LU* A II, 338–39; *Id.* I, § 98; *EPh.* I, Hua VII, 150ff.; *CM,* § 41, "Nachwort," Hua V, 154; *Kr.,* § 23.

158 Cf. John W. Yolton, *Perceptual Acquaintance,* Oxford: Blackwell, 1984, 135–42.

159 As Husserl says, Berkeley is a psychological idealist. *EPh.* I, Hua VII, 150
    (cf. however, 154–55 and "Nachwort," Hua V, 154); *Kr.*, §§ 13 and 23.

160 Berkeley, *Of the Principles of Human Knowledge,* I, §§ 29 and 146.

161 Hua III/1, 125 (=111)): "*Vernunftgründe für die Existenz eines außer-
    weltlichen 'göttlichen' Seins.*" Cf. § 51, Anm.

162 Not only to God and Freedom, as we have already seen, but also to
    Immortality. For, whereas I as a human being am mortal (*Phänom-
    enologische Psychologie,* Hua IX, 109), Husserl purports to prove that
    the transcendental stream of consciousness is "endless" in time: *Id.* I,
    §§ 81 and 82, especially Hua III/1, 184, ll. 18–21 (=[165]). This proof, of
    which Husserl says that it has great metaphysical import, is invalid, of
    course. We now see that Husserl's comparison of the transcendental
    reduction with a religious "conversion" should be taken seriously. Cf.
    Kr., § 35, in finem.

163 Cf., for instance, D.W. Hamlyn, *The Theory of Knowledge,* London:
    Macmillan, 1971, 12.

164 *LU* A/B I, 84–85, 133, 161, 231ff.

165 *Id.* I, §§ 7–10, 16, 62.

166 As Husserl says in *Crisis,* § 52, in the *epoché* we will be able to discover
    the "true ontological sense" of all objective being and truth (*der volle
    und wahre Seinssinn des objektiven Seins und so aller objektiven
    Wahrheit;* Hua VI, 179, ll. 26–28). Cf. *Id.* I, § 62, Hua III/1, 133, ll. 20–
    21 (=[118]): *die letzte Sinnesbestimmung des 'Seins' ihrer Gegen-
    stände*), and passim in the later works.

167 See *FTL,* §§ 55ff., *Erfahrung und Urteil,* §§ 63 and 64, and Hua VI, 365–
    86. I discussed Husserl's analysis in my Dutch book on Husserl, *De
    Fundering in de Logica in Husserl's 'Logische Untersuchungen'* (Lei-
    den: Labor Vincit, 1983), 230–50.

168 Cf. Descartes, *Dioptrics,* 5th discourse.

169 Gary C. Hatfield and William Epstein, "The Sensory Core and the
    Medieval Foundations of Early Modern Perceptual Theory," *Isis* 70
    (1979): 364.

170 Ibidem, 365. Hatfield and Epstein do not at all discuss the question
    as to how this "new metaphysical context" yields the principle of
    immanence.

171 Essential to my analysis is only that the incompatibility thesis and the
    principle of immanence are derived from a picture of the physical world
    (see below). It does not matter whether this picture is corpuscularian,
    mechanicist, or based on later theories of physics.

172 In Cartesian physics, this argument is convincing, because macro-
    scopic bodies are nothing but aggregates of corpuscles which are per-

fectly conjoined without interstices. But it is also accepted for modern physics by philosophers such as Russell or Wilfrid Sellars. See, for instance, W. Sellars, "Philosophy and the Scientific Image of Man," in his *Science, Perception, and Reality* (London: Routledge, 1963), 26–27 and 34–35.

173 This is the function of the Cartesian "judgement" in the perceptual act.

174 This point is argued in detail for Locke and Hume by Maurice Mandelbaum in *Philosophy, Science, and Sense Perception* (Baltimore: Johns Hopkins Press, 1964).

175 Cf. J. L. Austin, *Sense and Sensibilia* (Oxford: OUP, 1962); P. M. S. Hacker, *Appearance and Reality*, Oxford: Blackwell, 1987, and many other critiques. I argued in § 7 that Husserl's argument for the principle of immanence is inconclusive.

176 Cf. my paper on the latter, "The Absolute Network Theory of Language and Traditional Epistemology," *Inquiry* 33 (1990): 127–78.

177 Cf. M. Heidegger, *Sein und Zeit*, § 43a. Cf. also M. Merleau-Ponty, *La Phénoménologie de la Perception*.

178 As Heidegger says in *Die Frage nach dem Ding*, 2nd ed. (Tübingen: Niemeyer, 1975), 8, his philosophical questioning purports to prepare a *decision* as to whether science is the measure of knowledge, or whether there is a more fundamental kind of knowledge, in which the limits and the real import of scientific knowledge are determined. Clearly, Heidegger claims that there is such a more fundamental kind of knowledge, which is closer to both common sense and theology than to science.

179 Cf. *Kr.*, §§ 7, 15. It is now generally acknowledged that Husserl was not referring to himself when he said that the dream of a scientific philosophy had come to an end, but to the traditional project of a scientific philosophy, which had led to the crisis of the European sciences: Hua VI, 508.

180 Wittgenstein, *Philosophische Untersuchungen* I, § 104.

181 Hua VI, 49, l. 2.

182 *Kr.*, passim, see Hua VI, 108, 121, 136, 141, 165, 171, and 176.

183 *Kr.*, § 29, Hua VI, 114, ll. 20–21.

184. *Kr.*, § 29, Hua VI, 115, ll. 34–9.

7   Mind and body

I. THE MIND-BODY PROBLEM IN HUSSERL

Husserl is often read as an idealist, more like Kant than Berkeley, or else as a dualist, with epistemological motivations like those of Descartes. It would be only fitting for Husserl then to set aside the physical world and study pure consciousness. Phenomenology, the science of consciousness, would become the whole of philosophy.

However, when we look closely at what Husserl says about mind and body, when we read Husserl with an eye to the mind-body problem *per se*, his metaphysics looks very different. Husserl fashioned an intricate ontology of mind and body, coordinated with a rich phenomenology of our awareness of body and mind, as well as an epistemology of the kinds of evidence we have about body and mind. I propose to excavate and reconstruct Husserl's ontology of mind and body, along with the coordinate phenomenology. The result is a *monism* of substrata (individuals or events) and a *pluralism* of essences, as well as senses, of body and mind (which may apply to the same individuals or events). This many-aspect monism (not Husserl's term) is obscured by the superstructure of Husserl's "transcendental idealism," which does not set well on the monistic foundation. We shall remove (in a sense, deconstruct) that superstructure, revealing and restoring the underlying monism.

On Husserl's account, each concrete experience falls under two high-level essences or species, called Consciousness and Nature respectively, so that the mental and physical sides of the experience are two aspects of a single event. *Qua* acts of consciousness these events are defined primarily by their intentionality, their representing or being "directed" to something. *Qua* brain events they are

323

defined by natural laws of physics, biology, etc., which concern not intentionality but the physiology of neural activity. In Husserl's ontology, these two aspects are dependent parts, or "moments," of the same event, and the two parts instantiate respectively the very different essences Nature and Consciousness. Similarly, each human being – each I or self – falls under the two essences Nature and Consciousness, "my body" and "my mind" or "consciousness" being different aspects of the same individual *I*. This dual-aspect theory, Husserl believed, precludes the reduction of phenomenology to physics or neurophysiology or even naturalistic psychology.

Husserl ramified this dual-aspect ontology in interesting ways. The bodily aspect of a human being he divided into two aspects called the "physical body" (*Körper*) and the "living body" (*Leib*). The mental aspect he divided into three aspects called the "soul" (*Seele*) or "psyche" (*Psyche*), the "human being" (*Mensch*) or "spirit" (*Geist*), and the "pure I." My physical body, the material *I*, is my body *qua* physical: this body as defined by purely physical attributes of space, time, matter, and causality, and so instantiating the essence Nature. By contrast, my living body, the animate-organism *I*, is this body *qua* living: "my body" as defined by intentional attributes of volition and kinesthesis as well as spatiotemporal-material attributes, i.e., my body as that organ which I move by will and whose movement I am aware of kinesthetically. My soul or psyche, the psychological *I*, is then that aspect of my living body which "animates" it, what makes it a living body, a psychophysical animal. And my spirit or human I (*Ich-Mensch*) is then I *qua* human being: an embodied, personal, social being who belongs to the world-of-life, or "life-world" (*Lebenswelt*), the surrounding world as defined not by physics but by everyday life. The empirical *I*, the *I* of everyday experience, from which all philosophical reflection begins, is the human *I*. Finally, the pure *I* is I *qua* subject of intentional experiences or acts of consciousness.

These *I's* are not different substrata or substances. There is only one individual, I. But it has various aspects. The physical-body aspect instantiates the essence Material Nature, where the living-body aspect instantiates the essence Animal Nature, and the psychic aspect the psychological part of Animal Nature. Then the human aspect instantiates the essence Human Being, or its cognate Life-

World, while the pure-*I* aspect instantiates the essence Consciousness, or Subject of Consciousness.

Husserl's monism takes an incipient form in his recurrent example of seeing the same object from different sides or with very different properties. In a case of "exploding" perception, he holds, we see
numerically the same individual first as a human being, a woman
waving at us on the stair, and then, with a radical change of sense, as
a waxwork figure (we are in a waxworks museum).[1] That is, we see
the same object first as a person – with living body, soul, and
humanity – and then as a mere physical body. Monism, moving
from phenomenology to ontology, reifies these different aspects of
one and the same individual.

With this many-aspect doctrine Husserl distanced himself from
the familiar positions of materialism, Cartesian dualism, Berkeleyan
idealism, and Kantian transcendental idealism. Against Descartes,
he resisted the notion of the mind or soul as a distinct, purely mental substance. Moreover, he distinguished different aspects of the
human body, arguing that Descartes had reduced the body to a mechanical body whose essence is exhausted by the mathematics of
classical mechanics. Unlike Spinoza, however, he assumed there are
many substances or individual entities in the world, each with
bodily and mental aspects – and perhaps for that reason Husserl did
not use the term "monism." Against Berkeley, he resisted identifying material things with collections of ideas or sensations. Against
Kant, he rejected the conclusion that things-in-themselves are beyond the reach of all possible experience – though he borrowed the
label "transcendental idealism" for his own position. Against materialism, he criticized the "mathematization" of nature, and hence of
mind as a part of nature, on grounds that modern physics, as developed since Galileo, abstracts but one kind of essence of things
around us. Functionalism and the computer model of mind had not
yet taken root in Husserl's day, though Husserl's account of rules
governing mental processes might be modelled by algorithms defining a computer program (allowing perhaps fuzzy logic and connec-
tionist architecture). Nonetheless, Husserl would have rejected the
identification of mental processes with computational processes,
since syntactic rules for processing signs do not capture the content
and hence the "semantics" of mental acts. Moreover, Husserl's ac-

count of the "horizon" of meaning in intentional experience raises one form of the notorious "frame" problem in artificial intelligence: how can a digital computer program capture the open-endedness of our conceptions of the world around us? Finally, against recent forms of eliminative materialism, Husserl would have argued that neuroscience cannot reject or displace our phenomenological understanding of ourselves as conscious subjects of intentional experience, since phenomenology and neuroscience are not competing theories, but rather disciplines that study distinct aspects of our mental/neural activities. Moreover, our activities of theorizing in neuroscience themselves presuppose our everyday, life-world understanding of ourselves and of our surroundings, which is indispensable in the practice of science.

Husserl's ontology of body and mind, couched in his theory of "moments," is a highly articulate form of many-aspect monism. What is especially interesting and novel is the correlation between his ontology and his phenomenology. For his distinctions among various aspects of body and mind reflect phenomenological distinctions among different ways in which we know, experience, and conceive our bodies and our minds. There is nothing like this system of distinctions before Husserl, and nothing as articulate since. We have much to learn from Husserl's remarkable results, even if his ontology is too rich for some and his terminology even more so. Indeed, a more neutral ontology might accommodate Husserl's phenomenology of these several aspects of body and self. It is often said that, within the phenomenological tradition, first Heidegger and then Merleau-Ponty (in quite different ways) overcame or undercut the Cartesian mind-body/subject-object dualism supposed to be the foundation of Husserl's phenomenology. In fact, Husserl did not hold such a dualism: his distinction between nature and consciousness is a contrast of essences and moments, not substances. Moreover, the guiding motifs of the break with Cartesian dualism in Heidegger and in Merleau-Ponty are developments of insights detailed in Husserl's work and known to Heidegger and Merleau-Ponty, albeit worked out in their own arguably more radical terms.

Husserl's account of mind and body unfolded over four decades in his evolving system of ontology, phenomenology, and epistemology. His early *Logical Investigations* (1900–01) develops a detailed ontology that is, by most accounts, explicitly realist. By his middle period, in *Ideas* I (1913), there were variations on Kantian themes of "transcendental idealism," a form of idealism by some accounts. Yet the text begins with a reworking of the basic (realist) ontology of the *Investigations*, enhanced by a more explicit notion of formal categories and material "regions," including Nature and Consciousness. We shall begin our account with this reworked ontology, the foundation for his monism. Husserl's ontology of body and mind calls on his phenomenological distinctions among different ways of experiencing oneself, beginning with one's body and its place in nature. These distinctions are used in *Ideas* I and detailed in *Ideas* II and III (the Second and Third Books of *Ideas*, drafted in 1912 along with the First Book, but unpublished). They reappear in *Cartesian Meditations* (1913). And the ontology is enhanced in the *Crisis* (written in 1935–38), which focussed on the life-world and the mathematization of nature. The many aspects of body and mind, however, emerge most clearly in the exploratory *Ideas* II, which should be read in connection with his more familiar works. As we unfold Husserl's views about mind and body, we shall thus be tracing their development throughout his career.

Whether Husserl turned from realism in the *Investigations* to some form of idealism or antirealism in *Ideas* has been vigorously contested. Let us bracket that question (until section 13 following) and develop his ontology as realist. His analyses of various aspects of mind and body would have to be translated into the idealist ontology if he took that turn ("we have genuinely lost nothing" with the transcendental turn, says *Ideas* I, §50).[2] Moreover, there are difficulties in trying to reconcile idealism with other elements of Husserl's ontology to be explored here. Thus, I propose to remove the superstructure of idealism from Husserl's philosophy of body and mind, appraising his transcendental idealism (in Section 13) only on the foundation of his wider ontology of essences and moments and his special analyses of body and mind. In this way we shall gain a clear view of the underlying many-aspect monism, a monism that deserves our attention in its own right.

II. HUSSERL'S ONTOLOGY

In the *Logical Investigations* Husserl developed an ontology – inspired partly by Aristotle via Brentano and Stumpf – embracing the following formal ontological categories: Individual, Species, Quality, Relation, Part/Whole, Dependence, State of Affairs.[3] Locations in space and time are presumably qualities (perhaps relational properties). A state of affairs consists in an individual's having an instance of a quality or species, or two or more individuals' having an instance of a relation. Dependent parts are called "moments," and an instance of a quality- or relation-species in an individual is a moment of the individual. Husserl occasionally speaks of events, which have duration in time. An event that happens to an individual is a moment of the individual; alternatively, the individual is a part of, or partakes in, the event.

Among events are experiences (*Erlebnisse*), and most prominent among these are intentional experiences, those that are a consciousness *of* something. Every intentional experience, or "act," has a content, and that content is identified, in the *Investigations*, with the act-species. Species are "ideal," not in space or time, as opposed to "real," i.e., in space and/or time; however, the instance of the act-species exists in the act and thus in time (if not in space). If the act has an object, then it stands in an intentional relation to its object (a hallucination, for instance, has no visual relation to an object, but when a perceptual experience is a veridical perception *of* an object, the experience stands in an intentional relation to the object). Initially, Husserl agreed with Hume that there is no ego that performs the act: the unity of consciousness consists simply in the unity of the stream of experiences, without a substantial ego that has the experiences. Later, he would change his view, finding an ego at the source of intentional acts.

Human beings and their experiences are to be studied not only in the empirical sciences of psychology and biology, but in the new science that will become phenomenology. In particular, the contents of experiences are to be studied there, without concern for the causal history of the experience or its dependence on brain activity.

Ideas I opens (in §§ 1–16) with an ontology extending that of the *Investigations*. First comes the distinction of two realms: fact and essence (already distinguished in the *Investigations*). Later will be added the realm of meaning or sense (*Sinn*), or noema, i.e., intentional content, which is now distinguished from act-species (an important departure from the *Investigations*).

The realm of fact includes (as in the *Investigations*): concrete empirical individuals, e.g., trees and tables, and concrete empirical events, as well as concrete empirical states of affairs (*Sachverhalte*). States of affairs are "syntactically" or "categorially" formed from concrete individuals, or "substrata," and instances of essences in individuals. The state of affairs that this table is brown, for example, is formed from the table and its brownness, which is an instance of the essence Brown and is a "moment" of the table (not the universal Brown, shareable by other brown objects, but a particular element of that table). Among individuals are both independent individuals, e.g., tables, and moments of individuals, e.g., instances of colors in tables. The notion of moment is drawn from the *Logical Investigations*, where a *moment* is defined as a dependent part, one which cannot exist unless the whole of which it is a part exists (III, §17).[4]

The realm of essence, or eidos, includes species and also qualities and presumably relations. The realms of fact and essence – the concrete and the ideal – are inseparable, Husserl says. For individuals include instances of species (and qualities and relations) as dependent parts, or moments. In this respect Husserl is closer to Aristotle (or Medieval moderate realism) than to Plato. However, his postulation of a realm of essence is Platonic in spirit (as argued in the Prolegomena of the *Investigations*). Indeed, species are ideal, or nonreal, i.e., they do not exist in space or time. Concrete empirical individuals and states of affairs, however, are real, i.e., exist in space and time. Furthermore, the being of factual objects is contingent, while that of essences is necessary.

Species stand in genus-species hierarchies, as did biological species for Aristotle. At bottom, individuals instantiate species, and the infima species, or lowest species, under which an individual falls is an "eidetic singularity" or "individual essence." (Husserl seems to allow that two individuals might share the same individual essence, instantiated in different spatiotemporal locations in the two individuals. His notion of individual essence differs from that of Leibniz.) The highest species in a hierarchy – the highest "material genus" – is called a *region*. As we shall see, Husserl distinguishes the region Nature and the region Consciousness. The region Nature includes all things in nature and has subspecies such as Material Thing, Plant, Animal, etc. The region Consciousness includes all conscious experiences, with subspecies such as Perception, Judgment, Imagination, etc. *Ideas* III, we shall see, adds the region Spirit or Humanity, including entities formed by human affairs (human persons, cultural objects such as hammers or books, moral ideals, etc.).

Now, Husserl recognized both *formal* and *material* essences. Material essences – such as cited above – are the subject-matters of *material ontologies*, including the science of nature, which Husserl (the former mathematician) saw as a "mathematizable" science.[5] Formal essences, by contrast, are the subject-matter of *formal ontology*. They are the pure forms of "material" species or regions. These forms are called *categories*. The highest category is that of Object-In-General, and this subsumes the more special categories of: Individual, Essence (including Species, Quality, and Relation), State of Affairs, Unity, Plurality, Space, Time, etc. As these categories define the *form* of all objects in the world, they are also called "logical" categories. But Husserl defined logic more broadly than has the analytic tradition.[6] He distinguishes three types of categories: linguistic categories, e.g., those of name, predicate, and statement; meaning categories, e.g., of proposition, concept, etc.; and ontological categories, e.g., of individual, species, quality, and state of affairs. (Cf. §§10, 16, 124 *vis-à-vis* the linguistic forms discussed in the *Investigations*.) Our concern, however, will be with ontological categories. Husserl seems to have been the first philosopher to develop this conception of formal ontology, yet kindred notions of ontological form – especially forms of objects in facts or states of affairs – soon emerged in Bertrand Russell's doctrine of "logical atomism" (ca. 1917) and in Ludwig Wittgenstein's *Tractatus Logico-Philosophicus* (1922).

From the realms of fact and essence Husserl then distinguished the realm of meaning or sense (*Sinn*), including noemata and their components. (Cf. *Ideas* I, §§88–90, 128–31.) Meanings are, like essences, ideal, i.e., not in space or time. But they are not essences (*Ideas* III, §16); they are contents of intentional experiences, embodying ways in which objects are presented in consciousness. By virtue of its essence, each intentional experience has a content, or noema, the central part of which is called a sense (*Sinn*). The content of an experience presents or prescribes an object, and if there is such an object, that is the object of the experience. Thus, the object of an intentional experience is that which is prescribed by the content of the experience, and contents are meaning-entities which prescribe objects in the world outside consciousness. So, for Husserl, meaning is inseparable from consciousness, by virtue of the essence of consciousness. As noted, in *Logical Investigations* the intentional content of an experience was identified with the species of the experience, but in *Ideas* I these are distinguished.

Though there are differences between Husserl and Frege, Husserl's realm of noema in some ways resembles Frege's "third realm" of sense (*Sinn*). However, Frege's first two realms were the physical and the mental, while Husserl's were the concrete and the abstract, or fact and essence. Note that for Husserl propositions (*Sätze*) are a kind of senses (*Sinne*), not essences, and are distinct from states of affairs, which may be concrete, or real. It should be said that Husserl had his own semantics of sense and reference, developed with its own motivations and ontology, rather than one borrowed from Frege (as is sometimes assumed).

Husserl's basic ontology is summarized in Figure 1, where capitalized first letters indicate essences or species *per se*.

The realms of fact and essence Husserl called distinct domains (*Gebieten*) of knowledge. The realm of fact is the domain of the empirical sciences (physics, biology, psychology), and the realm of essence is the domain of the "eidetic" sciences (mathematics, logic, formal and material ontologies). The realm of meaning was, for Husserl, a third domain of knowledge, part of the domain of phenomenology – the new science of conscious experiences, their intentionality, and their contents. Of course, an empirical science such as physics seeks essential truths about physical things, placing them under appropriate essences, starting with the region Nature. And similarly, phenomenology seeks essential truths about experiences, placing them under appropriate essences, starting with the region Consciousness. However, concern with these essences *per se* – for instance, with their status as "ideal" entities – belongs to the ontology behind the science of physics or phenomenology.

Husserl's ontology of fact, essence, and meaning goes hand-in-hand with an epistemology and phenomenology of three species of intuition (*Anschauung*), which are the sources of evidence for our knowledge of these three domains. Entities in each domain are known through an appropriate kind of intuition. Thus, material things and events – in the realm of fact – are known through empirical intuition, i.e., sensory perception. Essences are known through eidetic intuition, or essential insight: I "see" what is essential to a

Fact (Concrete Entity)
  individuals
    independent individuals (substrates)
    dependent individuals (moments)
  states of affairs
  events
    experiences

Essence (Ideal Entity)
  Formal Essence
    Individual
    Species, Quality, Relation
    State of Affairs
  Material Essence
    Region (Highest Material Species)
      Nature
      Consciousness
      Spirit (Humanity)

Meaning or Sense (Content of Experience)
  senses of individuals
  predicative senses of species, qualities, relations
  propositions

Figure 1

species, Husserl says, by "eidetic variation," i.e., by imagining variations in the properties of instances of the species. And meanings or
senses, being contents of experiences, are known through phenomenological reflection on experiences: by "bracketing" the object of
my experience, the practice called *epoché*, I come to focus on the
way the object is given in the experience, and so in reflection I
apprehend the sense or noema of the experience.

Husserl finds the evidence for his ontology of fact, essence, and
meaning in these three kinds of intuition. However, our focus here
is on the ontology itself, not the corroborating epistemology and
phenomenology.

Within the above ontology, a doctrine of mind and body begins to take shape. In *Ideas* I, §33, Husserl says that each particular *I* or ego and each particular experience falls under two regions, the region Nature and the region Pure Consciousness. Accordingly, egos and experiences are known in different ways in empirical psychology, which studies them as natural objects (as neural activities or whatever), and in pure phenomenology, which studies them as conscious phenomena (as my-being-conscious-of-something). Here is the kernel of the many-aspect monism that unfolds in *Ideas* II.

Later sections of *Ideas* I (notably §§49–50) seem to adopt a strong form of idealism (the being of consciousness is "absolute" while the being of the spatiotemporal world is "relative" to, or "for," a consciousness). Such an idealism, we shall see, is incompatible with the ontology mapped out early in the work and expanded in *Ideas* II and III. One may respond that all these ontological structures will later be relativized to consciousness (in §§49–50), regrouped as mere phenomena of consciousness, so that idealism emerges only later in the work, after the "transcendental turn" effected by the *epoché*. However, another reading makes Husserl less of a Berkeleyan idealist and more of a Kantian realist for whom things-in-themselves lie outside consciousness. On that reading, we can experience things only through phenomena of consciousness, but neither the being nor the essence of these things is formed from acts or contents of consciousness. (These issues emerge in Section XIII following.)

III. NATURE AND CONSCIOUSNESS

When Husserl wrote the *Logical Investigations* (First Edition, 1900), he took his ontology and phenomenology to be compatible with both dualism and physicalism. "We must leave it completely open," he wrote (V, §4), "whether and how psychological and physical things are to be distinguished as equally justified coexistent thing-like unities." The choice between dualism and physicalism was to be determined by the course of scientific investigation, he declared (V, §7):[7]

[T]he objective unities of psychology and those of natural science are not identical, at least not, as in the position of first data, they await scientific elaboration. Whether the two sciences in their full development will still be separated, depends on whether they really concern separate, or at least relative-self-sufficient realities in their mutual relation. (Such self-sufficiency does not of course entail necessary separation of the two realities by any mystical abysses.) We can turn the matter round and say: If there is such a separation, we can only learn of it as both sciences develop.

By the time of *Ideas I* (1913), without waiting for the progress of science, Husserl had concluded that the same event or individual could carry both psychological and physical essences, distinguishing these "natural" essences from the essence of consciousness. In to-day's terms, he had taken a position of token identity and type/property dualism or pluralism. (Moreover, we shall see, the physical, psychological, and consciousness aspect of an individual are not self-sufficient but stand in relations of dependence.)

Having just introduced the phenomenological method of *epoché* in §32 of *Ideas* I, Husserl asks, in §33, what remains to be studied after we "bracket" the whole world of nature. The answer: a new region of being, the region Pure Consciousness. This will be the concern of the new science of phenomenology, whereas the region Nature is the concern of the natural sciences, including psychology. (In *Ideas* II, as we see below, Husserl characterizes both natural and cultural or "spiritual" aspects of the surrounding world, all bracketed by *epoché*. The region Consciousness will then be distinguished from both the region Nature and the region Spirit. Here in *Ideas* I, for pedagogic simplicity perhaps, Husserl focusses on Nature in contrast to Consciousness.)

Pure Consciousness is the region (the highest material genus) under which fall – in the realm of fact – both experiences and their subjects. A particular experience is an event that instantiates the essence Act of Consciousness, including as a moment an instance of the essence Act. And an experience essentially has a subject or ego. Thus, in having a particular experience, I instantiate the essence Subject of Consciousness or Pure Ego, including as a moment an instance of the essence Ego. When Husserl talks of "pure" or "transcendental" consciousness, or "pure" or "transcendental" ego, the word "pure" or "transcendental" simply means instantiating the essence Act or Ego, and hence the essence Consciousness, rather than the essence Nature. Phenomenology is concerned only with this Consciousness-aspect of experiences and subjects, not with any Nature-aspects thereof.

But now, one and the same experiential event (the same concrete event) falls under both the region Consciousness and the region Nature. And similarly one and the same ego or *I* (the same concrete individual) falls under both the region Consciousness and the region Nature. As Husserl writes (§33):

[S]ince the [region of] being to be pointed out is none other than what we refer to on essential grounds as "pure experiences [*Erlebnisse*]," "pure consciousness" with its pure "correlates of consciousness" [= contents or noemata], and on the other side its "pure I," we observe that it is from *the* I, *the* consciousness, *the* experience as given to us from the natural standpoint, that we take our start.

I am – I, the actual human being, a real object like others in the natural world. I carry out *cogitationes*, "acts of consciousness" in a wider and a narrower sense, and these acts are, as belonging to this human subject, events of the same natural reality.

We normally think of ourselves and our experiences, Husserl held, as part of nature, and this naturalistic presupposition carries over to psychology. However, after bracketing the world of nature, which means bracketing the region Nature, we can begin to study ourselves and our experiences – in phenomenology – as falling under the region Consciousness, which is a very different essence than Nature. Nonetheless, it is the same *I*, and likewise the same experience, that falls under both the region Nature and the region Consciousness: the same *I* and the same experience that is studied in both naturalistic, empirical psychology and non-naturalistic, pure or transcendental phenomenology.

Thus, when Husserl speaks of "the pure experience," he means "the experience *qua* act of consciousness," focussing on the Act-of-Consciousness aspect of the event itself. And when he speaks of "the pure *I*," he means "the *I qua* subject of consciousness," focussing on the Subject-of-Consciousness aspect of the individual. Moreover, drawing on his earlier work in *Logical Investigations*, Husserl had an articulate ontology of these *aspects:* they are moments or dependent parts of the experience and the *I* respectively. There is only one substratum *I*, but it has two aspects: the natural, bodily moment and the mental, experiential moment of the *I*. These moments are themselves distinct (dependent) parts of the *I*. This claim, which Husserl explicitly developed in *Ideas* II and in the *Crisis*, will be much discussed below.

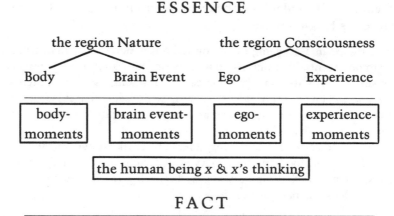

Figure 2

Much as Descartes distinguished the essence of mind (thought) from the essence of body (extension), so Husserl distinguished the essence of consciousness from the essence of nature. But whereas Descartes also distinguished the *I* or *res cogitans* from the body or *res extensa*, Husserl insisted that the "*I*" and the "body" are distinct aspects (moments) of a single individual – and likewise that, in the event of thinking, the "mental" event and the corresponding "natural" event are two aspects (moments) of a single event. Thus, while Descartes posited a dualism of both substance (mind versus body) and attribute (thought versus extension), Husserl posited a dualism of essence (Consciousness versus Nature) and a dualism of moments (instances of the essences), but an identity of substance or substratum. Husserl's ontology of mind and body is summarized in Figure 2. (As we shall see later, there are more than two such aspects of the *I*, so Husserl's wider position is not a dualism but a pluralism of aspects.)

Descartes found an incompatibility between the essence of mind (thought) and the essence of body (extension): bodies are essentially divisible (because extended in space), while minds are essentially indivisible (because not extended in space). Husserl found a similar difference in essence between Nature and Consciousness: things in nature are in their essence spatial, while acts and subjects of consciousness are not. However, Descartes held that no substance can have the attributes of both thought and extension, so that no substance could be both a body and a mind. Husserl held, to the contrary, that *the same* individual can be both spatial and thinking, that "body" and "mind" are not two kinds of individual but two aspects or moments in one individual, instances of the essences Nature and Consciousness respectively. For Husserl, these essences are different but they are not incompatible; they are not incapable of being instantiated in the same individual or event. (Cf. again *Ideas* I, §33, and *Ideas* II, discussed below.)

Husserl's ontology of essence and individual is largely Aristotelian, even in distinguishing instances of universals in individuals. Now Aristotle said the soul is the *form* of the body (which is then the "matter" of the individual stamped with that "form"). In effect, Husserl said the soul and the body are instances of *two distinct forms* – essences – in one individual. The difference in doctrines is important, because some philosophers of mind today have seen in Aristotle's doctrine an early form of functionalism. However, in Husserl's doctrine, the essence of consciousness does not reduce to the essence of brain activity – in either "form" (function) or "matter" (neural physiochemistry).

What then are the essences Nature and Consciousness? What properties belong to the essence of nature, and what properties belong to the essence of consciousness? The basic contrast is drawn in §42 of *Ideas* I.

Things in nature – material things – exist in space and time, in spacetime: they are in that sense "real" (*reale*). By contrast, experiences – events of consciousness – are temporal but not spatial and so are not "real." Their essence is that of being a consciousness *of* something, which does not entail their being spatial (§§34–36). Thus, the essence Nature includes the essence Spatiotemporal, while the essence Consciousness does not. However, acts of consciousness are temporal (and in that sense "*reell*": cf. §84). In the lectures gathered in *The Phenomenology of Internal Time-Consciousness* (1905–10), Husserl had distinguished "objective time" from "inner time," the former being the temporality of things in nature and the latter that of experiences in consciousness. Since space and space-time were "mathematized" in the work of Galileo and Descartes (within Cartesian geometry, in particular, followed quickly by the calculus), the essence Nature has been articulated in increasingly mathematical terms. As Husserl stressed in the *Crisis* (1935–38), this mathematizing has continued into the twentieth century – with ever new twists in the decades following Husserl's writing.

For Husserl, interestingly, the essence of something includes the ways in which it can be known or experienced (*Ideas* I, §42). A material thing can be perceived from only one side at a time. This property evidently derives from the essence of both the thing and the perceptual experience – a point of interaction between species subsumed under the essences Nature and Consciousness. By contrast, an experience cannot be perceived "from one side." Material things are known through perception, or empirical intuition, which is perspectival, presenting a thing like a tree from a spatial perspective; experiences are known or intuited (as pure experiences) not through sense-perception but through phenomenological reflection, which does not present experiences from spatial perspectives. Accordingly, Husserl calls material things "transcendent," meaning, first, that they are not a part of the stream of consciousness and, second, that they are perceivable only "one-sidedly" and thus incompletely. By contrast, he calls experiences "immanent," meaning that they are a proper part of the stream of consciousness. In this way the ontic essences Nature and Consciousness involve respectively these epistemic essences, Transcendence and Immanence.

Of course, I *qua* human being am a material thing (though not only that) and so perceivable from only one side. I *qua* pure ego, however, am a subject of experiences and, like the experiences themselves, intuited not in sense-perception but in phenomenological reflection, and in such reflection I am not given to myself from a spatial perspective.

Husserl did not argue directly for these principles about Nature and Consciousness. He held in general that through eidetic intuition we can "see" the validity of essential truths. This methodology led him to distinguish the essences Nature and Consciousness, and he then argued, in effect, by analyzing these essences. Specifically, in phenomenology we study the essence Consciousness, and by analyzing this essence we discover the intentionality of acts of consciousness.

IV. PURE CONSCIOUSNESS AND INTENTIONALITY

The natural sciences study the essence of nature, and Husserl counts psychology among them. Psychology studies the essences of experiences from a certain perspective, seeking an account of their role in nature – in Husserl's ontology, those of their essences that fall under the high-level essence or region Nature. Behavioral psychology would study behaviors of human beings, part of their naturalistic essence, forming theories about their experiences by probabilistic inferences from third-person observations of their behavior. By contrast, phenomenology studies the essences of experiences from a first-person perspective: one grasps essences of experiences through intuition of one's own experiences and their contents. Still, Husserl allowed that one part of psychology, called phenomenological psychology, can recount the same results as pure phenomenology (cf. *Ideas* III, Chapter 2, and the later *Phenomenological Psychology* (1925)). The difference is that phenomenological psychology would place experiences and egos under both the essences Nature and Consciousness, whereas pure phenomenology would bracket the essence Nature (or "moments" of things instantiating Nature) and thus the role of experiences and egos in nature.

The main theme of phenomenology, as noted, is intentionality: consciousness's being *of* something. *Ideas* I (1913) unfolds a basic account of intentionality via the noema of an experience. *Ideas* II (drafted in 1912) elaborates on kinesthetic awareness of one's own body and one's role as a human being in a social, human world. *Cartesian Meditations* (1931) expands on the role of horizon and the essence of the ego. Husserl's early lectures *Phenomenology of Internal Time-Consciousness* (1905–10) lay the foundation for studies of the temporality of consciousness and the ego.

It will be useful now to see in some detail how Husserl characterized the essence of consciousness, and how different it is from the essence of brain activity. In *Ideas* I (§§ 84–133) Husserl laid out a basic account of the essential structures of consciousness, which we may summarize as follows. Consciousness is spread out in time in the form of a stream of experiences. Each experience, or act of consciousness, is intentional: it is directed from an ego toward an object via a content. If there is no object, as in hallucination, the act is merely as if directed toward an object. The experience consists of a

noesis, or interpretive component, and if sensory a sensory component consisting of sensations or *hyletic data* (the "matter" that joins
with the "form" of noesis). The noetic component of the experience
bears the intentional content of the experience, its *noema.* The
noema includes two components: a thetic component and a *sense*
(*Sinn*). The thetic component qualifies the experience as of a perception, judgment, wish, or whatever (and more), while the sense component prescribes the object of the experience and the particular way
in which the object is given or presented in the experience. The
sense component is a broadly conceptual structure; in the case of an
act of thinking, it is a proposition (*Satz*). Following Brentano,
Husserl assumed that every experience includes also a secondary
intentionality, consisting in the ego's awareness of the experience
itself. This form of awareness is traditionally called apperception (a
term Husserl sometimes uses). It is part of what makes the experience conscious as opposed to unconscious (though Husserl rarely
mentioned the unconscious: one brief discussion is in *Experience
and Judgment,* § 67b).[8]

Accordingly, the basic structure of the property of intentionality –
fundamental to the essence of consciousness or experience – may be
depicted as follows:

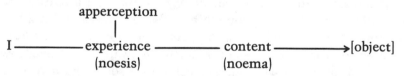

Of course, Husserl allowed that in some cases an intentional experience has no object. Thus, the existence of the object is bracketed in a
phenomenological study of the essence of the experience (the bracketing indicated here by the square brackets). This relational structure of the experience – its being "directed" from an ego through a
content toward an object – is the structure of intentionality, which
is the hallmark of the essence Consciousness.

A key player in the intentional relationship is the noema. As noted
earlier, in the *Logical Investigations* Husserl identified intentional
content with act-species, but in *Ideas* I he gave noemata their own
ontological type and status apart from species. Noemata are meanings
(*Sinne*), but they are act-meanings rather than linguistic meanings
(*Bedeutungen*). And meanings are their own kind of "ideal," "non-

real" entities: they are not essences, but meanings, Husserl stresses in *Ideas* III (§16). The essence of noemata consists largely in the role they play in intentional relationships, as outlined above.

Intentionality is defined by an experience's having both an "object-pole" and a "subject-pole." Whereas different experiences may be directed toward the same (putative) object, they may also be directed from the same ego. The principles that define these patterns of directedness define the essences Ego, Intentional Experience, and Noema, which articulate the essence Consciousness. The relations among the essences themselves are expounded in terms of what is "essential" to an ego, experience, and noema. an experience or act of consciousness is essentially intentional, i.e., essentially directed from an ego and via a noema and (if successful) to an object.

Furthermore, each experience is part of a stream of experiences, and it has a temporal duration and a temporal location in that stream. These temporal properties are defined in terms of "inner time," as opposed to "outer time," which is part of the essence Nature. Thus, each experience is part of a "temporal horizon" of experiences belonging to the same stream of consciousness. In *Cartesian Meditations* Husserl amplifies his account of the "horizon" of an experience. Each experience, he says, has a *horizon* of further possible experiences that present the same object in different ways – in the case of perception, these include possible perceptions of the object from different spatial perspectives. Horizon-analysis, he says, is a new kind of phenomenological analysis. It explicates the force of a noema in a different way, not by specifying the component meanings that are parts of the noema, but by specifying alternative noemata that present, or prescribe, the same object. These alternative noemata presuppose the ego's background assumptions about the given kind of object – further meanings that are not explicitly part of the noema but are intentionally associated with it in the "constitution" of objects of that type. In this way Husserl's theory of horizon ramifies his account of intentionality in terms of noemata.

Recall that we are assuming a realist reading of Husserl's ontology. The idealist reading is easily grafted on at this point. Simply drop the natural world and the objects of experience from this picture, leaving only the "pure" structures of consciousness: ego, experiences, their noemata, and their horizons, all mapping myriad patterns of intentionality – without an external world, but with a phenomenal world in which, from the ego's point of view, nothing is changed. Or, alternatively, pull the natural world into consciousness, by identifying natural objects with systems of phenomena or noemata.

Husserl said the essence Nature is mathematizable, as articulated by modern physics. Is the essence Consciousness mathematizable? Decades after Husserl died, computer models of the mind have assumed a positive answer: computer algorithms are held to articulate the essence of particular mental activities. Yet the computer model fails to capture important properties of experience, including sensory "qualia," emotional affect, volitional effect, and indeed intentionality – all essential features of certain kinds of experience according to Husserl's phenomenology. Indeed, Husserl's ontology of mind does not square with the functionalist model of recent artificial intelligence theory. Basically, what is mathematizable in the essence Consciousness are certain formal structures of noemata, part of the formal ontology of experiences. However, noemata have other properties such as their representing or prescribing certain objects. And those intentional or "semantic" properties are not captured by computer programs; at best they are described in further syntactic constructions with no intrinsic semantic properties. This is not to deny that a formal, mathematical model of those properties is possible, but the automata theory on which computer science is based does not and should not address those properties. The intentional properties of consciousness and noemata should be modelled instead in a formal intensional semantics developed in the broadly Fregean tradition (including – with possible-worlds variations – Tarski, Carnap, Hintikka, Kripke, Montague, Kaplan, Barwise and Perry, etc.).[9] We shall return to this question of "mathematizability," which Husserl took up in the *Crisis*. There Husserl criticized the very idea that all properties of things in our world – and indeed of our experiences – are mathematizable, or reducible to properties described by mathematical formulae that abstract from properties observed in everyday experience.[10]

V. THE PURE *I*

The essence of an *I* or ego consists in the ego's role in the complex of intentional relationships involved in a given stream of consciousness and the horizons associated with experiences in the stream.

Thus, the essence of the *I*, the "pure ego," is simply: the subject of intentional experiences – which stand in appropriate relationships with other experiences, noemata, and the objects those noemata prescribe in the world. It should be noted that Husserl included under experiences not only perceptions, judgments, etc., but also actions insofar as actions are intentional events rather than mere movements of the physical body. Thus, in *Ideas* II he spoke of volitional movements of the "living body" with kinesthetic awareness thereof. Accordingly, the *I* is not only a subject but also an "agent" (though Husserl does not use such a term). However, Husserl's account of action was at best sketchy in his central works, turning on the notion of "living body" developed in the posthumous *Ideas* II and in *Crisis*.[11]

In a stream of consciousness, there occur various concrete experiences, each had by the same *I* or ego. It is part of the essence Intentional Experience, or Act of Consciousness, that each experience is had by a particular ego. Thus, the ego itself instantiates the essence Subject of Consciousness, and in that way the essence Consciousness, precisely by virtue of playing this role of having intentional experiences. And the same individual, we saw, instantiates the essence Nature, by virtue of its role in various spatial, causal, and natural relationships involving its "body."

Husserl did not always acknowledge the pure *I*. In the First Edition of *Logical Investigations* (1900–01) he followed Brentano's model of "a 'psychology without a soul', i.e., a psychology that abandons all metaphysical presumptions in regard to the soul" (V, 67), including the assumption that there is a substantial ego that underlies experiences. Of the "pure ego" assumed by such neo-Kantian philosophers as his contemporary Paul Natorp, Husserl wrote (V, §8, 549):

I must frankly confess . . . that I am quite unable to find this ego, this primitive, necessary [subjective] centre of [intentional] relations.[11] The only thing I can take note of, and therefore perceive, are the empirical ego and its empirical relations to its own experiences, or to such external objects as are receiving special attention at the moment.

The pure ego is supposed to stand behind these phenomenal entities, as the subject that apprehends them, but Husserl's initial phenomenological search for such a subject came up short.

In the Second Edition of the *Investigations* (1913), however, Husserl took an about-turn, adding the famous footnote (p. 549):

I have since managed to find it, i.e. have learnt not to be led astray from a pure grasp of the given through corrupt forms of ego-metaphysic: cf. note to §6.

The note in §6 (p. 544) says that the First Edition

fails to do justice to the fact that the empirical ego is as much a case of transcendence as the physical thing. If the elimination of such transcendence . . . leaves us with no residual pure ego, there can be no real (adequate) self-evidence attaching to the "I am." But if there is really such an adequate self-evidence – who indeed could deny it? – how can we avoid assuming a pure ego? It is precisely the ego apprehended in *carrying out* a self-evident *cogito,* and the pure carrying out *eo ipso* . . . grasps it as the subject of a pure experience of the type *cogito.*

Husserl here concurs with Descartes' *cogito ergo sum* at least in the assumption that in carrying out a thought process one *eo ipso* grasps oneself as the subject of the thinking. Husserl does not spell out the argument explicitly. Each act of thinking, one might argue, is as if directed *from* an ego *toward* an object. Thus, the phenomenological structure of the act is "I think such-and-such." This structure is self-evident in the act of so thinking. Hence, the *ontological* structure of the act is given in self-evidence as that of an *I* doing the thinking and so, if the thinking is veridical, being in an intentional relation to an object. In short, there is an *I* at the source of the act. (Notice the interplay of the phenomenology, epistemology, and ontology of the *cogito.*)[12]

What is the "corrupt ego-metaphysics" Husserl thus rejects, and which he suggests was distracting him from the phenomenology of self-awareness? One such metaphysics was the phenomenalist, Humean view that identifies the self with the succession of perceptions that make up a person's consciousness.[13] While Husserl does not mention Hume here by name, his concern is phenomenalism regarding both ego and objects (cf. V, §7). But Husserl's fundamental ontology assumes an individual is distinct from its properties (cf. *Ideas* I (1913), Chapter 1). This principle would apply to the ego as much as to a physical thing, and he belatedly recognizes an ego that *has* experiences much as an object has properties. A related "corrupt metaphysics" would be a conception of the pure ego as a Kantian thing-in-itself beyond the reach of consciousness. This notion of things-in-themselves he rejects as nonsense (*Ideas* I, § 43), and so we might indeed grasp a pure *I* behind our experiences.

But there is more. Husserl's detailed reflections on the ego were drafted by this time though not released for publication; they belong to the posthumous Second Book of *Ideas* (1912). In that work Husserl stressed that there is just one entity that is I, but it has very different aspects, including those that qualify it as a subject and those that qualify it as an embodied, psychophysical organism, an "empirical ego." These views eventually appeared in *Cartesian Meditations* (1931). Despite the homage to Descartes (the text was delivered as lectures in Paris), Husserl's ontology of the ego is very different from that of Descartes.

In *Cartesian Meditations* (IV, §§30–37) Husserl elaborated on the essence of the *I* (*das Ich*) or ego (*ego*). The ego, he held, has different types of properties. Fundamentally, the ego is "inseparable from the processes [= experiences] making up his life." Thus, the ego is, first of all, "the I as identical pole of subjective processes," i.e., one and the same *I* who has the experiences in his stream of consciousness. Second, the ego is "the I as substrate of habitualities," i.e., one and the same *I* who has a variety of "habits" that give rise to a "personal character," including abiding opinions, decisions, values, and desires. Third, the ego is the *I* in "full concreteness," which Husserl calls a "monad," i.e., the *I* carrying all the actual experiences it has, in addition to the abiding habits of personality. These experiences and habitualities are unified by principles that define the ego's identity, including its identity through (inner) time. These properties define the essence Pure Ego, which is bound to the essence Consciousness.

Husserl distinguished the "pure" or "transcendental" ego from the "psychological" ego and the "mundane" "human ego" (§§11, 30ff). The psychological ego is the *I qua I* in nature, and the human ego is the *I qua* human being, *qua* psychophysical, social *I* in the human life-world (*Lebenswelt*). It is not that there are different individuals here; there are different aspects or moments of the one *I* or ego. In terms of the ontology of *Ideas* I, each individual *I* instantiates different essences. Most general are the essences Nature and Consciousness. More specific essences under the region Consciousness are those of Intentional Experience and Pure Ego. Under Intentional

Experience would fall the essences Perception, Judgment, Desire, etc., and under Ego would fall the essences Subject of Experiences, Substrate of Habitualities, and Monad. Corresponding to the essence Monad, but falling under the region Nature, would be the essence Psyche or Psychological Ego.

Husserl's account of the *I* differs in three main ways from Descartes's (as expressed in Husserlian terms). First, for Descartes the *I* instantiates the essence Consciousness but not the essence Body, whereas for Husserl it instantiates both. Second, for Descartes the *I* is a purely mental substance distinct from the body, which is a physical substance, whereas for Husserl the *I* is an individual that has both mental and physical aspects. So Descartes holds a dualism of substance as well as attribute, while Husserl, as noted, assumes a monism of the individual *I* but a dualism (or pluralism) of its attributes. Third, for Descartes there are causal interactions between the *I* and the body, or between the *I*'s thinking and certain of the body's activities, whereas for Husserl the "pure *I*" and the body are parts or moments of the same individual I and it is a category mistake – a "region" mistake – to hold that there are causal relations between these moments (see Section xi following). (For Husserl, there are causal relations between *other* parts or moments of the *I*, for instance, between events in my stomach and events in my brain or events in my mind as belonging to the natural world; these relations are studied in natural science as opposed to phenomenology. And, as we shall see, there are non-causal dependence relations among various moments of the *I*.)

VI. BODY, SOUL OR PSYCHE, AND SPIRIT OR
PERSON OR HUMAN *I*

Husserl distinguishes the "pure" *I*, then, from the "empirical" *I*: the embodied, psychophysical, human *I*. The distinction, we have seen, is one of different aspects of the same entity, I. The mind-body problem appears now as a problem of relations between different aspects of the *I*, including bodily and mental aspects.

Husserl's most fine-grained discussions of mind-body issues are in the Second Book of *Ideas* (1912), where Husserl distinguishes different ways of conceiving or experiencing both body and mind. The distinctions developed there, framed by the ontology of the First and

Third Books of *Ideas*, are later extended in the more famous *Crisis* (written during 1935–38), having shaped the distinctions in *Cartesian Meditations* (1931) among transcendental, psychological, and human ego. All three books of *Ideas* were drafted in 1912, but only *Ideas* I (1913) was released for publication in Husserl's lifetime. (*Ideas* II was revised, under Husserl's supervision, in 1916 and again in 1918 by Edith Stein and again in 1925 by Ludwig Landgrebe.) Nonetheless, Husserl's groundbreaking work in *Ideas* II, separating crucial aspects of mind and body as we experience them, was known to Heidegger and Merleau-Ponty. The influence of *Ideas* II is at work in the well-known views of Heidegger on the practical, social activities of the self (rechristened *Dasein*) and Merleau-Ponty on the human body and bodily intentionality – views which are commonly thought to be in opposition to Husserl's.[14]

Ideas II elaborates Husserl's analysis of the "constitution" of body and mind. The three main sections of the book concern the constitution of *material nature* (material things – and perhaps plants), *animal nature* (living animals), and the *human* or "*spiritual*" world. These analyses of constitution describe conceptual or intentional structures, i.e., structures of noemata, focussing on various "strata of sense" (cf. §4). The self or *I* as experienced in everyday life Husserl calls the empirical *I* (*empirisches Ich*) or, as he expounds, the human *I* (*Ich-Mensch*) (§§20, 27, 49, 57). On Husserl's analysis, our sense of human being, the sense "human *I*," has a stratified structure:

> "human *I*" or "spirit"
> "living body" *cum* "soul"
> "physical body" *qua* "material thing"

– where, as we shall see, the higher levels of sense depend or are founded on the lower levels. Thus, I experience myself fundamentally as having a physical body (*Körper*), which is a material thing with spatiotemporal location, material composition, and causal interaction. As a living organism or animal, however, I experience my physical body as "animated" (*beseelen*) by my soul (*Seele*) or psyche (*Psyche*), and thus as a living body (*Leib*), an animal organism. Furthermore, as a human being (*Mensch*) or human *I* (*Ich-Mensch*), or as·a person (*Person*), I take myself as having a spirit (*Geist*) insofar as I am a member of a social world, with a history, culture, and morality. These levels of sense concern not only oneself but others. By means of empathy (*Ein-*

fühlung), I experience other human beings as living human organisms with their own psyches or souls, and furthermore as fellow human persons with their own spirits or forms of humanity (§§ 43–47).

In drawing these distinctions Husserl is separating structures of *sense* or noema in virtue of which we experience ourselves as human, as living bodily organism, and as mere material object. These analyses of sense do not yet address the *essence* of a human being. For, as Husserl stresses in *Ideas* I, and emphatically in *Ideas* III (§16), noema and essence are different kinds of entity, so that a noema corresponding to an object is not the same thing as an essence of the object. A noema or noematic sense is the intentional content of an experience, whereas the essence of an object is an objective aspect of the object itself, transcendent to consciousness. (There is no essence Round Rectangle, Husserl notes, but in order to judge this there must be a noematic sense of "round rectangle." Analysis of sense structure belongs thus to phenomenology, while analysis of essence belongs to ontology. Nonetheless, it is evident throughout Husserl's discussions in *Ideas* II that he assumes there are parallel stratifications in the sense "human *I*" and in the essence Human *I*, hence in the concrete aspects or moments of the individual *I*.

In a diagram:

SENSE	ESSENCE	ASPECT
"human *I*" ("spirit")	Human *I* (Spirit)	as human being
"living body" *cum* "soul"	Living Body *cum* soul	as living body *cum* soul
"physical body"	Physical Body	as physical body

To reflect the regional category scheme described earlier, the parallel may be depicted as in Figure 3, where '*X* ⊢*Y*' means *Y* depends on *X*, or in Husserl's terms *Y* is "founded" on *X*, or *X* founds *Y*.

These three realms of essence reflect a refinement of Husserl's regional ontology. Thus, *Ideas* II and III amplify the distinction in *Ideas* I between the regions Nature and Consciousness. Three regions are now distinguished: Nature, Spirit, and Consciousness. And Nature has two subregions: Material Nature and Animal Nature. The "factual" entities of the world are characterized then by these high-level essences or regions, as in Figure 4. These ontological distinctions are meant to provide a foundation for the distinction Wilhelm Dilthey had drawn between the natural sciences and the human or cultural sciences

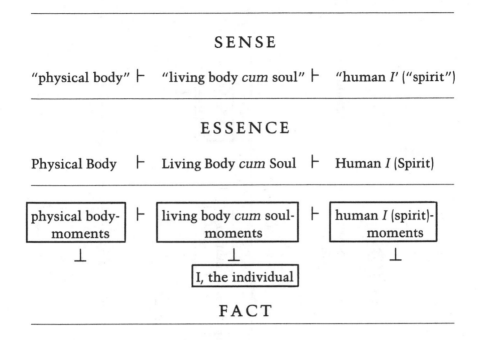

SENSE

"physical body" ⊢ "living body *cum* soul" ⊢ "human *I*' ("spirit")

ESSENCE

Physical Body ⊢ Living Body *cum* Soul ⊢ Human *I* (Spirit)

| physical body-moments | ⊢ | living body *cum* soul-moments | ⊢ | human *I* (spirit)-moments |

⊥   ⊥   ⊥

| I, the individual |

FACT

Figure 3

(*Naturwissenschaften* and *Geisteswissenschaften*). Nature is studied in the natural sciences, spirit in the human sciences, and consciousness in phenomenology. In the *Crisis* the region here called Spirit, the Spiritual or Personal World of the Human Being, will be called the Life-World, and the living body will belong to the Life-World.

Clearly, the region of Spirit should include not only human beings, but all personal, cultural beings (chimpanzees, extraterrestrials). Certainly we humans have some degree of empathy with many kinds of animals, and empathy is the way we understand both animal and "spiritual" beings (*Ideas* II, §§43ff., 46, 56e). Husserl's concrete concerns, though, are with human beings.

Both science and common sense assume that consciousness depends on brain activity and also on human cultural activity (as indicated in Figure 4). In Husserl's terminology, that is to say that the moments of the *I* which instantiate Consciousness are dependent on those that instantiate Nature and Spirit. Specifically, the soul depends on the physical body, for the soul is the psychic *I* that moves, i.e.,

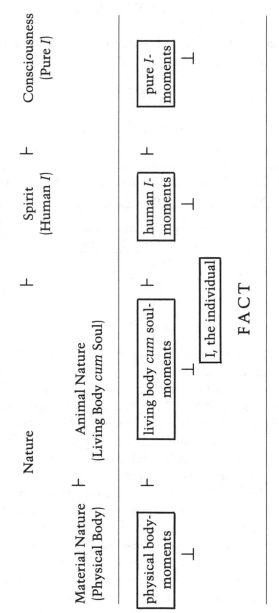

Figure 4

moves the physical body. And the human *I* depends on this psycho-physical *I*, the ensouled-embodied *I*, for the human *I* moves bodily and thereby acts in the "spiritual" human world, the life-world.[15]

Accordingly, consciousness is a proper part of the activities of the human *I* and the psychic or psychophysical *I*, as well as the pure *I*. For it is the same individual I who performs *pure* acts of consciousness, *human* actions in the life-world, and *living* bodily movements in animal nature. Thus, the human *I* is said to perform acts of consciousness (*Ideas* I, §33), and through the living body I am said to move, e.g., to lift or strike something (*Crisis*, §62). Moreover, the same event has the different aspects of being a physical bodily movement, a living bodily movement, a human action of lifting a box, and a pure act of willing to lift the box (cf. *Ideas* I, §33).

Pure consciousness is thus an abstraction from embodied consciousness in nature and encultured consciousness in the life-world: an abstractable moment or dependent part of the psychophysical *I* and the human *I*. The process of abstraction is *epoché* (as detailed in *Ideas* I, §§30–32). But the mind is not ontologically separated from the body, as in Cartesian dualism.

VII. THE SENSE OF BODY, SOUL, AND HUMAN *I*

Husserl's explorations of the constitution of body and mind are fascinating and original, marking a break with the Cartesian themes that had defined much of European philosophy since the Seventeenth Century. Most of the details are found in *Ideas* II, which is rich in the kind of close phenomenological analysis often wanting in Husserl's methodological discussions of the "new science" of phenomenology. Let us focus in on the points that bear most directly on the mind-body problem.

In Husserl's scheme, the lowest level of sense is that of "material thing" (*Ding*) or "physical body" (*Körper*) (§§11–13). One kind of material thing is the human body taken as mere "thing" or "physical body." The next level of sense is that of "animal" or "living [animated] body" (*Leib*) (§§19–20). An animal, human or otherwise, is experienced as having a soul (*Seele*) or psyche (*Psyche*) as well as a body. Husserl uses the terms "soul" and "psyche" interchangeably, so that the ancient notion of soul or *anima* as what animates (*beseelen*) a living body coincides with the notion of psyche as the proper object of study in psychology, which is a part of the natural sciences (as stressed in *Ideas* III). Thus, the sense "living body" includes the sense strata "physical body" and "soul," the latter founded upon the former. This is still the sense of an animal, not of a human being, which is a further level of sense. The sense of a human *I* (*Ich-Mensch*) is that of a person or "spiritual individual" who is a member of a social world. A human being has a living body, and therewith a soul or psyche, but also a spirit (*Geist*), a form of humanity or cultural identity. (Cf. §§49ff.) Thus, the sense "human *I*" includes the two sense strata "living body" and "spirit" or "human being" (*Mensch*), the latter founded upon the former.

The sense "material thing" itself breaks down into two strata. The first is that of a spatiotemporal or "real" (*reale*) object (§11), and the second that of a material object (§15). A "real" object is spatiotemporal, whereas a material thing is a real object that has materiality, which means it is substantial and enters into causal relations. Thus, a phantom is a spatiotemporal object that lacks materiality and so is not a material thing (§ 10). Interestingly, when one sees a ghost, Husserl notes, the ghost is constituted as a spatiotemporal object that looks like a human being but lacks materiality (§21). So the sense of materiality is founded on the sense of spatiotemporal reality. Importantly, spatiotemporal objects – material things and even phantoms and ghosts – are constituted as intersubjective objects (§§18f., 21), there for everyone and knowable by other *I*'s, other intentional subjects, other pure *I*'s.

An animal, as opposed to a physical body, is given or constituted as a living body, an animated organism. An animal has a body and a soul. The structure of Husserl's account is expressed in many passages, of which the following is typical (from §14):

The objects of nature in the second, enlarged, sense are . . . animal realities, characterized as living bodies [*Leiben*] with a soul. They are founded realities, which presuppose in themselves, as their lower stratum, material realities, so-called material bodies [*materiale Leiben*]. Furthermore, they have, and this is what is new about them, besides their specifically material determinations, still new systems of properties, the soulful [*seelische*] ones . . . In experience, these new properties we speak of are given as belonging to the living body in question, and it is precisely *because* of them that it is called living body or organism, i.e., an *"organ" for a soul* or for a spirit.

An animal's physical body (*Körper*) or corporeal aspect is its being material and spatiotemporal, while its soul or psychic aspect is its being animated or alive. The sense "soul" or "psyche" is thus a stratum of noemata that is founded on the sense "physical body," and the sense "living body" is that of an ensouled or animated physical body. Of course, the human body is of special concern, and Husserl has separated two ways in which we experience our bodily selves, as merely physical bodies and as living bodies (cf. specifically §41). This distinction between "physical body" and "living body" would later play a prominent role in Husserl's notion of the life-world as developed in the *Crisis*, and similar distinctions were prominent in writings by Sartre and Merleau-Ponty on the body.

For Husserl, a man or human being (*Mensch*) is experienced as having not only a body and a soul, but also a spirit. (Cf. §§48ff.) Accordingly, Husserl distinguishes soul and spirit as two *aspects* or moments of a human being, which he also calls a "human *I*," a "person," or a "spiritual individual." The distinction Husserl draws between soul and spirit is the distinction between the psychic or soulful *I*, which animates or moves the physical body, and the human *I*, "the *I as person* or *as member of a social world*" (§49). "As person [*Person*], I am what I am . . . as *subject of a surrounding world* [*Umwelt*]" (§50). This surrounding world would later be called the life-world (*Lebenswelt*), the surrounding world of everyday life. In this world, I find values and practicalities. Thus, I find a violin "beautiful" and a "work of art," and I find food as a "means of nutrition," or I find coal, choppers, hammers, etc., as "useful to me," for instance, coal as a heating material (continuing §50). These distinctions of meaning would be echoed fifteen years later in Heidegger's distinction between mere "things" and "tools," between things encountered as extant, or "present-at-hand," and tools encountered as for-use, or "ready-to-hand." Such "cultural" objects, given with value-qualities such as beauty and usefulness, belong to the cultural world in which the subject lives.

What Husserl calls the spiritual world is a region, a high-level essence: "Spirituality," if you will. Humanity, personhood, or spirituality is that aspect of a human being which involves, among other things, its belonging to a community of persons (§51). This community is both a factual and a moral community. As Husserl puts it (§51):

From a moral-practical standpoint, I am treating a human being as a mere thing if I do not take him as a person related to the moral, as a member of a moral association of persons in which the world of morals is constituted.... Again, analogously, I treat a human theoretically as a thing if I do not insert him in the association of persons with reference to which we are subjects of a common surrounding world ... He who sees everywhere only nature, nature in the sense of, and, as it were, through the eyes of, natural science, is precisely blind to the spiritual sphere, the special domain of the human sciences [*Geisteswissenschaften*]. Such a one does not see persons and does not see the Objects which depend for their sense on personal accomplishments, i.e., Objects of "culture."

One of the main differences for Husserl between the natural world and the spiritual world, i.e., between the essences of the natural and the human, is the order of connection in each domain. *Causation* connects events in material nature, but *motivation* connects events in the human or spiritual domain. Though we shall not pursue the details here, Husserl's notion of motivation is central to his account of the spiritual world (§56 in the chapter titled "Motivation as the Fundamental Law of the Spiritual world").[16] Motivation includes not only the motivation of behavior by emotion, but also the motivation of one belief by others in inductive reasoning and association. Moreover, Husserl characterizes *empathy* (*Einfühlung*) with other persons as understanding their motivations, both emotional and rational (§56e). Accordingly, the human sciences concern empathy. In this Husserl extends Dilthey's conception of the human sciences as distinct from the natural sciences, including naturalistic psychology as concerned with causation, rather than motivation, of behavior. Where the psyche or soul is to be studied in psychology as a part of nature, the human being or human *I* is to be studied in the human sciences as a part of the human or "spiritual" world, the life-world.

Empathy is not only the way in which we understand the actions of our fellow human beings in the life-world or "spiritual" world (§56e). It is also the way we understand the movements of other animate beings as living bodily movements (§§43–47). Husserl's conception of empathy in *Ideas* II has influenced, directly or indirectly, some of the most interesting phenomenological work of the century.

Edith Stein extended Husserl's rudimentary account in *On the Problem of Empathy* (1917): empathy consists in imaginatively putting oneself in the place of another *I*, reproducing in one's own imagination the form of the other's experience.[17] The notion of empathy in *Ideas* II set the agenda for later phenomenological accounts of "the other": in Heidegger's conception of being-with (*Mitsein*) in *Being and Time* (1927), Sartre's description of "the look of the other" in *Being and Nothingness* (1943), Merleau-Ponty's understanding of the other's body in *Phenomenology of Perception* (1945), and Simone de Beauvoir's account of the view of woman as "other" in *The Second Sex* (1948). Heidegger and Merleau-Ponty knew *Ideas* II, Sartre had read Heidegger, and Beauvoir and Sartre worked out their views in constant collaboration. Heidegger *et al.* sought anti-Cartesian accounts of self and other, but, needless to say here, Husserl's conception of empathy did not assume Cartesian dualism (one mental substance taking the place of another).

In contrast to one's body, soul, and spirit, on Husserl's account, stands one's pure ego, the pure *I*. When Husserl contrasts the pure or transcendental ego with the human ego and the psychological ego, in *Ideas* I and much later in *Cartesian Meditations*, these distinctions should be read against the characterizations of the same notions in *Ideas* II. In *Ideas* II, the transcendental ego is explicitly described as an aspect of the *I*. There is only one ego, one *I*, one entity that I am (as Husserl wrote in *Ideas* I, §33). But this substrate, I, has different aspects or moments: the human *I* or spirit, the psychological *I* or soul, the living body, the physical body, and – in contrast to all these – the pure or transcendental *I*. The pure *I* is merely the aspect of the *I* that consists in its being a subject of intentional experiences (§22, cf. §57). The properties that qualify it as corporeal, animal, and human are properties of a different order; they are not defined in terms of intentionality *per se*, but in other terms. And these distinctions of essence, bear in mind, parallel distinctions of sense, or ways in which the *I* is experienced.

VIII. THE ESSENCE OF BODY, SOUL, AND HUMAN BEING

Husserl's early views on mind-body issues, most articulate in *Ideas* II, were extended in his late work (of 1935–38) published posthumously as *The Crisis of the European Sciences and Transcendental Phenomenology.* Where *Ideas* II was focussed on structures of noema or sense, in the *Crisis* Husserl wrote more directly about the corresponding essences, and in a more appealing terminology. There (in §§62–67) he explicitly defines the physical body (*Körper*) and the soul (*Seele*) as abstractable parts, i.e., moments, of one and the same human being which is experienced in the life-world (*Lebenswelt*). One's body and soul are not, as Descartes had held, two substances (independently existing individuals) in causal interaction. Instead, they are "abstracta" (§66), in Husserl's technical sense of the term: a person's body and soul are two "real sides or strata" (§67) – moments, i.e., dependent or abstract parts – of one and the same human being.[18] They are separable from each other and from the human being only in the conceptual activity of abstraction, and never in reality – just as the color and shape of a thing are parts of it separable only in thought.

Prior to any such abstraction, we experience human beings as bodily and psychic or soulful beings in the world of everyday life, the life-world. In the practice of natural science (itself an intellectual and cultural practice carried out in the life-world), we abstract from all "things" their spatiotemporal bodily aspect, their "corporeity" (*Körperlichkeit*), described ideally in the mathematical terms of current physics. In the case of a human being, we abstract from the concrete individual his bodily "side": his body, as we say. A "complementary" abstraction – presupposing the abstraction of the body – yields his mind or "soul" (*Seele*). In Husserl's words (§66):

The natural science of the modern period, establishing itself as physics, has its roots in the consistent abstraction through which it *wants* to see, in the life-world, only corporeity. Each "thing" "*has*" corporeity even though, if it is (say) a human being or a work of art, it is not merely bodily but is only "embodied", like everything real [*reale*, i.e., in space-time]. . . .

Now what about human souls? It is human beings that are concretely experienced. Only after their corporeity has been abstracted – within the universal abstraction which reduces the world to a world of abstract [= abstracted] bodies – does the question arise, presenting itself now as so obvious, as to the "other side," that is, the complementary abstraction. Once the bodily "side" has become part of the general task of natural science. . . , the task of psychology is characterized as the "complementary" task, i.e., that of subjecting the psychic side to a corresponding theoretical treatment.

With "the division of man himself into two real sides or strata," we can then say what belongs to the psychic side: "it is a person, substrate of personal properties, of original or acquired psychic dispositions (faculties, habits)" (§67).

Husserl's ontology of essences in *Ideas* is still with him in the *Crisis* (as in his discussion of "species, genera, and regional categories of what is" in §48). On the view expressed above, each individual human being has (among others) the two sides or moments we call his body and his soul. His body side is an instance of the essence Human Body, which is a species of the genus Body, to be studied in physics and the other physical sciences. And his soul side is an instance of the essence Soul or Psyche, the essence to be studied in psychology and the social sciences. According to these essences, being a body entails being in space and time, and being a soul entails having personal properties and therewith being in time. Interestingly, Husserl says, being a soul also entails indirectly or "inauthentically" being in space, since a soul is part of an individual with a body side (*Crisis*, §62).

The essence Physical Body (*Körper*) clearly falls under the region Nature as characterized in *Ideas* I and II. Where does the essence Soul fall? The soul is not the pure *I*, that part or moment of the concrete human being which is an instance of the essence Subject of Pure Consciousness. Rather, the soul is the psychic side of the psychophysical human being, complementary to its physical bodily side, and is to be studied by the science of psychology, which Husserl takes to be a naturalistic science, unlike phenomenology. Thus, in *Ideas* II, the soul is that part of the human being which is an instance of the essence Soul or Psyche, which falls under the region Nature, under Animal Nature.

In the *Crisis* Husserl changes his categorization of both body and mind. The living body and the soul, we shall see, are characterized in similar terms as in *Ideas*, but they are classified under the region Life-World rather than Nature.

IX. THE PHYSICAL BODY, THE LIVING BODY, AND THE HUMAN AGENT

From the point of view of Husserl's ontology, the traditional mind-body problem looks hopelessly simplistic. Not only must we deal with relations between mind – indeed, consciousness, soul, spirit – and body. We must address different aspects of the body itself as living organism and as material thing. This *body-body* problem is suppressed in a Cartesian ontology that reduces the body to a mechanism in the sense of seventeenth-century physics, as Descartes sought to reduce all of physics to mechanics.

Ideas II introduces the distinction between the "living body" (*Leib*) and the "physical body" (*Körper*) of a human being (*Mensch*). This distinction runs through the *Crisis* (§§28, 62, and elsewhere), where its significance is heightened by Husserl's attack on the Galilean ideal of mathematizing physical bodies. Within the life-world are human beings, with animated living human bodies. Within nature, by contrast, are physical human bodies. The distinction between "living body" and "physical body" is thus crucial to Husserl's account of the life-world in the *Crisis*, where the notion or sense of physical object is a mathematical abstraction from that of objects in the life-world.

The living body is the body *qua* living human organ, through which I move or act by will: through which, as Husserl says, I "wield" (*walten:* intransitive in German) as I wield my body or objects at hand, with "kinesthesis" of my movement (*Crisis*, §28). By contrast, the physical body is not living, not moving volitionally and not moving with kinesthetic awareness. (The German *"Körper"* and the English "corpse" both derive from the Latin *"corpus"*; *"Leib"* is related to *"Leben,"* which means life or living.) As we have seen, the physical body is abstracted from the human being by physical science, leaving the soul (*Seele*) to be abstracted by psychology (§62). Then, *à la* Aristotle, it is the soul that animates the physical body, making it a living body. (In *Ideas* II and in *Cartesian Meditations* Husserl uses *"beseelen,"* or "animate," for what distinguishes animals from material things.)

In the *Crisis* Husserl writes (§62):

Everyone experiences the embodiment of souls in original fashion [i.e., in intuition] only in his own case. What properly and essentially makes up the character of a living body I experience only in my own living body, namely, in my constant and immediate wielding [of objects] through this physical body alone. . . . Through . . . striking, lifting, resisting, and the like, I act as ego across distances, primarily on the corporeal aspects of objects in the world. It is only *my* being-as-ego, as wielding [objects], that I actually experience as itself, in its own essence; and each person experiences only his own. All such wielding occurs in modes of "movement," but the "I move" in wielding [something] (I move my hands, touching or pushing something) is not in itself the spatial movement of a physical body, which as such could be perceived by everyone. My body – in particular, say, the bodily part "hand" – moves in space; the activity of wielding [something], "kinesthesis," which is embodied together with the body's movement, is not itself in space as a spatial movement but is only indirectly co-localized in that movement.

Others can perceive with their eyes the movement of my body, my living body, all in the life-world. But only I can directly experience my intentional movement: in kinesthesis I experience my volitional movement of my living body, also in the life-world. Interestingly, that kinesthesis itself, like my soul, is not in space; it is only "indirectly" in space, at the same place as my physical body, which is properly in space.

In *Ideas* II Husserl says the living body presents two faces: as the sensory or "aesthesiological" body and as the "body for the will" (§62). The sensory body is the body as we experience it in sensation: perceiving things around us in vision, touch, hearing, but also sensing our own bodily movement in kinesthesis. Kinesthetic sensations of bodily movement are a kind of perceptual experience in which we perceive our bodies not as in seeing ourselves in a mirror, but in sensing our movement, say, as we walk.

The human *I* is more than a living body. I move, willing my bodily movement and kinesthetically sensing it. But in so moving, I walk across the room, I pick up the telephone, I ask my friend to meet me at noon. That is to say, I perform these acts as activities in the human world, the life-world.

In a familiar English idiom, the human *I* can thus be defined as the human *agent*, the *I qua* subject of human *action*. But action involves intentional bodily movement – moving my living body by will, with kinesthetic awareness of my bodily movement – in a culturally significant way, e.g., in picking up the telephone. So the human *I* is not only *embodied* and *ensouled*, but also *encultured*. It includes as an aspect or moment the living body, which includes as aspects or moments the physical body and the soul that animates the physical body (cf. §62). Moreover, it includes as an aspect or moment the action of, say, telephoning a friend, which involves relations to *other* human *I*'s in the same culture. As a condition of such action, Husserl assumes, "I understand another physical body as a living body in which another *I* is embodied and wields [control over that body]" (§62), and this understanding is empathy.

In the *Crisis*, we noted, the living body and the soul are treated not as a part of nature, but as a part of the human or life-world: "what is given as physical and psychic in straightforward life-world experience" (§62). This shift from *Ideas* II attends Husserl's closer focus on the mathematization of the physical.

X. THE LIFE-WORLD AND THE SCIENTIFIC WORLD

When Husserl talks about the "world" in *Ideas* I, he speaks of the world of nature around us, given in everyday experience in the "natural attitude." In *Ideas* II he contrasts the "natural world" with the "spiritual world," the social, historical, human world. This latter notion is more memorably christened the "life-world" in the *Crisis*.

The life-world is "the everyday surrounding world of life" (*Crisis*, §28). It is the world of spatio-temporal "things," the "ground" and "horizon" of all human experiences, activities, and practices, including natural science. Of this world around us Husserl writes (*Crisis*, §37):

[T]he world is the universe of things ... – the spatiotemporal *onta*. Here would thus be found the task of a life-world ontology, understood as a ... doctrine of essence for these *onta*. ... [T]he life-world, for us who wakingly live in it, is always already there, existing in advance for us, the "ground" of all praxis whether theoretical or extratheoretical. The world is pregiven to us, the waking, ... not occasionally but always and necessarily as the universal field of all actual and possible praxis, as horizon. To live is always to live in certainty of the world. ... The world ... does not exist as *an* entity, as an object, but exists with such uniqueness that the plural makes no sense when applied to it. Every plural, and every singular drawn from it, presupposes the world-horizon.

So there is one world – the life-world – that surrounds us and includes everything there is (§34d). And among the "things" that populate this world are "stones, animals, plants, even human beings and human products" (§36).

But that world is not itself the world of modern science. "The objective-scientific world" is a kind of cultural artifact produced by scientists' theorizing, this activity being grounded in the life-world (§34e). Thus, "nature" is an abstraction from the one world in which we live, an abstraction beginning with "corporeity" (§66). In terms of Husserl's ontology, Nature is an essence defined by Corporeity, Space-time, etc., and under the essence Nature fall the myriad concrete "things" around us. Through eidetic intuition in scientific theorizing, we grasp this essence, which we abstract from the world of things around us. Our modern understanding of nature is expressed primarily in the mathematics of physics, the "mathematization" of nature beginning, Husserl says, with Galileo.

The world in itself is thus not identical with the world of nature. Nature is, rather, the world *qua* natural, or that part of the world that instantiates the essence Nature, an "abstractable" part of the world itself. Husserl's ontology is very different, then, from what today is called scientific realism – the doctrine that the world of science, especially physics, is the world in itself.

Yet the life-world is not the world-in-itself either. *The* world indeed includes us and our intentional and cultural activities. But the life-world is the world *qua* surrounding world of human life: it is that part of the world that instantiates the essence Life-World, as opposed to the essence Nature. Thus, the essence Life-World too is but one essence under which the world falls, and a very different essence than Nature or Natural World. While Husserl's concern with the life-world would primarily focus on the ways in which we experience things in the world of everyday life, his phenomenology of the life-world explicitly assumes his longstanding doctrine of essence and aims toward "an ontology of the life-world" (cf. §51 and also §§37 and 62 footnote).

For Husserl, our experience of nature presupposes – it is founded or dependent on – our experience of the life-world: the mathematical-scientific theorizing which abstracts "nature" from the world around us is founded on everyday experience, in which we experience the world in a more fundamental way as simply the world in which we live – for short, the life-world. Yet it would appear that, for Husserl, the essence Nature itself is also dependent in certain ways on the essence Life-World, as "nature" is an abstraction from the "world" around us. The core of this idea appeared already in *Ideas* II, §64, where Husserl said Nature is dependent on Spirit. The *Crisis* version, however, elaborates more fully the claim that the essence expressed mathematically is abstracted from the essence represented in everyday experience.

Husserl's ontology of the life-world, outlined in the *Crisis*, thus ramifies his ontology of mind and body in *Ideas* I–III. The region Life-World is distinguished from the region Nature or Natural World and from the region Consciousness, the essence Nature being a mathematically articulated structure. The living body and the soul now belong to the region of the life-world, while the physical body belongs to the region of nature, and the pure *I* to the region of consciousness, and all are parts or moments of the single concrete human being *I* which belongs to the region of the life-world. If there is a change from *Ideas* II on the living body, as seems the case, that is because both physical body and soul, hence animate organism, are abstractions from the concrete living human body.

The updated categorical ontology is schematized in Figure 5.

XI. ANOMALOUS MONISM

Husserl's monism is an ontologically more developed form of what has come to be known as *anomalous* monism.

The term comes from Donald Davidson's "Mental Events" (1970, 214):

Anomalous monism resembles materialism in its claim that all events are physical, but rejects the thesis, usually considered essential to materialism, that mental phenomena can be given purely physical explanations. Anomalous monism shows an ontological bias only in that it allows the possibility that not all events are mental, while insisting that all events are physical.

On Davidson's view, mental events are identical with physical events. More precisely, the events described by psychological theory are also described by physical theory. But there are no strict causal laws that relate the mental and the physical as such, no "bridge" laws that ascribe causal relations between events under mentalistic and physicalistic descriptions.

From Husserl's point of view, Davidson tilts mistakenly toward materialism. Those events we call mental are not in themselves physical: events in themselves are neither mental nor physical. It is

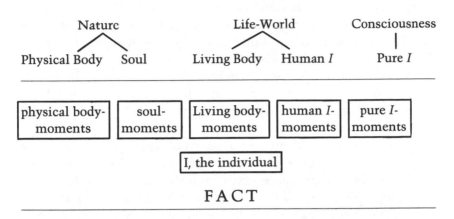

Figure 5

rather that physical theory captures certain essential features of those events, features belonging with the essence Nature. And phenomenological theory captures other essential features of those same events, notably intentionality, belonging with the essence Consciousness. Materialism would take only the natural essence of events as ultimately real, as actually instantiated; however, in Husserl's ontology, both the essences Nature and Consciousness are instantiated in moments that are parts of the given events.

Lest Davidson's formulation seem foreign to Husserl's thought, note that Davidson nods to Brentano (p. 211):

[T]he distinguishing feature of the mental is not that it is private, subjective, or immaterial, but that it exhibits what Brentano called intentionality. Thus intentional actions are clearly included in the realm of the mental along with thoughts, hopes, and regrets.

Husserl treated action as intentional, as a movement of the living body initiated by will and accompanied by kinesthetic awareness of movement (*Ideas* II, §38). Under the essence Consciousness, "acts" of will and kinesthesis are intentional; under the essence Living Body, they "animate" the physical body; and under the essence Human *I*, such movements have social and moral properties. Intentional "acts" of volition and kinesthesis are not intentional bodily *actions*, but components of human actions under the essence Living Body or Human *I*. So Husserl's scheme draws distinctions more fine-grained than Davidson's. Husserl would argue that Davidson has not clearly specified the locus of intentionality in action. To begin with, Davidson needs to distinguish clearly between the volition operative in an action and its background purpose or intention (allied with beliefs and desires) – between what John Searle, in a more Husserlian treatment, has called "intention in action" (better, volition) and "prior intention."[19]

Davidson's view is expressed in terms of language, viz., physical and psychological theory expressed in language. His monism thus finds the same events represented in descriptions drawn from disjoint ranges of theory. In *Pursuit of Truth* (1990) W.V.O. Quine "acquiesce[s] in what Davidson calls anomalous monism." In a departure from his long-standing skepticism about the intentional, Quine now finds it necessary to posit perception, belief, even empathy, in order to explain the acquisition of language. Skeptical still about intentional contents such as propositions, Quine, in effect, assumes language is the medium of intentionality, for in language we "posit" different kinds of entities. Anomalous monism thus involves a "linguistic dualism" of physicalistic and intentionalistic idioms, which represent mental events respectively as neural episodes and as beliefs or what have you. On Husserl's view, beginning in the *Logical Investigations*, language indicates or "intimates" intentional acts, expresses meaning (*Bedeutung*) that approximates noematic sense (*Sinn*), and thereby refers to objects and attributes them properties and essences. For Husserl, then, the distinction between the physical and the mental is drawn on four levels: in language, in intentional activity, in noematic sense, and in essence. Cutting across these levels are the distinctions among pure consciousness, nature, and life-world: the intentional, the natural, and the human. For philosophers like Quine and Davidson, for whom Husserl's ontology of sense and essence is too rich, Husserl's distinctions among the intentional, the natural, and the human would appear by proxy in disjoint ranges of language or theory: instead of the sense and essence of the intentional, natural and human, we would find three different forms of language about these phenomena. Husserl's monism would then find the same entities represented differently in these three ranges of language or theory.[20]

Davidson's aim was to dissolve the paradox Kant observed in our intuitive belief that human action is free yet everything in nature is caused. The paradox, in Davidson's terms (from p. 208), lies in combining three principles:

1. Some mental events interact causally with physical events.
2. Events related as cause and effect fall under strict deterministic laws.
3. There are no strict deterministic laws on the basis of which mental events can be predicted and explained.

Anomalous monism resolves the paradox because deterministic causal laws are restricted to physical theory and do not reach from naturalistic descriptions of events into mentalistic, intentionalistic descriptions of events. Events *qua* intentional actions are not caused by events *qua* neural episodes.

Husserl did not focus on the Kantian problem of freedom of action, but he explicitly assumed that actions are free and autonomous, initiated by will internal to action (*Ideas* II, §38). The living body is animated by the soul, by free acts of willing, which are part of the psychological realm under the essence Nature. The human *I* is a living body whose actions, initiated by free acts of will, are part of the "spiritual" realm of social, moral, historical humanity, under the essence Human *I*. Freedom or autonomy is traditionally cast as a problem of causation, whether something outside the action or the will causes the action. But in Husserl's ontology causation is strictly a relation in nature, falling under the essence Nature, and so it cannot bind acts of will, under the essence Consciousness. This much has a Kantian ring, except that the will is not in the realm of noumena or things in themselves, but in the realm of conscious aspects of things. It is not that volitions are things in themselves and bodily movements are phenomenal objects. Rather, volitional aspects (of events that are acts of consciousness) and bodily-movement aspects (of events that are actions) are different kinds of moments of things in themselves, and these moments – intentional and natural – do not stand in causal relations.

Indeed, there are different notions of causation in Husserl's ontology. Causation proper is part of the essence of the physical. Specifically, a material thing, in Material Nature, is constituted as having spatiotemporal, aesthetic (color, shape, etc.), substantial, and causal properties – dependent on one another in that order of foundation. And a living body, in Animal Nature, is constituted as "the organ of the will and seat of free movement" (*Ideas* II, §38). However, the human *I*, in Spirit, is constituted as performing actions that are "motivated" (§ 56), rather than caused. Thus, a human action in the life-world is motivated, but not caused, by its intention or volition. Even within animal nature a human organism's movement is not properly caused by psychological events in the soul. In terms that anticipate the *Crisis*, Husserl says in *Ideas* II (§32) that the thing in itself has mathematical properties including "mathematical causality-in-itself," whence:

If we . . . take the soul and borrow (as Kant did) the idea of *substance* from the mathematical thing, then we must undoubtedly say there is no soul-substance: the soul has no "in itself" the way "nature" has, nor does it have a mathematical nature as has the thing of physics . . . And as far as causality is concerned, we have to say that if we call *causality* that functional or lawful relation of dependence whch is the correlate of the constitution of persistent properties of a persistent real something of the type Nature, then *as regards the soul we cannot speak of causality at all.* . . . [T]he soul surely has its lasting soulful properties, which are expressions for certain regulated *dependencies of the soulful on the living bodily*. It is a being that is conditionally related to living bodily circumstances, to circumstances in physical nature. And, similarly, the soul is characterized by the fact that soulful events, in regulated fashion, have consequences in physical nature. . . . But *neither living body nor soul* thereby acquire "nature-properties" in the sense of logico-mathematical nature.

So there are relations of dependence between physical body and soul, but these are not properly called causality. The same point recurs in the *Crisis*. Having said that when "I move," with kinesthetic awareness of my movement, I "wield [power]," or wield my body, as soul moving my physical body, Husserl says (§62):

[C]ausality – if we remain within the life-world . . . – has in principle quite a different sense depending on whether we are speaking of natural causality or of "causality" among soulful [*seelische*] events or between the [physical] bodily and the soulful.

Husserl's monism is anomalous, then, in a more general sense than Davidson's. The point of Husserl's assumption that the three regions – Nature, Spirit, or Life-World, and Consciousness – are closed is that the essences are not "harmonious" in the sense that laws of essence bridge them. The guiding notion is not causal laws, but laws of essence, essential generalities about entities in the regions. Causal laws are a special case, among laws of the essence of nature. Where the defining features of consciousness are modes of intentionality, those of nature are spatiotemporal location, substance, and causal interaction, while those of the lifeworld or "spirit" are motivation and moral community. These essences simply do not mix, Husserl thinks. And so there are no essential laws that tie together the intentional, the physical, the psychophysical or animal, and the human as such. Thus, the plurality of regions or aspects in Husserl's monism are by essence islands unbridged by laws of essence.

This is not to say there are no relations between these different aspects or moments of the individual *I*. We have seen, for instance, that the soul aspect depends on the physical body aspect. So there is a dependence relation between these two moments of the *I*. For reasons not entirely clear, however, Husserl thinks this dependence is not a relation governed by laws of essence.

XII. HUSSERL *VIS-À-VIS* LATE TWENTIETH-CENTURY PHILOSOPHY OF MIND

Husserl's views on mind and body address issues central to more recent debates about mind, brain, and computer. Indeed, Husserl's views are more articulate in ontology as well as phenomenology than most of the familiar theories of recent decades. A brief comparison will place Husserl's views in the midst of contemporary philosophy of mind. This placement will help to indicate some of the issues that would have to be addressed in a thorough evaluation of the strengths and weaknesses of Husserl's complex ontology of mind and body – an enterprise beyond the scope of this already lengthy study.

In *Individuals* (1959) P. F. Strawson proposed that mental and physical predicates are predicates of the same things, namely, persons. Husserl would agree but would go beyond the linguistic claim to ask what phenomenological structures these predicates express and what essences (or moments) these predicates ascribe.

Donald Davidson's anomalous monism, in "Mental Events" (1970), we saw, held that *the same events* are described in two types of theory – physical theory and psychological theory – between which there are no "bridge laws," leaving the psychological sphere of the intentional a seamless whole unaddressed by physical theory. Now, Husserl distinguished phenomenology from natural theory, both physical and psychological theory, holding that the same events are described in different ways by these different types of theory. But he assumed an ontology of essences and moments (Davidson remained neutral on such issues), and he distinguished different aspects or moments of mental events which are ascribed by these different types of theory. In particular, according to Husserl, phenomenology describes the aspect of intentionality as a property of "pure" consciousness (bracketing physical properties of the mental event), psychology describes intentionality as a property of mental events in nature, and physical theory describes brain process. Assuming these are different aspects of the same event, would Husserl allow any "bridge laws" between these types of theory? Such laws would describe causal relations between the neural and intentional aspects or moments of a mental event. But for Husserl, we saw, causal relations are restricted to the natural aspects of an event. So Husserl would agree with Davidson only on condition that "psychological theory" be "pure" intentional psychology, i.e., phenomenology.

But would Husserl allow causal laws between "physical body" and "psyche" or "soul," between physical aspects and natural psychological aspect of the *I*? That is unclear. Since psychology abstracts the soul-aspect of the *I* (including intentionality as part of nature) only as a complementary aspect after the physical aspect is abstracted by physics, Husserl might hold that physical causation is restricted to the physical and does not reach into the psychological. However, Husserl would allow causal relations between the "living body" and intentional experiences, for I experience my volitions as causing my living body's movement. John Searle has called this kind of causation "intentional causation," in *Intentionality* (1983). If Husserl would allow *laws* about such causal relations, then these would be bridge laws relating the living body and volition.

With the rise of cognitive science in the 1970s, Jerry Fodor held that mental events and brain events are token-identical but type-distinct: the same events realize both mental and physical types.[21] Mental event types involve "representation" and are to be studied in the new post-behaviorist cognitive psychology, while brain event types are to be studied in neurophysiology and indeed physics. So far, Husserl would agree (Husserl's essences just are species or types, and §33 of *Ideas* I affirms token-identity). However, in pursuit of a physicalist ontology, Fodor went on to reduce the representational character of the mental – intentionality – to causal relations. Fodor analyzed particular mental event types in terms of (a) functional states within the thinking organism, defined by causal relations among beliefs, desires, etc., and (b) reference relations to things outside the organism, defined by causal relations between internal states of the organism and the environment. Fodor's "methodological solipsism" separated (a) from (b), much as Husserl's method of *epoché* bracketed the external world to describe consciousness. Nonetheless, Husserl would not agree with either phase of Fodor's reduction of the essence of the intentional. Husserl would not accept the reduction of the types of experiences to patterns of causal-functional relations among experiences, since mental events not only cause other mental events but often successfully intend things outside the flow of experiences. And on Husserl's account, the reference relations between experiences and their objects do not reduce to causal relations, since intentional relations involve the objects' satisfying the *contents* of experiences. In *Ideas*, at least, Husserl conceived contents as intrinsically conceptual entities or meanings (*Sinne*), and an object's satisfying a meaning is not a causal relation.

John Searle in *Intentionality* (1983) holds a similarly anti-functionalist view of intentional content, which Searle aligns with the "conditions of satisfaction" of an intentional state or its content. Indeed, Searle's account of intentionality is broadly Husserlian, carefully distinguishing an intentional state, its content, and its object. Unlike Husserl, however, Searle downplays the ontology of content and even type and token, and he has no inclination to idealism. For Searle, mental states are identical with brain states, and intentionality is a special, irreducible property of brains. Brains "secrete" intentionality, he says, just as naturally as the liver secretes bile. In *The Rediscovery of the Mind* (1992), Searle champions consciousness itself (still a feature of the neural activity), disclaiming the myriad unconscious processing posited by recent cognitive science as well as psychoanalysis. Rejecting materialism along with dualism and other "ism"s, Searle distinguishes different levels of description, including mental, intentional descriptions of the brain. His discussion carries the spirit of anomalous monism (still an ism), without the intricacies, for better or worse, of an ontology of aspects or moments.

To give consciousness this central place in the philosophy of mind is to press the importance of phenomenology against the prevailing materialist currents. When philosophers began to stress consciousness in the seventeenth century, whence cometh our English word "consciousness," they were onto something – as Alastair Hannay suggests in his *Human Consciousness* (1990), appraising our notion of consciousness in relation to contemporary philosophy of mind. Nor would all materialists disagree. David Armstrong, an early proponent of the mind-brain identity theory, has defended consciousness as "inner sense," the mind (= brain)'s perceiving its own mental activities (perception being itself a brain process). The notion of inner sense was defined phenomenologically by Brentano and Husserl, and, I have argued, is the defining trait of consciousness.[22]

Daniel Dennett, since the 1960s, has consistently separated the intentional from the physical.[23] He stressed the importance of the "stance" we take toward persons and their consciousness in treating them as intentional subjects and intentional processes. However, this "intentional stance" is all there is to the intentional, for Dennett: an appearance in the eyes of human beings, not a real part of nature. (Though a student of Gilbert Ryle, Dennett has attacked behaviorism, primarily B. F. Skinner's work.) Moreover, this appearance can be codified in computer programs that describe the behavior of human beings, Dennett holds, concurring with the research program of artificial intelligence. Husserl would welcome stressing the intentional stance: it is the stance of phenomenology. However, for Husserl, the intentional stance reveals the true nature or essence of experiences, especially their intentionality, which does not reduce to functional or computational properties, as assumed in artificial intelligence.

All the above theories are broadly materialist or naturalist in motivation, seeking to accommodate mind in the world of nature. A more radical position is the "eliminative materialism" of Paul Churchland and Patricia Churchland in the 1980s.[24] Intentional psychological theory, the Churchlands declare, is mere "folk psychology," a remnant of pre-scientific theorizing that attempts to explain human behavior in terms of "beliefs," "desires," and other propositional attitudes. They believe that ancient theory will be replaced by the advancing theory of neuroscience, which will find instead of such phenomena only neural activities in the human organism. Needless to say, Husserl would not agree. First, Husserl would say, the "theory" of belief, desire, etc., and their relation to behavior, is not a *theory* in the sense of a mere product of human beings trying to explain particular phenomena by positing particular entities like beliefs. Rather, for Husserl, beliefs, desires, etc., are an inescapable part of the world, and so central a part that they are unavoidable presuppositions on the basis of which we human beings formulate theories *per se*. This view Husserl elaborated in the *Crisis*. Second, the Churchlands acknowledge the existence of perception, introspection, and consciousness, but expect our folk-psychological conception of these phenomena to be reformed by neuroscience. The outstanding question is whether, after neuroscience has matured, human experience will retain much of the shape it has had for several hundred thousand years. Is there any reason, Husserl might ask, to think that human culture, marveling at the future results of neuroscience, will either want or be forced or even be able to eliminate the life-world level of self-understanding, centered as it presently is about the intentional? How could we want to eliminate (say) wanting?

Hilary Putnam was the founding father of modern functionalism, which flourished in the 1970s. His concern in the 1960s was to liberate the mental from the strict identification of mental events with brain events – physicalism in the form of the "identity theory." If an alien species from outer space had a different type of nervous system than Earth's *homo sapiens*, we would not want to preclude their having perceptions, beliefs, emotions, desires, etc. Accordingly, functionalism identified a mental type not with a particular neural pattern, but with the function of such an event in the organism's nervous system and environment. This model served the computer model of mind: describe the function of a mental event in appropriate algorithms or programs, and you define the mental event type itself. Putnam himself has since criticized functionalism, rejecting it on the grounds that it fails to capture the intentionality of mental phenomena.[25] We need to distinguish, he argues, at least three levels of theory about the mental: physical theory, functional theory, and intentional theory. Different types of physical system could realize the same functional type, and different functional types or programs could operationalize the same type of intentional event or experience. Thus, intentional experience types cannot reduce to functional types, and functional types cannot reduce to physical types of events.[26] Husserl, quite clearly, would have agreed.

Furthermore, Putnam has criticized the "scientific realism" that motivated physicalism, functionalism, and eliminative materialism (science was to tell us the real nature of the mind, the philosopher's problem being how – or whether – to accommodate the mental in a scientific image of the world). Putnam concurs with Husserl's analysis in the *Crisis*, which traced to Galileo the "objective-scientific" view of reality, described in the mathematical formulas of physics. Rejecting that kind of scientific realism, Putnam argues, dissolves the traditional problems of relating mind and body. Nor are we left with a Cartesian dualism, since, as Husserl observed, it was the Galilean "mathematization" of bodies that separated bodies from the world of everyday life and intentionality. Furthermore, we can no longer see the mind and its intentionality – for better or for worse – as a projection of scientific theory, because intentionality is presupposed and practiced in doing science itself.

Lest this *Crisis* analysis too easily dissolve the mind-body problem, we must dig deeper into the life-world conception of "body" (*Leib*) and experience and the *experienced* relations between them. The outstanding question then is whether more fundamental problems remain once the Galilean-Cartesian problem is dissolved.

XIII. TRANSCENDENTAL IDEALISM

So far we have bracketed the notorious problem of Husserl's "transcendental idealism" – the better to see the intricacies of his account of mind and body *sans* idealism. Again and again Husserl insisted that his "idealism" was not a "subjective" idealism like Berkeley's but a "transcendental idealism," borrowing Kant's label but rejecting the core claim of Kantian metaphysics, that things in themselves are beyond the reach of consciousness. What are we to make of Husserl's doctrine in light of the many-aspect monism we have reconstructed from *Ideas* I–III and the *Crisis*?

Three kinds of doctrine are candidates for Husserl's position of transcendental idealism:

1. Every object is identical with a system of intentional acts or, alternatively, intentional contents, i.e., noemata.
2. Every object is dependent in its being on a system of intentional acts or intentional contents.
3. Every object is known or intended only through a system of intentional acts or intentional contents.

The first option proposes ontological reduction, the second ontological dependence, and the third epistemic or intentional perspectivism. Dependence does not entail reduction, and perspectivism entails neither dependence nor reduction.

All three options are found in Husserl interpretation. Aron Gurwitsch read Husserl as resolving objects into systems of noemata. Thus, where Berkeley's idealism reduced material objects to bundles of ideas, or perceptual acts, Husserl's "idealism" would *reduce* them instead to ideal contents of intentional acts. Gurwitsch's Husserl would eschew Berkeley's "To be is to be perceived," since noemata are ideal entities that exist independently of particular acts of perception. Minimizing Husserl's differences from both Berkeley and Kant, Herman Philipse has argued that Husserl was committed to a form of idealism, even phenomenalism, whereby the world is a projection of and so *dependent* on consciousness. Dagfinn Føllesdal, however, has long argued what I am calling the perspectival interpretation, where Husserl held simply that we can intend objects only *through* noemata. There is no reduction of objects to noemata, or to perceptions, Føllesdal argues, since noemata are abstract ("ideal") meaning entities and perceptions are acts of consciousness, while material objects like trees are a completely different kind of thing. As Husserl remarks in *Ideas* I (§89), having just introduced the notion of noema (in §88):

The tree *simpliciter* can burn away, resolve itself into its chemical elements, and so forth. But the [noematic] sense – the sense of *this* perception, something that belongs necessarily to its essence – cannot burn away; it has no chemical elements, no forces, no real properties.

Nor, presumably, do trees depend for their existence on their being perceived or otherwise intended. Dallas Willard too has argued for a realist reading of Husserl, but on grounds of Husserl's conception of cognition (*Erkenntnis*) as a relation between consciousness and a transcendent object given in perception or intuition (*Anschauung*).[27]

An intermediate view would place noemata partly in the world with physical objects, somewhat as G. E. Moore took the red round sense datum to be the surface of the tomato one is seeing. Jaakko Hintikka has argued that, for Husserl, consciousness interfaces with the physical world precisely in perception, so that some aspects of a physical object one sees are "constituted" in perceptual experience, through interpretation, while some aspects of the object itself – the "given" aspects – are part of the intentional content of the perception: a part of the object is thus a part of the act.[28] On the latter point Hintikka's Husserl resembles Bertrand Russell, for Russell held that cognitive relations are direct relations to objects of appropriate type, sometimes universals and sometimes concrete particulars, with no mediating content. Robert Sokolowski too, joined by John Drummond, has construed Husserlian noemata as parts of objects in the world external to consciousness – somewhat as Hector-Neri Castañeda's quasi-Meinongian view takes objects as bundles of bundles-of-properties (or "guises") selections of which occur as contents of intentional acts. All these views are realist in that physical objects exist independently of consciousness.[29] Yet this group of ontologies all posit an interweaving of intentional contents themselves and objects in the world.

The monism we have unearthed in Husserl's writings, however, shifts the terms of debate. There is no question of reducing physical objects to systems of either intentional acts or their contents. All objects are known or intended only *in* intentional acts *through* their intentional contents. But material objects are not *composed* of either sensations or perceptions or noemata. *Qua* material objects under the essence Nature, they are in space-time and composed of matter or matter-energy. Yet brain/mind events, *qua* acts under the essence Consciousness, are not composed of matter-energy but are intentional. Generally, the same object has many aspects and may have very different essences, including Nature and Consciousness: whence monism. Moreover, the same object may be intended through different noemata that prescribe different aspects or essences of the object:

in that sense, perspectivism. This many-aspect monism calls for an intentional perspectivism without reduction. And this perspectivism defines Husserl's transcendental idealism *sans* reduction: all objects are intended through noemata ("pure" or "transcendental," "ideal" contents of consciousness) that specify aspects or essences of the objects. In a Kantian idiom, we know objects only *as* they appear in our acts of consciousness, though it is objects *in themselves* which we know in this way. Furthermore, nothing in this doctrine suggests that all objects are dependent for their being on consciousness. So perspectivism entails neither reduction to nor dependence on consciousness.

This perspectivism is the doctrine that fits best with the monism at work in *Ideas* I, notably in §33, and throughout *Ideas* II. Nonetheless, there are texts in which Husserl seems to endorse a strong form of idealism.[30] In *Ideas* I, § 49, Husserl says the being of spatiotemporal ("real") things is "relative" to consciousness, while the being of consciousness is "absolute." This language might suggest the weaker doctrine of perspectivism: so far as we can ever know natural objects, they are in *intentional relation* to our acts of consciousness. Yet Husserl explicitly advances a stronger doctrine of ontological dependence (*Ideas* I, §49):

[N]o *real thing . . . is necessary for the being of consciousness itself* (in the widest sense of the stream of experience) . . .

Immanent being is therefore without doubt absolute being in the sense that in principle nulla "re" indiget ad existendum [it needs nothing else to exist].

On the other hand, the world of the transcendent "res" is throughout [related] *to consciousness, and indeed not to a logically conceived but to actually shown* [consciousness].

So, Husserl proclaims, consciousness does not depend ontologically on spatiotemporal things, or on anything else. But spatiotemporal objects are ontologically dependent on consciousness: they have being only if actually intended by acts of consciousness. They have, Husserl will shortly say, "*mere intentional being, . . . a being for a consciousness.*"

The language of ontological dependence (including the term "absolute") belongs to Husserl's formal ontology of parts and wholes, drawn from the Third of the *Logical Investigations* (cf. §17). One object is said to be *founded* (*fundiert*) on another, and so dependent (*unselbstständig*), if the former could not exist unless the latter did (cf. §14). Husserl's examples of founded or dependent objects focus on dependent parts, or moments, including instances of color and shape in material things.[31]

Husserl explicitly calls on part-whole theory when he writes of consciousness and nature in *Ideas* I, §39:

> Individual consciousness is interwoven with the *natural world* in a *twofold* way: it is some *human's* [*Menschen*] or *animal's* consciousness, and it is, at least in a great number of cases, consciousness of this world. . . . *Yet thereby consciousness and* [material] *thinghood form a connected* physical and only thus concrete *whole*, connected in the single psychophysical unities which we call *animalia*, and above all connected in the *real* [spatiotemporal] *unity of the whole world*. Can the unity of a whole be other than unified through the proper essence of its parts, which therewith must have some *community of essence* instead of in principle heterogeneity?

Roman Ingarden surmised that it was precisely Husserl's formal ontology of parts and wholes that motivated Husserl's turn to transcendental idealism (to which the realist Ingarden, one of Husserl's ablest students, objected).[32] Husserl's motives were surely complex. In any event, Ingarden rightly took the closing question above as rhetorical. When a human or animal is conscious of a natural object such as a tree, there is one relation between him and his act of consciousness (he performs it) and a second relation between the act and its object (the act intends the object). These two relations tie the act of consciousness into the natural world, it would seem, making this act a *part* of the *whole* that is nature (along with the tree and the human or animal organism). Yet the essences of consciousness and nature are so heterogeneous, Husserl implies, that acts of consciousness and natural objects cannot be so united into a whole.

The point is more explicit in §49:

> [C]onsciousness (experience) and real [spatiotemporal] being are anything but coordinate ways of being, which live peacefully next to one another, circumstantially "related" to one another or "tied" with one another. Only things which are essentially related, each of which in the same sense has a proper essence, can in a true sense be tied together, form a whole.

Because the essences Consciousness and Nature do not properly jibe, Husserl holds, acts of consciousness and natural objects cannot combine to form a whole. Here is the precise form of Husserl's opposition to naturalism: consciousness is not a *part* of nature. Natural objects presumably form one kind of whole, nature, while acts of consciousness form another kind of whole, a stream of consciousness (there are many such streams). But these two kinds of wholes cannot combine to form a larger whole; nature and consciousness are mereologically disjoint. Nonetheless, acts of consciousness *intend* objects in the natural world, and are *performed* by human beings and animals in the natural world. Consequently, intentional and performance relations are not "real" relations in spacetime or in nature. Instead, these relations straddle a given stream of consciousness and the world of nature.

The mereological gap between nature and consciousness is, however, a gap between *moments* of individuals (or events), not individuals themselves. Given Husserl's ontology, what would combine into the relevant wholes are not essences but their concrete instances in individuals or events. So Husserl's claim is that *domains* of the regional essences Nature and Consciousness cannot, by virtue of the essences, combine into a whole. These domains are the world of nature, comprising all instances of Nature, and any given stream of consciousness, comprising instances of Consciousness. Instances of Nature and Consciousness are moments, or dependent parts, of underlying individuals or events. So the domains of Nature and Consciousness are wholes comprising, respectively, Nature moments and Consciousness moments. Also separated from these domains would be domains of the regional essence Human, given the analyses in *Ideas* II, since the human world involves peculiarly human (cultural or "spiritual") elements such as motivation; a human (or "spiritual") domain is a cultural community (there are many). Since moments are parts of individuals or events, we might expect the mereological gap between nature and consciousness to separate individuals or events, not just their moments. But given the monism in §33 of *Ideas* I, Nature moments and Consciousness moments, and Human moments too, may be moments of one and the same underlying individual or event. So it can only be such moments, not their substrata, that are separated as above.

If consciousness cannot be part of nature, by the above reasoning, neither can nature be part of consciousness. But then how can Husserl be an idealist? Enter dependence, a key player in his part-whole ontology.

Husserl does not say, in the argument of §49, that natural objects are *composed* of intentional acts or noemata; that would contradict their mereological separation. His idealist claim is rather that natural objects are ontologically *dependent* or *founded* on acts of consciousness. More precisely, given the monism in §33, the dependence holds not between individuals or events themselves, but between aspects or moments thereof: between a Nature (or Human) moment of an object and a Consciousness moment of an act or ego intending the object. So the dependence is not one of material substances on mental substances à *la* Berkeley, but of natural aspects of objects on mental aspects of egos or acts intending such objects. These relations of dependence or foundation bridge the gap between nature and consciousness. Notice that the dependence is between moments of distinct individuals – except, say, where I am seeing my own foot. (Whereas Husserl's usual concern is moments of a single individual, which are parts of the individual and are dependent on the individual but also may depend on each other.)

Husserl's "transcendental" idealism would thus say that the natural and human world is dependent or *founded* on ("pure" or "transcendental") consciousness. Precisely stated: every Nature or Human moment of any object is founded on some Consciousness moment of some event (an act of consciousness) intending that object. Of course, moments of individuals or events are founded on the individuals or events themselves. In a picture:

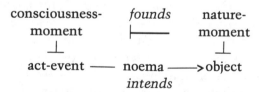

The dependence or foundation relation between act and object is one thing, the intentional relation another. The intentional relation holds between the event-in-itself and the object-in-itself, whereas the dependence relation holds between their moments or aspects. Yet the intentional relation obtains in virtue of these moments, as well as the act's content or noema. Here is Husserl's special form of idealism, detailed in terms of a complex ontology.

As §49 proceeds, Husserl adds a dimension of meaning or sense to the dependence:

Between consciousness and [spatiotemporal] reality [*Realität*] yawns a true abyss of sense [*Sinn*]. . . .

It is thus clear that in spite of all talk . . . of a real being of the *human I* and its conscious experiences *in* the world and of all that belongs thereto in any way in respect of "psychophysical" associations – that in spite of all this consciousness, considered in *"purity,"* has to be evaluated as an *association of being closed for itself,* as an association of *absolute being* into which nothing can penetrate and from which nothing can escape . . .

On the other side, the whole *spatio-temporal world,* which includes man and the human I as subordinate singular realities, is *according to its sense mere intentional being,* thus a being which has the merely secondary, relative sense of being *for* a consciousness . . . It is a being which consciousness posits in its experiences, . . . but *over and beyond* this, is just nothing at all.

So consciousness becomes the black hole of Husserl's universe, pulling everything else into itself: more precisely, pulling spatiotemporal, natural, and human moments into dependence on consciousness moments. §50 continues immediately:

Thus the ordinary sense of talk of being is inverted. The being which for us is the first, is in itself the second, i.e., it is what it is only in "relation" to the first. . . . Reality, reality of the thing taken singly and also reality of the whole world, essentially (in our strict sense) lacks independence. It . . . has no "absolute essence," it has the essentiality of something which is in principle *only* the intentional, *only* the consciously known.

Here Husserl says: the *sense* of natural objects is such that their *essence* is such that they have their *being* only intentionally, i.e., their being depends on their being intended in consciousness.

Could there be a more striking statement of idealism, or of what Hilary Putnam has called "internal realism"?[33] Yet this idealism is in tension with central elements in Husserl's work, including the practice of *epoché* and the underlying many-aspect monism in *Ideas* I–III.

First consider monism. In §49 of *Ideas* I Husserl speaks of spatiotemporal ("real") objects, animalia, man, and the human *I*. All these kinds of entities are explored in *Ideas* II, where Husserl says they are aspects or moments of objects, as distinct from substrata or things in themselves. The physical body, living body, soul, spirit, and pure ego are moments of one and the same individual, I, so Husserl's doctrine is a monism. Moreover, there are dependence relations among these aspects of the individual that is I. As noted: the soul aspect depends on the physical body aspect, the human aspect depends on the animal or living body aspect, and the consciousness aspect depends on the human, living body, and physical body aspects. Given this many-aspect monism, what could Husserl mean by "inversion" in §50 of *Ideas* I? In our everyday ontology, my consciousness aspect is dependent on my brain aspect, or on my human, psychic, and physical aspects. But in our enlightened phenomenological ontology, Husserl seems to say, all these dependencies are themselves dependent on my consciousness aspect. So the order of dependence detailed in *Ideas* II is inverted in §§49–50 of *Ideas* I. This inversion would define Husserl's "transcendental turn," taken as an ontological turn to idealism.[34]

Heidegger, and later Derrida, would follow the form of this turn, while reversing the dependence, so that modern philosophy's conception of consciousness depends on everyday language and practice and evolving cultural history. Interestingly, in *Ideas* II, §64, Husserl says the being of nature is "relative" to that of spirit (humanity), whose being is "absolute." To be consistent with *Ideas* I, he should say: nature is ontologically dependent on spirit, which is independent of nature, and spirit is ontologically dependent on consciousness, which is independent of both nature and spirit. That is precisely the structure of argument in the *Crisis*. The mathematical essence of nature is an abstraction from the essence of material objects in the life-world, and so natural aspects of objects are dependent on life-world aspects. But the life-world is dependent on pure consciousness. This structure of dependence gives Husserl the resolution of what he calls "the paradox of human subjectivity: being a subject [a pure *I*] for the world and at the same time being an object [a living body or human *I*] in the world" (*Crisis*, §§53–54). So Heidegger, whence Derrida, follows Husserl in the first step and rejects the second.

In Husserl's "transcendental" idealism, we have seen, the dependence of natural or cultural objects on consciousness would pertain to aspects or moments of individuals, not to individuals themselves. For Husserl, however, things in themselves exist independently of consciousness, even if their natural aspects or moments are dependent on consciousness moments. For Kant, as Husserl understands him, we can never know – our cognition can-

not reach – things in themselves. But against the Kantian view
Husserl writes (§43):

It is . . . an error in principle to suppose that perception . . . does not reach
the thing itself [*Ding selbst*]. The thing in itself [*an sich*] and in its being-in-
itself [*An-sich-sein*] would not be given to us. . . .
    But this view is nonsensical. It implies that there is no *essential differ-
ence* between the transcendent and the immanent . . . The spatial thing that
we see is, despite all its transcendence, the perceived, that which is consciously given in its *bodiliness* [*Leibhaftigkeit*].
    In immediate intuitive acts we intuit an "itself" ["*Selbst*"].

Husserl's stance here places him in opposition to any idealism holding that nothing exists beyond or independent of consciousness. Not
only do things in themselves exist in their own right, not dependent
on consciousness and not composed of acts or contents. But things
in themselves are the proper objects of perception, even though they
are given one-sidedly, through noemata, with sensory appearances,
as having spatiotemporal-material moments or aspects. This is how
Husserl answers the Kantian question of how knowledge of things in
themselves is possible: via noemata, sensory appearances, and relevant aspects.[35]
    Sartre's ontology in *Being and Nothingness* (1943) is similar and
indeed draws on Husserl's. For Sartre, trees and people, even the self,
are phenomena (or noemata) that float as a veneer on being itself.
The question of individuation remains. Is there but one substrate in
itself, or are there many? If one, the monism resembles Spinoza's.
However, Husserl often talks of our intending the same object in
different ways as having different aspects. He is clearly assuming
there is a plurality of substrata that may be intended in various
ways. Accordingly, intentionality involves our individuating objects
in consciousness. (See especially *Ideas* I, §§128–31.)[36]
    Husserl's ontology distinguishes among individuals themselves,
essences, instances of essences in individuals (moments), and noemata or senses through which we intend individuals as instantiating
essences. Essences and noemata, being "ideal" entities, are independent of both nature and consciousness, i.e., of instances of Nature
and Consciousness. But this Platonism or Platonic "idealism" is not
what is at stake in Husserl's "transcendental" idealism. Nor is the
issue one of dependence between the *essences* Nature and Con-

sciousness, or between the corresponding *senses* of nature and consciousness. At issue is the order of dependence between *instances* of these essences in individuals, viz., Nature moments and Consciousness moments.

Normally, monism is an alternative to idealism. However, Husserl's brand of "transcendental" idealism does not contradict but rather assumes the many-aspect monism we have sketched. What it does contradict is the order of dependencies sketched, assuming monism, in *Ideas* II. Thus, the traditional battleground between monism, idealism, materialism, and dualism – where issues of dependence and reduction are decided – is shifted from individuals to their moments or aspects.

Husserl's idealism does not graft easily onto his larger system, in spite of his claim that we have "lost nothing" with the idealist turn (*Ideas* I, §50). The problem is, Husserl has given two contradictory accounts of dependence: the order of dependence detailed in *Ideas* II, and the "inverted" order specified in §§49–50 of *Ideas* I. Husserl removes the paradox, we saw, by claiming the familiar order is itself dependent on consciousness: thus the inversion. How plausible is this maneuver? Why does Husserl push for the inverted order? While the conclusion is ontological, his reasoning is phenomenological.

As Husserl moves from the essence of natural objects to the noemata or senses through which we intend them, he moves from the ontology of nature to the phenomenology of our experience of nature. Questions of sense are questions of phenomenological structure, of how we know or intend or "constitute" things. So the inversion claim – "the ordinary sense of talk of being is inverted" (*Ideas* I, §50) – would mean that according to our ordinary sense of nature, in everyday experience, consciousness is dependent on nature, but according to its *proper* sense nature is dependent on consciousness. Presumably, we would come to intend nature as dependent on consciousness, reforming our everyday experience, after our "conversion" to idealism. But does phenomenological analysis support this inversion? Husserl presents no compelling phenomenological evidence for his claim that "the whole *spatio-temporal world* . . . is *according to its sense mere intentional being*" (*Ideas* I, §49), controverting his detailed analyses in *Ideas* II of our awareness of body, human *I*, and pure *I*.[37] Our ordinary sense of a natural object, in perception, entails not its dependence but its independence of our consciousness.

What *is* part of the structure of experiencing a natural object, however, is a certain *awareness of* our experiencing it.[38] This structure supports the doctrine of perspectivism, but not the dependence Husserl claims. Indeed, in a general way, Husserl's rich account of intentionality – whereby consciousness apprehends "transcendent" objects – does not set well with his turn toward idealism.[39]

A further problem for Husserl's idealist turn is methodological. The passages quoted from *Ideas* I, from §33 to §50, follow the introduction of the phenomenological method of *epoché* in §32: §33 launches the chapter "Consciousness and Natural Reality," in which the two regions are distinguished, and §§49–50, concerning the dependence of nature on consciousness, come in the following chapter "The Region of Pure Consciousness." To perform *epoché* is to bracket – to put out of use for methodological purposes – "the thesis of the natural standpoint," i.e., that there is a world around me including spatiotemporal, natural, and human and cultural objects (§§27ff.). With the being of the natural world in brackets, all I can say about the tree before me is that from my perspective in this act of seeing that tree, the tree has being *for me* in my seeing it. The tree may or may not exist in itself, and it may or may not depend for its existence on various other things, but these facts lie beyond the structure of my experience. On the minimalist interpretation urged by Føllesdal, the phenomenological method of *epoché* is designed to turn one's attention from the usual objects of experience, objects in one's surroundings, to the noematic content of one's experiences.[40] Indeed, it would seem that the practice of *epoché* precludes all ontological commitments, including those of idealism or dualism or materialism or what have you.[41] So it seems we are back to a doctrine of intentional perspectivism, with no idealist baggage: the idealist turn in § 49 goes beyond the practice of pure phenomenology, practiced via the *epoché*.

In fact, however, Husserl's introduction of *epoché* is couched in terms of a complex ontology. How does the method of *epoché* fit into that ontology? §33 opens with Husserl asking what is the utility of *epoché*. The goal of *epoché*, he then says, is "winning a new region of being," namely, the region Consciousness, which he proceeds to distinguish from the region Nature (as well as the region Spirit, alluded to in *Ideas* I but detailed in *Ideas* II and III). But *regions* are defined as high-level essences, not noemata. So Husserl appeals to

his ontology of essences to explain the deliverances of phenomenological reflection achieved by *epoché*. The question remains, why
the proclaimed inversion?

A plausible perspectivism, open to Husserl, would distinguish different kinds of dependence. Where Husserl said nature is ontologically dependent on consciousness, he might better say our *knowledge* or *experience* of natural objects, indeed all objects, is dependent
on acts of consciousness that intend them. The position would be
that while the *being* of natural objects does not depend on the being
of consciousness, their *being known or intended* does. There would
still be a stratification of physical body, living body, and human *I*,
with parallel levels of sense, essence, and aspects or moments. Objects would be intended as material, living, human, or whatever,
through appropriate noemata in appropriate experiences. But there
would be no idealist implosion, no black hole of consciousness.

This intentional perspectivism may seem a trivial doctrine. It is
indeed axiomatic, perhaps tautological, in a theory of intentionality
like Husserl's, where objects are intended through intentional contents. However, there are alternative views of intentionality, whereby *there are no contents* and intentional relations hold between act
and object with no mediation of content.[42] Further, it is not a trivial
claim that part of the essence of any object includes the ways in
which it can be known or experienced or indeed acted upon through
volition. The implications of this claim produce a complex, nontriv-
ial ontology of consciousness and world.[43]

Husserl struggled with issues of realism and idealism throughout
his career. His phenomenology *per se* should be compatible with
both (at least on most points, e.g., concerning the structure of seeing a tree). Indeed, it is profitable to read his works in order to see
how the doctrines of intentionality and many-aspect monism structure the issues of perspective, dependence, and reduction. The suggestion here is that transcendental idealism be renamed "intentional perspectivism" and developed as a many-aspect monism
coupled with a theory of intentionality via noemata: a discerning
analysis of epistemic perspective, putting sense and essence (and
language expressing both) in their proper places. If Husserl himself
took the plunge into idealism, we need not join him. He has shown
the way to the *Ding an sich*: through noema, essence, and moment.

BIBLIOGRAPHY

Husserl's works

The following works by Husserl are cited in the text, usually by title, date of first publication, and section number. Passages quoted in English translation follow the translations below as much as possible but with frequent changes.

Husserl, Edmund. *Logical Investigations, Volumes One and Two*, containing Investigations I–VI. Translated by J. N. Findlay. London and New York: Routledge & Kegan Paul, London and New York, 1970. German original, first published in 1900–01; second German edition, 1913, except Investigation VI in second German edition, 1921.

———. *The Phenomenology of Internal Time-Consciousness*. Edited by Martin Heidegger. Translated by James S. Churchill. Bloomington: Indiana University Press, 1964. German original, 1928, edited from lectures of 1905–1910.

———. *Ideas* [pertaining to a Pure Phenomenology and a Phenomenological Philosophy, First Book]: *General Introduction to Pure Phenomenology*. Translated by W. R. Boyce Gibson. London: George Allen & Unwin Ltd., and New York: Humanities Press, Inc., 1969. First English edition, 1931; German original, first published in 1913. Called *Ideas* I.

———. *Ideas pertaining to a Pure Phenomenology and a Phenomenological Philosophy, Second Book: Phenomenological Investigations of Constitution* [or as translated: *Studies in the Phenomenology of Constitution*]. Translated by Richard Rojcewicz and André Schuwer. Dordrecht and Boston: Kluwer Academic Publishers, 1991. German original, first published in 1952, drafted initially in 1912, revised in 1915 and again in 1928. Called *Ideas* II.

———. *Ideas pertaining to a Pure Phenomenology and a Phenomenological Philosophy, Third Book: Phenomenology and the Foundations of the Sciences*. Translated by Ted E. Klein and William E. Pohl. The Hague: Martinus Nijhoff, 1980. German original, first published in 1971, drafted initially in 1912. Called *Ideas* III.

———. *Phenomenological Psychology*. Translated by John Scanlon. The Hague: Martinus Nijhoff, 1977. German original text from lectures, Summer Semester, 1925.

———. *Cartesian Meditations*. Translated by Dorion Cairns. The Hague: Martinus Nijhoff, 1960. German original text, 1929; first published, in French translation, in 1931.

————. *The Crisis of European Sciences and Transcendental Phenomenology*. Translated by David Carr. Evanston: Northwestern University Press, 1970. German original, first published in 1936. Called the *Crisis*.

Other works

Armstrong, D. M., and Norman Malcolm. *Consciousness and Causality*. Oxford: Basil Blackwell, 1984.

Armstrong, D. M. *A Materialist Theory of the Mind*. London: Routledge & Kegan Paul, 1968.

Castañeda, Hector-Neri. "Perception, Belief, and the Structure of the World." *Synthese* 35 (1977): 285–352.

Churchland, Patricia S. *Neurophilosophy*. Cambridge: MIT Press, 1986.

Churchland, Paul M. *Matter and Consciousness*. Cambridge: MIT Press, 1984, 1988.

Davidson, Donald. "Mental Events." In Davidson, Donald, *Essays on Actions and Events*. Oxford: Oxford University Press, 1980, 1986. First published, 1970.

Dennett, Daniel C. *The Intentional Stance*. Cambridge: MIT Press, 1987.

————. *Consciousness Explained*. New York: Harper and Row, 1991.

Dreyfus, Hubert, Editor. *Husserl, Intentionality and Cognitive Science*. Cambridge: MIT Press, 1982.

Drummond, John J. *Husserlian Intentionality and Non-Foundational Realism: Noema and Object*. Dordrecht and Boston: Kluwer Academic Publishers, 1990.

Fodor, Jerry A. *The Language of Thought*. New York: Thomas Y. Crowell Company, 1975.

————. "Methodological Solipsism Considered as a Research Strategy in Cognitive Psychology." In Dreyfus (1982). First published, 1980.

Føllesdal, Dagfinn. "Husserl's Notion of Noema." In Dreyfus (1982). First published, 1969.

Gurwitsch, Aron. "Husserl's Theory of the Intentionality of Consciousness." In Dreyfus (1982). First published, 1967.

Hannay, Alastair. *Human Consciousness*. London: Routledge, 1990.

Heidegger, Martin. *The Basic Problems of Phenomenology*. Translated by Albert Hofstadter. Bloomington: Indiana University Press, 1988. German original, 1975. The text of a lecture course given in 1927.

Ingarden, Roman. *On the Motives which Led Husserl to Transcendental Idealism*. Translated from the Polish by Arnór Hannibalsson. The Hague: Martinus Nijhoff, 1975. Polish original, 1963.

McIntyre, Ronald. "Husserl and the Representational Theory of Mind." *Topoi* 5 (1986): 101–13.

Miller, Izchak. *Husserl, Perception, and Temporal Awareness.* Cambridge: MIT Press, 1984.

———. "Husserl on the Ego." *Topoi* 5 (1986): 157–62.

Putnam, Hilary. *The Many Faces of Realism.* La Salle: Open Court, 1987.

———. *Representation and Reality.* Cambridge: MIT Press, 1989.

———. *Realism with a Human Face.* Edited by James Conant. Cambridge: Harvard University Press, 1990.

Quine, Willard Van Orman. *Pursuit of Truth.* Cambridge: Harvard University Press, 1990.

Searle, John R. *Intentionality.* Cambridge: Cambridge University Press, 1983.

———. *The Rediscovery of the Mind.* Cambridge: The MIT Press, 1992.

Smith, Barry, Editor. *Parts and Moments: Studies in Logic and Formal Ontology.* Munich: Philosophia Verlag, 1982.

———. "Logic and Formal Ontology." In Mohanty, J. N., and William R. McKenna, editors, *Husserl's Phenomenology: a Textbook.* Washington, D.C.: Center for Advanced Research in Phenomenology and University Press of America, 1989: 29–67.

Smith, David Woodruff. "The Realism in Perception." *Noûs* XVI 1 (1982): 42–55.

———. "Mind and Guise." In James Tomberlin, editor, *Hector-Neri Castañeda.* Dordrecht and Boston: D. Reidel Publishing Company, 1986: 167–85.

———. *The Circle of Acquaintance: Perception, Consciousness, and Empathy.* Dordrecht and Boston: Kluwer Academic Publishers, 1989.

———. "Consciousness in Action." *Synthese* 90 (1992): 119–43.

———. "The Cogito *circa* A.D. 2000." *Inquiry* (1993): 225–254.

———. "How to Husserl a Quine – and a Heidegger Too." *Synthese* 98 1 (January, 1994): 153–173.

Smith, David Woodruff, and Ronald McIntyre. *Husserl and Intentionality: A Study of Mind, Meaning, and Language.* Dordrecht and Boston: D. Reidel Publishing Company, 1982.

Smith, David Woodruff, Charles W. Dement, and Peter M. Simons. *Manufacturing Metaphysics.* Forthcoming.

Sokolowski, Robert. *Husserlian Meditations.* Evanston: Northwestern University Press, 1974.

Stein, Edith. *On the Problem of Empathy.* Translated by Waltraut Stein. The Hague: Martinus Nijhoff, 1970. German original, doctoral dissertation, 1917.

Strawson, P. F. *Individuals.* London: Methuen, 1959.

Willard, Dallas. *Logic and the Objectivity of Knowledge.* Athens: Ohio University Press, 1984.

NOTES

1 The example occurs in *Logical Investigations*, V, §27. The metaphor of exploding perception is used in *Ideas* I, §138, and §151 discusses strata of sense where that of person is founded on that of material thing. The philosophical significance of perceptual "explosion" is explored in D. W. Smith, *The Circle of Acquaintance*, 1989, Chap. III.

2 The idealist reading is argued in detail in Herman Philipse, "Transcendental Idealism," in the present volume. On the idealist interpretation, the many-aspect monism to be detailed here would be a doctrine of "mundane" ontology, consonant with everyday experience and common sense (cf. Barry Smith, "Common Sense," in the present volume), but our mundane ontology, including this monism, would be radically altered when we adopt the "transcendental" attitude, leading into a form of idealism.

3 Cf. B. Smith, "Logic and Formal Ontology," 1989.

4 Husserl's notion of "moment" is laid out in *Logical Investigations*, 1900–01, Investigation III, summarized in §17. According to Husserl, a whole may have two kinds of parts. A part that could exist independently of the whole he called a *piece*, and a part that could not exist independently of the whole he called a *moment* or *abstract part* – "abstract" in the sense that it can be abstracted from the whole only conceptually. In one of Husserl's examples (§19), a tone in a melody is a part of the melody that could exist independently, while the intensity of the tone is a part of the tone that could not exist independently of the tone. These notions are discussed at length in B. Smith, editor, *Parts and Moments*, 1982, and in Kit Fine, "Part-Whole," in the present volume.

5 Husserl distinguishes sciences of facts from sciences of essence: cf. *Ideas* I, § 7. The geometer does not care whether the lines he draws on the chalkboard are instances of geometrical shapes described by geometry, but the student of nature expects things in nature to be actually as he experiences them and as the science of nature will describe them. In this way geometry is a science of essence while natural science is a science of facts. However, both offer material ontologies concerned with material essences and not merely with concrete facts.

Husserl relegates the term "metaphysics" for something still more special than material ontologies and sciences of facts. At the close of *Cartesian Meditations* he says, "[P]henomenology indeed *excludes every naïve metaphysics* that operates with absurd things in themselves, but *does not exclude metaphysics as such.*" He allows for metaphysics as concerned with "*all the problems of accidental facticity* [*Faktizität*], *of death, of fate,* of the possibility of a '*genuine*' human life" and so with "the *ethico-religious* problems."

6 Cf. B. Smith, "Logic and Formal Ontology," 1989.

7 These quotations are from the First Edition of *Logical Investigations*. The claim in §4 of Investigation V was excised in the Second Edition of 1913, and the passage from § 7 appears in the English translation of the Second Edition with the note that Husserl excised the whole section. Kevin Mulligan brought these passages to my attention.

8 This interpretation of Husserl's theory of intentionality is detailed in essays in Dreyfus, editor, *Husserl, Intentionality and Cognitive Science*, 1982 – which includes Føllesdal's seminal essay "Husserl's Notion of Noema," 1969 – and in Smith and McIntyre, *Husserl and Intentionality*, 1982. Within that interpretation the temporal structure of consciousness and its relation to perception are detailed in Miller, *Husserl, Perception and Temporal Awareness*, 1984. The feature of apperception is analyzed, within a similar framework, in Chapter II of D. W. Smith, *The Circle of Acquaintance*, 1989.

9 Some of these connections between intentionality theory and intensional logics or semantics are drawn in Smith and McIntyre, 1982.

10 Hubert Dreyfus has argued that Husserl took noemata to be formal structures of a kind that might be understood as informational content processed by digital computers, making Husserl the precursor of modern artificial intelligence theory. Ronald McIntyre has countered that Husserl's understanding of "formal" is quite different, and that Husserl's notion of noematic sense is a semantic notion that cannot be reduced to the syntactic "formal" notion required for the computational model of mind. Cf. Dreyfus' Introduction in his anthology, 1982, and McIntyre, "Husserl and the Representational Theory of Mind," 1986.

11 A Husserl-friendly analysis of action and its intentionality – including the roles of volition, kinesthesis, and background attitudes – is developed in D. W. Smith, "Consciousness in Action," 1992. A consonant account, drawing on Oxonian philosophy of action since Wittgenstein, is developed in Searle, *Intentionality*, 1983, Chap. 3. Compare the discussion of the everyday world in B. Smith, "Common Sense" (this volume).

12 The structure of consciousness *per se* involves just such an awareness of oneself in carrying out any process of thinking: see D. W. Smith, 1989, Chap. II. The core of the *cogito* argument can then be reconstructed without commitment to the characteristically Cartesian doctrines of dualism, rationalism, and incorrigibility of mind: see D. W. Smith, 1993. In the quotation above Husserl says the self-evidence of the *cogito* is "adequate" rather than apodictic or indubitable as Descartes claimed. Cf. the third of the *Cartesian Meditations*, where Husserl distinguishes three grades of "evidence" or self-evidence: "certain," "adequate," and "apodictic."

13 This is argued in Miller, "Husserl on the Ego," 1986.
14 For an account of the history of *Ideas* II, see the "Translators' Intro-
    duction" to the English edition, 1991. Merleau-Ponty, the translators
    recall, described his study of *Ideas* II as "une expérience presque
    voluptueuse." In *The Basic Problems of Phenomenology*, 1927, Hei-
    degger explicitly rechristens the traditional notion of self or subject,
    the human being, as "Dasein," with the aim of shedding *inter alia*
    suggestions of Cartesian dualism (§9 b). The intentionality of the
    Dasein's "comportments" (*Verhalten*) (§9a–b) has its foundation in
    Dasein's being-in-the-world, which involves Dasein's use of equip-
    ment, whose significance is grounded in social practices (§15). The
    social aspect of the human being is defined, according to Husserl in
    Ideas II, as part of the region Spirit or Humanity.
15 Husserl complicates this account of dependence in his doctrine of tran-
    scendental idealism. See Section XIII.
16 Cf. B. Smith, "Common Sense," this volume.
17 A consonant theory of the structure of empathy is developed in D. W.
    Smith, 1989, Chap. III.
18 See Husserl, *Logical Investigations*, 1900–01, III, §17, on dependent or
    abstract parts. Cf. B. Smith, editor, *Parts and Moments*, 1982.
19 Cf. D. W. Smith, "Consciousness in Action," 1992, and Searle, *Inten-
    tionality*, 1983, Chap. 3.
20. Cf. Quine, *Pursuit of Truth*, 1990. On Quine's view from a Husserlian
    perspective, see D. W. Smith, 1994. On Husserl's philosophy of lan-
    guage, see the essay by Peter Simons in the present volume, as well as
    the sections on language and meaning in Smith and McIntyre, 1982.
    Husserl's account of language features a theory of sense and reference
    and a theory of speech acts. Searle, 1983, sets his own earlier speech act
    theory in the wider context of a theory of intentionality, in a system
    quite like Husserl's.
21 Cf. Fodor, *The Language of Thought*, 1975, and "Methodological Solip-
    sism Considered as a Research Strategy in Cognitive Psychology," 1980.
22 Armstrong's argument is presented, in opposition to Malcolm's Wittgen-
    steinian resistance to talk of consciousness, in D. M. Armstrong and
    Norman Malcolm, *Consciousness and Causality*, 1984. His version of
    the identity theory was developed in *A Materialist Theory of the Mind*,
    1968. My discussion of consciousness is in Chapter II of *The Circle of
    Acquaintance*, 1989.
23 Cf. Dennett, *The Intentional Stance*, 1988, and *Consciousness Ex-
    plained*, 1991.
24 Cf. Paul M. Churchland, *Matter of Consciousness*, 1984, and Patricia S.
    Churchland, *Neurophilosophy*, 1986.

25 Cf. Putnam *The Many Faces of Realism*, 1987, *Representation and Reality*, 1988, and *Realism with a Human Face*, 1990.

26 Putnam, 1987, 14ff.

27 Cf. Gurwitsch, "Husserl's Theory of the Intentionality of Consciousness," 1967; Philipse, "Transcendental Idealism," in the present volume; Føllesdal, "Husserl's Notion of Noema," 1969; Willard, *Logic and the Objectivity of Knowledge*, 1984, and Willard, "Knowledge," in the present volume. Details of the realist, perspectivist interpretation are developed in Smith and McIntyre, *Husserl and Intentionality*, 1982, and in Miller, *Husserl, Perception and Temporal Awareness*, 1984.

28 See Hintikka, "The Phenomenological Dimension," in the present volume.

29 Cf. Sokolowski, *Husserlian Meditations*, 1974; Drummond 1990; Castañeda, "Perception, Belief, and the Structure of the World," 1977; and, on Castañeda's scheme *vis-à-vis* Husserlian themes, D. W. Smith, 1986.

30 Cf. Herman Philipse's extensive discussion of these texts in "Transcendental Idealism," in the present volume. My reading of Husserl differs in two ways from Philipse's. First, I think Husserl's overall (evolving) system does not entail idealism. The special form of idealism specified in §§49–50 of *Ideas* I is added onto the other parts of the system, and other parts push against idealism: not only the monism and perspectivism we noted, but also his Aristotelian basic ontology, his epistemology whereby we have increasing evidence of a transcendent world, and his theory of intentionality which sharply separates act and object. Second, I am unpersuaded that Husserl consistently held to a form of phenomenalism, a strong theme in Philipse's essay. §42 of *Ideas* I sharply separates a color in a material thing from the appearances (*Erscheinungen*) or adumbrations (*Abschattungen*) of the color, and both are distinguished from the hyle or sensory data that are part of the *reell* experience as explicated in §85. So Husserl has a kind of monism even for the so-called secondary qualities: the same quality presents different aspects to perceivers under different circumstances of lighting or perspective. These distinctions concerning perception are explored within a realist framework in Kevin Mulligan, "Perception," in the present volume (and in an unpublished essay by Ronald McIntyre and myself).

31 These notions are further explicated in Kit Fine, "Part-Whole," in the present volume, and in the essays in B. Smith, editor, *Parts and Moments*, 1982.

32 Cf. Ingarden, *On the Motives which Led Husserl to Transcendental Idealism*, 1963, 30ff.

33 Cf. Putnam, *The Many Faces of Realism*, 1987, *Representation and Reality*, 1989, and the title essay of *Realism with a Human Face*, 1990.

Though Putnam introduced the term "internal realism" earlier, it is in these works that he stresses the Kantian and Husserlian elements in his position.

34 This interpretation is argued in Philipse, "Transcendental Idealism," in the present volume.

35 That Husserl posed and answered such a Kantian question is argued in detail by Dallas Willard in "Knowledge," in the present volume.

36 These notions of individuation are explored at length in Smith and McIntyre, 1982.

37 A different line of reasoning, rooted in his theory of perception, would be Husserl's evolving phenomenalism, if Philipse is right in his analysis thereof: see Philipse, "Transcendental Idealism," in this volume. Realist interpretations of Husserl on perception or perceptual cognition are developed in Mulligan, "Perception," and Willard, "Knowledge," in this volume.

38 These two points I have argued in D. W. Smith, *The Circle of Acquaintance*, 1989. There I was not concerned with Husserl interpretation. However, Husserl's phenomenological analyses tend to support both points. His account of perception of "transcendent" objects suggests that we perceive objects as independent of our consciousness of them; his inversion doctrine would say that feature of everyday perception is, however, naive. Husserl follows Brentano's doctrine that every mental act includes a primary intention of its object and a secondary intention of the act itself: cf. *The Phenomenology of Internal Time-Consciousness*, 1905–10.

39 Cf. the reconstruction of Husserl's theory of intentionality in Føllesdal, "Husserl's Notion of Noema," 1969, Smith and McIntyre, *Husserl and Intentionality*, 1982, and Miller, *Husserl, Perception and Temporal Awareness*, 1984.

40 See Føllesdal, 1969 in Dreyfus, 1982. A similar conception of *epoché* is developed in Smith and McIntyre, 1982, and Miller, 1984.

41 Cf. Harrison Hall, "Was Husserl a Realist or an Idealist?," in Dreyfus, 1982: Hall's answer, "No." It has been remarked, by Lester Embree and J. N. Mohanty in conversation, that Husserl added the part of *Ideas* I preceding §27 (which launches discussion of *epoché*) only after writing the remainder of the work. This might suggest that the earlier part could and perhaps should be excised, leaving a project of pure phenomenological description, divested of all ontological commitment. In any event, Husserl added the first part, and that placed his project of pure phenomenology within his wider ontology.

42 The "content" and "object" approaches to intentionality are detailed (and the contrast coined) in Smith and McIntyre, 1982. Meinong's ap-

proach is for the most part an object approach. Russell argued explicitly against content, assuming the "cognitive" relation between knower and known is a two-term relation with no role for content: this point is explicated in D. W. Smith, 1989, Introduction.

43 Such an ontology is developed in Smith *et al.*, *Manufacturing Metaphysics* (forthcoming), concerning Ontek Corporation's knowledge-representation based computer system PACIS, a system designed for the management of large enterprises, such as manufacturing, that involve the integration of many large databases and their application in decision-making.

8   Common sense

I.   INTRODUCTION

Consider an experience that is free from all theory, an experience precisely as it is experienced, with no superadded interpretations (derived, for example, from physics or biology or myth or religion).[1] It is Husserl's thinking on this topic that will concern us in what follows. We shall set forth initially the main features of what we shall call *common-sense experience*.[2] We shall then, by way of contrast, set forth some parallel remarks on the nature and status of *physical theory*. Finally we shall examine Husserl's "phenomenological" account of the ways in which the worlds of common sense and of physics may each be conceived as reflections or products of certain special sorts of mental acts.

As basis for our inquiries we shall adopt the second book of Husserl's *Ideas*,[3] a work stemming largely from the period 1912–15 which presents above all an account of the fine structures of perceptual experience and of the world that is given in and through perception. We shall deal also with Husserl's *Crisis of European Sciences*,[4] a work that dates from around 1935 and presents a speculative history of the development of the scientific world-conception in its relation to what Husserl calls the "life-world" of common sense. *Ideas* II, which forms the hidden basis of the later work, was held back from publication in Husserl's lifetime. Our aim in what follows is not that of textual exegesis, however, nor is it one of presenting an account of the development of Husserl's thought. Rather, we seek to elucidate as clearly as possible the most important ingredients of Husserl's ideas on the topic of common-sense experience, and to show how they form a coherent whole from which much can still be learned.[5]

It must be pointed out immediately that Husserl himself does not use the expression "common sense" as a technical term of his philosophy. He does, however, use expressions, such as "life-world," "common surrounding world," "natural attitude," etc., which are closely related thereto and which will suffice to justify our exposition of Husserl's ideas on theory-free (or "original") experience by means of the terminology of common sense. Note that these ideas, especially in their final form, are themselves far from commonsensical. This is not, of itself, problematic, as is shown by the comparable case of Berkeley, who notoriously wanted to "save" common sense via the philosophy of immaterialism. A theory of common sense is open to criticism in this respect only to the extent that the *object* of this theory deviates from common sense itself. We must, however, be on our guard against the temptation faced by all philosophers concerned theoretically with common-sense experience to import into this experience factors which belong more properly elsewhere.

The Common-Sense World: The common-sense world is the world of what appears to us in everyday perceptual experience. It is the world as it appears to us directly – free of deliberations which would dig beneath the surface of appearances. It is a world in which people work, converse, judge, evaluate; a world of people, animals, tables, clothes, food, of red and green, hot and cold (and it goes without saying that these are not objects of the sort which are treated of, for example, in standard texts of mathematical physics). The common-sense world is above all a world of objects which we put to use for various practical purposes. Yet it is not itself there (or created) for some particular purpose. On the contrary: "Every end presupposes it." It is always on hand as the same, as nature "free from all theory, as it appears and is meant in this way or that, just as it enters into the personal life of mankind and determines this life in particular forms of practice."[6]

The common-sense world, the "actually intuited, actually experienced and experienceable world, in which our whole practical life takes place" is subject to a remarkable stability. It remains unchanged in its essential structures and in its causal style whatever we may do, and it retains its principal contours and frontiers from age to age and from generation to generation. The world of scientific theorizing changes and develops. The world of common sense, in contrast, "was always there for mankind . . . just as it continues its manner of being in the epoch of science."[7]

Primary and Secondary Theory: In his account of the world that is straightforwardly experienced in everyday life, Husserl anticipates the important distinction between primary and secondary theory drawn by the anthropologist R. Horton.[8] Horton points to empirical evidence to the effect that there is a primary core of beliefs and doctrines accepted by human beings across very many different cultures which is to a large degree invariant over time. "Secondary" theories of different degrees of sophistication become *attached* to this core. (In the western world, these secondary attachments are, above all, theories of the scientific sort.) The line between primary and secondary theory is difficult to draw. It is a line that is constantly crossed as a result of the fact that for example we in the west constantly employ theories about things, stuffs, natural kinds, and also theories about how things work (theories in engineering, geography, economics, etc.), when engaged in everyday planning and acting. What is important for our purposes here, however, are not theoretical extensions of common sense of these and related sorts. Rather, we are interested in the theory *of* common sense as such, or, in other words, in a secondary theory that would have primary theory as its subject-matter. This will be a theory in the strict and proper sense, and will employ theoretical instruments having a degree of sophistication in principle quite alien to that of common sense itself.

Such a theory can be developed as an empirical matter, for example, as a branch of psychology or anthropology. It might then be concerned with the contingent differences and similarities between, say, the beliefs about the world of an Eskimo and of a Trobriand Islander, and with the empirical question whether there are universal and culture-neutral core beliefs that can be allowed as constituting something like a primary theory in Horton's sense. Husserl, however, is concerned with common sense as an object of *philosophical* theorizing, with what belongs to the idea of common sense as such. Certainly the two sorts of question are not independent: for what belongs to common sense as such will therefore also be universally shared. The core beliefs and doctrines with which we shall deal in what follows will however have such an air of obviousness and even of triviality – thus for example they will consist of theses to the effect that persons exist or that bodies can move – that the thesis of universality will have much of the sting removed from its tail. (It is this triviality which accounts for the fact that the matters here presented have been often neglected in the past. Interestingly, it is a consequence of the fact that such matters are by no means trivial from the computer programmer's perspective that common sense has become, of late, an important area of research in the cognitive sciences.)

Historicists and relativists will of course balk at the idea of such a "core theory," objecting that it is sheer naivety to seek to display

a historical *a priori*, an absolute, supertemporal validity, after we have obtained such abundant testimony for the relativity of everything historical, of
all historically developed world-apperceptions, right back to those of the
"primitive" tribes. Every people, large or small, has its world in which, for
that people, everything fits well together, whether in mythical-magical or in
European-rational terms, and in which everything can be explained perfectly.
(*Crisis*, 373, Hua VI, 381f.)

Husserl has an answer to this objection, however, which rests on a consideration of what is involved in establishing just those historical facts that are held to support it:

Does not the undertaking of a humanistic science of "how it really was"
contain a presupposition taken for granted, a validity-ground never observed,
never made thematic, of a strictly unassailable self-evidence, without which
historical inquiry would be a meaningless enterprise? All questioning and
demonstrating which is in the usual sense historical presupposes history as
the universal horizon of questioning, not explicitly, but still as a horizon of
implicit certainty, which, in spite of all vague background-indeterminacy, is
the presupposition of all determinability, or of all intention to seek and to
establish determined facts.   (*Crisis*, 373, Hua VI, 382)

It is this "vague background-indeterminacy," which yet stands fast, as a rock beneath all our special inquiries and purposes, which will be our concern in what follows.

II. FEATURES OF THE COMMON-SENSE WORLD

Common sense is marked first of all by the feature of *systematic holism*. This turns on the fact that the various general concepts in terms of which common sense can be articulated, concepts such as *thing, mind, body, reality, perception, change, surroundings, cause, act, experience, belief, world,* are intertwined, each presupposing all the others in different, though systematic, ways – to the extent that it is difficult to know where exposition or investigation should begin.

The common-sense world is given as *real,* and this means, as Husserl sees it, that it is marked as a matter of necessity by two features: first is the feature of substantiality – the reality of the common-sense world is organized primarily around *things* (and not around sense-data);[9] and second there is the feature of *causal dependence in relational networks* – each real thing is as a matter of necessity such that its changes of state give rise in systematic ways to changes in correlated states of its neighbours.

The things of the common-sense world possess determinate real individual properties (of warmth, redness, heaviness, etc.). Each such property is, Husserl holds, of necessity changeable, or more precisely, exchangeable with other determinate real properties from the same family. It belongs to the essence of real things that they can move and be at rest, and that they can be subject to qualitative change and qualitative permanence.[10]

Real things exist further always *in situ,* which is to say in an environment of other real things, so that there are no causally isolated islands, cut off from all other realities: things are, in every case, embedded in wider circumstances of determinate sorts. To know a thing is to know, above all, its causal dependencies, which is to say, the ways in which its changes depend on changes in other real things. It is to know through experience or reasoning the sorts of stuffs it is made of, how it will change under given influences (for example, how it will behave when heated or bent). It is part of our common-sense understanding of reality that it manifests a limited repertoire of systematic regularities in these respects, in the sense that under similar circumstances similar series of changes occur. Again and again I can subject similar pieces of paper to the same series of bendings and foldings and observe and predict the same rule-governed effects in each case. The practical life of common sense to this extent involves constantly repeated inductions. This ordinary inductive knowledge is, however, "artless" compared to the "methodical" inductions made possible by natural science.[11]

We have to deal here with what Wittgensteinians call "ordinary certainty," or as Husserl puts it, with knowledge which constantly verifies itself from within. Such knowledge is "occasional" in that it is always tied to "the 'merely subjective-relative' intuition of pre-scientific world-life." And as Husserl points out, "this 'merely' has, as an old inheritance, the disdainful coloring of the *doxa*. In pre-scientific life itself, of course, it has nothing of this; there it is a realm of good verification and, based on this, of predicative cognitions which have proved themselves, and of truths which are just as secure as is necessary for the practical projects of life that determine their sense."[12]

The things of common sense "have, so to speak, their 'habits' – they behave similarly under typically similar circumstances." The common-sense world is thus a rule-governed (a reliable) world, a world whose denizens behave characteristically, and, for the most part, as we expect them to behave. Occasionally, of course, something happens that is strikingly new. We then immediately ask why, and look around us in order to find its cause in the things and events of our familiar environment. And even if we fail in this attempt, still we continue without hesitation to assume a universal, flawless causal regulation, or in other words to assume that this world is "not merely a totality but an all-encompassing unity, a whole (even though it is infinite)." Thus, in spite of the fact that we know comparatively little of what underlies particular causal dependencies, still we assume a universal causal style of our everyday world, and this makes possible (always typical and approximate) "hypotheses, inductions, predictions about the unknowns of its present, its past, and its future."[13]

Common-sense knowledge is spontaneously inductive knowledge – it is knowledge of how things will characteristically behave. But it is also knowledge of identity, or in other words knowledge of the respects in which a thing will remain the same through given series of changes. The things or substances of the common-sense world are given to us as unities through change: the same thing can survive even though, among its individual properties, radical changes have occurred.

The identity of the thing (and the corresponding "harmony" of our experience of things and processes) is explained by Husserl first of all by appeal to what he calls the "spatiotemporal skeleton," or in other words by the factor of *extension* which supports the qualities of the thing and which is experienced as identical in different sensory modalities. Indeed on Husserl's view the factor of extension is experienced as necessarily identical, where changes in the qualities themselves are merely "accidental" – even change from one quality to a contradictory quality does not prejudice the identity of the thing.[14]

Individual properties, too, can be conceived up to a certain point as unities through change – the same individual property of, say, elasticity in this tuning fork can change gradually yet remain for a time graspably the same real property. Thus, a patch of colour is a unity, as also is the corresponding area of the coloured surface. In this way it is as if the parts and moments within the thing constitute a series of strands overlapping in time. When a certain point is reached, when, for example, a coloured thing is bleached by the sun, then it is as if there is initiated a new segment of its being in virtue of the fact that it has a new colour-property in place of the old. What we have before us in such a case is a changed thing, one which preserves some properties, loses other properties and acquires new ones of a different type. It is because the overlapping segments in the duration of the thing form a dense fibre that we can grasp the thing as identical throughout its duration. That the thing does not break down into a succession of disjoint phases follows, in part, from the fact that the bulk of its properties are identical across any given temporal span: it has at every randomly selected stage in its existence a stock of lasting properties. (Later we shall discover that the mind, for Husserl, is a substance in a much stronger sense than this.)

Appearance: The things that are given to us in common-sense experience are given as distinct and distinguishable, but also as complete (thus, as completely determinate and also as well rounded in the sense that they appear, topologically speaking, as having one or other of a limited range of simple structures, generally the structure of a solid sphere). Each perceived thing is as it were present in the flesh as something which is three-dimensional, has surfaces, a (normally non-homogeneous) inside, a stuff or stuffs of which it is made. In any given case, however, only very little of the relevant whole contributes directly to the content of the relevant perceptual experience, and Husserl speaks here of the "aspects," "adumbrations" or "foreshortenings" which mark every perceptual experience of bodily objects. The perception of things is in this and other senses imperfect, and the kinds of imperfection are subject to intelligible regularities of their own. (Thus, there are different sorts of imperfections pertaining to the different kinds of things, e.g., to animals or men, to different perceptual conditions, and so on). Each such imperfection is given as in principle surmountable, however, in the sense that, while the perception of what is physical essentially includes features and dimensions that are left undetermined, it includes them *as determinable.*

It is in this context that there arises within the sphere of common sense the distinction between "appearance" and "reality." The former pertains to the presence of imperfections in perception, to cases of mismatch between adumbration and object, which are recognized as such. Thus common sense is in at least this sense not "naive": it is fully conscious of the distinction between the way things *are* (for commonsensical purposes) and the way things *appear to be* (to different subjects and under different circumstances).[15] Common-sense experience is, as Husserl puts it, an unceasing process of reciprocal adjustment:

each of us has his life-world, meant as the world for all. Each has it with the sense of a polar unity of subjectively, relatively meant worlds which, in the course of correction, are transformed into mere appearances of *the* world, the life-world for all, the intentional unity which always persists.

(*Crisis*, 245f., Hua VI, 258)

The duality of apperance and reality is seen by common sense as applicable through the whole external world, both to primary and also to secondary qualities. Thus, for example, we know that if all illumination were to cease, then colour-appearances would disappear. Yet still we believe that the real colours of the things themselves would remain as they are.[16] The duality is however applicable only locally: thus, it is not capable of being applied to the world as a whole, nor to that "horizon of implicit certainty" which is the background of all serious efforts to establish facts about reality.

Appearances are not real states or properties of the things. They are that through which such states or properties manifest themselves more or less imperfectly. Appearances are not states of the subject, either; they are transcendent with regard to our actual states, and most especially in regard to our intuitive experiences.[17] In fact, appearances are *relational entities,* dependent for their existence and nature upon both perceiving subject and appearing objects.

The perception of causes, too, is marked by imperfection, and thus also by the opposition between appearance and reality. For the cause of a manifest change need not itself become apparent, even though the change is itself experienced from the beginning as a causal change: the causal circumstance is then co-intended in an indeterminate way. Husserl is not asserting that cause or causal circumstances are necessarily in every case given perceptually – indeterminately or not. Rather, he is asserting that the world of common sense is *taken for granted*, in every normal perceptual experience, as a homogeneously meaningful and harmonious, causally organized, whole. Its changes are given as in principle understandable and explicable, as changes that happen reliably in correspondence to rules.[18]

Not everything that we perceive is a thing or sensible quality. We perceive also holes,[19] the gaps between things, and the media (for example water, smoke) in which things move.[20] We perceive shadows, rainbows, waves, and similar phenomena. And there are also perceived phantoms (faces which we seem to see in clouds or smoke); and while a perceived thing is unthinkable without sensuous qualification, such phantoms are thinkable without materiality or corporeality (though not without extension and thus also not without dimensionality). Thus there are experienced sensuous qualifications even where there are no thingly material objects.[21] Yet the converse does not hold; for the world that is given in straightforward perception is marked precisely by the fact that it is filled through and through by sensuous qualities. Within this sensuous array there are discriminable areas of organization, marked off by "boundary regions"[22] and separated by gaps. The world can in this sense be cleaved at its joints: it is organized into separate sensible things or bodies. Bodiliness and sensation in this way go hand in hand, since the bodily aspect of things exhibits itself perceptively only in visual, tactual, acoustical, and other such sensory aspects.[23]

When we perceive a thing, accordingly, then we are aware also of sensuous qualities and of a system of associated sensory surfaces. But the latter are not there as it were alongside the physical thing; what is there before us is a unity, something which has physical and sensible properties intertwined. Thus, the thing is experienced not as a bundle of properties or congeries of surfaces, but as one, single thing. And again: as far as our experience of real things and their manifest qualities is concerned, the content of our experience is as of *real transcendent properties*, not as of images or sense-data.[24]

My body, too, is, of course, like all other things in the world of common sense, a thing located in space, with a shape and a stock of qualities, and it is involved in causal dependencies. My body, too, remains identical through changes. The system of causalities into which my body is interwoven in normal experience is such that my body retains an identity of type through all its changes. Thus, my limbs return again and again to the same basic positions. They can again and again accomplish the same sorts of things (lifting, turning, running) in the same sorts of regular ways.[25]

Among the most important changes in or involving the body are those processes we call perceptual experiences. The network of such experiences is interwoven with other networks of changes in the body, above all with changes of bodily position and orientation. Husserl here anticipates J. J. Gibson's recognition of the crucial fact of the interwovenness of perception and bodily movements on the part of the perceiving subject:

if the eye turns in a certain way, *then* so does the "image"; if it turns differently in some definite fashion, then so does the image alter differently, in correspondence. We constantly find here this two-fold articulation . . . Perception is without exception a *unitary accomplishment* which arises essentially out of the playing together of two *correlatively related functions.*[26]

The body thereby plays a crucial role as concerns the spatial organization of the common-sense world. The body is that from out of which I grasp everything that is spatial and everything that is given to the senses: "each thing that appears has *eo ipso* an orienting relation to the body, and this refers not only to what actually appears but to each thing that is supposed to be able to appear."[27]

Inner Sensation: While perception is directed primarily to external objects in their external environments, this does not of course exclude the fact that we may also perceive, externally, certain parts of our own bodies: our legs, fingers, arms, etc.[28] In addition, however, the body is given in commonsensical experience also *from the inside,* in the sense that each case of external perception is correlated in systematic fashion with a sensation by the subject of the subject's own body. Material things can touch one another; but only when the body is involved do sensations occur. This is then always (as Husserl maintains) in such a way that we can talk of both inner and outer sensations, as also of inner and outer perceptions and feelings.[29] Thus, I see the apple and am simultaneously aware of my eyes and of myself as visually perceiving subject; I touch the table and am simultaneously aware of my own finger. Such bodily sensations are, of course, not normally attended to as such; they are rather experienced *on the side,* as part of a naturally unfolding system of regularities intertwined with the system of regularities unfolding on the side of the things perceived.

The organs of perception function in seeing, hearing, etc. always in such a way as to be bound together with an "I move" or an "I do" in a single comprehensive unity. As the experienced thing is given in successive series of aspects, so the body of the experiencing subject is given in successive kinaestheses, the two series running not simply alongside each other but being again such as to form a remarkable harmony.[30]

The Horizon of Perception: The two successive series are moreover in a precise sense open-ended. Each individual thing that is given in perception has the significance that it has for the perceiving subject through what Husserl calls an "open horizon" of possible perceptions, possible future continuations of the ways in which the object exhibits itself to the subject. As Husserl puts it,

a hidden intentional "if-then" relation is at work here: the exhibitings must occur in a certain systematic order; it is in this way that they are indicated in advance, in expectation, in the course of a harmonious perception. . . . This is the intentional background of every straightforward certainty of being of a presented thing.   (*Crisis,* 161f., Hua VI, 164)

In addition to the horizon of possible perceptions of the thing there is also what Husserl calls the "external horizon" of the thing as a thing within a field of things, something which points, in the end, to the whole world as perceptual world. Each perceptual experience picks out a certain group or field of simultaneously actually perceived things. Such a group is not given as isolated and as independently existing. Rather, the momentary field of perception, "always has the character for us of a sector 'of' the world, of the universe of things for possible perceptions."[31]

The world is pregiven to us, the waking, always somehow practically interested subjects, not occasionally but always and necessarily as universal field of all actual and possible practice, as horizon. To live is always to live-in-certainty-of-the-world.   (*Crisis,* 142, Hua VI, 145)

This horizon of perceptions, extending out from what is presently given to what is taken for granted (with "straightforward certainty") as capable of being given, has its analogue also in other spheres of experience. (Thus, the scientist experiences the world within the horizon determined by his theoretical end.)

The Continuum of Sense: The common-sense world, extending, in its horizons, out into infinity, has further the character of *multidimensionality:* in the unity which is the real thing, and in the totality of the experienced world at any given time, we can make out different strata of sensuous determinations corresponding to the different senses of vision, hearing, smell, etc. Each such stratum can be considered as homogeneous and as running its harmonious course and suffering characteristic types of alterations in and of itself. The different strata are, in terms of our access to them, separate, and essentially so, in the sense that colour, for example, is given perceptually only in seeing and never, for example, by means of hearing or touch. In themselves, however, the things we experience in common sense are not built out of separate or separable seen, heard and touched constituents, but are, rather, unities tied together by common strands. There is but one thing that is perceived as a unity along with its properties, "some of which are predominantly or exclusively (as, e.g., colours and their distinctions) grasped by vision, others by touch."[32]

On the subject side, too, the totality of inner sensations deriving from each of the different sensory modalities is similarly cemented together into a single harmonious unity, the "unity of consciousness":

As the image, *stream of experience* ... already indicates, the experiences, i.e., the sensations, perceptions, rememberings, feelings, affects, etc., *are not given to us in experience as annexes, lacking internal connection, of material bodies,* as if they were unified with one another only through the phenomenal link to the body. Instead, *they are one by means of their very essence.*   (Hua IV, 92)

Extension: The different strata are cemented together primarily through the fact that the boundaries of what is seen, touched or tasted come again and again into coincidence with each other in virtue of the existence of the common sensible of shape. For as we saw, the multidimensional sensory continuum is unified in the first place by the feature of extension. Extension is the axial determination of the thing in Husserl's eyes, and whatever other determinations the thing has, both as a whole and in its parts, it has these determinations across some relevant extent: "Every corporeal quality of a thing 'fills the spatial body'; the thing spreads itself out in the quality."[33] Thus the coloration of an opaque thing covers the entire outer surface of the thing in its specific fashion. Warmth fills the warm body in another, quite different fashion, and matters are different again as concerns hardness, texture, weight, and so on.[34] All such extensions are sub-extensions of the total infinite extension of the world.

The fact that the things of the common-sense world are extended and continuous, that they are not atoms or bundles of atoms, implies further that they can be subjected to actual or imagined *division into pieces*, the results of actual division being themselves such as to serve as things.[35] The parts of a thing do not exist merely side by side within the compass of the thing; they, too, are subject to systematic mutual relations of reciprocal action. The different parts are interlocked; they react in a unified way in face of external causal influences. In certain circumstances, however, this unity of reaction is lost and the thing "breaks up" (or "breaks down") into its parts. To divide a thing into pieces is, of course, to bring about also a corresponding fragmentation of its colouring and of its other real properties. This fragmentation applies not merely to the real determinations but also to the *appearances* of the thing and of its properties: for just as real colour and real extension are unthinkable in separation from each other, so also is their appearance.[36]

III. MIND AND BODY

One of the major components of common sense is what has been called "rational" or "folk" psychology, an area of "practical induction" which we treat here primarily from the point of view of ontology, or, in other words, in light of the question of the nature and status of the mind and of mental experience. The mind, for Husserl, is something that is affected by the outer world through perception and something from which acts issue forth. It is marked further by the fact that, as denizen of the common-sense world, it is tied to a certain body. Note that in his account of mind, Husserl adopts a conception of experience that rests on Cartesian dualistic assumptions which some (e.g., Heidegger or Ryle or Merleau-Ponty) would regard as alien to common sense. Thus Husserl talks of human souls as "animating" physical living bodies.[37] Husserl attempts, however, to minimize the force of these assumptions by stressing that the unity of man encompasses the two components of mind and body "not as two realities externally linked with one another but instead as most intimately interwoven and in a certain way mutually penetrating." Thus "one can understand that states and properties of either of these components count as ones of the whole, of the 'I as man' itself."[38]

Common sense is, one might say, *intrinsically underdetermined* in this respect, in that it leaves open the nature of this interwovenness of the two domains of mind and matter and is thus consistent with a variety of different positions as to their interrelation. Thus, common sense seems to be consistent also with Cartesian positions on this issue, though it would be an error to impute Cartesian dualism to common sense itself. Common sense is intrinsically underdetermined also in other respects. Thus, for example, despite our default assumption of universal causal regularity, the events within the world of common sense are marked by incomplete explainability (a lack of causal closure). Moreover common sense believes that material things can be divided into pieces, but it has no view as to whether, in this way, indivisibles will ultimately be arrived at. (This gives rise to the tricky problem of specifying the *limits* of common sense – of specifying the point or region where the determinations of primary theory come to an end and secondary theories must take over.)

Freedom: In planning manipulations of and interactions with other things we presuppose that our bodies, too, are things. Moreover, from external observation, mirrors, etc., we possess knowledge of our bodies' thingly qualities, and we also possess inner perceptions and inner feelings, e.g., of our hand and fingers when we grasp an apple. Through the experience we have as willing, acting subjects, however, we are in possession of knowledge of our bodies of a further kind. For our body is also given as a "freely moved totality of sense organs":

I know through experience that the parts of my body move in *that* special way which distinguishes them from all other things and motions of things (physical, mechanical motions); i.e., they have the character of subjective movement, of the "I move."   (Hua IV, 56, 259)

Each human ego

> experiences "its" physical body, not merely in general, as a particular physi-
> cal body, but in a quite peculiar way as "living body," as a system of its
> "organs" which it moves as an ego (in holding sway over them); how it thus
> "takes a hand" in its consciously given surrounding world as "I strike," "I
> push," "I lift" this and that, etc.   (*Crisis*, 211f., Hua VI, 215f.)

Each subject is "free" in the sense that it can change at will its (bodily)
position in relation to other things and other subjects. The body is a
self-moved mover which is at the same time somehow integrated into
the causal nexus of material nature. The body can be "freely" moved,
just as it can be affected also by passive bodily processes in which
freedom plays no part[39] (though common sense is underdetermined
also in this respect: that it has no precise understanding of the nature
of this "integration" – it has no *theory of freedom*).

Norm Kinds: The common-sense world, with its things, their real
states and appearances, is determined further by the following feature: there is a distinction that is drawn in all its spheres and dimensions between what is "*normal*" and what is to a greater or lesser
degree "*abnormal.*" This is, again, not a mere contingent matter in
Husserl's eyes, but belongs to the marks of the common-sense world
as such. Thus, there are abnormal experiences that occur, e.g., when
the different sensory strata fail to unify, or when sensation and judgment stand in contradiction to each other.[40] Common sense is then
marked crucially by the fact that it does not draw conclusions from
abnormal experiences which would lend it to reject its own central
principles. Common sense is in this sense not "fallibilistic." Rather
it is constantly self-verifying, excluding what does not harmonize
with its central principles as mere appearance.[41] Abnormal experiences are, as it were, passed over without comment, in the sense
that they are not held to yield data that is relevant to the understanding of the general, characteristic features of the common-sense
world (not such as to give rise to the need to change our global
understanding).

Consider the ways in which colour-appearances differ under different lighting conditions. Here "certain conditions prove to be the
'normal' ones: seeing in sunlight, on a clear day, without the influence of other bodies which might affect the colour appearance. The
'optimum' which is thereby attained then counts as the *colour it-*

self."[42] Appearances which fall outside the realm of what is normal are taken by common sense as secondary to or as deformations of that optimal appearance which alone counts as an appearance of reality. "The features which pertain to the thing 'itself' are the 'optimal' ones. This applies to all features, to the geometrical as well as to the sensuous qualities."[43]

In normal experience, then, we have access to (what count as) the real states themselves. What counts as real and what is real are for common sense identical (or the issue of their identity is reserved for the realm of what is left undetermined) – though this identity is qualified by the fact that common sense *is* fallibilistic in the sense that what counts as real at one time may at another time come to be seen, as a result of new experiences or of new information deriving from others' experiences, as having rested on error. Common sense is thus willing to subject itself to local but not to global revision (judgments as to individual matters of fact can be overturned in course of time, not however the general beliefs which stand fast, as it were, at the heart of common sense).[44]

The common-sense world is divided into "circles of similars": kinds or species, similar things, similar properties, similar events. All such kinds or species are subject to the opposition between normal (standard, typical) and abnormal (non-standard, non-typical) instances.[45] The normal instances of such species are marked by familiarity, they are part of what is taken for granted by common sense, both in regard to what they are and also in regard to what they will do (in regard to their regular patterns of behaviour in normal and regular circumstances).[46] Thus I perceive a door, or a leaf, *in one stroke*, and I know already the sorts of future ways in which this thing is likely to behave and to be perceivable in further acts. Normal instances are also stable: we can imagine them being deformed along different axes and yet as still remaining instances of the kinds in question. Abnormal instances, in contrast, are typically highly sensitive to deformations (as for instance a bluish red, on intensification of its blueness, may cease to be an instance of the colour red). Moreover, they may in different ways be assimilated in experience to the normal case (they may have normality thrust upon them, as it were), as when ambiguous figures, such as the duck-rabbit figure, are assimilated successively to one or other alternative "normal" reading.

We also have more or less abnormal *subjects* (in cases of colour-blindness and the like), and then the real thing of common sense is precisely the object that is given to the normal subject in relevant normal conditions.[47] The *real features* of the thing are those features which are experienced (in appropriate foreshortenings) by normal subjects in such normal conditions. Our bodies, too, are more or less normal or abnormal, and to talk of normal subjects is to talk also of bodies which are normal in relevant respects. Normal persons may, certainly, differ in their mental and bodily constitution, and such differences common sense allows for; but it allows for them along certain dimensions and to certain degrees only.

IV. CULTURE

The very existence of a stable structure called "common-sense world" carries with it the implication that this world appears to all normal persons in more or less identical ways. Differences of certain sorts do indeed make themselves apparent, e.g., when we compare the descriptions of the same event given by different individuals. But such differences can become apparent only because there is, as Husserl puts it, an underlying "intersubjective harmony of experience," a harmony, a general and unquestioned agreement, as to what sorts of features count as real, what sorts of conditions count as normal, in what sorts of ways given features can manifest themselves:

> normality is related to a multiplicity of persons in a communicating association, persons who, on the whole, in conformity with a predominating regularity, agree with one another in their experiences and consequently in their assertions about experience.[48]

The common-sense world includes not only my own body and various non-bodily things. It contains animals and plants; but more importantly it contains *other human bodies*, which is to say: material things of the same type as my own body. These I can perceive as I perceive other material things and as such they enjoy the same sorts of familiarity, normality, etc. Certainly our fellow human beings can surprise us in what they do, but not (characteristically) in the *types* of things they do, for these are restricted to the familiar repertoire of speaking, running, lifting, eating, killing, and so on. Human beings are of course not only material things: I can grasp them also (or so

Husserl argues) by means of a special mode of apprehension which he calls "*empathy*," the capacity to know how another person feels, what it is like to experience as this other is experiencing, etc. Through empathy I grasp – at least in normal circumstances – that these other bodies have a mind or ego like my own, along with everything that pertains thereto. Now it is a mark of those acts in which the common-sense world is given that they are characteristically and for the most part, *not subject to deliberation.* Empathy, too, is an act of this sort; automatically, as it were, it posits my and your consciousness and will as being of the same determinate and intelligible sort. My apprehension of the human being over there, as a whole human being with a life and mind very much like my own, spontaneously shapes and enlivens my perception of his body. There is an interesting parallel here to the way in which, in hearing words of a language which I thoroughly understand, my perception of the sounds is bound together completely with and is thoroughly shaped by my grasping of the associated meanings. As Husserl points out, "the word-sound is 'body' for the animating 'sense,' " the whole process spontaneously organizing itself in such a way that "each sense refers to a new sense and to new words in anticipation," in reflection of the ways the relevant words are joined together into sentences and other word-formations of higher order.⁴⁹

Empathy is a quite different matter from the grasping of natural causality in that it has both a physical and a psychic dimension. I grasp the other person as having mental and bodily behaviour and capacities like mine.⁵⁰ The two dimensions of empathy do not exist merely side by side, however. They are combined together in that special sort of unity which allows us to grasp a person as combining physical and psychic features in such a way that the latter are *brought to expression* in the former.⁵¹ Such expression is possible in virtue of the fact that our bodily movements are restricted to a certain familiar repertoire of types, and among these types (with their normal and abnormal instances) are those which are associated in rule-governed ways with corresponding psychic experiences.⁵²

Motivation: The totality of my experiences is bound together dynamically with the objects of the common-sense world. This holds first of all causally. There is a mechanical side to my experiences of the objects in the world and of the ways in which they impinge upon my own body and upon its sensory organs (and one possible criticism of recent research in "naive physics" is that its account of the dynamics of the common-sense world is restricted to features of this sort). But experiences and objects are bound together dynamically also in a second sense: the objects of this world, in being experienced, exert additional positive and negative forces upon me, subtle but compelling forces of attraction and repulsion, belonging not to the sphere of causality but to that of human (and animal) salience. When I perceive things and persons and surrounding circumstances I am determined (automatically, which is to say: non-deliberatively) by what Husserl calls a "web of motivations."[53] A skyscraper steers my regard onto itself through its special form. A butterfly draws attention to itself through its beautiful colour or texture. The noise of the cars out there makes me close the window. The glass of beer over here makes me reach out my arm to grasp it. "In short, in my theoretical, emotional, and practical behaviour – in my theoretical experience and thinking, in my position-taking as to pleasure, enjoyment, hoping, wishing, desiring, wanting – *I feel myself conditioned by the matter in question.*"[54] The object motivates the subject: it "intrudes on the subject" and stimulates him or her in a wide range of different though characteristically understandable and familiar ways. There are also examples of purely psychic motivation. Thus, I can be motivated to do this and that by an idea or a memory that occurs to me independently of my present experience of external objects. Indeed, as Husserl points out, everything that goes on in my mind is linked together through relations of motivation of this sort: through relations of significance. I *surmise* that A because I *know* that B. I *conclude* that D because I *discover* that E and F. I *desire* that G because I *learn* that H, and so on.[55]

To the causality which is the fundamental lawfulness of the purely material world, motivation now comes to be added as fundamental lawfulness of the world as this is determined by and for our mental life. And as in the case of physical causality so also here: the lawfulness turns on the fact that the similar motivates the similar under similar circumstances. The (normal) actions of (normal) subjects are *understandable* by other (normal) subjects in virtue of the similarity of motivations to which each of them is subjected in similar circumstances, as also in virtue of the similarity of the causal and bodily features involved.

Value: We can, if we exert ourselves, present to ourselves the objects of the common-sense world merely perceptually (as mere material targets of disinterested perception). As subjects of this world, however, we are not merely perceiving but also *acting* beings and are constantly subject to corresponding motivations. This means that under normal circumstances we automatically effect evaluations of the objects by which we are confronted in a way which amounts to a sort of *value-perception:* "the value-character itself is given in original intuition."[56] We directly (and thus pre-theoretically) experience the world as containing values and counter-values, and therewith also we acquire mediate and immediate goals. These give rise in turn to new motivational connections in light of the presuppositional connections between the sub-goals in whose realization we are at any given time engaged.

These values, goals, and motivations can now be seen (on the metacommonsensical, theoretical level) as a new dimension of being within the common-sense world itself. They are, of course, not commonsensical objects in the way that people, apples, houses are: but we can nonetheless pursue the theory of values and of rational practice as theoreticians of what belongs to the world of common sense in its total structure.

Our goals and values and the motivations which give rise to them lead us not least to transform the objects and stuffs of the common-sense world into new objects, the results of such transformation entering once more into the common-sense world as products or works. The world of objects of common sense is hereby marked by an intelligible opposition between natural things and *artifacts.* Such products may be recognized as valuable in different ways. They may serve as tools for further processes of production, leading us to new products and new evaluations as well as to new possibilities for future goals. And all of this is, as part of the human world of common sense, both familiar and understandable:

[E]ach work, each product, each action expresses an activity and is characterized as work, as act: one sees how the cigar is rolled, one discovers therein the expression of a manipulation and, on the other hand, the "visible" aim.
(Hua IV, 321; cf. 188)

The importance of Heidegger's *Being and Time* resides not least in its contribution to our understanding of these and related aspects of our common-sense experience (our experience of tools, of how they become extensions of our bodies, of how they work and fail to work).

Culture and Society: I am dependent in my behaviour on things, for example on their automatically (non-deliberatively) grasped pleasant or dangerous properties, their sweetness or bitterness, redness or greenness, on their usefulness as equipment, and so on. Tools, buildings, plants, animals motivate in different ways. They occasion and help to steer my behaviour. But I am dependent in an even more striking way on other *persons.* For human beings, too, exercise on one another immediate effects. They have "motivating power" for each other. Sometimes persons (or parts of human bodies) have effects on us in the same way as do physical things, i.e., through mere causality. And sometimes they have effects which involve both physical and mental components (for example in cases of sexual attraction). Persons influence each other also, however, in primarily mental ways, often via those deliberately constructed edifices of motivation we call uses of language. Persons direct their activities toward one another, "they perform acts with the intention of being understood by the other and of determining the other, via his understanding grasp of these acts, . . . to certain personal modes of behaviour."[57] There are, as Husserl tells us, *social acts,*

in which the ego turns to others and in which the ego is conscious of these others as ones toward which it is turning, . . . perhaps adjust their behaviour to it and reciprocate by turning toward that ego in acts of agreement or disagreement, etc. It is these acts, between persons who already "know" each other, which foster a higher unity of consciousness and which include in this unity the surrounding world of things as the surrounding world common to the persons who take a position in regard to it.[58]

Thus, there are not merely personal motivations in the narrow sense (ensuing, say, from this man who is my friend or from that man who strikes me as honest and reliable); there are also webs of motivation that pertain to communities of persons as such and hold social institutions together. Among these are what we might call *transcategorical* motivations, patterns of motivation that link together not only our mental and bodily experiences but also social and especially linguistic acts, laws, contracts, and so forth.

From all of this it follows that the persons in the common-sense world are determined by the fact that they belong to different personal unities of a higher order. The human being, as creature of the common-sense world, is a being marked by his dealings with others in relation to institutions, laws, morals, customs, etc., and human beings know each other as such:

The members of the community, of marriage and of the family, of the social class, of the union, of the borough, of the state, of the church, etc., "know" themselves as their members, find themselves dependent upon them in their consciousness and affect them in their consciousness in turn.[59]

To this extent, then, (and analogously to what holds in the case of values), institutions and related personal unities of higher order can be seen at least on the metacommonsensical (theoretical) level to constitute a new dimension of being within the common-sense world itself, analogous to the level of persons proper. Institutions have their own lives, they endure through time, despite acquiring or losing members; they have their own qualities and states, and their own ways of functioning in collaboration or in interaction with each other.[60] And like things on lower levels, they are through and through dependent on circumstances and are subject to more and less regular and intelligible patterns of change, to normality and abnormality.

Levels of Common Sense: In summary we can say that the common-sense world includes at least the following spheres or levels:

1. normal intuitive spatio-temporal nature, the earth and natural things and stuffs, both organic and inorganic, having real qualities and states and giving rise to sensations and also to practical motivations of various sorts;
2. people and animals, moving and behaving in determinate ways, at rest, thinking, working, speaking, writing;
3. artifacts, goods, implements, cultural objects, which presuppose deliberate, intelligent activity on the part of man;
4. values and goals affecting our behaviour and at the same time giving sense and structure to our activities over time;
5. morals and customs, languages, various social units and socially constituted entities with their particular norms and conventions.

The elements of (2) and (3) are grasped by common sense itself as standard constituents (denizens) of (1). There are elements of (4) and

(5), however, which seem to be distinguishable as such on the meta-commonsensical (theoretical) level only.

V. PHYSICS

So where does *theory* come from? Theory gets superadded to common sense in a variety of ways: we might use it in cooking, in building bridges, or for other practical purposes. Or we might use it as a way of making sense of natural calamities or of the history of our tribe. Husserl, however, is concerned not with theory as an ephemeral protagonist in the history of this or that society but in the idea of theory as such, with what makes theory theory, with the form which theory must take if it is to be theory in the most perfect sense.

What, then, does the idea of perfect theory involve? It involves, first of all, the idea of a total shareability of knowledge, of a knowledge for all, and for all times, as contrasted with the "occasional" knowledge of everyday existence. Second, it involves the idea of exactness, as contrasted with the vague forms – characterized by appearance, by normalcy and abnormalcy, and by the boundedness to sensory intuition – of common sense. Third, it is marked by the idea of total explainability (of closure under causal laws) and thereby of total prediction.

The goal of establishing a nature or reality valid for everybody arose at a certain point in the development of human culture. Each human being had until then taken for granted his own (his own society's) surrounding world, "with its traditions, its gods, its demons, its mythical powers, simply as the actual world." Then, however, there appeared a new idea of truth: "not tradition-bound, everyday truth, but an identical truth which is valid for all who are no longer blinded by traditions, a truth-in-itself."[61]

The goal of establishing such a truth-in-itself was fulfilled by making experienced *nature* thematic not as qualitative, but purely as *res extensa*. Nature became reduced to a mere mathematical manifold, each thing became reduced to a mere body, a mere extension. A garb of mathematical ideas, or of symbolic mathematical theories, came to be developed, which claimed by degrees to encompass the entirety of the everyday world and to represent all that is "objective" within it.

Where the common-sense world, then, is marked by empirical intuitable forms, the objective world yielded by the mathematical method (as Husserl conceives it) amounts to an infinite totality of ideal objects, pure extensions "which are determinable univocally, methodically, and quite universally for everyone ... an infinity which is determined, decided in advance, in itself, in respect to all its objects and all their properties and relations."

By means of pure mathematics and the practical art of measuring, one can produce, for everything in the world of bodies which is extended in this way, a completely new kind of inductive prediction; namely, one can "calculate" with compelling necessity, on the basis of given and measured events involving shapes, events which are unknown and were never accessible to direct measurement. Thus ideal geometry, estranged from the world, becomes "applied" geometry and thus becomes in a certain respect a general method of knowing the real.[62]

In making precise the common-sense world, two (Newtonian) principles are imposed upon it with methodical thoroughness: that similar consequences follow under similar circumstances, and that there is no change without cause. Natural science as Husserl conceives it orients itself strictly around these principles in such a way that the idea of necessary explainability is held to govern the world in all its aspects. Uncaused change is for Husserl ruled out by science *a priori*, even though a change that had no grounds might be possible *idealiter*.[63] The world of scientific theory is thus a world of self-enclosed causality in which everything that happens is determined in advance.

The sort of object which would be suitable for *theoretical* grasping in the fullest and most perfect sense is called by Husserl the "physicalistic" thing. The world of physicalistic things is grasped not via sensation but via theory, and it consists of entities all of whose properties are capable of being grasped with theoretical perfection. From this it follows, in Husserl's view, that there are no sense-qualities in the world of physicalistic things.[64] There are, certainly, physical facts which correspond to our qualitative distinctions of red and green, warm and cold, etc. But these physical facts are a matter of purely quantitative distinctions pertaining to reflectance, temperature, etc., and they serve merely as the basis on which qualitative appearances are produced by psychophysical processes of certain special sorts (these processes themselves being determinable with purely quantitative exactitude).[65]

The world of physicalistic things differs from the world of common sense in that the former is ruled entirely by causality. This relates always what is real to what is real, where the motivation which we encounter with causality in the common-sense world may involve what is not real, as for instance when I am moved by something that is merely remembered or even imagined. In this respect there is a fundamental distinction between real causal relations on the one hand and motivation-relations on the other: motivation is a matter of intentionality.[66]

The world of physicalistic things differs from the world of common sense further in that the former knows no opposition between the normal and the abnormal, and it is similarly free of values, and of all that belongs to the realm of practice:

Concepts such as the valuable, the beautiful, the amiable, the attractive, the perfect, the good, the useful, deed, work, etc., as well as, similarly, concepts like state, church, right, religion, and other concepts, that is, objectivities to whose constitution valuing or practical acts have essentially contributed – all these have no place in natural science, they are not concepts pertaining to nature.   (Hua IV, 25)

Exact vs. Morphological Science: The science of the common-sense world is a science of a different kind from physicalistic science. The latter is "exact," in Husserl's special sense, which is to say it is a theory built up logically from a small number of primitive concepts and axioms which together suffice to determine completely the entire domain of research. It is essential to this domain that the totality of all its possible constituent formations is determined "completely and unambiguously on lines of pure analytic necessity."[67] Such a domain – Husserl is thinking here above all of Euclidean geometry – is "mathematically exhaustively definable."

The science of the common-sense world is in contrast what Husserl calls a morphological science: it is a science which employs a large number of concepts of "vague Gestalt-types which can be apprehended only with the aid of sensory intuition"; it has to do with the "bodily shapes of rivers, mountains, buildings, etc."

The most perfect geometry and its most perfect practical control cannot help the descriptive student of nature to express precisely (in exact geometrical concepts) that which in so plain, so understandable, and so entirely suitable a way he expresses in the words: notched, indented, lens-shaped, umbelliform, and the like – simple concepts which are *essentially and not accidentally inexact,* and are *therefore* also unmathematical.[68]

Exact concepts are ideal; they express something one cannot (or not in normal circumstances) see, and they are built up from simple concepts in a strict hierarchical order. (We leave unexplored here the question of whether Husserl is right to conceive mathematical concepts as built up in this sense.) Morphological concepts, in contrast, are grasped via direct intuitive experience and bear within themselves a sort of "occasional" or "indexical" component; they are concepts of this world, of the here and now of human beings. They are not capable of being exhaustively grasped in axioms or laws of any theory. Moreover, they are related to each other not hierarchically but holistically, i.e., in networks of mutual dependence. Thus they are not reducible to one another, and the bulk of the laws governing their interrelations are synthetic rather than analytic in nature.[69] Finally, and again in contrast to exact concepts, morphological concepts are subject to normal and abnormal instances.

The causality of nature as this is determined by the natural sciences under Husserl's conception can be expressed in exact and exceptionless laws (called "laws of nature"), and on the basis of these laws we can determine in principle what has to follow from given initial conditions. Exact prediction, then, and the sort of explanation which goes hand in hand with prediction as its converse (*p* happened *because q, r and s* had happened earlier) are at the heart of the physicalistic conception of reality.

The motivation which is allied with causality in the sphere of common sense (and in the sphere of the human sciences, which have the theory of common sense as their presupposition) is in contrast not exact and can be captured in no exact mathematical laws. Moreover, in common-sense experience both causality and motivation are always only partially and imperfectly apprehended. While, certainly, causality holds sway also in the human world of common sense, still, human scientists can make no exact predictions but can at best (for example) clarify motivations; thus they can make intelligible how given individuals or groups came to behave in such and such ways under such and such circumstances.[70]

From the perspective of the natural scientist it is only what can be grasped exactly, and mathematically, that is truly real. Only as far as concerns the primary qualities of mass, shape, motion, etc. can we grasp the real states of things. Our experience of secondary qualities, in contrast, corresponds to nothing truly real in the physical sense at all. From this perspective, indeed, *the entire common-sense world is reduced to the level of mere appearance* – an appearance of true, physicalistic nature – and this is the case even though there is an opposition between "appearance" and "reality" running through the common-sense world itself.

Qualitative Physics: The physicalistic world is a world denuded of that sort of intuitive and emotional richness which characterizes our everyday experience. Above all sensory qualities are excluded from the realm of physicalistic nature since they cannot be directly treated by the methods of the natural sciences. Instead, the place of tones, colours, etc., is taken by tone-vibrations, warmth-vibrations, etc., i.e., by events belonging to the world of shapes. As Husserl points out, the thickness, tension, etc., of a vibrating string are all measurable factors. It is such factors which allow us to adapt the common-sense world to the just-mentioned "well-fitting garb of ideas":

through a method which (as we hope) can be really carried out in every particular and constantly verified, we first construct numerical indices for the actual and possible sensible plena of the concretely intuited shapes of the life-world, and in this way we obtain possibilities of predicting concrete occurrences in the intuitively given life-world, occurrences which are not yet or no longer actually given. And this kind of prediction infinitely surpasses the accomplishment of everyday prediction. (*Crisis*, 51, Hua VI, 51)

As a result of this process of adaptation, however, the thing, formerly given intuitively, becomes reduced to an empty something determined exclusively through the forms of space and time and through the associated primary qualities of energy, motion, etc. It becomes an X awaiting determinations of the sort which are capable of being established in the course of natural-scientific investigations.[71] The fact that real physical determinations are always a matter of mathematically exact functional connections between one thing and another, and the fact that the world of physicalistic nature is exhausted by such determinations, together imply a variety of functionalism as concerns the objects of this world. The latter are what they are only in reference to other such objects in the interweavings of causality. The thing as object of theoretical physics is nothing other than a node in a system of causalities, and physical reality itself is a system of functional relations (a "system of relativities" in Husserl's terms). From this, however, it follows that real nature is in a certain sense anonymous: *no physicalistic thing has individuality in itself. "The physical thing of the natural science has only a formal essence; it has only its formula."*[72] Physical things (for example electrons, quanta of energy) are mere *examples* of species; they are fungible, substitutable one for another, repeatable at will.

Anchorage: What is it, now, which brings this "anonymous" relational framework into connection with the world of common-sense experience? And how can our will and practical actions become related to the physical world thus conceived? How, furthermore, can the mind be entwined in physical causality through its relation to the body and to its physiological processes? Two answers to these questions have been floated already:

1. the physical world is a *making precise* of the common-sense world that arises via processes of theorizing; it is a *product* of theorizing activity (of a sort which takes place, alongside other activities, within the everyday world of common sense);

2. the physical world is the *reality* of which common sense is the *appearance*. "The quantitative is not merely in the appearing extensional processes; the quantitative is also therein something indicated by what is merely qualitative. And it is possible that the quantitative be subsequently exhibited sensibly through sensible manners of appearance (somehow 'clothed' qualitatively)."[73]

Husserl draws these two seemingly incompatible strands together by introducing a new perspective, the perspective of the *subject*. Only subjects engage in processes of theorizing, and only in relation to the subject are there "appearances" of any sort. Only subjects engage in "producing" activity, and only subjects can provide a point of orientation in relation to which the framework of time, space and motion can acquire a necessary anchor.

What distinguishes two things that are alike is the real-causal nexus, which presupposes the here and now. And with that we are led back necessarily to an individual subjectivity, whether a solitary or an intersubjective one, with respect to which alone determinateness is constituted in the positing of location and of time.   (Hua IV, 299)

The subject is, if you like, absolute individuator. Subjects (and subjects alone) are not mere *examples of universals.*

Thus, where analytical philosophers have only in recent years learned to ask questions about the nature of internal experience and of the individuating role of subjects (for example when Nagel asks what it is like to be a bat, or when Perry talks of the "essential indexical") – conceiving subjects (quite naturally, given the fundamentally materialistic perspective which forms the background of their work) as an incidental extra, from the perspective of German idealist philosophy the subject (or "subjectivity," "spirit" or *Geist*) stands at the very beginning of the philosophical enterprise. Husserl's move to place the subject at the starting-point of his philosophizing – where in the first edition of his *Logical Investigations* the subject plays no role at all – therefore amounts to an emigration into the German tradition.

From Husserl's new perspective, everything which affects and determines the mind as a natural reality is exemplary and universal. Subjects may thus enjoy similar experiences, yet each subject remains "ineluctably distinct from every other by means of an abyss."[74]

Husserl's account of this individuality is difficult to follow. First, it is held to reside in the fact that the mind is itself given in mental experience. It is not (like physical things) given as the individual that it is *only in relation to other individuals:* rather it is self-given, with evidence, as something unique. It is however difficult to see how this epistemological fact should have implications of the ontological sort which are involved in individuation. Second, the mind is held by Husserl to be unlike any mere node in a network of causalities in that it is an active centre, a source of freedom: "it has *its motivation in itself.* It does not have individuality only by being in a determinate place in the world."[75] Third, Husserl offers a transcendental argument to the effect that subjects must be more than mere interchangeable nodes of the sort that can be made the objects of theoretical natural science:

Subjects cannot be dissolved into nature, for in that case what gives nature its sense would be missing. Nature is a field of what is through and through relative, and it can be so because these are always in fact relative to an absolute, the mind, which consequently is what sustains all the relativities [relatives].   (Hua IV, 297)[76]

From this metaphysical perspective, the subject (mind or ego) is not a substance in the sense in which this is true of physical or material things: it is not an X available for exact theoretical determinations, and neither is it an object of sense, a mere bearer of qualities; "it has neither a mathematical nature in the manner of the thing of physics, nor a nature like the one of the thing of intuition."[77] The mind endures as something self-identical. It affects the body and thereby also has effects in and is affected by the world of physical nature. Its identity is manifested also in the regular patterns of its sensations, behaviour, feelings, etc. But the mind or subject is, in Husserl's eyes, a substance also in a much stronger (metaphysical) sense. Not merely is it a source of intentionalities in its own right. It is also essentially such as to have a history. For the mind undergoes "a continuous new formation or re-formation of dispositions under the familiar titles of: association, habit, memory, motivated change of meaning, motivated change of convictions, of direction of feeling . . . and will," etc. This occurs always in a cumulative fashion, i.e., always in such a way that my present stock of experiences is a totality dependent on my earlier experiences. Thus, "it pertains to the essence of *psychic reality* that as a matter of principle it *cannot* return to the same total psychic state."[78] Physicalistic things, in contrast (at least as Husserl conceives them), are in a certain sense history-less realities (they are subject, if you like, to the law of eternal return).

VI. CONSTITUTIVE PHENOMENOLOGY

Recall the holistic embranglement which we mentioned at the beginning of this essay and which echoed and re-echoed throughout the pages which followed. This holism gives rise to quite peculiar problems, problems which Husserl sought to resolve, we can now say, by appeal to a conception of the subject as "constituting ego" (hence the sub-title of Book II of Husserl's *Ideas: Studies in the Phenomenology of Constitution*).

The basic axiom of constitutive phenomenology is this: *All ob-*

*jects refer back to corresponding acts in which they are (or can be)
given.* All entities, on whatever level, are correlates of corresponding
acts. Only from the perspective of this basic axiom will we be in a
position to understand Husserl's thesis to the effect that not only
the physicalistic world but also the world of everyday appearances
"require" the subject. Note that this basic axiom leaves open the
issue as to whether the constitution of the world is or is not a matter
of creation (as an idealist might suppose). This issue will be resolved
in due course.

"A correlate as such," as Husserl says, "has its support in persons
and in their experiences."[79] The absolute being of the latter precedes
the relative being of the former. Above all, the individuation of the
correlates as such – of "appearances" – depends on the absolute
individuation of the subject and its experiences. On the other hand,
however, a subject, with its acts, is thereby directed towards correlates in its turn, indeed toward a world of correlates, for: "As person
I am what I am (and each other person is what he is) as *subject of a
surrounding world.* The concepts of ego and surrounding world are
related to one another inseparably."[80]

From the basic axiom it follows that physical things, too, can be
nothing other than the correlates of certain acts, namely of the theoretical acts of physicists. Physical nature is then itself the common
"surrounding world" of physicists, precisely as they know of it in
their theories and conceived as extended *in infinitum* and in perfect
regularity. Other such special "surrounding worlds" can be distinguished also, including private worlds (of dreams, etc.) as well as the
stable, public worlds which are of interest to us here. For there are
different sorts of relations of mutual understanding through which a
conscious mutual relation of persons is produced, different sorts of
normal institutional groups and associated normal attitudes which
involve also a corresponding relation to a precisely suited world of
objects. Thus, for example, there are the ideal worlds of mathematical or legal objects, of financial instruments, folk tales, chess, and so
on. Each such realm of objects is an interpersonal, cultural accomplishment, presupposing a certain association of human beings.[81]

The world of common-sense, too, is an accomplishment of a community of persons recognizing each other (or better: taking each
other for granted) as normal, as similar, as in agreement. And again,
the things of the common-sense world, taken exactly in the way

they present themselves to us in this world, are not anonymous objects as in the case of the natural sciences, mathematics, or chess. Rather, they are direct correlates of intuitive experiences, "things we see, grasp, and touch, just as we, and other people, see them, grasp them, etc."[82] But more, the common-sense world is the most general world; it corresponds to the most general community of persons, and serves as the presupposed background of all the special, institutional worlds which may arise. The theory of the common-sense world is accordingly "a universal morphology of the natural world as the common world of a people, of any society whatever."[83] This theory is an important part of the foundations of the human sciences in general (including history, as we have seen).

If the world of physicalistic nature presupposes the subject, however, and if the latter comes along only hand in hand with this "common surrounding world," then mere common sense – the *doxa* so often disparaged in the course of philosophical history – "now suddenly claims the dignity of a foundation for science, for *episteme*."[84] Philosophers have, in general, not thought through the consequence of the fact that human beings live in the world of common sense and can put all their practical and theoretical questions only to it, a fact which serves as the necessary presupposition of all of natural science. For it implies that all our scientific knowledge, all knowledge of laws,

could be knowledge only of predictions, grasped as lawful, *about occurrences of actual or possible experiential phenomena*, predictions which are indicated when experience is broadened through observations and experiments penetrating systematically into unknown horizons, and which prove themselves in the manner of inductions. To be sure, everyday induction grew into induction according to scientific method, but that changes nothing of the essential meaning of the pregiven world as the horizon of all meaningful inductions. It is this world that we find to be the world of all known and unknown realities. To it, the world of actually experiencing intuition, belongs the form of space-time together with all the thingly shapes incorporated in it; it is in this world that we ourselves live, in accord with our bodily, personal way of being. But here we find nothing of geometrical idealities, no geometrical space or mathematical time with all their shapes. (*Crisis*, 50, Hua VI, 50)

All empirical inquiries of the natural scientist presuppose visible measuring scales, scale-markings, etc. They rest on the premise of something "which actually exists in the life-world, as something valid."[85] The scientific world is a purposeful structure – a structure made by human beings, and like every practical world, it presupposes the world of common sense.

Natural Sciences and Human Sciences: As a result of the activities of different specialized communities of persons (scientists, artists, mathematicians, etc.), the common-sense world comes to be extended in correspondingly specialized ways. From this perspective "the natural sciences, as sciences, are enclosed within the human sphere, the sphere of the mind."[86] They are a part of human culture. But now we have another twist of the wheel: by the basic axiom of constitutive phenomenology, they must be constituted as such in special acts – the acts of human scientists.

From the perspective of natural science there are no persons, no culture, no personal and cultural accomplishments such as theories and works of art. Human sciences, in contrast, posit persons, culture, works, theories, as dependent not on physicalist nature but on the world of common sense – on acts and on the "normal" surrounding world of persons, objects for use, etc. The natural sciences, too, are parts of this human world. This implies in turn, however, that these very sciences, as really existing institutional creations, must fall short of the ideal of perfection that is their guiding principle.

Physicalistic nature is a theoretical and rational construction. It is a mathematically objective nature, which enjoys only an asymptotic reality; it is "an idea lying in the infinite," an idea to which we, in an infinite historical process, strive by degrees to approximate.[87] Natural science falls short of its intended perfection in a number of ways. Above all it is affected by a sort of routinization, which inevitably comes into play as the same methods are repeated over and over again and which implies that scientific validations with true evidential force are no longer sought for systematically.[88] Assertions are taken over merely passively, meanings are combined together in empty association, whereby it often happens that

a meaning arises which is apparently possible as a unity – i.e., can apparently be made self-evidence through a possible reactivation – whereas the attempt at actual reactivation can reactivate only the individual members of the combination, while the intention to unify them into a whole, instead of being fulfilled, comes to nothing.   (*Crisis*, 361, Hua VI, 372)

Psychophysics: Hence, according to Husserl, we should not (or not without much further ado) take the haphazard productions of the natural sciences for realities. Such productions are at best soundings from the depths, *abstractions* yielded up by the application of a method. In light of this, however, the old problem of mind and body takes on new meaning. It raises in new form the question whether we could even in principle succeed in determining mind as part of nature understood in the natural-scientific sense after the manner of psychophysics. The latter starts out from the thesis that the mind, too, is a unity of dependencies in the sense that the mental is dependent on things and events in the physical world – not only via perceptual experience but also via other bodily processes (sleep, the intake of chemicals, etc.) which affect our conscious life:

the psychic is given as localized in the body and as temporalized in the unity of natural time. If we investigate this real unity thematically, specifically aiming at a knowledge "valid for everyone," then we have to determine the body as a physical-chemical, biological thing and determine the soul in relation to this physicalistic corporeality. (Hua IV, 391)

Such a view is now seen to be incoherent – it is defeated by the realization that the world of physicalistic things is itself a world of abstracta: "the last residuum of the Cartesian theory of two substances is defeated simply because abstracta" – the ideal products of the exact, mathematical method – "are not 'substances'."[89]

Contrast, now, the "human" science of mind. This is not a natural science, but it embraces within its subject-matter all the sciences of nature themselves as cognitive and cultural formations, accomplishments of determinately ordered cognitive communities with determinate human goals. Like all human sciences, it deals not in exact explanations but in descriptions formulated in "morphological" terms and resting on data that is intuitive in nature.

But there is a still more radical science of mind, the science of phenomenology, whose basic axiom asserts that every variety of object has a certain sort of conscious act correlated with it. More precisely, we can distinguish a range of varieties of act-object correlation, from the (ideally) most perfect sort of givenness to that sort of more or less empty directedness which is effected via language (via meanings built upon meanings in more or less associative fashion).

All such acts, together with the objects posited in them, become for Husserl the subject-matter of a new type of scientific investigation:

all the species of acts which the researcher of any kind of science accomplishes, all the species of meanings which in such acts mediate the relation to objectivities, all the modes of appearances in which these objectivities enter into the researcher's consciousness, all the modes of thoughtful grasping and noetical qualification which emerge therewith – all these become in phenomenology theoretical objects. Phenomenology does not investigate the objects investigated by the researcher in other sciences; on the contrary, it investigates the total system of possible acts of consciousness, of possible appearances and meanings related to precisely those objects.   (Hua IV, 312)

Human science is concrete and historical; it is marked by its concern with this specific case: the world of you and me. Phenomenology, in contrast, is the investigation of constitutive subjectivity in general, a science directed to lawful universality; it is concerned with *world as such, experience as such, theory as such*, wherever these might be realized.

Dissolution: We said that motivation can involve also what is not real, as for example when I experience fear in relation to an object which I merely imagine. And now – in a final twist of the wheel – it turns out that from the perspective of constitutive phenomenology the object-pole of motivation *always* has this unreal character:

If we examine the structure of the consciousness that constitutes a thing, then we see that all of nature, with space, time, causality, etc., is completely dissolved into a web of immanent motivations. In the unity of the lived total experience, which comprises consciousness of a thing there and of an ego here with its body, we find distinguishable objectivities of many kinds, and we also find functional dependencies which are not dependencies of an actual thing on the actual body and the actual ego in the world, which, in short, are not natural-scientific psychic and psychophysical dependencies. But then neither are they dependencies of subjective appearances . . . on real objectivities that are posited or received as real.   (Hua IV, 226f)

There are experiences of an ego, experiences which stand to each other in relations of motivation. There occurs within the stream of consciousness a procession of positings, regulated by strict rules. But there is, as Husserl sees things, *nothing else*. There is a certain harmonious play of motivations, unfolding itself consequentially, but there is no "world" of common sense, and no world of physics either.

Husserl's much-mooted *epoché* amounts, indeed, to the over-throw of common sense:

Every interpretation of . . . , every opinion about "the" world, has its ground in the pregiven world. It is from this very ground that I have freed myself through the epoché; I stand *above* the world, which has now become for me, in a quite peculiar sense, a *phenomenon*.   (*Crisis*, 152, Hua VI, 155)

And the *epoché* takes away from physics, too, its claim to objective reference. Earlier we said that the physicalistic thing "has only its formula." From the perspective of the *epoché*, the essence of the physicalistic thing turns out to lie in this: that it is an intentional unity, regulated *according to this very formula*, of an infinite variety of appearances "of all men."[90] Admittedly, Husserl seeks to thwart the obvious objections which here arise by placing this *"aller Menschen"* in quotation marks. He succeeds thereby, however, only in drawing inadvertant attention to the problematic character of this most "radical" of standpoints. For the problem with all transcendental idealist views is of course the problem of *intersubjectivity* – of accounting for the existence of harmony among the different worlds which arise when "world" is relativized to your and my subjective appearances and of accounting for the possibility of a single universal science which would govern the modes and manners of such appearing. In a review of *Ideas* II, Alfred Schutz reports that Husserl held back from publishing this work precisely because of problems in this respect.[91] Husserl's attempts to resolve these problems, above all in the *Cartesian Meditations*, are brilliant indeed. Unfortunately however they fall far short of what would be needed if the ontology of transcendental idealism – of "constitutive" phenomenology – were to acquire a firm foundation.

NOTES

1 Prepared as part of research projects sponsored by the Swiss National Foundation (SNF) and the Austrian Fund for Scientific Research (FWF). Thanks are due to Roberto Casati, to Herman Philipse, to Karl Schuhmann, and also to the co-editor of this volume, for helpful comments.

2 This terminology and focus are adopted for two reasons: (1) We hold that an important reason why Husserl was neglected for so long by Anglo-Saxon philosophers lies in the fact that those responsible for the translation and exegesis of his work in English have made too little effort to

counteract the effects of Husserl's idiosyncratic terminology; (2) We would like to exploit Husserl's work on the structures of common sense as a contribution to the exploration of this topic within the context of work on folk psychology and on artificial intelligence. See, on this, my "The Structures of the Commonsense World," in A. Pagnini and S. Poggi, eds., *Gestalt Psychology. Its Origins, Foundations and Influence* (Florence: Olschky, 1994); P. J. Hayes, "The Second Naive Physics Manifesto," in J. R. Hobbs and R. C. Moore, eds., *Formal Theories of the Common-sense World* (Norwood: Ablex, 1985), 1–36; and D. W. Smith, C. Dement, and P. M. Simons, *Manufacturing Metaphysics* (forthcoming).

3 References are given to the Husserliana edition, the pagination of which is included also in the English translation by R. Rojcewicz and A. Schuwer: *Ideas Pertaining to a Pure Phenomenology and to a Phenomenological Philosophy*, Second Book (Dordrecht/Boston/London: Kluwer Academic Publishers, 1989).

4 Edmund Husserl, *The Crisis of European Sciences and Transcendental Phenomenology. An Introduction to Phenomenology*, translated by David Carr (Evanston: Northwestern University Press, 1970). References are given also to the Husserliana edition.

5 On the historical and textual background, see the chapter "Husserls Göttinger Lebenswelt," in Manfred Sommer, *Lebenswelt und Zeitbewusstsein* (Frankfurt: Suhrkamp, 1990), 59–90, and Bernhard Rang, *Husserls Phänomenologie der materiellen Natur* (Frankfurt a. M.: Klostermann, 1990).

6 *Crisis*, 382, 319, Hua VI, 461, 298f. Cf. Hua IV, 186, 285f. and also Husserl's *Experience and Judgment*, § 10.

7 *Crisis*, 50f., 123, Hua VI, 51, 125.

8 See his "Tradition and Modernity Revisited," in M. Hollis and S. Lukes, eds., *Rationality and Relativism* (Oxford: Blackwell, 1982), esp. 227ff.

9 So central are things to the common-sense world that Kotarbiński was led to propound the doctrine that common-sense is "reist" in the sense of a doctrine which accepts only things as entities. See his "The Humanities without Hypostases," in T. Kotarbiński, *Gnosiology. The Scientific Approach to the Theory of Knowledge* (Oxford: Pergamon Press, 1966), 481–91.

10 "A thing can, e.g., be unmoved and unchanged *de facto*, but it would be countersensical to claim that it is unmovable and unchangeable in principle" (Hua IV, 36).

11 *Crisis*, 51, Hua VI, 51. The regularity of changes in the world, the fact that things fall within a limited repertoire of familiar and recognizable

types, goes hand in hand with the fact that this world and *language* "are inseparably intertwined" (*Crisis*, 359, Hua VI, 370). Thus, it is a mark of things that they can serve as objects of judgments which involve a claim to being *true* of the corresponding things. (Cf. Hua IV, 82)

12 *Crisis*, 125, Hua VI, 127f.
13 *Crisis*, 31, Hua VI, 28f. Such reasoning has been dealt with at length in recent work in folk psychology; for an overview of the literature see Ernest Davis, *Representations of Commonsense Knowledge* (San Mateo, Cal.: Morgan Kaufmann, 1990).
14 Cf. *Crisis*, 307, Hua VI, 285.
15 It goes without saying that standard representations of "naive realism" are in need of reconsideration in this light. See, on this, the discussion of Thomas Reid in L. Forguson, *Common Sense*, London: Routledge, 1989, 38, and also S. A. Grave, *The Scottish Philosophy of Common Sense* (Oxford: Clarendon Press, 1960), 108.
16 Cf. Hua IV, 71.
17 Cf. Hua IV, 201.
18 Cf. Hua IV, 48.
19 See R. Casati and A. Varzi, *Holes and Other Superficialities* (Cambridge, Mass.: MIT Press, 1994), chap. 10.
20 See Fritz Heider, "Thing and Medium," in Heider, *On Perception, Event-Structure and Psychological Environment, Psychological Issues*, I, No. 3, 1959.
21 It is, as Husserl points out, "a mere phantom that faces us when we learn, in a stereoscope, to bring fitting organizations into corporeal fusion. We are then seeing [Husserl means: seeming to see] a *spatial body*, regarding which meaningful questions can be raised about its [apparent] form, its colour, and even about it smoothness, and other, similarly classified, determinations." (Hua IV, 36)
22 These are regions of accumulation of sensory qualities, where "accumulation" is to be understood in the topological sense: see J. Petitot and B. Smith, "New Foundations for Qualitative Physics," in J. E. Tiles, G. T. McKee, and C. G. Dean, eds., *Evolving Knowledge in Natural Science and Artificial Intelligence* (London: Pitman Publishing, 1990) 231–49, and also "Physics and the Phenomenal World" in R. Poli and P. M. Simons, *Formal Ontology* (Dordrecht: Reidel, forthcoming). Compare B. Russell, *Human Knowledge. Its Scope and Limits* (London: George Allen and Unwin, 1948), especially Russell's "Postulate IV" (510f.).
23 Cf. *Crisis*, 106, Hua VI, 108.
24 Cf. Hua IV, 43, 176.
25 Cf. Hua IV, 61, 68.
26 Hua IV, 58. Cf. J. J. Gibson, *The Senses Considered as Perceptual Sys-*

tems (Boston: Houghton-Mifflin, 1966), 56f. The similarity between Husserl and Gibson becomes even more clearly apparent in Husserl's lectures on "Thing and Space," for example, in the following passage: "All spatiality is constituted and comes to givenness in motion, in the motion of the object itself and in the motion of the 'I,' with the change of orientation that is given thereby." (*Ding und Raum*, Hua XVI, 154.) See also *Analysen zur passiven Synthese*, Hua XI, e.g., 13f.) See also the considerable philosophical literature on the unity of action and perception, e.g., B. O'Shaughnessy, "The Diversity and Unity of Action and Perception," in T. Crane, ed., *The Contents of Experience* (Cambridge: Cambridge University Press, 1992), 216–66, and G. Evans, *The Varieties of Reference* (Oxford: Clarendon Press, 1982), 154ff. Cf. also Evans' essay "Molyneux's Question", in his *Collected Papers* (Oxford: Clarendon Press, 1985), 383ff. (on the concept of "behavioural space").

27 Hua IV, 56.

28 The ways in which our bodies can appear to us externally are restricted in a very definite way:

certain of my corporeal parts can be seen by me only in a peculiar perspectival foreshortening, and others (e.g., the head) are altogether invisible to me. The same body which serves me as means for all my perceptions obstructs me in the perception of it itself and is a remarkably imperfectly constituted thing. (Hua IV, 159)

Compare the famous drawing on p. 19 of Mach's *Analysis of Sensations* (New York: Dover, 1959).

29 Cf. Hua IV, 146 and also the extended treatment in Part One of Merleau-Ponty's *Phenomenology of Perception* (London: Routledge and Kegan Paul, 1962).

30 Cf. *Crisis*, 106, Hua VI, 108.

31 *Crisis*, 162, Hua VI, 165. Cf. *Crisis*, 35, Hua VI, 33, on the "total form" of the world as universal configuration of all bodies with their individual constituent forms.

32 Hua IV, 70, cf. 39f. The thing itself does not have a visual element which it could gain or lose. Moreover (against Berkeley): "It makes no sense to assign to each sense its property-complexes as separate components of the thing, any more than it makes sense to claim that the 'primary' properties [of size, shape, etc.] are somehow *doubled* when grasped by the different senses" (Hua IV, 70).

33 Hua IV, 30.

34 We can conceive each real property of a thing as a single ray of the thing's being. The extension of a thing, in contrast, is not a ray of being in this sense; rather, as Husserl puts it (and now we can pause to note a

first element of Cartesianism in Husserl's approach to common sense): "it is an essential form of all real properties" (Hua IV, 31).

35 The treatment of matter or stuff would belong here too: stuffs are, we might suppose, what remains of objects when they are subjected to a process of maximal division and to related operations of blending, grinding, mixing.

36 There is an analogue of continuity, extension and fragmentation also on the subject side: a sensation-content is, as Husserl puts it, "unified with the moment of spread (we do not here mean spatial extension, talk of which makes no sense with regard to sensation-contents)" (Hua IV, 154). Brentano draws in this connection a distinction between what is *continuously many* (e.g., the surface of a disk divided into continuously many segments of different colours) and what is *continuously manifold* (e.g., the central point of this disk, a boundary shared in common by each of the given segments). An experience of a complex colour array is not itself spatially extended; but it has an analogue of such extension nonetheless. The mind, Brentano concludes, is a continuously manifold zero-dimensional entity which endures through time. See F. Brentano, *Philosophical Investigations on Space, Time and the Continuum* (London: Croom Helm, 1988), 32ff.

37 *Crisis*, 211f., Hua VI, 215.

38 Hua IV, 94.

39 Cf. Hua IV, 159.

40 Here a range of perceptual illusions has its place (as, e.g., in the case of the stick that appears bent when immersed in water).

41 See *Crisis*, 124, Hua VI, 126. Compare P. K. Feyerabend, "In Defence of Aristotle: Comments on the Condition of Content Increase," in G. Radnitzky and G. Andersson, eds., *Progress and Rationality* (Dordrecht: Reidel, 1978), 143–80.

42 Hua IV, 59.

43 Hua IV, 77.

44 See Avrum Stroll, "How I See Philosophy: Common Sense and the Common Sense View of the World," in *Certainty and Surface in Epistemology and Philosophical Method*, eds., A. P. Martinich and M. J. White (Lewiston/Queenstown/Lampeter, The Edwin Mellen Press, 1991), 185–201. Compare also G. Evans, Commentary on Fodor's "Methodological Solipsism":

although the statement "it seems to S as though there is food to the right, in front of him" entails nothing about S's current environment, it could not be true if S did not eat, and if S's movement in the world, forward or backward, to the left or to the right, were not systematically dependent upon information from its environment. (Evans, *Collected Papers*, Oxford: Clarendon Press, 1985, 402)

45 Cf. the concept of "norm kind" introduced by N. Wolterstorff in his *Works and Worlds of Art* (Oxford: Clarendon Press, 1980), 56f.

46 Our remarks here are related to recent work on the (still relatively little understood) role of prototypes in early learning, as also to work of Gestalt psychologists on the notion of "*Prägnanz*" (see, e.g., G. Kanizsa, *Organization in Vision: Essays on Gestalt Perception* (New York: Praeger, 1979)) and the discussion of typicality in A. Schutz, "Type and Eidos in Husserl's Late Philosophy," in his *Collected Papers*, Vol. III (The Hague: Nijhoff), 92–115.

47 Cf. Hua IV, 60, 82. From this it follows that the *qualities* of material things as objects of the common-sense world are dependent on the nature of the body of the normal subject and on its normal sensibility.

48 Hua IV, 207, cf. 315f. The later Wittgenstein, again, caught something of what is involved in this thesis. See, e.g., *Philosophical Investigations*, (Oxford: Blackwell, 1953), Part I, para. 242, *On Certainty*, (Oxford: Blackwell, 1969), e.g., paras. 156f.

49 Hua IV, 240f.

50 Thus I grasp the other as having a body that is located in the same common surrounding space, our respective locations being in principle interchangeable. Cf. Hua IV, 202 and also § 51 of the *Cartesian Meditations*.

51 In fact, the other's mind or ego exists as object of nature available for determination in theoretical operations *only* as something that is expressed in the human body.

52 One should not suppose that we have to do here with a simple dichotomy between man and thing (only the former being subject to empathy). For there may be a sort of empathy also in relation to other animate entities, and (as D. Dennett has stressed) even to machines. Human beings stand out, however; so much so "that mere animals have ontic meaning only by comparison to them, as variations of them," (*Crisis*, 277, Hua VI, 230).

53 *Ideas* I (Hua III, 1), 101.

54 Hua IV, 140, cf. also 219. Cf. the Gestalt-theoretical notion of "requiredness" discussed by Wolfgang Köhler in his *The Place of Value in a World of Facts* (New York: Liveright, 1938), 250ff.

55 Cf. Hua IV, 230. Note that the causal intervolvement of mind and body is quite different from the motivational relations here discussed:

the physiological processes in the sense organs, in the nerve cells and in the ganglia, do not motivate me . . . What I do not "know," what does not stand over against me in my lived experiences, in my representing, think-

ing and acting, as the represented, perceived, remembered, thought, etc.,
does not "determine" me as a mind. And what is not intentionally included in my experiences, even if unattended or implicit, does not motivate me, not even unconsciously. (Hua IV, 230f.)

56 Hua IV, 186.

57 Hua IV, 192.

58 Hua IV, 194. The theory of such social acts, which corresponds in certain
respects to modern speech act theory, was worked out in detail by Adolf
Reinach as part of a general *a priori* ontology of social interaction. See
his "The A Priori Foundations of Civil Law," first published in 1913,
Eng. trans. by J. Crosby, in *Aletheia* 3 (1983): 1–142, and compare also K.
Mulligan, ed., *Speech Act and Sachverhalt. Reinach and the Foundations of Realist Phenomenology* (Dordrecht: Nijhoff, 1987). A view of
social ontology in many ways parallel to that of Reinach is defended in
M. Gilbert, *On Social Facts* (New York: Routledge, Chapman and Hall,
1989).

59 Hua IV, 182, cf. 141, 315f. As the phenomenologist Aurel Kolnai points
out, a human society

is not only composed of various parts – it is composed of various parts in a
multiplicity of ways; and consequently its component parts cannot but
overlap. In other words, it consists ultimately of individuals, but only in
the sense that it divides into a multitude of individuals across several
social subdivisions, such that it comprehends the same individual over
and over again in line with his various social affiliations, – some of them
factual, natural and "statistical," some of them largely or wholly a result
of voluntary choice.

See A. Kolnai, "Identity and Division as a Fundamental Theme of Politics," in B. Smith, ed., *Structure and Gestalt. Philosophy and Literature
in Austria-Hungary and Her Successor States* (Amsterdam: John Benjamins, 1981), 317–46, 319.

60 On this, see K. Schuhmann, *Husserls Staatsphilosophie* (Munich: Alber,
1988), Chap. 1.

61 *Crisis*, 286, Hua VI, 332.

62 *Crisis*, 32f., Hua VI, 30f. Cf. Hua IV, 41ff., 47f., 353. This is another
example of the Cartesianism at the root of Husserl's thinking. See also
Beilage VIII to Husserl's *Formale und transzendentale Logik* (Hua XVII),
444.

63 Cf. Hua IV, 52.

64 It could be argued that Husserl here falls victim to a confusion between
sense qualities and *appearances thereof*, for even if sense qualities are
dependent upon sense organs for their appearance, this does not imply

that they have no place in the physicalistic world. For a defence of a realist view of colour see D. Hilbert, *Color and Color Perception* (Stanford: CSLI, 1987).

65 Cf. Hua IV, 84, and compare Petitot and Smith, "New Foundations for Qualitative Physics," *op. cit.*

66 Cf. Hua IV, 233.

67 Hua III, 1, 152.

68 Hua III, 1, 155; *Crisis*, 27f., Hua VI, 24f.

69 See W. Żełaniec, "Fathers, Kings, and Promises: Husserl and Reinach on the A Priori," *Husserl Studies*, 9, 1992, 147–77.

70 Cf. Hua IV, 229. A similar opposition has been drawn within the philosophy of the social sciences, for example, by F. A. Hayek in his "Degrees of Explanation" (see Hayek, *Studies in Philosophy, Politics and Economics*, (London: Routledge and Kegan Paul, 1967), 3–21).

71 Cf. Hua IV, 88, 355.

72 Hua IV, 376, cf. 298f.

73 *Crisis*, 308, Hua VI, 286.

74 Hua IV, 309.

75 Hua IV, 299.

76 As Husserl puts it: "The mind, and indeed only the mind, exists in itself and for itself, is self-sufficient; and in its self-sufficiency, and only in this way, can it be treated truly rationally, truly and from the ground up scientifically." (*Crisis*, 297, Hua VI, 345)

77 Hua IV, 345.

78 Hua IV, 136f. Thus also there is, "for essential reasons, no zoology of peoples. They are spiritual unities; they do not have, and in particular the supranational unity of Europe does not have, a mature shape that has ever been reached or could be reached as a shape that is regularly repeated." (*Crisis*, 275, Hua VI, 320)

79 Hua IV, 302.

80 Hua IV, 185.

81 Such associations are conceived by Husserl as being such that all persons are in principle able to partake in them. Compare the essay on "The Origin of Geometry," where Husserl points out that geometrical existence

does not exist as something personal within the personal sphere of consciousness; it is the existence of what is objectively there for "everyone" (for actual and possible geometers, or those who understand geometry) (*Crisis*, 356, Hua VI, 367).

82 Hua IV, 287.

83 Hua IV, 376.

84 *Crisis*, 155f., Hua VI, 158.

85 *Crisis*, 126, Hua VI, 129. This was stressed by Sellars, too, in his account of the relation between the "scientific" and "manifest" image; see "Philosophy and the Scientific Image of Man," in W. F. Sellars, *Science, Perception and Reality* (London: Routledge and Kegan Paul, 1963), 1–40.

86 Hua IV, 392.

87 Hua IV, 353, cf. 372. From the perspective of constitutive phenomenology the idea of true being goes hand in hand with the idea of a personality that would sustain itself, in principle, into the infinite, either as an endless community of persons (Hua IV, 363) or as an infinite God (cf. M. Scheler, *Formalism in Ethics and Non-Formal Ethics of Values* (Evanston: Northwestern University Press, 1973), 396f.)

88 Cf. *Crisis*, 48, Hua VI, 48.

89 *Crisis*, 229, Hua VI, 232.

90 Hua IV, 376f. See also *Ideas* I (Hua III, 1), 100f.; *Cart. Med.* (Hua I), 89ff., 138; *Crisis*, 179, cf. 220, Hua VI, 182f, 223f.

91 See A. Schutz, "Edmund Husserl's Ideas, Volume II," *Philosophy and Phenomenological Research* 13, 1953, as repr. in Schutz, *Collected Papers*, Vol. III (The Hague: Nijhoff, 1975), 15–39, 17.

9 Mathematics

Husserl began to publish on problems in the philosophy of mathematics and logic soon after he received his Ph.D. in mathematics in 1881, and he continued to publish on them throughout his lifetime. Although much has happened in the foundations of mathematics since the turn of the century, many of Husserl's ideas are still relevant to recent issues in the philosophy of mathematics. In this essay, I argue that a number of the views on mathematics that are part of Husserl's transcendental phenomenology are more compelling than current alternative views in the philosophy of mathematics. In particular, I indicate how Husserl's views can be used to solve some basic problems in the philosophy of mathematics that arise for (naive) Platonism, nominalism, fictionalism, Hilbertian formalism, pragmatism and conventionalism.

I. A PRÉCIS OF PROBLEMS IN THE PHILOSOPHY OF MATHEMATICS

Many of the basic problems in the philosophy of mathematics center around the positions just mentioned. It will not be possible to discuss these problems in any detail here, but at least some general indications can be given.

A major difficulty for Platonism has been to explain how it is possible to have knowledge of immutable, acausal, abstract entities like numbers, sets, and functions. Once it is argued that these entities are abstract and mind-independent, there seems to be no way to establish an epistemic link with them that is not utterly mysterious. The apparent insurmountability of this problem might persuade one to abandon Platonism altogether in favor of some form of nominalism. The nominalist will at least not have the problem of explaining how knowledge of abstract entities or universals is possible, because on this view there simply are no abstract entities or universals. There are only concrete spatio-temporal particulars, and it is argued that however one ends up construing these, there will be no great mystery about how we could come to know about them. One could work quite naturally, for example, with a causal account of knowledge.

The problems for nominalism lie elsewhere. Nominalism just does not appear to do justice to actually existing parts of mathematics, and especially to set theory. Mathematical statements do not appear, *prima facie*, to be about concrete spatio-temporal particulars, even though they may in some cases be applied to such entities. The language of mathematics does not itself mention such objects. So one of the first problems for the nominalist is to explain how and why mathematics is really so much different from the way it appears to be, and from the way it is taken to be by practicing mathematicians. For example, it is a fundamental assumption of different mathematicians at different times and places that they are discussing the *same number* (e.g., the number π) in their research. Mathematical practice suggests that *there is* an identity through difference here, but how could this be possible on a nominalist view?

We are also supposed to believe that we are systematically misled by the language of mathematics but not, for some reason, by language that refers to physical objects, or to concrete spatio-temporal particulars. Nominalist enterprises are reductive, for they propose schemes for reducing the language of mathematics to the language of concrete spatio-temporal particulars. The reductive schemes proposed even for elementary number theory, however, have either turned out to employ notions that resist nominalistic treatment or to be rather far-fetched. A major barrier to a nominalistic treatment of mathematics lies in the fact that many mathematical propositions are about infinite sets of objects, like the set of natural numbers, but it is difficult to see how such propositions could be reduced to a language in which only spatio-temporal particulars are mentioned. The assumption that there is an infinite number of spatio-temporal particulars goes beyond what is needed in physical theory and may, in fact, be false. On the other hand, one might try to introduce modal notions into the reductive scheme to provide for at least a potential infinity of natural numbers. Here too there are problems. A coherent nominalist account of modality must be provided, but no such account has been forthcoming.

Should the problems of nominalism be enough to make one rebound into Platonism? Not according to fictionalists. Fictionalism, roughly speaking, is the view that assimilates the language of mathematics to the language of fiction. Arguments for fictionalism have recently been brought back into circulation in some of the work of Hartry Field.[1] Like nominalism, it denies that there are mind-independent, abstract objects. Mathematical objects are fictions, albeit sometimes convenient fictions. Unlike nominalism, it need not attempt to reduce the language of mathematics to a language of concrete spatio-temporal particulars. A fictionalist can argue that we understand mathematics independently of any such reductive scheme, just as we understand fiction independently of such a scheme. There are many problems with fictionalism and I shall return to them below.

Hilbertian formalism, as an attempt to secure the foundations of mathematics via finitist consistency proofs, is also beset with many problems. In particular, Gödel's incompleteness theorems show that we will not be able to have consistency proofs for interesting parts of mathematics, even for elementary number theory, if these proofs are to be based, as Hilbert wished, on only the immediate intuition of concrete, 'meaningless' finite sign-configurations. Consistency proofs for interesting mathematical theories will evidently have to involve reflection on or analysis of the *meanings* of the sign configurations, or will have to introduce more "abstract" elements (e.g., objects that cannot be encoded in the natural numbers) into our thinking, such as the elements we find in the Gödel and Gentzen consistency proofs for number theory. Traditional Hilbertian formalism has no place for such meaning-theoretic considerations or for such abstract elements. On the other hand, modifications of Hilbert's program that allow for such considerations, or for abstract objects like primitive recursive functionals, take a decisive step away from strict formalism. The reliability or security of mathematics that is supposed to be based on metamathematical consistency proofs must now rest on insights of a different character.[2]

Hilbert's emphasis on the role of "meaningless" syntax is also related to other problems of formalism, like the problem of why mathematicians are so interested in some systems of sign-configurations but not others. This difference must have something to do with the meaning or reference of the sign-configurations. Moreover, how is the strict formalist to account for the understanding we have of the applications of mathematics?

Another perspective on mathematics is provided by pragmatism. In some of its formulations pragmatism appears to be simply anti-mathematical. For example, if we are not to accept any distinction which does not make a difference to practice it would appear that we ought not to accept large parts of "pure" or theoretical mathematics. Pragmatists do not recognize any form of evidence intrinsic to mathematics that is supposed to support our mathematical beliefs. Our mathematical beliefs are to be judged solely on the basis of their fruitfulness, not on whether or not they are faithful to some intuitive or informal mathematical concept that we believe we are developing. On Quine's view, for example, we are justified in believing axioms of mathematical theories only insofar as they form part of our best-confirmed scientific theories. But then what of unapplied parts of mathematics? One might wonder why mathematics should be beholden in this way to the natural sciences.

Another problem for the Quinean view has been pointed out by Charles Parsons.[3] Quine's view avoids the difficulties of earlier, cruder forms of empiricism about mathematics by assimilating mathematics to the most theoretical part of natural science, the part farthest removed from observation. But then how can it account for the obviousness of elementary mathematics? Are we really to believe that "$7 + 5 = 12$" is a highly theoretical assertion, one which is even more rarified than the highly theoretical assertions of the physical sciences?

Finally, a consideration of how mathematics is actually done, of mathematical practice, shows that pragmatism simply does not respect the facts of mathematical experience. Fruitfulness does not always figure into which definitions, rules, or axioms are accepted by mathematicians. There are many examples in mathematics of efforts to be faithful to some intuitive or informal mathematical concept that is under investigation, examples of what Georg Kreisel has called "informal rigor."[4] One of the best recent examples of such informal but rigorous concept analysis can be found in Zermelo's description of an iterative concept of set, which has since been extended by set theorists.[5] Efforts to settle open problems in set theory (e.g., the continuum hypothesis) by adopting new axioms have not been focused only on the question of which axioms are most fruitful. Another very recent example of informal rigor in constructive mathematics can be found in the descriptions of the concept of lawless sequences that Troelstra and van Dalen use to obtain axioms for the intuitionistic theory of these objects.[6]

Conventionalism about definitions, rules and axioms is subject to similar objections about informal rigor. It too fails to recognize any form of evidence unique to mathematics. It fails to do justice to the way open problems are approached and solved in practice. For conventionalism there is no question of trying to be faithful to some intuitive mathematical concept that we are developing, because in no particular case is there such a concept. Conventionalism is, in fact, unable to recognize any intrinsic constraints on mathematical concepts, as though concepts can be changed at will and solutions to problems adopted by decree. There are, in addition, many other objections that can be raised to conventionalism.

Husserl's position in the philosophy of mathematics, or at least the part of it that is worth saving, cuts across the various positions we have been discussing. It comprises an effort to avoid the kinds of problems described above and to arrive at a more refined view, and at the same time to do justice to mathematics as it is actually given and practiced.

II. THE BACKGROUND OF HUSSERL'S VIEW:
OBJECTIVITY AND SUBJECTIVITY IN MATHEMATICS

Husserl, having been trained in mathematics late in the nineteenth century, was witness to advances in formalization, generalization, and abstraction that were unprecedented in the history of mathematics.[7] He was evidently deeply impressed through his own work in the field with the "objective" nature of mathematics. Early on, in the *Philosophie der Arithmetik*, we find him attempting to reconcile the "psychological" or subjective aspects of our mathematical experience with the "logical" or objective aspects. The relationship between the subjective and objective aspects of our experience in mathematics and logic was to become a central theme in his work, from the earliest to the latest stages of his career.[8] In Section 2 of the

Introduction to the second volume of the *Logical Investigations* (*LI*), for example, we find him asking,

> How can that which is intrinsically objective become a presentation, and thus, so to speak, something subjective? What does it mean to say that an object exists both "in itself" and "given" in knowledge? How can the ideal nature of what is universal, [for example] a concept or a law, enter the stream of real mental events and become an item of knowledge for a thinking person?

Husserl's questions here bear a striking parallel to questions that had been discussed earlier by Bolzano and that were also being confronted by Husserl's great contemporary, Frege. In "The Thought," we find Frege trying to answer exactly the same questions about timeless and immutable "thoughts."[9] Recently, we find a similar concern in Gödel's effort to explain how we could have knowledge of transfinite sets that "clearly do not belong to the physical world."[10] The tenor of Husserl's questions suggest the perspective of a Platonist, although, as we shall see, he is not a classical metaphysical Platonist, and he wishes to avoid the plight of the Platonist mentioned above. While it is as important for Frege and Gödel to answer these kinds of questions as it is for Husserl, we find that Husserl devoted far more effort to the project and obtained far better results. Husserl's answer to the questions show that he is also not a nominalist, fictionalist, or formalist, and that he disagrees with pragmatism and conventionalism about mathematics. At the center of his approach lies the concept of intentionality.

III. INTENTIONALITY

It takes no great insight to notice that our mathematical beliefs are always *about* something. They are about certain objects like numbers, sets, functions, or groups, or they are directed to states of affairs concerning such objects. This "aboutness" or "directedness" of mathematical beliefs is referred to as the "intentionality" of such beliefs. That is, intentionality is just the characteristic of "aboutness" or "directedness" possessed by various kinds of cognitive acts, like acts of believing, knowing, remembering, imagining, willing, desiring, and so on.

It is curious that while the intentionality of cognition is widely recognized and discussed in other areas of philosophy, there has been a veritable blind spot about it in the literature in the philosophy of mathematics. As a consequence, it has been easier for philosophers of mathematics to ignore what appear to be insurmountable problems in the efforts to naturalize intentionality.

A standard (if simplified) way to analyze the concept of intentionality is to say that an act of cognition is directed toward, or refers to an object (or state of affairs) by way of the "content" of the act, where the object (or state of affairs) the act is about may or may not exist. Historically, a variety of terms have been used in place of the term "content," e.g., "idea," "concept," "intention," and in Husserl's later technical terminology, "noematic nucleus."[11] We can picture the general structure of the intentionality of our acts in the following way:

$$\text{act (content)} \longrightarrow \text{[object]},$$

where we "bracket" the object in the sense that we do not assume that the object of an act always exists. Husserl is famous for suggesting that we bracket the object and then focus our attention on the act and act-content, where we think of an act as directed toward a particular object by way of its content.

The contents of acts can be determined by considering "that"-clauses in attributions of beliefs and other cognitive states to persons. Consider, for example, the following expressions:

Mathematician M believes that $7 + 5 = 12$,
M knows that there is no largest prime number,
M believes that if $n > 2$, then the equation $x^n + y^n = z^n$ cannot be solved in the positive integers x, y, z, with $x,y,z \neq 0$ (Fermat's last theorem).

Or consider an example from Zermelo-Fränkel (ZF) set theory:

M remembers that $(\forall x)(x \neq \phi \to (\exists y)(y \in x \And y \cap x = \phi))$ (the axiom of foundation).

Or a belief about extending ZF:

M believes that a supercompact cardinal exists.

In these examples, the contents of a mathematicians' acts are expressed by the propositions following the word "that." Different act-characters are also indicated: believing, knowing, remembering. Thus, a mathematician might have different types of acts with the same content, or acts of the same act-character with different contents. Note also the various differences in the contents expressed here. We have, respectively, a simple singular proposition about natural numbers, a theorem, a conjecture, an axiom, and a proposed axiom. Also, the propositions may be expressed in a formal language or not, and may be, for example, singular or universal, and so forth.

Different sets of considerations would be brought to bear in the phenomenological analysis of these propositions, depending on the features we have noted, but on Husserl's view what they have in common, as expressions of intentions, is that they are *about* numbers or sets, and properties of or relations between these objects. They are not directed toward other kinds of objects, like physical aggregates or strings of signs. Husserl's view comports well with the ordinary view that the grammar and logic of mathematical language is not somehow deceptive and radically different from other parts of language. In fact, we can avoid from the outset the nominalist's problem, and all of the related problems, of having to explain how and why mathematics is really so much different from the way it appears to be and from the way it is actually taken to be in practice.[12] On Husserl's view we are to take mathematical language at face value, and to take mathematical theorems as true.

It should be noticed that we are, of course, taking these expressions of content to have a meaning. On Husserl's view language is, in fact, meaningful only insofar as it expresses intentions.[13] We can think of the content of an act as the meaning of the act by virtue of which we refer to an object or state of affairs. As Husserl puts it: "Under content we understand the 'meaning' of which we say that in it or through it consciousness refers to an object as its own" (*Ideas I*, §129). Intentionality and meaning theory thus go hand-in-hand. Husserl, in fact, calls for just the kind of reflection on or analysis of the meaning of sign-configurations for which there is no place in Hilbertian formalism but which Gödel's incompleteness theorems suggest we cannot avoid. Husserl thought it possible to do a good deal of phenomenology on the basis of reflecting on the content of our acts without being concerned about whether objects or referents of the acts existed or not. For example, we could seek to clarify descriptively the content (meaning) of our acts through genetic or "origins" analysis or through a procedure that Husserl called "free variation in imagination."[14] I shall have more to say about Husserl's views on the descriptive clarification of meaning below.

Husserl also has an account of the reliability of mathematics that is untouched by Gödel's theorems. I shall briefly describe this below. And on this view it is precisely by virtue of the meaning of sign-configurations that mathematicians are so interested in some systems of sign-configurations and not others. None of this, of course, means that formalization is not possible. Husserl was, in fact, quite favorably disposed toward efforts to formalize mathematical theories. It is only a matter of properly understanding what we are doing.[15] The effort to develop formalized mathematical languages can be viewed as an attempt to express what is essential to the form of the "noematic nucleus" of the acts, depending on various background assumptions.

The way that meaning is built up in our mathematical acts is also linked to the applications of mathematics. Husserl has an analysis of the "origins" of mathematical content according to which mathematical acts and contents are founded on more immediate perceptual acts and contents. To say they are "founded" means that they depend on such underlying acts and contents, which could exist even if there were no mathematics.[16] Husserl says that

[w]hat we have are acts which . . . *set up new objects*, acts in which something *appears as actual and self-given*, which was not given, and could not have been given, as what it now appears to be, in these foundational acts alone. *On the other hand, the new objects are based on the older ones, they are related to what appears in the basic acts.*   (*LI* VI §46)

Then it is a condition of the possibility of mathematical knowledge that there be acts of reflection on and abstraction from our basic sensory experience. Mathematical knowledge would not be possible without such acts. While formalist and fictionalist views get stuck on the problem of applications, Husserl could argue that parts of mathematics have applications because mathematics has its origins in our everyday experience in the first place. It is just that some of our idealizations, abstractions and formalizations in mathematics are quite far removed from their origins.

IV. MATHEMATICAL OBJECTS

If mathematical language is to be taken at face value, then on Husserl's theory of intentionality our mathematical beliefs are evidently about objects like numbers, sets, and functions, and not about objects of any other type. This fact, taken together with what Husserl says about the "ideal" nature of mathematical objects, suggests that we must confront the Platonists' problem of explaining how it is possible to know about ideal or abstract objects. Husserl's solution to this vexing problem is quite interesting. Let us approach it by considering his view of mathematical objects.

Perhaps the single most important thing to say about the conception of objects of cognition in Husserl's transcendental phenomenology, whether the objects be mathematical or physical, is that they are to be understood in terms of the "invariants" or "identities" in our experience. Many aspects of our experience are variable and in a constant state of flux and out of this flux, or against this background of variation, we find that certain invariants emerge.[17] Physical objects are identities that emerge for us through various sensory experiences or observations. Facts about such objects, obtained by empirical induction and expressed in empirical laws, are to be understood in the same way. Now Husserl argues that we also find invariants or regularities in our mathematical experience, although in mathematics the facts are not established, strictly speaking, by empirical induction. Mathematicians are not satisfied, for example, with establishing the truth of Goldbach's conjecture or Fermat's last theorem on the basis of inductive generalizations from specific numerical instances of these propositions. Rather, a mathematical proof is required.

In mathematics we suppose that different mathematicians are reasoning about the same number, or the same set, or the same function at different times and in different places, and if it were not the *same* object we were reasoning about in all these different circumstances, it would be very difficult to see how the science of mathematics would be possible at all. Mathematics would be utterly fragmented. No two statements of a theorem (or of theorems) could be about the same objects. But this is absurd. There are facts about mathematical objects, expressed in axioms and theorems, that constitute invariants across our experience with these objects. Note that this conception of an object is rather minimal compared to some conceptions, but this is perfectly appropriate given Husserl's plea that we not let our views be clouded from the outset with various philosophical presuppositions.[18]

Invariants may simply emerge as we gain more experience with objects, much as this happens in ordinary sense experience, or we may try to make them emerge through conscious and systematic efforts of the sort that are embodied in the methods of the sciences. Husserl argues that while both mathematical and physical objects are "invariants" in our experience, the meanings under which we think such objects are quite different.[19] Mathematical objects are not meant as "real" but, rather, they are meant as "abstract" or "ideal," and this meaning is derived from several sources. They could not be objects (identities) of sense experience, because objects of sense experience occur and change in space and time and interact causally with one another and with us. They could not be mental in nature, because what is mental occurs and changes in time. If mathematical objects were objects of either of these types, there would be no stability in mathematics. The ground would constantly be shifting beneath us. Husserl's extensive arguments against psychologism, nominalism, and other forms of empiricistic reductionism in the *Logical Investigations* and many other places are meant to ward off efforts to assimilate mathematical objects to the objects of "inner" or "outer" perception. Mathematical objects also cannot be assimilated to social or cultural objects, because social and cultural objects are bound to times and places. Thus, Husserl says that mathematical objects are not "bound idealities" but, rather, they are "free idealities."[20]

Objects like numbers are also identities that transcend consciousness in the sense that there are indefinitely many things we do not know about them at a given time, on the analogy with our knowledge of perceptual objects, but at the same time we can extend our knowledge of them by solving open problems, devising new methods, and so on. They transcend consciousness in the same way that physical objects do. And, similarly, we cannot will them to be anything we like, nor can we will anything to be true of them. They are mind-independent. On Husserl's view, unlike some empiricist or pragmatist views, it is not a puzzle that experimental methodologies in the physical sciences are different from methodologies in pure mathematics. Husserl was attempting to account for the fact, for example, that theorems of mathematics are not expressed probabilistically, and that we do not find in pure mathematics any statements referring to the space-time properties of the objects under consideration. Husserl's view also explains differences in the dynamics of the growth of the natural sciences and pure mathematics.

The abstractness of mathematical objects, on Husserl's view, implies and is implied by the fact that mathematical objects are unchanging, omnitemporal, and acausal. As we just noted, there is also a sense in which mathematical objects are mind-independent and transcendent. Husserl's position is nonetheless different from classical or naive platonism in a number of important respects. Husserl's is a phenomenological (and a transcendental) view of objects, not a classical metaphysical view. This means that objects are to be understood as invariants *in the phenomena* or in our actual experience in mathematics. The response to the nominalist is that the existence of mathematics presupposes that *there are* identities through difference, except that these are now simply understood as identities through the multiplicities of our own cognitive acts and processes. They are not anything more ultimate than that, not anything "metaphysical" lying behind the phenomena. This view is very much like what Kant has to say about empirical objects and empirical realism, except that now it is also applied to mathematical experience. On the *object* side of his analysis, Husserl can still claim to be a kind of realist about mathematical objects, for mathematical objects are not our own ideas. On the analogy with Kant's view of empirical objects, mathematical objects are not mental entities, nor are they fictions.

This view takes much of the sting out of standard nominalist objections to abstract objects, for such objections are directed toward naive metaphysical Platonism. But how can the nominalist object to a *phenomenological* account of the "invariants" in our mathematical experience without failing to respect that experience? Nominalism is just a kind of skepticism about abstract objects or universals. Skepticism about metaphysical objects that are supposed to somehow lie behind given phenomena is indeed warranted, but it would simply be disingenuous to doubt that there are invariants in mathematical experience. The latter kind of doubt is inconsistent with the daily practice of mathematicians. Let us go further in our response to nominalism by filling in the account of mathematical knowledge.

V. KNOWLEDGE OF MATHEMATICAL OBJECTS

We have already said enough about how "abstract" objects should be understood to go a considerable distance toward solving the problem of how knowledge of abstract objects is possible. This problem has figured centrally in the recent philosophy of mathematics, in part due to a particular formulation of it by Paul Benacerraf.[21] On Benacerraf's formulation, our best account of truth for mathematical statements, Tarski's, calls for the assignment of numbers to number terms, sets to set terms, functions to function terms, properties or relations to predicate terms, and the like. Since it is numbers, sets, functions, etc., that we are assigning, and not other objects that might be understood as concrete, the concept of truth for mathematical languages seems to require objects to which subjects could not stand in causal relations. Our best hope in epistemology, Benacerraf argues, is some form of a causal theory of knowledge. A causal theory of knowledge requires that for M to know that S there must be a causal relation between M and the referents of the names in S, or at least that there must have once been such a relation for someone. On these premises it is a deep puzzle as to how we could have any mathematical knowledge at all.

Almost no one now believes in the causal theory of knowledge in the exact form in which it was formulated by Benacerraf. That there is still a lingering problem, even for newer reliabilist accounts of knowledge, is shown by the literature in the philosophy of mathematics since Benacerraf's paper was published. Certain kinds of empiricists continue to think that some kind of causal link to objects is a condition at least for noninferential knowledge of objects. This has led some philosophers to go to rather extreme lengths, from a Husserlian perspective, to solve the puzzle. In recent work by Penelope Maddy and Jaegwon Kim, for example, it is argued that at least some abstract mathematical objects – sets of physical objects – exist in space and time, and hence are themselves the kinds of objects to which we can be causally related.[22] On the views of Maddy and Kim, we literally sense these *sets*, using the same kinds of neural mechanisms that we use to sense insects, even though we cannot sense other kinds of mathematical objects, like the set of real numbers or the empty set. The problem for these views is that they either equivocate on the notion of sensory perception or on the notion of

what counts as a mathematical object. It would presumably be a
mistake in mathematics itself, for example, to suppose that a set has
a color. If sets never have colors, what could it mean to say that they
are objects in the physical world that we sense through various
neural mechanisms? Husserl would object that these views do not
do justice to the nature of mathematical objects or to mathematical
knowledge. It could not be the case that some kinds of abstract,
mathematical objects are located in space and time, are subject to
causal interactions with other physical objects, are changeable, and
so on, while other abstract, mathematical objects do not have these
characteristics. From Husserl's viewpoint, attempts to solve the puzzle along these lines amount to imposing on mathematics a predeter-
mined philosophical position which simply does not fit the data.
One ends up twisting things out of shape to make the theory fit.

We can make some progress on the problem, however, if we start
with the relatively harmless idea of mathematical objects as invariants that persist across acts carried out by different mathematicians
at different times and places. Now even in the case of ordinary sense
perception it can be pointed out that the only way to identify a
perceptual object to which we believe we are causally related at a
stage in our experience is through ongoing perceptions which either
correct or fail to correct that identification. So the focus of our account will be on the sequences of acts through which evidence for
mathematical objects (invariants) is acquired, and on this basis we
can give an account of how we come to reject some propositions in
mathematics but to accept others. Let us first briefly consider the
analysis of how we reject propositions.

Mathematical objects and facts have a stability over time in our
mathematical experience. In mathematical experience, as in ordinary perceptual experience, it can happen that what is believed to be
an object at one stage of our experience is later seen to be an illusion.
Thus, suppose we have an axiom from which we can derive the
existence of a particular object, like the set that contains all and only
those sets that do not contain themselves. Then at a later stage of
our experience we see that in believing that such a set exists we are
led to a contradiction. Thus, at the earlier stage of our experience we
were under an illusion about the existence of this "object," and
about the "axiom" or "fact" from which its existence was derived.
This is an "object" which does not persist over time, which does not

have any stability in our mathematical experience. Husserl says that the experience in which such an object is intended as existing "explodes," due to the discovered contradiction.[23] (This is something that Frege may have experienced first-hand.) Many other examples could be used to illustrate the same point. For example, round squares are not regarded as mathematical objects and there are no positive existence statements about them in mathematics because the assumption that they exist leads to contradiction, even though the expression "round square" does, of course, have a meaning. Likewise, there can be no (universal) Turing machine which determines whether an arbitrary Turing machine running on an arbirary input halts or not. We now know that there could be no such mathematical object, although there was uncertainty about this at earlier stages of our experience with the concept of a mechanical procedure or recursive function.

So much for the basic idea of how we come to reject certain kinds of propositions in mathematics. The account of how we come to accept propositions in mathematics is more complex, for there are, in effect, different types and degrees of acceptance depending on the kinds of evidence that we might acquire in multiplicities of acts. A justified belief in the existence of an object toward which an act is directed will depend on what Husserl calls the *fulfillment*, partial or otherwise, of an (empty) intention directed toward the object, and one cannot have evidence for existence independently of this.[24] There is no room for any mysterious source of knowledge on this account. Husserl distinguished different types and degrees of evidence. Thus, one might or might not have evidence that is apodictic, adequate, clear, and distinct.[25] Briefly put, apodictic evidence is evidence of necessity, while adequate evidence is evidence in which every possible act required to make the knowledge of an object complete would be carried out. Since infinitely many acts would be required for perfect knowledge, Husserl regards perfect adequacy as an ideal. There are only degrees of adequacy/inadequacy. There are also degrees of clarity and distinctness of evidence.

Husserl uses the idea of the fulfillment of an empty intention to define intuition: we (partially) intuit an object when our intention toward the object is (partially) fulfilled. The basic distinction between an empty and a fulfilled intention is straightforward. An intention is fulfilled when the object intended is actually experienced, and is fulfillable when the object could be experienced. If existence proofs in mathematics are supposed to be expressions of the *knowledge* that *objects* of our intentions exist, then we must evidently actually experience the object, or at least possess the means for coming to experience it, and not merely produce a contradiction from the assumption that the object does not exist. In the latter case, we have only the bare contradiction. We are not presented with or do not see the object, even partially, nor are we given any means to find the object. It may be that our reasoning in a particular domain of research stabilizes over time as we build up more propositions on the basis of indirect proofs, and we may even hold that this is a way of "filling in" our mathematical knowledge, but this is still not the same thing as being presented with an object, or with having an intention toward an object be fulfillable. Husserl's view of the presence or absence of objects like numbers, sets, functions, and so on, thus takes on a "constructivist" slant. This is already suggested above by our talk about objects being invariants *in our experience*. Saying that *objects* are invariants in our experience must be counted as different from saying that sets of thoughts-about-objects have some stability in our experience.

Other elements of Husserl's view on cognitive acts and processes in mathematics, and on the genetic analysis of mathematical concepts, also point to an epistemology of mathematical objects that is constructivist or "critical" in a Kantian sense. In fact, these ideas have struck a chord in a number of logicians and mathematicians who have studied Husserl's work, including Hermann Weyl, Oskar Becker, Arend Heyting, and Per Martin-Löf.[26] Indeed, Becker and Heyting straightforwardly identified fulfilled mathematical intentions with constructions. Husserl's views on mathematics do share a number of themes with traditional intuitionism, as a consequence of the fact that both views are concerned with mathematical cognition, but it is clear that Husserl would be critical of the strains of subjective idealism, solipsism, extreme anti-formalism, and psychologism that can be found in Brouwerian intuitionism. Husserl also has a more sophisticated philosophical view of meaning and mathematical objects than can be found in traditional intuitionism, and I do not think that one could argue for the actual rejection of parts of mathematics on phenomenological grounds.[27] One could account for non-constructive parts of mathematics on the basis of

Husserl's views about idealization, abstraction, and formalization. Intuitionism, however, is a form of constructivism that recognizes some abstract objects, e.g., objects that cannot be encoded in the natural numbers, and this is one respect in which it is similar to Husserl's view.[28] Gödel has also suggested a position in the philosophy of mathematics that combines epistemological constructivism with abstract objects.[29]

Like Kant's transcendental philosophy, Husserl's transcendental phenomenology contains a critique of knowledge. Unlike Kant, however, Husserl was in a position to see what this meant in the case of modern mathematics and to carry the idea further in the case of mathematical knowledge. Husserl's view strikes a balance between criticisms of mathematical knowledge that are too restrictive, like those of ultrafinitism or finitism, and completely uncritical views on mathematical knowledge, like those of naive Platonism or naive rationalism. On the phenomenological view, mathematics will be reliable to the extent that our intentions toward mathematical objects are fulfillable in different degrees. Indeed, an analysis of processes of fulfillment might even be offered as an account of the "reliable processes" sought by reliabilism. Parts of mathematical experience in which we do not have fulfillable intentions to objects will be reliable to the extent that they have at least stabilized over time in such a way as to allow for the development of new propositions, new methods, and so on. None of this, however, gives us absolute security. There are only degrees of security.

As is the case in other areas of cognition, mathematical intentions are to be viewed as expectations about objects or states of affairs, where these expectations are a function of the knowledge we have acquired up to the present time. They have their associated "horizons" in which the possibilities of filling in our knowledge are determined by the meaning of the act.[30] Husserl says that these possibilities depend on structures of cognition that are governed by rules. Our expectations can then either be realized, partially realized, or can fail to be realized. Now, as suggested above, Husserl was well aware of the fact that there are limitations on intuition, and, hence, on the kind of direct evidence we can have in mathematics. We cannot, for example, complete an infinite number of intuitions. In a section of *Formal and Transcendental Logic* on the "idealizing presuppositions of logic and the constitutive criticism of them," he says, for example, that the subjective correlate of "reiterational infinity" is that one can carry out an infinite sequence of acts. He says that "this is plainly an idealization," since, in fact, no one has such an ability (*FTL*, §74). The limitations on human knowledge are clearly noted in his discussions of types and degrees of evidence, and in other places where he recognizes the finiteness in time and space of human experience. Husserl therefore says that there is no such thing as absolute evidence which would correspond to absolute truth. All truth is "truth within its horizons" (*FTL*, §105).

Now in a Tarskian theory of truth, invoked by Benacerraf, we are in effect dealing with a dead or frozen relationship between a formal language and mathematical objects. The relationship can be highly idealized if "truth" is abstracted from the horizons of subjects who know about truth or if, as Husserl says, it is detached from the "living intentionality" of human subjects. The way to solve Benacerraf's problem, and indeed the problem of the relation of the subjective to the objective in mathematics posed earlier by Husserl, can be summed up as follows. We can agree that mathematical objects are "abstract" and that number terms, function terms, and so on, refer to such objects. But what we mean by this is that these terms refer to the invariants or identities found in the multiplicities of our mathematical acts and processes. We *know* about these invariants in the way indicated above, that is, through sequences of acts in which we have evidence for their existence, even if we know about them only partially or incompletely. Otherwise, they are merely intended, in the sense that an intention directed toward an object exists even if we do not experience the object itself, and these intentions may have some stability in our experience. Note that at no point in this argument for how mathematical knowledge is possible do we suppose that we are causally related to mathematical objects.

VI. AGAINST FICTIONALISM

Many basic objections to fictionalism about mathematical objects, and to assimilating mathematics to fiction, fall out of what has already been said above. We have seen that Husserl does not wish to be understood as a "naive" realist or platonist about mathematical objects, but he is also not a fictionalist. Husserl says:

It is naturally not our intention to put the *being of what is ideal* on a level with the *being-thought-of which characterizes the fictitious or the nonsensical.*   (*LI* II §8)

Let us consider some of the objections that can be raised to fictionalism. Our intentions toward some mathematical objects are fulfillable, but it is not clear what it could mean for intentions to fictional objects to be fulfillable. Even where our intentions to mathematical objects are not presently fulfillable we should hesitate to assimilate these intentions to intentions expressed in fiction. Generally, the idea that mathematical objects are fictions runs contrary to the way that these objects are intended in the science of mathematics. For example, various kinds of existence statements abound in mathematics texts, and it is not the business of the philosopher of mathematics to explain these away. They are to be taken at face value, and it is the business of the philosopher to explain how they are possible. In texts concerning fictional objects, we do not, however, find statements asserting the existence of objects. If the concept of existence even appears in such a context, it is subject to various anomalies that are not present in mathematical language. A very substantial difference between mathematics and fiction is suggested by Husserl's discussion of reason and actuality[31]: a sustained belief in the existence of fictional objects, as distinct from merely imagining such objects, is a sign of irrationality. It is a psychopathological phenomenon. On the other hand, belief in the existence of mathematical objects, in the sense in which one believes existence theorems one has read in a mathematics text, is not at all a sign of irrationality. On the contrary, mathematics is usually taken to be one of the finest achievements of reason.

Other differences are also manifest. The idea of obtaining contradictions from the assumption of the existence of certain objects, which shows how such "objects" do not have any stability in our mathematical experience, has no analog in our understanding of fiction. There is also a disanalogy concerning questions of the development of knowledge and of the determinacy of mathematical intentions when compared to intentions in fiction. Thus, when we ask "Was Hamlet over 6' tall or not?," we find that no determinate answer could be given. Of course, we could extend the story of Hamlet however we like so that we get a determinate answer, but this is not at all how open problems are solved in the discipline of mathematics. It could also be argued that mathematics ought not to be assimilated to fiction because mathematics has extremely rich and fruitful applications. It is not clear how this would be possible if mathematics were nothing but fiction. We might generalize from the point Kant made about empirical objects: mathematical objects ought not to be construed as "fictions" just because we have no God's-eye view of them, or because it would be wrong to understand them as noumenal "things-in-themselves."

VII. DESCRIPTIVE CLARIFICATION OF THE MEANING OF MATHEMATICAL CONCEPTS

We just said that we do not solve problems in mathematics by extending the mathematical "story" any way we like. On Husserl's view, there is a kind of evidence that is intrinsic to mathematics. Husserl's mature conception of the phenomenological method includes the idea of descriptive clarification of the content (meaning) of our acts through the procedure of free variation in imagination and through the analysis of the "origins" of content. I do not have the space to discuss Husserl's ideas on genetic analysis and free variation here, but I would like to note that what lies behind these ideas is the belief in the kind of informal rigor mentioned at the beginning of this paper. The idea of informal rigor is that one obtains definitions, rules, and axioms by analyzing informal, intuitive concepts and putting down their properties. On Husserl's view informal, intuitive concepts in mathematics are assumed to be significant, and it is believed that we can extend our knowledge of such concepts, make them precise, and gain insight into the fundamental relations that hold among them through genetic analysis and free variation.

This helps us to account for the problem the pragmatist has of explaining why mathematicians are not gripped only by considerations of fruitfulness in their research. As the example of the continuum hypothesis shows, set theorists are concerned about whether proposed axioms are faithful to an intuitive, iterative concept of set. There is evidence that is unique to mathematics which supports our beliefs in certain axioms. Moreover, we can solve the Quinean problem of explaining the obviousness of elementary mathematics precisely on the basis of the concept of mathematical intuition described above. There is, within mathematics itself, a distinction between more observable and more theoretical parts of research, and between what is closer to and farther from its origins in the "life-world" of everyday perceptions and practices.[32] Husserl's view also helps us to solve problems of conventionalism and formalism. We cannot make the invariants in our mathematical experience be anything we want them to be. Mathematical theories are not arbitrary creations but rather we are "forced" in certain ways in the development of mathematical knowledge. We do not, for example, solve open problems by convention.

It is important that Husserl is advocating a descriptive method for clarification of the meaning of mathematical concepts. A good deal of philosophical methodology, especially in the analytic tradition of philosophy, is concerned with offering arguments for the truth of various assertions. There is clearly a problem in trying to apply this methodology to elucidate primitive terms and to justify axioms of mathematical theories since with it one only succeeds in backing the problem up a step by depending on other unanalyzed concepts and propositions. As an alternative, Husserl's philosophy suggests that it is possible to understand the meaning of some mathematical assertions not only through argument but also through careful, detailed description of a concept, like the iterative concept of set. Husserl's work thus suggests that there is a way out of the old philosophical problem of how we should understand the meanings of the primitive terms and axioms of mathematical theories.

VIII. CONCLUSION

The views described above are framed in Husserl's later philosophy by a variety of interconnected arguments against empiricism, naturalism, nominalism, and psychologism in mathematics. It is clear from comments in the "Prolegomena to Pure Logic" and other places in the *Logical Investigations* that Husserl sees nominalism and psychologism as species of empiricism or naturalism about mathematics. They are forms of empiricistic reductionism, and Husserl is generally opposed to reductionism in the philosophy of mathematics. In his critique in *Philosophie der Arithmetik* of Frege, who is certainly no empiricist about mathematics, we see Husserl pointing out that Frege's extensional definition of number also amounts to a kind of reductionism about the meaning of the concept of number.[33] Husserl is concerned that any of the above-mentioned views do not do justice to our mathematical intentions and to the way in which mathematical objects are intended in our acts. The views simply do not do justice to what we know in the science of mathematics. For the same general reasons, his view would be opposed to conventionalism, and to any kind of strict formalism about mathematics. His views on formalism do not entail that formalization in mathematics has no value. On the contrary, formalization of our mathematical concepts is quite important. However, from everything that Husserl says about intentionality, meaning, formal (as opposed to transcendental) logic, the idealizations and abstractions from experience required by formal systems, and the kind of informal rigor which makes mathematics possible, it is clear that Husserl is not a Hilbertian formalist.

Husserl thus gives us a way to solve the Platonists' problem while avoiding the problems of nominalism and fictionalism. His call for a "transcendental" foundation of mathematics is unaffected by Gödel's incompleteness theorems and the problems of "meaningless" syntax, but it also avoids the problems that result from the pragmatic overemphasis on fruitfulness and from supposing that mathematics is nothing but convention.[34]

NOTES

1 See Hartry Field, *Realism, Mathematics and Modality*, (Oxford: Basil Blackwell, 1989).

2 Gödel links these claims directly to Husserlian phenomenology in "The Modern Development of the Foundations of Mathematics in the Light of Philosophy." This is an unpublished translation by E. Köhler and H. Wang of a 1961 shorthand draft of a lecture that was never given. To appear in *Kurt Gödel: Collected Works*, Volume III.

3 See Parsons, "Mathematical Intuition," *Proceedings of the Aristotelian Society* 80 (1980): 151.

4 See Georg Kreisel, "Informal Rigour and Completeness Proofs," in Imre Lakatos, ed., *Problems in the Philosophy of Mathematics*, (Amsterdam: North-Holland, 1967, 138–86).

5 Zermelo's earliest description is in "Über Grenzzahlen und Mengenbereiche," *Fundamenta Mathematicae* 16 (1930):29–47.

6 See Troelstra, Anne, and van Dalen, Dirk, *Constructivism in Mathematics*, Vol. II, (Amsterdam: North-Holland, 1988), 645–57).

7 For some of the background of Husserl's mathematical training, see especially J. P. Miller, *Numbers in Presence and Absence*, (The Hague: Nijhoff, 1982). Also, Dieter Lohmar, *Phänomenologie der Mathematik*, (Dordrecht: Kluwer, 1989). Other works on or related to Husserl's philosophy of mathematics are Guillermo Rosado-Haddock, "Husserl's Epistemology of Mathematics and the Foundation of Platonism in Mathematics," *Husserl Studies* 4 (1987):81–102, Gian-Carlo Rota, "Husserl and the Reform of Logic" and "Husserl," in M. Kac, G-C. Rota, and J. Schwartz, eds., *Discrete Thoughts*, (Boston: Birkhäuser, 1986), Roger Schmit, *Husserls Philosophie der Mathematik. Platonistische und konstruktivistische Momente in Husserls Mathematikbegriff*, (Bonn: Grundmann, 1981), Thomas Seebohm, Dagfinn Føllesdal, and Jitendra Nath Mohanty, eds., *Phenomenology and the Formal Sciences*, (Dordrecht: Kluwer, 1991), Richard Tieszen, *Mathematical Intuition: Phenomenology and Mathematical Knowledge*, (Boston: Kluwer, 1989), Robert Tragesser, *Phenomenology and Logic*, (Ithaca, New York: Cornell University Press, 1977), and *Husserl and Realism in Logic and Mathematics*, (Cambridge: Cambridge University Press, 1984), Dallas Willard, *Logic and the Objectivity of Knowledge*, (Athens, Ohio: Ohio University Press, 1984).

8 See, for example, Husserl's *Philosophie der Arithmetik*, Husserliana Vol. XII, (The Hague: Nijhoff, 1970); "Philosophy as Rigorous Science," in P. McCormick, and F. Elliston, eds., *Husserl: Shorter Works*, (Notre Dame, Indiana: Notre Dame University Press, 1977), 172); *Formal and Transcendental Logic*, (The Hague: Nijhoff, 1969, §100); *The Crisis of European Sciences and Transcendental Phenomenology*, (Evanston, Ill.: Northwestern University Press, 1970, Appendix VI). We refer to this latter work hereafter as the *Crisis*. Also, *Experience and Judgment*, (Evanston, Ill.: Northwestern University Press, 1973), §§3–4).

9 See Gottlob Frege, "The Thought," in *Mind* 65 (1956):289–311.

10 Kurt Gödel, "What is Cantor's Continuum Problems?," in Feferman, Solomon, et al., eds., *Kurt Gödel: Collected Works*, Vol. II, (Oxford: Oxford University Press, 1990), 483. See also Richard Tieszen, "Kurt Gödel and Phenomenology," *Philosophy of Science* 59 (1992):176–94.

11 See especially Edmund Husserl, *Ideas Pertaining to a Pure Phenomenology and to a Phenomenological Philosophy*, (The Hague: Nijhoff, 1983), §§36–37, 84, 87–102, 128–35). We refer to this work hereafter as *Ideas I*. Also, *Logical Investigations*, Investigations I and V, (London: Routledge and Kegan Paul, 1970).

12 For Husserl's specific criticisms of nominalism, see especially the *Logical Investigations*, Investigation II, §§2, 7–8, 14, 26 speak to the issue of

taking language about mathematical objects and universals at face value. See also the *Ideas I*, §§1–26.

13 See the *Logical Investigations*, Investigations I and V; and the *Ideas I*, §§87–91 and 128–33.

14 On "free variation," see "Philosophy as Rigorous Science," *Experience and Judgment*, §§87–93; and *Ideas*, §§67–72.

15 Husserl's views on formalization and formalism are scattered throughout the *Logical Investigations*, *Ideas I*, *Formal and Transcendental Logic*, and various unpublished writings and letters. For my remarks here, see especially *Formal and Transcendental Logic*, §§73–93, 101–7; and the *Logical Investigations*, Investigation I, §20.

16 The themes of genetic analysis, founding and founded acts, and acts of reflection and abstraction are found throughout Husserl's work. See, for example, *Logical Investigations*, Investigation VI, §§40–58; *Formal and Transcendental Logic*, §§70–71, 82–91; *Experience and Judgment*; and the *Crisis*, Appendix VI, "The Origin of Geometry." See also Richard Tieszen, *Mathematical Intuition* (note 7 above).

17 See, e.g., *Formal and Transcendental Logic*, §§61–63; *Cartesian Meditations*, §§17–18, 21 (The Hague: Nijhoff, 1970); and *Experience and Judgment*, §§13, 64–65.

18 See, e.g., *Ideas I*, §§19–23, and "Philosophy as Rigorous Science."

19 See, e.g., *Logical Investigations*, "Prolegomena to Pure Logic," Investigation II, Investigation VI, §§40–58; *Formal and Transcendental Logic*, §§55–68, 82–87; *Ideas I*, §§1–26; *Experience and Judgment*, §§63–65.

20 See *Experience and Judgment*, §65.

21 Paul Benacerraf, "Mathematical Truth," in Paul Benacerraf, and Hilary Putnam, eds., *Philosophy of Mathematics: Selected Readings* (2nd edition), (Cambridge: Cambridge University Press, 1983), 403–20.

22 Penelope Maddy, *Realism in Mathematics*, (Oxford: Oxford University Press, 1990), Chap. 2. Also, Jaegwon Kim, "The Role of Perception in *A Priori* Knowledge," *Philosophical Studies* 40 (1981): 339–54.

23 *Ideas I*, §§138, 151.

24 See *Logical Investigations*, Investigation VI, §§1–29, 36–48; *Ideas I*, §§136–41.

25 *Formal and Transcendental Logic*, §§58–60, 69, 78–80, 82–91, 105–7; *Cartesian Meditations*, §6; *Ideas I*, §§67–71, §§238.

26 See Hermann Weyl, *Das Kontinuum*, (Leipzig: Veit, 1918), and "Comments on Hilbert's Second Lecture on the Foundations of Mathematics," in Jan van Heijenoort, ed., *From Frege to Gödel*, (Cambridge, Mass.: Harvard University Press, 1977), 480–84. Oskar Becker, *Mathematische Existenz: Untersuchungen zur Logik und Ontologie mathematischer Phänomene*, (Halle: Niemeyer, 1927), Arend Heyting, "The Intuitionist

Foundations of Mathematics," in Paul Benacerraf and Hilary Putnam, eds., 1983, 52–61. Per Martin-Löf, "Truth of a Proposition, Evidence of a Judgment, Validity of a Proof," *Synthese* 73 (1987): 407–20. Also, Richard Tieszen, "Review of D. Lohmar, *Phänomenologie der Mathematik,*" *Husserl Studies* 7 (1991):199–205, and "What is a Proof?," in Michael Detlefsen, ed., *Proof, Logic and Formalization,* (London: Routledge, 1992), 57–76.

27 See Richard Tieszen, "What is the Philosophical Basis of Intuitionistic Mathematics?," forthcoming in D. Prawitz, B. Skyrms, and D. Westerståhl, eds., *Logic, Methodolgoy and Philosophy of Science IX,* (Amsterdam: North-Holland).

28 See Richard Tieszen, "Mathematical Intuition and Husserl's Phenomenology," *Noûs* 18 (1984):395–421.

29 Kurt Gödel, "On an Extension of Finitary Mathematics Which Has Not Yet Been Used," in Feferman, Solomon, et al., eds., 1990, 271–80.

30 On the concept of the "horizon" of an act, see *Ideas I,* §§27, 44, 47, 63, 69, 82–83, 142; *Experience and Judgment,* §8; *Cartesian Meditations,* §22.

31 *Ideas,* §§136, 138.

32 The concept of the "lifeworld" in Husserl's later philosophy is an outgrowth of his earlier ideas on founding and founded acts, genetic analysis, and related themes. See especially the *Crisis,* §§9, 33–38, and Appendix VII.

33 See Richard Tieszen, "Husserl and Frege on Number," *Ratio* (New Series) 3 (1990):150–64.

34 I would like to thank Barry Smith for helpful editorial comments and suggestions.

10 Part-whole

Husserl's third *Logical Investigation* is perhaps the most significant treatise on the concept of part to be found in the philosophical literature.[1] In it Husserl attempts to analyze the notion of dependent part, to lay down the principles governing its use, and to relate it to more general considerations concerning the nature of necessity and unity.

He begins his study with the consideration of objects in the psychological sphere. A typical example of the kind of object he has in mind is that of a visual datum, a red patch, let us say, and its various aspects or "moments" – its colour, say, or its extension. He takes each of these moments to be peculiar to the object in question; no other datum, no matter how great its resemblance to the original datum, will have the very same moments. He also takes the moments to be, in a suitably broad sense, part of the given object; they are thought to be actually present in it.

Now Husserl is struck, as was his teacher Stumpf, by a peculiar ontological difference between the datum and its moments. The moments are, in a certain sense, *dependent* objects; they cannot stand on their own. The datum, on the other hand, is independent, capable of standing on its own. Husserl is, therefore, concerned to pin down this distinction, to state exactly in what it consists.

But although Husserl begins his study with examples from the psychological sphere, he intends his conclusions to have universal validity and to be applicable to all objects whatever, whether psychological or not. Thus no appeal is to be made to those features that are peculiar to the examples at hand, but only to those that are properly generalizable.

The resulting account contains many interesting ideas concerning the concept of part. For Husserl has a keen eye for the complexity and structure that results from this broader perspective on the concept. He sees that different kinds of dependency can hold among the parts of an object (466–76); he recognizes that the notion of part can, in a significant sense, be iterated, with the "moments" themselves having pieces or moments as parts (467–68); and he realizes that the resulting hierarchy of parts embodies a well-defined notion of level (470–72). He is also able to frame a "glueless" theory of the unity of an object in terms of the interlocking of its dependent parts (476–81).

The account is interesting in other ways as well. Husserl has a clear conception of an objective and metaphysical sense of necessity, as opposed to a subjective or empirical sense (446). He is clear on the *de re/de dicto* distinction (§11, 456–57) and held the currently topical view that *de re* necessary truths are rooted in the essence of things (§6, 445–46 passim). He considered it an important task for ontology to lay out these *de re* truths and regarded his own work on part-whole as merely part of this larger project (482).

The incidental remarks are also often very insightful – for example, those concerning the notion of boundary in §17, 468, and the notion of the specious present in §13, 461. Such is the range of the work that it is with a growing sense of excitement that one discovers the riches that lie beneath its rough and seemingly impenetrable exterior.

My aim in the present essay is to clarify certain formal aspects of Husserl's thought. I have here and there inserted some critical comments; but my main concern has been to say what the views are, and not to say whether or not they are right. Husserl himself took the formalization of his ideas to be not only possible, but highly desirable. He writes (§24, 484):

a proper working out of the pure theory we here have in mind would have to define all concepts with mathematical exactness and to deduce all theorems by *argumenta in forma*, i.e., mathematically. . . . That this end can be achieved has been shown by the small beginnings of a purely formal treatment in our present chapter. In any case, the progress from vaguely formed to mathematically exact concepts and theories is here, as everywhere, the precondition for full insight into *a priori* connections and an inescapable demand of science.

Thus the present paper can be regarded as an attempt to carry though the project that he began.

Unfortunately, his own "small beginnings" are rather feeble by modern standards and do not even compare well with other formal work which was being done at the time. A general difficulty in his approach is that he mixes up the generic and the objectual formulation of foundational facts. The locution "an *A* is founded on a *B*" may either be taken to indicate a relation between two individuals, which happen to be of the respective species *A* and *B*, or to indicate a relation between the two species *A* and *B* themselves.

Husserl himself is quite clear on the difference. He writes (§7a, 448):

Our distinctions have first of all related to the being of particular individuals thought of in "ideal universality," i.e., of such individuals treated purely as instances of Ideas. But they obviously carry over to Ideas themselves, which can, in a corresponding, if somewhat modified sense, be spoken of as "independent" and "non-independent."

All the same, it is often not clear, in particular passages, whether he has the objectual or the generic notions in mind. To take but one example from many, when he writes (§21, 473), "*A content of the species A is founded upon a content of the species B*, if an *A* can in its essence . . . not exist, unless a *B* also exists," it would appear as if the generic relation is being defined. But later when he talks of how "the same whole can be interpenetrative in relation to certain parts, and combinatory in relation to others," it would appear from the context that he has the objectual notion in mind. So somehow he has made the transition from the one notion to the other. But it is not clear from the passage either when the transition is made or how it is to be legitimated.

It is clear that Husserl thinks that the objectual notions are somehow to be understood in terms of the generic ones; and it is for this reason that he generally prefers to invoke reference to the species. But the theory of species and of their connection with objects is best guided by the much simpler and less problematic theory of objects; and, for this reason, it seems advisable to begin with the theory of objects. Such a procedure will still be compatible with a reduction of the objectual to the generic; but the reduction will emerge as a consequence of, rather than as precondition for, the formal development.

That part of Husserl's theory which concerns only the relations of foundation and part among objects I call the *core*. My main concern in this work is with the core, although I do sketch the principal ways in which the core might be extended.

Various other philosophers have taken up the task of formalizing Husserl's theory. The first attempt was made by Simons (1982), and a subsequent attempt was made by Null (1983). An overview of the different approaches, including my own, is given in Simons (1987); and I refer the reader to that work for details.

The systems from my notes, as presented in Simons (1987), are somewhat different from the systems presented here. The present paper also contains a more delicate discussion of the "six theorems" and includes supplementary material on a variety of different topics.

I. THE SIX THEOREMS

We adopt the following notational conventions: the letters x, y and z and variants thereof are used as variables for objects; the letters α, β and τ and variants are used as variables for species; $\leq$ is used for the relation of part to whole, F for the relation of foundation, and I for the relation of membership between an object and species. We also use $\square_{x,\alpha}$ to stand in for the locution: x as an α is such that.[2]

Let us first deal with Husserl's six propositions (§14, 463–65). We may be brief, since the matter has been very satisfactorily covered by Simons (1982). Our aim is to uncover the basis in the core for the propositions which Husserl wishes to assert.

The most natural formulation of his first proposition is as follows:

P1. $\exists x(xI\alpha \;\&\; \square_{x,\alpha}\exists y(yI\beta \;\&\; xFy)) \rightarrow \forall x^+(\exists x(xI\alpha \;\&\; x \leq x^+) \;\&\; \neg\exists y(yI\beta \;\&\; y \leq x^+)) \rightarrow \exists y(yI\beta \;\&\; x^+Fy))$.

In other words, if an α as such is founded upon a β, then every whole containing an α but not a β as a part is founded upon a β.

Husserl takes this proposition to be an axiom or, at least, "axiomatically self-evident" (464); and so the problem which arises for the proponent of the core is whether there is a reasonable basis for this proposition, i.e., of whether there is a core proposition which is as reasonable as the given proposition and from which it follows.

I maintain that there is such a proposition, viz.:

A1. $(xFy \;\&\; x \leq x^+ \;\&\; \neg(y \leq x^+)) \rightarrow x^+Fy$.

That is to say, if one object is founded upon another, then so is every object containing the first as long as it does not already contain the second.

We may derive P1 from A1 in the following way. Let the antecedent of P1 be ϕ and its consequent be ψ. Let ϕ' be the statement: $\forall x(xI\alpha \rightarrow \exists y(yI\beta \,\&\, xFy))$. (This is a kind of non-modal version of ϕ; and it is interesting that Husserl's gloss on P1 at p. 464 is more suggestive of the non-modal claim.) Then it is readily shown that $\phi' \rightarrow \psi$ is a logical consequence of A1. Now let us also make the reasonable assumption that truths as such are generalizable, i.e.:

B1. $\Box_{x,\alpha}\chi \rightarrow \forall x(xI\alpha \rightarrow \chi)$.

If an α as such χ's then every α χ's. (Indeed, B1 should probably, in its turn, be based upon the following two propositions:

$\Box_{x,\alpha}\chi \rightarrow \forall x(xI\alpha \rightarrow \Box_{x,\alpha}\chi)$
(if an α as such χ's, then every α as such χ's);
$\Box_{x,\alpha}\chi \rightarrow \chi$
(if an α as such χ's then it χ's).)

ϕ' can then be deduced from ϕ; and so P1 $= \phi \rightarrow \chi$ can be deduced from $\phi' \rightarrow \chi$.

Moreover, A1 appears to be as reasonable as P1. Indeed, it is hard to see how anyone could accept P1 except on the basis of A1. We have here then a simple illustration of how reference to species and essence has muddied the conceptual waters.

For the formulation of Husserl's second proposition, we need to define the notions of dependent part, independent whole and relativized dependent part:

D1. $DP(x) =_{df} \exists x(xFy)$;
D2. $IW(x) =_{df} \neg DP(x)$;
D3. $DP_z(x) =_{df} (\exists y \leq z)(xFy)$.

The natural formulation of the second proposition is then as follows:

P2. $(x \leq x^+ \,\&\, xFy \,\&\, \neg\, y \leq x^+) \rightarrow$
       $DP(x^+) \,\&\, \forall z(x \leq z \,\&\, x^+ \leq z \,\&\, IW(z) \rightarrow$
       $DP_z(x^+))$.

If one object is founded upon another, then any object containing the first but not the second is dependent both absolutely and relatively to any independent whole which contains the two given objects.

Husserl takes this proposition to be a corollary of the first, i.e., P1. But as Simons points out (1982), 128–30), the argument does not go through. However, T2 does follow from A1; and this is further evidence that Husserl treats A1 as a basis for T1. It is also significant in this regard that the other propositions are formulated directly in terms of objects (or "contents") and not in terms of species and essence. This suggests that the purpose of the reference to species in the first axiom was to bring out the ontological ground behind a purely objectual principle.

To formulate the third proposition, we need the notion of independent part:

$$D4. \quad xIPy =_{df} x \leq y \ \& \ \neg \ (\exists y' \leq y)(xFy').$$

(Independent parts of a whole are parts not founded on any part of the whole.) The third proposition then becomes:

$$P3. \quad xIPy \ \& \ yIPz \rightarrow xIPz.$$

The proof uses the transitivity of part-whole:

$$A2. \quad x \leq y \ \& \ y \leq z \rightarrow x \leq z;$$

and is rather nice. Suppose $xIPy$ and $yIPz$. Then $x \leq y$ and $y \leq z$. So by A2, $x \leq z$. Suppose for reductio that not $xIPz$. Then for some u, xFu and $u \leq z$. If $u \leq y$, then not $xIPy$. So not $u \leq y$. Since also $x \leq y$ and xFu, yFu by A1. But since $u \leq z$, not $yIPz$ after all.

Essentially the same proof is given by Husserl.[3]

The relation of dependent part may be defined by:

$$D5. \quad xDPy =_{df} x \leq y \ \& \ (\exists z \leq y)(xFz).$$

Husserl's fourth proposition is then:

$$P4. \quad xDPy \ \& \ y \leq z \rightarrow xDPz.$$

This proposition is a trivial consequence of the transitivity of $\leq$ (A2). The fifth proposition (without its second part) may be rendered as:

P5. $DP_y(x) \rightarrow DPx$.

This is a trivial consequence of the definitions.

Relative independence may be defined by:

D6. $I_z(x) =_{df} \neg(\exists y \leq z)(xFy)$.

Proposition 6, namely:

P6. $xIPz \ \& \ yIPz \rightarrow I_y(x)$

is then a trivial consequence of the definitions and A2.

II. WEAK AND STRICT FOUNDATION

The proofs of Husserl's six propositions make very little use of the fundamental properties of part and foundation. The first two propositions are straightforward consequences of axiom A1; propositions 4 and 6 are trivial consequences of axiom A2; proposition 5 is analytic; and proposition 3, which is the only interesting result, is a consequence of both the axioms. It is therefore natural to wonder what other axioms should be laid down.

I conjecture that the following axioms constitute a reasonable basis for the kind of theory Husserl had in mind:

Axioms for Part

AP1.	(Reflexivity)	$x \leq x$;
AP2.	(Transitivity)	$x \leq y \ \& \ y \leq z \rightarrow x \leq z$;
AP3.	(Anti-symmetry)	$x \leq y \ \& \ y \leq x \rightarrow x = y$;

Axioms for Foundation

AF1.	(Apartness)	$xFy \rightarrow \neg \ y \leq x$;
AF2.	(Qualified transitivity)	$xFy \ \& \ yFz \ \& \ \neg \ x \leq z \rightarrow xFz$;
AF3.	(Addition on the left)	$xFy \ \& \ x \leq x^+ \ \& \ \neg \ y \leq x^+ \rightarrow x^+Fy$;

AF4.   (Subtraction on the right) $xFy \ \& \ y' \leq y \ \& \ \neg \ y' \leq x \rightarrow xFy'$;
AF5.   (Integrity) $\exists y(xFy) \rightarrow \exists y(xFy \ \& \ x \leq y \ \&$
                                                     $\forall z(xFz \rightarrow z \leq y))$;

The first of the foundational axioms, AF1, states that no object is founded on any of its parts. The second states that if one object is founded on a second and the second on a third, then the first is founded on the third as long as the third is not part of the first. The next two axioms state that if one object is founded on another then any whole containing the first is founded on the second and the first is founded on any part of the second, again subject to the qualification that the second of the resulting objects should not be part of the first. The final axiom states that if one object is founded on another then it is founded on an object which contains the given object and all of the other objects upon which it is founded.

I have stated the theory with minimal assumptions concerning the notion of part. But in some ways a more natural system is obtained by also assuming the existence of arbitrary sums:

> for any non-empty set X of objects, there exists a
> least upper bound $z = \cup X$ (defined by the condition
> $\forall y((\forall x \ \varepsilon \ X)(x \leq y) \leftrightarrow z \leq y))$.

It will also be helpful to consider a reformulation of the system with a different primitive in place of F. Husserl uses the term "foundation" in two different senses. In what one might call its strict sense, an object cannot be founded upon its parts; while in the weak or neutral sense, an object is always founded upon its parts.[4] The weak notion is in some sense simpler and, as we shall see, leads to a more natural axiom-system. On the other hand, the strict notion serves to isolate the cases of weak foundation which are of distinctive ontological interest, viz. those in which an object is founded on something outside of itself.

Using WF as a primitive for the weak notion, we obtain the following axiom-system:

> AP1–3. As before.
> AWF1. (Parts) $y \leq x \rightarrow xWFy$;
> AWF2. (Transitivity) $xWFy \ \& \ yWFz \rightarrow xWFz$;
> AWF3. (Integrity) $\exists y(xWFy \ \& \ \forall z(xWFz \rightarrow z \leq y))$;

The reader may readily verify that we have the following theorems in the system:

T1. $xWFx$;
T2. $xWFy \ \& \ x \leq x^+ \rightarrow x^+WFy$;
T3. $xWFy \ \& \ y' \leq y \rightarrow xWFy'$;

and with the existence of arbitrary sums, we also have:

T4. $(\forall i \ \varepsilon \ I)(xWFy_i) \rightarrow xWF \cup \{y_i: i \ \varepsilon \ I\}$.

Strict foundation may be defined in terms of the weak notion:

D(F/WF). $xFy =_{df} xWFy \ \& \ \neg \ y \leq x$.

And weak foundation may be defined in terms of strict foundation:

D(WF/F). $xWFy =_{df} xFy \ \lor \ y \leq x$.

Under these two definitions the two systems are then deductively equivalent.[5]

What is the evidence that Husserl would have accepted these axioms? The principles concerning part are completely unproblematic and there is no reason to suppose that he would not have accepted them. Indeed, as we have seen, the proof of two of his propositions would seem to presuppose transitivity. It is not clear to me whether Husserl would have accepted the existence of arbitrary sums. However, there is some evidence that he would have accepted the existence of some "artificial" sums. For example, in attempting to find a case of a proper part which is immediate in the sense that it is not a proper part of any other proper part, he considers the case (§21, 469) in which "we emphasize in a visual intuition the unified combination formed by all such internal 'moments' as remain identical despite all change of place."

The axiom AF3 is the same as A1; and as we have seen, there is direct textual evidence that he would have supported it.

In regard to AF1, we may argue as follows. Either the notion of foundation is such that it is always true that an object is founded on its parts or such that it is never true. Now, in the former case, it would have been unnecessary for Husserl in his formulation of A1 to add the condition $\neg\ y \leq x^+$; and so we may conclude that the latter case obtains.

The main evidence for AF2 comes from his discussion of mediate foundation. He writes in §16, 467, "if A_o is immediately founded on B_o, but mediately on C_o (in so far as B_o is immediately founded on C_o)." This suggests that the foundation relation should be transitive: $x\mathrm{F}y\ \&\ y\mathrm{F}z \rightarrow x\mathrm{F}z$. But since x and y can be founded upon one another (see §16), x would then be founded upon x, contrary to AF1. So we must at least require that z not be a part of x. The only question which would then seem to arise is whether there might not be some other mereological relationship between x and z which would be incompatible with their being in a foundational relationship. Could it not be necessary for x and z to be disjoint, for example, or for x not to be a part of z? But the only mereological constraint mentioned in axiom A1 was that the founded object not be a part of the founding object; and if that constraint was good enough for that case, it is hard to see why it should not be good enough for the present case. Indeed, it is hard to see how any other constraint could be compatible with A1. For could not a foundational fact be such that an application of A1 would lead to a violation of the constraint?

There is, as far as I know, no direct textual evidence for AF4; but it is hard to see how Husserl could have regarded it as unacceptable.

The main evidence for AF5 comes from Husserl's insistence that an object and the objects upon which it is founded combine together to form a whole. Thus in §5, 443, he writes:

The content is by its nature bound to other contents, it cannot be, if other contents are not there together with it. We need not emphasize the fact that they form a unity with it, for can there be essential coexistence without connection or "blending" (*Verschmelzung*), however loose?

Husserl does not go on to say that the content is founded upon this unity; but it is clear from his examples that he does take the content to be founded on the unifying object in such a case.

There is also some indirect evidence for supposing that Husserl would have accepted our axioms for weak foundation. For at various places in the text, he suggests a definition of weak foundation in essentialist terms. For example, at §21, 475, where he writes:

A content of the species A is founded upon a content of the species B if an A can by its essence (i.e., legally, in virtue of its specific nature) not exist unless a B also exists.

And at §21, 443, he writes:

The sense of non-independence lies likewise in the positive thought of *dependence*. The content is by its nature bound to other contents.

Now these and other passages are somewhat hard to interpret. But one thing they suggest is the following criterion (where $\square_x$ is used for "it is true in virtue of the essence of x that" and *Ex* is used for "x exists")[6]:

$$\text{(CWF)} \quad x\text{WF}y \leftrightarrow \square_x (Ex \rightarrow Ey).$$

Given some fairly plausible assumptions concerning the behaviour of $\square_x$, the various axioms for weak foundation then follow. This makes it hard to see how he could have accepted the criterion but not the axioms.[7]

III. INDEPENDENCE AND CLOSURE

There are two other formulations of the system that are worth considering. The first takes as primitive the notion of being an independent object, one not founded upon anything (except its parts). There is then one axiom:

$$\text{AI}1. \quad \exists y(Iy \ \& \ y \leq x \ \& \ \forall z(Iz \ \& \ z \geq x \rightarrow y \leq z).$$

This says that there always exists a smallest independent object containing a given object.

In the presence of arbitrary sums, we may instead adopt the following two axioms:

AI1′. The universal object is independent;
AI1″. The non-empty intersection of arbitrarily many independent objects is independent.

Independence can be defined in terms of weak foundation by:

$$Ix \leftrightarrow \forall y(xWFy \rightarrow y \leq x);$$

or, in terms of strict foundation, by:

$$Ix \leftrightarrow \neg \; \exists y(xFy).$$

On the other hand, weak foundation can be defined in terms of independence by:

$$xWFy \leftrightarrow \forall x^+(Ix^+ \; \& \; x \leq x^+ \rightarrow y \leq x^+).$$

(One object is weakly founded upon another just in case every independent whole containing the one contains the other). Under these definitions, the present system is equivalent to the previous two.

It is interesting to note that Husserl gives a somewhat similar definition of foundation in terms of independent wholes. He writes (§14, 463):

If a law of essence means that an *A* cannot as such exist except in a more comprehensive unity which associates it with an *M*, we say that an *A as such requires foundation by an M*.

It seems reasonable to assume that the "comprehensive unity" is what we have called an independent object, though there is some unclarity as to what Husserl means by association. If it is merely a question of both being parts of the same whole, then we get our definition once the reference to essences is removed.

Natural as these definitions are, they are not in my view correct. Let us deal only with the definition of independence in terms of foundation, since similar considerations apply to the definition in the other direction. Suppose one holds an Aristotelian conception of properties according to which they require the existence of *some instance or another*. Properties would then be dependent in the intuitive philosophical sense, even though they did not require the existence of any particular object (other than their parts).

Of course, such a criticism would only require Husserl to give up the proposed definition of independence; and sometimes he does seem to have in mind the weaker notion of not requiring the existence of *some nonpart or another*. But even though the notion might then be correct, the axiom (AI1) would not be. For given an Aristotelian property, there is no object which one can sensibly take to be the smallest independent object which contains it.[8] Thus one must either give up the theory or its intended interpretation.

The other formulation of the theory is in terms of the concept of the foundational closure $f(x)$ of an object x. There are three axioms:

Af1. $x \le f(x)$;
Af2. $f(f(x)) \le f(x)$;
Af3. $x \le y \to f(x) \le f(y)$.

The concepts of closure and of weak foundation are interdefinable:

$f(x) = y \leftrightarrow x\mathrm{WF}y \,\&\, \forall z(x\mathrm{WF}z \leftrightarrow z \le y)$;
$x\mathrm{F}y \leftrightarrow y \le f(x)$.

Under these definitions, the two systems are equivalent.

The above axioms define a well-known algebraic structure, viz. a pre-closure algebra.[9] It is, therefore, perhaps no exaggeration to claim that, once all the extraneous material is removed, the mathematical structure underlying Husserl's theory of foundation is that of a pre-closure algebra.

It is interesting in this connection to note Husserl's remarks on relativization in §13 and elsewhere. He is obviously aware that the central concepts of his theory can be relativized, though to what extent he is aware of the possibility of a thorough-going relativization – of both concepts and theorems – is not so clear. All the same, his remarks do seem to contain some sort of dim foreshadowing of the notion of a relative closure algebra (which is the algebraic analogue of the notion of a relative topological space).

IV. FRAGMENTATION

Given that Husserl accepts the axioms for a pre-closure algebra, it is natural to wonder whether he would have accepted the additional additivity axiom for a closure algebra. His theory could then be seen to be essentially topological in character.

In this regard, his discussion at §25, 484–89, is especially revealing. He thinks that he has got hold of a general principle which is valid in the phenomenological sphere but not in the physical sphere. He expresses this principle in the following words (at 485):

The fragmentation of a dependent "moment" conditions a fragmentation of the concrete whole, in so far as the mutually exclusive "pieces," without themselves entering into a foundational relation with one another, attract new "moments" to themselves in virtue of which they are singly distributed to "pieces" of the whole.

What does this mean? A dependent moment is an object x for which it is true that:

(i) $f(x) \neq x$.

A fragmentation of an object x is constituted by objects x_i, $i \in I$, for which it is true that:

(ii) $\cup x_i = x$;
(iii) x_i and x_j are disjoint for $i \neq j$;
(iv) any common part of $f(x_i)$ and of x is a part of x_i.

Clause (ii) here is unproblematic. Clause (iv) is definitional of what it is for x_i to be a *piece* of x (cf. the account of piece in §17, 467). Clause (iii) is unproblematic for some sense of "disjoint," but there are apparently two different things that the word could mean. It could be used to convey that x_i and x_j have no piece of x in common or, simply, that they have no part in common, whether or not it be a piece of x. Husserl distinguishes carefully between the two notions and argues that they are not co-extensive (§17, 468).[10] But he is mistaken on this point; and so we may shift freely between either notion.

The fragmentation x_i, $i \in I$, is then meant to determine a fragmentation $f(x_i)$, $i \in I$, of the concrete whole $f(x)$. In other words:

(v) $\cup f(x_i) = f(x)$ ($= f(\cup x_i)$);
(vi) $f(x_i)$ and $f(x_j)$ are disjoint for $i \neq j$.

Thus, Husserl is asserting that (v) and (vi) follow from (i)–(iv).

Condition (i) may be dropped, since the implication is trivial if $f(x) = x$, i.e., if x is independent. It is not clear whether Husserl would allow I to be infinite. But if I is required to be finite, we can reduce the general case of fragmentation to a splitting, i.e., a fragmentation into two pieces. Let us say that x and y are *reciprocally independent* if x, $f(y)$ and y, $f(x)$ are both disjoint pairs. Then the special case is equivalent to the following two claims:

(vii)   If x_1 and x_2 are reciprocally independent, then
$f(x_1)$ and $f(x_2)$ are disjoint;

(viii)   If x_1 and x_2 are reciprocally independent,
then $f(x_1 \cup x_2) = f(x_1) \cup f(x_2)$.

The second of them, we may note, is a special case of the characteristic axiom for a closure algebra or topological space, viz. $f(x_1 \cup x_2) = f(x_1) \cup f(x_2)$; and it is plausible to suppose that anyone who accepts this special case would also be prepared to accept the unrestricted axiom.[11]

Moreover, Husserl may have his own reasons for endorsing the unrestricted axiom, quite apart from his endorsement of the special case. For any violation of it would make it hard to see how the particular foundational facts could be grounded in generic laws of foundation. We may also note that Husserl's counter-example to the principle of fragmentation within the physical realm is actually to the first of these clauses, not to the second, and therefore gives us no reason to doubt its application in the wider realm.[12]

I also suspect that Husserl's endorsement of the *first* of these clauses is based upon an over-hasty generalization from the example in hand. He is really thinking of what he earlier calls extensive wholes. But it is not clear that the principle holds generally in the psychological realm. For suppose that I have mixed feelings towards someone. Then that complex of feelings may be taken to consist of a presentation x of the person and of two attitudinal moments, y_1 and y_2 – one of love, let us say, and the other of hate. Now y_1 and y_2 are reciprocally independent: for the closure of y_1 is a feeling of love towards the person and hence is disjoint from y_2, the attitude of hate; and similarly for y_2. But the closures of y_1 and of y_2 are not disjoint, since they have the presentation x in common.

V. FURTHER DEVELOPMENTS

A matter for urgent consideration is which further concepts and principles should be added to our existing formalism in order adequately to represent Husserl's thought. I should like here to outline some suggestions.

1. We should introduce a new primitive relation which is to hold between two objects when they are of the same lowest species (even if ultimately we define such a relation in terms of the objects being instances of a common species). Let us designate such a relation by $\approx$ and call it *uniformity*. Then, for certain purposes, we may identify a lowest species of the object x with the equivalence class $|x| = \{y: y \approx x\}$; and foundation between lowest species can be defined by: α F β *iff* $(\forall x \; \varepsilon \; \alpha) \; (\exists y \; \varepsilon \; \beta) \; (x \; F \; y)$.

Husserl assumes that uniform objects are uniform with respect to foundation, i.e., $xFy \; \& \; x \approx x' \rightarrow \exists y'(y' \approx y \; \& \; x' \; F \; y')$. From this assumption, it then follows that the foundational relationships between objects are mirrored at the level of species, i.e., $xFy \rightarrow |x|F|y|$. Husserl would probably wish to subscribe to other uniformity assumptions, e.g., the principle that like objects have like parts, i.e., $x \leq y \; \& \; y \approx y' \rightarrow (\exists x')(x' \approx x \; \& \; x' \leq y')$. There consequently arises the task of constructing a reasonable theory of uniformity.

2. Let us say that a set B of objects is a *mereological basis* (for the universe) if every object in the universe is the union of objects in B. Thus an atomic mereology is one in which the atoms, the objects without proper pieces, constitute a mereological basis.

In terms of the uniformity relation it is possible to define plausible mereological bases, even in the absence of atoms. For example, let us say that an object is *simple* if it is uniform with any of its pieces; and let us say that an object is *absolutely simple* if it is uniform with any of its parts. Given the assumption that no object is uniform with any of its dependent parts, it follows that any absolutely simple object has no dependent parts, it is "momentless." And given the further assumption that any independent object has dependent parts,[13] it follows that absolutely simple objects are themselves moments. Thus, the two assumptions together guarantee that absolute simples are momentless moments.

It is quite plausible to suppose that the Husserlian ontology is one for which the simples, or even the absolute simples, constitute a mereological basis. In any case, it would be of interest to investigate the different kinds of basis which can be defined with the help of the uniformity relation.

3. Let us say that a set B of objects is a *foundational basis* (for the

universe) if for any object x of the universe, $f(x) = \cup \{z \; \varepsilon \; B$: for some $y \; \varepsilon \; B$, $y \le x$ & $y\mathrm{WF}z\}$). Husserl would appear to have an interest in foundational bases. For he seems to presuppose that all foundational relationships derive somehow from relationships of immediate foundation; and he also seems to presuppose that relationships of immediate foundation only hold among certain sorts of object. The objects of those sorts would then appear to constitute a foundational basis.

Let it be supposed that general additivity holds for the objects of a mereological basis B, i.e., for any objects $x_1, x_2, \ldots$ of B, $f(x_1 \cup x_2 \cup \ldots)$ $= f(x_1) \cup f(x_2) \cup \ldots$. Then any mereological basis is a foundational basis. For any object x is the union $x_1 \cup x_2 \cup \ldots$ of objects $x_1, x_2, \ldots$ in the basis B. So $f(x) = f(x_1 \cup x_2 \cup \ldots) = f(x_1) \cup f(x_2) \cup \ldots$. But each $f(x_i)$ is, in its turn, the union $x_{i_1} \cup x_{i_2} \cup \ldots$ of objects in the basis. Hence $f(x)$ is the union $(f(x_{1_1}) \cup f(x_{1_2}) \cup \ldots) \cup (f(x_{2_1}) \cup f(x_{2_2}) \ldots \cup \ldots) \ldots$, with each x_i weakly founded on each of the x_{ij}. It therefore follows that our considerations concerning mereological bases are directly relevant to the determination of foundational bases as well.

4. In §17 at 468, Husserl introduces the important concept of an extended object. He writes:

When a whole permits the sort of "piecing" in which the pieces essentially belong to the same lowest Genus as is determined by the undivided whole, we speak of it as an *extended whole*, and of its pieces as *extended parts*. Here belongs, e.g., the division of an extent into extents, in particular of a spatial stretch into spatial stretches, of a temporal stretch into temporal stretches etc.

Let us say that an object x is *divisible* if it is the union of pieces y and z which are both distinct from x; and let us say that x is *indefinitely divisible* if any piece of x is divisible. The above passage then suggests that we should define an extended object as one which is simple (i.e., uniform with its pieces) and indefinitely divisible. In terms of such a definition, we can then develop a theory of extended objects.[14]

Any such theory, if it is to do justice to Husserl's thinking on the subject, must show how the extended objects at different levels are coordinated. Given an extended object u, let P_u be the set of its pieces; and given any object x, let f_x be the relative closure with respect to x, i.e. $f_x(y) = f(y) \cap x$. The coordination principle then states that for any two extended objects u and v, with $u \le v$, the restriction of f_v to P_u is a mereological isomorphism from P_u to P_v, i.e. f_v is a one-one map from P_u onto P_v and, for $u_1, u_2 \, \varepsilon \, P_u$, $u_1 \le u_2$ iff $f_v(u_1) \le f_v(u_2)$.

5. In §16 at 466–67, Husserl introduces the distinction between immediate and mediate foundation. One naturally supposes that immediate foundation is simply foundation which is not mediated: that is, x is immediately founded on y iff x is founded on y and for no z is x founded on z and z founded on y. But such a definition will not work. For take a case in which a colour moment x is immediately found on an extension moment y; and let y' be a proper piece of y. Then x is founded on $x \cup y'$ and $x \cup y'$ is founded on y. Indeed, I am convinced that is impossible to define immediate foundation in terms of foundation (even with the help of the uniformity relation) and that it should therefore be taken as a primitive.

It is clear that Husserl supposes that all of the foundational facts can somehow be generated from the relationships of immediate foundation; and consequently there arises the question of determining the sense in which the one might be taken as a basis for the other.[15] The obvious way of generating the foundational facts is by chains of relationships of immediate foundation. But this will not do. For a particular colour is founded not just on the corresponding particular extension, but also on the pieces of that extension; and a particular hue is founded not just on a particular brightness and saturation, taken separately, but also on the combination of the two. But the chains which are forged from the relationships of immediate foundation will only hold between *corresponding* moments and hence will be incapable of generating these other ties. Some method, which takes into account the possibility of generating unions and parts, must therefore be given.

6. In §19 at 470–72, Husserl introduces the important concept of the distance of a part from its whole. Whereas the pieces of a piece will always be at the same distance from the whole, the moments of a part will, in general, be at a further distance from the whole. How is this concept of distance to be defined? As in the case of immediate foundation, it is hard to see how the relevant notion of distances can be defined in terms of foundation. For consider his case (p. 471) in which "the moment of colour or shape that inheres in an extended part of what is visually intuited as such, is primarily attached to this part, only secondarily to the intuited whole." We cannot say that the

colour moment x is a primary part of the extended part y in virtue of the fact that it is not a proper part (or dependent part) of anything which is a proper part (or dependent part) of y. For x is a dependent part of the union of the colour moment and the shape moment, which is, in its turn, a dependent part of y. But then how else could the notion be defined?

I suggest that it be defined in terms of immediate foundation. To take a critical case, x will be a primary dependent part of z if z is of the form $x \cup y_1 \cup y_2 \cup \ldots \cup y_n$, where x is immediately founded on $y_1, y_2, \ldots, y_n$. But one would also like to assign a distance to every part of a whole. Suppose, for example, that the part is the fusion of one piece of an extended whole and the moment of another piece. Then what is its distance from the whole? This is not a kind of case which Husserl considers; but it is of interest to see to what extent a reasonable notion of distance can be defined for such cases.

7. Other key concepts can be defined in terms of the notion of immediate foundation. For example, at 475 of §21, Husserl introduces the concept of a *pregnant whole*:

One can give the following noteworthy definition of the *pregnant concept of whole* by way of the *notion of foundation*: by a whole we understand a range of contents which are all covered *by a single foundation* without the help of further contents. The contents of such a range we call its parts. Talk of the *singleness of the foundation* implies that *every content is foundationally connected, whether directly or indirectly, with every other content.*

The obvious way of understanding this definition is that a pregnant whole is the union of two or more objects, any two of which are foundationally connected. But what is meant by foundational connection? Most expositors take the foundational connection between two objects to consist in something like one being founded on the other. But this makes nonsense of the intention behind the definition. Take a belief x of mine and a love y of yours. Suppose, for simplicity, that x is the union of a presentation x_1 of what is believed and a moment x_2 of belief and that y is the union of a presentation y_1 of the beloved and a moment y_2 of love. Then the non-pregnant whole $x \cup y$ is the union of $x_1 \cup y_1$ and $x_2 \cup y_2$, where $x_2 \cup y_2$ is founded upon $x_1 \cup y_1$. Insist, however, on the foundational connection being mediate (i.e., given by a chain of relationships of immediate foundation) and the difficulty does not arise.

I also suspect that in his talk at 468 of §17 of a proximate or relative concretum, Husserl is struggling with the idea of an object which is, in an absolute sense, relatively complete. Thus, a colour moment or a shape moment will, in this sense, be relatively complete, since they will only require supplementation at a "higher level." On the other hand, the union of the two moments will not be relatively complete. Again, it is plausible that such a notion should be defined in terms of the notion of immediate foundation.

8. Husserl wishes to derive all particular foundational facts from general laws of foundation and from statements specifying the species of the various objects. His views on immediate foundation and immediate part are very relevant to the formulation of the laws; for they serve to constrain both which species will be mentioned and which will be related. However, there is a problem in deriving the particular foundational facts which he never faces. A law for him will be something like: any object of species α is founded on an object of species β. Suppose now that x is an object of species α (a shape moment, let us say) and that it is founded on an object of species β (a colour moment, let us say). Then all one can derive from the law is that x is founded on an object of species β; it will be impossible to show that x is founded on a particular object y of species β. To do this, it appears that both the laws and the specifications of the species must be modified. The law must now be something like: any object of species α is founded on any "coincident" object of species β; and in specifying the essence of x and y, we must include the relational fact that x and y coincide. Given these modifications, however, a derivation of the sort that he envisages would appear to be possible; and it would be of interest to see exactly how it would proceed, especially in the light of the various constraints which might be imposed on the structure of foundation.

REFERENCES

Fine, K. "The Concept of Essence." In *Philosophical Perspectives*, 8, *Logic and Language*; Ed. by J. Tomberlin. 1994a.
———. "The Logic of Essence". Forthcoming in the *Journal of Philosophical Logic*, 1994b.
Ginsberg, E. "On the Concepts of Existential Dependence and Independence". Translated from the Polish and reprinted in Smith 1982.

Husserl, E. *Logische Untersuchungen,* 1st ed. Halle: Niemeyer, 1900–01; 2nd edition, 1913/21. Both now available as *Husserliana* XVIII–XIX, The Hague: Nijhoff, 1975, 1984. English translation, *Logical Investigations,* J. N. Findlay. London: Routledge, 1970. The page references are to the Findlay edition, though the translation has occasionally been emended.

Null, G. T. A "First-Order Axiom System for Part-Whole and Foundation Relations." In *Phenomenological Essays in Memory of Aron Gurwitsch.* Edited by L. Embree. Lanham, Md.: University Press of America, 1984.

Ore, O. "Some Studies on Closure Relations." *Duke Mathematical Journal* 10 (1943): 761–85.

———. "Combinations of Closure Relations." *Annals of Mathematics,* 47: 514–33.

———. "Mappings of Closure Relations," *Annals of Mathematics,* 1946 47: 56–72.

Simons, P. M. "The Formalization of Husserl's Theory of Parts and Wholes." In *Parts and Moments: Studies in Logic and Formal Ontology,* Edited by B. Smith. Munich: Philosophia, 1982.

———. *Parts: A Study in Ontology.* Oxford: Clarendon Press, 1982.

Smith, B. *Parts and Moments: Studies in Logic and Formal Ontology.* Munich: Philosophia, 1982.

NOTES

1 This paper is based on work I did about fifteen years ago. I am very grateful to Barry Smith for his general encouragement and for writing up a much expanded version of my notes. Most of the material on immediate foundation and levels of part has here been suppressed, though I do hope to present it elsewhere.

2 It is natural to suppose that $\Box_{x,\alpha}\ \phi(x)$ means something like: $\Box(\forall y)\ (y I\alpha \rightarrow \phi(y))$, where $\Box$ is a form of analytic necessity.

3 But the two W's on p. 464 in the translation are a muddle and should be F's.

4 The qualification in proposition 1 at §14 and the unifying role of foundation mentioned in §22, 478, suggest the strict notion; while the essentialist criterion for foundation in §21, 475, suggests the weak notion. See Simons 1982, 113 and 115.

It might be worth considering other part-theoretic constraints on the weak notion. For example, it may be required, if x is to be founded on y, not only that y not be a part of x but also that x not be a part of y. However, there is no guarantee, once further restrictions are imposed, that the weak notion will be recoverable. Indeed, I suspect that it will not be for foundation as defined above.

5 The proofs of this and of other meta-logical results are fairly straightforward and are therefore omitted.

6 In my notes, I considered defining weak foundation by $\Box(Ex \rightarrow Ey)$; and Simons considers the same proposal in his book 1987, 316. But I now believe that there are serious philosophical and exegetical reasons against understanding $\Box_x \phi$ as $\Box(Ex \rightarrow \phi)$ and consequently against treating the two definientia $\Box_x (Ex \rightarrow Ey)$ and $\Box(Ex \rightarrow Ey)$ as equivalent. The philosophical reasons are briefly discussed in my paper 1994a; and the logic of the operator $\Box_x$ is developed in 1994b. As to the exegetical issue, the question is how to connect the reference to essence and species. Husserl seems to want to identify the essence of an object x with its lowest species $\sigma(x)$; and this suggests that he would be willing to understand $\Box_x \phi$ as $\Box_{x,\sigma(x)} \phi$. The proper definition of $\Box_x \phi$ is therefore $\Box(\forall y)$ $(yI\sigma(x) \rightarrow \phi(y))$ rather than $\Box(Ex \rightarrow \phi)$.

7 The weak point in the derivation concerns Integrity; for this requires us to accept that if it is true in virtue of the essence of x that each of x_1, x_2, . . . exists if x exists, then it is true in virtue of the essence of x that the union of x_1, x_2, . . . exists if x exists. But it is true in virtue of the essence of the set $\{x_1, x_2, . . .\}$ that each of its members x_1, x_2, . . . exists if it does, but not true in virtue of the essence of the set that their union exists if it does. Still, it is plausible to suppose that Husserl would not have been aware of this somewhat subtle point.

8 A somewhat similar criticism is made in §5 of the perceptive critique of Ginsberg 1982.

9 For some early work on these algebras, see the references under Ore.

10 He writes "pieces that have no piece identically in common are called *exclusive* (disjoined) pieces. . . . Two such pieces may still have a common identical "moment": their common boundary, e.g., is an identical "moment" of the adjoining pieces of the divided continuum. Pieces are said to be *isolated* when they are disjoined in the strict sense, when they therefore also have *no identical moments.*" However, we may show that if the pieces x_i and x_j of x have a part y in common then they also have a piece z of x in common. For let $z = f(x_i \cap x_j) \cap x$. Then it is readily verifed that z is a piece of x and that it is a part of both x_i and x_j. (I might note that even if the general existence of intersections is regarded as problematic, the existence of the relevant intersections in this case is relatively unproblematic).

In relation to the example of the boundary, this argument shows that either the boundary is a piece or that it is part of a common piece of the two sections. What makes Husserl's example so persuasive is the fact that the boundary may in an intuitive sense be regarded as a dependent part of the continuum. But this is the sense in which it depends for its existence upon *some* section which has that boundary, not any particular section; and this is a sense of dependence which, as I have argued, Husserl is unable to capture.

11 In this regard it should be noted that the unrestricted principle follows from its restriction to independent objects: for $f(x \cup y) = f(f(x) \cup f(y)) = f(f(x)) \cup f(f(y)) = f(x) \cup f(y)$.

12 It is actually somewhat misleading to regard the counter-example as one which lies within the physical realm; for the counter-example is obtained by modifying the sense of "nature." Would not a similar modification in the sense of nature also produce a counter-example in the phenomenological sphere?

13 C.f. the remark at §17, 468, that "each absolutely independent content possesses abstract parts."

14 An alternative approach is to take the notion of an extended object as primitive. Uniformity on extended objects (though not on all objects) may then be defined by the condition that u is uniform with v iff $u \cup v$ is an extended object with u and v as pieces.

15 There is a clear connection here with the topological notion of basis – a point which further underscores the topological character of Husserl's thought.

BIBLIOGRAPHY

I. HUSSERL'S PRINCIPAL PUBLICATIONS

Beiträge zur theorie der Variationsrechnung, Dissertation. Vienna, 1882.

Über den Begriff der Zahl. Psychologische Analysen. Habilitationsschrift, Halle a. d. S., 1887.

Philosophie der Arithmetik. Psychologische und logische Untersuchungen. Erster Band, Halle a. d. S.: C. E. M. Pfeffer (R. Stricker), 1891.

Logische Untersuchungen. Erster Theil: Prolegomena zur reinen Logik, Halle a. d. S.: Max Niemeyer, 1900; 2nd ed. 1913.

Logische Untersuchungen. Zweiter Theil: Untersuchungen zur Phänomenologie und Theorie der Erkenntnis, Halle a. d. S.: Max Niemeyer, 1901; 2nd ed. in two parts, 1913/22.

"Philosophie als strenge Wissenschaft." *Logos* 1 (1911): 289–341.

"Ideen zu einer reinen Phänomenologie und phänomenologischen Philosophie." *Jahrbuch für Philosophie und phänomenologische Forschung* 1 (1913): 1–323. Published simultaneously as Separatum.

"Vorlesungen zur Phänomenologie des inneren Zeitbewusstseins." Ed. by M. Heidegger. *Jahrbuch für Philosophie und phänomenologische Forschung* 9 (1928): VIII–X and 367–498. Published simultaneously as Separatum. Halle: Max Niemeyer.

"Formale und transzendentale Logik. Versuch einer Kritik der logischen Vernunft." *Jahrbuch für Philosophie und phänomenologische Forschung* 10 (1929): V–XIII and 1–298. Published simultaneously as Separatum.

Méditations cartésiennes. Introduction à la phénoménologie. Translated from the German by G. Pfeiffer and E. Levinas. Paris: Librairie Armand Colin, 1931.

"Die Krisis der europäischen Wissenschaften und die transzendentale Phänomenologie. Eine Einleitung in die phänomenologische Philosophie." *Philosophia* 1 (1936): 77–176.

Erfahrung und Urteil. Untersuchungen zur Genealogie der Logik. L. Landgrebe, ed. Prague: Akademia Verlagsbuchhandlung, 1939.

487

II. WORKS PUBLISHED IN THE
HUSSERLIANA EDITION

This critical edition of Husserl's works was founded by Herman Leo Van Breda in 1950. Since 1976 it has been edited under the auspices of Samuel Ijsseling. The series was first published by Nijhoff (The Hague), since 1989 by Kluwer Academic Publishers (Dordrecht/Boston/London).

Hua I: *Cartesianische Meditationen und Pariser Vorträge.* S. Strasser, ed. 1950, 2nd ed., 1973.

Hua II. *Die Idee der Phänomenologie: Fünf Vorlesungen.* W. Biemel, ed. 1950, revised and expanded edition 1973.

Hua III. *Ideen zu einer reinen Phänomenologie und phänomenologischen Philosophie. Erstes Buch: Allgemeine Einführung in die reine Phänomenologie.* W. Biemel, ed. 1950. Revised edition in two parts by K. Schuhmann, 1976.

Hua IV. *Ideen zu einer reinen Phänomenologie und phänomenologischen Philosophie. Zweites Buch: Phänomenologische Untersuchungen zur Konstitution.* M. Biemel, ed. 1952, repr. 1984.

Hua V. *Ideen zu einer reinen Phänomenologie und phänomenologischen Philosophie. Drittes Buch: Die Phänomenologie und die Fundamente der Wissenschaften.* M. Biemel, ed. 1952, repr. 1971.

Hua VI. *Die Krisis der europätschen Wissenschaften und die transzendentale Phänomenologie. Eine Einleitung in die phänomenologische Philosophie.* W. Biemel, ed. 1954.

Hua VII. *Erste Philosophie (1923–1924). Erster Teil: Kritische Ideengeschichte.* R. Boehm, ed. 1956.

Hua VIII. *Erste Philosophie (1923–1924). Zweiter Teil: Theorie der phänomenologischen Reduktion.* R. Boehm, ed. 1959.

Hua IX. *Phänomenologische Psychologie. Vorlesungen Sommersemester 1925.* W. Biemel, ed. 1962.

Hua X. *Zur Phänomenologie des inneren Zeitbewusstseins (1893–1917).* R. Boehm, ed. Revised ed. 1966, repr. 1969.

Hua XI. *Analysen zur passiven Synthese. Aus Vorlesungs- und Forschungsmanuskripten (1918–1926).* M. Fleischer, ed. 1966.

Hua XII. *Philosophie der Arithmetik. Mit ergänzenden Texten (1890–1901).* L. Eley, ed. 1970.

Hua XIII. *Zur Phänomenologie der Intersubjektivität. Texte aus dem Nachlass. Erster Teil: 1905–1920.* I. Kern, ed. 1973.

Hua XIV. *Zur Phänomenologie der Intersubjektivität. Texte aus dem Nachlass. Zweiter Teil: 1921–1928.* I. Kern, ed. 1973.

Hua XV. *Zur Phänomenologie der Intersubjektivität. Texte aus dem Nachlass. Dritter Teil: 1929–1935.* I. Kern, ed. 1973.

Hua XVI. *Ding und Raum. Vorlesungen 1907.* U. Claesges, ed. 1973.

Hua XVII. *Formale und transzendentale Logik. Versuch einer Kritik der logischen Vernunft.* P. Janssen, ed. 1974.

Hua XVIII. *Logische Untersuchungen. Erster Band: Prolegomena zur reinen Logik.* E. Holenstein, ed. 1975.

Hua XIX. *Logische Untersuchungen. Zweiter Band: Untersuchungen zur Phänomenologie und Theorie der Erkenntnis.* U. Panzer, ed. In two volumes, 1984.

Hua XX. *Logische Untersuchungen. Ergänzungsband zur Umarbeitung der VI. Untersuchung. Texte aus dem Nachlass (1911–1917).* F. Belussi, ed. in preparation.

Hua XXI. *Studien zur Arithmetik und Geometrie. Texte aus dem Nachlass (1886–1901).* I. Strohmeyer, ed. 1983.

Hua XXII. *Aufsätze und Rezensionen (1890–1910).* B. Rang, ed. 1979.

Hua XXIII. *Phantasie, Bildbewusstein, Erinnerung. Zur Phänomenologie der anschaulichen Vergegenwärtigungen. Texte aus dem Nachlass (1898–1925).* E. Marbach, ed. 1980.

Hua XXIV. *Einleitung in die Logik und Erkenntnistheorie. Vorlesungen 1906/07.* U. Melle, ed. 1984.

Hua XXV. *Aufsätze und Vorträge (1911–1921).* T. Nenon and H. R. Sepp, eds. 1987.

Hua XXVI. *Vorlesungen über Bedeutungslehre. Sommersemester 1908.* U. Panzer, ed. 1987.

Hua XXVII. *Aufsätze und Vorträge (1922–1937).* T. Nenon and H. R. Sepp, eds. 1989.

Hua XXVIII. *Vorlesungen über Ethik und Wertlehre (1908–1914).* U. Melle, ed. 1988.

III. PRINCIPAL ENGLISH TRANSLATIONS

"Phenomenology," *Encyclopedia Britannica* (London), 14th ed., vol. 17 (1929):699–702. New complete translation by R. E. Palmer, *Journal of the British Society for Phenomenology* 2 (1971): 77–90.

The Idea of Phenomenology. Translated by W. P. Alston and G. Nakhnikian. The Hague: Nijhoff, 1964.

"Philosophy as Rigorous Science" and "Philosophy and the Crisis of European Man," In Q. Lauer, ed. *Phenomenology and the Crisis of Philosophy.* New York, Harper, 1965, 71–147 and 149–92.

Formal and Transcendental Logic. Translated by D. Cairns. The Hague: Nijhoff, 1969.

The Crisis of European Sciences and Transcendental Phenomenology: An

Introduction to Phenomenological Philosophy. Translated by David Carr. Evanston, Ill.: Northwestern University Press, 1970.

"On the Concept of Number: Psychological Analyses." Translated by D. Willard. *Philosophia Mathematica* 9 (1972): 44–52, 10 (1973): 37–87.

Logical Investigations. Translation of the 2nd edition by J. N. Findlay. London: Routledge and Kegan Paul, 1973.

Experience and Judgment. Investigations in a Genealogy of Logic. English translation by J. S. Churchill and K. Ameriks. London: Routledge and Kegan Paul, 1973.

Introduction to the Logical Investigations. A Draft of a 'Preface' to the 'Logical Investigations'. Translated with an Introduction by P. J. Bossert and C. H. Peters. The Hague: Nijhoff, 1975.

The Paris Lectures. Translated with an Introductory Essay by P. Koestenbaum. The Hague: Nijhoff, 1975.

Phenomenological Psychology. Lectures, Summer Semester 1925. Translated by J. Scanlon. The Hague: Nijhoff, 1977.

Ideas Pertaining to a Pure Phenomenology and to a Phenomenological Philosophy. Third Book: Phenomenology and the Foundations of the Sciences. Translated by T. E. Klein and W. E. Pohl. Dordrecht/Boston/London: Kluwer, 1980.

Husserl. Shorter Works. P. McCormick and F. Elliston, eds. Notre Dame: University of Notre Dame Press, 1981.

Ideas Pertaining to a Pure Phenomenology and to a Phenomenological Philosophy. First Book: General Introduction to a Pure Phenomenology. Translated by F. Kersten. The Hague: Nijhoff, 1982.

Cartesian Meditations. An Introduction to Phenomenology. Translated by D. Cairns. Dordrecht/Boston/London: Kluwer, 1988.

Ideas Pertaining to a Pure Phenomenology and to a Phenomenological Philosophy. Second Book: Studies in the Phenomenology of Constitution. Translated by R. Rojcewicz and A. Schuwer. Dordrecht: Kluwer, 1989.

On the Phenomenology of the Consciousness of Internal Time (1893–1917). Translated by J. B. Brough. Dordrecht/Boston/London: Kluwer, 1990.

Early Writings in the Philosophy of Logic and Mathematics. Translated by Dallas Willard. Dordrecht/Boston/London: Kluwer, 1994.

IV. BIOGRAPHICAL WORKS

De Boer, Theodore. *The Development of Husserl's Thought.* The Hague: Nijhoff, 1978. Slightly abridged English Translation of the Dutch original: *De Ontwikkelingsgang in het denken van Husserl.* Assen: Van Gorcum, 1966.

Schuhmann, K. *Husserl-Chronik. Denk- und Lebensweg Edmund Husserls.* The Hague: Nijhoff, 1977.

Edmund Husserl und die phänomenologische Bewegung. Zeugnisse in Text und Bild. Ed. by H. R. Sepp. Freiburg/München: Alber, 1988, 465 pp. Includes short memoirs by H.-G. Gadamer, L. Landgrebe, M. Haga, E. Levinas, M. Müller and H. Spiegelberg.

Husserl, Edmund *Briefwechsel.* Edited by Karl Schuhmann in collaboration with Elisabeth Schuhmann. Dordrecht: Kluwer Academic Publishers, 1994. This critical edition of Husserl's correspondence is in ten volumes, as follows:

> *Band I: Die Brentanoschule*
> *Band II: Die Münchener Phänomenologen*
> *Band III: Die Göttinger Schule*
> *Band IV: Die Freiburger Schüler*
> *Band V: Die Neukantianer*
> *Band VI: Philosophenbriefe*
> *Band VII: Wissenschaftlerkorrespondenz*
> *Band VIII: Institutionelle Schreiben*
> *Band IX: Familienbriefe*
> *Band X: Einführung und Register*

V. BIBLIOGRAPHIES

Allen, J. "Husserl Bibliography of English translations." *The Monist* 59 (1975): 133–37.

Eley, Lothar. "Husserl-Bibliographie 1945–1959", *Zeitschrift für philosophische Forschung,* 13 (1959):357–67, 475.

Heismann, G. "Austrian, German and Swiss Dissertations on Edmund Husserl, 1912–1976." *Phenomenological Information Bulletin* 3 (1979): 95–104.

Lapointe, F. H. *Edmund Husserl and His Critics. An International Bibliography (1884–1979).* Bowling Green: Philosophy Documentation Center, 1980.

Maschke, G. and I. Kern. "Husserl-Bibliographie." *Revue Internationale de Philosophie* 19 (1965):153–202.

Patočka, Jan. "Husserl-Bibliographie." *Revue Internationale de Philosophie* 1 (1939):374–97.

Raes, J. "Husserl-Bibliographie." *Revue Internationale de Philosophie* 4 (1950):460–61, 469–75.

Schmitz, Manfred. "Bibliographie der bis zum 8. April 1989 veröffentlichten Schriften Edmund Husserls." *Husserl Studies* 6 (1989):205–26.

VI. GENERAL SURVEYS AND INTRODUCTIONS

Bell, David. *Husserl* (Arguments of the Philosophers Series). London: Routledge, 1989.

Bernet, Rudolf, Iso Kern, Eduard Marbach. *An Introduction to Husserlian Phenomenology* (Studies in Phenomenology and Existential Philosophy). Evanston, Ill.: Northwestern University Press, 1993.

Edie, James M. *Edmund Husserl's Phenomenology: A Critical Commentary.* Bloomington: Indiana University Press, 1987.

Elliston, Frederick and Peter McCormick, eds. *Husserl: Expositions and Appraisals.* Notre Dame: University of Notre Dame Press, 1977.

Farber, Marvin. *The Aims of Phenomenology. The Motives, Methods and Impact of Husserl's Thought.* New York: Harper and Row, 1966.

———. *The Foundations of Phenomenology. Edmund Husserl and the Quest for a Rigorous Science of Philosophy.* 3rd rev. ed. Albany: State University of New York Press, 1968.

Ingarden, Roman. *Einführung in die Phänomenologie Edmund Husserls. Osloer Vorlesungen 1967* (Ingarden Gesammelte Werke 4). G. Häfliger, ed. Tübingen: Niemeyer, 1992.

Künne, Wolfgang. "Edmund Husserl: Intentionalität." In J. Speck, ed., *Grundprobleme der grossen Philosophen, Philosophie der Neuzeit IV.* Göttingen: Vandenhoeck and Ruprecht, 1986, 165–215.

Natanson, Maurice. *Edmund Husserl: Philosopher of Infinite Tasks.* Evanston: Northwestern University Press, 1973.

Pivčević, Edo. *Husserl and Phenomenology.* New York and London: Hutchinson University Library, 1970.

Ricoeur, Paul. *Husserl: An Analysis of His Phenomenology.* Evanston, Ill.: Northwestern University Press, 1967.

Sajama, Seppo and Matti Kamppinen. *A Historical Introduction to Phenomenology.* London/New York/Sydney: Croom Helm, 1987.

Sokolowski, Robert. *The Formation of Husserl's Concept of Constitution.* The Hague: Martinus Nijhoff, 1970.

———. *Husserlian Mediations.* Evanston: Northwestern, 1974.

Spiegelberg, Herbert. *The Context of the Phenomenological Movement.* The Hague: Nijhoff, 1981.

———. *The Phenomenological Movement. A Historical Introduction.* 3rd revised and enlarged edition with the collaboration of Karl Schuhmann. The Hague/Boston/Lancaster: Martinus Nijhoff, 1982.

VII. SECONDARY LITERATURE

We have concentrated in what follows primarily on more recent English-language material, and on material that is of direct relevance to the problems and concerns of analytic philosophy.

Baldwin, Thomas. "Phenomenology, Solipism and Egocentric Thought." *Proceedings of the Aristotelian Society. Supplementary Volume* 62 (1988):27–43.

Bar-Hillel, Y. "Husserl's Conception of a Purely Logical Grammar." *Philosophy and Phenomenological Research* 17 (1956):362–69.

Baruss, I. "Categorical Modelling of Husserl's Intentionality." *Husserl Studies* 6 (1989):25–42.

Becker, Oskar. "The Philosophy of Edmund Husserl." In R. O. Elveton, ed., *The Phenomenology of Husserl: Selected Critical Readings*. Chicago: Quadrangle Books, 1970.

Bell, David A. "Phenomenology, Solipsism and Egocentric Thought." *Proceedings of the Aristotelian Society. Supplementary Volume* 62 (1988):45–60.

———. "Reference, Experience, and Intentionality." In Leila Haaparanta, ed. *Mind, Meaning and Mathematics. Essays on the Philosophical Views of Husserl and Frege*. Dordrecht/Boston/London: Kluwer (1994), 185–209.

Bergmann, Gustav. "The Ontology of Edmund Husserl." In G. Bergmann, *Logic and Reality*. Madison: University of Wisconsin Press, 1964, 193–224.

Bernet, Rudolf. "Husserl's Theory of Signs Revisited." *Edmund Husserl and the Phenomenological Tradition. Essays in Phenomenology*. Edited by Robert Sokolowski. Washington D. C.: Catholic University of America Press, 1988, 1–24.

———. "Husserl's Concept of the World." In A. B. Dallery *et al.*, eds. *Crises in Continental Philosophy*. Albany: State University of New York Press, 1990, 3–22.

———. "Husserls Begriff des Noema." In Samuel Ijselling, ed. *Husserl-Ausgabe und Husserl-Forschung*. Dordrecht/Boston/London: Kluwer, 1990, 61–80.

Brough, John B. "Husserl on Memory," *The Monist* 59 (1975):40–62.

———. "Art and Artworld: Some Ideas for a Husserlian Aesthetic." *Edmund Husserl and the Phenomenological Tradition. Essays in Phenomenology*. Edited by Robert Sokolowski. Washington D. C.: Catholic University of America Press, 1988, 25–45.

———. "Husserl's Phenomenology of Time-Consciousness." In *Husserl's Phenomenology: A Textbook*. J. N. Mohanty and W. R. McKenna, eds.

Lanham: The Center for Advanced Research in Phenomenology and University Press of America, 1989, 249–90.

Brown, Charles S. "Husserl, Intentionality, and Cognitive Architecture." *Southwest Philosophy Review* 6 (1990):65–72.

———. "Problems with the Fregean Interpretation of Husserl." *Journal of the British Society for Phenomenology* 22 (1991):53–64.

Bruzina, Ronald. *Logos and Eidos. The Concept in Phenomenology.* The Hague/Paris: Mouton, 1970.

Butts, R. E. "Husserl's Critique of Hume's Notion of 'Distinctions of Reason.'" *Philosophy and Phenomenological Research* 20 (1959/60):213–21.

Carr, David. *Interpreting Husserl. Critical and Comparative Studies.* Dordrecht/Boston/Lancaster: Nijhoff (Phaenomenologica 106), 1987.

———. "The Life-World Revisited." In *Husserl's Phenomenology: A Textbook.* J. N. Mohanty and W. R. McKenna, eds. Lanham: The Center for Advanced Research in Phenomenology and University Press of America, 1989, 291–308.

Carr, Lloyd J. "Husserl's Philosophy of Language." In *Husserl's Phenomenology: A Textbook.* J. N. Mohanty and W. R. McKenna, eds. Lanham: The Center for Advanced Research in Phenomenology and University Press of America, 1989, 107–46.

Casebier, Allan. *Film and Phenomenology: Toward a Realist Theory of Cinematic Representation.* Cambridge and New York: Cambridge University Press, 1991.

Cataldo, Peter J. "Husserl on Galileo's Intentionality." *The Thomist* 51 (1987):680–98.

Cavallin, Jens. *Content and Object. Husserl, Twardowski and Psychologism.* Stockholm: Akademitryck AB, 1990.

Cesarz, G. L. "Meaning, Individuals, and the Problem of Bare Particulars; A Study in Husserl's *Ideas.*" *Husserl Studies* 2 (1985):157–68.

Chisholm, Roderick M., ed. *Realism and the Background of Phenomenology.* Glencoe, Ill.: The Free Press, 1960.

Chokr, N. "Mind, Consciousness, and Cognition: Phenomenology vs. Cognitive Science." *Husserl Studies* 9 (1992):179–98.

Cobb-Stevens, Richard. "Being and Categorical Intuition." *The Review of Metaphysics* 44 (1990):43–66.

———. *Husserl and Analytic Philosophy* (Phaenomenologica 116). Dordrecht/Boston/Lancaster: Kluwer, 1990.

Crowell, Steven Galt. "Husserl, Lask and the Idea of Transcendental Logic." *Edmund Husserl and the Phenomenological Tradition. Essays in Phenomenology.* Edited by Robert Sokolowski. Washington D. C.: Catholic University of America Press, 1988, 63–85.

———. "Husserl, Heidegger, and Transcendental Philosophy: Another Look at the *Encyclopedia Britannica* Article." *Philosophy and Phenomeno-logical Research* 50 (1990):501–19.

Davie, George. "Husserl and Reinach on Hume's 'Treatise'." In *Speech Act and Sachverhalt: Reinach and the Foundations of Realist Phenomenology (Primary Sources in Phenomenology* 1). Edited by Kevin Mulligan. Dordrecht/Boston/London, Nijhoff, 1987, 257–74.

Dennett, Daniel C. *Consciousness Explained.* Boston: Little, Brown, and Co., 1991.

Dreyfus, H. L. "Husserl's Perceptual Noema." In Dreyfus, H. L., ed. *Husserl, Intentionality and Cognitive Science.* Cambridge, Mass.: MIT Press, 1982, 97–123.

Drost, Mark P. "The Primacy of Perception in Husserl's Theory of Imagining." *Philosophy and Phenomenological Research,* 50 (1990):569–82.

Drummond, John J. "On the Nature of Perceptual Appearances, or Is Husserl an Aristotelian?" *New Scholasticism* 52 (1978): 1–22.

———. "The Perceptual Roots of Geometric Idealizations." *Review of Metaphysics* 37 (1983/84):785–810.

———. "Frege and Husserl: Another Look at the Issue of Influence." *Husserl Studies* 2 (1985):245–66.

———. "Realism *Versus* Anti-Realism: A Husserlian Contribution." *Edmund Husserl and the Phenomenological Tradition. Essays in Phenomenology.* Edited by Robert Sokolowski. Washington D.C.: Catholic University of America Press, 1988, 87–106.

———. *Husserlian Intentionality and Non-Foundational Realism: Noema and Object* (Contributions to Phenomenology 4). Dordrecht/Boston/London: Kluwer, 1990.

Dummett, Michael. "Thought and Perception: The Views of Two Philosophical Innovators." In D. A. Bell and N. Cooper, eds. *The Analytic Tradition. Meaning, Thought and Knowledge.* Oxford: Blackwell, 1990, 83–103.

———. *Frege: Philosophy of Mathematics.* Cambridge, Mass.: Harvard University Press, 1991, chap. 12, "Frege and Husserl," 141–54.

———. *On the Origins of Analytic Philosophy.* London: Duckworth and Cambridge, Mass.: Harvard University Press, 1993.

Durfee, Harold A., ed. *Analytic Philosophy and Phenomenology.* The Hague: Martinus Nijhoff, 1976.

Edie, James M. *William James and Phenomenology.* Bloomington: Indiana University Press, 1987.

Embree, Lester. "Some Noetico-Noematic Analyses of Action and Practical Life." In *The Phenomenology of the Noema.* John Drummond and Lester Embree, eds. Dordrecht: Kluwer Academic Publishers, 1992, 157–210.

Evans, J. Claude. "Phenomenological Deconstruction: Husserl's Method of *Abbau.*" *Journal of the British Society for Phenomenology* 21 (1990): 14–25.

———. *Strategies of Deconstruction: Derrida and the Myth of the Voice.* Minneapolis and Oxford: University of Minnesota Press, 1991.

———. "The Myth of Absolute Consciousness." In A. B. Dallery *et al.*, eds. *Crises in Continental Philosophy.* Albany: State University of New York Press, 1990, 35–44.

Findlay, J. N. "Husserl's Analysis of the Inner Time-Consciousness." *The Monist* 59 (1975):3–20.

Føllesdal, Dagfinn. *Husserl und Frege. Ein Beitrag zur Beleuchtung der Entstehung der phänomenologischen Philosophie.* Oslo: Aschehoug, 1958. English translation "Husserl and Frege: A Contribution to Elucidating the Origins of Phenomenological Philosophy." In Leila Haaparanta, ed. *Mind, Meaning and Mathematics. Essays on the Philosophical Views of Husserl and Frege.* Dordrecht/Boston/London: Kluwer (1994), 3–47.

———. An Introduction to Phenomenology for Analytic Philosophers." In R. E. Olson and A. M. Paul, *Contemporary Philosophy in Scandinavia.* Baltimore and London: The Johns Hopkins Press (1972), 417–29.

———. "Husserl's Theory of Perception." *Ajatus* 36 (1976):95–105.

———. "Brentano and Husserl on Intentional Objects of Perception." *Grazer Philosophische Studien* 5 (1978):83–94.

———. "Husserl's Notion of *Noema.*" *The Journal of Philosophy* 66 (1969):680–87. Reprinted in Dreyfus, H. L., ed. *Husserl, Intentionality and Cognitive Science.* Cambridge, Mass.: MIT Press, 1982, 73–80 and 93–96.

———. "Husserl and Heidegger on the Role of Actions in the Constitution of the World." In E. Saarinen, *et al.*, eds. *Essays in Honour of Jaakko Hintikka.* Dordrecht: Reidel (1979), 365–78.

———. "Husserl on Evidence and Justification." *Edmund Husserl and the Phenomenological Tradition. Essays in Phenomenology.* Edited by Robert Sokolowski. Washington D. C.: Catholic University of America Press, 1988, 107–29.

———. "Noema and Meaning in Husserl." *Philosophy and Phenomenological Research* 50 (1990):263–71.

———. "The Justification of Logic and Mathematics in Husserl's Phenomenology." In *Phenomenology and the Formal Sciences.* T. Seebohm, *et al.*, eds. Dordrecht/Boston/Lancaster: Kluwer Academic Publishers 1991, 25–34.

Frege, Gottlob. "Rezension von E. G. Husserl, Philosophie der Arithmetik. I." *Zeitschrift für Philosophie und philosophische Kritik.* N. F. 103 (1894):313–32. Translated by E.-H. W. Kluge in *Mind* 81 (1972):321–37.

García-Baró, Miguel. "Ideal Objects and Skepticism: A Polemical Point in *Logical Investigations.*" *Analecta Husserliana* 29 (1990):73–90.

Garrison, James W. "Husserl, Galileo and the Processes of Idealization." *Synthese* 66, (1986):329–38.

Gier, Nicolas F. *Wittgenstein and Phenomenology. A Comparative Study of the Later Wittgenstein, Husserl, Heidegger, and Merleau-Monty.* Albany: State University of New york Press, 1981.

Grieder, Alfons. "Husserl and the Origins of Geometry." *Journal of the British Society for Phenomenology* 20 (1989):277–89.

Gurwitsch, Aron. "The Last Work of Edmund Husserl." *Philosophy and Phenomenological Research* 16 (1955/56):380–99, 17 (1956/57):370–98.

———. *The Field of Consciousness.* Pittsburgh: Duquesne University Press, 1964.

———. "Edmund Husserl's Conception of Phenomenological Psychology." *Review of Metaphysics* 19 (1965/66):689–727.

———. *Studies in Phenomenology and Psychology.* Evanston: Northwestern University Press, 1966.

Haaparanta, Leila. "Analysis as the Method of Logical Discovery: Some Remarks on Frege and Husserl." *Synthese* 77 (1988):73–97.

———. "Intentionality, Intuition and the Computational Theory of Mind." In Leila Haaparanta, ed. *Mind, Meaning and Mathematics. Essays on the Philosophical Views of Husserl and Frege.* Dordrecht/Boston/London: Kluwer (1994), 211–33.

Hall, Harrison. "Husserl's Realism and Idealism." In *Husserl's Phenomenology: A Textbook.* J. N. Mohanty and W. R. McKenna, eds. Lanham: The Center for Advanced Research in Phenomenology and University Press of America (1989):429–44.

Hardy, Lee and Lester Embree, eds. *Phenomenology of Natural Science* (Contributions to Phenomenology). Dordrecht: Kluwer, 1993.

Hart, James G. "A Précis of a Husserlian Philosophical Theology." In Steven W. Laycock and James G. Hart, eds. *Essays in Phenomenological Theology.* Albany: State University of New York Press, 1986, 134–42.

———. "I, We, and God: Ingredients of Husserl's Theory of Community." In Samuel Ijsseling, ed. *Husserl-Ausgabe and Husserl-Forschung* (Phaenomenologica 115). Dordrecht/Boston/London: Kluwer Academic Publishers, 1990, 125–49.

Harvey, Charles W. "Husserl's Phenomenology and Possible Worlds Semantics: A Reexamination." *Husserl Studies* 3 (1986):191–208.

———. "Husserl and the Problem of Theoretical Entities." *Synthese* 66, no. 2 (1986):291–309.

———. *Husserl's Phenomenology and the Foundations of Natural Science*

(Studies in Continental Thought, 15). Athens, Ohio: Ohio University Press, 1989.

Harvey, Charles and Jaakko Hintikka. "Modalization and modalities." In *Phenomenology and the Formal Sciences*. T. Seebohm, *et al.*, eds. Dordrecht/Boston/Lancaster: Kluwer Academic Publishers 1991, 79–91.

Heelan, Patrick. A. *Space Perception and the Philosophy of Science*. Berkeley and Los Angeles: University of California Press, 1988.

———. "Husserl, Hilbert, and the Critique of Galilean Science." *Edmund Husserl and the Phenomenological Tradition. Essays in Phenomenology*. Edited by Robert Sokolowski. Washington D. C.; Catholic University of America Press, 1988, 157–73.

———. "Husserl's Philosophy of Science." In *Husserl's Phenomenology: A Textbook*. J. N. Mohanty and W. R. McKenna, eds. Lanham: The Center for Advanced Research in Phenomenology and University Press of America, 1989, 387–428.

Hill, Claire Ortiz. *Word and Object in Husserl, Frege and Russell. The Roots of Twentieth-Century Philosophy*. Athens, Ohio: Ohio University Press, 1991.

Hintikka, Jaakko. *The Intentions of Intentionality and Other New Models for Modalities*. Dordrecht: Reidel, 1975.

Holenstein, Elmar. *Roman Jakobson's Approach to Language: Phenomenological Structuralism*. Bloomington and London: Indiana University Press, 1975.

Holmes, Richard H. "The World According to Husserl and Heidegger." *Man and World* 18 (1985):373–87.

Hutcheson, Peter. "Husserl's Alleged Private Language." *Philosophy and Phenomenological Research* 47 (1986):133–36.

———. "Husserl, Analogy and Other Minds." *Journal of the British Society for Phenomenology* 18 (1987):285–89.

———. "Transcendental Phenomenology and Possible Worlds Semantics." *Husserl Studies* 4 (1987):225–42.

Ingarden, Roman. "What is New in Husserl's *Crisis?*" *Analecta Husserliana* 2 (1982):23–47.

———. "A priori knowledge in Kant versus a priori knowledge in Husserl." *Dialects and Humanism*. Autumn 1973: 5–18.

———. *On the Motives which led Husserl to Transcendental Idealism*. Translated from the Polish by A. Hannibalsson. The Hague: Martinus Nijhoff, 1975.

Johansson, Ingvar. *Ontological Investigations. An Inquiry into the Categories of Nature, Man and Society*. London: Routledge, 1989.

Kalinowski, G. "La logique des valeurs d'Edmund Husserl." *Archives de*

Philosophie du Droit 13 (1968):267–82 and in G. Kalinowski, *Etudes de logique déontique*, Paris, 1972, 237–56.

———. "La logique des normes d'Edmund Husserl." in G. Kalinowski, *Etudes de logique déontique*. Paris, 1972, 111–22.

Kerszberg, Pierre. "The Phenomenological Analysis of Earth's Motion." *Philosophy and Phenomenological Research* 48 (1987):177–208.

Kidder, Paul. "Husserl's Paradox." *Research in Phenomenology* 17 (1987): 227–42.

Kim, Sang-Ki. "Marvin Farber and Husserl's Phenomenology." *Analecta Husserliana* 26 (1989):3–15.

Kitchen, F. L. *An Investigation of Husserl's Relevance to Carnap's Early Philosophy.* Ann Arbor: University Microfilms, 1983.

Küng, Guido. *Ontology and the Logistic Analysis of Language,* Dordrecht: Reidel, 1967.

———. "The World as Noema and as Referent." *Journal of the British Society for Phenomenology* 3 (1972):15–26.

———. "Husserl on Pictures and Intentional Objects." *Review of Metaphysics* 26 (1973):670–80.

———. "The Phenomenological Reduction as 'Epoché' and Explication." *The Monist* 59 (1975):63–80.

Künne, Wolfgang. "The Nature of Acts: Moore on Husserl." In D. A. Bell and N. Cooper, eds. *The Analytic Tradition. Meaning, Thought and Knowledge.* Oxford: Blackwell, 1990, 104–16.

Kuroda, S. Y. "Edmund Husserl, *Grammaire générale et raisonnée,* and Anton Marty," *Foundations of Language* 10 (1973): 169–75.

Kusch, Martin. *Language as Calculus vs. Language as Universal Medium. A Study in Husserl, Heidegger and Gadamer* (Synthese Library, 207). Dordrecht: Kluwer, 1989.

———. "Husserl and Heidegger on Meaning." *Synthese* 77 (1988):99–127.

———. "The Criticism of Husserl's Arguments against Psychologism in German Philosophy 1901–1920." in Leila Haaparanta, ed. *Mind, Meaning and Mathematics. Essays on the Philosophical Views of Husserl and Frege.* Dordrecht/Boston/London: Kluwer (1994), 51–84.

Langsdorf, Lenore. "The Noema as Intentional Entity: A Critique of Føllesdal." *The Review of Metaphysics* 37 (1984):757–84.

Langsdorf, Lenore and Harry Reeder. "A Phenomenological Exploration of Popper's 'World 3'." In *The Horizons of Continental Philosophy. Essays on Husserl, Heidegger, and Merleau-Ponty.* Edited by Hugh J. Silverman, Algis Mikunas, Theodore Kisiel, and Alphonso Lingis. Dordrecht/Boston/Lancaster: Nijhoff (1988), 93–129.

Laycock, Steven. W. "Bergmannian Meditations." *Noûs* 21 (1987):135–60.

Levin, David Michael. *Reason and Evidence in Husserl's Phenomenology.* Evanston: Northwestern University Press.

Lübbe, Hermann "Positivismus and Phänomenologie (Mach und Husserl)." In *Beiträge zu Philosophie und Wissenschaft. Wilhelm Szilasi zum 70. Geburtstag.* Munich: Francke, 1960, 161–84.

Macnamara, John. *A Border Dispute: The Place of Logic in Psychology.* Cambridge, Mass.: MIT Press, 1986.

Marbach, Eduard. "How to Study Consciousness Phenomenologically or Quite a Lot Comes to Mind." In *Journal of the British Society Phenomenology* 19 (1988):252–68.

———. *Mental Representation and Consciousness. Towards a Phenomenological Theory of Representation and Reference.* Dordrecht/Boston/London: Kluwer, 1993.

McInerney, Peter K. "What is still valuable in Husserl's analyses of inner time-consciousness?" *Journal of Philosophy* 85 (1988): 605–16.

———. *Time and Experience.* Philadelphia: Temple University Press, 1991.

McIntyre, Ronald. "Intending and Referring." In Dreyfus, H. L., ed. *Husserl, Intentionality and Cognitive Science.* Cambridge, Mass.: MIT Press, 1982, 215–31.

———. "Husserl and Frege." *Journal of Philosophy* 84 (1987):528–35.

———. "Husserl and the Representational Theory of Mind." *Topoi* 5 (1986):101–14.

McIntyre, Ronald and David Woodruff Smith. "Theory of Intentionality." In *Husserl's Phenomenology: A Textbook.* J. N. Mohanty and W. R. McKenna, eds. Lanham: The Center for Advanced Research in Phenomenology and University Press of America, 1989, 147–80.

McKenna, William R. "Husserl's Theory of Perception." In *Husserl's Phenomenology: A Textbook.* J. N. Mohanty and W. R. McKenna, eds. Lanham: The Center for Advanced Research in Phenomenology and University Press of America, 1989, 181–212.

Mahnke, D. "From Hilbert to Husserl. First Introduction to Phenomenology, Especially that of Formal Mathematics." *Studies in History and Philosophy of Sciences* 8 (1977):71–84.

Mall, R. A. *Experience and Reason. The Phenomenology of Husserl and its Relation to Hume's Philosophy.* The Hague: Martinus Nijhoff, 1973.

Mays, Wolfe and Barry Jones. "Was Husserl a Fregean?" *Journal of the British Society for Phenomenology* 12 (1981):76–80.

Mensch, James Richard. "Phenomenology and Artificial Intelligence: Husserl learns Chinese." *Husserl Studies,* 8 (1991):107–28.

Miller, Izchak. *Husserl, Perception and Temporal Awareness.* Cambridge, Mass.: MIT Press, 1984.

———. "Husserl and Sartre on the Self." *The Monist* 69 (1986):534–45.

———. "Husserl on the Ego." *Topoi* 5 (1986):157–62.

———. "Perceptual Reference." *Synthese* 66 (1986):35–60.

Miller, J. P. *Numbers in Presence and Absence: A Study of Husserl's Philosophy of Mathematics* (Phaenomenologica 90). The Hague/Boston/London: Nijhoff, 1982.

Mohanty, J. N. "Husserl's Theory of Meaning." in F. A. Elliston and P. McCormick, eds., *Husserl: Expositions and Appraisals*. Notre Dame: University of Notre Dame Press, 1977, 18–37.

———. "Intentionality and Noema." *Journal of Philosophy* 78 (1981):706–17.

———. *Husserl and Frege*. Bloomington: Indiana University Press, 1982.

———. "Perceptual Meaning." *Topoi* 5 (1986):131–36.

———. *Transcendental Phenomenology. An Analytic Account*. Oxford: Blackwell, 1989.

———. "Husserl's Formalism." In *Phenomenology and the Formal Sciences*. T. Seebohm, *et al.*, eds. Dordrecht/Boston/Lancaster: Kluwer Academic Publishers, 1991, 93–105.

Moreland, James Porter. *Universals, Qualities, and Quality-Instances. A Defense of Realism*. Lanham/New York/London: University Press of America, 1985.

———. "Was Husserl a Nominalist?" *Philosophy and Phenomenological Research* 49 (1989):661–74.

Mulligan, Kevin. "Promisings and Other Social Acts: Their Constituents and Structure." In K. Mulligan, ed., *Speech Act and Sachverhalt*. Dordrecht/Boston/Lancaster, Kluwer, 1987, 29–90.

———. "How Not to Read: Derrida on Husserl." *Topoi* 10 (1991): 199–208.

Mulligan, Kevin and Barry Smith. "A Husserlian Theory of Indexicality." *Grazer Philosophische Studien* 28 (1986):133–63.

———. "Husserl's Logical Investigations." *Grazer Philosophische Studien* 27 (1986):199–207.

Münch, Dieter. *Intention und Zeichen. Untersuchungen zu Franz Brentano und zu Edmund Husserls Frühwerk*. Frankfurt: Suhrkamp, 1993.

Murphy, Richard T. *Hume and Husserl. Towards Radical Subjectivism*. The Hague/Boston/London: Martinus Nijhoff, 1980.

———. "Husserl and British Empiricism (1886–1895)." *Research in Phenomenology* 16 (1986):121–37.

———. "Husserl and Hume: Overcrowding Scepticism." *Journal of the British Society for Phenomenology* 22 (1991):30–44.

Naess, Arne. "Husserl on the Apodictic Evidence of Ideal Laws." *Theoria* 20 (1954):53–63.

Natanson, Maurice. "Descriptive Phenomenology." In *Descriptions*. Edited by Don Ihde and Hugh J. Silverman. Albany: State University of New York Press, 1985, 2–13.

Null, Gilbert T. "Husserl's Doctrine of Essence." In *Husserl's Phenomenology: A Textbook*. J. N. Mohanty and W. R. McKenna, eds. Lanham: The Center for Advanced Research in Phenomenology and University Press of America, 1989, 69–106.

Parret, H. "Husserl and the Neo-Humboldtians on Language." *International Philosophical Quarterly* 12 (1972):43–68.

Patočka, Jan. "Edmund Husserl's Philosophy of the Crisis of Science and His Conception of a Phenomenology of the 'Life-World'." *Husserl Studies* 2 (1985):129–56.

———. *Le Monde naturel et le mouvement de l'existence humaine* (Phaenomenologica 110). Dordrecht/Boston/London: Kluwer, 1988. German trans. *Die natürliche Welt als philosophisches Problem (Phänomenologische Schriften I)*. Edited by K. Nellen and J. Němec. Translated by E. and R. Melville. Stuttgart: Klett-Cotta, 1990.

Pepp, Dane. "A Husserlian Response to Derrida's Early Criticisms of Phenomenology." *Journal of the British Society for Phenomenology* 18 (1987):226–44.

Peruzzi, Alberto. "Towards a Real Phenomenology of Logic." *Husserl Studies* 6 (1989):1–24.

Philipse, Herman. "The Problem of Occasional Expressions in Edmund Husserl's *Logical Investigations*." *Journal of the British Society for Phenomenology* 13 (1982):168–85.

———. "The Concept of Intentionality. Husserl's Development from the Brentano Period to the *Logical Investigations*." *Philosophy Research Archives* 12 (1986–87):293–328.

———. "Psychologism and the Prescriptive Function of Logic." *Grazer Philosophische Studien* 29 (1987):13–33.

Pietersma, Henry. "Husserl's Concept of Existence." *Synthese* 66 (1986): 311–28.

———. "The Problem of Knowledge and Phenomenology." *Philosophy and Phenomenological Research* 50 (1989):27–68.

———. "Truth and The Evident." In *Husserl's Phenomenology: A Textbook*. J. N. Mohanty and W. R. McKenna, eds. Lanham: The Center for Advanced Research in Phenomenology and University Press of America, 1989, 213–48.

Reinach, Adolf. "Concerning Phenomenology." *The Personalist* 50 (1969): 194–211. English translation by Dallas Willard of a lecture given in Marburg in 1914. See Reinach 1989, 531–50.

———. *Sämtliche Werke. Kritische Ausgabe mit Kommentar*, Band I: *Die Werke*, Teil I: *Kritische Neuausgabe (1905–1914)*, Teil II: *Nachgelassene Texte (1906–1917)*; Band II: *Kommentar und Textkritik*. Edited by Karl Schuhmann and Barry Smith. Munich and Vienna: Philosophia, 1989.

Rollinger, R. D. "Husserl and Brentano on Imagination." *Archiv für die Geschichte der Philosophie* 75 (1993):195–210.

———. *Meinong and Husserl on Abstraction and Universals. From Hume Studies I to Logical Investigations II* (Studien zur Österreichischen Philosophie XX). Amsterdam/Atlanta: Rodopi, 1993.

Rosado Haddock, G. E. *Edmund Husserls Philosophie der Logik und Mathematik im Lichte der gegenwärtigen Logik und Grundlagenforschung.* Dissertation, Bonn University, 1973.

———. "Remarks on Sense and Reference in Frege and Husserl." *Kant-Studien* 73 (1982):425–39.

———. "Husserl's Epistemology of Mathematics and the Foundations of Platonism in Mathematics." *Husserl Studies* 4 (1987):81–102.

Rota, Gian-Carlo. "Edmund Husserl and the Reform of Logic." In D. Carr and E. S. Casey, eds. *Explorations in Phenomenology.* The Hague: Nijhoff, 1973.

———. "*Fundierung* as a Logical Concept." *The Monist* 72 (1989):70–77.

Rouse, Joseph. "Husserlian Phenomenology and Scientific Realism." *Philosophy of Science* 54 (1987):222–32.

Ryle, Gilbert. "Phenomenology." *Proceedings of the Aristotelian Society. Supplementary Volume* 11 (1932):63–83. Reprinted in Ryle, *Collected Papers.* London: Hutchinson, 1971, Vol. 1, 167–78.

———. "Review of Marvin Farber, 'The Foundations of Phenomenology'." *Philosophy* 21 (1946):263–69. Reprinted in Ryle, *Collected Papers.* London: Hutchinson, 1971, Vol. 1, 215–24.

———. "Phenomenology versus 'The Concept of Mind'." In Ryle, *Collected Papers.* London: Hutchinson, 1971, Vol. 1, 179–96.

Salmon, C. V. "The Central Problem of David Hume's Philosophy. An Essay towards a Phenomenological Interpretation of the First Book of the Treatise of Human Nature." *Jahrbuch für Philosophie und phänomenologische Forschung.* 10 (1929):299–449.

Scanlon, John. "Husserl's *Ideas* and the Natural Concept of the World." *Edmund Husserl and the Phenomenological Tradition. Essays in Phenomenology.* Edited by Robert Sokolowski. Washington D. C.: Catholic University of America Press, 1988, 217–33.

———. "Phenomenological Psychology." In *Husserl's Phenomenology: A Textbook.* J. N. Mohanty and W. R. McKenna, eds. Lanham: The Center for Advanced Research in Phenomenology and University Press of America, 1989, 445–64.

———. "«Tertium non datur». Husserl's conception of a definite multiplicity." In *Phenomenology and the formal sciences.* Seebohm, *et al.,* eds. 1991, 139–47.

Schuhmann, Karl. " 'Phänomenologie': Eine begriffsgeschichtliche Reflexion." *Husserl Studies* 1, 1984, 31–68.

———. "Husserl und Reinach." In *Speech Act and Sachverhalt: Reinach and the Foundations of Realist Phenomenology (Primary Sources in Phenomenology* 1). Edited by Kevin Mulligan. Dordrecht/Boston/Lancaster: Nijhoff, 1987, 239–56.

———. "Husserl and Masaryk." In *On Masaryk. Texts in English and German.* Edited by Josef Novák (*Studien zur Österreichischen Philosophie,* Vol. 13). Rodopi: Amsterdam, 1988, 129–56.

———. *Husserls Staatsphilosophie.* Freiburg i. Br.: Alber, 1988.

———. "Husserl's Concept of the Noema: A Daubertian Critique." *Topoi* 8 (1989):53–61.

———. "Husserl's Concept of Philosophy." *Journal of the British Society for Phenomenology* 21 (1990):274–83.

———. "Husserl's Yearbook." *Philosophy and Phenomenological Research* 50, Supplement (1990):1–25.

———. "Husserl's Theories of Indexicals." F. M. Kirkland and D. P. Chattopadhyaya, eds. *Phenomenology – East and West.* Dordrecht: Kluwer, 1993, 111–27.

———. "Husserl and Twardowski." In F. Coniglione, R. Poli, and J. Wolenski, eds. *Polish Scientific Philosophy. The Lvov-Warsaw School.* Amsterdam/Atlanta: Rodopi, 1993, 41–58.

Schuhmann, Karl and Barry Smith. "Against Idealism: Johannes Daubert vs. Husserl's *Ideas* I." *Review of Metaphysics* 39 (1985):763–93.

———. "Two Idealisms: Lask and Husserl." *Kant-Studien* 84 (1993), 448–66.

Schutz, Alfred. "Edmund Husserl's *Ideas,* volume II." *Philosophy and Phenomenological Research* 13 (1952/53): 394–413. Reprinted in Schutz, *Collected Papers,* Vol. III.

———. "Edmund Husserl's *Ideas,* volume III." *Philosophy and Phenomenological Research* 13 (1952/53):506–14. Reprinted in Schutz, *Collected Papers,* Vol. III.

———. "Type and Eidos in Husserl's Late Philosophy." *Philosophy and Phenomenological Research* 20 (1959/60):147–65. Reprinted in Schutz, *Collected Papers,* Vol. III.

———. *Collected Papers,* vol. III. *Studies in Phenomenological Psychology.* The Hague: Martinus Nijhoff, 1975.

Seebohm, Thomas M. "Phenomenology of Logic and the Problem of Mo-
dalizing." *Journal of the British Society for Phenomenology* 19 (1988):
235–51.

———. "Transcendental Phenomenology." In *Husserl's Phenomenology: A
Textbook*. J. N. Mohanty and W. R. McKenna, eds. Lanham: The Center
for Advanced Research in Phenomenology and University Press of
America, 1989, 345–86.

———. "Psychologism revisited." In *Phenomenology and the Formal Sciences*. T. Seebohm, *et al.*, eds. Dordrecht/Boston/Lancaster: Kluwer Academic Publishers, 1991, 149–82.

Seebohm, T. M., D. Føllesdal, and J. N. Mohanty, eds. *Phenomenology and
the Formal Sciences*. Dordrecht/Boston/Lancaster: Kluwer, 1991.

Shelton, Jim. "Schlick and Husserl on the Foundation of Phenomenology."
Philosophy and Phenomenological Research 49 (1988):557–61.

Simons, Peter M. "The Formalisation of Husserl's Theory of Wholes and
Parts." In B. Smith, ed., *Parts and Moments*, Munich: Philosophia Verlag, 1982, 113–59.

———. *Philosophy and Logic in Central Europe from Bolzano to Tarski.
Selected Essays.* Dordrecht: Kluwer, 1992.

Small, R. "Ryle and Husserl." *Journal of the British Society for Phenomenology* 12 (1981):195–210.

Smid, R. N. "An Early Interpretation of Husserl's Phenomenology. J.
Daubert and the 'Logical Investigations'." *Husserl Studies* 2 (1985):
267–90.

Smith, Barry. "Logic, Form and Matter." *Proceedings of the Aristotelian
Society, Supplementary Volume* 55 (1981):47–63.

———. "Husserl, Language and the Ontology of the Act." In D. Buzzetti and
M. Ferriani, eds. *Speculative Grammar, Universal Grammar, and the
Philosophical Analysis of Language*. Amsterdam: John Benjamins,
1987, 205–27.

———. "Logic and Formal Ontology." In *Husserl's Phenomenology: A Textbook*. J. N. Mohanty and W. R. McKenna, eds. Lanham: The Center for
Advanced Research in Phenomenology and University Press of America, 1989, 29–68.

———. "Husserl's Theory of Meaning and Reference." In L. Haaparanta, ed.
*Mind, Meaning and Mathematics. Essays on the Philosophy of Husserl
and Frege*. Dordrecht/Boston/Lancaster: Kluwer, 1994, 163–183.

———. *Austrian Philosophy. The Legacy of Franz Brentano.* La Salle: Open
Court, 1994.

Smith, Barry, ed. *Parts and Moments: Studies in Logic and Formal Ontology.* Munich: Philosophia Verlag, 1992.

Smith, David Woodruff. "The Realism in Perception." *Noûs* 16 (1982): 42–55.

———. "Husserl on Demonstrative Reference and Perception." In Dreyfus, H. L., ed. *Husserl, Intentionality and Cognitive Science*. Cambridge, Mass.: MIT Press, 1982, 193–213.

———. "Husserl's Philosophy of Mind." In G. Floistad, ed., *Contemporary Philosophy: A New Survey*, Vol. 4, *Philosophy of Mind*. The Hague: Martinus Nijhoff, 1983, 249–86.

———. "The Structure of (Self-) Consciousness." *Topoi* 5 (1986):149–56.

———. *The Circle of Acquaintance. Perception, Consciousness and Empathy*. Dordrecht/Boston/Lancaster: Kluwer, 1989.

Smith, David Woodruff and Ronald McIntyre. *Husserl and Intentionality*. Dordrecht/Boston: Reidel, 1982.

Soffer, Gail. "Phenomenology and Scientific Realism: Husserl's Critique of Galileo." *The Review of Metaphysics* 44 (1990):67–94.

———. *Husserl and the Question of Relativism* (Phaemenologica 122). Dordrecht: Kluwer, 1991.

Sokolowski, Robert. "The Logic of Parts and Wholes in Husserl's Logical Investigations." *Philosophy and Phenomenological Research* 28 (1967/8):537–53. Reprinted in J. N. Mohanty, ed. *Readings on Edmund Husserl's Logical Investigations*. Haag: Nijhoff, 1977, 94–111.

———. "The Structure and Content of Husserl's Logical Investigations." *Inquiry* 14 (1971):318–47.

———. *Presence and Absence. A Philosophical Investigation of Langauge and Being*. Bloomington and London: Indiana University Press, 1978.

Spiegelberg, Herbert. "Is the Reduction Necessary for Phenomenology? Husserl's and Pfänder's Replies." *Journal of the British Society for Phenomenology* 4 (1973):3–15.

Sprigge, T. L. S. "The Self and its World in Bradley and Husserl." In A. Manser and G. Stock, eds. *The Philosophy of F. H. Bradley*. Oxford: Clarendon, 1984, 285–302.

Stella, Giuliana. *I Giuristi di Husserl. L'Interpretazione fenomenologica del diritto*. Milan: A. Giuffre, 1990.

Stephens, James Whyte. *Phenomenology and Realism: An Essay on Husserl's 'Logical Investigations'*, Dissertation, Princeton University, 1978 (Ann Arbor: University Microfilms).

Ströker, Elisabeth. *Husserlian Foundations of Science*. Edited by Lee Hardy. Lanham: University Press of America, 1987.

———. "Husserl and the Philosophy of Science." In *Journal of the British Society for Phenomenology* 19 (1988):221–34.

———. "Phenomenology as First Philosophy: Reflections on Husserl." *Ed-*

mund Husserl and the Phenomenological Tradition. Essays in Phenomenology. Edited by Robert Sokolowski. Washington D. C.: Catholic University of America Press, 1988, 249–63.

Sukale, Michael. *Comparative Studies in Phenomenology.* The Hague: Martinus Nijhoff, 1976.

Tieszen, Richard L. "Phenomenology and Mathematical Knowledge." *Synthese* 75 (1988):373–403.

———. *Mathematical Intuition. Phenomenology and Mathematical Knowledge.* Dordrecht/Boston/Lancaster: Kluwer, 1989.

Tito, Johanna Maria. *Logic in the Husserlian Context.* Evanston: Northwestern University Press, 1990.

Tragesser, Robert S. *Husserl and Realism in Logic and Mathematics.* Cambridge: Cambridge University Press, 1984.

Tuedio, James "Merleau-Ponty's Refinement of Husserl." *Philosophy Today* 29 (1985):99–109.

———. "The Source and Nature of Edmund Husserl's Transcendental Turn", *Philosophy Today,* 30 (1986):191–209.

Wallner, Ingrid M. "In Defense of Husserl's Transcendental Idealism: Roman Ingarden's Critique Re-Examined." *Husserl Studies* 4 (1987):3–44.

White, A. "Reconstructing Husserl: A Critical Response to Derrida's *Speech and Phenomena.*" *Husserl Studies* 45–62.

Willard, Dallas. "The Paradox of Logical Psychologism: Husserl's Way Out." *American Philosophical Quarterly* 19 (1972): 94–100. Reprinted in *Husserl. Expositions and Appraisals.* Edited by F. Elliston and P. McCormick. Notre Dame: University of Notre Dame Press, 1977, 10–17.

———. "Husserl on a Logic that Failed." *Philosophical Review* 89 (1980): 46–64.

———. *Logic and the Objectivity of Knowledge.* Athens, Ohio: University of Ohio Press, 1984.

———. "On Discovering the Difference between Husserl and Frege." *Analecta Husserliana* 26 (1989):393–97.

———. "The Concept of Number." In *Husserl's Phenomenology: A Textbook.* J. N. Mohanty and W. R. McKenna, eds. Lanham: The Center for Advanced Research in Phenomenology and University Press of America, 1989, 1–28.

———. "Sentences which are true in virtue of their color." In *Phenomenology and the Formal Sciences.* T. Seebohm, *et al.,* eds. Dordrecht/Boston/Lancaster: Kluwer Academic Publishers, 1991, 225–42.

———. "The Integrity of the Mental Act: Husserlian Reflections on a Fregian Problem." In Leila Haaparanta, ed. *Mind, Meaning and Mathe-*

matics. Essays on the Philosophical Views of Husserl and Frege. Dordrecht/Boston/London: Kluwer, 1994, 235–62.

Williams, Forrest. "Intersubjectivity: A Brief Guide." In *Husserl's Phenomenology: A Textbook.* J. N. Mohanty and W. R. McKenna, eds. Lanham: The Center for Advanced Research in Phenomenology and University Press of America, 1989, 309–44.

Żełaniec, Wojciech. "Fathers, Kings, and Promises: Husserl and Reinach on the A Priori." *Husserl Studies* 9 (1992):147–77.

INDEX

509